Lecture Notes in Computer Science 14168

Founding Editors

Gerhard Goos
Juris Hartmanis

The series Lecture Notes in Computer Science (LNCS), including its subseries Lecture Notes in Artificial Intelligence (LNAI) and Lecture Notes in Bioinformatics (LNBI), has established itself as a medium for the publication of new developments in computer science and information technology research, teaching, and education.

LNCS enjoys close cooperation with the computer science R & D community, the series counts many renowned academics among its volume editors and paper authors, and collaborates with prestigious societies. Its mission is to serve this international community by providing an invaluable service, mainly focused on the publication of conference and workshop proceedings and postproceedings. LNCS commenced publication in 1973.

Abdelrahaman Aly · Mehdi Tibouchi
Editors

Progress in Cryptology – LATINCRYPT 2023

8th International Conference on Cryptology
and Information Security in Latin America, LATINCRYPT 2023
Quito, Ecuador, October 3–6, 2023
Proceedings

Editors
Abdelrahaman Aly ⓘ
Technology Innovation Institute
Abu Dhabi, United Arab Emirates

Mehdi Tibouchi ⓘ
NTT Social Informatics Laboratories
Tokyo, Japan

ISSN 0302-9743 ISSN 1611-3349 (electronic)
Lecture Notes in Computer Science
ISBN 978-3-031-44468-5 ISBN 978-3-031-44469-2 (eBook)
https://doi.org/10.1007/978-3-031-44469-2

This Springer imprint is published by the registered company Springer Nature Switzerland AG
The registered company address is: Gewerbestrasse 11, 6330 Cham, Switzerland

Paper in this product is recyclable.

Preface

This book contains the proceedings of the 8th International Conference on Cryptology and Information Security in Latin America, LATINCRYPT 2023. The conference was held in Quito, Ecuador on October 3–6, 2023. This event was organized in cooperation with the International Association for Cryptologic Research.

The 19 accepted papers collected in this volume and presented at the conference were carefully selected by the Program Committee (PC), after a double-blind peer review process, from 59 submissions by researchers from 27 different countries. The PC co-chairs were supported in this matter by a PC consisting of 47 leading experts on all aspects of cryptologic research. 24 external reviewers also provided invaluable input for the selection of papers. Each submission received around 4 reviews from the committee, or 5 reviews for papers co-authored by a PC member. Strong conflict of interest rules ensured that papers were not handled by PC members with a close personal or professional relationship with the authors. The two program chairs were not allowed to submit a paper.

Alongside the presentations of the accepted papers, the program of LATINCRYPT 2023 featured three excellent invited talks. Furthermore, leading up to the conference, the ASCrypto school in cryptography took place on the two previous days, and included numerous expository talks on some of the topics covered in the technical program. ASCrypto was chaired by Sofia Celi and Diego Aranha.

The conference proceedings volume contains the revised versions of the 19 papers that were selected. The final revised versions of papers were not reviewed again and the authors are responsible for their contents.

Many people contributed to the success of LATINCRYPT 2023. We would like to thank the authors for submitting their research results to the conference. We are very grateful to the PC members and external reviewers for contributing their knowledge and expertise, and for the tremendous amount of work involved in reviewing papers and contributing to the discussions. We are greatly indebted to Walter Fuertes, the General Chair, for his efforts and overall organization. The same can be said of the Local Organizing Committee. We also thank the steering committee for their direction and advice throughout the preparation of the conference, and Springer for handling the publication of these conference proceedings. Special thanks go to Francisco Rodríguez-Henríquez for his indefatigable guidance and support.

October 2023

Abdelrahaman Aly
Mehdi Tibouchi

The originally published version of the front matter was revised: The names of Sofia Celi and Diego Aranha have been included under the preface.

Organization

General Chair

Walter Fuertes
Universidad de las Fuerzas Armadas - ESPE, Ecuador

Local Organizing Committee

Sonia Cardenas
Universidad de las Fuerzas Armadas - ESPE, Ecuador

Efraín. R. Fonseca C.
Universidad de las Fuerzas Armadas - ESPE, Ecuador

Tatiana Gualotuña
Universidad de las Fuerzas Armadas - ESPE, Ecuador

Jorge Edison Lascano
Universidad de las Fuerzas Armadas - ESPE, Ecuador

Mauricio Loachamín
Universidad de las Fuerzas Armadas - ESPE, Ecuador

Diego Marcillo
Universidad de las Fuerzas Armadas - ESPE, Ecuador

Geovanny Ninahualpa
Universidad de las Fuerzas Armadas - ESPE, Ecuador

Marcelo Rea
Universidad de las Fuerzas Armadas - ESPE, Ecuador

Freddy Tapia
Universidad de las Fuerzas Armadas - ESPE, Ecuador

Program Committee Chairs

Abdelrahaman Aly
CRC-TII, UAE

Mehdi Tibouchi
NTT Social Informatics Laboratories, Japan

Steering Committee

Michel Abdalla
CNRS and DI/ENS, Université PSL, France

Diego Aranha
Aarhus University, Denmark

Paulo Barreto	University of Washington, Tacoma, USA
Ricardo Dahab	Universidade Estadual de Campinas, Brazil
Alejandro Hevia	Universidad de Chile, Chile
Kristin Lauter	Meta, USA
Julio López	Universidade Estadual de Campinas, Brazil
Daniel Panario	Carleton University, Canada
Francisco Rodríguez-Henríquez	CRC-TII, UAE
Nicolas Thériault	Universidad de Santiago de Chile, Chile
Alfredo Viola	Universidad de la República de Uruguay, Uruguay

Program Committee

Miguel Ambrona	Nomadic Labs, France
Elena Andreeva	TU Wien, Austria
Diego Aranha	Aarhus University, Denmark
Ero Balsa	Cornell Tech, USA
Gustavo Banegas	Qualcomm, France
Paulo Barreto	University of Washington, Tacoma, USA
Ward Beullens	IBM Zurich, Switzerland
Charlotte Bonte	Zama, France
Alejandro Cabrera-Alday	Tampere University, Finland
Fabio Campos	Radboud University, Netherlands
Sofía Celi	Brave, USA
Céline Chevalier	University Pantheon-Assas, France
Jesús-Javier Chi-Domínguez	CRC-TII, UAE
Bernardo David	University of Copenhagen, Denmark
Luca De Feo	IBM Zurich, Switzerland
Daniel Escudero	JP Morgan, USA
Maria Isabel González-Vasco	Carlos III University of Madrid, Spain
Debayan Gupta	Ashoka University, India
Minki Hhan	Korean Institute of Advanced Studies, Korea
Elena Kirshanova	CRC- TII, UAE
Nadim Kobeissi	Nym Technologies, Switzerland
Hilder Vitor Lima Pereira	imec-COSIC, KULeuven, Belgium
Patrick Longa	Microsoft Research, USA
Julio López	University of Campinas, Brazil
Eleftheria Makri	University of Leiden, Netherlands
Victor Matteu	CRC- TII, UAE
Svetla Nikova	University of Bergen, Norway
Anca Nitulescu	Protocol Labs, France

Miyako Ohkubo	National Institute of Information and Communication Studies, Japan
Elena Pagnin	Chalmers University, Sweden
Daniel Panario	University of Carleton, Canada
Octavio Pérez-Kempner	NTT Social Informatics Laboratories, Japan
Peter Pessl	Infineon Technologies, Germany
Carla Ràfols	Universitat Pompeu Fabra, Spain
Joost Renes	NXP Semiconductors, Netherlands
Peter Scholl	Aarhus University, Denmark
Peter Schwabe	Max Planck Institute for Security and Privacy, Germany and Radboud University, Netherlands
Tjerand Silde	NTNU, Norway
Chao Sun	Kyoto University, Japan
Titouan Tanguy	imec-COSIC, KU Leuven, Belgium
Nicolas Thériault	Universidad de Chile, Chile
Javier Verbel	CRC-TII, UAE
Frederick Vercauteren	KU Leuven, Belgium
Alfredo Viola	Universidad de la República de Uruguay, Uruguay
Fernando Virdia	Independent Researcher, Argentina
Yang Yu	Tsinghua University, China
Arantxa Zapico	Ethereum Foundation, USA

Additional Reviewers

Gora Adj
Marc Beunardeau
Marco Calderini
Viola Campos
Wonseok Choi
Heewon Chung
Siemen Dhooghe
David Gerault
Akiko Inoue
Yan Ji
Nikolay Kaleyski
Changmin Lee

Semyon Novoselov
Ivan Oleynikov
Adrián Ranea
Magnus Ringerud
Yusuke Sakai
Mahdi Sedaghat
Koutarou Suzuki
Sharwan Kumar Tiwari
Nicola Tuveri
Senpeng Wang
Zachary Welch
Gustavo Zambonin

Contents

Symmetric-Key Cryptography

On the Algebraic Immunity of Weightwise Perfectly Balanced Functions

Agnese Gini$^{(\boxtimes)}$ ⓘ and Pierrick Méaux ⓘ

University of Luxembourg, Esch-sur-Alzette, Luxembourg
{agnese.gini,pierrick.meaux}@uni.lu

Abstract. In this article we study the Algebraic Immunity (AI) of Weightwise Perfectly Balanced (WPB) functions. After showing a lower bound on the AI of two classes of WPB functions from the previous literature, we prove that the minimal AI of a WPB n-variables function is constant, equal to 2 for $n \geq 4$. Then, we compute the distribution of the AI of WPB function in 4 variables, and estimate the one in 8 and 16 variables. For these values of n we observe that a large majority of WPB functions have optimal AI, and that we could not obtain a WPB function with AI 2 by sampling at random. Finally, we address the problem of constructing WPB functions with bounded algebraic immunity, exploiting a construction from [12]. In particular, we present a method to generate multiple WPB functions with minimal AI, and we prove that the WPB functions with high nonlinearity exhibited in [12] also have minimal AI. We conclude with a construction giving WPB functions with lower bounded AI, and give as example a family with all elements with AI at least $n/2 - \log(n) + 1$.

Keywords: Boolean functions · algebraic immunity · weightwise perfectly balanced functions · FLIP

1 Introduction

Among the different criteria of Boolean functions analyzed during the last years, those targeting Boolean functions with restricted input sets have been increasingly studied after the work of Carlet, Méaux, and Rotella [6]. The authors introduced cryptographic criteria of Boolean functions with restricted input for the cryptanalysis of FLIP stream cipher [22], whose specificity is that its filter function is evaluated on sets of Boolean vectors having constant Hamming weight. Therefore, considering functions with good properties also when restricted is crucial for investigating its security. Properties on sets of constant Hamming weight arise also in other contexts, such as side channel attacks where it is common to obtain information on the Hamming weight of inputs (*e.g.* [18,32]).

One property of main interest is the balancedness, as in most cryptographic contexts using balanced functions prevents biased output distributions, it is desirable for applications like FLIP to work with functions balanced when

© The Author(s), under exclusive license to Springer Nature Switzerland AG 2023
A. Aly and M. Tibouchi (Eds.): LATINCRYPT 2023, LNCS 14168, pp. 3–23, 2023.
https://doi.org/10.1007/978-3-031-44469-2_1

restricted to the slices $\mathsf{E}_{k,n} = \{x \in \mathbb{F}_2^n \,|\, \mathsf{w}_\mathsf{H}(x) = k\}$ of the Boolean hypercube $\mathbb{F}_2^n$. In this context Carlet *et al.*[6] presented the concept of Weightwise Perfectly Balanced (WPB) functions, $f \colon \mathbb{F}_2^n \to \mathbb{F}_2$, such that $|\{x \in \mathsf{E}_{k,n} \,|\, f(x) = 0\}| = |\{x \in \mathsf{E}_{k,n} \,|\, f(x) = 1\}|$ for each $1 \le k \le n - 1$, f globally balanced, and $f(0_n) = 0$. These functions are at maximal distance from the set of symmetric functions, deeply studied in the context of cryptography *e.g.*[1–3], analogously to the bent functions (*e.g.*[24,30]) from the set of affine functions. Diverse methods for constructing WPB functions have been proposed since 2017 *e.g.*[10–15,17,19,25–27,33–35,37]. The main cryptographic properties that have been studied on WPB functions so far are the weightwise nonlinearity (*i.e.*nonlinearity restricted on the slices) such as in [10,15,27], and more recently the (global) nonlinearity such as in [12,17]. Other relevant cryptographic properties on Boolean functions have not been studied deeply on the set of WPB functions, such as the algebraic immunity.

The concept of Algebraic Immunity (AI) appeared in [7] in the context of algebraic attacks on stream ciphers. In the attack described by Courtois and Meier, instead of focusing on the system of equations given by a filter function f (a Boolean function in n variables), they consider a system of equations potentially simpler to solve, obtained by the annihilators of f. They show that even if f has a high degree (close to n), f or $f + 1$ always admits an annihilator of degree at most $\lceil (n+1)/2 \rceil$, allowing the attacker to reduce the attack to solving an algebraic system of the annihilator's degree. The notion of algebraic immunity has been formalized later in [23], as $\mathsf{AI}(f) = \min_{g \ne 0}\{\deg(g) \mid fg = 0 \text{ or } (f+1)g = 0\}$. Due to its high impact on the security of stream ciphers, the algebraic immunity has been thoroughly studied since 2003. For WPB functions the AI is only known for a few constructions. The family exhibited by Tang and Liu [33], and later the families from [26,27] are designed to have optimal AI. Then, all the other results are experimental, computing the AI of WPB functions in 4, 8 or 16 variables such as in [11,25,35].

Hence, the goal of this article is to further study the algebraic immunity of WPB functions. First we investigate the extreme values of the AI inside the class of WPB functions, and the AI distribution in a small number of variables. Since families with optimal AI have been exhibited, we focus on the minimal value that can reach a WPB function, and show lower bounds for two former secondary constructions (from [6] and [37]). Contrarily to the degree that is at least $n/2$, we show that the minimal AI of a WPB function is constant, equal to 2 for $n \ge 4$. We compute the distribution of the AI of WPB functions in 4 variables, and estimate the one in 8 and 16 variables, following the model established by [10] for the weightwise nonlinearities. For these values of n we observe that a large majority of WPB functions have optimal AI, and that we could not obtain an WPB function with AI 2 by sampling at random. Then, we address the problem of constructing WPB functions with bounded algebraic immunity. We use the construction from [12] to build functions with upper bounded AI. In particular, we present a method to generate multiple WPB functions with minimal AI, and we prove that the WPB functions with high nonlinearity exhibited in [12] also have minimal AI. We finish with a construction giving WPB functions with lower bounded AI, and give as example a family with all elements with AI at least $n/2 - \log(n) + 1$.

2 Preliminaries

For readability we use the notation $+$ instead of $\oplus$ to denote the addition in $\mathbb{F}_2$ and $\sum$ instead of $\bigoplus$. We denote by $[a, b]$ the subset of all integers between a and b: $\{a, a+1, \ldots, b\}$. For a vector $v \in \mathbb{F}_2^n$ we use $\mathsf{w_H}(v)$ to denote its Hamming weight $\mathsf{w_H}(v) = |\{i \in [1, n] \mid v_i = 1\}|$. For two vectors v and w of $\mathbb{F}_2^n$ we denote $\mathsf{d_H}(v, w)$ the Hamming distance between v and w, that is $\mathsf{d_H}(v, w) = \mathsf{w_H}(v + w)$.

2.1 Boolean Functions and Weightwise Considerations

In this part we recall general concepts on Boolean functions and their weightwise properties we use in this article. For a deeper introduction on Boolean functions and their cryptographic parameters we refer to the survey of [4] and to [6] for the weightwise properties, also called properties on the slices. For $k \in [0, n]$ we denote $\mathsf{E}_{k,n}$ the set $\{x \in \mathbb{F}_2^n \mid \mathsf{w_H}(x) = k\}$ and call it slice of the Boolean hypercube (of dimension n). Accordingly, the Boolean hypercube is partitioned into $n + 1$ slices where the elements have the same Hamming weight.

Definition 1 (Boolean Function). *A Boolean function f in n variables is a function from $\mathbb{F}_2^n$ to $\mathbb{F}_2$. The set of all Boolean functions in n variables is denoted by $\mathcal{B}_n$, and we denote by $\mathcal{B}_n^*$ the set without the null function.*

To denote when a property or a definition is restricted to a slice we use the subscript k. For example, for a n-variable Boolean function f we denote its support $\mathsf{supp}(f) = \{x \in \mathbb{F}_2^n \mid f(x) = 1\}$ and we denote $\mathsf{supp}_k(f)$ its support restricted to a slice, that is $\mathsf{supp}(f) \cap \mathsf{E}_{k,n}$.

Definition 2 (Balancedness). *A Boolean function $f \in \mathcal{B}_n$ is called balanced if $|\mathsf{supp}(f)| = 2^{n-1} = |\mathsf{supp}(f + 1)|$. For $k \in [0, n]$ the function is said balanced on the slice k if $||\mathsf{supp}_k(f)| - |\mathsf{supp}_k(f + 1)|| \leq 1$. In particular when $|\mathsf{E}_{k,n}|$ is even $|\mathsf{supp}_k(f)| = |\mathsf{supp}_k(f + 1)| = |\mathsf{E}_{k,n}|/2$.*

Definition 3 (Weightwise (Almost) Perfectly Balanced Function (WPB and WAPB)). *Let $m \in \mathbb{N}^*$ and f be a Boolean function in $n = 2^m$ variables. It will be called Weightwise Perfectly Balanced (WPB) if, for every $k \in [1, n-1]$, f is balanced on the slice k, that is $\forall k \in [1, n-1], |\mathsf{supp}_k(f)| = \binom{n}{k}/2$, and $f(0, \ldots, 0) = 0$ and $f(1, \ldots, 1) = 1$. The set of WPB functions in 2^m variables is denoted $\mathcal{WPB}_m$.*
When n is not a power of 2, other weights $k \notin \{0, n\}$ give slices of odd cardinality, in this case we call $f \in \mathcal{B}_n$ Weightwise Almost Perfectly Balanced (WAPB) if $|\mathsf{supp}_k(f)| = (|\mathsf{E}_{k,n}| \pm (|\mathsf{E}_{k,n}| \mod 2))/2$. The set of WAPB functions in n variables is denoted $\mathcal{WAPB}_n$.

Definition 4 (Walsh transform and restricted Walsh transform). *Let $f \in \mathcal{B}_n$ be a Boolean function, its Walsh transform W_f at $a \in \mathbb{F}_2^n$ is defined as: $W_f(a) := \sum_{x \in \mathbb{F}_2^n} (-1)^{f(x)+a \cdot x}$. Let $f \in \mathcal{B}_n$, $S \subset \mathbb{F}_2^n$, its Walsh transform restricted to S at $a \in \mathbb{F}_2^n$ is defined as: $W_{f,S}(a) := \sum_{x \in S} (-1)^{f(x)+ax}$. For $S = \mathsf{E}_{k,n}$ we denote $W_{f,\mathsf{E}_{k,n}}(a)$ by $\mathcal{W}_{f,k}(a)$, and for $a = 0_n$ we denote $\mathcal{W}_{f,k}(a)$ by $\mathcal{W}_{f,k}(0)$.*

Definition 5 (Nonlinearity). *The nonlinearity $\mathsf{NL}(f)$ of a Boolean function $f \in \mathcal{B}_n$, where n is a positive integer, is the minimum Hamming distance between f and all the affine functions in $\mathcal{B}_n$: $\mathsf{NL}(f) = \min_{g, \deg(g) \le 1}\{\mathsf{d_H}(f,g)\}$, where $g(x) = a \cdot x + \varepsilon$, $a \in \mathbb{F}_2^n, \varepsilon \in \mathbb{F}_2$ (where $\cdot$ is an inner product in $\mathbb{F}_2^n$, any choice of inner product will give the same value of $\mathsf{NL}(f)$).*

Definition 6 (Non Perfect Balancedness ([12] Definition 11)). *Let $m \in \mathbb{N}^*$, $n = 2^m$, and f an n-variable Boolean function, the non perfect balancedness of f, denoted $\mathsf{NPB}(f)$ is defined as $\mathsf{NPB}(f) = \min_{g \in \mathcal{WPB}_m} \mathsf{d_H}(f,g)$.*

Property 1 (NPB and restricted Walsh transform ([12], Proposition 2)). *Let $m \in \mathbb{N}^*$, $n = 2^m$, and $f \in \mathcal{B}_n$, the following holds on its non perfect balancedness:*

$$\mathsf{NPB}(f) = \frac{2 - \mathcal{W}_{f,0}(0) + \mathcal{W}_{f,n}(0)}{2} + \sum_{k=1}^{n-1} \frac{|\mathcal{W}_{f,k}(0)|}{2}.$$

Definition 7 (Algebraic Normal Form (ANF) and degree). *We call Algebraic Normal Form of a Boolean function f its n-variable polynomial representation over $\mathbb{F}_2$ (i.e. belonging to $\mathbb{F}_2[x_1, \ldots, x_n]/(x_1^2 + x_1, \ldots, x_n^2 + x_n))$: $f(x_1, \ldots, x_n) = \sum_{I \subseteq [1,n]} a_I \left(\prod_{i \in I} x_i\right)$ where $a_I \in \mathbb{F}_2$. The (algebraic) degree of f $\deg(f)$ is either $\max_{I \subseteq [1,n]} \{|I| \mid a_I = 1\}$ if f is not null, or $\deg(f) = 0$, otherwise.*

Property 2 ([6], Proposition 4). *If f is a WPB Boolean function of n variables, then the ANF of f contains at least one monomial of degree $n/2$.*

Definition 8 (Algebraic Immunity). *The algebraic immunity of a Boolean function $f \in \mathcal{B}_n$ is $\mathsf{AI}(f) = \min_{g \ne 0}\{\deg(g) \mid fg = 0 \text{ or } (f+1)g = 0\}$, where $\deg(g)$ is the algebraic degree of g. The function g is called an annihilator of f (or $f + 1$). Additionally, we denote $\mathsf{AN}(f) = \min_{g \ne 0}\{\deg(g) \mid fg = 0\}$.*

Property 3. *If $g \in \mathcal{B}_n^*$ is an annihilator of f and h another function such that $\mathsf{supp}(h) \subseteq \mathsf{supp}(g)$, then $hf = 0$.*

2.2 Families of WPB Functions

In this section we recall families of WPB functions exhibited in former works, they will be used as examples or building blocks.

Definition 9 (CMR WAPB construction (adapted from [6], Proposition 5)). *Let $n \in \mathbb{N}, n \geq 2$, the WAPB function f_n is recursively defined by $f_2(x_1, x_2) = x_1$ and for $n \geq 3$:*

$$f_n(x_1, \ldots, x_n) = \begin{cases} f_{n-1}(x_1, \ldots, x_{n-1}) & \text{if } n \text{ odd}, \\ f_{n-1}(x_1, \ldots, x_{n-1}) + x_{n-2} + \prod_{i=1}^{2^{d-1}} x_{n-i} & \text{if } n = 2^d; d > 1, \\ f_{n-1}(x_1, \ldots, x_{n-1}) + x_{n-2} + \prod_{i=1}^{2^d} x_{n-i} & \text{if } n = p \cdot 2^d; p \text{ odd}. \end{cases}$$

Re-indexing the variables the subfamily of WPB functions (when n is a power of 2) can be written as $f(x_1, x_2, \ldots, x_{2^m}) = \sum_{a=1}^{m} \sum_{i=1}^{2^{m-a}} \prod_{j=0}^{2^{a-1}-1} x_{i+j2^{m-a+1}}$.

Definition 10 (TL WPB construction (adapted from [33], Construction 1)). *Let $m \in \mathbb{N}^*$ and $n = 2^m \geq 4$ be an integer. A TL WPB Boolean function g on n-variable is such that:*

- *$g(0_n) = 0$ and $h(1_n) = 1$.*
- *$g(x, y) = 0$ if $\mathsf{w_H}(x) < \mathsf{w_H}(y)$, where $x, y \in \mathbb{F}_2^{m-1}$.*
- *$g(x, y) = 1$ if $\mathsf{w_H}(x) > \mathsf{w_H}(y)$, where $x, y \in \mathbb{F}_2^{m-1}$.*
- *the cardinality of $U_i = \mathsf{supp}(g) \cap \left\{(x, y) \in \mathbb{F}_2^{2^{m-1}} \times \mathbb{F}_2^{2^{m-1}} : \mathsf{w_H}(x) = \mathsf{w_H}(y) = i\right\}$ is exactly $\binom{2^{m-1}}{j}^2/2$ for all $0 < j < 2^{m-1}$.*

Remark 1. Despite Definition 10 may appear quite different respect the original paper, it is equivalent when applying the constrains from the definitions we consider. Namely, here we consider only the case where n is a power of two. Referring to Construction 1 of [33], this implies that the coefficients $c_1, \ldots, c_{k-1}$ must be zero. Moreover, in [33] $g(0_n) = 0$ and $g(1_n) = 1$ is not required for weightwise perfectly balancedness, differently from Definition 3. This implies that in this context we can only instantiate the construction with $(-1, 0, .., 0, 1)$ as input sequence, *i.e.* as in Definition 10.

Property 4 (TL WPB functions properties [33]). *Let $m \in \mathbb{N}^*$ and $n = 2^m$, a n-variable TL function g_n has optimal algebraic immunity $\mathsf{AI}(g_n) = \frac{n}{2}$.*

2.3 Symmetric Functions and Krawtchouk Polynomials

The n-variable Boolean symmetric functions are those that are constant on each slice $\mathsf{E}_{k,n}$ for $k \in [0, n]$. This class has been thoroughly studied in the context of cryptography, see *e.g.*[1–3, 5, 20, 29, 31]. The set of n-variable symmetric functions is denoted $\mathcal{SYM}_n$, and $|\mathcal{SYM}_n| = 2^{n+1}$. In this article we mainly consider two families of symmetric functions, which are both bases of the symmetric functions' vector space:

Definition 11 (Elementary symmetric functions). *Let $i \in [0, n]$, the elementary symmetric function of degree i in n variables, denoted $\sigma_{i,n}$, is the function which ANF contains all monomials of degree i and no monomials of other degrees.*

Definition 12 (Slice indicator functions). *Let $k \in [0, n]$, the indicator function of the slice of weight k is defined as: $\forall x \in \mathbb{F}_2^n$, $\varphi_{k,n}(x) = 1$ if and only if $\mathsf{w}_{\mathsf{H}}(x) = k$.*

Property 5 (Properties of elementary symmetric functions). *Let $n \in \mathbb{N}^*$, $d \in [0, n]$:*

- *The function $\sigma_{d,n}$ takes the value $\binom{k}{d}$ mod 2 on the elements of $\mathsf{E}_{k,n}$.*
- *The function $\sigma_{2,n}$ takes the value 1 only on the slices $\mathsf{E}_{k,n}$ such that $k = 2$ mod 4 or $k = 3$ mod 4.*
- *For n even the function $\sigma_{n/2,n}$ has algebraic immunity $n/2$ (e.g.[1, Theorem 9]).*

Property 6 [11, Proposition 4]. *Let $n \in \mathbb{N}^*$, $k \in [0, n]$ and $f \in \mathcal{B}_n$, the following holds on $f + \varphi_{k,n}$: $\forall a \in \mathbb{F}_2^n, \forall i \in [0, n] \setminus \{k\}, \mathcal{W}_{f+\varphi_{k,n},i}(a) = \mathcal{W}_{f,i}(a)$, and $\mathcal{W}_{f+\varphi_{k,n},k}(a) = -\mathcal{W}_{f,i}(a)$.*

We give two results relatively to Krawtchouk polynomials we will use in the article. We refer to *e.g.* [16] for more details on these polynomials and their properties.

Definition 13 (Krawtchouk polynomials). *The Krawtchouk polynomial of degree k, with $0 \leq k \leq n$ is given by: $\mathsf{K}_k(\ell, n) = \sum_{j=0}^{k} (-1)^j \binom{\ell}{j} \binom{n-\ell}{k-j}$.*

Property 7 (Krawtchouk polynomials relations). *Let $n \in \mathbb{N}^*$ and $k \in [0, n]$, the following relations hold:*

- $\mathsf{K}_k(\ell, n) = \sum_{x \in \mathsf{E}_{k,n}} (-1)^{a \cdot x}$, *where $a \in \mathbb{F}_2^n$ and $\ell = \mathsf{w}_{\mathsf{H}}(a)$,*
- *[9, Proposition 5] For n even, $k \in [0, n]$ $\mathsf{K}_k(n/2, n) = (-1)^{k/2} \binom{n/2}{k/2}$ if k is even, and null otherwise.*

3   General Results on the Algebraic Immunity of WPB Functions

In this section we give general results on the algebraic immunity of weightwise perfectly balanced functions, and give constructions in Sect. 4. First, we discuss the bounds on the algebraic immunity known from former constructions. Then, we focus on lower bounds of the algebraic immunity. In Sect. 3.1 we show a lower bound on the algebraic immunity of a secondary constructions of WPB functions, that encompasses CMR WPB functions. The lower bound result is also extended to the construction of WAPB functions from [37]. Then, in Sect. 3.2 we study the minimal algebraic immunity a WPB function can take. Finally, in Sect. 3.3 we complete this general investigation by experimentally determining the AI of WPB functions chosen at random in a small number of variables.

The algebraic immunity of a WPB function can reach the optimal value (of an n-variable Boolean function, $i.e. n/2$). It has been proven by Tang and Liu in [33] where they gave the first construction of WPB functions with optimal algebraic immunity (see Property 4). Since then the constructions presented in [26,27] generalize this construction and also have optimal algebraic immunity. No lower bound have been exhibited so far, only experimental results show that not all WPB functions have optimal algebraic immunity. The algebraic immunity of constructions (following the idea of modifying low degree functions slightly weightwise unbalanced, as pioneered in [25]) in respectively 4, 8 and 16 variables are provided in [14,34], reaching respectively an AI of 2, 3 and 3. In [11], the algebraic immunity of secondary constructions is provided in 8 and 16 variables. The secondary construction seeded with CMR functions result in functions of AI 3 in 8 variables and between 4 and 6 in 16 variables (the AI of f_8 itself is 3 and the one of f_{16} equals 4). The secondary construction seeded with Boolean functions from [15] give WPB functions with AI 4 and 7 in 8 and 16 variables respectively.

3.1   Lower Bound on the Algebraic Immunity of Secondary Constructions

The experimental results inventoried above show that not all WPB functions have optimal algebraic immunity, and in particular for the first values of n the AI of CMR function grows logarithmically in n. In the following we show that $\mathsf{AI}(f_{2^m})$ is at least m. To do so we first specify a secondary construction, at the same time a subfamily of the secondary construction presented in [6] and encompassing CMR functions. The secondary constructions of WPB functions from [6] is the following:

Definition 14 (Adapted from [6], Theorem 2). *Let* $m \in \mathbb{N}^*$, $n = 2^m$, f, f' *and* g *be* n-variable WPB functions and g' an arbitrary n-variable function. We define the $2n$ WPB function h as: $h(x, y) = f(x) + \prod_{i=1}^{n} x_i + g(y) + (f(x) + f'(x))g'(y)$ where $x, y \in \mathbb{F}_2^n$.

We focus on the restriction where g' is the null function, and iterate the construction with WPB functions in a different number of variables.

Definition 15. *Let* $m \in \mathbb{N}^*$, $n = 2^m$, f *and* g_0 *be two* n-variable WPB functions. Let $t \in \mathbb{N}$ and for $i \in [1, t]$ g_i be a 2^{m+i} WPB function. We define the 2^{m+t+1} WPB function $S(f, g_0, \ldots, g_t)$ as:

$$S(f, g_0, \ldots, g_t)(x, y^{(0)}, \ldots, y^{(t)}) = f(x) + g_0(y^{(0)}) + \prod_{j=1}^{n} y_j^{(0)} + \cdots + g_t(y^{(t)}) + \prod_{j=1}^{2^{m+t}} y_j^{(t)},$$

where $x, y^{(0)} \in \mathbb{F}_2^n$, and for $i \in [1, t]$ $y^{(i)} \in \mathbb{F}_2^{2^{m+i}}$.

Note that CMR function, f_{2^m}, is obtained in [6] from this construction, taking $f_2 = x_1$ in 2 variables, $f = f_2 = g_0$ and iterating.

Contrarily to the secondary construction of Definition 14, the one from Definition 15 can be written as a direct sum of functions (that is, a sum of functions acting on different variables). We use this structure to give a lower bound on the algebraic immunity of any function built as $S(f, g_0, \ldots, g_t)$, and an upper bound for CMR functions. We first recall a result on the algebraic immunity of direct sums from [21].

Property 8 (Adapted from [21], Lemma 6). *Let* $t \in \mathbb{N}^*$, *and* $f_1, \ldots, f_t$ *be* t *Boolean functions, if for* $r \in [1, t]$ *there exists* r *different indexes* $i_1, \ldots, i_r$ *of* $[1, t]$ *such that* $\forall j \in [1, r], \deg(f_{i_j}) \geq j$ *then* $\mathsf{AI}(\mathsf{DS}(f_1, \ldots, f_t)) \geq r$, *where* $\mathsf{DS}(f_1, \ldots, f_t)$ *denotes the direct sum of* f_1 *to* f_t.

Proposition 1. *Let* $m \in \mathbb{N}^*$, $n = 2^m$, f *and* g_0 *be two* n-*variable WPB functions. Let* $t \in \mathbb{N}$ *and for* $i \in [1, t]$ g_i *be a* 2^{m+i}-*variable WPB function, then* $\mathsf{AI}(S(f, g_0, \ldots, g_t)) \geq t + 2$.

Proof. First, we remark that $S(f, g_0, \ldots, g_t)$ is the direct sum of $t + 2$ functions, f and $g_i' = g_i + \prod_{j=0}^{2^{m+i}} y_j^{(i)}$ for i in $[0, t]$. f has degree at least 1 since it is a WPB function, and for all i in $[0, t]$ the function g_i' has degree 2^{m+i}. The latter comes from the fact that g_i has degree at most $2^{m+i} - 1$ since it is WPB and therefore balanced, and then the addition with the degree 2^{m+i} monomial makes g_i' a 2^{m+i}-degree function. Then, for $i \in [0, t]$ we have $\deg(g_i') = 2^{m+i} \geq 2 + i$, it allows to apply Property 8 and to conclude $\mathsf{AI}(S(f, g_0, \ldots, g_t)) \geq t + 2$.

We recall a result form [8] on the number of annihilators of f and $f + 1$ when f is a direct sum with a linear part.

Property 9 (Adapted from [8], Proposition 9). *Let* $f \in \mathcal{B}_n$ *be the direct sum of a linear function* g *in* $k > 0$ *variables and* h *in* $n - k$ *variables then:* $\forall d \in [0, n]$, $N_d^0 = N_d^1$, *where* N_d^ε *for* $\varepsilon \in \{0, 1\}$ *denotes the number of (linearly) independent annihilators of* $f + \varepsilon$ *of degree at most* d.

Proposition 2. *Let* $m \in \mathbb{N}^*$, *and* f_{2^m} *be the* 2^m-*variable CMR function (Definition 9), then* $\mathsf{AI}(f_{2^m}) \geq m$, *and for* $m > 3$, $\mathsf{AI}(f_{2^m}) \leq 2^{m-2}$

Proof. The bound $\mathsf{AI}(f_{2^m}) \geq m$ is a consequence of Proposition 1. Since $\mathsf{AI}(f_2) = 1$, $\mathsf{AI}(f_4) = 2$, and by construction for $m > 2$ we have $f_{2^{m+1}} = S(f_2, f_2, f_4, \ldots, f_{2^m})$ and $\mathsf{AI}(S(f_2, f_2, f_4, \ldots, f_{2^m})) \geq m + 1$ by Proposition 1, a direct induction gives $\mathsf{AI}(f_{2^m}) \geq m$.

The bound $\mathsf{AI}(f_{2^m}) \leq 2^{m-2}$ comes from the upper bound on the algebraic immunity of a direct sum, the AI of the direct sum cannot be greater than the sum of the two AIs (*e.g.* [4], Section 9.1.4). We show the result by induction. For $m = 4$ since $\mathsf{AI}(f_m) = 4$, $\mathsf{AI}(f_{2^m}) \leq 2^{m-2}$ holds. Then for $m + 1 > 4$ we can write $f_{2^{m+1}}$ as $S(f_{2^m}, f_{2^m})$ which is the direct sum of f_{2^m} and $g = f_{2^m} + \prod_{i=1}^{2^m} y_i$. By hypothesis $\mathsf{AI}(f_{2^m}) \leq 2^{m-2}$, and by construction g differs from f_{2^m} only in the value 1_{2^m} therefore an annihilator of f_{2^m} is also an annihilator of g since $f_{2^m}(1_{2^m}) = 1$ (since f is WPB). Since f_{2^m} can be written as the direct sum of the linear function f_2 and a $2^m - 2$ variable function, from Property 9 for each annihilator of f_{2^m} of degree d there is an annihilator of $1+f_{2^m}$ of the same degree, it guarantees that $\mathsf{AI}(g) \leq \mathsf{AI}(f_{2^m})$. Therefore, $\mathsf{AI}(f_{2^{m+1}}) \leq 2 \cdot \mathsf{AI}(f_{2^m}) \leq 2^{m-1}$.

With a similar approach we can bound the algebraic immunity of the secondary construction of WAPB functions from Zhu and Su [37].

Definition 16 (Adapted from [37], Theorem 2). *Let $t \in \mathbb{N}^*$ and $n_1, \ldots, n_t$ be different powers of 2, and for $i \in [1,t]$, f_i be a WPB function in n_i variables. We call ZS construction the function f in $\sum_{i=1}^{t} n_i$ variables the direct sum $ZS(f_1, \ldots, f_t) = \sum_{i=1}^{t} f_i$.*

Proposition 3. *Let $t \in \mathbb{N}^*$ and $n_1, \ldots, n_t$ be different powers of 2, and for $i \in [1,t]$, f_i be a WPB function in n_i variables. The function $f = ZS(f_1, \ldots, f_t)$ is such that:*

$$\mathsf{AI}(f) \geq \begin{cases} t-1 & \text{if } \exists j, k \in [1,t] \text{ such that } n_j = 1 \text{ and } n_k = 2, \\ t & \text{otherwise,} \end{cases}$$

and $\mathsf{AI}(f) \leq \left\lceil \sum_{i=1}^{t} n_i/2 \right\rceil$.

Proof. The upper bound comes from the fact that any n-variable function has its AI upper bounded by $\lceil n/2 \rceil$. Relatively to the lower bound, since an n-variable WPB function has algebraic degree at least $n/2$ (see Property 2), we can apply Property 8 on the f_i. When there are both an f_j in 1 variable and an f_k in 2 variables, we can only guarantee to find a chain of $t - 1$ indexes r_1 to r_{t-1} such that $\deg(f_{r_i}) \geq i$ since both f_j and f_k could have degree 1. Since, apart from $n_j = 1$ and $n_k = 2$, the different powers of 2, n_i, ensure that the condition $\deg(f_{r_i}) \geq i$ can be fulfilled, we obtain $\mathsf{AI}(f) \geq t - 1$. $\qquad\square$

3.2   Minimal Algebraic Immunity of WPB Functions

In the previous parts we showed that there exist WPB functions which algebraic immunity cannot be higher than 2^{m-2} (Proposition 2), and we saw examples close to $\log m$ or less for small values of m. In the following, we demonstrate that for $m \geq 2$ the minimal AI that a WPB function can reach is in fact a constant.

We begin by defining the minimal degree of annihilator (non null) a 2^m-variable WPB function (or its complement) can have, and give an alternative expression of this quantity.

Definition 17 (Minimal degree of annihilator reachable by a 2^m-variable WPB function). *Let $m \in \mathbb{N}^*$ and $\varepsilon \in \{0,1\}$, we denote d_m^ε the quantity:*

$$\mathsf{d}_m^\varepsilon = \min\{\mathsf{AN}(f + \varepsilon) \mid f \in \mathcal{WPB}_m\}.$$

Lemma 1. *Let $m \in \mathbb{N}^*$, $n = 2^m$ and $g \in \mathcal{B}_{2^m}^*$ such that $\mathcal{W}_{k,g}(0) \geq 0 \; \forall k \in [1, 2^m - 1]$.*

1. If $\mathcal{W}_{n,g}(0) \geq 0$, then there exists $f \in \mathcal{WPB}_m$ such that g is an annihilator of f.
2. If $\mathcal{W}_{0,g}(0) \geq 0$, then there exists $f \in \mathcal{WPB}_m$ such that g is an annihilator of $1 + f$.

Proof. Since $\mathcal{W}_{k,g}(0) \geq 0$ there are at least $\binom{n}{k}/2$ elements of Hamming weight k not in the support of g for $k \in [1, n-1]$. Therefore, we can build a function h such that $|\mathsf{supp}_k(h)| = \frac{\binom{n}{k}}{2}$ and $\mathsf{supp}_k(h) \supseteq \mathsf{supp}_k(g)$ for all $k \in [1, n-1]$. We have two cases:

a. Suppose $\mathcal{W}_{n,g}(0) \geq 0$. This implies that $g(1_n) = 0$. Then, we can set $h(1_n) = 0$ and $h(0_n) = 1$, in order to get a function $h \in \mathcal{B}_{2^m}^*$ such that $\mathsf{supp}(1 + h) \subseteq \mathsf{supp}(1 + g)$ and $(1 + h) \in \mathcal{WPB}_m$.
b. Suppose $\mathcal{W}_{0,g}(0) \geq 0$. This implies that $g(0_n) = 0$. Then, that we can set $h(1_n) = 1$ and $h(0_n) = 0$, in order to get $\mathsf{supp}(1 + h) \subseteq \mathsf{supp}(1 + g)$ and $h \in \mathcal{WPB}_m$.

To conclude it is sufficient to notice that $1 + g$ is an annihilator of g. Indeed, Property 3 implies that $g(h + 1) = 0$, *i.e.* in both cases g is a non constant annihilator of $1 + h$. Therefore, 1. and 2. follow by setting $f = 1 + h$ and $f = h$, respectively.

Proposition 4 (Equivalent characterization of d_m^ε). *Let $m \in \mathbb{N}^*$ and $\varepsilon \in \{0, 1\}$. It holds $\mathsf{d}_m^\varepsilon = \min\{\deg(f), f \in \mathcal{B}_{2^m}^* \,|\, \forall k \in [1 - \varepsilon, 2^m - \varepsilon], \mathcal{W}_{k,f}(0) \geq 0\}$.*

Proof. We denote $n = 2^m$. First we prove $\mathsf{d}_m^\varepsilon \geq \min\{\deg(f), f \in \mathcal{B}_n^* \,|\, \forall k \in [1 - \varepsilon, n - \varepsilon], \mathcal{W}_{k,f}(0) \geq 0\}$. We take $f \in \mathcal{WPB}_m$, and g an annihilator (not null) of f of degree d_m^0. Since f is WPB, f has exactly $|\mathsf{E}_{k,n}|/2$ elements of Hamming weight k (for $k \in [1, n-1]$) in its support and one in $\mathsf{E}_{n,n}$, therefore g takes the value 0 over all these elements. Consequently, $\forall k \in [1, 2^m]$:

$$\mathcal{W}_{k,g}(0) = \sum_{\substack{x \in \mathsf{E}_{k,n}}} (-1)^{g(x)} = \sum_{\substack{x \in \mathsf{E}_{k,n} \\ g(x)=0}} 1 - \sum_{\substack{x \in \mathsf{E}_{k,n} \\ g(x)=1}} 1 \geq \frac{\binom{n}{k}}{2} - \sum_{\substack{x \in \mathsf{E}_{k,n} \\ g(x)=1}} 1 \geq 0.$$

Similarly, if we consider g an annihilator (not null) of $1 + f$ of degree d_m^1. Since f is WPB $|\mathsf{supp}_k(f)| = |\mathsf{supp}_k(f+1)|$ for all $k \in [1, 2^m - 1]$ and $|\mathsf{supp}_0(1+f)| = 1$, we obtain that $\mathcal{W}_{k,g}(0) \geq 0$ for $k \in [0, 2^m - 1]$.

Then, we prove $\mathsf{d}_m^\varepsilon \leq \min\{\deg(f), f \in \mathcal{B}_n^* \,|\, \forall k \in [1 - \varepsilon, n - \varepsilon], \mathcal{W}_{k,f}(0) \geq 0\}$. We take g_0, g_1 two 2^m-variable functions of minimum degree such that $\mathcal{W}_{k,g_\varepsilon}(0) \geq 0$ for all $k \in [1 - \varepsilon, n - \varepsilon]$. From Lemma 1 we can build two functions f_ε for $\varepsilon \in \{0, 1\}$, such that f_ε are WPB, and g_ε is a non null annihilator of $f_\varepsilon + \varepsilon$ by construction. This allows to conclude. □

As a first remark, since the algebraic immunity of a function f is the minimum between $\mathsf{AN}(f)$ and $\mathsf{AN}(f + 1)$ (Definition 8), we have that $\min\{\mathsf{d}_m^0, \mathsf{d}_m^1\}$ is the minimal AI a WPB function can have. Then, since for any function f its complement $1 + f$ is an annihilator, for each WPB function it gives an annihilator of the same degree, therefore d_m^ε is upper bounded by the minimal degree of a 2^m-variable WPB function, that is 2^{m-1} for $m \geq 1$ (see Property 2). In the following we show that $d_1^\varepsilon = 1$, but $d_m^\varepsilon > 1$ for $m > 1$.

Lemma 2. *Let $m \in \mathbb{N}^*$, $n = 2^m$ and $\varepsilon \in \{0,1\}$, then $d_1^\varepsilon = 1$ and for $m > 1$ $d_m^\varepsilon > 1$.*

Proof. We start with the particular case $m = 1$. In this context, denoting x_1 and x_2 the 2 variables, there are only two WPB functions: $f = x_1$ and $g = x_2$. They are respectively annihilated by the degree-1 function $1 + x_1$ and $1 + x_2$, and not by the constant function equal to 1, which allows to conclude $d_1^0 = 1$. Furthermore, the two complementary functions of 2-variable WPB are $1 + x_1$ and $1 + x_2$, similarly annihilated by a degree 1 function and not by the constant function equal to one, so in this case $d_1^1 = 1$. This implies that 1 is also the minimum on the algebraic immunity.

For $m > 1$, we show that no affine function f can satisfy the characterisation of d_m^ε from Proposition 4. If f is constant, f cannot be the null function by definition of d_m^ε, and the constant function equal to one is such that $\mathcal{W}_{k,f}(0) < 0$ for all $k \in [1,n]$. Then, any non constant affine function is balanced, therefore: $W_f(0) = 0 = \sum_{i=0}^n \mathcal{W}_{f,k}(0)$. The condition in the definition of d_m^0 form Proposition 4 for $k = n$ forces $\mathcal{W}_{f,n}(0) = 1$ and therefore the restriction on the other coefficients can be only satisfied if $\mathcal{W}_{f,0}(0) = -1$, and for all $k \in [1, n-1]$, $\mathcal{W}_{f,k}(0) = 0$. This implies that f is balanced on all slices, and more precisely that $f + 1$ is a weightwise perfectly balanced function. Similarly, if we consider the condition in the definition of d_m^1 form Proposition 4, we obtain that f should be a weightwise perfectly balanced function. Since a WPB function has degree at least 2^{m-1} by Property 2, both these cases are impossible. □

We show that in fact d_m^0 is constant in m, more precisely that for $m \geq 2$ there are always 2^m-variable WPB functions that are annihilated by quadratic functions.

Proposition 5. *Let $m \in \mathbb{N}$, for all $m \geq 2$, $d_m^0 = 2$.*

Proof. We denote $n = 2^m$ for readability. We show that there exist degree-2 functions $g \in \mathcal{B}_n$ such that $\forall k \in [1,n]$, $\mathcal{W}_{g,k}(0) \geq 0$ or equivalently $\forall k \in [1,n]$, $|\mathsf{supp}_k(g)| \leq \binom{n}{k}/2$. More precisely we consider the functions with algebraic normal form $x_i x_j + x_i x_k$ where $i, j, k \in [1,n]$ and $i \neq j \neq k$, without lost of generality we take $g = x_1(x_2 + x_3)$. In the following we consider the size of the support of g on each slice.

- If $k \in [0,1]$, g takes only the value 0 hence $|\mathsf{supp}_k(g)| \leq \binom{n}{k}/2$.
- For $k = 2$, $g(x) = 1$ only when $x_1 = x_2 = 1$ or $x_1 = x_3 = 1$, therefore $|\mathsf{supp}_2(g)| = 2 \leq 2^{m-2}(2^m - 1) = \binom{n}{2}/2$.
- For $k \geq 3$, we split $x \in \mathbb{F}_2^n$ as (y, z) where $y \in \mathbb{F}_2^3$ and $z \in \mathbb{F}_2^{n-3}$, and determine the number of elements such that $g(x) = 1$ based on the value of y. The function g takes the value 1 only when $x_1(x_2 + x_3) = 1$ that is when

$y = (1,1,0)$ or $y = (1,0,1)$, thereafter for $x \in E_{k,n}$ it corresponds to 2/3 of the cases where $\mathsf{w_H}(y) = 2$ and none when $\mathsf{w_H}(y) \neq 2$. It allows us to get the cardinal of $\mathsf{supp}_k(g)$:

$$|\mathsf{supp}_k(g)| = 2\binom{n-3}{k-2}.$$

Then, we have to compare this value to $\binom{n}{k}/2$:

$$2\binom{n-3}{k-2} \leq \frac{\binom{n}{k}}{2} \Leftrightarrow$$

$$4\binom{n-3}{k-2} \leq \binom{n-3}{k-3} + 3\binom{n-3}{k-2} + 3\binom{n-3}{k-1} + \binom{n-3}{k},$$

$$\Leftrightarrow \binom{n-3}{k-2} \leq \binom{n-3}{k-3} + 3\binom{n-3}{k-1} + \binom{n-3}{k}.$$

Since $n-3$ is odd the binomial coefficient $\binom{n-3}{k-2}$ is lower than or equal to one of the two binomial coefficients $\binom{n-3}{k-1}$ and $\binom{n-3}{k-3}$, Therefore $|\mathsf{supp}_k(g)| \leq \binom{n}{k}/2$ that is $\mathcal{W}_{k,g}(0) \geq 0$.

It allows to conclude $\mathsf{d}_m^0 \leq 2$ from Proposition 4, and since for $m \geq 2$ $\mathsf{d}_m^0 > 1$ from Lemma 2, we obtain $\mathsf{d}_m^0 = 2$.

Theorem 1. *Let $m \in \mathbb{N}$, for all $m \geq 2$, $\min\{\mathsf{AI}(f) : f \in \mathcal{WPB}_m\} = 2$.*

Proof. From Lemma 2 and Proposition 5 we have $\min\{\mathsf{AI}(f) : f \in \mathcal{WPB}_m\} = \min\{\mathsf{d}_m^0, \mathsf{d}_m^1\} = 2$. □

Corollary 1. *If $f \in \mathcal{WPB}_2$, then $\mathsf{AI}(f) = 2$.*

Proof. For every n-variable Boolean function f we have that $\mathsf{AI}(f) \leq \lceil n/2 \rceil$ and $\mathsf{AI}(f) \geq 2$ from Theorem 1. This implies $\mathsf{AI}(f) = 2$ for all $f \in \mathcal{WPB}_2$. □

Additionally, in Sect. 4.2 we give a construction to build WPB functions with minimal algebraic immunity, and study its properties.

3.3   Algebraic Immunity Distribution

To conclude this section we perform an experimental investigation on the algebraic immunity distribution for WPB functions in a small number of variables, following the same principle as in [10,12]. Exhausting $\mathcal{WPB}_2$, we found that all the WPB function in 4 variables have algebraic immunity 2, it is indeed coherent with Corollary 1. For $m = 3$, we extrapolated an approximation of the algebraic immunity distribution from a sample of size larger than 2^{23}. As shown by Table 1, 8-variable WPB functions with non-optimal algebraic immunity are rare. In fact, for 16 variables we were not able to collect a sample sufficiently large to get at least a function with AI lower than 8.

Table 1. Approximation of the algebraic immunity distribution in $\mathcal{WPB}_3$ via sampling elements of $\mathcal{WPB}_3$ uniformly at random: $\tilde{p}_{\mathsf{AI}}(x) = \{f \in S \colon \mathsf{AI}(f) = x\} / |S|$ where S is a sample of size larger than 2^{23}.

x	3	4
$\tilde{p}_{\mathsf{AI}}(x)\%$	0.004	99.996
#	353	8427167

4 Constructions of WPB Functions with Bounded Algebraic Immunity

In this section we exploit GM construction [12, Construction 1] in order to produce WPB functions with bounded algebraic immunity and prescribed nonlinearity. First, we focus on constructions with upper bounded AI in Sect. 4.1. More specifically, in Sect. 4.2 we construct WPB functions reaching the lowest algebraic immunity, the lower bound from Theorem 1. We refer to these particular functions with AI 2 as *porcelain* functions, since independently of their aesthetic, we do not advise to use them when implementing a cipher. Then, we prove that the WPB family of functions with almost optimal nonlinearity described in [12] has also minimal algebraic immunity. Finally, in Sect. 4.4 we show how to build WPB functions with lower bounded AI from GM construction. As an example we give a family of WPB functions with AI at least $2^{m-1} - m + 1$.

4.1 Construction with Upper Bounded AI

We describe here a method to construct WPB functions with upper bounded algebraic immunity and prescribed nonlinearity. The main idea is to construct a WPB function forcing a suitable function f of degree d to be an annihilator. We observed that we can efficiently built WPB functions as in Lemma 1 by seeding with certain functions the construction proposed by Gini and Méaux in [12] recalled in Construction 1. Indeed, their algorithm produces a WPB function from any Boolean function in 2^m variables by modifying the support of the input function on each slice to make it perfectly balanced, in such a manner that can be compatible with our method.

We first summarize some useful properties of Construction 1 extending Theorem 2 of [12]:

Proposition 6. *Let $m \in \mathbb{N}$, $m \geq 2$ and $n = 2^m$. Any function h given by Construction 1 with input g is weightwise perfectly balanced. For $k \in [1, n-1]$:*

- *If $g \in \mathcal{B}_n^*$ is such that $\mathcal{W}_{k,g}(0) \leq 0$. Then $\mathsf{supp}_k(h) \subseteq \mathsf{supp}_k(g)$.*
- *If $g \in \mathcal{B}_n^*$ is such that $\mathcal{W}_{k,g}(0) \geq 0$. Then $\mathsf{supp}_k(h) \supseteq \mathsf{supp}_k(g)$.*

Additionally, $\mathsf{NL}(h) \geq \mathsf{NPB}(g) - \mathsf{NL}(g)$.

Construction 1. Construction 1 from [12]

Input: Let $m \in \mathbb{N}$, $m \geq 2$, $n = 2^m$ and g a n-variable function.
Output: $h \in \mathcal{WPB}_m$.
1: Initiate the support of h to $\mathsf{supp}(g)$.
2: If $0_n \in \mathsf{supp}(g)$ remove 0_n from $\mathsf{supp}(h)$.
3: If $1_n \notin \mathsf{supp}(g)$ add 1_n to $\mathsf{supp}(h)$.
4: **for** $k \leftarrow 1$ to $n-1$ **do**
5:     Compute $C_{k,n} = \mathcal{W}_{g,k}(0)/2$,
6:     **if** $C_{k,n} < 0$ **then**
7:         remove $|C_{k,n}|$ elements from $\mathsf{supp}_k(h)$,
8:     **else**
9:         **if** $C_{k,n} > 0$ **then**
10:             add $C_{k,n}$ new elements to $\mathsf{supp}_k(h)$,
11:         **end if**
12:     **end if**
13: **end for**
14: **return** h

Proof. The first part (g is WPB) comes from Theorem 2 of [12]. Then, if for $k \in [1, n-1]$ $\mathcal{W}_{k,g}(0) \leq 0$, we get $C_{k,n} \leq 0$ in Construction 1. Hence, from step 7 we have that $\mathsf{supp}_k(h) \subseteq \mathsf{supp}_k(g)$. While, if $\mathcal{W}_{k,g}(0) \geq 0$, we get $C_{k,n} \geq 0$. Hence, from step 10 we have that $\mathsf{supp}_k(h) \supseteq \mathsf{supp}_k(g)$. Finally, for the nonlinearity, if a is an affine function, $\mathsf{NL}(g) \leq \mathsf{d_H}(g, a) \leq \mathsf{d_H}(g, h) + \mathsf{d_H}(h, a)$. This implies that $\mathsf{NL}(h) \geq \mathsf{NL}(g) - \mathsf{NPB}(g)$, since $\mathsf{d_H}(g, h) = \mathsf{NPB}(g)$ from Theorem 2 of [12]. □

Thus, combining Proposition 6 with arguments similar to Lemma 1 we obtain that seeding Construction 1 with suitable functions we can obtain WPB functions with upper bounded algebraic immunity.

Theorem 2. *Let $m \in \mathbb{N}$, $m \geq 2$ and $n = 2^m$. Let function $g \in \mathcal{B}_n^*$ such that $\mathcal{W}_{k,g}(0) \geq 0$ for all $k \in [1, n]$. Any function f given by Construction 1 seeded with $g + 1$ has the following properties:*

1. $f \in \mathcal{WPB}_m$,
2. $\mathsf{AI}(f) \leq \deg(g)$,
3. $\mathsf{NL}(f) \geq \mathsf{NL}(g) - \mathsf{NPB}(g)$.

Proof. From Proposition 6 we have that $f \in \mathcal{WPB}_m$, $\mathsf{NL}(f) \geq \mathsf{NL}(g + 1) - \mathsf{NPB}(g + 1) = \mathsf{NL}(f) \geq \mathsf{NL}(g) - \mathsf{NPB}(g)$ and $\mathsf{supp}_k(f) \subseteq \mathsf{supp}_k(1 + g)$ for all $k \in [1, n-1]$. Moreover, since $\mathcal{W}_{n,g}(0) \geq 0$, $(1 + g)(1_n) = 1$. This implies that $\mathsf{supp}(f) \subseteq \mathsf{supp}(1 + g)$. Since $(1 + g)$ is an annihilator of g, from Property 3 we obtain that $gf = 0$. Namely, g is a non constant annihilator of f. Therefore, $\mathsf{AI}(f) \leq \deg(g)$. □

Theorem 3. *Let $m \in \mathbb{N}$, $m \geq 2$ and $n = 2^m$. Let function $g \in \mathcal{B}_n^*$ such that $\mathcal{W}_{k,g}(0) \geq 0$ for all $k \in [0, n-1]$. Any function f given by Construction 1 seeded with g has the following properties:*

1. $f \in \mathcal{WPB}_m$,
2. $\mathsf{AI}(f) \leq \deg(g)$,
3. $\mathsf{NL}(f) \geq \mathsf{NL}(g) - \mathsf{NPB}(g)$.

Proof. From Proposition 6 we have that $f \in \mathcal{WPB}_m$, $\mathsf{NL}(f) \geq \mathsf{NL}(g) - \mathsf{NPB}(g)$ and $\mathsf{supp}_k(f) \supseteq \mathsf{supp}_k(g)$ for all $k \in [1, n-1]$. Moreover, since $\mathcal{W}_{n,g}(0) \geq 0$, $g(0_n) = 0$. This implies that $\mathsf{supp}(1+f) \subseteq \mathsf{supp}(1+g)$. Since $(1+g)$ is an annihilator of g, from Property 3 we obtain that $g(1+f) = 0$. Namely, g is a non constant annihilator of $1+f$. Therefore, $\mathsf{AI}(f) \leq \deg(g)$. □

4.2   Porcelain WPB Functions

Using the characterization of d_m^0 in Sect. 3.2 we proved that for any $m \geq 2$ there exist WPB functions having algebraic immunity 2. Via Construction 1 we can explicitly construct many of them. We consider as primary material, for producing porcelain WPB functions, any *kaolin* function $\kappa_n = x_i(x_j + x_\ell)$ where i, j, ℓ are distinct. In fact, in the proof of Proposition 5 we showed that functions of this kind satisfy the hypotheses of Theorem 2. Thus, we have that any function h given by Construction 1 seeded by κ_n has the following properties: h is a WPB function and $\mathsf{AI}(h) \leq 2$, hence $\mathsf{AI}(h) = 2$. Moreover, we remark that kaolin functions are very peculiar, as their nonlinearity and their non perfect balancedness coincide:

Proposition 7. *Let $m \in \mathbb{N}$, $m \geq 2$ and $n = 2^m$, let $\kappa_n \in \mathcal{B}_n$ denote a function of the form $x_i(x_j + x_\ell)$ such that $i \neq j \neq \ell$. The following holds:*

$$\mathsf{NPB}(\kappa_n) = 2^{n-2}, \quad and \quad \mathsf{NL}(\kappa_n) = 2^{n-2}.$$

Proof. We begin with the non perfect balancedness, using Property 1 we get:

$$\mathsf{NPB}(\kappa_n) = \frac{2 - \mathcal{W}_{\kappa_n,0}(0) + \mathcal{W}_{\kappa_n,n}(0)}{2} + \sum_{k=1}^{n-1} \frac{|\mathcal{W}_{\kappa_n,k}(0)|}{2}.$$

Following the proof of Proposition 5 we get:

- $\mathcal{W}_{\kappa_n,0}(0) = 1$ and $\mathcal{W}_{\kappa_n,1}(0) = n$ since $|\mathsf{supp}_k(\kappa_n)| = 0$ for $k \in [0, 1]$,
- $\mathcal{W}_{\kappa_n,2}(0) = \binom{n}{2} - 4$ since $|\mathsf{supp}_2(\kappa_n)| = 2$ for $k \in [0, 1]$,
- $\mathcal{W}_{\kappa_n,k}(0) = \binom{n}{k} - 4\binom{n-3}{k-2}$ for $k \in [3, n]$ since $|\mathsf{supp}_k(\kappa_n)| = 2\binom{n-3}{k-2}$.

Hence we obtain:

$$\mathsf{NPB}(\kappa_n) = \frac{2-1+1}{2} + \frac{1}{2}\left(n + \binom{n}{2} - 4 + \sum_{k=3}^{n-1}\binom{n}{k} - 4\binom{n-3}{k-2}\right),$$

$$= \frac{1}{2}\left(\sum_{k=0}^{n}\binom{n}{k} - 4\binom{n-3}{k-2}\right) = 2^{n-1} - 2\sum_{k=0}^{n}\binom{n-3}{k-2},$$

$$= 2^{n-1} - 2^{n-2} = 2^{n-2}.$$

Then, we determine the nonlinearity of κ_n. First we give the nonlinearity of κ_3. Since the function κ_3 has degree 2 it is not affine hence $\mathsf{NL}(\kappa_3) > 0$, its degree is not maximal hence the nonlinearity cannot be odd, and since κ_3 has weight 2 we can conclude $\mathsf{NL}(\kappa_3) = 2$. Then, in n variables κ_n can be written as the direct sum of κ_3 and the null function in $n-3$ variables, using the formula of the nonlinearity of direct sums (e.g. [4], Section 7.1.9.I.B), $\mathsf{NL}(\kappa_n) = \mathsf{NL}(\kappa_3) \cdot 2^{n-3} + \mathsf{NL}(0) \cdot 2^3 - 2 \cdot \mathsf{NL}(0) \cdot \mathsf{NL}(\kappa_3) = 2 \cdot 2^{n-3} + 0 \cdot 2^3 - 2 \cdot 0 \cdot 2 = 2^{n-2}$. □

We compute now the number of porcelain WPB functions that can be generated by one kaolin function κ_n. Equation (9) from [12] gives the number of WPB functions that can be produced by Construction 1 for a fixed seed g:

$$\mathfrak{F}_n(g) = \prod_{k=1}^{n-1} \binom{\frac{1}{2}\binom{n}{k} + |C_{k,n}|}{|C_{k,n}|}, \tag{1}$$

where $C_{k,n} = \mathcal{W}_{g,k}(0_n)/2$. Notice that, although Corollary 1 of [12] is for a specific input, the proof of the value of $\mathfrak{F}_n$ holds in general. From the proof of Proposition 7 the following holds: $C_{k,n} = \mathcal{W}_{\kappa_n,k}(0_n)/2$. Namely,

$$\mathfrak{F}_n(\kappa_n) = \binom{n}{\frac{n}{2}} \binom{\binom{n}{2} - 2}{\frac{1}{2}\binom{n}{2} - 2} \prod_{k=3}^{n-1} \binom{\binom{n}{k} - 2\binom{n-3}{k-2}}{\frac{1}{2}\binom{n}{k} - 2\binom{n-3}{k-2}}$$

For instance, $\mathfrak{F}_8(\kappa_8) > 2^{152}$ and $\mathfrak{F}_{16}(\kappa_{16}) > 2^{44521}$.

4.3   WPB Functions from [12]

The authors of [12] apply their construction to produce a family of WPB functions with high nonlinearity. The used seed function is $g_n = \sigma_{2,n} + \ell_{n/2}$, where $\ell_{n/2} = \sum_{i=1}^{n/2} x_i$. We now prove that this function satisfies the hypotheses of Theorem 3, which implies that all WPB functions from Construction 1 seeded with g_n have algebraic immunity 2 since the function g_n has degree 2.

Proposition 8. Let $m \in \mathbb{N}$, $m \geq 2$ and $n = 2^m$. $\forall k \in [0, n-1]$, $\mathcal{W}_{k,g_n}(0) \geq 0$.

Proof. First, we determine the values of $\mathcal{W}_{g_n,k}(0)$. Since $\ell_{n/2}$ is a linear function of $n/2$ terms using Property 7 Item 1 we have:

$$\mathcal{W}_{\ell_{n/2},k}(0) = \sum_{x \in \mathsf{E}_{k,n}} (-1)^{x \cdot (1_{n/2}, 0_{n/2})} = \mathsf{K}_k(n/2, n).$$

Then, using Property 7 Item 2 we obtain:

- For $k = 0 \mod 4$, $\mathcal{W}_{\ell_{n/2},k}(0) = \binom{n/2}{k/2} \geq 0$;
- for $k = 1 \mod 4$ and $k = 3 \mod 4$, $\mathcal{W}_{\ell_{n/2},k}(0) = 0$,
- for $k = 2 \mod 4$, $\mathcal{W}_{\ell_{n/2},k}(0) = -\binom{n/2}{k/2} \leq 0$.

Then, we can determine the sign of $\mathcal{W}_{g_n,k}(0)$ using Property 6, since $g_n = \ell_{n/2} + \sigma_{2,n}$ we get $\mathcal{W}_{g_n,k}(0) = \mathcal{W}_{\ell_{n/2},k}(0)$ when $\sigma_{2,n}$ takes the value 0 on $\mathsf{E}_{k,n}$ and $\mathcal{W}_{g_n,k}(0) = -\mathcal{W}_{\ell_{n/2},k}(0)$ when $\sigma_{2,n}$ takes the value 1 on $\mathsf{E}_{k,n}$. Using Property 5 Item 2, the sign changes only when $k = 2 \mod 4$ or $k = 3 \mod 4$. Therefore we obtain:

- For $k = 0 \mod 4$, $\mathcal{W}_{g_n,k}(0) = \mathcal{W}_{\ell_{n/2},k}(0) = \binom{n/2}{k/2} \geq 0$,
- for $k = 1 \mod 4$, $\mathcal{W}_{g_n,k}(0) = \mathcal{W}_{\ell_{n/2},k}(0) = 0$,
- for $k = 2 \mod 4$, $\mathcal{W}_{g_n,k}(0) = -\mathcal{W}_{\ell_{n/2},k}(0) = \binom{n/2}{k/2} \geq 0$,
- for $k = 3 \mod 4$, $\mathcal{W}_{g_n,k}(0) = -\mathcal{W}_{\ell_{n/2},k}(0) = 0$.

It allows us to conclude $\forall k \in [0, n-1]$, $\mathcal{W}_{k,g_n}(0) \geq 0$. $\qquad \square$

4.4 Functions with Lower Bounded AI

We show how Construction 1 can be used to build WPB functions with lower bounded algebraic immunity. First we recall a result from Mesnager and Tang:

Property 10 (Adapted from [28], Proposition 12). *Let* $k,d \in \mathbb{N}$, *let* $f \in \mathcal{B}_n$ *such that* $\mathsf{AI}(f) = k$, *and* $h \in \mathcal{B}_n$ *such that* $\mathsf{w_H}(h) < \min(2^{n-k}, 2^{d+1} - 1)$, *then* $|\mathsf{AI}(f + h) - \mathsf{AI}(f)| \leq d$.

This result shows that modifying few elements of the support has a limited impact on the algebraic immunity of the function. It allows to derive the following bound regarding Construction 1.

Theorem 4. *Let* $m \in \mathbb{N}^*$, $m \geq 2$ *and* $n = 2^m$. *Let* $f \in \mathcal{B}_n$ *such that* $\mathsf{NPB}(f) < 2^{n/2}$. *Any (WPB) function* g *given by Construction 1 seeded with* f *has the following property:* $\mathsf{AI}(g) \geq \mathsf{AI}(f) - \lfloor \log(\mathsf{NPB}(f) + 1) \rfloor$.

Proof. By construction g can be written as $f + h$ where $\mathsf{w_H}(h) = \mathsf{NPB}(f)$. Since $\mathsf{w_H}(h) < 2^{n/2}$ we have $\mathsf{w_H}(h) < 2^{n-\mathsf{AI}(f)} \leq 2^{n/2}$, and taking $d = \lfloor \log(\mathsf{NPB}(f) + 1) \rfloor$ we get $\mathsf{NPB}(f) < 2^{d+1} - 1$. Therefore, we can apply Property 10, $\mathsf{AI}(g) \geq \mathsf{AI}(f) - \lfloor \log(\mathsf{NPB}(f) + 1) \rfloor$. $\qquad \square$

Accordingly to the theorem, seeding Construction 1 with functions with high algebraic immunity and low non perfect balancedness allows to get WPB functions with relatively high AI. In the next proposition, we show how low degree functions (hence functions with low AI) with low non perfect balancedness can also be used to produce WPB functions with lower bounded AI.

Proposition 9. *Let* $m \in \mathbb{N}^*$, $m \geq 2$ *and* $n = 2^m$. *Let* $f \in \mathcal{B}_n$ *such that* $\mathsf{NPB}(f) < 2^{n/2}$ *and* $\deg(f) < n/2$. *Any (WPB) function* g *given by Construction 1 seeded with* $f + \sigma_{n/2,n}$ *has the following property:* $\mathsf{AI}(g) \geq \frac{n}{2} - \deg(f) - \lfloor \log(\mathsf{NPB}(f) + 1) \rfloor$.

Proof. Since the non perfect balancedness is not changed by the addition of a symmetric function null in 0 and 1_n (see Property 6), $\mathsf{NPB}(f + \sigma_{n/2,n}) = \mathsf{NPB}(f) < 2^{n/2}$. It allows to use Theorem 4, giving $\mathsf{AI}(g) \geq \mathsf{AI}(f + \sigma_{n/2,n}) - \lfloor \log(\mathsf{NPB}(f) + 1) \rfloor$.

Then, we bound the algebraic immunity of $f + \sigma_{n/2,n}$. Since $\mathsf{AI}(\sigma_{n/2,n}) = n/2$ (Property 5 Item 3) and since the algebraic immunity decreases by at most d when adding a degree-d function (*e.g.*[4], Proposition 139), we obtain $\mathsf{AI}(f + \sigma_{n/2,n}) \geq \frac{n}{2} - \deg(f)$.   □

In particular, using Proposition 9 with low degree function with (known) low NPB allows to build WPB functions with relatively high AI. We illustrate it with the examples of truncated CMR functions, which weightwise support has been recently studied in [36].

Property 11 (Adapted from [36], Theorem 1). *Let* $m \in \mathbb{N}^*$, $m \geq 2$ *and* $n = 2^m$. *Let* $d \in \mathbb{N}^*$, $d < m$, *and let* $f_{d,m} \in \mathcal{B}_n$ *the function which ANF contains only the terms of degree at most* 2^{d-1} *of the CMR function* f_n *(Definition 9), the following holds for* $0 \leq k \leq n$:

$$|\mathsf{supp}_k(f_{d,m})| = \begin{cases} \frac{1}{2}\binom{n}{k} & \text{if } k \not\equiv 0 \mod 2^d, \\ \frac{1}{2}\binom{n}{k} - \frac{(-1)^{k/2^d}}{2}\binom{2^{m-d}}{k/2^d} & \text{if } k \equiv 0 \mod 2^d. \end{cases}$$

Proposition 10. *Let* $m \in \mathbb{N}^*$, $m \geq 2$ *and* $n = 2^m$. *Let* $d \in \mathbb{N}^*$, $d < m$, *and let* $f_{d,m} \in \mathcal{B}_n$ *the function which ANF contains only the terms of degree at most* 2^{d-1} *of the CMR function* f_n *(Definition 9), any (WPB) function* g *given by Construction 1 seeded with* $f_{d,m} + \sigma_{n/2,n}$ *has the following property:*

$$\mathsf{AI}(g) \geq \frac{n}{2} - 2^{d-1} - m + d + 1.$$

Proof. First, we compute the NPB of $f_{d,m}$. Using Property 1, we get:

$$\mathsf{NPB}(f_{d,m}) = \frac{2 - \mathcal{W}_{f_{d,m},0}(0) + \mathcal{W}_{f_{d,m},n}(0)}{2} + \sum_{k=1}^{n-1} \frac{|\mathcal{W}_{f_{d,m},k}(0)|}{2}.$$

Using Property 11 since $\mathcal{W}_{f,k}(0) = |E_{k,n}| - 2|\mathsf{supp}_k(f)|$ it gives:

$$\mathsf{NPB}(f_{d,m}) = \frac{2 - 1 + 1}{2} + \frac{1}{2} \sum_{t=1}^{2^{m-d}-1} \binom{2^{m-d}}{t} = 1 + 2^{m-d-1} - 1 = 2^{m-d-1}.$$

Then, since $2^{m-d-1} < 2^{n/2}$, we can apply Proposition 9, which gives

$$\mathsf{AI}(g) \geq \frac{n}{2} - \deg(f_{d,m}) - \lfloor \log(\mathsf{NPB}(f_{d,m}) + 1) \rfloor = 2^{m-1} - 2^{d-1} - m + d + 1.$$

    □

In particular for $d = 1$ (in this case $f_{1,m}$ corresponds to $\ell_{n/2}$), it gives WPB functions with algebraic immunity at least $2^{m-1} - m + 1$.

5   Conclusion and Open Questions

In this article we performed the first study on the algebraic immunity of WPB function, the values it can take, and presented constructions reaching a low, or high value. In Sect. 3 we focused on the maximal and minimal values the AI can take inside this family, and the general distribution of this parameter. We showed a lower bound on the AI of two secondary constructions, and then proved the existence of WPB functions of AI only 2 for all m greater than 2. The experimental study that we performed in 8 and 16 variables showed that such functions are rare, whereas most WPB functions have optimal AI.

On the constructive side, in Sect. 4 we showed how GM Construction (Construction 1) can be used to generate WPB functions with bounded AI. In a first time we proved how to build WPB functions with lower bounded AI, one main example being the porcelain functions, an entire family with AI 2. We also demonstrated that the WPB functions with very high nonlinearity exhibited in [12] have in fact minimal AI. In a second time we used the construction to generate functions with upper bounded AI, together with an example of family with AI at least $2^{m-1} - m + 1$.

Different open questions arose from this study. First, since the GM construction allows to derive WPB functions with proven very high nonlinearity ([12]), but minimal AI or proven high AI when used with different seeds, it would be interesting to determine if the results can be combined to find seeds generating WPB functions with both proven high nonlinearity and AI. Then, we notice that in both cases the seeds used rely on a symmetric function with optimal nonlinearity in the first case and algebraic immunity in the second case. This leads to question if investigating the properties of WPB functions up to addition of symmetric functions could lead to WPB functions with good parameters for all the cryptographic criteria. Finally, the experimental tests and former results on WPB families show that WPB functions have high AI in general. It would be interesting to see if this property propagates to the criterion of weightwise algebraic immunity, AI_k, measuring the resistance to algebraic attacks when the Hamming weight is fixed.

References

1. Braeken, A., Preneel, B.: On the algebraic immunity of symmetric boolean functions. In: Maitra, S., Veni Madhavan, C.E., Venkatesan, R. (eds.) INDOCRYPT 2005. LNCS, vol. 3797, pp. 35–48. Springer, Heidelberg (2005). https://doi.org/10.1007/11596219_4
2. Canteaut, A., Videau, M.: Symmetric Boolean functions. IEEE Trans. Inf. Theory **51**, 2791–2811 (2005)
3. Carlet, C.: On the degree, nonlinearity, algebraic thickness, and nonnormality of boolean functions, with developments on symmetric functions. IEEE Trans. Inf. Theory **50**(9), 2178–2185 (2004)
4. Carlet, C.: Boolean Functions for Cryptography and Coding Theory. Cambridge University Press, Cambridge (2021)

5. Carlet, C., Méaux, P.: A complete study of two classes of boolean functions: direct sums of monomials and threshold functions. IEEE Trans. Inf. Theory **68**(5), 3404–3425 (2022)
6. Carlet, C., Méaux, P., Rotella, Y.: Boolean functions with restricted input and their robustness; application to the FLIP cipher. IACR Trans. Symmetric Cryptol. **2017**(3) (2017)
7. Courtois, N.T., Meier, W.: Algebraic attacks on stream ciphers with linear feedback. In: Biham, E. (ed.) EUROCRYPT 2003. LNCS, vol. 2656, pp. 345–359. Springer, Heidelberg (2003). https://doi.org/10.1007/3-540-39200-9_21
8. Couteau, G., Dupin, A., Méaux, P., Rossi, M., Rotella, Y.: On the concrete security of Goldreich's pseudorandom generator. In: Peyrin, T., Galbraith, S. (eds.) ASIACRYPT 2018. LNCS, vol. 11273, pp. 96–124. Springer, Cham (2018). https://doi.org/10.1007/978-3-030-03329-3_4
9. Dalai, D.K., Maitra, S., Sarkar, S.: Basic theory in construction of boolean functions with maximum possible annihilator immunity. Des. Codes Cryptogr. **40**, 41–58 (2006)
10. Gini, A., Méaux, P.: On the weightwise nonlinearity of weightwise perfectly balanced functions. Disc. Appl. Math. **322**, 320–341 (2022)
11. Gini, A., Méaux, P.: Weightwise almost perfectly balanced functions: secondary constructions for all n and better weightwise nonlinearities. In: Isobe, T., Sarkar, S. (eds.) Progress in Cryptology - INDOCRYPT. Lecture Notes in Computer Science, vol. 13774, pp. 492–514. Springer, Heidelberg (2022). https://doi.org/10.1007/978-3-031-22912-1_22
12. Gini, A., Méaux, P.: Weightwise perfectly balanced functions and nonlinearity. In: El Hajji, S., Mesnager, S., Souidi, E.M. (eds.) C2SI 2023. LNCS, vol. 13874, pp. 338–359. Springer, Cham (2023). https://doi.org/10.1007/978-3-031-33017-9_21
13. Guo, X., Su, S.: Construction of weightwise almost perfectly balanced boolean functions on an arbitrary number of variables. Disc. Appl. Math. **307**, 102–114 (2022)
14. Li, J., Su, S.: Construction of weightwise perfectly balanced boolean functions with high weightwise nonlinearity. Disc. Appl. Math. **279**, 218–227 (2020)
15. Liu, J., Mesnager, S.: Weightwise perfectly balanced functions with high weightwise nonlinearity profile. Des. Codes Cryptogr. **87**(8), 1797–1813 (2019)
16. MacWilliams, F., Sloane, N.: The Theory of Error-Correcting Codes, 2nd edn. North-holland Publishing Company, Amsterdam (1978)
17. Mandujano, S., Ku Cauich, J.C., Lara, A.: Studying special operators for the application of evolutionary algorithms in the seek of optimal boolean functions for cryptography. In: Pichardo Lagunas, O., Martínez-Miranda, J., Martínez Seis, B. (eds.) MICAI 2022. LNCS, vol. 13612, pp. 383–396. Springer, Cham (2022). https://doi.org/10.1007/978-3-031-19493-1_30
18. Mangard, S., Oswald, E., Popp, T.: Power Analysis Attacks - Revealing the Secrets of Smart Card. Springer, Boston (2007). https://doi.org/10.1007/978-0-387-38162-6
19. Mariot, L., Picek, S., Jakobovic, D., Djurasevic, M., Leporati, A.: Evolutionary construction of perfectly balanced boolean functions. In: 2022 IEEE Congress on Evolutionary Computation (CEC), pp. 1–8. IEEE Press (2022)
20. Méaux, P.: On the fast algebraic immunity of threshold functions. Cryptogr. Commun. **13**(5), 741–762 (2021). https://doi.org/10.1007/s12095-021-00505-y
21. Méaux, P.: On the algebraic immunity of direct sum constructions. Disc. Appl. Math. **320**, 223–234 (2022). https://doi.org/10.1016/j.dam.2022.05.021

22. Méaux, P., Journault, A., Standaert, F.-X., Carlet, C.: Towards stream ciphers for efficient FHE with low-noise ciphertexts. In: Fischlin, M., Coron, J.-S. (eds.) EUROCRYPT 2016. LNCS, vol. 9665, pp. 311–343. Springer, Heidelberg (2016). https://doi.org/10.1007/978-3-662-49890-3_13

23. Meier, W., Pasalic, E., Carlet, C.: Algebraic attacks and decomposition of boolean functions. In: Cachin, C., Camenisch, J.L. (eds.) EUROCRYPT 2004. LNCS, vol. 3027, pp. 474–491. Springer, Heidelberg (2004). https://doi.org/10.1007/978-3-540-24676-3_28

24. Mesnager, S.: Bent Functions, vol. 1. Springer, Heidelberg (2016). https://doi.org/10.1007/978-3-319-32595-8

25. Mesnager, S., Su, S.: On constructions of weightwise perfectly balanced boolean functions. Cryptogr. Commun. **13**, 951–979 (2021)

26. Mesnager, S., Su, S., Li, J.: On concrete constructions of weightwise perfectly balanced functions with optimal algebraic immunity and high weightwise nonlinearity. In: Boolean Functions and Applications (2021)

27. Mesnager, S., Su, S., Li, J., Zhu, L.: Concrete constructions of weightwise perfectly balanced (2-rotation symmetric) functions with optimal algebraic immunity and high weightwise nonlinearity. Cryptogr. Commun. **14**(6), 1371–1389 (2022)

28. Mesnager, S., Tang, C.: Fast algebraic immunity of boolean functions and LCD codes. IEEE Trans. Inf. Theory **67**(7), 4828–4837 (2021)

29. Qu, L., Feng, K., Liu, F., Wang, L.: Constructing symmetric boolean functions with maximum algebraic immunity. IEEE Trans. Inf. Theory **55**, 2406–2412 (2009). https://doi.org/10.1109/TIT.2009.2015999

30. Rothaus, O.: On bent functions. J. Comb. Theory Ser. A **20**(3), 300–305 (1976)

31. Sarkar, P., Maitra, S.: Balancedness and correlation immunity of symmetric boolean functions. In: Discrete Mathematics, pp. 2351–2358 (2007)

32. Standaert, F.: Introduction to side-channel attacks. In: Verbauwhede, I.M.R. (ed.) Secure Integrated Circuits and Systems. Integrated Circuits and Systems, pp. 27–42. Springer, Heidelberg (2010). https://doi.org/10.1007/978-0-387-71829-3_2

33. Tang, D., Liu, J.: A family of weightwise (almost) perfectly balanced boolean functions with optimal algebraic immunity. Cryptogr. Commun. **11**(6), 1185–1197 (2019)

34. Zhang, R., Su, S.: A new construction of weightwise perfectly balanced boolean functions. Adv. Math. Commun. **17**(4), 757–770 (2023)

35. Zhao, Q., Jia, Y., Zheng, D., Qin, B.: A new construction of weightwise perfectly balanced functions with high weightwise nonlinearity. Mathematics **11**(5), 1193 (2023)

36. Zhao, Q., Li, M., Chen, Z., Qin, B., Zheng, D.: A unified construction of weightwise perfectly balanced boolean functions. Disc. Appl. Math. **337**, 190–201 (2023)

37. Zhu, L., Su, S.: A systematic method of constructing weightwise almost perfectly balanced boolean functions on an arbitrary number of variables. Disc. Appl. Math. **314**, 181–190 (2022)

ACE-HoT: Accelerating an Extreme Amount of Symmetric Cipher Evaluations for (High-order) Avalanche Tests

Emanuele Bellini[1], Juan Grados[1], Mohamed Rachidi[1(✉)], Nitin Satpute[1],
Joan Daemen[2], and Solane El Hirch[2]

[1] Cryptography Research Center, Technology Innovation Institute, Abu Dhabi, UAE
{emanuele.bellini,juan.grados,mohamed.rachidi,nitin.satpute}@tii.ae
[2] Radboud University, Nijmegen, The Netherlands
joan@cs.ru.nl, solane.elhirch@ru.nl

Abstract. In this work, we tackle the problem of estimating the security of iterated symmetric ciphers in an efficient manner, with tests that do not require a deep analysis of the internal structure of the cipher. This is particularly useful during the design phase of these ciphers, especially for quickly testing several combinations of possible parameters defining several cipher design variants.

We consider a popular statistical test that allows us to determine the probability of flipping each cipher output bit, given a small variation in the input of the cipher. From these probabilities, one can compute three measurable metrics related to the well-known full diffusion, avalanche and strict avalanche criteria.

This highly parallelizable testing process scales linearly with the number of samples, i.e., cipher inputs, to be evaluated and the number of design variants to be tested. But, the number of design variants might grow exponentially with respect to some parameters.

The high cost of Central Processing Unit (CPU)s makes them a bad candidate for this kind of parallelization. As a main contribution, we propose a framework, ACE-HoT, to parallelize the testing process using multi-Graphics Processing Units (GPUs). Our implementation does not perform any intermediate CPU-GPU data transfers.

The diffusion and avalanche criteria can be seen as an application of discrete first-order derivatives. As a secondary contribution, we generalize these criteria to their *high-order* version. Our generalization requires an exponentially larger number of samples, in order to compute sufficiently accurate probabilities. As a case study, we apply ACE-HoT on most of the finalists of the National Institute of Standards and Technologies (NIST) lightweight standardization process, with a special focus on the winner ASCON.

Keywords: GPU · CUDA programming · Avalanche tests · Symmetric ciphers · Statistical tests

© The Author(s), under exclusive license to Springer Nature Switzerland AG 2023
A. Aly and M. Tibouchi (Eds.): LATINCRYPT 2023, LNCS 14168, pp. 24–43, 2023.
https://doi.org/10.1007/978-3-031-44469-2_2

1   Introduction

In this work, we describe how to perform a security assessment of encryption and authentication algorithms by means of statistical tests. These tests require a large amount of computations to be executed. We show how to perform these tests on Graphics Processing Units.

1.1   Background and Motivation

The cryptographic community is constantly trying to design more secure and better-performing ciphers. Several public selections took place to determine the best cryptographic primitives for standardization. Some notable examples by the American NIST are the Advanced Encryption Standard selection process [24] started in 1997, the Secure Hash Algorithm of third generation (SHA-3) competition [19] started in 2007, and the NIST lightweight cryptography standardization process [20] started in 2018 and terminated in 2023 with the selection of ASCON, a permutation-based hash and authenticated encryption cipher. Other examples include the eSTREAM competition [21] for stream ciphers, and the CAESAR competition [1] for Authenticated Encryption.

In order for these competitions to evaluate the candidates more fairly, it is important to establish a common framework that allows evaluation of the security of each primitive. One possible approach to establishing the quality of a round function is to define a certain measurable property, observe its variation across the rounds, and then compare it with the computational cost of the round function itself (which depends on the platform).

Avalanche Tests. A common way of performing this assessment is by measuring some statistical properties observed after evaluating the cipher under scrutiny over samples with certain characteristics. This work focuses on a particular type of statistical test, namely the avalanche tests and on their higher order version introduced in this work. The main challenge in performing high-order avalanche tests is the large number of samples that they require. For example, the most costly high-order avalanche test we perform requires $2^{49.29} \approx 10^{14.83}$ cipher evaluations.

Parallel Computing. Graphics Processing Units (GPUs) can perform thousands of computations in parallel depending on the availability of the number of cores on the Streaming Multiprocessors (SMs) [10,12,17]. The computations are distributed on GPUs when the CPU launches an application in the form of a kernel. There are many challenges with regard to the multi-GPU implementation of avalanche tests, especially when these tests have to be executed for an extremely high number of variants of a cipher (during its design phase), or in their high-order version. These challenges are categorized in terms of CPU-bottleneck during iterative kernel calling, inter-block GPU synchronization, which is taken care of by iterative kernel calling, inter-GPU communication during the processing of avalanche tests and memory-based implementation of avalanche tests for random samples.

One of the ways to overcome the above challenges is to effectively parallelize the computations on the GPUs using the Compute Unified Device Architecture (CUDA) programming framework. Typically, CPU acts as a host and launches a device kernel with a required number of computation blocks on the GPU. The GPU schedules the computation blocks for the kernel on the SMs. Each SM can handle one or more computation blocks. The GPU resource manager schedules and allocates resources for each compute block. The blocks communicate and synchronize via a device memory on the GPU. Threads in a block execute in groups called warps and share a common memory in that block. Each warp uses the resources of the SM based on its register memory requirements. The ratio between the number of warps in process and the maximum number of warps defines the occupancy of the GPU [4,14]. It is important to maintain a high occupancy of the GPU to achieve maximum computing performance. In order to efficiently utilize the hardware, it is essential to understand the computation and communication resources. Based on the availability of the CPU-GPU resources, the tasks from an application can be scheduled and allocated efficiently.

1.2   Our Contribution

In this work, we provide a framework, ACE-HoT, to perform avalanche tests requiring an extremely high number of cipher evaluations exploiting GPUs. This can be useful during the design phase of a cipher, when a very high number of parameters have to be quickly evaluated against differential properties. We also generalize avalanche tests to a high-order version. This generalization requires a very large amount of cipher executions that can be easily handled by our framework. As a case study, we provide a detailed analysis of our new test on the winner of the NIST lightweight standardization process [20], namely the ASCON permutation [6]. Due to space constraints, we provide a less detailed analysis of the other finalists.

We refer to our new test as *high order avalanche test*. When the order d is known, we say *avalanche test of order d* or *d-order (or d-th order) avalanche test*. The contributions of the paper are presented below in more detail:

1. A framework to perform avalanche tests requiring an extremely high number of cipher evaluations exploiting GPUs.
2. We introduce a new high-order avalanche test for the assessment of a symmetric cipher in the black box scenario, i.e. where no knowledge is assumed of the internal structure of the cipher except its input/output bit size. From a cryptographic point of view, the already known first-order test allows to retrieve information about the applicability of certain attacks, such as impossible differentials [2] and truncated differentials [15]. With our generalization, we have information that might lead to the discovery of higher-order differentials distinguishers [15,16].

3. We provide an accelerated implementation of the avalanche tests of orders 1, 2, 3 and 4 for the ASCON permutation and show that the avalanche criteria (defined under 3 different metrics) are met after 4 rounds with avalanche tests of order 1 and 2 and after 5 rounds for order 3 and 4.

4. To the best of our knowledge, this is the first work towards multi-GPU acceleration for high-order avalanche tests to study the trend of avalanche metrics with respect to the number of samples and rounds. The proposed implementation includes efficient utilization of hardware resources without any intermediate CPU-GPU data transfers and no inter-GPU communications.

5. The 3rd order avalanche test requires 14 s (approx.) for 2,000 samples on 8xTITAN GPUs. The implementation on 4xA100 Ampere GPUs is generally faster compared to the implementation on 8xTITAN GPUs. Notice that in this case, $\binom{320}{3} = 5,410,240 \approx 2^{22.36}$ differences need to be evaluated.

6. The 4th order avalanche test requires 49.55 s and 40.30 min for 2,000 and 100,000 samples respectively on 4xA100 Ampere GPUs. Notice that in this case, $\binom{320}{4} = 428,761,520 \approx 2^{28.67}$ differences need to be evaluated, which corresponds to $\approx 2^{46.29}$ 5-round Ascon evaluations in the case of $100,000$ samples per difference. To highlight the potential of the framework, we note that 2^{47} 5-round Ascon evaluations on a single core CPU are estimated to last on average 113 days on an i9 Intel macOS laptop, which shows a significant reduction in timing by using GPUs. Additionally, we verified all the Ascon distinguishers presented by Raghvendra Rohit and Santanu Sarkar [22] in minutes, while for them, it took weeks (especially for 7-round Ascon distinguisher).

7. We release our source code to the community for future research (GitHub: Link Anonymous[1]).

1.3   Related Works

In this subsection, we give an insight into some of the works that have been done previously. The notion of avalanche tests applied on ciphers was raised from the ideas of completeness and avalanche effect first introduced by Kam and Davida [11] and Feistel [8], respectively. A cipher is said *complete* (or that it reached *full diffusion*) when each of its output bits depends on all of the input bits. The avalanche effect of a cryptographic algorithm is observed when an average of one half of the output bits change whenever a single input bit is flipped. Webster and Tavares [26] explain how to build what are called perfect 4×4 S-Boxes by using the strict avalanche criterion. Later, Joan Daemen, Seth Hoffert, Gilles Van Assche and Ronny Van Keer [5] report in their paper on the performance of the cipher Xoodoo with respect to these criteria. Avalanche tests can be seen as a special case of statistical tests where the randomness of the output of a cipher is examined. One of the most frequently used test batteries is the NIST Statistical Test Suite [23]. In 2021, Kim and Yeom [13] propose a GPU based parallel implementation of the most time-consuming part of the

---

[1] We can provide the source code to the reviewers if requested.

entropy estimation in these tests and demonstrate that their implementation is about 3 to 25 times faster than that of the NIST package (measured on two different hardware configurations, see reference for details). While in this work we introduce the notion of high order avalanche test for a symmetric cipher, the notion of high order Strict Avalanche Criterion has already been known for a long time in the case of small Boolean functions [9].

1.4   Outline of this Work

The remainder of this paper is structured as follows. Section 2 and Sect. 3 describe high-order avalanche tests and criteria. Section 4 and Sect. 5 provide framework for multi-GPU acceleration for high-order avalanche tests. Sections 6 to 8 explains the evaluation methodology and presents the detailed experimental results and discussions. Finally, we conclude the paper in Sect. 9.

2   Avalanche Tests

We denote by $GF(2)$ the binary field with 2 elements, and with $GF(2)^n$ the n-dimensional vector space over $GF(2)$. Block ciphers are functions with inverse and they are iterated. That is, block ciphers apply an map repeatedly over a series of rounds. In other words, given a set of r maps $F_i : GF(2)^n \times GF(2)^m \to GF(2)^n$ with $i = 0, \ldots, r-1$, that takes as input a n bits block and a m bits subkey, an iterated block cipher F is such that $F = F_{r-1} \circ \ldots \circ F_0$.

Three tests to measure the avalanche properties of a symmetric iterated block cipher are presented in [5]. These tests evaluate the cipher with respect to three different criteria: the *full diffusion*, the *avalanche*, and the *strict avalanche* criteria. The goal of these tests is to measure the quantitative diffusion power of the round function. Note that the common behavior of an iterated cipher is not to meet the criterion for the first rounds and then to meet it for all the remaining ones.

2.1   The Avalanche Probability Vector

The tests are performed by computing the so-called Avalanche Probability Vector (APV) $P_{\Delta F}$ of a cryptographic primitive F for an input difference Δ. The i-th component of the APV is the probability that bit i of the output of F flips due to the input difference Δ, or, equivalently, the probability that bit i of $F(x) + F(x + \Delta)$ equals 1. After M samples, the expected standard deviation of the elements of $P_{\Delta F}$ is $1/\sqrt{M}$. So for high precision, M must be chosen large enough. In [5] experiments $M = 250,000$ was used. In this work, we observe the behavior of the tests for smaller values of M.

2.2   Avalanche Criteria

The APV is used to derive 3 metrics, where $p_i = P_{\Delta F_i}$:

- **Avalanche dependence**: number of output bits that may flip, defined as $D_{av}(F, \Delta) = b - \sum_i \delta(p_i)$, with $\delta(x)$ equal to 1 if $x = 0$ and 0 otherwise. The **full diffusion** criterion is satisfied if $D_{av}(F, \Delta) = b$ for all Δ with Hamming weight 1.
- **Avalanche weight**: expected Hamming weight of the output difference, defined as $W_{av}(F, \Delta) = \sum_i p_i$. Given a certain threshold t, the **avalanche** criterion is satisfied if $b/2 - t \leq W_{av}(F, \Delta) \leq b/2 + t$ for all Δ with Hamming weight 1.
- **Avalanche entropy**: uncertainty about whether output bits flip, defined as an entropy: $H_{av}(F, \Delta) = \sum_i (-p_i \log_2(p_i) - (1 - p_i) \log_2(1 - p_i))$. Given a certain threshold t, the **strict avalanche** criterion (SAC) is satisfied if $b - t \leq H_{av}(F, \Delta) \leq b + t$ for all input differences Δ with Hamming weight 1.

The three metrics have values in the range $[0, \ldots, b]$ and for a random transformation F we have that for any input difference Δ then $D_{av}(F, \Delta) \approx b$, $W_{av}(F, \Delta) \approx b/2$ and $H_{av}(F, \Delta) \approx b$. We actually report on the minimum value over all first order input differences.

Algorithm 1. avalanche probability vector of order d

Require: a transformation F over $GF(2)^b$, a vector space $\mathcal{V}$ of length b and dimension d generated by a basis of 1-bit vectors (sometimes called *unit vectors*), and number of samples M.
Ensure: p, the avalanche probability vector of order d.
1: Initialize a b-bit vector p of probabilities p_i to all zeroes.
2: **for** M randomly generated states x **do**
3:      Compute $B = \sum_{v \in \mathcal{V}} F(x + v)$
4:      **for** all state bit positions i **do**
5:          $p_i = p_i + B_i/M$
6:      **end for**
7: **end for**

---

3   High-Order Avalanche Tests

In [5], the metrics are computed for all Δ of Hamming weight 1, i.e. for all 1st order input differences of the cipher. This is equivalent to say that the APV is computed for the first order derivative of the n-bit vectorial Boolean function F with respect to the points Δ of Hamming weight 1. Such derivative is defined as $D_\Delta(x) = F(x) + F(x + \Delta)$, with $x, \Delta \in GF(2)^b$ [3]. The same approach can be easily extended to higher order derivatives of F with respect to a vector space

$\mathcal{V}$ of length b and dimension d, i.e. $D_{\mathcal{V}}(x) = \sum_{v \in \mathcal{V}} F(x + v)$. Our technique is somewhat similar to computing higher order derivatives [16], however, the metrics which we evaluate in this work are completely different. For example, a traditional d-order derivative is utilized in integral/cube attacks to check the presence or absence of a superpoly and then later used for recovering key bits. In our case, we use the d-order derivative to generalize the first-order avalanche tests. In what follows, we first describe metrics of high-order avalanche tests and then discuss their computational challenges.

3.1   High-Order Avalanche Probability Vector

More precisely, the *avalanche probability vector* $P_{\Delta F}$ of order d of a cryptographic primitive F for a vector space $\mathcal{V}$ of length b and dimension d and generated by a basis of single-bit vectors, is the vector whose i-th component is the probability that bit i of the output of $\sum_{v \in \mathcal{V}} F(x + v)$ equals 1. The high-order APV can be computed following Algorithm 1.

3.2   High-Order Avalanche Criteria

The avalanche dependence, weight and entropy are then computed as for the first order and the three criteria are defined as follows.

- The **full diffusion** criterion of order d is satisfied if $D_{av}(F, \mathcal{V}) = b$ for all vector spaces $\mathcal{V}$ of length b and dimension d generated by a basis of single-bit vectors.
- Given a certain threshold t, the **avalanche** criterion of order d is satisfied if $b/2 - t \leq W_{av}(F, \mathcal{V}) \leq b/2 + t$ for all vector spaces $\mathcal{V}$ of length b and dimension d.
- Given a certain threshold t, the **strict avalanche** criterion of order d is satisfied if $b - t \leq H_{av}(F, \mathcal{V}) \leq b + t$.

4   Parallelization Strategies and Multi-GPU Implementation

In this section, we discuss two parallelization strategies that are well-known in machine learning training, namely, *data* and *model*-level parallelization (see, e.g., [7, Section 5.1, 5.2]). We also provide a discussion on how to select the most appropriate strategy with reference to concrete use cases. In particular, for ease of explanation (and because it was never done before), we focus our description on the case of computing high-order avalanche probability vectors and their corresponding criteria. We briefly discuss how the same technique can be also applied in other use cases.

4.1 Determining the Workload

Let us now focus on the case of computing high-order avalanche probability vectors and their corresponding criteria.

Recall that b is the bit size of the cipher input and $\mathcal{V}$ is a vector space over $GF(2)$ of dimension d, length b and whose basis is made of d 1-bit vectors. The number of samples needed for each vector space is indicated by M. Also, recall from Sect. 3.2 that in order to compute the metrics avalanche dependence, avalanche weight, and avalanche entropy, we need to compute first the APV for a specific vector space $\mathcal{V}$. Furthermore, to compute an APV, we need to compute the sum B for every random sample (see Algorithm 1). Finally, recall that once we have the metrics, we can compute the full-diffusion, avalanche, and strict avalanche criteria.

From the description above, note that our main workload comes from cipher evaluations $F(\cdot)$ to compute B. Thus, to compute B for an APV of order d, we need $|\mathcal{V}|$ cipher evaluations. In turn, to compute this APV, we need M random samples. Thus, to compute the avalanche metrics for all vector spaces (i.e., $\binom{b}{d}$) in a d order derivative of a cipher, we need a total of $\binom{b}{d} \cdot |V| \cdot M$ cipher evaluations.

4.2 Parallelization Techniques Overview

To parallelize the workload of the high-order avalanche test, we explore two options: *data-level* and *model-level* parallelization. Essentially, these two techniques differ in how a dataset is distributed to the processing units, or CUDA threads in the case of GPUs. More in detail, in the high-order avalanche test, the two techniques differ as follows:

- *Data-level Parallelism*: Each CUDA thread is assigned a b-bit random sample x and it is responsible of computing $B = \sum_{v \in \mathcal{V}} F(x+v)$ for the *single* sample x. In this scenario, the same vector space is used across multiple threads until the right number of samples is exhausted.
- *Model-level Parallelism*: Each CUDA thread is assigned a vector space and computes $B = \sum_{v \in \mathcal{V}} F(x+v)$ for *all* M samples $x \in GF(2)^b$.

In data-level parallelism, the number of threads depends on the number of samples needed to compute the avalanche criteria. On the other hand, in model-level parallelism, the number of threads only depends on the number of vector spaces.

4.3 Choosing the Parallelization Technique

Choosing which type of parallelism technique to adopt might not be trivial. In particular, for the case of avalanche tests, it seems natural to distribute the samples over each thread. This might turn out to be a good solution for the case of first-order avalanche tests, since the number of vector spaces (determined by weight 1 differences) is very small, i.e., b. However, for higher dimensions, the number of vector spaces quickly outnumbers the number of samples, and model-level parallelization becomes more useful. Another factor in deciding which technique to exploit is the number of physical cores available in the machine. For example, in our experiments with high-order avalanche tests, we used two types of GPUs: TITAN RTX, with a capability of 18432 CUDA cores, and A100-SXM4, with a capability of 27648 CUDA cores per GPU). If the number of samples is $\approx 10^4$, then not all cores will be used in both cases. Finally, distributing the samples over the processing units, requires some communication cost among the units, to compute the value B of the summation. This is not the case in model-level parallelization, where the generation of the elements of the vector space $\mathcal{V}$, the computation of B, the APVs, and the metrics are all computed in the same thread. Note that all these operations have a relatively low cost for a GPU.

For the case of high-order avalanche tests, and for all the reasons stated in the paragraphs above, we decided to use model-level parallelism instead of data-level parallelism.

4.4   Use Cases

Another important use case for applying model-level parallelization is when evaluating first-order avalanche tests for a high number of variants of a cipher. This highly parallelizable testing process scales linearly with the number of samples, i.e., cipher inputs, to be evaluated and the number of design variants to be tested. But, the number of design variants might grow exponentially with respect to some parameters. For example, in ASCON, freeing the 10 rotation offsets in the linear layer gives $63^5 \cdot 62^5 \approx 2^{60}$ possible variants of the cipher.

One third use case for applying model-level parallelization is when evaluating first-order avalanche tests for input differences with Hamming weight greater than one. This would be useful to have a preliminary understanding of the resistance of the cipher against differential cryptanalysis with a low Hamming weight initial difference. Notice that is very common for high probability differential trails to start with low Hamming weight differences. Nevertheless, such a test cannot replace automated differential trail search techniques, which, on the other hand, require quite heavy computations and dedicated modeling of the cipher.

A fourth scenario where model-level parallelization is beneficial is in the evaluation of high-order truncated differentials. Specifically, consider an APV $P_{\Delta F}$ of order d for a cryptographic primitive F. Each entry ρ in $P_{\Delta F}$ represents the probability of a d-order truncated differential, starting with the vectors used to compute $P_{\Delta F}$, and ending at the index indicated by ρ. We will leave the implementation of this scenario as future work.

5   Implementation Challenges

In this section, we describe the main practical challenges in implementing model-level parallelization in GPUs, and how we overcame them.

5.1   Avoiding CPU Bottleneck

The logical number of threads might be different from the actual number of CUDA cores. We already mentioned that when the number of threads is smaller than the number of cores, there is a poor utilization of the GPU resources. On the other hand, when the number of threads is greater than the number of cores, then the threads are divided into batches and executed one batch at a time. This iteration is concretized through an iterative call of the kernel from the CPU. The CPU assigns workloads to the GPU through iterative calls, which is time-consuming due to CPU-GPU communication. To optimize performance, we used the so-called *grid-stride loop* technique to execute the iterative task solely on the GPU without CPU intervention, enhancing performance [18].

In CUDA programming, a *grid-stride loop* is a common technique used to efficiently parallelize certain operations on NVIDIA GPUs. It involves breaking down a large data set or computational task into smaller chunks and assigning each chunk to a different thread block. The threads within each block then process elements of the data in a loop.

The term grid in CUDA refers to the collection of thread computational blocks that are launched to execute a kernel function on the GPU. Stride in a *grid-stride loop* refers to the distance between consecutive elements that each thread processes. It allows multiple threads to work on non-contiguous elements in memory simultaneously. By using a stride, threads can efficiently load and process data, minimizing memory access conflicts and improving memory coalescing. Here's a brief overview of how a *grid-stride loop* is typically implemented:

- Determine the grid and block dimensions: The data or task is divided into a grid of thread blocks. The grid and block dimensions are chosen based on the problem's requirements and the available GPU resources.
- *Calculate the global thread index*: Each thread is assigned a unique global index that represents its position within the entire grid of thread blocks.
- *Calculate the stride*: Stride is often computed as the total number of threads in the grid multiplied by the number of elements each thread should process.
- *Perform the grid-stride loop*: Each thread enters a loop and processes the data or computation assigned to it based on its global thread index and the calculated stride. The loop continues until all elements have been processed.

Grid-stride loop is particularly useful when the data or task involves irregular memory access patterns or when the data set is too large for a single thread block to handle. *Grid-stride loops* help achieve better performance by maximizing parallelism and minimizing memory access conflicts. In particular, we use grid-stride loop in high-order test to efficiently compute B (see Algorithm 1), APVs, and metrics for multiple vector spaces. Instead of assigning a single CUDA thread to handle the computations associated with a single vector space, we map a thread to a group of vector spaces in a stride way.

5.2   Synchronization and Communication

In the context of parallel programming, synchronization refers to the coordination of parallel resources to avoid race conditions or to ensure the correct order of operations, and communication refers to the transfer of data between parallel resources. For example, moving data between different memory spaces, such as transferring data from the host memory to the GPU memory or between different GPUs. In our implementation, we basically have the following parallel resources, CUDA threads, CUDA blocks, GPUs, and CPUs.

As mentioned in Sect. 2, a cipher is considered to meet the criteria if the values of each metric, namely avalanche dependence, avalanche weight, and avalanche entropy, are b, $b/2$, and b, respectively, for all vector spaces $\mathcal{V}$ of dimension d and length b. This means that the cipher meets the criteria if the minimum values (worst-case scenario) for each metric are approximately b, $b/2$, and b, respectively. Thus, besides the computations of the APVs and metrics (as stated in Sect. 4.2), we compute the minimum value of each metric by using an atomic operation. This minimum value is computed in each GPU and communicated to the CPU to perform the final computation to obtain the criteria.

By utilizing model-level parallelism, communication among the parallel resources can be significantly reduced. As mentioned in Sect. 4.2, we use model-level parallelism to assign each thread a unique vector space and compute the corresponding metrics independently. The only communication required is limited to 1) the initial transfer of avalanche test configurations from the CPU to the GPU, and 2) the transmission of the minimum metric values from the GPUs to the CPUs to compute the avalanche criteria.

Two methods can be used to achieve inter-block synchronization in the GPU: atomic operations or transferring control to the CPU. In our approach, we use the former method to compute the minimum value of each metric and check if a cipher meets the criteria. We do not require inter-GPU synchronization since we send the minimum value computed from each GPU to the CPU. However, synchronization at the CPU is necessary to determine the resultant minimum value after receiving the minimum values from corresponding GPU.

5.3   Distributing the Workload

Below we describe the tasks of high-order avalanche tests on the CPU. Specifically, we describe the tasks to distribute the main workload. The proposed implementation takes the following inputs: the cipher, the order d of the test (e.g., 1st, 2nd, 3rd, and 4th order), the number of samples M, the number of rounds of the cipher, and the number of GPUs. The number of computational threads and blocks are evaluated dynamically at runtime, and the workload is assigned to each GPU by considering that we need to distribute $|\mathcal{V}| \cdot \binom{n}{d} \cdot M$ cipher evaluations among these resources.

A high-order avalanche test kernel is launched with the number of parallel threads and blocks on each GPU. To compute the number of parallel threads and blocks, we use the CUDA API. Specifically, we use the function `cudaOccupancyMaxPotentialBlockSize`, which returns the grid and block size that achieves maximum potential occupancy for a device function. In our case, this device function is the kernel high-order test.

As previously mentioned, a cipher performs well with respect to the high-order avalanche tests if the following scores are satisfied for each vector space: the avalanche dependence must be $\approx b$, the weight must be $\approx b/2$, and the entropy must be $\approx b$. Otherwise, the respective criterion is not satisfied. CPU evaluates the resultant worst-case values of the avalanche metrics received from all the GPUs.

The device kernel executes the following steps:

1) it generates vectors $v \in \mathcal{V}$,
2) generates a seed,
3) uses the seed to generate random samples for evaluating avalanche metrics,
4) the cipher is evaluated on the random samples and vectors v to compute, B, the APV and the metrics,
5) the minimum values of avalanche metrics amongst threads on a GPU are obtained using atomic operation in CUDA. These minimum values from each GPU are communicated to the CPU.

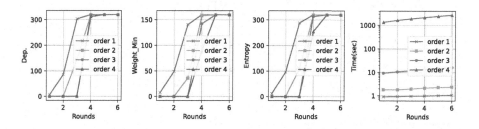

The avalanche criteria are satisfied when Dep. $\approx$ 320, Weight_Min $\approx$ 160 and Entropy $\approx$ 320.

Fig. 1. High-order Avalanche Test for ASCON on 4xA100 Ampere GPUs for 100,000 samples. The above metrics are computed from the vector space that gives the worst values of the corresponding criterion.

6   Detailed Results in the ASCON Use Case

Due to the page limit and because it is the winner of the NIST lightweight standardization process, we have decided to perform a detailed report on the performance of ASCON with respect to each criterion and for each different number of rounds. We will summarize the results of other primitives in the next Sect. 7.

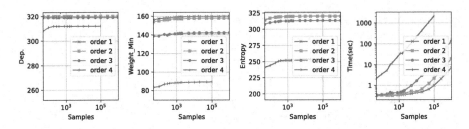

Fig. 2. High-order Avalanche Test for ASCON 4 rounds on 4xA100 Ampere GPUs *Note: 4ᵗʰ order test is not included for more than 100,000 samples due to linearly increasing time dependency for evaluating all differences.*

Specifically, this section presents a report for up to the 4th order and for different rounds. There are two aspects to analyze the results: 1) evaluate whether ASCON performs well or not the tests along the rounds and 2) timings and speedup of the experiments with respect to the number of rounds and the order of the tests. We evaluated our approaches on the following platforms: 4xA100 GPUs and 8xTITAN GPUs. In Sect. 6.1, we present experiments we did for aspect 1) and in Sect. 6.2, we present experiments we did for aspect 2). Also, here, we make a comparison of our implementations with respect to the aforementioned platforms (4xA100 GPUs and 8xTITAN).

6.1 High-Order Avalanche Tests on ASCON

We evaluate three avalanche metrics: avalanche dependence, weight, and entropy. In order to perform well with respect to the criteria associated with these metrics, ASCON must satisfy the following scores for their respective criterion:

1. avalanche dependence must be equal to 320
2. avalanche weight must be approximately[2] 160 and
3. avalanche entropy must be approximately 320.

We evaluate these tests for the variations in the number of rounds when the sample size is constant. Secondly, we assess the avalanche metrics for the variations in the number of samples for a given number of rounds.

Avalanche Properties Versus the Number of Rounds. We evaluate three avalanche tests with respect to the number of rounds and the sample sizes. We show the results corresponding to 100,000 samples in Fig. 1. We observe the following in terms of avalanche tests:

1. **Full diffusion criterion:** For all orders, 1st, 2nd, 3rd and 4th order, this criterion needs 100 samples before saturation (when the values of the metric increase with very slow rate). Regarding the numbers of rounds, 1st and 2nd order need 4 rounds to meet the criterion, while 3rd and 4th order require five rounds.

---

[2] A certain threshold has to be fixed.

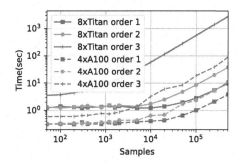

Fig. 3. Performance Comparison of Avalanche Tests for ASCON - on 4xA100 and 8xTITAN RTX GPUs.

2. **Avalanche criterion:** Similar behaviour is observed here. For all orders, 800 samples are needed to reach 158 value and 2,000 samples to reach 159 value and then saturates. Regarding the numbers of rounds, 1st and 2nd need four rounds, and 3rd and 4th require five rounds.
3. **Strict Avalanche criterion:** Here again, for all orders, 400 samples are enough to reach 319 value and then saturates. Similarly to both previous cases, 1st and 2nd need four rounds, and 3rd and 4th require five rounds.

For each criterion, the 3rd and 4th order tests require at least 5 rounds to reach it. An important point to note is that our framework can also spot the state bits for which the criteria are not satisfied for 4-round Ascon.

Avalanche Metrics Versus the Number of Samples. In what follows, we observe the evolution of the values of the metrics with respect to the number of samples. We evaluate the three avalanche metrics for 4 rounds of Ascon with different number of samples as it is shown in Fig. 2^3. We have not included 4th order avalanche test for more than 100,000 samples (equivalent to $\approx 2^{46.29}$ 5-rounds evaluations) due to linearly increasing time dependency. We observe from Fig. 2 that the values of the criteria are almost similar whether using 10^3 or 10^5 samples. To be more specific, Fig. 6 shows how accurate the values of the criteria are according to the chosen number of samples.

6.2   Time and Speedup of 4 x A100 w.r.t. 8xTITAN GPUs

We measure evaluation time on 4xA100 GPUs and 8xTITAN GPUs and observe the following:

1. **Execution time** for the 3rd order avalanche test requires 14 s for 2,000 samples on 8xTITAN GPUs. However, the implementation on 4xA100 GPUs is generally faster in comparison to the 8xTITAN GPUs as shown in Fig. 3. The

---

[3] We recall that we report on the minimum value of each metric. This is why all metrics are monotonically non-decreasing.

number of multiprocessors per GPU is more in A100 (i.e. 108) in comparison to the TITAN RTX (i.e. 72). Ampere A100 have more cores (6912) and higher FLOPS (single and double) in comparison to the TITAN RTX (4608 cores).

2. **Speedup** The performance of 4xA100 GPUs is generally faster in comparison to the 8xTITAN GPUs as shown in Fig. 3. The range of speedup varies depending upon the order of the tests.

6.3 Note on the Inverse of ASCON

We have seen that in the 1st order case, the 3 criteria are reached after 4 rounds of ASCON. The inverse of ASCON reaches the 3 criteria even faster, as we can see in Fig. 4. Each cell of this figure is green if the probability of flipping of the underlying bit is close to $\frac{1}{2}$ with a 0.01 bias due to a single input bit difference, red otherwise. We can see that after the 2nd round, all cells are green, meaning that at this round, the weight criterion is satisfied.

This behavior is common on ciphers with a linear layer whose inverse is more dense than its forward operation. For instance, it is well known that one bit difference in the input of the inverse of Ascon linear layer affects at least 31 output bits, while it affects only 3 output bit for the forward linear layer. In most cases, the inverse of a linear layer is chosen to be complex and therefore allows a better diffusion, which prevent successful backward extension of linear or differential trails for example.

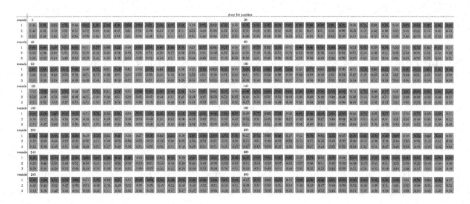

Fig. 4. Weight criterion for the inverse of ASCON. Input bit difference injected in position 0.

7   Results for the Most Popular Ciphers

In this section, we decided to focus our attention on the permutations of the finalists of the NIST lightweight standardization process, plus some of the most famous block ciphers and cipher underlying permutations. More specifically, we focused on the following primitives shown in Table 1:

Table 1. Selected primitives for our analysis and their respective plaintext and key bit sizes.

Primitives	plaintext size	key size	rounds
Ascon-p	320	–	12
Xoodoo	384	– ·	12
Gift	128	128	40
Keccak-f[400]	400	–	20
Photon	256	–	12
Skinny	128	384	40
Speck	128	128	32
AES	128	128	10
Chacha	512	–	20
DES	64	64	16
Present	64	80	31

From our experiments, we observed that the selected primitives had a similar behavior than Ascon, that is satisfying all the 3 criteria for the 3rd and 4th orders one round after they get satisfied for the 1st and 2nd orders.

Due to the page limit, we could not display the comparison between all the previous ciphers for each of the 3 criteria. We had to choose one and we believe that the most important criterion is the strict avalanche criterion based on the avalanche entropy. The comparison is shown in Fig. 5, where we display the percentage of the number of rounds needed to reach the strict avalanche criterion over the total number of rounds. We show this value for 1st, 2nd, 3rd, and 4th orders. We notice that a more interesting comparison, rather than the number of rounds, would take into account the number of gates in the implementation on a specific platform. On the other hand, this metric is not easy to measure, and we leave it for future work.

8   Discussion

In this paper, we propose and evaluate high-order avalanche tests on multi-GPU platforms. We apply our new test to the selected candidate of the NIST lightweight standardization process, namely the ASCON permutation, a round-based cipher. We conclude the following in terms of avalanche metrics and execution time from the experimental analysis:

1. **Full diffusion criterion** needs 100 samples enough for full diffusion (see Sect. 6.1).
2. **Avalanche criterion** needs 800 samples (see Sect. 6.1) to reach 158 (around 160) value and 2,000 samples to reach 159 (around 160) value and then saturates (increases with very slow rate).

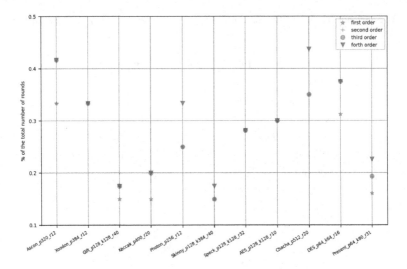

Fig. 5. Avalanche entropy comparison: percentage of number of rounds needed to reach the entropy criterion over the total number of rounds, for 1st, 2nd, 3rd, and 4th order.

3. **Strict Avalanche criterion** needs 400 samples (see Sect. 6.1) to reach 319 (around 320) value and then saturates.
4. **Execution time** for the 3rd order avalanche test requires 14 s for 2,000 samples on 8xTITAN GPUs.
5. Following analysis can be made in order to satisfy all avalanche metrics:
   (a) 1st and 2nd order avalanche tests require at least 4 rounds to satisfy all criteria.
   (b) 3rd and 4th order avalanche tests require at least 5 rounds to satisfy all criteria.
6. **Generalization of the number of threads required for performing n-th order tests in parallel:** Our initial implementation requires memory for seeds corresponding to each thread in order to generate the number of random samples for each thread. The memory requirements increase with the increase in the number of threads corresponding to each combination difference. The memory dependency with respect to the number of computational threads is detailed as follow: i-th order test requires at least $\binom{320}{i} \cdot 48$ KB memory and $\binom{320}{i}$ threads.
   However, the above memory dependency has been successfully removed in our memory-less implementation for high-order avalanche tests.
7. **Statistical Analysis of the Results.** We use a confidence level of 99% and a population of 2^{320} input samples (for ASCON) as shown in Fig. 6. It can be seen that already from samples $= 100$, for 1st order difference, 3 rounds is outside the confidence interval. This cannot be observed only for 10 samples. However, we will not worry too much as these are really very few samples. The result can be interpreted as follows: given

(a) a Confidence Level of 99%

(b) a Confidence Interval C (a positive integer). Note that C is a function of the sample size, population size and the confidence level.

(c) an input difference D of 1st order,

then 99% of all possible plaintexts P will generate a pair $(P, P + D)$ for which the Avalanche Weight will fall inside the confidence interval of $[160 - C, 160 + C]$. For example, for a sample size of 20,000, we have $C = 0.91216$. We see that at round 4, the avalanche weight is always inside the interval $[160 - 0.91216, 160 + 0.91216]$, so we can consider the test passed at round 4 as shown in Fig. 7.

8. **Scalability:** The model level implementation supports scalability in terms of (the large) number of vector spaces computed per GPU. As the number of GPUs increases, the total number of vector spaces computed per GPU decreases and hence decreasing the total evaluation time. It will provide flexibility to process high-order avalanche tests (where order ≥ 4) in lesser time. Our implementation performs reasonably well for up to 4-th order tests. Of course, adding or removing CUDA cores would improve or diminish the performances in a trivial way. The main challenge, which for now remains an open problem, is to perform 5-th order tests. If one would want to implement the same tests over CPUs, the main issue he would face is the cost of purchasing several cores. For comparison, we used around 100,000 CUDA cores. The CPUs are efficient when the total number of vector spaces to be processed is reasonable. The CPUs are limited by the number of cores and the number of operations drastically increases when the order of tests increases. CPUs under-performs already for 3-th order avalanche tests.

Confidence Interval	Sample size needed
0.1	1664100
0.91216	20,000
1	16641
2.8845	2,000
3.724	1,200
10	166
12.9	100
40	10

Fig. 6. Confidence Interval for the Sample Sizes for Confidence Level 99% on population 2^{320}

Samples	Rounds	Weight_Min	Weight_Max	Confidence Interval
10	3	131.1	160.0	40
10	4	150.2001	160.0	40
100	3	137.63	160.0	12.9
100	4	157.49	161.9	12.9
1,200	3	139.7333	160.0	3.724
1,200	4	159.3608	160.7158	3.724
2,000	3	139.8149	160.0	2.8845
2,000	4	159.4271	160.6405	2.8845
20,000	3	140.4578	160.0	0.91216
20,000	4	159.8024	160.1752	0.91216

Fig. 7. Analysis of Confidence Intervals for Various Sample Sizes on 1st order Avalanche Tests

9 Conclusion

In this paper, we propose and evaluate high-order avalanche tests on multi-GPU platforms through our ACE-HoT framework. This framework is general and can be easily adapted to test other block ciphers and permutations on several GPU models.

We provided a detailed analysis of the permutation of the ASCON cipher and a comparison of how different ciphers perform under this test. We showed that for some ciphers (e.g. ASCON) the avalanche criteria are reached at a later round when considering higher orders than 1.

The main challenge of this test was the huge number of cipher evaluations that need to be performed, especially for order 4 tests. We leave for future work to optimize the code and reach even higher orders and to study how the newly found biases could be exploited as a base to mount new or improve existing attacks.

Another open challenge for future work is to explore the use of this generic framework for other applications of cryptanalysis like the work that has been done for the first collision of full SHA-1 [25].

References

1. Authors, V.: CAESAR: competition for authenticated encryption: security, applicability, and robustness (2014). https://competitions.cr.yp.to/caesar.html. Accessed 14 Apr 2022
2. g Biham, E., Biryukov, A., Shamir, A.: Cryptanalysis of skipjack reduced to 31 rounds using impossible differentials. In: Advances in Cryptology-EUROCRYPT'99: International Conference on the Theory and Application of Cryptographic Techniques Prague, Czech Republic, 2–6 May 1999 Proceedings 18, pp. 12–23. Springer, Heidelber (1999). https://doi.org/10.1007/3-540-48910-x_2
3. Carlet, C., Crama, Y., Hammer, P.L.: Vectorial boolean functions for cryptography. In: Crama, Y., Hammer, P.L. (eds.) Boolean Models and Methods in Mathematics, Computer Science, and Engineering, pp. 398–470. Cambridge University Press, Cambridge (2010). https://doi.org/10.1017/cbo9780511780448.012
4. Corp., N.: Dynamic parallelism in CUDA (2012). https://goo.gl/KhEhve
5. Daemen, J., Hoffert, S., Assche, G.V., Keer, R.V.: The design of Xoodoo and Xoofff. IACR Trans. Symm. Cryptol. 2018(4), 1–38 (2018). https://doi.org/10.13154/tosc.v2018.i4.1-38
6. Dobraunig, C., Eichlseder, M., Mendel, F., Schläffer, M.: Ascon v1.2 submission to nist. Technical report, NIST (2021). https://ascon.iaik.tugraz.at/files/asconv12-nist.pdf
7. Fedus, W., Zoph, B., Shazeer, N.: Switch transformers: scaling to trillion parameter models with simple and efficient sparsity. J. Mach. Learn. Res. 23, 120:1–120:39 (2022)
8. Feistel, H.: Cryptography and computer privacy. Sci. Am. 228(5), 15–23 (1973)
9. Forrié, R.: The strict avalanche criterion: spectral properties of boolean functions and an extended definition. In: Goldwasser, S. (ed.) CRYPTO 1988. LNCS, vol. 403, pp. 450–468. Springer, New York (1990). https://doi.org/10.1007/0-387-34799-2_31
10. Hetherington, T.H., Lubeznov, M., Shah, D., Aamodt, T.M.: Edge: event-driven gpu execution. In: 2019 28th International Conference on Parallel Architectures and Compilation Techniques (PACT), pp. 337–353. IEEE Computer Society, Los Alamitos (2019). https://doi.org/10.1109/PACT.2019.00034

11. Kam, J.B., Davida, G.I.: Structured design of substitution-permutation encryption networks. IEEE Trans. Comput. **28**(10), 747–753 (1979)
12. Kim, J., Hur, S., Lee, E., Lee, S., Kim, J.: Nlp-fast: a fast, scalable, and flexible system to accelerate large-scale heterogeneous nlp models. In: 2021 30th International Conference on Parallel Architectures and Compilation Techniques (PACT), pp. 75–89. IEEE Computer Society, Los Alamitos (2021). https://doi.org/10.1109/PACT52795.2021.00013
13. Kim, Y., Yeom, Y.: Accelerated implementation for testing IID assumption of NIST SP 800–90B using GPU. PeerJ Comput. Sci. **7**, e404 (2021)
14. Kirk, D.B., Hwu, W.M.W.: Programming Massively Parallel Processors: A Hands-on Approach, 3rd edn. Morgan Kaufmann Publishers Inc., San Francisco (2016)
15. Knudsen, L.R.: Truncated and higher order differentials. In: Preneel, B. (ed.) FSE 1994. LNCS, vol. 1008, pp. 196–211. Springer, Heidelberg (1995). https://doi.org/10.1007/3-540-60590-8_16
16. Lai, X.: Higher order derivatives and differential cryptanalysis. In: Communications and Cryptography, pp. 227–233. Springer, Heidelberg (1994). https://doi.org/10.1007/978-1-4615-2694-0_23
17. Liu, G., Wang, S., Bao, Y.: Seer: a time prediction model for CNNs from GPU kernel's view. In: 2021 30th International Conference on Parallel Architectures and Compilation Techniques (PACT), pp. 173–185. IEEE Computer Society, Los Alamitos (2021). https://doi.org/10.1109/PACT52795.2021.00020
18. Mark, H.: CUDA Pro Tip: Write Flexible Kernels with Grid-Stride Loops (2013)
19. NIST: SHA-3 Competition (2007). https://csrc.nist.gov/projects/hash-functions/sha-3-project. Accessed 14 Apr 2022
20. NIST: Lightweight Cryptography Standardization Process (2018). https://csrc.nist.gov/Projects/lightweight-cryptography. Accessed 14 Apr 2022
21. Preneel, B., Robshaw, M., Johansson, T., Bosselaers, A.: eSTREAM: the ECRYPT Stream Cipher Project (2005). https://www.ecrypt.eu.org/stream/. Accessed 14 Apr 2022
22. Rohit, R., Sarkar, S.: Diving deep into the weak keys of round reduced Ascon. In: IACR Transactions on Symmetric Cryptology, pp. 74–99 (2021)
23. Rukhin, A., Soto, J., Nechvatal, J., Smid, M., Barker, E.: A statistical test suite for random and pseudorandom number generators for cryptographic applications. Technical report, Booz-allen and hamilton inc mclean va (2001)
24. Smid, M., Foti, J.: Development of the advanced encryption standard (2021). https://doi.org/10.6028/jres.126.024. https://tsapps.nist.gov/publication/get_pdf.cfm?pub_id=931014
25. Stevens, M., Bursztein, E., Karpman, P., Albertini, A., Markov, Y.: The first collision for full SHA-1. In: Katz, J., Shacham, H. (eds.) CRYPTO 2017. LNCS, vol. 10401, pp. 570–596. Springer, Cham (2017). https://doi.org/10.1007/978-3-319-63688-7_19
26. Webster, A., Tavares, S.E.: On the design of s-boxes. In: Conference on the theory and Application of Cryptographic Techniques, pp. 523–534. Springer, Linz (1985). https://doi.org/10.1007/3-540-39799-x_41

Multi-party Computation

On Fully-Secure Honest Majority MPC Without n^2 Round Overhead

Daniel Escudero[1(✉)] and Serge Fehr[2]

[1] J.P. Morgan AI Research & J.P. Morgan AlgoCRYPT CoE, New York, USA
daniel.escudero@protonmail.com
[2] CWI Amsterdam, Amsterdam, The Netherlands

Abstract. Fully secure multiparty computation (or guaranteed output delivery) among n parties can be achieved with perfect security if the number of corruptions t is less than $n/3$, or with statistical security with the help of a broadcast channel if $t < n/2$. In the case of $t < n/3$, it is known that it is possible to achieve linear communication complexity, but at a cost of having a round count of $\Omega(\mathsf{depth}(C) + n)$ in the worst case. The number of rounds can be reduced to $O(\mathsf{depth}(C))$ by either increasing communication, or assuming some correlated randomness (a setting also known as the preprocesing model). For $t < n/2$ it is also known that linear communication complexity is achievable, but at the cost of $\Omega(\mathsf{depth}(C) + n^2)$ rounds, due to the use of a technique called dispute control. However, in contrast to the $t < n/3$ setting, it is not known how to reduce this round count for $t < n/2$ to $O(\mathsf{depth}(C))$, neither allowing for larger communication, or by using correlated randomness.

In this work we make progress in this direction by taking the second route above: we present a fully secure protocol for $t < n/2$ in the preprocessing model, that achieves linear communication complexity, and whose round complexity is only $O(\mathsf{depth}(C))$, without the additive n^2 term that appears from the use of dispute control. While on the $t < n/3$ such result requires circuits of width $\Omega(n)$, in our case circuits must be of width $\Omega(n^2)$, leaving it as an interesting future problem to reduce this gap. Our $O(\mathsf{depth}(C))$ round count is achieved by avoiding the use of dispute control entirely, relying on a different tool for guaranteeing output. In the $t < n/3$ setting when correlated randomness is available, this is done by using error correction to reconstruct secret-shared values, but in the $t < n/2$ case the equivalent is robust secret-sharing, which guarantees the reconstruction of a secret in spite of errors. However, we note that a direct use of such tool would lead to *quadratic* communication, stemming from the fact that each party needs to authenticate their share towards each other party. At the crux of our techniques lies a novel method for reconstructing a batch of robustly secret-shared values while involving only a linear amount of communication per secret, which may also be of independent interest.

© The Author(s), under exclusive license to Springer Nature Switzerland AG 2023
A. Aly and M. Tibouchi (Eds.): LATINCRYPT 2023, LNCS 14168, pp. 47–66, 2023.
https://doi.org/10.1007/978-3-031-44469-2_3

1   Introduction

Secure multiparty computation (MPC) is a set of techniques that enable a set of parties $P_1, \ldots, P_n$, each P_i having a private input x_i, to securely compute a function $z = f(x_1, \ldots, x_n)$ while only involving communication among each other, in such a way that they learn the output z, and not even an *adversary* corrupting a subset of t parties can learn any information about the inputs x_i from non-corrupted/honest parties, besides from what is inherently leaked by the result z.

Multiple MPC protocols exist depending on different factors like the power of the adversary, or the level of security required. A first important distinction is whether the adversary is *passive*, meaning that the behavior of corrupt parties is not affected (*i.e.* they follow the protocol specification), or whether he is *active*, meaning that the corrupt parties can deviate arbitrarily from the protocol execution. In this work we only consider active security, so from now on we assume the adversary under consideration is malicious, or active. Also, security can be computational, meaning that it is based on the hardness of some computational problem, or it can be information-theoretic, which means that security holds even against computationally unbounded adversaries. In the information-theoretic case there is a further distinction between perfect and statistical security, where the latter allows for a negligible error probability while the former achieves zero error probability.

Different techniques are used—and different results can be obtained—conditioning on the amount of parties t that the adversary is assumed to corrupt. If $t < n/3$ then we can achieve very efficient MPC with perfect security and with guaranteed output delivery (also abbreviated G.O.D., which means that the honest parties are guaranteed to receive the correct output z in spite of arbitrary adversarial behavior) [BTH08], and if $t < n/2$ then we can achieve the same but with statistical security, assuming a broadcast channel, which can be shown to be necessary [GSZ20]. Finally, if we do not assume any bound on t, then we must rely on computational assumptions, and the G.O.D. property (or even fairness, where the honest parties get the output *if* the adversary gets it) cannot be obtained in general. The focus of this work is the setting $t < n/2$, also known as *honest majority*. Furthermore, we assume the maximal case $n = 2t + 1$. From now on, whenever we refer to the setting $t < n/2$, we mean statistical security with an assumed broadcast channel, while for $t < n/3$ we mean perfect security without broadcast. In both cases we require full security, or G.O.D.

Several works have studied MPC in the honest majority setting. As we have mentioned, it is known that in this case G.O.D. with statistical security is attainable, with the help of a broadcast channel. Furthermore, this can be done while maintaining a total communication complexity of $O(n|C|)$, where $|C|$ is the size of the circuit to be computed (measured in the number of multiplication gates) [GSZ20]. This means that the total communication scales linearly with the number of parties, or put differently, the communication per party (*i.e.* after dividing by n) is constant in n. This is crucial for scalability, since this ensures each party does not communicate more as more parties join. Unfortunately, there is a major drawback of these works: the round complexity is given by $\Omega(\mathsf{depth}(C) + n^2)$. In contrast, weaker notions such as security with abort in the honest majority setting allow for a round complexity of $O(\mathsf{depth}(C))$, without any dependency in n. This is good for cases where the underlying communication has high latency, and the number of parties is large enough so that n^2 extra rounds become too much of an overhead.

Dispute Control. To understand where this additive term of n^2 originates from, it is worth discussing at a high level the core ideas involved in existing G.O.D. constructions like [GSZ20, BSFO12, BTH06]. In short, these works operate by letting the parties compute the circuit in a gate-by-gate fashion, where the parties maintain the invariant that for each wire they hold secret-shares of the underlying value. Multiplication gates require interaction, and a malicious party may cause an error by misbehaving. To ensure that the computation can recover from this failure, a technique called dispute control, introduced in [BTH06], is used. With this method, upon detecting a failure, the parties execute a "localization" protocol whose purpose is to identify a pair of parties $\{P_i, P_j\}$ where at least one is guaranteed to be corrupt (we say that P_i and P_j are *dispute* with each other). At this point, the computation is attempted once again, but this time some machinery is put on top so that it is ensured that either (1) the computation succeeds, or (2) a *new* dispute is identified, that is, the same pair $\{P_i, P_j\}$ will not fall in a dispute again.

The techniques used for securely computing multiplication gates require linear communication complexity $O(n)$ per gate, with interaction at each layer of the circuit, so in particular if there are no failures, the total communication is $O(n|C|)$ distributed across $O(\mathsf{depth}(C))$ rounds. Unfortunately, an active adversary can cause all new attempts to fail, generating the maximal number of disputes, which is $\Omega(n^2)$. This would lead to a communication of $n^2 \cdot \Omega(n|C|) = \Omega(n^3|C|)$ and $n^2 \cdot \Omega(\mathsf{depth}(C))$ rounds, but fortunately this can be addressed by partitioning the circuit into segments and verifying the correctness of each of them, instead of checking the whole circuit. This way, at most n^2 segments are repeated, and by choosing segments of size $|C|/n^2$ we see that the overall communication remains $O(n|C|)$. In terms of round count, letting d be the depth of each segment, the number of rounds is $O(\mathsf{depth}(C))$ from the optimistic case, plus $\Omega(n^2 d)$ from the possible n^2 segments that are repeated in the worse case. Hence, the round complexity in the worst case becomes $\Omega(\mathsf{depth}(C) + n^2)$. We note that this is particularly prohibitive when n is moderately large, with the overhead being more and more noticeable for not so large values of $\mathsf{depth}(C)$ (in particular when $\mathsf{depth}(C) = o(n^2)$).

On the $< n/3$ Setting. We recall that honest majority protocols that achieve weaker notions such as security with abort achieve a round complexity of $O(\mathsf{depth}(C))$. Currently, it is not known whether G.O.D. protocols with $O(\mathsf{depth}(C)) + o(n^2)$ rounds exist, which shows that, in the honest majority case, there is an efficiency gap between security with abort and guaranteed output delivery. In contrast, the landscape turns out to be different for the $t < n/3$

case. There it is also possible to achieve linear communication complexity by making use of a tool called player elimination. This is similar to dispute control (and in fact, player elimination predates dispute control), with the difference that when a pair $\{P_i, P_j\}$ with at least one corrupt party is identified, both of these parties can be removed from the computation, before a reattempt.[1] This way, a segment is repeated at most $O(n)$ times (since for every iteration there is one less corrupt party), so by taking segments of size $|C|/n$, linear communication is achieved with a round count of $\Omega(\mathsf{depth}(C) + n)$ in the worst case.

In stark contrast with the honest majority case, for $t < n/3$ it is actually possible to remove the overhead in n in the round complexity to obtain a protocol with $O(\mathsf{depth}(C))$ rounds, and this can be done in two different ways:

1. Pay more in terms of communication, leading to works such as [AAPP22, AAY21] that have superlinear communication.[2]
2. Maintain linear communication, but assume correlated randomness, or in other words, consider a protocol in the preprocessing model.

The second approach above is based on the observation that, in player-elimination-based protocols such as [BTH08], the adversary can only cause the repetition of a segment in a preprocessing phase in which some correlated randomness is established. Once this is completed, the online phase is guaranteed to provide output "in one go", without the need of repeating any segment (or splitting the remaining of the computation into segments, for that matter). We emphasize again that it is not known how to achieve $O(\mathsf{depth}(C))$ round count for the honest majority case, not even giving up on linear communication complexity, or even assuming correlated randomness. Hence, this motivates the following question:

> *Can we design fully secure honest majority MPC protocols with statistical security that require $O(\mathsf{depth}(C))$ rounds to securely compute a circuit C, either by having superlinear communication or assuming correlated randomness?*

1.1   Our Contribution

As previously mentioned, for the $t < n/3$ setting with perfect security, such result is only known to be achievable by either allowing for superlinear communication complexity, or having linear communication but assuming correlated randomness. In this work we take the second route in the question above, and

---

[1] This is not possible in the case of $n = 2t + 1$ since one out of the $t + 1$ honest parties may end up being removed, and the t remaining honest parties cannot "keep the state" of the computation (since otherwise the set of t corrupt parties should be able to also determine such state).

[2] In fact, the very recent work of [AAPP23] shows how to obtain *expected* $O(\mathsf{depth}(C))$ rounds while still achieving linear communication complexity, for certain class of circuits. We do not discuss this work further since our interest is on deterministic $O(\mathsf{depth}(C))$ rounds.

we present a statistically and fully secure MPC protocol for honest majority, that has a round complexity $O(\mathsf{depth}(C))$ that is independent of n, and has *linear* communication complexity. One drawback of our protocol is that the claimed linear communication holds for circuits of width $\Omega(n^2)$, while in the $t < n/3$ case this width requirement is a factor of n smaller. We leave it as interesting future work to further extend our techniques to tolerate circuits of width $\Omega(n)$, hence narrowing down the gap between results for $t < n/2$ and $t < n/3$.

In more detail, we present an MPC protocol to securely compute a circuit $|C|$ over a finite field $\mathbb{F}$, that has the following features:

- The protocol is set in the *preprocessing model* where the parties have access to some *correlated randomness*;
- The communication complexity is $O(n|C| + n^3\mathsf{depth}(C))$, which is linear if $\mathsf{depth}(C) = O(|C|/n^2)$, that is, each layer should contain $\Omega(n^2)$ multiplication gates.
- The round complexity is $O(\mathsf{depth}(C))$.

Our result is achieved by introducing novel ideas that remove the need of using dispute control techniques, in the preprocessing model. Qualitatively speaking, our approach offers several advantages with respect to protocols based on dispute control: the protocol proceeds in a gate-by-gate fashion (batching multiplication gates in the same layer), and handling each gate is guaranteed to be completed "in one go", without the need of checking its correctness or repeating its computation. Furthermore, our protocol is also arguably simpler than dispute-control-based protocols, as it does not need to localize and handle disputes, repeat segments, or incur in any of the related complexities of using dispute control. In fact, one important advantage of our protocol we only require a broadcast channel for the input phase, while the rest of the computation can happen over point to point channels; in contrast, dispute-control-based protocols like [BTH06] require a broadcast channel throughout the whole computation.

At the heart of our techniques lies a new and non-trivial technique for reconstructing a batch of n^2 values that are secret-shared in a robust manner, while involving a communication complexity of $O(n^3)$, which ultimately leads to a communication of $O(n)$ per reconstructed value. This may find several other applications in contexts where robust secret-sharing is used, like secure distributed storage.

1.2 Related Work

We already discussed some related work above, but here we present a more thorough discussion on relevant literature. In [HMP00], which is set in the $t < n/3$ setting, the idea of splitting the circuit into segments, together with the tool of player elimination, were introduced. This work makes use of verifiable secret-sharing and re-sharing á la [BOGW88, GRR98] in order to securely compute a given arithmetic circuit. This was later improved in [BTH08] by making use of multiplication triples, which, on top of achieving linear communication complexity, pushes the use of player elimination to the offline phase thanks to the use of error-correction techniques for the online phase. Any work that uses player elimination introduces an additive overhead of $\Omega(n)$ in terms of the number of rounds, stemming from the need of re-running each segment every time a new semi-corrupt pair (a pair of parties where at least one of them is guaranteed to be corrupt) is identified. If one wishes to avoid this overhead, works such as [AAPP22, AAY21] achieve a round count of $O(\mathsf{depth}(C))$, albeit with super-linear communication complexity. Substantial progress towards improving this trade-off was made in [AAPP23], where a perfectly secure protocol for $t < n/3$ with linear communication complexity (for certain class of circuits) and *expected* $O(\mathsf{depth}(C))$ rounds was given.

In [BTH06] the dispute control framework, which is inspired by the player elimination framework, is introduced for the setting of $t < n/2$. This time, instead of removing an identified semi-corrupt pair, a mechanism is set in place so that these parties can keep participating in the protocol, and subsequent cheating leads to a *new* semi-corrupt pair being identified. To enable the identification of semi-corrupt pairs whenever cheating takes place, the secret-sharing structure must be enhanced by letting the parties hold shares of their shares, along with extra additional information in the form of tags under a message authentication code (MAC). Similarly to the player elimination technique, the use of dispute control introduces an additive overhead in terms of the number of rounds, this time of n^2, which corresponds to the maximum number of disputes that can occur.

The protocol in [BTH06] achieves a communication complexity of $O(|C|n^2\kappa)$ (ignoring non-dominant terms and broadcast calls), where κ is the statistical security parameter. This was later improved in [BSFO12] to $O(|C|(n + \kappa))$.[3] Concrete constants (plus certain quadratic term that is affected by the depth of the circuit) are further improved in [GSZ20]. We remark, however, that these two works still make use of the core ideas introduced in [BTH06] regarding dispute control, splitting the circuit into segments and repeating each of these in case of cheating. As a result, they suffer from a n^2 overhead in terms of the number of rounds. This also holds for the work of [BGIN20], which is based on replicated secret-sharing.

Another important work is [IKP+16], where a transformation that takes a semi-honest honest majority protocol together with a fully-secure protocol with a potentially smaller threshold, and produces a fully-secure honest majority protocol, is presented. This achieved by adapting the IPS compiler [IKP+16] from the computational to the information-theoretic setting. However, their approach once again makes use of similar ideas as player elimination and dispute control, and hence they incur in an additive overhead of $\mathsf{poly}(n)$ in terms of the number of rounds.[4]

---

[3] Here we count the number of field elements, although the only constructions known in the literature require a field whose size grows linearly with the number of parties.

[4] Interestingly, here the overhead if n instead of n^2, since the authors do not use dispute control but instead a technique that is closer to player elimination.

1.3   Overview of Our Techniques

For aiding in terms of readability, we provide a high level overview of our techniques.

A Protocol for $t < n/3$ in the Preprocessing Model. In order to motivate our protocol, we begin by presenting a G.O.D. protocol (with perfect security) in the $t < n/3$ setting, that achieves linear communication complexity and only requires $O(\text{depth}(C))$ number of rounds. This is a simplified version of the protocol from [BTH08]. First, we introduce some notation: we consider a finite field $\mathbb{F}$, and use $[\![x]\!]_d$ to denote Shamir secret-sharing with degree d. At a high level, the protocol proceeds as the majority of secret-sharing-based protocols: the parties start with degree-t sharings of the inputs of the computation, and then they proceed in a gate-by-gate fashion by computing shares of the result of each gate, until shares of the output are obtained, which can then be reconstructed. Addition gates are processed locally with the help of the linearity properties of Shamir secret-sharing. For multiplication gates, the parties make use of the preprocessing model in the following way: given $[\![x]\!]_t$ and $[\![y]\!]_t$ to be multiplied, and given correlated randomness of the form $([\![a]\!]_t, [\![b]\!]_t, [\![a \cdot b]\!]_t)$, where $a, b \in \mathbb{F}$ are uniformly random, (1) the parties compute locally $[\![d]\!]_t = [\![x]\!]_t - [\![a]\!]_t$ and $[\![e]\!]_t = [\![y]\!]_t - [\![b]\!]_t$, (2) they reconstruct these values to obtain d and e, and (3) the parties compute locally $[\![xy]\!]_t = e[\![a]\!]_t + d[\![b]\!]_t + [\![ab]\!]_t + de$.

The protocol is private given that a (and b) entirely hides x (and y) when reconstructing d (and e). Communication-wise, the complexity depends on how d and e are reconstructed. One way of doing this is letting each party announce their share of $[\![d]\!]_t$ (and $[\![e]\!]_t$) to each other party, who then reconstruct d (and e) from the received shares. A crucial property of Shamir secret-sharing with degree t is that, if $t < n/3$, then the t potentially incorrect shares provided by the corrupt parties can be error-corrected, and the receiving parties are guaranteed to be able to reconstruct the right underlying secret. In particular, every gate is guaranteed to succeed, so no repetitions are required and hence the number of rounds is $O(\text{depth}(C))$.

Getting Linear Communication Complexity. The approach sketched above, however, suffers from one major issue: since each party sends a share to every other party, communication is $\Omega(n^2)$. We are interested in linear communication, so a different approach is required. A common idea to achieve linearity when reconstructing secret-shared values is to use a "relay": all parties send their shares to a chosen party, say P_1, who reconstructs and forwards the result to the other parties. Unfortunately nothing prevents a corrupt P_1 from forwarding an incorrect value of their choice to the other parties. To handle this, a clever solution is given in [DN07], which consists of using multiple relays in such a way that, intuitively, there is always at least one honest relay who is guaranteed to reconstruct the right secret. However, special care is needed to really reduce communication to linear.

To do this reconstruction efficiently—while also guaranteeing successful reconstruction—the trick is to batch a collection of $t + 1$ values to be reconstructed $[\![s_0]\!]_t, \ldots, [\![s_t]\!]_t$, define the polynomial $f(\mathsf{Z}) = \sum_{\ell=0}^{t} s_\ell \cdot \mathsf{Z}^\ell$, compute (locally) $[\![f(j)]\!]_t$ for $j \in [n]$, and reconstruct each $f(j)$ towards each party P_j, who then relays this reconstructed value to the other parties. The main observation is that the parties can again apply error correction to $(f(1), \ldots, f(n))$ in order to recover the polynomial $f(\mathsf{Z}) = \sum_{\ell=0}^{t} s_\ell \cdot \mathsf{Z}^\ell$, from which they can recover the secrets $s_0, s_1, \ldots, s_t$. Notice that communication is still quadratic in n, but crucially, $t + 1$ values have been reconstructed. Hence, if $t + 1 = \Theta(n)$ (e.g. if $n = 3t + 1$), then this is $O(n^2/(t + 1)) = O(n)$ communication per secret, as desired. One can interpret $(f(1), \ldots, f(n))$ as "Shamir sharings", except that we are not interested in the zero point $f(0)$, but rather in the polynomial $f(\mathsf{Z})$ itself.

A First $\Omega(n^2|C|)$ Protocol for Honest Majority. With the ideas for G.O.D. with $t < n/3$ in the preprocessing model, we are ready to tackle the $t < n/2$ case. We begin by presenting a construction that achieves quadratic communication, and then discuss how we improve this initial protocol to achieve linear communication complexity. First, we follow a similar template as the protocol above: the parties start with Shamir sharings $[\![\cdot]\!]_t$ of each input, proceed in a gate-by-gate manner, handling addition gates locally and multiplication gates using triples $([\![a]\!]_t, [\![b]\!]_t, [\![ab]\!]_t)$, and finally reconstruct the output. Recall that, with this paradigm, a major bottleneck is the reconstruction of a secret-shared value $[\![s]\!]_t$, which in the $t < n/3$ setting is done while exploiting the error-correcting properties of Shamir secret-sharing. Unfortunately, for $t < n/2$, degree-t Shamir sharings do not satisfy error correction, and instead they only satisfy error detection, which ensures that either the correct secret is reconstructed by the receiver, or possibly no secret is reconstructed at all. At this point, one can obtain a protocol with abort, but it is not clear how to leverage this for G.O.D., besides making use of dispute control techniques to identify disputes and re-run some computation, which we want to avoid in order to only use $O(\mathsf{depth}(C))$ rounds.

Our first observation towards solving this issue is that, even though in the honest majority setting it is not possible to perform error correction, there is a related notion that provides a similar functionality, and this is *robust secret-sharing*. In a robust secret-sharing scheme there is a share algorithm that enables the distribution of a secret into multiple shares, and there is a rec(onstruction) algorithm that, on input n shares among which t of them are potentially maliciously modified, outputs the correct underlying secret, with overwhelming probability. There are multiple robust secret-sharing constructions in the literature (*cf.* [BPRW16,FY19]). Normally, these schemes operate by letting each party obtain Shamir shares of the secret s, together with some authentication tags that enable each share owner to prove to the intended receiver that the share they send is correct. To check correctness of the received shares and tags, each party also receives some keys. Let us abstract this notion and denote by $\langle x \rangle$ when a value x is robustly secret-shared. It is common that these constructions satisfy some notion of linearity, meaning that the parties can locally compute $\langle x + y \rangle$ from $\langle x \rangle$ and $\langle y \rangle$. We will make use of this in what follows.

We can use $\langle \cdot \rangle$ as a building block instead of plain Shamir $[\![\cdot]\!]_t$ in the template above to obtain an honest majority G.O.D. protocol, where the preprocessing produces correlations of the form $(\langle a \rangle, \langle b \rangle, \langle ab \rangle)$. In its basic form, reconstruction would be done by letting the parties use the rec procedure towards every other party, which enables each party to successfully reconstruct each value needed for handling multiplication gates.[5] However, this basic protocol is insufficient for our goals here, simply due to the reason that the resulting communication complexity is $\Omega(n^2|C|)$. This stems from the fact that, whenever a shared value must be learned by all parties (which again, happens for every single multiplication gate), each single party must send their share and tags to each other single party.

Reducing to $O(n|C|)$ for $t < n/2$. Our core contribution consists of improving the approach from above, that achieves G.O.D. in the preprocessing model using quadratic communication via robust secret-sharing, to linear communication. $\Omega(n^2)$ communication stems from the need of reconstructing a robustly-shared value towards all parties. Recall that a similar issue was faced when we sketched the protocol for $t < n/3$, and in page 53 we discussed a solution to this problem originating in the ideas from [DN07]. Hence, our first approach is to try and adapt this idea from the secret-sharing scheme used there, namely plain Shamir secret-sharing $[\![\cdot]\!]$, to the robust scheme $\langle \cdot \rangle$ used here. Such adaptation would look like this: to reconstruct $t+1$ robustly-shared values $\langle s_0 \rangle, \ldots, \langle s_t \rangle$, (1) the parties define the polynomial $f(\mathsf{Z}) = \sum_{\ell=0}^{t} s_\ell \cdot \mathsf{Z}^\ell$, (2) they compute $\langle f(j) \rangle$ for $j \in [n]$ (which can be done using the homomorphic properties of $\langle \cdot \rangle$), (3) they reconstruct each $f(j)$ towards each party P_j, who successfully reconstructs this $f(j)$ using the robustness properties of $\langle \cdot \rangle$. At this point, P_j is supposed to send $f(j)$ to the other parties, who then recover $f(\mathsf{Z})$ from these received values. However, here we face a fundamental issue: while this works in the $t < n/3$ case due to error correction, in our $t < n/2$ case the polynomial $f(\mathsf{Z})$ cannot necessarily be recovered from the values $(f(1), \ldots, f(n))$! This is precisely why robust secret-sharing was introduced: in order to guarantee reconstruction.

Our idea is to ensure that the parties are able to get not only "Shamir shares of $f(\mathsf{X})$", as above, but actual "robust shares of $f(\mathsf{X})$". In a bit more detail, our approach is to ensure the parties can obtain authentication information on the "Shamir shares" $(f(1), \ldots, f(n))$, which guarantees that each receiver can successfully filter out incorrect $f(i)$'s, and hence reconstruct the polynomial $f(\mathsf{Z})$, and with it the secrets $s_0, \ldots, s_t$. An important problem here, however, is that we would need to devise a way to enable each P_j to obtain tags on $f(j)$, one for each receiver P_k. We now discuss at an intuitive level how this is addressed in our work.

Providing P_j with Authentication Information. Recall that P_j holds $f(j)$, which is a "Shamir share" of the polynomial $f(\mathsf{Z})$, and P_j sends $f(j)$ to every other recipient P_k. We are missing a method by which P_k can check the correctness of this $f(j)$. To this end, imagine that $(f(1), \ldots, f(n))$ were *robust* sharings.

---

[5] We note that this is the approach taken in, for example, Bedoza [BDOZ11], which is set in the dishonest majority setting $t < n$.

of $f(\mathsf{Z})$, that is, in addition to the share $f(j)$, each party P_j also holds a set of authentication tags $(\tau_{1j}, \ldots, \tau_{nj})$ on $f(j)$. To reconstruct, P_j provides P_k with $f(j)$ and τ_{kj}, and P_k uses τ_k to verify the correctness of $f(j)$. Now, in our setting $f(j)$ is not a "sharing" per se, as it is not the result of a dealer distributing robust shares, or linear combinations of these. Instead, P_j obtained $f(j)$ via a robust reconstruction of $\langle f(j) \rangle$.

Our idea is to enhance the robust secret-sharing scheme to allow for "nested" reconstruction: we let the parties also hold shares of $(\langle \tau_{1j} \rangle, \ldots, \langle \tau_{nj} \rangle)$, which can be reconstructed towards P_j so that this party can obtain the tags $(\tau_{1j}, \ldots, \tau_{nj})$ on $f(j)$, and hence prove correctness of $f(j)$ to each other party P_k. The problem with this approach is that communication grows to n^3, given that each party must reconstruct n values towards each other party.

To alleviate this issue, consider a larger number of shares to be reconstructed, say n groups of $t+1$ sharings each (hence, there are $O(n^2)$ total shared values). If we first apply the idea above to each of the n groups, we obtain a communication of n^4, or $n^4/n^2 = n^2$ per reconstruction. However, here we make the crucial observation that, among these n^4 messages, the amount related to transmitting shares not related to authentication is n^3. Indeed, if authentication was not an issue, for each group, each P_j would receive one share from each other party P_i, and each P_j would send one share to each P_k, leading to n^2 elements, which is n^3 when the number of groups is factored in. As a result, the n^4 overhead is only coming from the transmission of authentication-related information. In the notation of the sketch above, this is originating from the reconstruction of the authentication tags $(\langle \tau_{1j} \rangle, \ldots, \langle \tau_{nj} \rangle)$ towards P_j (one for each group), whose sole purpose is to enable P_j to prove the correctness of $f(j)$ towards P_k.

To achieve linear communication complexity, we note that *all authentication information can be compressed across the n groups using random linear combinations*, or in other words, the parties can distribute the authentication data of the n groups at the same cost of one single group. This results in n^3 communication in total for the n^2 reconstructions, or $n^3/n^2 = n$ per reconstruction, as desired. One must be careful when developing this idea in detail. First, a corrupt party can easily overcome a check that uses random linear combinations if he/she knows the random coefficients before adding the errors. To address this, in contrast to vanilla robust secret-sharing where each party can send their Shamir share at the same time as the authentication information, we require each party to "commit" to their errors by first sending their Shamir shares before sampling the random coefficients, and only then they distribute the associated authentication data. However, this new approach introduces another complication, which is that the random linear combination used to convince each P_j of the reconstruction of $f(j)$ cannot be the same as the one P_j will use to convince each P_k of the correctness of $f(j)$. To this end, after P_j has sent $f(j)$ to each P_k, new random coefficients are sampled, and the parties robustly reconstruct towards P_j the necessary authentication data (using these coefficients) to convince P_k of the correctness of $f(j)$.

This high level idea is materialized in detail in Sect. 3, where we show how to efficiently and robustly reconstruct secret-shared values. The robust secret-sharing scheme we use is introduced in Sect. 2.

1.4 Notation

We let $\mathbb{F}$ be a finite field with $|\mathbb{F}| > \mathsf{poly}(n) \cdot 2^\kappa$, where κ is the statistical security parameter. We use $[k]$ to denote the set $\{1, \ldots, k\}$. $\mathbb{F}_{\leq d}[\mathsf{X}]$ denotes the vector space of polynomials over $\mathbb{F}$ of degree at most d, on the variable X. For security definitions in MPC we refer the reader to standard references such as [CDN15].

2 Robust Secret-Sharing

The main tool we make use of in our work is that of robust secret-sharing, which enables the properties of error correction, a secret to be distributed into multiple shares. Concretely, we introduce the following construction.

Definition 1. *We define the sharing $\langle x \rangle$ for a secret $x \in \mathbb{F}$ to consist of*

- *a random sharing polynomial $F_0(\mathsf{X}) \in \mathbb{F}_{\leq t}[\mathsf{X}]$ subject $F_0(0) = x$,*
- *random randomizer polynomials $F_1(\mathsf{X}), \ldots, F_t(\mathsf{X}) \in \mathbb{F}_{\leq t}[\mathsf{X}]$*
- *random key polynomials $A_0(\mathsf{Y}), \ldots, A_t(\mathsf{Y}) \in \mathbb{F}_{\leq t}[\mathsf{Y}]$, and*
- *the checking polynomial $C(\mathsf{X}, \mathsf{Y}) \in \mathbb{F}_{\leq t, \leq t}[\mathsf{X}, \mathsf{Y}]$ given by*

$$C(\mathsf{X}, \mathsf{Y}) = F_0(\mathsf{X}) \cdot A_0(\mathsf{Y}) + F_1(\mathsf{X}) \cdot A_1(\mathsf{Y}) + \cdots + F_t(\mathsf{X}) \cdot A_t(\mathsf{Y}). \tag{1}$$

Every party P_i is given $F_0(i), F_1(i), \ldots, F_t(i)$ and $A_0(i), A_1(i), \ldots, A_t(i)$ as well as the (coefficients of the) polynomial $C(\mathsf{X}, i)$.

With the definition above, we note that the view of party P_i is given by

$$\mathsf{view}_i(\langle x \rangle) = \big(A_0(i), A_1(i), \ldots, A_t(i), F_0(i), F_1(i), \ldots, F_t(i), C(\mathsf{X}, i)\big);$$

similarly, $\mathsf{view}_{\mathcal{A}}(\langle x \rangle)$ denotes the joint view of a set $\mathcal{A}$ of parties. For *multiple* secrets, their sharings are defined as above, but with *the same* key polynomials $A_0(\mathsf{Y}), \ldots, A_t(\mathsf{Y})$ yet random and independent sharing and randomizer polynomials. In other words, the key polynomials $A_0(\mathsf{Y}), \ldots, A_t(\mathsf{Y})$ are sampled uniformly at random once and for all, and the sharing and randomizer polynomials are sampled freshly for each x uniformly at random subject to the given constraint, i.e., $F_0(0) = x$.

To have simpler notation and more concise expressions, we introduce the *polynomial vectors* $\boldsymbol{F}(\mathsf{X}) = \big(F_0(\mathsf{X}), \ldots, F_t(\mathsf{X})\big) \in \mathbb{F}_{\leq t}[\mathsf{X}]^{t+1}$ and $\boldsymbol{A}(\mathsf{X}) = \big(A_0(\mathsf{Y}), \ldots, A_t(\mathsf{Y})\big) \in \mathbb{F}_{\leq t}[\mathsf{Y}]^{t+1}$, which allows us to re-write (1) very compactly as

$$C(\mathsf{X}, \mathsf{Y}) = \boldsymbol{F}(\mathsf{X}) \cdot \boldsymbol{A}(\mathsf{Y}). \tag{2}$$

A sharing $\langle x \rangle$ is then a random triple $\big(A(\texttt{Y}), F(\texttt{X}), C(\texttt{X}, \texttt{Y})\big)$ subject to $F_0(0) = x$ and (2), and the view of P_i (and similar for a set of parties) becomes $\mathsf{view}_i(\langle x \rangle) = \big(A(i), F(i), C(\texttt{X}, i)\big)$.

It follows immediately from (2) and the fact that $A(\texttt{Y})$ is reused for different sharings, that linear functions can be computed on shared values by obvious local computations. We will use the notation $\langle x + y \rangle \leftarrow \langle x \rangle + \langle y \rangle$ for local additions, and similarly for more general affine combinations.

Lemma 1 below ensures that a sharing $\langle x \rangle$ of a secret x leaks no information on x to any t parties, except with negligible probability.

Lemma 1. *For any set $\mathcal{A}$ of t (or fewer) parties, and for a random key polynomial vector $A(\texttt{Y})$, the following holds except with probability $1/|\mathbb{F}|$ over the choice of $A(\texttt{Y})$: The distribution of $\mathsf{view}_{\mathcal{A}}(\langle x \rangle)$ conditioned on $A(\texttt{Y})$ does not depend on the value of x.*

Proof. Without loss of generality, we may assume $\mathcal{A} = \{P_1, \dots, P_t\}$. We consider an arbitrary but fixed choice of $A(\texttt{Y})$, and we show the claimed independence to hold unless the $(t \times t)$-matrix with entries $A_i(j)$ for $i, j \in [t]$ is singular, which happens with probability $1/|\mathbb{F}|$ for a random $A(\texttt{Y})$.

Let $K_0(\texttt{X}) \in \mathbb{F}_{\leq t}[\texttt{X}]$ be the (unique) polynomial with $K_0(0) = 1$ yet $K_0(1) = \dots = K_0(t) = 0$. Also, let $K_1(\texttt{X}), \dots, K_t(\texttt{X})$ be such that also here $K_\ell(1) = \dots = K_\ell(t) = 0$ for $\ell \in [t]$, but now $K_1(0) \cdot A_1(j) + \dots + K_t(0) \cdot A_t(j) = -A_0(j)$ for $j \in [t]$. This exists due to the assumption on $A(\texttt{Y})$. The above conditions ensure that $K_1(\texttt{X}) \cdot A_1(j) + \dots + K_t(\texttt{X}) \cdot A_t(j) = -K_0(\texttt{X}) \cdot A_0(j)$, and thus $K(\texttt{X}) \cdot A(j) = 0$, for $j \in [t]$. Then, for any $\delta \in \mathbb{F}$, the pair consisting of $F'(\texttt{X}) := F(\texttt{X}) + \delta \cdot K(\texttt{X})$ and $C'(\texttt{X}, \texttt{Y}) := F'(\texttt{X}) \cdot A(\texttt{Y})$, together with $A(\texttt{Y})$, forms a sharing $\langle x' \rangle$ for the secret $x' = x + \delta$, for which the parties $P_1, \dots, P_t$ have the same view; namely $F'(i) := F(i)$ and $C'(\texttt{X}, i) = \big(F(\texttt{X}) + \delta \cdot K(\texttt{X})\big) \cdot A(i) = F(\texttt{X}) \cdot A(i) = C(\texttt{X}, i)$ for all $i \in [t]$. Furthermore, the above mapping from $\big(F(\texttt{X}), C(\texttt{X}, \texttt{Y})\big)$ to $\big(F'(\texttt{X}), C'(\texttt{X}, \texttt{Y})\big)$ is bijective, which proves the claim of the statement. $\square$

Recall that P_i's *share vector* $s_i = F(i)$ satisfies $s_i \cdot A(j) = C(i, j)$, and so any *incorrect* share vector $s_i' \neq s_i$ satisfies $s_i' \cdot A(j) = C(i, j)$ if and only if $(s_i - s_i') \cdot A(j) = 0$, which happens with probability $1/|\mathbb{F}|$ only when $A(j)$ is random. Thus, Lemma 2 below implies that the set $\mathcal{A}$ of corrupt parties will find an incorrect share vector that will be accepted by honest P_j with probability $1/|\mathbb{F}|$ only, even if they get to see the entire sharing polynomial vector $F(\texttt{X})$. Hence, any honest P_j can filter out all incorrect share vectors $s_i' \neq s_i$, allowing him to reconstruct the polynomial vector $F(\texttt{X})$, and thus $F(0)$ and the actual secret $x = F_0(0)$.

Lemma 2. *For any set $\mathcal{A}$ of t (or fewer) parties, for any $j \notin \mathcal{A}$, and for any $x \in \mathbb{F}$, the key vector $A(j)$ is uniformly random and independent of the pair $\big(\mathsf{view}_{\mathcal{A}}(\langle x \rangle), F(\texttt{X})\big)$.*

Proof. Again, we may assume $\mathcal{A} = \{P_1, \dots, P_t\}$. Let $K(\texttt{Y}) \in \mathbb{F}_{\leq t}[\texttt{Y}]$ be such that $K(1) = \dots = K(t) = 0$ and $K(j) = 1$. Then, for any vector $\delta \in \mathbb{F}^{t+1}$ the triple consisting of $A'(Y) = A(Y) + K(Y) \cdot \delta$, $F(X)$ and $C'(X,Y) = F(X) \cdot A'(Y)$ forms a sharing $\langle x \rangle$ of x for which the parties $P_1, \ldots, P_t$ have the same view, but now with P_j having key vector $A'(j) = A(j) + \delta$. Furthermore, the above mapping from $\big(A(Y), F(X), C(X,Y)\big)$ to $\big(A'(Y), F(X), C'(X,Y)\big)$ is bijective, which proves the claim of the statement. $\square$

From the above, we see that a secret-shared value $\langle x \rangle$ can be reconstructed towards a given receiver P_j, in such a way that P_j is guaranteed to obtain the correct secret. More precisely, each party P_i sends their share vector $s_i = F(i)$ to the receiver P_j, who checks that $s_i \cdot A(j) = C(i,j)$ for every $i \in [n]$. There are at least $t+1$ honest shares s_i that will pass the check, and due to Lemma 2 above, any incorrect share will fail the check with overwhelming probability. Hence, P_j will have sufficient correct shares to reconstruct the right secret: from the $\geq t+1$ shares $s_i = (F_0(i), \ldots, F_t(i))$ that pass the check, P_j uses the corresponding $F_0(i)$'s to reconstruct the secret $x = F_0(0)$. We call this procedure $\pi_{\mathsf{QuadRec}}(\langle x \rangle)$.

3   Efficient Reconstruction

It is possible to securely evaluate any arithmetic circuit over $\mathbb{F}$ with using our robust secret-sharing solution and multiplication triples $(\langle a \rangle, \langle b \rangle, \langle ab \rangle)$ from the preprocessing model: to add two robustly shared values the parties use the linearity properties of $\langle \cdot \rangle$, and to multiply they make use of the multiplication triples by first opening $d \leftarrow \langle x \rangle - \langle a \rangle$ and $e \leftarrow \langle y \rangle - \langle b \rangle$, and then computing locally $\langle xy \rangle \leftarrow e \langle a \rangle + d \langle b \rangle + \langle ab \rangle + de$. Reconstruction is guaranteed to result in the correct d and e, which ensures correctness, which is also the same property that guarantees the final output can be reconstructed correctly.

Since our goal is to achieve linear communication, we must design a way of reconstructing a series of shared values robustly and with linear communication per secret, which is precisely what we discuss in this section. Jumping ahead, our protocol will reconstruct n^2 secrets with $O(n^3)$ communication per secret, which means $O(n)$ per secret amortized. In the MPC protocol sketched above[6] each multiplication gate requires two reconstructions, and all reconstructions corresponding to multiplication gates in a single layer can be batched together. This means we need $n^2/2 = O(n^2)$ multiplication gates per layer (in average) to get the linear communication benefits from our reconstruction procedure, which is where the circuit width requirements of our results come from.

3.1   Towards Efficient Reconstruction

The naive approach of reconstructing a shared value by every party sending their share to every other party has quadratic complexity even when ignoring additional information, like tags etc., that are needed to filter out incorrect shares. In other words, just communicating the actual Shamir shares produces

---

[6] Even though this approach is quite standard in the literature, we provide a formal description and a security proof in the full version.

a too large overhead. For passive security, one can reconstruct a Shamir-shared value by sending the shares to a single party, who reconstructs and acts as a relay by sending the result to the other parties. In the actively secure setting, the work of [DN07] introduces a technique to achieve linear communication when reconstructing a batch of Shamir-shared values, essentially by using a different honest party to reconstruct each different value. However, for guaranteed output delivery this trick requires error correction, which is possible when $t < n/3$, but does not work in the $t < n/2$ regime, where only error detection is possible.

Here, we show how to reconcile the trick from [DN07] with the sharing $\langle x \rangle$ introduced above so that the (amortized) communication of the actual Shamir shares $s_i = F_0(i)$ becomes *linear*. However, the resulting reconstruction approach will still involve quadratic communication, but crucially, the super-linear overhead will be "only" due to the tags, *i.e.*, the remaining coordinates of $\boldsymbol{F}(i)$. We address this in Sect. 3.2, where we show how this quadratic communication can be taken care of. This is done, in essence, by batching together sufficiently many openings and using a single set of tags to verify a random linear combination.

Consider $t + 1$ sharings $\langle x^{(0)} \rangle, \ldots, \langle x^{(t)} \rangle$ that need to be reconstructed. They are given by $t + 1$ triples $\big(\boldsymbol{A}(\mathtt{Y}), \boldsymbol{F}^{(\ell)}(\mathtt{X}), C^{(\ell)}(\mathtt{X}, \mathtt{Y})\big)$ with the same $\boldsymbol{A}(\mathtt{Y})$ and with $C^{(\ell)}(\mathtt{X}, \mathtt{Y}) = \boldsymbol{F}^{(\ell)}(\mathtt{X}) \cdot \boldsymbol{A}(\mathtt{Y})$. Inspired by the basic idea from [DN07], we consider $\boldsymbol{F}(\mathtt{X}, \mathtt{Z}) = \sum_{\ell=0}^{t} \mathtt{Z}^{\ell} \cdot \boldsymbol{F}^{(\ell)}(\mathtt{X})$ and $C(\mathtt{X}, \mathtt{Y}, \mathtt{Z}) = \sum_{\ell=0}^{t} \mathtt{Z}^{\ell} \cdot C^{(\ell)}(\mathtt{X}, \mathtt{Y})$ which satisfy $C(\mathtt{X}, \mathtt{Y}, \mathtt{Z}) = \boldsymbol{F}(\mathtt{X}, \mathtt{Z}) \cdot \boldsymbol{A}(\mathtt{Y})$. The reconstruction then proceeds as follows:

1. Each P_i sends $\boldsymbol{F}(i, j) = \sum_{\ell} j^{\ell} \boldsymbol{F}^{(\ell)}(i)$ to P_j.
2. Each P_j checks that $C(i, j, j) = \boldsymbol{F}(i, j) \cdot \boldsymbol{A}(j)$ for $i \in [n]$, and P_j reconstructs $\boldsymbol{F}(0, j)$ from the values that pass the check.
3. Each P_j sends to each P_k the vector $\boldsymbol{F}(0, j)$.
4. Each P_k checks that $C(0, k, j) = \boldsymbol{F}(0, j) \cdot \boldsymbol{A}(k)$ for each $j \in [n]$, and then P_k reconstructs $\boldsymbol{F}(0, \mathtt{Z})$ from the values $\boldsymbol{F}(0, j)$ that pass the check. From $\boldsymbol{F}(0, \mathtt{Z})$ one can then read out $\boldsymbol{F}^{(0)}(0), \ldots, \boldsymbol{F}^{(t)}(0)$ and thus $x^{(0)}, \ldots, x^{(t)}$.

The key idea in our protocol above is the following. When P_j receives the vec- · tors $\boldsymbol{F}(1, j), \ldots, \boldsymbol{F}(n, j)$ in step 1, P_j can filter out incorrect shares and hence reconstruct $\boldsymbol{F}(0, j)$, so in particular P_j obtains the "secret" $F_0(0, j)$, which is relayed to each other party P_k. However, the main observation is that P_j also obtained as a "byproduct" the other points $(F_1(0, j), \ldots, F_t(0, j))$, and it turns out these can be used for P_j to convince each receiver P_k of the correctness of $F_0(0, j)$. In a bit more detail, we make the crucial observation that $\boldsymbol{F}(\mathtt{X}, j)$ are the share vectors corresponding to the sharing $\big(\boldsymbol{A}(\mathtt{Y}), \boldsymbol{F}(\mathtt{X}, j), C(\mathtt{X}, \mathtt{Y}, j)\big)$. So, from the discussion before Lemma 2, an honest P_j will indeed be able to recover $\boldsymbol{F}(0, j)$. Similarly the $\boldsymbol{F}(0, j)$'s sent to P_k in step 3. are the share vectors corresponding to the sharing $\big(\boldsymbol{A}(\mathtt{Y}), \boldsymbol{F}(0, \mathtt{Z}), C(0, \mathtt{Y}, \mathtt{Z})\big)$, allowing each P_k to recover $\boldsymbol{F}(0, \mathtt{Z})$.

3.2 Batched Verification

Unfortunately, the above reconstruction still has quadratic amortized complexity. This originates in the fact that, in the first (and third) step, each party sends a length-$(t+1)$ vector to each other party. However, the crucial observation is that if we do *not* count the information that is "only" sent for checking purposes, e.g., if in step 1. we only count the first coordinate $F_0(i,j)$ of $\boldsymbol{F}(i,j)$, then we actually *have* linear amortized complexity.

Due to this observation, we can get the aspired amortized linear complexity by doing the verification in batches, that is, compressing the checking information of a number of reconstructions without increasing the associated communication costs. Concretely, we consider the reconstruction of n groups of $t+1$ secrets each: $\langle x^{(m,0)} \rangle, \ldots, \langle x^{(m,t)} \rangle$ for $m \in \{0, \ldots, n-1\}$. Intuitively, our protocol with linear communication complexity is obtained by running, for each $m \in \{0, \ldots, n-1\}$, the solution from the previous section, but ignoring the checking information. That is, step 1. from the previous section is modified by letting each P_i compute $\boldsymbol{F}^{(m)}(i, \mathsf{Z}) = \sum_{\ell=0}^{t} \mathsf{Z}^\ell \boldsymbol{F}^{(m,\ell)}(i)$, but P_i only sends the first coordinate $F_0^{(m)}(i,j)$ to P_j. For each other coordinate $h \in [t]$, P_i sends a *compressed* version $F_h(i,j) = \sum_{m=0}^{n-1} \xi^m F_h^{(m)}(i,j)$, where $\xi \in \mathbb{F}$ is a fresh uniformly random value known by all parties.[7] This can still be used by P_j to filter out incorrect shares and hence reconstruct $F_0^{(m)}(0,j)$ for $m \in \{0, \ldots, n-1\}$. Then, P_j relays these values to each other party P_k.

The challenge now is that, to interpolate $F_0^{(m)}(0, \mathsf{Z})$ and hence learn the reconstructed secrets, P_k requires certain checking information to verify the validity of the values $F_0^{(m)}(0,j)$ sent by P_j. In step 3. from Sect. 3.1, such information corresponds to $(F_1^{(m)}(0,j), \ldots, F_t^{(m)}(0,j))$, but P_j does not have the means to send this to P_k as P_j only received $(F_1(0,j), \ldots, F_t(0,j))$, which is a compressed version of these values (and moreover, even if P_j had this data, sending it to each P_k would be too costly). The solution once again is to apply compression. A first thought would be to let P_j send $(F_1(0,j), \ldots, F_t(0,j))$ to P_k, who can use these values to check the correctness of $F_0^{(0)}(0,j), \ldots, F_0^{(n-1)}(0,j)$ by verifying the correctness $F_0(0,j) = \sum_{m=0}^{n-1} \xi^m F_0^{(m)}(0,j)$ instead. However, this does not work since P_j already knows ξ before sending each $F_0^{(m)}$, so P_j can correct any error present in these terms.

The solution here is to sample a new fresh random challenge ω, after P_j has "committed" to the values $F_0^{(m)}$ by sending them to each P_k, and use the compressed check as above but with this new term for the linear combination. The problem now is that, for $h \in [t]$, P_j holds $F_h(0,j) = \sum_{m=0}^{n-1} \xi^m F_h^{(m)}(0,j)$, but not the necessary $F_h'(0,j) = \sum_{m=0}^{n-1} \omega^m F_h^{(m)}(0,j)$ to convince each receiver P_k. To address this we simply let the parties run the "checking part" of the first part of the protocol above but using the challenge ω instead of ξ. More precisely, each P_i sends $F_h'(i,j) = \sum_{m=0}^{n-1} \omega^m F_h^{(m)}(0,j)$ to P_j, who uses this values to interpolate $F_h'(0,j)$, which P_j sends to P_k. The details of this protocol are provided below.

---

[7] This is done by reconstructing, using the procedure π_{QuadRec} from Sect. 3.1, a pre-shared random $\langle \xi \rangle$ provided by the preprocessing functionality.

π_{LinRec}: **Reconstruction with linear communication**

Input: $(t+1) \cdot n$ secrets $(\langle x^{(m,\ell)} \rangle)$, for $\ell \in \{0,\ldots,t\}$ and $m \in \{0,\ldots,n-1\}$, each given by polynomials $(\boldsymbol{A}(\mathrm{Y}), \boldsymbol{F}^{(m,\ell)}(\mathrm{X}), C^{(m,\ell)}(\mathrm{X},\mathrm{Y}))$.

Output: Each party P_k learns all $(x^{(m,\ell)})_{m,\ell}$.

Preprocessing: A functionality $\mathcal{F}_{\mathsf{Prep}}$ that distributes sharings $\langle r \rangle$, where $r \in \mathbb{F}$ is uniformly random and unknown to the adversary.

For each $j \in [n]$, each P_k obtains $\{F_0^{(m)}(0,j)\}_{m=0}^{n-1}$:

1. For $m \in \{0,\ldots,n-1\}$, each P_i computes $\boldsymbol{F}^{(m)}(i,\mathrm{Z}) = \sum_{\ell=0}^{t} \mathrm{Z}^\ell \boldsymbol{F}^{(m,\ell)}(i)$, and P_i sends $F_0^{(m)}(i,j)$ to each P_j.

2. The parties call $\mathcal{F}_{\mathsf{Prep}}$ to obtain $\langle \xi \rangle$, where $\xi \in \mathbb{F}$ is uniformly random and unknown to any party, and the parties execute the procedure $\pi_{\mathsf{QuadRec}}(\langle \xi \rangle)$, so that all parties learn ξ.

3. For $\ell \in \{0,\ldots,t\}$ and $h \in [t]$, each P_i computes $F_h(i,\mathrm{Z}) = \sum_{m=0}^{n-1} \xi^m F_h^{(m)}(i,\mathrm{Z})$, and sends to each P_j the vector $(F_1(i,j),\ldots,F_t(i,j))$.

4. Each P_j computes, for $i \in [n]$, $F_0(i,j) = \sum_{m=0}^{n-1} \xi^m F_0^{(m)}(i,j)$, and upon receiving $(F_1(i,j),\ldots,F_t(i,j))$ from P_i, P_j checks that

$$\boldsymbol{F}(i,j) \cdot \boldsymbol{A}(j) = \sum_{m=0}^{n-1} \sum_{\ell=0}^{t} \xi^m j^\ell \cdot C^{(m,\ell)}(i,j).$$

5. Let $\mathcal{I} \subseteq [n]$ be the set of indexes i's for which the check above did not fail. P_j interpolates $\boldsymbol{F}(\mathrm{X},j)$ from $(\boldsymbol{F}(i,j))_{i \in \mathcal{I}}$.

6. Each P_j sends $\{F_0^{(m)}(0,j)\}_{m=0}^{n-1}$ to each P_k.

Each P_j receives checking information:

7. The parties call $\mathcal{F}_{\mathsf{Prep}}$ to obtain $\langle \omega \rangle$, where $\omega \in \mathbb{F}$ is uniformly random and unknown to any party, and the parties execute the procedure $\pi_{\mathsf{QuadRec}}(\langle \omega \rangle)$, so that all parties learn ω.

8. Each P_i computes $F_h'(i,\mathrm{Z}) = \sum_{m=0}^{n-1} \omega^m F_h^{(m)}(i,\mathrm{Z})$ for $h \in [t]$. Then P_i sends $(F_1'(i,j),\ldots,F_t'(i,j))$ to each P_j.

9. Each P_j computes, for $i \in [n]$, $F_0'(i,j) = \sum_{m=0}^{n-1} \omega^m F_0^{(m)}(i,j)$, and upon receiving $(F_1'(i,j),\ldots,F_t'(i,j))$ from P_i, P_j checks that

$$\boldsymbol{F}'(i,j) \cdot \boldsymbol{A}(j) = \sum_{m=0}^{n-1} \sum_{\ell=0}^{t} \omega^m j^\ell \cdot C^{(m,\ell)}(i,j).$$

10. Let $\mathcal{I} \subseteq [n]$ be the set of indexes i's for which the check above did not fail. P_j interpolates $\boldsymbol{F}'(\mathrm{X},j)$ from $(\boldsymbol{F}'(i,j))_{i \in \mathcal{I}}$.

Each P_j sends checking information to each P_k, who then reconstruct:

11. Each P_j sends $(F_1'(0,j),\ldots,F_t'(0,j))$ to each P_k.
12. Upon receiving these values, each P_k computes $F_0'(0,j) = \sum_{m=0}^{n-1} \omega^m \cdot F^{(m)}(0,j)$ and checks that

$$\boldsymbol{F}'(0,j) \cdot \boldsymbol{A}(j) = \sum_{m=0}^{n-1} \sum_{\ell=0}^{t} \omega^m j^\ell \cdot C^{(m,\ell)}(0,j),$$

for each $j \in [n]$
13. Let $\mathcal{J} \subseteq [n]$ be the set of indexes j's for which the check above did not fail. For each $m \in \{0,\ldots,n-1\}$, P_k interpolates $F_0^{(m)}(0,\mathsf{Z}) = \sum_{\ell=0}^{t} x^{(m,\ell)} \mathsf{Z}^\ell$ from $(F_0^{(m)}(0,j))_{j \in \mathcal{J}}$, and outputs $(x^{(m,\ell)})_{m,\ell}$.

Theorem 1. *After executing procedure* π_{LinRec} *on input* $(\langle x^{(m,\ell)} \rangle)_{\ell \in \{0,\ldots,t\}, m \in \{0,\ldots,n-1\}}$, *each party P_k outputs the correct secrets $x^{(m,\ell)}$, except with probability $3t(n+1)/|\mathbb{F}|$. Moreover, the protocol requires linear communication complexity and makes use of a constant number of rounds.*

Proof. The claim on the number of rounds is verified by inspection. It is also easy to check that the total communication is $\Theta(n^3)$, and when we divide by the $(t+1)n = \Theta(n^2)$ elements being reconstructed, we obtain an amortized communication of $\Theta(n)$ per secret, as required.

Now, we prove the correctness and security of the protocol. To this end, we begin with the following claim.

Claim. In step 5, each P_j interpolates the correct $\boldsymbol{F}(\mathsf{X},j)$, except with probability $t(n+1)/|\mathbb{F}|$.

Proof (of claim). Let us consider a malicious party P_i who sends incorrect $\{F_0^{(m)}(i,j) + \epsilon_0^{(m)}\}_{m=0}^{n-1}$, and $(F_1(i,j) + \epsilon_1, \ldots, F_t(i,j) + \epsilon_t)$, to P_j. Assume that at least one $\epsilon_0^{(m)}$ is not zero. The check that P_j performs is

$$\sum_{h=0}^{t} (F_h(i,j) + \epsilon_h) \cdot A_h(j) = \sum_{m=0}^{n-1} \sum_{\ell=0}^{t} \xi^m j^\ell \cdot C^{(m,\ell)}(i,j),$$

where $\epsilon_0 = \sum_{m=0}^{n-1} \xi^m \epsilon_0^{(m)}$. Notice that the distribution of $\{\epsilon_0^{(m)}\}_{m=0}^{n-1}$ is independent of ξ since P_i sent $\{F_0^{(m)}(i,j) + \epsilon_0^{(m)}\}_{m=0}^{n-1}$ to P_j before the value ξ was opened. Hence, since at least one $\epsilon_0^{(m)}$ is not zero, Schwartz-Zippel lemma implies that ϵ_0 is also not zero except with probability at most $(n-1)/|\mathbb{F}|$.

It can be checked that the right hand side is equal to $\sum_{h=0}^{t} F_h(i,j) \cdot A_h(j)$, so in particular the check passes if and only if $\sum_{h=0}^{t} \epsilon_h \cdot A_h(j) = 0$. From the above, except with probability at most $|\mathbb{F}|^{-1}$, the vector $\boldsymbol{\epsilon}$ is not zero. Furthermore, from

Lemma 2 we have that, except with probability $|\mathbb{F}|^{-1}$, the vector $\boldsymbol{A}(j)$ looks uniformly random to the adversary. Hence, we see that except with probability $(n-1)/|\mathbb{F}| + 1/|\mathbb{F}| = n/|\mathbb{F}|$, the adversary passes the check if and only if a dot product between a random vector and a non-zero vector results in zero. This can happen only with probability $1/|\mathbb{F}|$. Hence, except with probability $1-(n+1)/|\mathbb{F}|$, the shares received by P_i are rejected.

From the above we see that the probability that P_j accepts an incorrect share is at most $(n+1)/|\mathbb{F}|$. Since there are at most t malicious parties, we have that the probability that there is at least one incorrect share accepted by P_j is at most $t(n+1)/|\mathbb{F}|$. Since the check for every honest party passes, and there are at least $t+1$ honest parties, P_j successfully reconstructs the correct $\boldsymbol{F}(\mathtt{X}, j)$, except with the probability above. This completes the proof of the claim.

With the claim at hand, we see that with overwhelming probability, every honest party P_j sends the correct $F_0^{(m)}(0, j)$ to each P_k in step 6. In a completely similar way as the proof of the claim above, we can prove the following:

Claim. In step 10, each P_j interpolates the correct $\boldsymbol{F}'(\mathtt{X}, j)$, except with probability $t(n+1)/|\mathbb{F}|$.

Proof (of claim). We proceed in the same way as in the claim above, but replacing ξ by ω, and $(F_1(i, j)+\epsilon_1, \ldots, F_t(i, j)+\epsilon_t)$ by $(F_1'(i, j)+\delta_1, \ldots, F_t'(i, j)+\delta_t)$, where δ_h are the possible errors introduced by P_i in step 8. The same proof works given that, as before, the error $\epsilon_0^{(m)}$ on $F_0^{(m)}$ is chosen by the adversary before sampling ω. We do not write down the rest of the details.

This claim shows then that, with overwhelming probability, each honest P_j will send to each P_k the correct $(F_1'(0, j), \ldots, F_t'(0, j))$ in Step 11, so in particular P_k receives at least $t+1$ correct shares. This turns out to be enough for an honest P_k to interpolate $F_0^{(m)}(0, \mathtt{Z})$ correctly since, as the following claim illustrates, P_k can filter out incorrect shares with overwhelming probability.

Claim. In step 13, P_k interpolates the correct $F_0^{(m)}(0, \mathtt{Z})$, except with probability at most $t(n+1)/|\mathbb{F}|$.

Proof (of claim). The proof is similar to that of the previous two Lemmas 1 and 2. Consider a malicious P_j who sends $\{F_0^{(m)}(0, j) + \delta_0^{(m)}\}_{m=0}^{n-1}$ to P_k in step 6, and also $(F_1'(0, j) + \delta_1, \ldots, F_t'(0, j) + \delta_t)$ in step 11. The check that P_k carries out is then

$$\sum_{h=0}^{t}(F_h'(0, j) + \delta_h) \cdot A_h(j) = \sum_{m=0}^{n-1}\sum_{\ell=0}^{t}\omega^m j^\ell \cdot C^{(m,\ell)}(0, j),$$

where $\delta_0 = \sum_{m=0}^{n-1}\omega^m \delta_0^{(m)}$. The right-hand side equals $\sum_{h=0}^{t} F_h'(0, j) \cdot A_h(j)$, so the check passes if and only if $\sum_{h=0}^{t}\delta_h \cdot A_h(j) = 0$. Here, we proceed as with the proofs of the previous claims, noticing that $\{\delta_0^{(m)}\}_{m=0}^{n-1}$ is chosen by the adversary before seeing the challenge ω, so $\delta_0 \neq 0$ with probability at least

$1 - (n-1)/|\mathbb{F}|$. Following similar steps as the previous proofs, we obtain that P_k accepts an incorrect share with probability at most $(n+1)/|\mathbb{F}|$. Hence, the probability that P_k reconstructs an incorrect $F_0^{(m)}(0, \mathsf{Z})$ is at most $t(n+1)/|\mathbb{F}|$, as stated in the claim.

Putting together what we have seen above, we obtain that, except with probability $3t(n+1)/|\mathbb{F}|$, each P_k reconstructs the correct secrets. Thus, the theorem is proven. □

Acknowledgments. This paper was prepared in part for information purposes by the Artificial Intelligence Research Group and the AlgoCRYPT CoE of JPMorgan Chase & Co and its affiliates ("JP Morgan") and is not a product of the Research Department of JP Morgan. JP Morgan makes no representation and warranty whatsoever and disclaims all liability, for the completeness, accuracy, or reliability of the information contained herein. This document is not intended as investment research or investment advice, or a recommendation, offer, or solicitation for the purchase or sale of any security, financial instrument, financial product, or service, or to be used in any way for evaluating the merits of participating in any transaction, and shall not constitute a solicitation under any jurisdiction or to any person, if such solicitation under such jurisdiction or to such person would be unlawful. 2023 JP Morgan Chase & Co. All rights reserved.

References

[AAPP22] Abraham, I., Asharov,G., Patil, S., Patra, A.: Asymptotically free broadcast in constant expected time via packed vss. In: Kiltz, E., Vaikuntanathan, V. (eds.) Theory of Cryptography: 20th International Conference, TCC 2022, Chicago, IL, USA, 7–10 November 2022, Proceedings, Part I, pp. 384–414. Springer, Heidelberg (2022). https://doi.org/10.1007/978-3-031-22318-1_14

[AAPP23] Abraham, I., Asharov, G., Patil, S., Patra, A.: Detect, pack and batch: perfectly-secure mpc with linear communication and constant expected time. In: Hazay, C., Stam, M. (eds.) Advances in Cryptology-EUROCRYPT 2023: 42nd Annual International Conference on the Theory and Applications of Cryptographic Techniques, Lyon, France, 23–27 April 2023, Proceedings, Part II, pp. 251–281. Springer, Heidelberg (2023). https://doi.org/10.1007/978-3-031-30617-4_9

[AAY21] Abraham, I., Asharov, G., Yanai, A.: Efficient perfectly secure computation with optimal resilience. In: Nissim, K., Waters, B. (eds.) TCC 2021. LNCS, vol. 13043, pp. 66–96. Springer, Cham (2021). https://doi.org/10.1007/978-3-030-90453-1_3

[BDOZ11] Bendlin, R., Damgård, I., Orlandi, C., Zakarias, S.: Semi-homomorphic encryption and multiparty computation. In: Paterson, K.G. (ed.) EUROCRYPT 2011. LNCS, vol. 6632, pp. 169–188. Springer, Heidelberg (2011). https://doi.org/10.1007/978-3-642-20465-4_11

[BGIN20] Boyle, E., Gilboa, N., Ishai, Y., Nof, A.: Efficient fully secure computation via distributed zero-knowledge proofs. In: Moriai, S., Wang, H. (eds.) ASIACRYPT 2020. LNCS, vol. 12493, pp. 244–276. Springer, Cham (2020). https://doi.org/10.1007/978-3-030-64840-4_9

[BOGW88] Ben-Or, M., Goldwasser, A., Wigderson, A.: Completeness theorems for non-cryptographic fault-tolerant distributed computation. In: Proceedings of the Twentieth Annual ACM Symposium on Theory of Computing, pp. 1–10 (1988)

[BPRW16] Bishop, A., Pastro, V., Rajaraman, R., Wichs, D.: Essentially optimal robust secret sharing with maximal corruptions. In: Fischlin, M., Coron, J.-S. (eds.) EUROCRYPT 2016. LNCS, vol. 9665, pp. 58–86. Springer, Heidelberg (2016). https://doi.org/10.1007/978-3-662-49890-3_3

[BSFO12] Ben-Sasson, E., Fehr, S., Ostrovsky, R.: Near-linear unconditionally-secure multiparty computation with a dishonest minority. In: Safavi-Naini, R., Canetti, R. (eds.) CRYPTO 2012. LNCS, vol. 7417, pp. 663–680. Springer, Heidelberg (2012). https://doi.org/10.1007/978-3-642-32009-5_39

[BTH06] Beerliová-Trubíniová, Z., Hirt, M.: Efficient multi-party computation with dispute control. In: Halevi, S., Rabin, T. (eds.) TCC 2006. LNCS, vol. 3876, pp. 305–328. Springer, Heidelberg (2006). https://doi.org/10.1007/11681878_16

[BTH08] Beerliová-Trubíniová, Z., Hirt, M.: Perfectly-secure MPC with linear communication complexity. In: Canetti, R. (ed.) TCC 2008. LNCS, vol. 4948, pp. 213–230. Springer, Heidelberg (2008). https://doi.org/10.1007/978-3-540-78524-8_13

[CDN15] Cramer, R., Damgård, I.B., Nielsen, J.B.: Secure Multiparty Computation. Cambridge University Press, Cambridge (2015)

[DN07] Damgård, I., Nielsen, J.B.: Scalable and unconditionally secure multiparty computation. In: Menezes, A. (ed.) CRYPTO 2007. LNCS, vol. 4622, pp. 572–590. Springer, Heidelberg (2007). https://doi.org/10.1007/978-3-540-74143-5_32

[FY19] Fehr, S., Yuan, C.: Towards optimal robust secret sharing with security against a rushing adversary. In: Ishai, Y., Rijmen, V. (eds.) EUROCRYPT 2019. LNCS, vol. 11478, pp. 472–499. Springer, Cham (2019). https://doi.org/10.1007/978-3-030-17659-4_16

[GRR98] Gennaro, R., Rabin, M.O., Rabin, T.: Simplified vss and fast-track multiparty computations with applications to threshold cryptography. In: Proceedings of the Seventeenth Annual ACM Symposium on Principles of Distributed Computing, pp. 101–111 (1998)

[GSZ20] Goyal, V., Song, Y., Zhu, C.: Guaranteed output delivery comes free in honest majority MPC. In: Micciancio, D., Ristenpart, T. (eds.) CRYPTO 2020. LNCS, vol. 12171, pp. 618–646. Springer, Cham (2020). https://doi.org/10.1007/978-3-030-56880-1_22

[HMP00] Hirt, M., Maurer, U., Przydatek, B.: Efficient secure multi-party computation. In: Okamoto, T. (ed.) ASIACRYPT 2000. LNCS, vol. 1976, pp. 143–161. Springer, Heidelberg (2000). https://doi.org/10.1007/3-540-44448-3_12

[IKP+16] Ishai, Y., Kushilevitz, E., Prabhakaran, M., Sahai, A., Yu, C.-H.: Secure protocol transformations. In: Robshaw, M., Katz, J. (eds.) CRYPTO 2016. LNCS, vol. 9815, pp. 430–458. Springer, Heidelberg (2016). https://doi.org/10.1007/978-3-662-53008-5_15

Privacy-Preserving Edit Distance Computation Using Secret-Sharing Two-Party Computation

Hernán Vanegas[1], Daniel Cabarcas[1], and Diego F. Aranha[2(✉)]

[1] Universidad Nacional de Colombia, Medellín, Colombia
{hdvanegasm,dcabarc}@unal.edu.co
[2] Aarhus University, Aarhus, Denmark
dfaranha@cs.au.dk

Abstract. The edit distance is a metric widely used in genomics to measure the similarity of two DNA chains. Motivated by privacy concerns, we propose a 2PC protocol to compute the edit distance while preserving the privacy of the inputs. Since the edit distance algorithm can be expressed as a mixed-circuit computation, our approach uses protocols based on secret-sharing schemes like Tinier and $SPDZ_{2^k}$; and also daBits to perform domain conversion and edaBits to perform arithmetic comparisons. We modify the Wagner-Fischer edit distance algorithm, aiming at reducing the number of rounds of the protocol, and achieve a flexible protocol with a trade-off between rounds and multiplications. We implement our proposal in the MP-SPDZ framework, and our experiments show that it reduces the execution time respectively by 81% and 54% for passive and active security with respect to a baseline implementation in a LAN. The experiments also show that our protocol reduces traffic by two orders of magnitude compared to a BMR-MASCOT implementation.

Keywords: edit distance · secure MPC · secret-sharing schemes

1 Introduction

Given an alphabet of symbols Σ, the edit distance between two strings in Σ^* is the minimum cost of a sequence of editing operations (insertions, deletions, or substitutions) to transform one string into the other [28]. Intuitively, the smaller the edit distance between two strings, the more similar they are. Algorithms to compute the edit distance have been studied for many years and the most popular are based on dynamic programming, such as the Wagner-Fischer algorithm [29]. Such algorithms are useful in genomics, where the similarity between two gene sequences is used in disease diagnosis and treatment [32]. On a typical scenario, millions of *reads* from a subject's DNA are compared to a reference for alignment, with read lengths ranging from a few hundred to a few million bases [23].

Despite the benefits of computing similarities in genomic data, there are risks that come from revealing such information. One of the main risks is called *re-identification*, where a subject can be identified from its genomic data [21]. There

The author was partially supported by the CyTeD program grant 522RT0131.

are other concerns like *ancestry identification*, where an individual can identify their ancestors from genomic data; and the so-called *attribute disclosure attacks via DNA*, where an attacker can detect a sensible attribute about someone from their DNA sample and a database of attribute-related samples [13].

These concerns motivate the application of privacy-preserving computation in the following scenario: Alice and Bob are connected via a secure communication channel and each has a DNA chain represented as a list of nucleotides. They want to compute the edit distance of both chains, but without revealing their chain to each other. We will accomplish this task by evaluating the Wagner-Fischer (WF) algorithm without revealing the inputs. The WF algorithm is a dynamic programming solution to find the edit distance $d(A, B)$ between two chains $A = (a_1, \ldots, a_n)$ and $B = (b_1, \ldots, b_m)$. The core of the algorithm is to compute a matrix D for which the recursion holds (for $1 \leq i \leq n$ and $1 \leq j \leq m$):

$$D(i,j) = \min \begin{cases} D(i-1,j) + 1, \\ D(i,j-1) + 1, \\ D(i-1,j-1) + t(i,j) \end{cases}, \text{ with } t(i,j) \stackrel{\text{def}}{=} \begin{cases} 1 & \text{if } a_i \neq b_j \\ 0 & \text{otherwise} \end{cases}.$$

In this algorithm, two operations have high relevance for security: (i) the computation of t requires a secure equality test between a pair of symbols in the chains; (ii) the computation of the minimum requires secure comparison between integers, which in turn needs the extraction of their most significant bit.

These challenges can be solved using various cryptographic techniques. Particularly, we will focus on *secure multi-party computation* (MPC). In an MPC protocol, a set of parties, each one holding part of the input of a function, want to compute such function while preserving the privacy of the inputs. To achieve their goal, the parties exchange messages and perform local computations. In the end, the parties may obtain the correct result, and the messages exchanged between them are guaranteed not to reveal any information about their inputs.

Most previous works in secure computation of edit distance employ garbled circuits as the MPC protocol because of their good performance in bit-wise operations [12,18,31]. Another class of MPC protocol based on *secret-sharing schemes* (SSS) is efficient for arithmetic operations [14], but it was rarely used for this problem [26]. Since recent advances in protocols based on SSS allow efficient transformation between an arithmetic and a binary domain [1,11,14,25], and since the WF algorithm has significant mixed computation, designing an efficient MPC solution based on secret-sharing should be possible.

Related Work. Most current and past research in secure computation of edit distance are based on homomorphic encryption (HE) and garbled circuits (GC) (see surveys at [12] and [22]). In the case of HE, Zheng et al. [32] propose an architecture where the data owners outsource the computation of edit distance. They ensure privacy by using a modified version of the Paillier cryptosystem [5], but their protocol allows one of the parties to know the DNA chain of the other party and compute the edit distance between blocks in the clear to improve performance. For dynamic programming approaches, Rane and Sun [24] compute the minimum between three elements using HE. Cheon et al. [7] take the idea further and compute the minimum of a list of numbers to reduce circuit depth. However, they do not prove correctness and optimality of all their techniques, and focus on same-length strings. We extend their strategy to solve both problems.

Another technique actively used to compute edit distance is GC, and protocols derived from Yao's GC are widely used to implement dynamic programming approaches [12]. Jha et al. [18] is among the first works, and they use one circuit for each basic operation in the algorithm: increment, minimum, and equality test. Further theoretical and practical work in [12,31] improves security, memory usage, communication complexity, and specialized hardware to increase parallelism. More recently, Zhu and Huang [33] use GC to compute the edit distance in both active and passive threat models, and claim to outperform the best previous GC-based protocols. As in our work, they consider the secure computation of the WF algorithm and exploit the structure of the minimization problem to find better bounds to improve performance, but they do not report performance measurements in the actively secure setting. Other works consider an approximation version of the edit distance problem to improve performance [3].

Compared to HE and GC, protocols based on secret-sharing techniques are less common for edit distance. Rane and Sun [24] use additive secret-sharing alongside HE, but they do not rely on secret-sharing to perform the operations. EPISODE by Schneider et al. [26] is the closest to our techniques. They use ideas from [2] to compute an approximation of the edit distance using the ABY framework [11]. ABY allows designing protocols using mixed-circuit computation against passive adversaries, so they can compute parts of their protocol in binary or arithmetic domains, moving secrets from one domain to another. There are significant differences between this and our work: (i) they only consider security against passive adversaries, while we also explore active adversaries; (ii) they improve performance by approximating the edit distance, while we focus on the exact problem; (iii) they consider a different security setup, aligning multiple sequences to a publicly known reference genome.

Contributions. We propose a 2PC protocol to compute the edit distance privately. More parties are possible, but the scenario naturally suggests two parties. We apply recently developed MPC protocols based on secret-sharing schemes such as $SPDZ_{2^k}$ [9] and Tinier [15], and protocols such as daBits [25] and edaBits [14]. To the best of our knowledge, we are the first to propose a solution to secure edit distance using these techniques. We divide the WF algorithm into two parts: the preamble in charge of computing the matrix t, and the arithmetic section to compute the matrix D. We optimize each part separately.

For the computation of t, we encode the nucleotides using a binary representation, and we propose a protocol to compute the equality test between a pair of nucleotides through bit-wise operations using Tinier. Once we compute t, we obtain binary shares of each possible value of the function, and we use daBits to transform such binary shares into arithmetic shares for the arithmetic section.

For the arithmetic part, we generalize the ideas presented by Cheon et al. [7] in two directions. First, we expand the recursions from the WF algorithm to compute D not as the minimum of three numbers, but of a longer list of numbers. This allows us to divide D into sub-boxes, such that it takes fewer rounds to compute them. However, this strategy also increases the number of multiplications and comparisons in the protocol, raising a trade-off between execution time and communication. This trade-off is studied both theoretically and empirically. For comparison, Cheon et al. consider a sub-box that matches the size of D and focus only on equal-length chains. We generalize their work for sub-boxes of arbitrary size, which works for DNA chains with different lengths.

As part of this generalization, we propose an algorithm to automatically generate the equations to compute each sub-box. This algorithm arises from representing the recursions of the WF algorithm as a graph. Using this representation, we prove both the correctness and the optimality of the generation. We must point out that Cheon et al. use a different graphical method to compute their own equations, for which they do not prove correctness or optimality.

We perform experimental evaluations of our method using the MP-SPDZ framework, and analyze the performance trade-off as the size of the sub-box increases. We show that our algorithm has a significant reduction in the execution time in a LAN compared to a naive implementation of the WF algorithm. Additionally, we find that our protocol is competitive with the techniques currently used to solve the edit distance problem, like Yao's garbled circuits, and outperforms techniques like HE and BMR [4]. Moreover, we empirically show that protocols in $\mathbb{Z}_{2^k}$ are best-suited for our implementation and we give supporting arguments. Our complete source code can be found in a GitHub repository[1].

Organization. Section 2 covers a formal definition of edit distance, the WF algorithm, a background on MPC and other building blocks. In Sect. 3, we compute edit distance using MPC protocols based on secret-sharing and perform complexity analysis. In Sect. 4, we show an algorithm based on graph theory to obtain the minimal number of terms as parameters of the minimum function to compute edit distance correctly. Finally, in Sect. 5, we present a performance evaluation of our solution and compare it with the current state-of-the-art.

2 Preliminaries

2.1 The Edit Distance Problem

The edit distance is the minimum-weight series of operations that transforms one string into the other. Formally, let $A \overset{\text{def}}{=} (a_1, \ldots, a_n)$ be a string over an alphabet Σ. We define the possible *editing operations* on A:

1. *delete* the i-th position to obtain $(a_1, \ldots, a_{i-1}, a_{i+1}, \ldots, a_n)$.
2. *insert* $b \in \Sigma$ at position $(i+1)$ to obtain $(a_1, \ldots, a_i, b, a_{i+1}, \ldots, a_n)$.
3. *change* position i to $b \in \Sigma$ to obtain $(a_1, \ldots, a_{i-1}, b, a_{i+1}, \ldots, a_n)$.

---

[1] https://github.com/hdvanegasm/sec-edit-distance.

Given $A, B \in \Sigma^*$, the *edit distance problem* consists in finding the sequence of editing operations to transform A into B that minimizes the sum of the costs of the operations. We assume that each editing operation costs 1, and we are only interested in computing the minimum cost, and not in the operations.

To solve this problem, Wagner and Fischer propose a dynamic programming algorithm [29]. Let $A \stackrel{\text{def}}{=} (a_1, \ldots, a_n)$ and $B \stackrel{\text{def}}{=} (b_1, \ldots, b_m)$ be two strings in Σ^*. For $i \in [n]$ the set $\{1, 2, \ldots, n\}$, denote the sub-string $A^{(i)} \stackrel{\text{def}}{=} (a_1, a_2, \ldots, a_i)$ and the edit distance between $A^{(i)}$ and $B^{(j)}$ by $D(i, j)^2$. The goal is thus to find $D(n, m)$. Wagner and Fischer propose Algorithm 1 and prove its correctness.

Algorithm 1 Edit distance algorithm

Input: two chains $A = (a_1, \cdots, a_n)$ and $B = (b_1, \cdots, b_m)$.
Output: an integer value with the edit distance between the chains A and B.

1: Let t be an $n \times m$ matrix with indexes starting from one.
2: **for** $(i, j) \in [n] \times [m]$ **do**
3:     **if** $a_i \neq b_j$ **then** $t(i, j) = 1$
4:     **else** $t(i, j) = 0$
5: Let D be an $(n+1) \times (m+1)$ zero-initialized matrix, indexes starting from zero.
6: **for** $i = 0$ to n **do** $D(i, 0) = i$
7: **for** $j = 0$ to m **do** $D(0, j) = j$
8: **for** $i = 1$ to n **do**
9:     **for** $j = 1$ to m **do**
10:
$$D(i, j) = \min \begin{cases} D(i-1, j) + 1, \\ D(i, j-1) + 1, \\ D(i-1, j-1) + t(i, j) \end{cases} \tag{1}$$

11: **return** $D(n, m)$

2.2 Multi-party Computation and Secret-Sharing Schemes

In a secure multi-party computation (MPC) protocol, parties $P_1, \ldots, P_n$ jointly compute the value of $f(x_1, \ldots, x_n)$, where f is a fixed publicly known function and P_i holds the value x_i. During the computation, parties exchange messages and perform local computations such that there is no leakage of information about the parties' inputs, except for the function output.

The security of an MPC protocol can be stated and proven using techniques like universal composability (UC) [6]. One assumes the existence of an adversary that corrupts a subset of parties. An adversary can be *passive* or *active*. In the former, it tries to learn information from the exchanged messages but it does not deviate from the protocol specification. In the latter, the adversary can deviate from the protocol to obtain information about the parties' inputs or to prevent the honest parties from learning the correct output of the function.

---

² We will occasionally replace the parentheses with a subscript for the matrices D and t. That is, $D(i, j)$ will be written as $D_{i,j}$ and $t(i, j)$ as $t_{i,j}$.

A particular type of MPC protocols are those based on SSS, where a secret s is split into n parts, called *shares*, such that any subset of at most t shares reveal no information about s, but s can be completely reconstructed from any set of at least $t+1$ shares [8]. If s is secret-shared among the parties using shares $s^{(1)}, \ldots, s^{(n)}$, where P_i holds $s^{(i)}$, we denote this by $[\![s]\!] \overset{\text{def}}{=} (s^{(1)}, \ldots, s^{(n)})$.

Even though our edit distance solution can be instantiated in various ways[3], we concretely consider two particular SSS-based MPC protocols: SPDZ_{2^k} [9] with algebraic domain $\mathbb{Z}_{2^k}$, and Tinier [15] with algebraic domain $\mathbb{Z}_2$. To make clear the domain of computation in which the shares live, we distinguish shares of SPDZ_{2^k} from those of Tinier by respectively denoting them as $[\![s]\!]_{2^k}$ and $[\![s]\!]_2$. Both secret-sharing schemes are linear, meaning that additions and multiplications by public constants can be done without communication. However, the product of secret values is more involved, requiring communication among the parties and calls to subprotocols (like OPEN to reveal values to other parties). For security against active adversaries, both protocols use information-theoretic MACs to authenticate secret-shared values.

To securely compute a function f using a protocol based on an SSS, the function is considered as an arithmetic circuit. Initially, the parties distribute shares of their inputs. Then, using the protocols mentioned above, the parties evaluate the circuit so that each party holds a secret-shared value of the intermediate steps. At the end, the parties reconstruct the final result of the computation.

2.3 Domain Conversions and Comparisons

In our protocol for the edit distance, we need to compute two main operations securely: domain conversion and integer comparisons. These two operations can be done efficiently using daBits and edaBits. In the domain conversion, the goal is to convert binary Tinier shares $[\![x]\!]_2$ into arithmetic SPDZ_{2^k} shares $[\![x]\!]_{2^k}$, where $x \in \{0,1\}$. For that case, we use a daBit, which is a tuple $([\![r]\!]_2, [\![r]\!]_{2^k})$, where $r \in \mathbb{Z}_2$ is chosen at random. In [25], they propose a protocol to generate daBits that is secure against malicious adversaries, which is improved later in [1]. We can perform a domain conversion using techniques presented in [10] which can be adapted to the case where daBits are generated in a pre-processing phase.

To compute integer comparisons efficiently, we use edaBits. An edaBit is a tuple of m binary secret-shared random bits $([\![r_{m-1}]\!]_2, \ldots, [\![r_0]\!]_2)$ along with shares $[\![r]\!]_{2^k}$, such that $r = \sum_{i=0}^{m-1} r_i \cdot 2^i$. In [14], a protocol is proposed to generate edaBits that is secure against active adversaries. Also, a protocol is presented to compare integers using edaBits by expressing comparisons in terms of the extraction of the most significant bit of their binary representation.

It is worth mentioning that although SPDZ_{2^k} and Tinier are different protocols, they are compatible to compute domain conversions and comparisons using daBits and edaBits. This is because the protocols used to generate such random material model the MPC protocols as an arithmetic black box. Also, the protocols to generate daBits and edaBits are independent of the methods used by the MPC protocols based on secret-sharing schemes to authenticate shared values.

---

[3] Any MPC protocol that implements an $\mathcal{F}_{\text{edaBits}}$ functionality as described in [14].

3   A Privacy-Preserving Solution Using Secret Sharing

In this section, we present an efficient strategy to compute the edit distance using an SSS-based MPC protocol. Although the strategy works for any protocol based on linear secret-sharing schemes, we will aim at schemes whose computation domain is $\mathbb{Z}_{2^k}$. We build our protocol upon MPC schemes that implement an $\mathcal{F}_{\text{edaBits}}$ functionality, thus, its security follows from the security of the underlying scheme. We divide the task into two distinctive parts of the Algorithm 1, the *preamble* (lines 1–4), and the *arithmetic* part (lines 5–10).

The preamble of Algorithm 1 computes matrix t by comparing every pair of nucleotides. We propose to compare nucleotides in an efficient way using a binary domain. We will encode the nucleotides of a DNA chain using two elements of $\mathbb{Z}_2$ as $A \mapsto 00$, $C \mapsto 01$, $G \mapsto 10$, and $T \mapsto 11$. We denote the sharing of the nucleotide $N = \langle b_0, b_1 \rangle \in \mathbb{Z}_2^2$ as $[\![N]\!]_2 \stackrel{\text{def}}{=} \langle [\![b_0]\!]_2, [\![b_1]\!]_2 \rangle$. We extend the XOR operations to nucleotides $N = \langle b_0, b_1 \rangle$ and $N' = \langle b'_0, b'_1 \rangle$ by $N \oplus N' \stackrel{\text{def}}{=} \langle b_0 \oplus b'_0, b_1 \oplus b'_1 \rangle$, and extend it to shares in a natural way. Notice that $N = N'$ iff $N \oplus N' = 0$. To determine if a nucleotide is zero, we use the logical OR among its components. Denoting by $S(N) \stackrel{\text{def}}{=} b_0 \vee b_1 = (b_0 + b_1 + b_0 b_1) \mod 2$, we have that $N = N'$ iff $S(N \oplus N') = 0$. Hence, denoting by $N \stackrel{?}{=} N'$ a bit that indicates whether $N = N'$ or not, we can obtain a Boolean share of the assertion as

$$\left[\!\!\left[N \stackrel{?}{=} N' \right]\!\!\right]_2 = 1 - [([\![b_0]\!]_2 + [\![b'_0]\!]_2) + ([\![b_1]\!]_2 + [\![b'_1]\!]_2)$$
$$+ ([\![b_0]\!]_2 + [\![b'_0]\!]_2)([\![b_1]\!]_2 + [\![b'_1]\!]_2)].$$

Using this approach, we can compute the matrix t using mn multiplications in $\mathbb{Z}_2$. In total, we need to transmit $4nm$ bits through invocations of the OPEN protocol. Since the computation of each entry of t is independent of all other entries, we can compute them in parallel and the computation of the matrix only costs one round. Once the matrix t is computed, each entry is a binary share, so we will have to transform it to an arithmetic share for the next part.

3.1   Arithmetic Part

After computing the matrix t, we use daBits to transform its entries into arithmetic shares. For the arithmetic part, we thus assume that the parties hold shares $[\![t(i,j)]\!]_{2^k}$ for each index (i,j). Also, following Algorithm 1, $D(i,0) = i$, for all $i \in [n]$, and $D(0,j) = j$, for all $j \in [m]$. Our goal is to compute shares of the bottom-right corner of the matrix D, namely, $[\![D(n,m)]\!]_{2^k}$.

It is possible to compute the entries of D using well-known protocols to compute comparisons between two signed integers (c.f [10]). The problem of this approach is the sequential dependency between the positions of the matrix. This dependency prevents us from parallelizing the process, which increases the number of rounds. To overcome this limitation we compute only some selected entries of the matrix. Our approach builds upon the ideas in [7] to compute the edit distance using homomorphic encryption. We generalize their idea, fixing some issues, and we apply it to secret-sharing based protocols.

Let A and B be two DNA chains with lengths n and m, respectively. The matrix D will then have $n+1$ rows and $m+1$ columns. Applying Eq. (1) from Algorithm 1 recursively for $D(i-1,j)$, $D(i,j-1)$, and $D(i-1,j-1)$, and removing identical formulas, we obtain that $D(i,j)$ is equal to the minimum of

$$
\begin{array}{ll}
D(i-2,j)+2, & D(i-2,j-1)+t(i-1,j)+1, \\
D(i-2,j-1)+3, & D(i-1,j-2)+3, \\
D(i-2,j-2)+t(i-1,j-1)+2, & D(i,j-2)+2, \\
D(i-1,j-2)+t(i,j-1)+1, & D(i-2,j-1)+t(i,j)+1, \\
D(i-1,j-2)+t(i,j)+1, & D(i-2,j-2)+t(i,j)+t(i-1,j-1).
\end{array}
$$

We can then remove some redundant formulas, which can be proven to be greater or equal to some other formula in the set. After systematically removing all of them, we obtain that $D(i,j)$ is equal to the minimum of the following list:

$$
\begin{array}{ll}
D(i-2,j)+2, & D(i-2,j-1)+t(i-1,j)+1, \\
D(i-2,j-1)+t(i,j)+1, & D(i-2,j-2)+t(i-1,j-1)+t(i,j), \\
D(i,j-2)+2, & D(i-1,j-2)+t(i,j-1)+1, \\
D(i-1,j-2)+t(i,j)+1. &
\end{array}
$$

We will explain this process further in Sect. 4. Notice that by systematically substituting occurrences of $D(i-1,j-1)$, we completely removed it from the equation. We can repeat recursively to write $D(i,j)$ in terms of formulas that include the value of positions of the matrix that lie on the border of a rectangle inside the matrix which bottom right corner is $D(i,j)$. More specifically and following the notation of [7, Section 4.3], define the $(\tau+1)$-box for $D(i,j)$ as the set comprised of the union of the following sets, with τ a positive integer:

$$
\mathcal{T} \overset{\text{def}}{=} \{D_{i-\tau,j-\tau}, D_{i-\tau,j-\tau+1}, \ldots, D_{i-\tau,j}\}, \quad \mathcal{B} \overset{\text{def}}{=} \{D_{i,j-\tau}, D_{i,j-\tau+1}, \ldots, D_{i,j}\},
$$

$$
\mathcal{L} \overset{\text{def}}{=} \{D_{i-\tau,j-\tau}, D_{i-\tau+1,j-\tau}, \ldots, D_{i,j-\tau}\}, \quad \mathcal{R} \overset{\text{def}}{=} \{D_{i-\tau,j}, D_{i-\tau+1,j}, \ldots, D_{i,j}\}.
$$

With these definitions, not just $D(i,j)$ but all the elements in $\mathcal{B} \cup \mathcal{R}$ can be written as the minimum of formulas that depend on positions in $\mathcal{T} \cup \mathcal{L}$. Figure 1a shows the positions in the $(\tau+1)$-box, with the sets $\mathcal{T}$, $\mathcal{R}$, $\mathcal{B}$ and $\mathcal{L}$ highlighted.

Continuing with the example for $\tau=2$ and using the new notation for the borders of the box, we can compute positions $D(i-1,j)$ and $D(i,j-1)$ as for $D(i,j)$ using the following equations in terms of the positions in $\mathcal{T} \cup \mathcal{L}$:

$$
D(i-1,j) = \min \begin{cases} D(i-2,j)+1 \\ D(i-2,j-1)+t(i-1,j) \\ D(i-2,j-2)+t(i-1,j-1)+1 \\ D(i-1,j-2)+2 \end{cases}, \tag{2}
$$

$$
D(i,j-1) = \min \begin{cases} D(i,j-2)+1 \\ D(i-1,j-2)+t(i,j-1) \\ D(i-2,j-2)+t(i-1,j-1)+1 \\ D(i-2,j-1)+2 \end{cases}. \tag{3}
$$

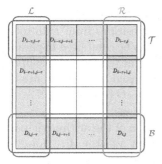

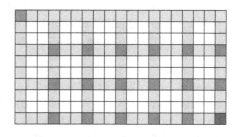

(a) Positions inside a $(\tau + 1)$-box.

(b) Division of the edit distance matrix into boxes.

Fig. 1. Positions in a $(\tau + 1)$-box relative to $D(i, j)$ and its use to divide the edit distance matrix into boxes.

In [7], the authors use only one $(\tau + 1)$-box, with $\tau = n$, to compute the edit distance of two chains of the same length. Going beyond the ideas in [7] we leave τ as a hyperparameter that can be specified by the user allowing a trade-off between the number of rounds and the data sent during the secure computation. Figure 1b shows an example of the complete matrix D divided into boxes. The green position corresponds to $D(0, 0)$ and the blue position corresponds to $D(n, m)$. The light red positions are the positions that are needed to compute the position $D(n, m)$, and the dark red positions are the most expensive position to compute inside each $(\tau + 1)$-box. Our approach also allow us to compute the edit distance between two DNA chains that do not have the same length.

To compute each minimum, we use the protocol MIN_q proposed in [10, 27]. It computes the minimum of a list of q numbers in $O(\log_2 q) \cdot (c_r + 2)$ rounds, where c_r is the number of rounds of a comparison. It requires $q - 1$ comparisons and $2q - 2$ multiplications. As an example, for $\tau = 2$, we can compute securely a share of the position $D(i, j)$ by executing MIN_7 with the following list of arguments:

$$\begin{array}{ll}
[\![D(i-2, j)]\!]_{2^k} + 2, & [\![D(i-2, j-1)]\!]_{2^k} + [\![t(i-1, j)]\!]_{2^k} + 1 \\
[\![D(i-2, j-1)]\!]_{2^k} + [\![t(i, j)]\!]_{2^k} + 1, & [\![D(i-2, j-2)]\!]_{2^k} + [\![t(i-1, j-1)]\!]_{2^k} + [\![t(i, j)]\!]_{2^k} \\
[\![D(i, j-2)]\!]_{2^k} + 2, & [\![D(i-1, j-2)]\!]_{2^k} + [\![t(i, j-1)]\!]_{2^k} + 1 \\
[\![D(i-1, j-2)]\!] + [\![t(i, j)]\!]_{2^k} + 1
\end{array}$$

The shares $[\![D(i-1, j)]\!]_{2^k}$ and $[\![D(i, j-1)]\!]_{2^k}$ can be written similarly following the Eqs. (2) and (3), and using the protocol MIN_4.

Our method traverses left-to-right and top-to-down the $(\tau + 1)$-boxes, computing, for each box, the positions in $\mathcal{B} \cup \mathcal{R}$ from the positions in $\mathcal{T} \cup \mathcal{L}$. At the end of the protocol, the parties will hold shares $[\![D(n, m)]\!]_{2^k}$, which is the share of the edit distance. They can then reveal it using the OPEN protocol.

We analyze the complexity of the arithmetic part of the protocol, assuming the stated complexity of the MIN_q functionality [27, Section 13.1.1]. In Sect. 4, we will present a method to calculate the formulas in each minimum computation and we will prove that the number of formulas in the minimum computation is bounded by $O(\tau \cdot 2^{3\tau})$. Assuming that τ divides both m and n, we need to compute nm/τ^2 boxes. Given that we need to compute $2\tau - 1$ positions in each $(\tau + 1)$-box, we are required to compute $\frac{nm}{\tau^2} \cdot (2\tau - 1)$ positions from D in total.

Note that all the positions in $\mathcal{B} \cup \mathcal{R}$ within one box can be computed in parallel since there is no dependency between them. This makes the term $2\tau - 1$ disappear from the round count. For two DNA chains of lengths n and m, we compute the edit distance in $O\left(\frac{nm}{\tau^2} \cdot (3\tau + \log_2 \tau) \cdot (c_r + 2)\right)$ rounds, $O\left(\frac{nm}{\tau^2} \cdot (\tau^2 \cdot 2^{3\tau} - \tau)\right)$ comparisons, and $O\left(\frac{nm}{\tau^2} \cdot (\tau^2 \cdot 2^{3\tau+1} - 2\tau)\right)$ multiplications.

In comparison with a straightforward implementation of the arithmetic part, we find that our method reduces the number of rounds by a factor of τ. However, the higher the τ, the higher the number of multiplications and comparisons, which increases the data sent in the protocol execution. This is a trade-off that should be considered according to the specific protocol and the network speed.

4   Automatic Generation of Formulas for Edit Distance

In this section, we present an algorithm to produce a correct and minimal set of formulas necessary to compute any positions in $\mathcal{B} \cup \mathcal{R}$ of the $(\tau + 1)$-box in terms of the positions in the sets $\mathcal{T} \cup \mathcal{L}$. For example, with $\tau = 2$, applying Eq. (1) recursively without removing any formula inside the minimum, we obtain the equation in Sect. 3.1, which contains the formulas

$$D(i - 2, j - 1) + t(i - 1, j) + 1 \quad \text{and} \quad D(i - 2, j - 1) + 3.$$

Since $t(i - 1, j) \in \{0, 1\}$, for any $D(i - 2, j - 1)$ and $t(i - 1, j)$, it holds that

$$D(i - 2, j - 1) + t(i - 1, j) + 1 \leq D(i - 2, j - 1) + 3.$$

Hence, we can remove $D(i - 2, j - 1) + 3$ from the set of formulas without changing the overall result of the minimum function.

We use a directed labeled graph with colored edges to represent the direct dependencies among the entries of the matrix D as shown in Fig. 2a. The vertices are the entries of the matrix and each edge represents the dependency given by Eq. (1), labeled by the term to add in the formula. We color an edge black if the label is 1, and red otherwise. We will refer to the graph G constructed in this way for a $(\tau + 1)$-box as the *dependency graph*. A similar abstraction was considered by Ukkonen in [28, Section 2] without colors.

The formulas inside a minimum to compute one entry of $\mathcal{B} \cup \mathcal{R}$ in terms of one in $\mathcal{T} \cup \mathcal{L}$ correspond to paths in the dependency graph.

Definition 1. *Let $V \in \mathcal{B} \cup \mathcal{R}$, $W \in \mathcal{T} \cup \mathcal{L}$ and P a path from W to V. The formula induced by P, is $f_P \stackrel{def}{=} W + a$, where a is the sum of all the labels of the edges in the path P. Each formula f_P will be called an unrolled formula from W to V and the set of all such formulas will be called the set of unrolled formulas from W to V.*

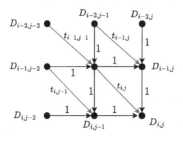

(a) Dependency graph for $\tau = 2$.

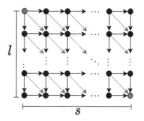

(b) Delanoy graph.

Fig. 2. Graphs used in the automatic generation of formulas.

We can compute the position $V \in \mathcal{B} \cup \mathcal{R}$ in the matrix D as

$$V = \min\{f_P \mid P \text{ is a path from } W \text{ to } V \text{ in } G, \ \forall W \in \mathcal{T} \cup \mathcal{L}\},$$

which gives an equivalent representation of the unrolled formulas.

We now define the quantities that are key for removing redundant formulas.

Definition 2. *Let P and Q be two paths in the dependency graph G. We define $r_{P,Q}$ as the number of red edges in P that are not in Q. Also, we define b_P as the number of black edges in the path P.*

The following proposition states a criterion for removing redundant formulas.

Proposition 1. *Let $U \in \mathcal{T} \cup \mathcal{L}$, $W \in \mathcal{B} \cup \mathcal{R}$, let $\mathcal{P}_{U,W}$ be the set of all paths form U to W in a dependency graph G, and let P be any path in $\mathcal{P}_{U,W}$. We can remove the formula induced by P from the set of unrolled formulas from U to W without changing the overall value of the minimum, if $r_{Q,P} + b_Q \leq b_P$, for some $Q \in \mathcal{P}_{U,W} \setminus \{P\}$.*

Proof. Let $P \in \mathcal{P}_{U,W}$ be any path, and suppose there exists some $Q \in \mathcal{P}_{U,W} \setminus \{P\}$ such that $r_{Q,P} + b_Q \leq b_P$. We can write the formula induced by P as

$$f_P \overset{\text{def}}{=} D_U + \sum_i t_i + \sum_{i=1}^{r_{P,Q}} t_i^{(P)} + b_P.$$

The terms denoted by t_i are the red labels shared by both P and Q, and the terms denoted by $t_i^{(P)}$ are the red labels that are in P but not in Q. Similarly, denoting by $t_i^{(Q)}$ the terms that are in Q but not in P, we can write the formula induced by Q, and it follows that:

$$f_Q \stackrel{\text{def}}{=} D_U + \sum_i t_i + \sum_{i=1}^{r_{Q,P}} t_i^{(Q)} + b_Q \leq D_U + \sum_i t_i + r_{Q,P} + b_Q$$

$$\leq D_U + \sum_i t_i + \sum_{i=1}^{r_{P,Q}} t_i^{(P)} + r_{Q,P} + b_Q$$

$$\leq D_U + \sum_i t_i + \sum_{i=1}^{r_{P,Q}} t_i^{(P)} + b_P = f_P.$$

Hence, we can remove the formula induced by P without changing the overall value of the minimum over the set of unrolled formulas.

Using Proposition 1, we can formulate an algorithm to produce a subset of the set of unrolled formulas for $W \in \mathcal{B} \cup \mathcal{R}$ without changing the result of the minimum. The details of the algorithm are presented in Algorithm 2.

Algorithm 2 Optimal set of paths

Input: a dependency graph G, two endpoints $U \in \mathcal{T} \cup \mathcal{L}$ and $W \in \mathcal{B} \cup \mathcal{R}$.
Output: a reduced set of paths $\mathcal{S}$ such that the minimum over all the formulas induced by paths in $\mathcal{S}$ is equal to the minimum over all the formulas induced by paths in $\mathcal{P}_{U,W}$.

1: Generate the set $\mathcal{P}_{U,W}$.
2: $\mathcal{S} \leftarrow \emptyset$.
3: **for** $P \in \mathcal{P}_{U,W}$ **do**
4:      $r \leftarrow$ True
5:      **for** $Q \in \mathcal{P}_{U,W} \setminus \{P\}$ **do**
6:          **if** $r_{Q,P} + b_Q \leq b_P$ **then**
7:              $r \leftarrow$ False
8:              **break**
9:      **if** $r =$ True **then** Append P to $\mathcal{S}$
10: **return** $\mathcal{S}$

To generate the expression to compute $D(i', j') \in \mathcal{B} \cup \mathcal{R}$ in a $(\tau + 1)$-box, we run the algorithm several times, with $D(i', j')$ fixed as the end point and for each of the vertices in $\mathcal{T} \cup \mathcal{L}$ as end points, and then we take the union of the resulting formulas as argument of the minimum function. Note that when we change the starting point of the paths, the induced formulas are not comparable, because they depend on different entries of the matrix D that can take any value.

We prove that Algorithm 2 is optimal with respect to the following definition.

Definition 3. *(Optimality).* Let $U, W \in V(G)$. A set $\mathcal{S} \subseteq \mathcal{P}_{U,W}$ is optimal if, for all $P \in \mathcal{S}$, there exists an assignment of the red variables $(t_{i,j})$ such that, for all $Q \in \mathcal{S} \setminus \{P\}$, it holds that $f_P < f_Q$.

Proposition 2. *(Optimality of Algorithm 2). Let $U, W \in V(G)$ be such that $U \in \mathcal{T} \cup \mathcal{L}$ and $W \in \mathcal{B} \cup \mathcal{R}$. Algorithm 2 returns an optimal set of paths $\mathcal{S} \subseteq \mathcal{P}_{U,W}$ (in the sense of Definition 3) such that the minimum over all the formulas induced by paths in $\mathcal{S}$ is the same as the minimum over all the formulas in the set of unrolled formulas from U to W.*

Proof. From Proposition 1, we know that the algorithm returns a set of paths whose induced formulas does not change the result of the minimum function. It remains to show that this set is optimal[4].

Let $\mathcal{S} \subseteq \mathcal{P}_{U,W}$ be the set of paths returned by Algorithm 2. Let $P \in \mathcal{S}$ be an arbitrary path. We can write f_P as

$$f_P = D_U + \sum_i t_i^{(P)} + b_P, \tag{4}$$

where $t_i^{(P)}$ are the labels of the red edges in P. Let us consider the following assignment of the red variables $(t_k) \in \{0,1\}^*$ for the dependency graph G: if the edge labeled as t_k is in the path P, set $t_k = 0$, and otherwise set $t_k = 1$. Given this assignment, it holds that

$$f_P = D_U + \sum_i t_i^{(P)} + b_P = D_U + b_P. \tag{5}$$

Now, let $Q \in \mathcal{S} \setminus \{P\}$. We can similarly expand f_Q with t_i being the labels of the red edges that are in both P and Q, and $t_i^{(Q)}$ the labels of the red edges that are in Q but not in P. It follows that

$$f_Q = D_U + \sum_i t_i + \sum_{i=1}^{r_{Q,P}} t_i^{(Q)} + b_Q = D_U + r_{Q,P} + b_Q > D_U + b_P = f_P. \tag{6}$$

The last inequality follows since both P and Q are paths returned by the algorithm, when the paths P and Q were selected in the iterations, the path P was not removed. Therefore, it holds that $r_{Q,P} + b_Q > b_P$. This shows that the algorithm is optimal in the sense of Definition 3. □

To compute an upper bound for the number of formulas generated by our approach, we consider the graph presented in Fig. 2b. This graph is similar to the dependency graph in a $(\tau + 1)$-box, but it has some additional edges. The number of all paths from the top-left corner to the bottom-right corner of this graph is given by the Delanoy number [30, Definition 1.2.8]:

$$\mathcal{D}(l,s) = \sum_{i=0}^{\min\{l,s\}} \binom{l}{i}\binom{s}{i} \cdot 2^i. \tag{7}$$

---

[4] We will not consider here the case $|\mathcal{P}_{U,W}| = 1$, since Algorithm 2 returns the only path in $\mathcal{P}_{U,W}$, which is trivial. Henceforth, we will consider only $|\mathcal{P}_{U,W}| > 1$. The case $\mathcal{P}_{U,W} = \emptyset$ is also not considered due to the definition of optimality.

This is an upper bound on the number of paths from the top-left corner to the bottom-right corner of the dependency graph because the dependency graph is a subgraph of the graph in Fig. 2b. Since the number of paths is maximum for bottom-right corner of the box, it follows that an upper bound for the number of formulas inside the minimum function to compute $D(i,j)$ in a $(\tau+1)$-box is

$$\sum_{k=1}^{\tau} [\mathcal{D}(\tau, \tau - k) + \mathcal{D}(\tau - k, \tau)] + \mathcal{D}(\tau, \tau). \tag{8}$$

Furthermore, it can be proven that

$$\sum_{k=1}^{\tau} [\mathcal{D}(\tau, \tau - k) + \mathcal{D}(\tau - k, \tau)] + \mathcal{D}(\tau, \tau) = O(\tau \cdot 2^{3\tau}). \tag{9}$$

5   Experiments

We now evaluate the performance of our private edit-distance solution. All the experiments were implemented in the MP-SPDZ framework [19] and were executed on a single AWS EC2 instance of type `c6a.4xlarge`[5], which has an AMD EPYC 7R13 Processor with 16 virtual cores and 32 GB of RAM. Some of the experiments were run without network limitation, so the communication speed is close to running the processes in the same machine. In order to measure the impact of the network, we simulate a local area network (LAN) architecture with 1.6 GBps of bandwidth and 0.3 milliseconds of latency, using the `tc`[6] command from the Linux operating system. For all of our experiments, we consider a bit-length of 16, which allows 16-bit integer computations. We select such number of bits because the edit distance between two chains of length n is upper-bounded by n. Hence, 16 bits is the least number of bits multiple of 8 that allows us to represent the integer numbers needed for the computation. Additional results can be found in the full version of the paper available on the IACR ePrint Archive.

We also compared the performance of the computation of the preamble in a binary domain with respect to a traditional implementation using an arithmetic domain. For two DNA chains of length 1,000, using Semi2^k for passive security, it reduces the data sent by approximately 18.68%, and using SPDZ$_{2^k}$ for active security, it reduces the data sent by approximately 18.48%. These are percentages of the total data sent of the whole algorithm, including the arithmetic part.

We compared the performance of our solution on a field-domain protocol and a ring-domain protocol. For the ring-domain, we use SPDZ$_{2^k}$ which has active security, and Semi2^k as its corresponding passive secure version. For the field-domain, we use MASCOT [20] to guarantee active security and Semi as its corresponding passive secure version. As an example, on a 1020 long DNA-chain Semi2^k sends 85% less data than Semi and SPDZ$_{2^k}$ sends 86% less data than

---

[5] https://aws.amazon.com/ec2/instance-types/c6a/.
[6] https://man7.org/linux/man-pages/man8/tc.8.html.

MASCOT.[7] This improvement is explained by the advantages of $\mathbb{Z}_{2^k}$ protocols to perform operations like truncations and reductions modulo 2^k.

5.1   The Effect of the Box Size, τ

As we saw in Sect. 3.1, the size of the $(\tau + 1)$-box affects the number of rounds, multiplications, and comparisons. We evaluate this trade-off by measuring data sent and the execution time of the protocol. We tested for DNA chains of length 1,020, on the passively secure protocol Semi2^k and on the actively secure one SPDZ$_{2^k}$. We execute each protocol for $\tau \in \{1, 2, 3, 4, 5\}$. We report performance of the whole protocol (including pre-processing) and of the online phase alone.

Table 1 and Fig. 3a present the results. Since MPC protocols are sensitive to the network speed, we repeated the box size experiments simulating a LAN network as discussed at the beginning of this section. Table 2 shows the results of the LAN experiments and Fig. 3b the corresponding graphical representation.

Table 1. Effect of changing τ on our solution without any network limitations.

Security	τ	Preprocessing+online		Online phase only	
		Data [MB]	Time [s]	Data [MB]	Time [s]
Passive (Semi2^k)	1	1,214.0	389.5	54.4	338.0
	2	1,794.3	186.1	60.7	144.2
	3	2,641.2	113.3	78.9	97.2
	4	4,207.0	154.6	106.7	90.4
	5	7,110.3	172.0	167.6	83.6
Active (SPDZ$_{2^k}$)	1	166,629	3,114.9	695.5	821.4
	2	241,689	3,407.9	348.8	391.3
	3	350,062	4,474.0	309.9	285.5
	4	551,783	6,366.6	389.3	275.8
	5	924,881	9,665.0	546.4	269.7

The results confirm the analysis in Sect. 3. The number of rounds decreases as an inverse linear function of τ, while the number of multiplications increases exponentially as a function of τ. The execution time is thus the sum of two functions of τ, an inverse linear induced by the number of rounds, and an exponential induced by the number of multiplications. The specific constants depend on the protocol and on the network, and they affect differently the offline and the online phase. For example, for the actively secure protocol, if we consider the offline phase (Fig. 3a), the exponential term dominates the execution time, suggesting no benefit for increasing τ. However, looking only at the online phase (Fig. 3a), as τ increases, the execution time decreases and eventually seems to

---

[7] All these experiments use daBits and edaBits and box-size $\tau = 3$.

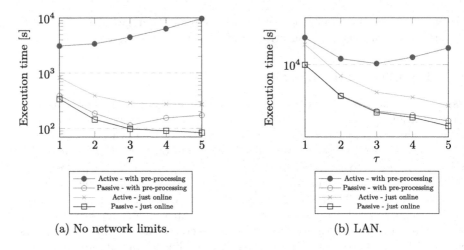

(a) No network limits.   (b) LAN.

Fig. 3. Effect of the box size τ.

Table 2. Effect of τ on our solution on a LAN.

Security	τ	Preprocessing+online		Online phase only	
		Data [MB]	Time [s]	Data[MB]	Time[s]
Passive (Semi2^k)	1	1,214.0	9,941.0	54.4	9,923.5
	2	1,794.3	3,891.9	60.7	3,837.8
	3	2,641.2	2,429.5	78.9	2,342.2
	4	4,207.0	2,155.8	106.7	2,008.3
	5	7,110.3	1,813.7	167.6	1,552.7
Active (SPDZ$_{2^k}$)	1	166,629	22,552.1	695.5	18,298.5
	2	241,689	11,925.8	348.8	7,044.2
	3	350,062	10,300.2	309.9	4,300.1
	4	551,783	12,474.0	389.3	3,689.2
	5	924,881	16,482.1	546.4	2,864.7

flatten. The effect of the rounds in the total time is even more acute for the passively secure protocol (Fig. 3a), where the execution time first decreases and then increases with an optimal value on $\tau = 3$. This is because multiplications are relatively cheap for such protocol, yet we expect the graph to eventually increase because the effect of the exponential part induced by the number of multiplications dominates asymptotically. The positive effect of increasing τ is also enhanced on a slower network, as shown on the simulated LAN results in Fig. 3b.

Considering both the online and offline phases together, selecting the best value of τ for the passive and active security setting in the LAN configuration respectively reduces the execution time by 81% and 54% in comparison with a baseline implementation using $\tau = 1$.

5.2 Comparison Between Garbled Circuits and Secret-Sharing

We compare the performance of our implementation using garbled circuits and using protocols based on secret-sharing schemes with $\mathbb{Z}_{2^k}$ domain. Due to the constraints of the AWS EC2 instance, we use DNA chains of length 210 for this experiment. As previously, we use a bit-length of 16 and we consider both a network with no limitations and a simulated LAN. We set $\tau = 1$ for garbled circuits and $\tau = 3$ for the protocols based on secret-sharing schemes, because garbled circuits have better performance when $\tau = 1$, as observed in a preliminary exploration. As τ increases, the number of formulas inside the minimum function grows exponentially and the number of addition gates increases too, which is specially costly for GC-based protocols.

Table 3 presents the results of the experiment. Notice that the secret-sharing based protocols perform better than the GC protocols regarding the data sent. In particular, they send approximately 67–99% less data than the GC protocols. This is due to the high number of arithmetic operations of the algorithm, which implies a high number of gates to garble and send through the network.

For passively secure protocols, the higher data sent of the GC protocols is compensated by their constant-round communication. This can be observed in the similar execution time without network limitations, and even more acutely in the faster execution on LAN.

Table 3. Performance of our solution using GC and SSS-based protocols.

Network	Security	Protocol	Time [s]	Data sent [MB]
No limit	Passive	Yao's GC	2.6	345.8
		Semi2^k	4.9	113.1
	Active	BMR-MASCOT	5,968.6	2.09×10^6
		SPD$\mathbb{Z}_{2^k}$	140.1	14,893.8
LAN	Passive	Yao's GC	2.7	345.8
		Semi2^k	103.0	113.1
	Active	BMR-MASCOT	9,034.0	2.09×10^6
		SPD$\mathbb{Z}_{2^k}$	368.5	14,893.8

For actively secure protocols, GC is one order of magnitude slower than the protocols based on secret-sharing schemes, and the former sends two orders of magnitude more data than the latter. This can be explained by the edit distance algorithm and by the mechanism to provide active security in BMR[8]. The edit distance algorithm has a heavy arithmetic component and many additions that require AND gates. In the case of BMR, the underlying MPC protocol to

---

[8] Although there are other alternatives for actively secure GC protocols, we choose BMR because it is the only available GC-based protocol for malicious adversaries in MP-SDPZ. This allows us to make comparisons in the same "ground".

compute the offline phase is MASCOT [20], which uses MACs to ensure security against malicious adversaries. So, garbling an AND gate needs to compute multiplications with the assistance of MASCOT which requires the generation of multiplication triples and puts an additional overhead. This overhead does not appear in protocols based on secret-sharing schemes because additions do not need communication.

5.3   Comparison with Protocols Based on Homomorphic Encryption

We compare the results of our experiments with a relevant homomorphic encryption (HE) solution. In [7], Cheon et al. consider experiments with DNA chains of length 8 at 80 bits of security. According to the results in Table 6 in that paper, their method spends 27.54 s on key generation and 16.45 s on encryption on an Intel Xeon i7 2.3 GHz, 192 GB. In their report, they state that it takes 27.5 s to obtain the edit distance using the Halevi-Shoup library (HElib) [17] along with the techniques presented in [16]. In our case, considering both the pre-processing and the online phase on a LAN, using $\tau = 2$, we can compute the edit distance of two chains of length 8 in 0.3 s using Semi2^k protocol for passive security and in 5.92 s using the SPDZ$_{2^k}$ protocol for active security. Furthermore, Cheon et al. estimate that their method for DNA chains of length 100 with a security parameter of 62 bits, computes the edit distance in 1 day and 5 h. Our method computes the edit distance of two chains of length 100 in 96.69 s on a LAN using the SPDZ$_{2^k}$ protocol. In terms of security, a 62 bits for HE is insufficient for the current recommended security levels in cryptography.

6   Conclusion

We presented an MPC approach based on secret sharing to securely compute the edit distance via the Wagner-Fischer algorithm. Our method leverages the equations in the algorithm to compute selected positions of the edit distance matrix as minimum of several integers. This modification reduces the number of rounds but increases the number of multiplications and comparisons, inducing a performance trade-off. Using graph theory, we develop an algorithm to automatically generate all the equations needed to compute the required positions in the matrix. We prove that the algorithm returns correct and optimal equations. Our solution is competitive with GC-based solutions on a passive security model, and much faster if active security is required, demonstrating the effectiveness of the secret-sharing approach for bit-wise computations.

We identify two research problems for future work. The first is to find an optimal box size, given environment parameters such as bandwidth, latency, chain lengths, and local computational power. The second is to generalize the graph theory techniques from Sect. 4 to other dynamic programming problems.

References

1. Aly, A., Orsini, E., Rotaru, D., Smart, N.P., Wood, T.: Zaphod: efficiently combining LSSS and garbled circuits in scale. Cryptology ePrint Archive, Paper 2019/974 (2019)
2. Asharov, G., Halevi, S., Lindell, Y., Rabin, T.: Privacy-preserving search of similar patients in genomic data. In: PETS 2018, pp. 104–124 (2018)
3. Aziz, M.M.A., Alhadidi, D., Mohammed, N.: Secure approximation of edit distance on genomic data. BMC Med. Genom. **10**, 55–67 (2017)
4. Beaver, D., Micali, S., Rogaway, P.: The round complexity of secure protocols (extended abstract). In: STOC, pp. 503–513. ACM (1990)
5. Bresson, E., Catalano, D., Pointcheval, D.: A simple public-key cryptosystem with a double trapdoor decryption mechanism and its applications. In: Laih, C.-S. (ed.) ASIACRYPT 2003. LNCS, vol. 2894, pp. 37–54. Springer, Heidelberg (2003). https://doi.org/10.1007/978-3-540-40061-5_3
6. Canetti, R.: Universally composable security: a new paradigm for cryptographic protocols. In: FOCS, pp. 136–145. IEEE (2001)
7. Cheon, J.H., Kim, M., Lauter, K.: Homomorphic computation of edit distance. In: Brenner, M., Christin, N., Johnson, B., Rohloff, K. (eds.) FC 2015. LNCS, vol. 8976, pp. 194–212. Springer, Heidelberg (2015). https://doi.org/10.1007/978-3-662-48051-9_15
8. Cramer, R., Damgård, I.B., Nielsen, J.B.: Secure Multiparty Computation. Cambridge University Press, Cambridge (2015)
9. Cramer, R., Damgård, I., Escudero, D., Scholl, P., Xing, C.: SPDZ$_{2^k}$: efficient MPC mod 2^k for dishonest majority. In: Shacham, H., Boldyreva, A. (eds.) CRYPTO 2018. LNCS, vol. 10992, pp. 769–798. Springer, Cham (2018). https://doi.org/10.1007/978-3-319-96881-0_26
10. Damgård, I., Escudero, D., Frederiksen, T.K., Keller, M., Scholl, P., Volgushev, N.: New primitives for actively-secure MPC over rings with applications to private machine learning. In: IEEE Symposium on Security and Privacy, pp. 1102–1120. IEEE Computer Society (2019)
11. Demmler, D., Schneider, T., Zohner, M.: ABY - a framework for efficient mixed-protocol secure two-party computation. In: NDSS. The Internet Society (2015)
12. Dugan, T.M., Zou, X.: A survey of secure multiparty computation protocols for privacy preserving genetic tests. In CHASE, pp. 173–182. IEEE (2016)
13. Erlich, Y., Narayanan, A.: Routes for breaching and protecting genetic privacy. Nat. Rev. Genet. **15**(6), 409–421 (2014)
14. Escudero, D., Ghosh, S., Keller, M., Rachuri, R., Scholl, P.: Improved primitives for MPC over mixed arithmetic-binary circuits. In: Micciancio, D., Ristenpart, T. (eds.) CRYPTO 2020. LNCS, vol. 12171, pp. 823–852. Springer, Cham (2020). https://doi.org/10.1007/978-3-030-56880-1_29
15. Frederiksen, T.K., Keller, M., Orsini, E., Scholl, P.: A unified approach to MPC with preprocessing using OT. In: Iwata, T., Cheon, J.H. (eds.) ASIACRYPT 2015. LNCS, vol. 9452, pp. 711–735. Springer, Heidelberg (2015). https://doi.org/10.1007/978-3-662-48797-6_29
16. Gentry, C., Halevi, S., Smart, N.P.: Homomorphic evaluation of the AES circuit. In: Safavi-Naini, R., Canetti, R. (eds.) CRYPTO 2012. LNCS, vol. 7417, pp. 850–867. Springer, Heidelberg (2012). https://doi.org/10.1007/978-3-642-32009-5_49
17. Halevi, S., Shoup, V.: Design and implementation of Helib: a homomorphic encryption library. Cryptology ePrint Archive, Paper 2020/1481 (2020)

18. Jha, S., Kruger, L., Shmatikov, V.: Towards practical privacy for genomic computation. In: IEEE Symposium on Security and Privacy, pp. 216–230. IEEE (2008)
19. Keller, M.: MP-SPDZ: a versatile framework for multi-party computation. In: CCS, pp. 1575–1590. ACM (2020)
20. Keller, M., Orsini, E., Scholl, P.: MASCOT: faster malicious arithmetic secure computation with oblivious transfer. In: CCS, pp. 830–842. ACM (2016)
21. Oestreich, M., et al.: Privacy considerations for sharing genomics data. EXCLI J. **20**, 1243–1260 (2021)
22. Ohata, S.: Recent advances in practical secure multi-party computation. IEICE Trans. Fundam. Electron. Commun. Comput. Sci. **103–A**(10), 1134–1141 (2020)
23. Payne, A., Holmes, N., Rakyan, V., Loose, M.: BulkVis: a graphical viewer for Oxford nanopore bulk FAST5 files. Bioinformatics **35**(13), 2193–2198 (2018)
24. Rane, S., Sun, W.: Privacy preserving string comparisons based on levenshtein distance. In: WIFS, pp. 1–6. IEEE (2010)
25. Rotaru, D., Wood, T.: MArBled circuits: mixing arithmetic and Boolean circuits with active security. In: Hao, F., Ruj, S., Sen Gupta, S. (eds.) INDOCRYPT 2019. LNCS, vol. 11898, pp. 227–249. Springer, Cham (2019). https://doi.org/10.1007/978-3-030-35423-7_12
26. Schneider, T., Tkachenko, O.: EPISODE: efficient privacy-preserving similar sequence queries on outsourced genomic databases. In: AsiaCCS, pp. 315–327. ACM (2019)
27. Toft, T.: Primitives and Applications for Multi-party Computation. Ph.D. thesis. Aarhus University (2007)
28. Ukkonen, E.: Algorithms for approximate string matching. Inf. Control **64**(1–3), 100–118 (1985)
29. Wagner, R.A., Fischer, M.J.: The string-to-string correction problem. J. ACM **21**(1), 168–173 (1974)
30. West, D.B.: Combinatorial Mathematics. Cambridge Uni Press, Cambridge (2020)
31. Zhao, C., et al.: Secure multi-party computation: theory, practice and applications. Inf. Sci. **476**, 357–372 (2019)
32. Zheng, Y., Lu, R., Shao, J., Zhang, Y., Zhu, H.: Efficient and privacy-preserving edit distance query over encrypted genomic data. In: WCSP, pp. 1–6. IEEE Computer Society (2019)
33. Zhu, R., Huang, Y.: Efficient and precise secure generalized edit distance and beyond. IEEE Trans. Dependable Secur. Comput. **19**(1), 579–590 (2022)

Broadcast-Optimal Two Round MPC with Asynchronous Peer-to-Peer Channels

Ivan Damgård[1], Divya Ravi[1(✉)], Luisa Siniscalchi[2], and Sophia Yakoubov[1]

[1] Aarhus University, Aarhus, Denmark
{ivan, divya,sophia.yakoubov}@cs.au.dk
[2] Danish Technical University, Lyngby, Denmark
luisi@dtu.dk

Abstract. In this paper we continue the study of two-round broadcast-optimal MPC, where broadcast is used in one of the two rounds, but not in both. We consider the realistic scenario where the round that does not use broadcast is *asynchronous*. Since a first asynchronous round (even when followed by a round of broadcast) does not admit any secure computation, we introduce a new notion of asynchrony which we call (t_d, t_m)-asynchrony. In this new notion of asynchrony, an adversary can delay or drop up to t_d of a given party's incoming messages; we refer to t_d as the *deafness threshold*. Similarly, the adversary can delay or drop up to t_m of a given party's outgoing messages; we refer to t_m as the *muteness threshold*.

We determine which notions of secure two-round computation are achievable when the first round is (t_d, t_m)-asynchronous, and the second round is over broadcast. Similarly, we determine which notions of secure two-round computation are achievable when the first round is over broadcast, and the second round is (fully) asynchronous. We consider the cases where a PKI is available, when only a CRS is available but private communication in the first round is possible, and the case when only a CRS is available and no private communication is possible before the parties have had a chance to exchange public keys.

1 Introduction

Round complexity is an important metric of the efficiency of a secure computation (MPC) protocol. When MPC is run over a high latency network, each round of communication can take a long time. Two rounds has been shown to be optimal; one round of communication is clearly not enough for secure computation, since it leaves the protocol vulnerable to *residual function attacks*, where the adversary can recompute the function with the same honest party inputs

D. Ravi—Funded by the European Research Council (ERC) under the European Unions's Horizon 2020 research and innovation programme under grant agreement No. 803096 (SPEC).
S. Yakoubov—Funded by the Danish Independent Research Council under Grant-ID DFF-2064-00016B (YOSO).

A. Aly and M. Tibouchi (Eds.): LATINCRYPT 2023, LNCS 14168, pp. 87–106, 2023.
https://doi.org/10.1007/978-3-031-44469-2_5

and different corrupt party inputs simply by preparing different messages on the corrupt parties' behalf.

However, optimal round complexity is only the first step towards efficient use of resources. *Broadcast*, which, in practice, requires either multiple rounds of peer-to-peer communication or special channels (which use, e.g., physical assumptions or blockchains), is itself an expensive resource. Most known two-round MPC protocols either use broadcast in both rounds [7,13,14], or only achieve the weakest security guarantee (selective abort) [3]. Cohen *et al.* [9], Damgård *et al.* [10] and Damgård *et al.* [11] explore the tradeoffs between the security of two-round MPC protocols and their use of broadcast (where broadcast can be used in the first round only, in the second round only, in both rounds, or in neither round). Cohen *et al.* focus on the dishonest majority setting; Damgård *et al.* [10] focus on the honest majority setting; and Damgård *et al.* [11] additionally remove the use of PKI and private peer-to-peer channels in the first round from the previous works. All three of these papers gave tight characterizations of the security guarantees that can be achieved in the different settings.

1.1 Our Contributions

In this paper, we focus on the realistic setting where the rounds that do not use broadcast are also not fully synchronous. Since fully asynchronous MPC has been studied in the literature extensively [5,6,15], we limit ourselves to the case where at least one of the two rounds uses a synchronous broadcast channel.

Asynchrony in the First Round. If the first round is fully asynchronous, the adversary can prevent a party from communicating anything to any of the honest parties in the first round; since correctness demands that the protocol produce an output even in the event of adversarial message scheduling, this means that either that party's input cannot influence the output (this is known as *input deprivation*), or that the protocol is vulnerable to residual function attacks (since the adversary can, like in one-round protocols, recompute the second-round messages on behalf of a corrupt party who no-one heard from in the first round).

So, we introduce a new flavor of asynchrony, where the adversary is only able to delay *up to a certain threshold of* messages to and from any one party. We call it (t_d, t_m)-asynchrony. In (t_d, t_m)-asynchrony, at most t_m of any party's messages can be arbitrarily delayed or dropped, where t_m is the *muteness threshold*. Similarly, at most t_d of the messages to a given party can be arbitrarily delayed or dropped, where t_d is the *deafness threshold*. We allow the adversary to be *rushing* i.e. determine which messages to delay or drop based on the messages she sees during the round. By setting t_m, we ensure that each party communicates to sufficiently many parties in the first round, enabling us to sidestep the problem of input deprivation.

This new notion of asynchrony is a contribution in and of itself. It is incomparable to the standard notion of asynchrony, where the adversary can arbitrarily delay—*but not drop*—any number of the messages[1].

We now summarize our findings about two-round MPC where the first round is (t_d, t_m)-asynchronous (over peer-to-peer channels), and the second round uses synchronous broadcast. Let n be the number of participants, and t be the corruption threshold. We show that, if a PKI is available, no such secure two-round MPC is possible if $n \leq t + t_m$. When $t + t_m < n \leq 2t + t_m$, the best achievable guarantee is *unanimous abort*, where honest parties either all learn the output, or abort. When $2t + t_m < n$, identifiable abort—where in the event of an abort, honest parties agree on the identity of a corrupt party—is additionally achievable. (Stronger guarantees have already been ruled out if broadcast is not available in the first round, as long as $t > 1$ [10].) Our constructions that rely on a PKI use one-or-nothing secret sharing [10] (which is a flavor of secret sharing that allows a dealer to share a vector of secrets, among which at most one secret would be reconstructed).

If a PKI is not available, but parties are able to send one another private messages in the first round, as before no such secure two-round MPC is possible if $n \leq t + t_m$. Additionally, nothing is achievable if $n \leq t + 2t_d$ and $n \leq t + 2t_m$. However, the rest of the time, unanimous abort is possible. Identifiable abort is unachievable if $n \leq 3t + t_m$; we show that it is achievable if $3t + t_m < n$ and $\min(t_d, t_m) \leq t$, but we leave what happens without that last requirement as an open problem.

If neither a PKI nor private channels are available in the first round, we show that no such secure two-round MPC is possible if $n \leq t + t_d + t_m$. However, the rest of the time, unanimous abort is achievable. As before, identifiable abort is unachievable if $n \leq 3t + t_m$; we show that it is achievable if $3t + t_m < n$ and $3t + t_d < n$, but we leave what happens without that last requirement as an open problem.

We give several constructions that do not rely on a PKI. For somewhat looser bounds, we show constructions that rely on standard assumptions by generalizing the one-or-nothing secret sharing with intermediaries introduced by Damgård *et al.* [11]. We provide also new constructions with the tightest bounds of t, t_d and t_m that rely on differing-inputs obfuscation to demonstrate feasibility, or, rather, the infeasibility of a negative result. (The obfuscation-based constructions that achieve identifiable abort are additionally limited to a constant number of parties.)

Asynchrony in the Second Round. If the first round uses fully synchronous broadcast, security is possible even if the second round is asynchronous in the classical

---

[1] Our notion is also incomparable to the notion of send/receive-omission corruptions of [20] which considers an adversary who can send-corrupt *some* parties whose (any number of) sent messages may be dropped and/or receive-corrupt *some* parties that may not receive (any of the) messages sent to them. This is different from our notion where a *bounded* number of outgoing and incoming messages for *each* party is blocked.

sense; that is, the adversary can arbitrarily delay (but not drop) any number of the second-round messages. In this setting, we show that if a PKI is available, no secure MPC is possible if $n \leq 2t$. However, the strongest guarantee—guaranteed output delivery—is achievable otherwise, as shown by a simple observation by Rambaud and Urban [19].

If a PKI is not available, but parties are able to send one another private messages in the first round, selective abort is achievable as long as $2t < n$. No stronger guarantee is achievable, by the lower bounds of Patra and Ravi [18] and Damgård et al. [11].

If neither a PKI nor private channels are available in the first round, we show that no secure MPC is possible for any corruption threshold $t \geq 1$.

1.2   Terminology

We characterize our protocols in terms of (a) the kinds of communication channels used in each round, (b) the security guarantees they achieve, (c) the setup they require, and (d) the corruption threshold t they support. We will use shorthand for all of these classifications to make our discussions less cumbersome.

Communication Structure. We consider different kinds of channels:

Broadcast Channels (BC), where each broadcast message recipient has the guarantee that all other recipients received the same message.
Peer to Peer Channels (P2P), where recipients have no guarantee of consistency.

When a PKI is available, or when the parties have already had a chance to exchange encryption keys, *private* communication is possible over both BC and P2P channels. However, when this is not the case (that is, when a PKI is not available, and this is the first round), it makes sense to break these up into the following:

Public Peer to Peer Channels (PubP2P), where recipients don't have the guarantee that all others see the same message (nor do they have a guarantee of privacy).
Private Peer to Peer Channels (PrivP2P), where recipients don't have the guarantee that all others see the same message, but parties can communicate messages privately.
Public Broadcast Channels (PubBC), where a party can either broadcast a message *or* communicate it over public peer to peer channels. (Note that using a broadcast channel is strictly stronger than using a public peer to peer channel; the only reason to choose to use a public peer to peer channel instead of a broadcast channel is efficiency.)
Broadcast with Private Channels (PrivBC), where a party can either broadcast a message *or* communicate it privately.

We use a concatenation of two channel names to denote the communication structure of a protocol. As an example, PrivP2P-BC denotes a protocol whose first round is over private peer to peer channels, and whose second round is over broadcast. (Private messages are also possible in the second round, since the parties can exchange public keys in the first round.)

Security Guarantees. An MPC protocol can achieve one of five notions of security. These are described below, from weakest to strongest (with the exception that fairness and identifiable abort are incomparable).

Selective Abort (SA): Every honest party either obtains the output, or aborts.

Unanimous Abort (UA): Either *all* honest parties obtain the output, or they all (unanimously) abort.

Identifiable Abort (IA): Either all honest parties obtain the output, or they all (unanimously) abort identifying one corrupt party.

Fairness (FAIR): Either all parties obtain the output, or none of them do. (An adversary should not be able to learn the output if the honest parties do not.)

Guaranteed Output Delivery (GOD): All honest parties will learn the computation output no matter what the adversary does.

Setup. We consider two kinds of setup: either only a common reference string (CRS), where parties have access to a common string generated in a trusted way, or both a CRS and a (trusted) PKI, where parties additionally know one another's public keys before the protocol starts.

1.3   Technical Overview

We consider protocols with and without a PKI. With a PKI, we consider the P2P-BC and BC-P2P settings; without a PKI, we consider the PrivP2P-BC, PubP2P-BC, PrivBC-P2P and PubBC-P2P settings. We explore what security guarantees are achievable when the P2P and PrivP2P rounds are asynchronous.

Asynchrony in the First Round. As we explained earlier, in the P2P-BC and PrivP2P-BC settings, no security guarantee is achievable when the adversary can schedule the first-round messages arbitrarily. However, if we make some restrictions on the message scheduling, some notions of security become achievable for some thresholds. To this end, we introduce (t_d, t_m)-asynchrony, where the adversary can drop or delay only t_d incoming messages for each party, and t_m outgoing messages for each party.

Prior works [8,10] show that even in the synchronous setting (with $t_d = t_m = 0$) and given a PKI, no P2P-BC or PrivP2P-BC protocol can achieve fairness or

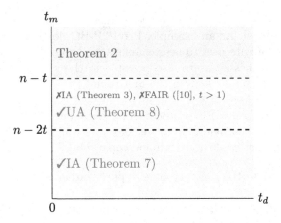

Fig. 1. Partial Asynchrony Feasibility and Impossibility Results in the P2P-BC setting, with a PKI and CRS

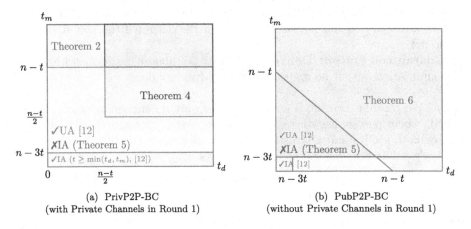

Fig. 2. Partial Asynchrony Feasibility and Impossibility Results with a CRS. (Some of our results appear in full version [12].)

GOD[2]. Figures 1 and 2 describe our findings about the feasibility of SA, UA and IA when a PKI is available, when a PKI is not available but private channels in the first round are, and when neither a PKI nor private channels in the first round are available.

Lower Bounds. Most of our negative results follow a common blueprint. We start by showing (in Theorem 1) that if there is a group of parties A whose second-round messages do not depend on messages from a disjoint group B,

---

[2] The impossibility holds for more general settings such as when $t > 1$ or $n \leq 3t$. However, it is possible to achieve GOD for the special case when $t = 1$ and $n \geq 4$ [16,17] (even in the P2P-P2P synchronous setting with no CRS or PKI). We leave open the question of weakening the synchrony assumptions for these special cases.

and if the adversary has all the information she needs in order to recompute the first and second round messages of B and other messages that *depend* on messages from B (while keeping the messages—and thus inputs—of A fixed), then the adversary is able to execute a residual function attack by recomputing the function with different inputs on behalf of B. We then show how adversarial network scheduling and corruption strategies can lead to such groups in various settings. Specifically, we use this strategy to show that:

1. In the P2P-BC, PKI setting, no secure computation is achievable if $t_m \geq n - t, t_d \geq 1$ (Theorem 2);
2. In the P2P-BC, PKI setting, no secure computation *with identifiable abort* is achievable if $t_m \geq n - 2t, t_d \geq 1$ (Theorem 3);
3. In the PrivP2P-BC, CRS setting, no secure computation is achievable if $n \leq t + 2t_d$, $n \leq t + 2t_m$ (Theorem 4);
4. In the PubP2P-BC, CRS setting, no secure computation is achievable if $n \leq t + t_d + t_m$ (Theorem 6).

The PrivP2P-BC, IA, CRS, $n \leq 3t + t_m$ setting is the only one for which we use a different blueprint. This proof follows the proof of Damgård *et al.* [11], which shows that in the fully synchronous PrivP2P-BC, IA, CRS, $n \leq 3t$, IA cannot be achieved. They do this by showing how t corrupt parties can get away with sending first round messages computed on different inputs to two disjoint sets of honest parties; they show that the protocol must yield output on *both* inputs, since the honest parties may not be able to identify a cheater. We show that the presence of an additional t_m parties, all of who may not have heard a given first round message due to network scheduling, does not help matters. This shows that in this setting, IA cannot be achieved (Theorem 5).

Upper Bounds. Our upper bounds in the presence of a PKI follow the blueprint of the constructions of Cohen *et al.* [9], Damgård *et al.* [10] and Damgård *et al.* [11]. Damgård *et al.* introduce one-or-nothing secret sharing; for our constructions with PKI, we simply tweak the reconstruction thresholds of one-or-nothing secret sharing to account for the adversary's ability to drop t_m of each party's outgoing messages.

When a PKI is *not* available, we show protocols using variant of one-or-nothing secret sharing defined by Damgård *et al.* [11], which is called *one-or-nothing secret sharing with intermediaries*. Here we adjust the privacy as well as reconstruction thresholds to adapt them to the (t_d, t_m)-asynchronous setting. Unfortunately, these constructions without PKI are not tight with respect to our lower bounds. This led us to bring our study forward and investigate if it was possible to obtain tighter lower bounds or alternatively, design matching upper bounds that are based on stronger assumptions (as this would give evidence that proving a tighter lower bound is not possible).

Towards this, we provide completely new constructions based on differing-inputs obfuscation (diO) [1,4]. These constructions rely on a CRS in the form of an obfuscated program the code of which hides a secret decryption key. In the first round, each party encrypts her input to the corresponding public encryption key, generates a signing - verification key pair, signs her ciphertext, and sends the ciphertext, verification key and signature to all of her peers. In the second round, the parties echo everything they heard in the first round over the broadcast channel; these echos then serve as input to the obfuscated program. The program checks that the echos are consistent enough before decrypting the ciphertexts and evaluating the function. If the echos are *not* consistent enough, it aborts; to achieve identifiable abort it is possible to use the conflict graph that it derives from the echos to identify a cheater. One difficulty is that we must make sure that the adversary cannot copy and reuse an honest party's ciphertext (with a fresh verification key). We do this by introducing a new primitive which we call *puncturable public key encryption*. Here, the sender uses her own public key as an input to the encryption algorithm, so that the resulting ciphertext is bound to the sender. The receiver's public key can be *punctured* at one or more senders' public keys, so that ciphertexts produced by those senders no longer carry any information about the messages used.

Of course, diO is wildly impractical, and as mentioned previously, our results which use diO should be seen as feasibility results (or rather, as evidence of the infeasibility of proving a tighter lower bound).

Asynchrony in the Second Round. For BC-P2P protocols, the classical notion of asynchrony in the second round does not preclude secure computation, so we stick to that. We summarize our findings about asynchronous BC-P2P protocols in Table 1. The details of these results appear in the full version [12].

In this setting, we show that for $n \leq 2t$, a BC-P2P protocol cannot even achieve selective abort, even if a PKI is available[3]. This follows from the fact that parties can't wait for more than $n - t \leq t$ second-round messages before computing output, since the remaining $\leq t$ parties may be corrupt and may not have sent messages. So, parties must be able to compute output even if they only received second-round messages from corrupt parties; this allows the adversary to recompute the output based on different corrupt parties' inputs, in what is an effective residual function attack.

For $2t < n$, given a PKI, a BC-P2P protocol can achieve the strongest notion of security—GOD. This follows from an observation in [19] that shows that the BC-P2P construction of Damgård *et al.* [10] works even if the second round is asynchronous.

Without a PKI, a PrivBC-P2P protocol can achieve selective abort as long as $2t < n$, which is the best guarantee we can hope for (see footnote 2). (Nothing is possible in the PubBC-P2P setting). For our SA construction, we rely on certain properties of synchronous schemes to extend them to this setting. We show that any *synchronous* protocol that is PrivBC-P2P SA CRS $2t < n$ could be also executed with an asynchronous second round as long as it is easy to determine whether second-round messages are "valid", the inputs can be extracted from first-round messages, and $n - t$ valid second-round messages are sufficient to

---

[3] It already followed from the work of Cohen *et al.* that unanimous abort is unachievable in this setting.

Table 1. Feasibility and impossibility of partially-asynchronous BC-P2P MPC with different guarantees. The first-round broadcast and peer-to-peer communication is synchronous and second round communication is asynchronous. Existing impossibility results in the BC-P2P setting where the second round is synchronous extend to the BC-P2P setting where the second round is asynchronous. Arrows indicate implication: the possibility of a stronger security guarantee implies the possibility of weaker ones in the same setting, and the impossibility of a weaker guarantee implies the impossibility of stronger ones in the same setting. (Our results appear in the full version [12].)

t	Setup & Communication Pattern	selective abort	unanimous abort	identifiable abort	fairness	guaranteed output delivery
$n \leq 2t$	CRS + PKI, BC-P2P	✗[12]	✗[9] ——→✗		✗[8] ——→✗	
$2t < n$	CRS + PKI, BC-P2P	✓ ←	✓ ←	✓ ←	✓ ←	✓ [19]
$2t < n$	CRS, PrivBC-P2P	✓[12]	✗[18], [11] ——→✗ ——→✗ ——→✗			
$2t < n$	CRS, PubBC-P2P	✗[12] ——→✗ ——→✗ ——→✗ ——→✗				

recover the output. We then adapt the construction of Ananth *et al.* [2], using commitments and NIZKs, to provide an instantiation of the starting PrivBC-P2P synchronous protocol.

1.4 Organization

We use the standard ideal/real world paradigm, the formal definitions of which are in the full version. In Sect. 2, we describe our lower and upper bounds for the setting when the first round is over (t_d, t_m)-asynchronous channels. Our obfuscation-based constructions in the (t_d, t_m)-asynchronous setting and the results for the setting when the second round is asynchronous appear in the full version [12].

2 P2P-BC

In this section, we assume that the first round of communication occurs over peer-to-peer channels with (t_d, t_m)-asynchrony (and the peer-to-peer and broadcast communication in the second round is fully synchronous). We determine the feasibility of various notions of security, in three settings: (1) when a PKI is available, (2) when no PKI is available, but a CRS and private peer-to-peer channels are, and (3) when no PKI or private channels are available in the first round, but a CRS is. Our results are summarized in Figs. 1 and 2.

2.1 Lower Bounds

Before describing our lower bounds, we present a theorem that is useful for our lower bound arguments. In this theorem, we identify what type of protocol design makes it vulnerable to a residual attack by the adversary i.e. allows the adversary to obtain the output on multiple inputs of her choice, while keeping the inputs of a subset of honest parties fixed.

Theorem 1. *Consider an n-party two-round protocol Π. Let E be the event that the parties can be assigned to three sets A, B and C with the following properties:*

1. *A contains a subset of honest parties.*
2. *C contains the set of corrupt parties, where $1 \leq |C| \leq t$.*
3. *$|A|, |B| \geq 1$, and A is disjoint from $B \cup C$ (but B and C are not necessarily disjoint).*
4. *The second-round messages of parties in A do not depend on the first-round messages of parties in B.*
5. *The adversary (controlling the parties in C) has access to the communication from A to B as well as private information that parties in B receive from the setup (if any).*
6. *The adversary obtains the output (computed on honest parties' inputs).*

If Π allows the above event E to occur with non-negligible probability, then there exists functions f such that Π can not securely compute f.

Proof. We use the function f_{mot}. Let the input of P_n be a pair of strings $x_n = (z_0, z_1)$, where $z_0, z_1 \in \{0,1\}^\lambda$, and let the input of every other party P_i ($i \in \{1, \ldots, n-1\}$) be a single bit $x_i \in \{0,1\}$. f_{mot} allows everyone to learn z_c where $c = \oplus_{i=1}^{n-1} x_i$. Towards a contradiction, we assume that the two-round secure protocol Π computes f_{mot} securely. Suppose that event E (described in the theorem) occurs during an execution of Π and results in the adversary obtaining the output (computed on honest parties' inputs).

We observe that, since the second-round messages of parties in A do not depend on the first round messages of parties in B, these are independent of the inputs of parties in B. This makes Π susceptible to the following residual attack: the adversary can use different choices of inputs on behalf of the parties in B and recompute their first and second round messages, while keeping the messages of parties in A fixed. The adversary also keeps the first-round messages of parties in $C \setminus B$ fixed and recomputes their second-round messages (based on the recomputed first-round messages of B).

Note that recomputing messages on behalf of parties in B (based on chosen inputs) requires (a) the private information (if any) that parties in B receive from the setup, and (b) the first-round messages that parties in B received from parties in A and C. Since the adversary has access to all of this (based on the assumptions and the fact that the adversary controls C), it is possible for the adversary to recompute messages on behalf of parties in B (using chosen inputs). It is now easy to see that this will allow the adversary to obtain multiple evaluations of the function, for different choices of inputs of parties in B while the inputs of other parties remain fixed. This contradicts the security of Π. More concretely, suppose $P_n \in A$. Then, this "residual attack" breaches the privacy property of the protocol, as it allows the adversary to learn both input strings of an honest P_n (which is not allowed in an ideal realization of f_{mot}).

Corollary 1. *Assume a setup with PKI or correlated randomness and the existence of a protocol Π where properties (1), (2), (3), (4) and (6) of E described in Theorem 1 are satisfied with non-negligible probability. If $B \subseteq C$ holds, then there exists functions f such that Π cannot securely compute f.*

Proof. We observe that when $B \subseteq C$, property (5) of Theorem 1 automatically holds – as the adversary controlling the parties in B has access to their private information received as a part of the setup and incoming messages. Hence, the corollary holds.

Corollary 2. *Assume a setup with CRS, a network with private peer-to-peer channels and the existence of a protocol Π where properties (1), (2), (3), (4) and (6) of E described in Theorem 1 are satisfied with non-negligible probability. If there is no communication from parties in A to parties in B, then there exist functions f such that Π cannot securely compute f.*

Proof. It is easy to see that if there is no communication from parties in A to B and the setup is public, then property (5) of Theorem 1 is satisfied by default. Hence, the corollary holds.

Corollary 3. *Assume a setup with CRS, a network with public peer-to-peer channels and the existence of a protocol Π where properties (1), (2), (3), (4) and (6) of E described in Theorem 1 are satisfied with non-negligible probability. Then, there exist functions f such that Π cannot securely compute f.*

Proof. Property (5) of Theorem 1 must also hold since the setup is public and the public peer-to-peer channels enable the adversary to learn the incoming messages of parties in B. Hence, the corollary holds.

With PKI. In this section, we assume the availability of a PKI. We adopt the same proof approach in each of our negative results in this section: we describe an adversarial strategy and message scheduling that results in the occurrence of the event E described in Corollary 1. We then invoke the impossibility result of Corollary 1 to complete the proof.

Theorem 2 (P2P-BC, SA, PKI, $t_m \geq n - t$, $t_d \geq 1$). *There exist functions f such that no n-party two-round protocol can compute f with selective abort if $t_m \geq n - t$ and $t_d \geq 1$; where the first round communication is over peer-to-peer channels with (t_d, t_m)-asynchrony and the second round communication is over synchronous broadcast and peer-to-peer channels.*

Proof. We use the function $f_{\mathtt{mot}}$ described in Theorem 1. Towards a contradiction, we assume a protocol Π computing $f_{\mathtt{mot}}$ with selective abort exists, whose first round communication is over peer-to-peer channels with (t_d, t_m)-asynchrony and second round communication is over synchronous broadcast and peer-to-peer channels.

Consider a scenario where the adversary passively corrupts the parties in a set C (where $|C| = t$) and A denotes the set of honest parties. Since the first round is over peer-to-peer channels with (t_d, t_m)-asynchrony, the adversary can schedule the first round messages of a party in C, say P_i, such that they are received by only corrupt parties. Such a scheduling is allowed, since the messages of P_i are delivered to parties in C where $|C| = t \geq n - t_m$ parties, and each honest party hears from $n - 1 \geq n - t_d$ parties. The correctness of Π (which must hold as everyone including the passively controlled parties behaved honestly) dictates that this execution must result in output computation. However, since none of the parties in A received the first round messages of P_i, it is easy to see that their second-round messages are independent of P_i's first round message. Setting $B = \{P_i\} \subseteq C$, it is easy to check that each of the conditions of Corollary 1 hold. It now directly follows from Corollary 1 that Π cannot securely compute f_{mot}, completing the proof.

Theorem 3 (P2P-BC, IA, PKI, $t_m \geq n - 2t$, $t_d \geq 1$). *There exist functions f such that no n-party two-round protocol can compute f with identifiable abort if $t_m \geq n - 2t$ and $t_d \geq 1$; where the first round communication is over peer-to-peer channels with (t_d, t_m)-asynchrony and the second round communication is over synchronous broadcast and peer-to-peer channels.*

Proof. We use the function f_{mot} described in Theorem 1. Towards a contradiction, we assume a protocol Π computing f_{mot} with identifiable abort exists, whose first round communication is over peer-to-peer channels with (t_d, t_m)-asynchrony and second round communication is over synchronous broadcast and peer-to-peer channels. Consider a partition of the set of parties into three disjoint sets S_0, S_1 and S_2, where $|S_0| = t_m$, $|S_1| = t$ and $|S_2| \leq t$. The adversary schedules the first round messages of a party in S_1, say P_i, such that they are not received by parties in set S_0. Such a scheduling is allowed, since the messages of P_i are delivered to everyone except the t_m parties in S_0 and each party hears from at least $n - 1 \geq n - t_d$ parties. We now consider two scenarios:

> **Scenario 1:** Adversary controls the party P_i in S_1 who behaves as per protocol specifications except the following:
>   - In the first round, P_i does not send first-round messages to honest parties in S_2.
>   - In the second round, P_i pretends as if she did not receive first-round messages from parties in S_2. In other words, P_i sends second-round messages based on protocol specifications when P_i did not receive first-round messages from parties in S_2.
>
> **Scenario 2:** Adversary controls the parties in S_2 (where $|S_2| \leq t$) who behave as follows:
>   - In the first round, parties in S_2 behave honestly, except that they do not send their first-round message to P_i.
>   - In the second round, parties in S_2 pretend as if they did not receive the first-round message from P_i.

The honest parties in S_0 cannot distinguish between the above two scenarios, since in both scenarios P_i and parties in S_2 claim that they have not received first-round messages from each other. Since the honest parties in S_0 do not know whom to blame (P_i or the parties in S_2, where $|S_2| \leq t$), it must be the case that both the above scenarios result in output computation (i.e. does not result in an abort).

Consider an execution of Π where the adversary controls the parties in S_1 who behave honestly except a single party $P_i \in S_1$ who behaves as per Scenario 1. Since none of the honest parties in $S_0 \cup S_2$ received the first round messages of P_i, it is easy to see that their messages are independent of P_i's input. Based on the above argument, this scenario must result in output computation. This output must also be learnt by the adversary since its view subsumes the view of an honest P_i in Scenario 2 (who learns the output).

Setting $A = S_0 \cup S_2$ as the set of honest parties, $B = \{P_i\}$ and $C = S_1$ (where $B \subseteq C$), one can check that each of the conditions of Corollary 1 holds. It now directly follows from Corollary 1 that Π cannot securely compute $f_{\mathtt{mot}}$, completing the proof.

Without PKI, with Private Channels. In this section, we present two negative results for the setting when PKI is not available but the peer-to-peer channels are private. For the first negative result, just like in the previous section, we adopt the approach of describing an adversarial strategy and message scheduling that results in the occurrence of the event E described in Corollary 2. We then invoke the impossibility result of Corollary 2 to complete the proof. The second negative result shows impossibility of identifiable abort when $n \leq 3t + t_m$. This proof is a slight modification of the proof of Damgård *et al.* [11], which shows the impossibility of identifiable abort in the synchronous P2P-BC setting when $n \leq 3t$.

Theorem 4 (PrivP2P-BC, SA, CRS, $n \leq t + 2t_d$, $n \leq t + 2t_m$). *There exist functions f such that no n-party two-round protocol can compute f with selective abort if $n \leq t + 2t_d$ and $n \leq t + 2t_m$; where the first round communication is over private peer-to-peer channels with (t_d, t_m)-asynchrony and the second round communication is over synchronous broadcast and peer-to-peer channels.*

Proof. We use the same function $f_{\mathtt{mot}}$ used in the proof of Theorem 1. Towards a contradiction, we assume a PrivP2P-BC, SA, CRS protocol Π with $n \leq t + 2t_d$ and $n \leq t + 2t_m$ securely computing $f_{\mathtt{mot}}$ exists, whose first-round communication is over peer-to-peer channels with (t_d, t_m)-asynchrony and second-round communication is over synchronous broadcast and peer-to-peer channels.

Consider a partition of the parties into three disjoint sets A, B and C, where $|A| = \frac{n-t}{2}$, $|B| = \frac{n-t}{2}$, and $|C| = t$, respectively. Consider an execution of Π where the adversary *passively* corrupts the t parties in C and schedules the messages in the first round so that no messages from B are delivered to A, and vice versa. Such a scheduling is permitted based on the assumption that $t_m \geq \frac{n-t}{2}$ and $t_d \geq \frac{n-t}{2}$.

The correctness of Π (which must hold as everyone including the passively controlled parties behaved honestly) dictates that this execution must result in output computation. However, we note that second-round messages of parties in A do not depend on the first-round messages of parties in B (as parties in A did not receive any first-round messages from parties in B). Furthermore, since there is no first-round communication from parties in A to parties in B as well, we observe that all the conditions of Corollary 2 are satisfied. It now directly follows from Corollary 2 that Π cannot securely compute f_{mot}, completing the proof.

Theorem 5 (PrivP2P-BC, IA, CRS, $n \leq 3t+t_m, t_d \geq 1$). *There exist functions f such that no n-party two-round protocol can compute f with identifiable abort if $n \leq 3t + t_m$; where the first round communication is over private peer-to-peer channels with (t_d, t_m)-asynchrony and the second round communication is over synchronous broadcast and peer-to-peer channels.*

We prove Theorem 5 in the full version [12], which is a slight modification of the proof of Damgård *et al.* [11], (that shows the impossibility of identifiable abort in the synchronous P2P-BC setting when $n \leq 3t$).

Without PKI, Without Private Channels. In this section, we assume that the first-round peer-to-peer channels are public. We show that selective abort is impossible to achieve when $n \leq t + t_d + t_m$. This proof follows the approach of the previous results, where we describe an adversarial strategy and scheduling that reduces the argument to Corollary 3.

Theorem 6 (PubP2P-BC, SA, CRS, $n \leq t+t_d+t_m$). *There exist functions f such that no n-party two-round protocol can compute f with selective abort if $n \leq t + t_d + t_m$; where the first round communication is over public peer-to-peer channels with (t_d, t_m)-asynchrony and the second round communication is over synchronous broadcast and peer-to-peer channels.*

Proof. We use the same function f_{mot} used in the proof of Theorem 1. Towards a contradiction, we assume a PubP2P-BC, SA, CRS protocol Π with $n \leq t+t_d+t_m$ securely computing f_{mot} exists, whose first-round communication is over public peer-to-peer channels with (t_d, t_m)-asynchrony and second-round communication is over synchronous broadcast and peer-to-peer channels.

Consider a partition of the parties into three disjoint sets A, B and C, where $|A| = t_m$, $|B| = t_d$, and $|C| = t$, respectively. Consider an execution of Π where the adversary *passively* corrupts the t parties in C and schedules the messages in the first round so that no messages from B are delivered to A.

The correctness of Π (which must hold as everyone including the passively controlled parties behaved honestly) dictates that this execution must result in output computation. Note that the second-round messages of parties in A do not depend on the first-round messages of parties in B (as parties in A did not receive any first-round messages from parties in B). It is now easy to see that all the conditions of Corollary 3 are satisfied. It now directly follows from Corollary 3 that Π cannot securely compute f_{mot}, completing the proof.

2.2   Upper Bounds

With PKI. In this section, we present two upper bounds for the setting where a PKI is available, the first-round communication is over peer-to-peer channels with (t_d, t_m)-asynchrony, and the second-round communication is over synchronous peer-to-peer and broadcast channels.

An important tool in our constructions is one-or-nothing secret sharing, introduced in Damgård *et al.* [10], which we describe briefly below.

One-or-Nothing Secret Sharing (1or0). One-or-nothing secret sharing is a special kind of secret sharing that allows a dealer to share a vector of secrets. As the name suggests, at most one among these secrets is eventually reconstructed. Once the shares are distributed, each receiver votes on the index of the value to reconstruct by producing a "ballot". If the receiver is unsure which index to vote for, she can publish a special equivocation ballot instead. Damgård *et al.* define a non-interactive variant of such a secret sharing, which supports parties being able to vote even if they have not received the shares. Informally, the properties required from a one-or-nothing secret sharing scheme are as follows.

> δ-**Correctness.** This property requires that if at least δ parties produce their ballot using the same index v (and the rest produce their ballot with $\perp$ i.e. the special equivocation ballot), then the secret at index v is reconstructed.
>
> **Privacy.** If no honest party produced their ballot using v, then the adversary learns nothing about the secret at index v.
>
> **Contradiction-privacy.** If two different honest parties produce their ballots using different votes (i.e. vote for different indices), then the adversary learns nothing at all.

While the definition in Damgård *et al.* defined correctness with respect to $\delta = n - t$, we consider a more general version of the same to adapt it to our setting with (t_d, t_m)-asynchrony. Their work presents a construction of a non-interactive one-or-nothing secret sharing scheme with $(n - t)$-correctness when $n > 2t$. We observe that, more generally, the same construction (with a minor tweak) serves as a non-interactive one-or-nothing secret sharing scheme with δ-correctness when $\delta > t$ holds. We defer the formal details of this construction to the full version [12].

Looking ahead, in our upper bounds, we use a non-interactive one-or-nothing secret sharing scheme with (1) $(n - t - t_m)$-correctness when $n > 2t + t_m$, and (2) $(n - t_m)$-correctness when $n > t + t_m$.

Protocol Overview of P2P-BC, ID, PKI, 2t < n [10]. Since both our upper bounds are constructed by slight modifications to the fully synchronous P2P-BC, ID, PKI, $2t < n$ construction of Damgård *et al.*, we give an overview of their construction below (we refer to [10] for the formal description). Their work presents a compiler that transforms a fully synchronous BC-BC, ID, PKI protocol Π_{bc} to a fully synchronous P2P-BC, ID, PKI, $2t < n$ protocol Π_{p2pbc}. The following steps are executed in Π_{p2pbc}: In the first round over synchronous peer-to-peer channels, the parties send their first-round message of Π_{bc} along with a signature to each of their peers. In the second round (over broadcast), the parties do the following:

1. Compute and broadcast a garbling of their next-message function (that has hardcoded input and randomness of a party, takes as input the first-round messages of Π_{bc} from all parties and computes the second-round message of the party according to Π_{bc});
2. Use the non-interactive 1or0 scheme with $(n-t)$-correctness to share all the input labels for their garbled circuit;
3. Based on the first-round messages received, "vote"[4] for which labels to reconstruct corresponding to everyone's garbled circuit (vote for $\bot$ in case no or invalid first-round message was received);
4. Compute a zero-knowledge proof to prove correctness of the actions taken in the second round; and
5. Echo all the first-round messages of Π_{bc} with the corresponding signatures received from the other parties in the first round.

During output computation, parties first verify the zero-knowledge proofs and signatures and catch the relevant party in case anyone's proof fails or there exist distinct first-round messages with valid signatures from the same party. They then proceed to reconstruct the appropriate labels of the garbled circuits of all parties. A party P_i is blamed if the reconstruction of the label corresponding to her first-round message fails. If all the labels are reconstructed successfully, the parties proceed to evaluating the garbled circuits and obtain the second round messages of Π_{bc} for all parties; which is subsequently used to obtain the output.

Intuitively, the protocol achieves identifiable abort when $n > 2t$. This is because, to avoid being caught, a corrupt party needs to send her first-round message with a valid signature to at least one honest party (otherwise $n - t > t$ parties would claim to have a conflict with her and she would be implicated). Further, she cannot afford to send different first-round messages to different honest parties with valid signatures (otherwise the contradictory signatures would implicate her). Contradiction privacy of one-or-nothing secret sharing ensures that in such a case the adversary does not learn any of the labels. Next, the zero-knowledge proof in the second round ensures that every corrupt party garbles and shares its garbled circuit labels correctly. Lastly, if no party is caught,

---

[4] Note that the one-or-nothing secret sharing is non-interactive; thereby "share" and "vote" can be executed in the same round.

it must hold each party's first-round message is echoed by at least $(n - t)$ parties who would vote accordingly. The $(n - t)$-correctness of one-or-nothing secret sharing ensures that in such a case, exactly one label from each label pair is reconstructed, which enables the underlying protocol Π_{bc} to be carried out.

Adapting to (t_d, t_m) asynchrony. We note that when the first-round communication is over peer-to-peer channels with (t_d, t_m)-asynchrony, we can implicate a party as being a cheater only if her message is echoed by fewer than $n - t - t_m$ parties (this ensures that an honest party whose first round message may be dropped to t_m honest parties and t corrupt parties may pretend to have not received her first-round message sent over peer-to-peer channels is not implicated). Therefore, to ensure that reconstruction is successful when no one is identified, we require a one-or-nothing secret sharing with $(n - t - t_m)$-correctness instead, for our construction with IA. For our construction with UA, we require $(n - t_m)$-correctness to ensure output computation when everyone behaves honestly (because in such a case, an honest party's message may be echoed by only $(n - t_m)$ parties). We state the formal theorems below and defer their proofs to the full version [12].

Theorem 7. (P2P-BC, IA, PKI, $2t + t_m < n$). *Let f be an efficiently computable n-party function and let $2t + t_m < n$. Let Π_{bc} be a BC-BC, ID, PKI protocol that securely computes f with the additional constraint that the straight-line simulator can extract inputs from corrupt parties' first-round messages. Assume the existence of a secure garbling scheme, digital signature scheme, non-interactive one-or-nothing secret sharing scheme [10], non-interactive key agreement scheme and non-interactive zero-knowledge proof system. Then, there exists a P2P-BC, ID, PKI protocol that securely computes f over two rounds, the first of which is over peer-to-peer channels with (t_d, t_m)-asynchrony, and the second of which is over a synchronous broadcast and peer-to-peer channel.*

Theorem 8. (P2P-BC, UA, PKI, $t + t_m < n$). *Let f be an efficiently computable n-party function and let $t + t_m < n$. Let Π_{bc} be a BC-BC, UA, PKI protocol that securely computes f with the additional constraint that the straight-line simulator can extract inputs from corrupt parties' first-round messages. Assume the existence of a secure garbling scheme, non-interactive one-or-nothing secret sharing scheme [10], non-interactive key agreement scheme and non-interactive zero-knowledge proof system. Then, there exists a P2P-BC, UA, PKI protocol that securely computes f over two rounds, the first of which is over peer-to-peer channels with (t_d, t_m)-asynchrony, and the second of which is over synchronous broadcast and peer-to-peer channels.*

Without PKI, Without Private Channels, from One-or-Nothing Secret Sharing with Intermediaries. In this section, we present two constructions for the CRS setting where the first-round communication is over public peer-to-peer channels with (t_d, t_m)-asynchrony and the second round communication is over synchronous peer-to-peer and broadcast channels. In contrast to the obfuscation-based constructions in the full version [12], these can be built from standard assumptions and for any polynomial number of parties. However, the bounds on t, t_d and t_m they achieve are looser.

An important tool in our constructions is one-or-nothing secret sharing with intermediaries, introduced in Damgård *et al.* [11], which we describe briefly below. (It is somewhat different from one-or-nothing secret sharing, which we used in our upper bounds with PKI; we'll elaborate on the differences below.)

One-or-Nothing Secret Sharing (1or0wi). Similar to the one-or-nothing secret sharing scheme with PKI (1or0) described in Sect. 2.2, 1or0wi is a kind of secret sharing that allows a dealer to share a vector of secrets, among which at most one is eventually reconstructed. Each share recipient is allowed to 'vote' for the index she wishes to reconstruct or abstain from voting. When a PKI is absent, it becomes more difficult to establish verifiable/reliable communication from the dealer to an intended share recipient. To address this concern, 1or0wi relies on a set of intermediaries to enable this share transfer. We recall (informally) the properties required from a one-or-nothing secret sharing with intermediaries scheme below.

ϵ-**privacy:** Informally, this property requires that when fewer than ϵ honest parties produce their ballot using the same index v, then the adversary learns nothing about the secret at index v.

α-**identifiability:** Informally, this property requires that when at least α parties produce their ballot using the same v, either the secret at index v is reconstructed or a corrupt party is identified.

β-**correctness:** Informally, this property requires that when all algorithms are executed honestly, if at least β parties produce their ballot using the same v, the secret at index v is reconstructed.

While the definition in Damgård *et al.* [11] defined privacy with respect to $\epsilon = n - 2t$ and identifiability with respect to $\alpha = n - t$, we consider a more general version of the same to adapt it to our setting with (t_d, t_m)-asynchrony. Furthermore, Damgård *et al.* does not consider correctness explicitly, as β-correctness is implied by β-identifiability (since it corresponds to the case when there are no cheaters). However, we consider the correctness property since it is useful in one of our constructions where identifiability is not required. At a very high-level, for our IA upper bound, we first show how the construction of 1or0wi in [11] can be modified to achieve $(n - t_m - t)$-identifiability and $(n - 2t - t_m)$-privacy when $n > 3t + t_m + t_d$ and $n > 3t + 2t_m$. Next, we observe that plugging in this (malicious secure) 1or0wi with modified parameters of privacy and identifiability in the compiler of [11] yields P2P-BC IA upper bounds tolerating (t_d, t_m)-asynchrony in the first round for certain range of thresholds. Similarly, for our UA upper bound, we first show how the construction of 1or0wi in [11] can be modified to achieve $(n - t_m)$-correctness and $(n - t - t_m)$-privacy when $n > t + t_m + t_d$ and $n > t + 2t_m$. Next, we observe that plugging in this (malicious secure) 1or0wi with modified parameters of privacy and correctness in the compiler of [11] yields P2P-BC UA upper bounds tolerating (t_d, t_m)-asynchrony in the first round for certain range of thresholds. We elaborate on these results in the full version [12].

References

1. Ananth, P., Boneh, D., Garg, S., Sahai, A., Zhandry, M.: Differing-inputs obfuscation and applications. Cryptology ePrint Archive, Report 2013/689 (2013). https://eprint.iacr.org/2013/689
2. Ananth, P., Choudhuri, A.R., Goel, A., Jain, A.: Round-optimal secure multiparty computation with honest majority. In: Shacham, H., Boldyreva, A. (eds.) CRYPTO 2018, Part II. LNCS, vol. 10992, pp. 395–424. Springer, Cham (2018). https://doi.org/10.1007/978-3-319-96881-0_14
3. Ananth, P., Choudhuri, A.R., Goel, A., Jain, A.: Two round information-theoretic MPC with malicious security. In: Ishai, Y., Rijmen, V. (eds.) EUROCRYPT 2019, Part II. LNCS, vol. 11477, pp. 532–561. Springer, Cham (2019). https://doi.org/10.1007/978-3-030-17656-3_19
4. Barak, B., et al.: On the (Im)possibility of obfuscating programs. In: Kilian, J. (ed.) CRYPTO 2001. LNCS, vol. 2139, pp. 1–18. Springer, Heidelberg (2001). https://doi.org/10.1007/3-540-44647-8_1
5. Ben-Or, M., Canetti, R., Goldreich, O.: Asynchronous secure computation. In: 25th ACM STOC, pp. 52–61. ACM Press (1993)
6. Ben-Or, M., Kelmer, B., Rabin, T.: Asynchronous secure computations with optimal resilience (extended abstract). In: Anderson, J., Toueg, S. (eds.) 13th ACM PODC, pp. 183–192. ACM (1994)
7. Benhamouda, F., Lin, H.: k-round multiparty computation from k-round oblivious transfer via garbled interactive circuits. In: Nielsen, J.B., Rijmen, V. (eds.) EUROCRYPT 2018, Part II. LNCS, vol. 10821, pp. 500–532. Springer, Cham (2018). https://doi.org/10.1007/978-3-319-78375-8_17
8. Cleve, R.: Limits on the security of coin flips when half the processors are faulty (extended abstract). In: 18th ACM STOC, pp. 364–369. ACM Press (1986)
9. Cohen, R., Garay, J., Zikas, V.: Broadcast-optimal two-round MPC. In: Canteaut, A., Ishai, Y. (eds.) EUROCRYPT 2020, Part II. LNCS, vol. 12106, pp. 828–858. Springer, Cham (2020). https://doi.org/10.1007/978-3-030-45724-2_28
10. Damgård, I., Magri, B., Ravi, D., Siniscalchi, L., Yakoubov, S.: Broadcast-optimal two round MPC with an honest majority. In: Malkin, T., Peikert, C. (eds.) CRYPTO 2021. LNCS, vol. 12826, pp. 155–184. Springer, Cham (2021). https://doi.org/10.1007/978-3-030-84245-1_6
11. Damgård, I., Ravi, D., Siniscalchi, L., Yakoubov, S.: Minimizing setup in broadcast-optimal two round MPC. In: Hazay, C., Stam, M. (eds.) EUROCRYPT 2023. LNCS, vol. 14005, pp. 129–158. Springer, Cham (2023). https://doi.org/10.1007/978-3-031-30617-4_5
12. Damgård, I., Ravi, D., Siniscalchi, L., Yakoubov, S.: Broadcast-optimal two round MPC with asynchronous peer-to-peer channels. Cryptology ePrint Archive, Paper 2023/1187 (2023)
13. Garg, S., Srinivasan, A.: Two-round multiparty secure computation from minimal assumptions. In: Nielsen, J.B., Rijmen, V. (eds.) EUROCRYPT 2018, Part II. LNCS, vol. 10821, pp. 468–499. Springer, Cham (2018). https://doi.org/10.1007/978-3-319-78375-8_16
14. Dov Gordon, S., Liu, F.-H., Shi, E.: Constant-round MPC with fairness and guarantee of output delivery. In: Gennaro, R., Robshaw, M. (eds.) CRYPTO 2015, Part II. LNCS, vol. 9216, pp. 63–82. Springer, Heidelberg (2015). https://doi.org/10.1007/978-3-662-48000-7_4

15. Dov Gordon, S., Liu, F.-H., Shi, E.: Constant-round MPC with fairness and guarantee of output delivery. In: Gennaro, R., Robshaw, M. (eds.) CRYPTO 2015. LNCS, vol. 9216, pp. 63–82. Springer, Heidelberg (2015). https://doi.org/10.1007/978-3-662-48000-7_4

16. Ishai, Y., Kumaresan, R., Kushilevitz, E., Paskin-Cherniavsky, A.: Secure computation with minimal interaction, revisited. In: Gennaro, R., Robshaw, M. (eds.) CRYPTO 2015, Part II. LNCS, vol. 9216, pp. 359–378. Springer, Heidelberg (2015). https://doi.org/10.1007/978-3-662-48000-7_18

17. Ishai, Y., Kushilevitz, E., Paskin, A.: Secure multiparty computation with minimal interaction. In: Rabin, T. (ed.) CRYPTO 2010. LNCS, vol. 6223, pp. 577–594. Springer, Heidelberg (2010). https://doi.org/10.1007/978-3-642-14623-7_31

18. Patra, A., Ravi, D.: On the exact round complexity of secure three-party computation. In: Shacham, H., Boldyreva, A. (eds.) CRYPTO 2018, Part II. LNCS, vol. 10992, pp. 425–458. Springer, Cham (2018). https://doi.org/10.1007/978-3-319-96881-0_15

19. Rambaud, M., Urban, A.: Almost-asynchronous MPC under honest majority, revisited. Cryptology ePrint Archive, Paper 2021/503 (2021). https://eprint.iacr.org/2021/503

20. Zikas, V., Hauser, S., Maurer, U.: Realistic failures in secure multi-party computation. In: Reingold, O. (ed.) TCC 2009. LNCS, vol. 5444, pp. 274–293. Springer, Heidelberg (2009). https://doi.org/10.1007/978-3-642-00457-5_17

Isogeny-Based Cryptography

Effective Pairings in Isogeny-Based Cryptography

Krijn Reijnders[(✉)]

Radboud University, Nijmegen, The Netherlands
krijn@cs.ru.nl

Abstract. Pairings are useful tools in isogeny-based cryptography and have been used in SIDH/SIKE and other protocols. As a general technique, pairings can be used to move problems about points on curves to elements in finite fields. However, until now, their applicability was limited to curves over fields with primes of a specific shape and pairings seemed too costly for the type of primes that are nowadays often used in isogeny-based cryptography. We remove this roadblock by optimizing pairings for highly-composite degrees such as those encountered in CSIDH and SQISign. This makes the general technique viable again: We apply our low-cost pairing to problems of general interest, such as supersingularity verification and finding full-torsion points, and show that we can outperform current methods, in some cases up to four times faster than the state-of-the-art. Furthermore, we analyze how pairings can be used to improve deterministic and dummy-free CSIDH. Finally, we provide a constant-time implementation (in Rust) that shows the practicality of these algorithms.

1 Introduction

In the event that quantum computers break current cryptography, post-quantum cryptography will provide the primitives required for digital security. Isogeny-based cryptography is a field with promising quantum-secure schemes, offering small public keys in key exchange (CSIDH [9]), and small signatures (SQISign [17]). The main drawback of isogeny-based cryptography is speed, as it requires heavy mathematical machinery in comparison to other areas of post-quantum cryptography. In particular, to ensure security against real-world side-channel analysis, the requirements for constant-time and leakage-free implementations cause a significant slowdown. Trends in current research in isogenies are, therefore, looking at new ideas to improve constant-time performance [1,2,6,10–12,21,30,31,33], and analyzing side-channel threats [3,7,8,25].

This work was done in large while the author was on an internship at the Cryptographic Research Centre of the Technology Innovation Institute, Abu Dhabi, UAE. In particular, the author thanks Francisco Rodríguez-Henríquez and Michael Scott for their warm support and excellent advice on the performance of these pairings. A full version of this paper is available at https://eprint.iacr.org/2023/858.

Surprisingly, although pairings were initially considered in SIDH and SIKE to improve the cost of key compression [14,15], they have received little attention for optimizing CSIDH or later isogeny-based protocols. There are clear obstructions that heavily affect the performance of pairings: we have no control over the Hamming weight of p for the base fields (in CSIDH or SQISign), we are likely to compute pairings of highly-composite degree, and many optimizations in the pairing-based literature require different curve models than the ones we consider in isogeny-based cryptography. Nevertheless, the field of pairing-based cryptography is rich in ideas and altogether many small improvements can make pairings efficient even for unpractical curves. As a general technique, we can use pairings to analyze certain properties of *points on elliptic curves* by a pairing evaluation as *elements of finite fields*. In this way, a single pairing can be used to solve a curve-theoretical problem with only field arithmetic, which is much more efficient. Hence, even a relatively expensive pairing computation can become cost-effective if the resulting problem is much faster to solve "in the field" than "on the curve".

Our Contributions. Our main contribution is combining an optimized pairing with highly-efficient arithmetic in $\mu_r \subseteq \mathbb{F}_{p^2}^*$ to solve isogeny problems faster. To achieve this, we first optimize the pairing and then apply this low-cost pairing to move specific problems from curves to finite fields. Specifically,

1. we optimize pairings on supersingular curves: in Miller's Algorithm, we first reduce the cost of subroutines Dbl and Add and then reduce the total number of subroutines using non-adjacent forms and windowing techniques.
2. we analyze the asymptotic and concrete cost of single and multi-pairings, in particular for supersingular curves over p512 (the prime used in CSIDH-512).
3. we apply these low-cost pairings to develop alternative algorithms for supersingularity verification, verifying full-torsion points, and finding full-torsion points, using highly-efficient arithmetic available for pairing evaluations.
4. we discuss the natural role these algorithms have when designing 'real-world' isogeny-based protocols, in particular, CSIDH-variants that are deterministic and secure against side-channel attacks.
5. we provide a full implementation of most of these algorithms in Rust, following the "constant-time" paradigm, that shows such algorithms can immediately be used in practice to speed up deterministic variants of CSIDH.

Our implementation is available at:

https://github.com/Krijn-math/EPIC

Related Work. This work can partly be viewed as a natural follow-up to [6, 10,11], works that analyze CSIDH as a real-world protocol, that is, removing randomness and dummy operations. Independent work by Lin, Wang, Xu, and Zhao [26] applies pairings to improve the performance of SQISign [17]. This shows the potential of pairings in isogeny-based cryptography and we believe this work can contribute to improving performance even further.

2   Preliminaries

Notation. Throughout, p denotes a large prime used with the base field $\mathbb{F}_p$, and quadratic extension $\mathbb{F}_{p^2}$, realized as $\mathbb{F}_p(i)$ with $i^2 = -1$. Both ℓ and ℓ_i denote a small odd prime that divides $p + 1$. A (supersingular) elliptic curve E_A is assumed to be in Montgomery form

$$E_A : y^2 = x^3 + Ax^2 + x, \quad A \in \mathbb{F}_p,$$

although our work also applies to other curve forms (most notably Edwards). μ_r denotes the set of r-th roots in $\mathbb{F}_{p^2}^*$. In particular, μ_{p+1} can be seen as $\mathbb{F}_{p^2}^*/\mathbb{F}_p^*$, the elements in $\mathbb{F}_{p^2}$ of norm 1, and μ_r for $r \mid p + 1$ is a subgroup of μ_{p+1}.

Finite field operations are denoted as **M** for multiplications, **S** for squarings, and **A** for additions. Inversions (**I**) and exponentiation (**E**) are expressed in **M**, **S** and **A** as far as possible. We use a cost model of $1\mathbf{S} = 0.8\mathbf{M}$ and $1\mathbf{A} = 0.01\mathbf{M}$ to compare performance in terms of finite field multiplications.

2.1   Isogeny-Based Cryptography

This work deals with specific problems in isogeny-based cryptography. We assume a basic familiarity with elliptic curve arithmetic, e.g. Montgomery ladders and addition chains. A great introduction is given by Costello and Smith [16].

The Prime p. We specifically look at supersingular elliptic curves over $\mathbb{F}_p$, where $p = h \cdot \prod_{i=1}^n \ell_i - 1$, with h is a suitable cofactor and the ℓ_i are small odd primes. We refer to these ℓ_i as *Elkies primes* [9]. We denote the set of Elkies primes as L_χ[1] and write $\ell_\chi = \prod_{\ell_i \in L_\chi} \ell_i$. Hence, $\log p = \log h + \log \ell_\chi$. If h is large, the difference in bit-size between ℓ_χ and $p + 1$ can be significant, and this can impact performance whenever an algorithm takes either $\log \ell_\chi$ or $\log p$ steps. For p512, h is only 4 and so we do not differentiate between the two.

Torsion Points. Let E be a supersingular elliptic curve over $\mathbb{F}_p$, then E has $p + 1$ rational points. Such points $P \in E(\mathbb{F}_p)$ therefore have order $N \mid p + 1$. When $\ell_i \mid N$, we say P has ℓ_i-torsion. When P is of order $p + 1$, we say P is a *full-torsion* point. The twist of E over $\mathbb{F}_p$ is denoted by E^t, and E^t is also supersingular. Rational points of E^t can also be seen as $\mathbb{F}_{p^2}$-points in $E[p + 1]$ of the form (x, iy) for $x, y \in \mathbb{F}_p$. Using x-only arithmetic, we can do arithmetic on *both* $E(\mathbb{F}_p)$ and $E^t(\mathbb{F}_p)$ using only these rational x-coordinates.

CSIDH. We briefly revisit CSIDH [9] to show where full-torsion points appear, and refer to [9,31,33] for more details. CSIDH applies the class group action of $\mathrm{Cl}(\mathcal{O})$ on supersingular elliptic curves E_A over $\mathbb{F}_p$ whose rational endomorphism ring $\mathrm{End}_p(E_A) \cong \mathcal{O}$ to create a non-interactive key exchange. Given a starting

---

[1] pronounced "ell-kie".

curve E_0, Alice's private key is an ideal class $[\mathfrak{a}] \in Cl(\mathcal{O})$ and her public key is $E_A := \mathfrak{a} * E_0$, and equivalent for Bob with $[\mathfrak{b}]$ and $E_B := \mathfrak{b} * E_0$. Both can derive the shared secret $E_{AB} := \mathfrak{a} * E_B = \mathfrak{b} * E_A$, given only the other's public key. In reality, we cannot sample random ideal classes $[\mathfrak{a}] \in Cl(\mathcal{O})$. Instead, we generate $\mathfrak{a}$ as a product of small ideals $\mathfrak{l}_i = (\ell_i, \pi - 1)$ and $\mathfrak{l}_i^{-1} = (\ell_i, \pi + 1)$ (the decomposition of (ℓ_i) into prime ideals), e.g., $\mathfrak{a} := \prod \mathfrak{l}_i^{e_i}$, where the e_i are secret.

Evaluating $\mathfrak{a} * E$ is done by the factorization of $\mathfrak{a}$ into $\mathfrak{l}_i$, where each $\mathfrak{l}_i^{\pm 1}$ can be evaluated using Vélu's formulas [41] if we have a point $P \in \ker(\pi \pm 1) \cap E[\ell_i]$. This requirement comes down to P being a rational point of order ℓ_i, with $\pi P = P$, hence $P \in E(\mathbb{F}_p)$ and $\mathfrak{l}_i^{+1} * E$ is evaluated as $E \to E/\langle P \rangle$, or $\pi P = -P$, hence P lives on the twist E^t and $\mathfrak{l}_i^{-1} * E$ is evaluated as $E^t \to E^t/\langle P \rangle$.

By sampling random points $P \in E(\mathbb{F}_p)$ and $Q \in E^t(\mathbb{F}_p)$ of order ℓ_i, we can use the right scalar multiple of either P or Q to compute the action of $\mathfrak{l}_i$ resp. $\mathfrak{l}_i^{-1}$ whenever ℓ_i divides $Ord(P)$ resp. $Ord(Q)$. The original points P and Q can then be pulled through the isogeny and used again as a new set of points on the co-domain [9,31,33]. By repeating this procedure and sampling new points P, Q when necessary, we compute the full action of $\mathfrak{a} * E$. As P and Q are sampled randomly, they have probability $\frac{\ell_i - 1}{\ell_i}$ that ℓ_i divides their order.

Deterministic CSIDH. The probabilistic nature of the evaluation of $\mathfrak{a} * E$, stemming from the random sampling of points P, Q, causes several issues, as randomness makes constant-time implementations difficult [1,6,11], leaks secret information through physical attacks [3], and requires a good source of entropy, which can be expensive or difficult on certain devices.

One way to avoid this random nature of $\mathfrak{a} * E$ is to ensure that both P and Q are *full-torsion points*, e.g., we have $Ord(P) = Ord(Q) = p + 1$. For a point P that is not a full-torsion point, we say P *misses* some torsion ℓ_i and we denote the *missing torsion* for P by $Miss(P)$. Note that $Miss(P) \cdot Ord(P) = p + 1$. By restricting coefficients e_i to $\{-1, +1\}$, CSIDH implementations avoid randomness and dummy operations [6,10,11].

2.2   Building Blocks in Isogeny-Based Cryptography

We list several general routines in isogeny-based cryptography that will be analyzed in more detail in later sections. These routines are posed as general problems, with their role in CSIDH specified afterward.

1. Finding the order of a point: Given $P \in E(\mathbb{F}_p)$, find the order $Ord(P)$.
2. Verifying supersingularity: Given $A \in \mathbb{F}_p$, verify E_A is supersingular.
3. Verifying full-torsion points: Given two points $P \in E(\mathbb{F}_p)$, $Q \in E^t(\mathbb{F}_p)$ verify P and Q are full-torsion points.
4. Finding full-torsion points: Given a curve E_A, find two full-torsion points $P \in E(\mathbb{F}_p)$ and $Q \in E^t(\mathbb{F}_p)$.

It is easy to see that these problems are related. For example, verifying supersingularity is usually done by verifying that E_A has order $p + 1$, by showing that there is a $\mathbb{F}_p$-rational point of order $N \geq 4\sqrt{p}$. This implies $N \mid \#E_A(\mathbb{F}_p)$ and hence we must have $\#E(\mathbb{F}_p) = p+1$ as $p+1$ is the only possible remaining value in the Hasse interval.

All variants of CSIDH use a supersingularity verification in order to ensure a public key E_A is valid. dCSIDH [6] includes full-torsion points (P, Q) in the public key to speed up the shared-secret computation. This requires finding full-torsion points in key generation and, given the public key, verifying such points (P, Q) are full-torsion before deriving the shared secret.

2.3   Pairing-Based Cryptography

One of the goals in pairing-based cryptography is to minimize the cost of computing a Weil or Tate pairing. We assume a basic familiarity with pairings up to the level of Costello's tutorial [13]. Other great resources are Galbraith [19] and Scott [36]. We focus only on the reduced Tate pairing, as it is more efficient for our purposes. We build on top of the fundamental works [4,5,32,42].

The Reduced Tate Pairing. In this work, we are specifically focused on the reduced Tate pairing of degree r for supersingular elliptic curves with embedding degree $k = 2$, which can be seen as a bilinear pairing

$$e_r : E[r] \times E(\mathbb{F}_{p^2})/rE(\mathbb{F}_{p^2}) \to \mathbb{F}_{p^2}^*/(\mathbb{F}_{p^2}^*)^r.$$

In the *reduced* Tate pairing, the result $\zeta = e_r(P, Q)$ is raised to the power $k = (p^2 - 1)/r$, which ensures ζ^k is an r-th root of unity in μ_r. In this work, we want to evaluate the Tate pairing on points $P \in E(\mathbb{F}_p)$ and $Q \in E^t(\mathbb{F}_p)$ of order r. For supersingular curves over $\mathbb{F}_p$ and $r \mid p+1$, such points generate all of $E[r]$. From the point of view of pairings, $E(\mathbb{F}_p)$ is the *base-field subgroup* and $E^t(\mathbb{F}_p)$ is the *trace-zero subgroup* of $E[p+1]$. Using the bilinear properties of the Tate pairing, we can compute $e_r(P, Q)$ from its restriction to $E(\mathbb{F}_p) \times E^t(\mathbb{F}_p)$.

Computing the Tate Pairing. There are multiple ways to compute the Tate pairing [27,28,32,39]. Most implementations evaluate e_r in three steps.

1. compute the Miller function f_{rP}, satisfying $\mathrm{div}(f_{rP}) = r(P) - r(\mathcal{O})$,
2. evaluate f_{rP} on an appropriate divisor D_Q,
3. raise $f_{rP}(D_Q)$ to the appropriate power, $\frac{p^2-1}{r}$, i.e., $e_r(P, Q) = f_{rP}(D_Q)^{p-1}$.

In practice, f_{rP} is a function in x and y of degree r, where r is cryptographically large, and therefore infeasible to store or evaluate. Miller's solution is a bitwise computation and direct evaluation of f_{rP} on D_Q to compute $f_{rP}(D_Q)$ in $\log(r)$ steps. By the work of Barreto, Kim, Lynn, and Scott [4, Theorem 1], we are in the fortunate situation that we can choose $D_Q = Q$. The Hamming weight of r is a large factor in the cost of computing $f_{rP}(Q)$ as a single step in Miller's loop takes close to twice the computational cost if the bit is 1. For our purposes, $r = p+1$ or $r = \ell_\chi$, and thus we have little control over the Hamming weight of r. The last step is also known as *the final exponentiation*. Algorithm 1 describes Miller's Algorithm before applying any optimizations, where $l_{T,T}$ and $l_{T,P}$ denote the required line functions (see [13, § 5.3]). We refer to the specific subroutines in Line 3 as Dbl and Line 5 as Add.

Algorithm 1. Miller's Algorithm

Input: $P \in E(\mathbb{F}_p)$, $Q \in E^t(\mathbb{F}_p)$, r of embedding degree $k = 2$, with $r = \sum_{i=0}^{t} t_i \cdot 2^i$
Output: The reduced Tate pairing $e_r(P, Q) \in \mu_r$
1: $T \leftarrow P$, $f \leftarrow 1$
2: **for** i from $t - 1$ to 0 **do**
3:     $T \leftarrow 2T$, $f \leftarrow f^2 \cdot l_{T,T}(Q)$ // Dbl
4:     **if** $t_i = 1$ **then**
5:         $T \leftarrow T + P$, $f \leftarrow f \cdot l_{T,P}(Q)$ // Add
6: **return** f^{p-1}

More generally, the value f is updated according to the formula

$$f_{(n+m)P} = f_{nP} \cdot f_{mP} \cdot \frac{l}{v} \tag{1}$$

where l and v are the lines that arise in the addition of nP and mP. Miller's Algorithm uses $n = m$ to double $T = nP$, or $m = 1$ to add $T = nP$ and P.

2.4   Field Arithmetic

The result of the reduced Tate pairing is a value $\zeta \in \mu_r \subseteq \mathbb{F}_{p^2}^*$ of norm 1, as it is an r-th root of unity. We require two useful algorithms from finite field arithmetic: Lucas exponentiation and Gauss's Algorithm to find primitive roots.

Gauss's Algorithm. An algorithm attributed to Gauss [29, p. 38] to find primitive roots of a certain order in a finite field is given in the full version, specialized to the case of finding a generator α for a finite field $\mathbb{F}_q$. It assumes a subroutine Ord computing the order of any element in the finite field.

Gauss's Algorithm is easy to implement and finds generators quickly. The main cost is computing the orders. We can adapt Gauss's Algorithm to elliptic curves to find generators for $E(\mathbb{F}_p)$, simply by replacing the rôles of α, β by rational points P, P' until P reaches $\text{Ord}(P) = p + 1$. Intuitively, one could say we "add" the torsion that P is missing using the right multiple of P'.

Lucas Exponentiation. Lucas exponentiation provides fast exponentiation for $\zeta \in \mathbb{F}_{q^2}$ of norm 1. They are used in cryptography since 1996 [22] and specifically applied to pairings by Scott and Barreto [37]. We follow their notation.

Let $\zeta = a + bi \in \mathbb{F}_{p^2}$ be an element of norm 1, i.e. $a^2 + b^2 = 1$, then ζ^k can be efficiently computed using only $a \in \mathbb{F}_p$ for every $k \in \mathbb{N}$ using Lucas sequences, based on simple laddering algorithms. We denote these sequences by $V_k(a)$ and $U_k(a)$ but often drop a for clarity. The central observation is

$$\zeta^k = (a + bi)^k = V_k(2a)/2 + U_k(2a) \cdot bi, \quad \text{for } \zeta \in \mu_{p+1},$$

where

$$V_0 = 2, \quad V_1 = a, \quad V_{k+1} = a \cdot V_k - V_{k-1},$$
$$U_0 = 0, \quad U_1 = 1, \quad U_{k+1} = a \cdot U_k - U_{k-1}.$$

Given V_k, we can compute U_k by $(a \cdot V_k - 2 \cdot V_{k-1})/(a^2 - 4)$. An algorithmic description is given in [37, App. A]. For this work, we only require the value of $V_k(2a)$. As such, exponentiation of norm-1 elements is much more efficient than general exponentiation in $\mathbb{F}_{p^2}^*$: the former requires $1\mathbf{S} + 1\mathbf{M}$ per bit of k, whereas the latter requires roughly $2\mathbf{S} + \frac{5}{2}\mathbf{M}$ per bit of k, assuming the Hamming weight of k is $\log(k)/2$. In our cost model, this is an almost 60% improvement. We denote the cost of exponentiation per bit for norm-1 elements by C_{Lucas}.

This arithmetic speed-up is key to the applications in this work: as the required pairings have evaluations of norm 1, we can apply Lucas exponentiation to the results to get very fast arithmetic. In comparison to x-only arithmetic on the curve, we are between five and six times faster per bit. Hence, if the cost of the pairing is low enough, the difference in cost between curve arithmetic and Lucas exponentiation is so large that it makes up for the cost of the pairing.

3   Optimizing Pairings for Composite Order

In this section, we apply several techniques to decrease the cost of Miller's Algorithm, specifically for pairings of degree $r \mid p + 1$, and points $P \in E(\mathbb{F}_p)$, $Q \in E^t(\mathbb{F}_p)$, with E supersingular and $p = h \cdot \ell_\chi - 1$. This is a different scenario than pairing-based literature usually considers: we have no control over the Hamming weight of $p+1$, and we compute pairings of composite degree.

We first give an abstract view and then start optimizing Miller's Algorithm. In Sect. 3.2, we decrease the cost per subroutine Dbl/Add with known optimizations that fit our scenario perfectly. In Sect. 3.3, we decrease the number of subroutines Dbl/Add using non-adjacent forms and (sliding) window techniques, inspired by finite field exponentiation and elliptic curves scalar multiplication.

3.1   An Abstract View on Pairings

Silverman [38], views the reduced Tate pairing as a threefold composition

$$E[r] \to \operatorname{Hom}(E[r], \mu_r) \to \mathbb{F}_{p^2}^* / \mathbb{F}_{p^2}^{*,r} \xrightarrow{z \mapsto z^{(p^2-1)/r}} \mu_r(\mathbb{F}_{p^2}) \qquad (2)$$

similar to the one described in Sect. 2.3. Namely, for $r = p + 1$, we can reduce the first map to $E(\mathbb{F}_p) \to \mathrm{Hom}(E^t(\mathbb{F}_p), \mu_r)$ to get

$$\Psi : E(\mathbb{F}_p) \to \mathrm{Hom}(E^t(\mathbb{F}_p), \mu_r), \quad P \mapsto e_r(P, -),$$

which can be made concrete as the Miller function $P \mapsto f_{rP}$. By composing with its evaluation on Q, we get $f_{rP}(Q) = e_r(P, Q)$ (unreduced). To $f_{rP}(Q)$, we apply the final exponentiation $z \mapsto z^{(p^2-1)/r}$. In the case of $r = p + 1$, we thus get the reduced Tate pairing $e_{p+1}(P, Q)$ as $\zeta = f_{(p+1)P}(Q)^{p-1}$.

From this point of view, identifying full-torsion points $P \in E(\mathbb{F}_p)$ is equivalent to finding points P that map to isomorphisms $f_{rP} \in \mathrm{Hom}(E^t(\mathbb{F}_p), \mu_r)$. We make this precise in the following lemma.

Lemma 1. *Let E be a supersingular curve over $\mathbb{F}_p$. Let $P \in E(\mathbb{F}_p)$ and $r = p+1$. Then f_{rP} as a function $E^t(\mathbb{F}_p) \to \mu_r$ has kernel*

$$\ker f_{rP} = \{Q \in E^t(\mathbb{F}_p) \mid \mathsf{Ord}(P) \text{ divides } \mathsf{Miss}(Q)\}.$$

Hence, $|\ker f_{rP}| = \mathsf{Miss}(P)$. Thus, if P generates $E(\mathbb{F}_p)$, the kernel is trivial.

Proof. See full version.

Note that, given a full-torsion point $P \in E(\mathbb{F}_p)$, we can thus identify full-torsion points $Q \in E^t(\mathbb{F}_p)$ as points where $e_r(P, Q)$ is a primitive root in μ_r. In light of Lemma 1, we can try to tackle the routines sketched in Sect. 2.2 using properties of f_{rP}, $f_{rP}(Q)$ and $\zeta = f_{rP}(Q)^{p-1}$. For example, we can find $\ker f_{rP}$ by evaluating f_{rp} on multiple points Q_i, and finding the orders of the resulting elements ζ_i. In the language of pairing-based cryptography, we compute multiple pairings $e_r(P, Q_i)$ for the same point P. Hence, we need to minimize the cost of several evaluations of the Tate pairing for fixed P but different points Q_i.

3.2 Reducing the Cost per Subroutine of Miller's Loop

We now optimize the cost per Dbl and Add in Miller's Algorithm. We assume that $P \in E(\mathbb{F}_p)$ is given by $\mathbb{F}_p$-coordinates $x_P, y_P \in \mathbb{F}_p$, and $Q \in E^t(\mathbb{F}_p)$ can be given by $\mathbb{F}_p$-coordinates $x_Q, y_Q \in \mathbb{F}_p$ (we implicitly think of Q as $(x_Q, i \cdot y_Q)$).

Some of these techniques were used before in SIDH and SIKE [14,15], in a different situation: in SIDH and SIKE, these pairings were specifically applied for $p = 2^{e_2} \cdot 3^{e_3} - 1$, whereas we assume $p = h \cdot \ell_\chi - 1$. Thus, we have much more different $\ell_i \mid p + 1$ to work with, and we cannot apply most of their techniques.

Representations. For T, we use projective coordinates to avoid costly inversions when doubling T, adding P and computing $\ell_{T,T}$ and $\ell_{T,P}$. For Q, as we only evaluate Q in $\ell_{T,T}$ and $\ell_{T,P}$, we leave Q affine. $f = a + bi$ is an $\mathbb{F}_{p^2}$-value represented projectively as $(a : b : c)$, with $a, b, c \in \mathbb{F}_p$ and c as the denominator. Although x-only pairings exist [20], they seem unfit for this specific scenario.

The Final Exponentiation. As established before, after computing $f_{rP}(Q) \in \mathbb{F}_{p^2}$ we perform a final exponentiation by $p-1$. This is beneficial for two reasons:

1.) Raising to the power p is precisely applying Frobenius $\pi : z \mapsto z^p$ in $\mathbb{F}_{p^2}$, and so $\pi : a + bi \mapsto a - bi$. Hence we can compute $z \mapsto z^{p-1}$ as $z \mapsto \frac{\pi(z)}{z}$. The Frobenius part is 'free' in terms of computational cost. In $\mathbb{F}_{p^2}$, $z \mapsto z^{-1}$ is simply $(a+bi)^{-1} = \frac{(a-bi)}{a^2+b^2}$. Hence, the $\mathbb{F}_p$-inversion of $a^2 + b^2$ is the dominating cost of the final exponentiation. In constant-time, this costs about $\log p$ multiplications. When a and b are public, we use faster non-constant-time inversions. In comparison to prime pairings, this final exponentiation is surprisingly efficient.

2.) Raising z to the power $p-1$ for $\mathbb{F}_{p^2}$-values gives the same as $\alpha \cdot z$ for $\alpha \in \mathbb{F}_p^*$, as $(\alpha \cdot z)^{p-1} = \alpha^{p-1} \cdot z^{p-1} = z^{p-1}$. Hence, when we compute $f_{rP}(Q) \in \mathbb{F}_{p^2}$, we can ignore or multiply by $\mathbb{F}_p$-values [4], named "denominator elimination" in pairing literature. That is, we ignore the denominator c in the representation $(a : b : c)$ of f in the Miller loop, and similarly in evaluating $l_{T,T}(Q)$ and $l_{T,P}(Q)$, saving several $\mathbb{F}_p$-operations in Dbl/Add

Reusing Intermediate Values. In Dbl, computing $T \leftarrow 2T$ shares many values with the computation of $l_{T,T}$ and in Add computing $T \leftarrow T+P$ shares values with $l_{T,P}$. Reusing such values saves again several $\mathbb{F}_p$-operations in Dbl/Add.

Improved Doubling Formulas. As shown in [16, §4.1], the subroutine Dbl in Miller's Algorithm is more efficient when using a projective representation of $T \in E(\mathbb{F}_p)$ as (X^2, XZ, Z^2, YZ), although this requires a slight adjustment of the formulas used in Add. Overall, this reduces the cost for Dbl to $5\mathbf{S} + 15\mathbf{M}$ and the cost for Add becomes $4\mathbf{S} + 20\mathbf{M}$, for an average of $7\mathbf{S} + 25\mathbf{M}$ per bit.

3.3 Reducing the Number of Subroutines in the Miller Loop

Next to reducing the cost for a single Dbl/Add, we apply techniques to reduce the total number of Adds. Usually in pairing-based cryptography, we do so by using primes p of low Hamming weight. Here we do not have this freedom, thus we resort to techniques inspired by exponentiation in finite fields.

Non-adjacent Form. With no control over the Hamming weight of $p + 1$, we assume half of the bits are 1. However, in Miller's Algorithm, it is as easy to add $T \leftarrow T + P$ as it is to subtract $T \leftarrow T - P$ (which we denote Sub), with the only difference being a negation of y_P. Hence, we use *non-adjacent forms* (NAFs [34]) to reduce the number of Add/Subs. A NAF representation of $p + 1$ as $\sum_{i=0}^{n} t_i \cdot 2^i$, $t_i \in \{-1, 0, 1\}$, reduces the Hamming weight from $\log(p)/2$ to $\log(p)/3$, and thus decrease the number of expensive Add/Subs in Miller's Algorithm by $\log(p)/6$. We get an average cost of $6\frac{1}{3}\mathbf{S} + 21\frac{2}{3}\mathbf{M}$ per bit, a saving of about 10%.

Algorithm 2 gives a high-level overview of the Miller loop with the improvements so far, for general p. Note that, as the output $\zeta \in \mathbb{F}_{p^2}$ will have norm 1, we only require the real part of ζ. See the full version for the specific algorithms Dbl, Add and Sub, which are implemented in `bignafmiller.rs`.

Algorithm 2. Miller's algorithm, using NAFs

Input: $x_P, y_P, x_Q, y_Q \in \mathbb{F}_p$, $p + 1 = \sum_{i=0}^{t} t_i \cdot 2^i$
Output: The real part of $e_r(P, Q) \in \mu_{p+1}$
1: $T = (X^2, XZ, Z^2, YZ) \leftarrow (x_P^2, x_P, 1, y_P)$
2: $f \leftarrow (1, 0)$
3: **for** i from $t - 1$ to 0 **do**
4:     $(T, f) \leftarrow \mathsf{Dbl}(T, f, x_Q, y_Q)$
5:     **if** $t_i = 1$ **then**
6:         $(T, f) \leftarrow \mathsf{Add}(T, f, x_P, y_P, x_Q, y_Q)$
7:     **if** $t_i = -1$ **then**
8:         $(T, f) \leftarrow \mathsf{Sub}(T, f, x_P, y_P, x_Q, y_Q)$
9: $a \leftarrow f[0]$, $b \leftarrow f[1]$
10: **return** $\frac{a^2 - b^2}{a^2 + b^2}$ // The final exponentiation

---

For Specific Primes. For specific primes p, such as p512, we can improve on the NAF representation by using windowing techniques [23, 24]. This allows us to decrease even further the times we need to perform Add or Sub, at the cost of a precomputation of several values.

In short, windowing techniques allow us to not only add or subtract P but also multiples of P during the loop. To do so, we are required to precompute several values, namely $iP, -iP, f_{iP}$ and f_{-iP}. We need the multiples $\pm iP$ to perform $T \leftarrow T \pm iP$, and the line values f_{iP} to set $f \leftarrow f \cdot f_{\pm iP} \cdot \ell_{T,iP}(Q)$ in Add/Sub. We first precompute the required iP in projective form, and we keep track of f_{iP}. We use Montgomery's trick to return the points iP in affine form at the cost of a single inversion and some multiplications. Using affine form decreases the cost of $T \leftarrow T \pm iP$ during Add/Sub.

We note that iP gives $-iP$ for free, simply by negating y_{iP}. Furthermore, from $f_{iP} = a + bi$ we can obtain f_{-iP} as $f_{iP}^{-1} = \frac{a - bi}{a^2 + b^2}$. However, as $a^2 + b^2 \in \mathbb{F}_p^*$, we can ignore these (thanks to the final exponentiation) and simply set $f_{-iP} = a - bi$. Altogether, these sliding-window techniques reduce the number of Add/Subs from $\log(p)/3$ down to about $\log(p)/(w + 1)$. See `bigwindowmiller.rs` for the implementation of this algorithm.

For the prime p512, we found the optimum at a window size $w = 5$. This requires a precomputation of $\{P, 3P, \ldots, 21P\}$. Beyond $w = 5$, the cost of additional computation does not outweigh the decrease in Add/Subs. Altogether this gives another saving of close to 10% for this prime.

3.4   Multiple Pairing Evaluations

The previous sections attempt to optimize a single pairing $e_r(P,Q)$. However, in many scenarios, including the ones in Sect. 4, it is beneficial to optimize the cost of multiple pairings, in particular multiple pairings $e_r(P,Q_1),\ldots e_r(P,Q_k)$ for the same point P. This is known as the "one more pairing" problem in pairing literature. We quickly sketch two methods to do so. Firstly, assuming the set $\{Q_1,\ldots,Q_k\}$ is known in advance and we minimize the overall cost of these k pairings. Secondly, assuming we want to compute additional pairings $e_r(P,Q_{k+1})$ after having already computed $e_r(P,Q_1),\ldots,e_r(P,Q_k)$.

Evaluating a Fixed Set $Q_1, Q_2, \ldots, Q_k$. Optimizing k pairings $e_r(P,Q_i)$ for an already known set $Q_1,\ldots,Q_k$ is easy: only f depends on Q_i, hence we can easily adapt Algorithm 2 for an array of points $[Q_1,\ldots,Q_k]$ to keep track of a value $f^{(i)}$ per Q_i, and we return an array $\zeta^{(1)},\ldots,\zeta^{(k)}$. All evaluations share (per bit) the computations of T, $l_{T,T}$ and $l_{T,P}$. Our additional cost per extra point Q_i thus comes down to the evaluations $l_{T,T}(Q_i)$, $l_{T,P}(Q_i)$ and updating $f^{(i)}$. In total, this is 7**M** per Dbl, and 5**M** per Add/Sub, plus $2\mathbf{S}+\mathbf{I}$ to compute $\zeta^{(i)}$ given $f^{(i)}$ (the final exponentiation) per point Q_i. See `bigmultimiller.rs` for the implementation of this algorithm.

Evaluating Additional Points $Q_1, Q_2, \ldots$ It is more difficult when we want to compute $e_r(P,Q')$ *after* the computation of $e_r(P,Q)$. I.e., in some applications we compute $e_r(P,Q)$ first, and, based on this evaluation, compute another $e_r(P,Q')$. In practice, this seems to require another full pairing computation.

Scott [35] observed that one can achieve a time/memory trade-off, by dividing Miller's Algorithm into three distinct subalgorithms: one to compute f_{rP}, one to evaluate $f_{rP}(Q_i)$ per Q_i and one for the final exponentiation. Paradoxically, this brings us back to the original three-step process from Sect. 2.3, where we argued that the degree of f_{rP} is too large to store f_{rP} in full. However, Scott notes, $f_{rP}(Q)$ can be computed from the set of all line functions $l_{T,T}$ and $l_{T,P}$ and Q. Up to $\mathbb{F}_p$-invariance, all such line functions l can be written as

$$l(x,y) = \lambda_x \cdot x + \lambda_y \cdot y + \lambda_0, \quad \lambda_i \in \mathbb{F}_p,$$

and we get a line function per Dbl, Add, and Sub. Thus, at a memory cost of

$$\underbrace{(\log(p) + 1/3 \log(p))}_{\#\text{subroutines}} \cdot \underbrace{3 \cdot \log(p)}_{\text{bits per } l} = 4 \cdot \log(p)^2$$

(the factor $1/3$ can be decreased using windowing) we can store a representation of f_{rP} as an array of line functions. Hence, we can split up Algorithm 2 into three subroutines Construct, Evaluate, and Exponentiate, which coincide precisely with the decomposition of the Tate pairing given in Eq. (2). We refer to the composition of these subalgorithms as Scott-Miller's algorithm. See the full version for an algorithmic description.

3.5 Summary of Costs

We summarize Sect. 3 in terms of $\mathbb{F}_p$-operations for pairings of degree $r = p + 1$.

General primes. Miller's Algorithm has $\log p$ steps and each step performs 1 Dbl. Using the techniques from Sect. 3.3 decreases the number of Add/Subs[2]:

1. each Dbl costs $15\mathbf{M} + 5\mathbf{S} + 7\mathbf{A}$, we always perform $\log p$ Dbls
2. each Add or Sub costs $20\mathbf{M} + 4\mathbf{S} + 9\mathbf{A}$,
   (a) in a naïve approach, we perform $\frac{1}{2}\log p$ Adds and Subs
   (b) using NAFs, we perform $\frac{1}{3}\log p$ Adds and Subs
   (c) using windowing, we perform $\frac{1}{w+1}\log p$ Adds and Subs

For CSIDH-512. For p512, Table 1 gives the number of $\mathbb{F}_p$-operations to compute a pairing, and shows the effectiveness of the optimizations: a reduction of 40% compared to unoptimized pairings.

Table 1. Concrete cost of the Miller loop for p512 for a pairing of degree $r = p + 1$. 'Total' gives the number of $\mathbb{F}_p$-operations, with cost model $1\mathbf{S} = 0.8\mathbf{M}$ and $1\mathbf{A} = 0.01\mathbf{M}$.

	M	S	A	Total
Original Miller's Algorithm	28498	2621	39207	30987
Optimized step (Sect. 3.2)	12740	3569	12230	15717
Using NAFs (Algorithm 2)	11152	3254	11125	13866
Using windows ($w = 5$)	9963	2960	10592	12436
Additional pairing	4410	2	5704	4468

For an additional pairing, if the points are known beforehand, we require only slightly more memory cost for each additional pairing. If we need to compute a multipairing for variable points, this takes $4 \cdot \log(p)^2$ bits of memory to store the representation of f_{rP}, using Scott-Miller's algorithm (Sect. 3.4).

Remark 1. In Table 1, we consider the cost for a pairing of degree $r = p + 1$. An alternative for primes $p = h \cdot \ell_\chi - 1$ with large cofactor h is to consider pairings of degree $r = \ell_\chi$ on $E[\ell_\chi]$. In many applications, such as [6], this contains all the necessary torsion information needed. The loop, then, has $\log \ell_\chi = \log p - \log h$ steps. The cost of such a pairing can be deduced from the given estimates.

4 Applications of Pairings to Isogeny Problems

In this section, we apply the optimized pairing from Sect. 3 to the isogeny problems described in Sect. 2.1. The core design idea is clear: the pairing is now cheap enough to move isogeny problems from curves to finite fields, where we have highly efficient Lucas exponentiation.

---

[2] These techniques are inspired by finite field exponentiation and scalar multiplication, and have been analyzed previously for pairing-based cryptography [23,24].

4.1 Verification of Full-Torsion Points

We start with the following problem: Given $P \in E(\mathbb{F}_p)$ and $Q \in E^t(\mathbb{F}_p)$, verify both points have full-torsion, for a supersingular curve E over $\mathbb{F}_p$[3].

Current Methods. Current methods to verify full-torsion points compute $[\frac{p+1}{\ell_i}]P \neq \mathcal{O}$ to conclude p has ℓ_i-torsion for every $\ell_i \mid p+1$ and hence is a full-torsion point. In a naïve way, this can be done per ℓ_i for the cost of a scalar multiplication of size $\log p$, using either Montgomery ladders or differential addition chains, at a total complexity of $\mathcal{O}(n \log p)$. Concretely, this comes down to a cost of $C_{\text{curve}} \cdot n \log p$ where C_{curve} is the cost of curve arithmetic per bit.

Using product trees this drops down to $\mathcal{O}(\log n \log p)$, taking $\mathcal{O}(\log n)$ space. Product-tree-based order verification is the method used [6] to verify a given basis (P, Q). For both P and Q, this comes down to $2 \cdot C_{\text{curve}} \cdot \log n \log p$ operations.

Torsion Bases. We can improve on the previous verification matter by two easy observations. Firstly, whenever a pair of points $P \in E(\mathbb{F}_p)$ and $Q \in E^t(\mathbb{F}_p)$ generates all of $E[p+1] \subseteq E(\mathbb{F}_{p^2})$, the pair (P, Q) is a torsion basis for the $(p+1)$-torsion. As proposed in SIDH/SIKE [14,15], we can verify such a torsion basis using the result that $\zeta = e_{p+1}(P, Q) \in \mu_{p+1}$ must be a $(p+1)$-th primitive root in $\mathbb{F}_{p^2}$. Secondly, this situation is ideal for our pairing: P has both rational coordinates, and Q has rational x and purely imaginary y-coordinate. As noted before, ζ is an element of norm 1 in $\mathbb{F}_{p^2}$, which allows us to apply fast Lucas exponentiation to compute ζ^k. The following lemma is our key building block.

Lemma 2. *Let $P \in E(\mathbb{F}_p)$ and $Q \in E^t(\mathbb{F}_p)$. Let $\zeta = e_{p+1}(P, Q) \in \mu_{p+1}$. Then*

$$\zeta^{\frac{p+1}{\ell_i}} \neq 1 \Leftrightarrow [\frac{p+1}{\ell_i}]P \neq \mathcal{O} \text{ and } [\frac{p+1}{\ell_i}]Q \neq \mathcal{O}.$$

Proof. This is a direct application of Lemma 1. $\qquad\qquad\qquad\qquad\square$

Hence, instead of verifying that both P and Q have ℓ_i-torsion, we verify that the powers $\zeta^{\frac{p+1}{\ell_i}}$ do not vanish. Furthermore, as ζ and its powers have norm 1, we simply verify that $\text{Re}(\zeta^k) \neq 1$ which implies $\zeta^k \neq 1$. In terms of Lucas sequences, this is equal to $V_k(2a) \neq 2$ for $\zeta = a + bi$. Per bit, Lucas exponentiation is much more efficient than curve arithmetic, which allows us to compute every $\zeta^{\frac{p+1}{\ell_i}}$ (again using product trees) very efficiently at a similar complexity $\mathcal{O}(\log n \log p)$, and a concrete cost of $1 \cdot C_{\text{Lucas}} \cdot \log n \log p$[4].

This approach is given in Algorithm 3. Order uses a product-tree approach to compute the order of ζ using Lucas exponentiation. See `bigpairingfo.rs` for an implementation of Algorithm 3.

---

[3] We treat *finding* full-torsion points in Sect. 4.3.

[4] To compute using Lucas exponentiation we use a constant-time laddering approach. Interesting future work would be to use (differential) addition chains to reduce costs.

Algorithm 3. Verification of torsion basis

Input: $P \in E(\mathbb{F}_p)$, $Q \in E^t(\mathbb{F}_p)$
Output: True or **False**
1: $\zeta \leftarrow \mathsf{Re}(e_{p+1}(P, Q))$, $m \leftarrow \mathsf{Order}(\zeta)$
2: **if** $m = p + 1$ **then return True, else return False**

Further Improvements. As stated before, working in μ_{p+1} has the added benefit that we work in same subgroup of $\mathbb{F}_{p^2}$, independent of the curve E_A. This can be used to speed up the cost of torsion basis verification even more, at the cost of $\log p$ additional bits next to the pair (P, Q), as follows.

The scalars $\Lambda := \mathbb{Z}_{p+1}^*$ of invertible elements in $\mathbb{Z}_{p+1}$ act faithfully and free on both the group of full-torsion points of E_A, as well as on exact primitive roots in $\mu_{p+1} \subseteq \mathbb{F}_{p^2}$. This means that we can write any full-torsion point T relative to another full-torsion point T' as $T = [\lambda]T'$ with $\lambda \in \Lambda$. Similarly for primitive roots, this implies we can pick a system parameter ζ_0 as the "standard" primitive root, and can find $\lambda \in \Lambda$ such that for $\zeta = e_{p+1}(P, Q)$ we get $\zeta = \zeta_0^\lambda$.

By including λ next to (P, Q), we do not have to verify the complete order of ζ. Instead, we simply verify that $\lambda \in \Lambda$, compute $\zeta = e_{p+1}(P, Q)$ and verify that $\zeta = \zeta_0^\lambda$ which implies that ζ is an exact $(p + 1)$-th root of unity. Compared to the algorithm sketched before this means that instead of $\mathcal{O}(\log n \log p)$ to verify the order of ζ, we use a single Lucas exponentiation $\mathcal{O}(\log p)$ to verify ζ.

Remark 2. The addition of the discrete log λ such that $\zeta = e_{p+1}(P, Q) = \zeta_0^\lambda$ might be unnecessary depending on the specific application. Namely, for a pair (P, Q), we get another pair $(P, \lambda^{-1}Q)$ that is a torsion basis, with

$$e_{p+1}(P, \lambda^{-1}Q) = e_{p+1}(P, Q)^{\lambda^{-1}} = \zeta^{\lambda^{-1}} = \zeta_0.$$

As ζ_0 is a public parameter, verification requires no extra λ. However, the choice of P and Q might have been performed carefully, e.g. to make sure both have small x-coordinates to reduce communication cost. It thus depends per application if a modified torsion basis $(P, \lambda^{-1}Q)$ reduces communication cost.

Remark 3. The above algorithm not only verifies that P and Q are full-torsion points, but includes the supersingularity verification of E_A, as it shows E_A has points of order $p + 1$. This can be useful for applications, e.g. those in [6].

4.2   Pairing-Based Supersingularity Verification

Supersingularity verification asks us to verify that E_A is a supersingular curve. A sound analysis of the performance of different algorithms was made by Banegas, Gilchrist, and Smith [2]. They examine **(a.)** a product-tree based approach to find a point of order $N \geq 4\sqrt{p}$, **(b.)** Sutherland's algorithm [40] based on isogeny volcanoes, and **(c.)** Doliskani's test [18] based on division polynomials. They conclude that Doliskani's test is best for Montgomery models over $\mathbb{F}_p$, as it requires only a single scalar multiplication over $\mathbb{F}_{p^2}$ of length $\log p$ followed by $\log p$ squarings in $\mathbb{F}_{p^2}$. The algorithms we propose resemble the product-tree approach, but move the computation of the orders of points from the curve to the field. There are two ways to apply the pairing approach here:

Approach 1. Sample random points $P \in E(\mathbb{F}_p)$ and $Q \in E^t(\mathbb{F}_p)$, compute $\zeta = e_r(P,Q)$ for $r = p + 1$, and compute $\mathsf{Ord}(\zeta)$ using a product-tree up until we have verified $\mathsf{Ord}(\zeta) \geq 4\sqrt{p}$.

Approach 2. Divide L_χ into two lists L_1 and L_2 such that $\ell^{(1)} := \prod_{\ell_i \in L_1} \ell_i$ is slightly larger than $4\sqrt{p}$. Sample again two random points $P \in E(\mathbb{F}_p)$ and $Q \in E^t(\mathbb{F}_p)$, and multiply both by $\frac{p+1}{\ell^{(1)}} = h \cdot \ell^{(2)}$ so that $P, Q \in E[\ell^{(1)}]$. Then, compute the pairing of degree $r = \ell^{(1)}$ and verify that $\zeta \in \mu_r$ has $\mathsf{Ord}(\zeta) \geq 4\sqrt{p}$.

Approach 1 is essentially Algorithm 3, where we cut off the computation of $\mathsf{Ord}(\zeta)$ early whenever we have enough torsion. Approach 2 uses the fact that we do not have to work in all of μ_{p+1} to verify supersingularity. This reduces the number of steps in the Miller loop by half, $\frac{1}{2}\log p$ compared to $\log p$, but requires two Montgomery ladders of $\log(p)/2$ bits to kill the $\ell^{(2)}$-torsion of P and Q. Note that we must take L_1 a few bits larger than $4\sqrt{p}$ to ensure with high probability that random points P, Q have enough torsion to verify or falsify supersingularity. In practice, the fastest approach is highly dependent on the prime p and the number of factors ℓ_i, as well as the size of the cofactor 2^k. Approach 2 is summarized in Algorithm 4. See the folder `supersingularity` for the implementations of these algorithms.

Algorithm 4. Verification of supersingularity

Input: $A \in \mathbb{F}_p$, where $p = h \cdot \ell^{(1)} \cdot \ell^{(2)} - 1$
Output: **True** or **False**
1: $(P, Q) \xleftarrow{\$} E(\mathbb{F}_p) \times E^t(\mathbb{F}_p)$
2: $P \leftarrow [4 \cdot \ell^{(2)}]P,\ Q \leftarrow [h \cdot \ell^{(2)}]Q$
3: $\zeta \leftarrow \mathrm{Re}(e_{\ell^{(1)}}(P, Q)),\ m \leftarrow \mathsf{Order}(\zeta)$
4: **If** $m \geq 4\sqrt{p}$ **then return True, else** repeat

---

Remark 4. Line 4 of Algorithm 4 computes the order of ζ using product-trees to verify (a) $\zeta' := \zeta^{\frac{p+1}{\ell_i}} \neq 1$ and (b) $\zeta'^{\ell_i} = 1$. At any time, if (a) holds but not (b), the curve is *ordinary*. As in [9, Alg. 1], we then return **False**.

Remark 5. Note that in an approach where torsion points (P, Q) are given, together with a discrete log λ, so that $e_{p+1}(P, Q) = \zeta_0^\lambda$, or even the variant where $(P, \lambda^{-1}Q)$ is given as in Remark 2, the cost of supersingularity verification is essentially that of a single pairing computation, or that of a pairing computation together with a Lucas exponentiation of length $\log \lambda \approx \log p$. For CSIDH-512, this beats Doliskani's test as we will see in Sect. 4.4

4.3   Finding Full-Torsion Points

Finding full-torsion points is more tricky. Current implementations [6,11] simply sample random points and compute their order until they find a full-torsion point. The curve-equivalent of Gauss's Algorithm already improves this approach, yet still requires a lot of curve arithmetic. We apply pairings again to improve performance. We specifically need Scott-Miller's algorithm (Sect. 3.4) to compute a variable number of pairings for a given P.

Abstract Point-of-View. From the abstract point of view, sketched in Sect. 3.1, we want to identify a full-torsion point P as an isomorphism $f_{rP} : E^t(\mathbb{F}_p) \to \mu_r$, using Lemma 1. Scott-Miller's algorithm allows us to compute a representation of f_{rP} and to evaluate f_{rP} efficiently on points $Q \in E^t(\mathbb{F}_p)$.

Starting from random points $P_1 \in E(\mathbb{F}_p)$ and $Q_1 \in E^t(\mathbb{F}_p)$, we compute $\zeta_1 := f_{rP_1}(P_1, Q_1)^{p-1}$ and $\mathsf{Ord}(\zeta_1)$. The missing torsion $m_1 = \mathsf{Miss}(\zeta_1)$ is then equal to $\mathrm{lcm}(\mathsf{Miss}(P), \mathsf{Miss}(Q))$. If $m_1 = 1$, then we know both P_1 and Q_1 are full-torsion points. If $m_1 \neq 1$, we continue with a second point Q_2. Compute ζ_2 and $m_2 = \mathsf{Miss}(\zeta_2)$. Let $d = \gcd(m_1, m_2)$. If $d = 1$, that is, m_1 and m_2 are co-prime, then P_1 is a full-torsion point, and we can apply Gauss's Algorithm to compute a full-order point Q, given Q_1 and Q_2.

For $d > 1$, it is most likely that $d = |\ker f_{rP_1}| = \mathsf{Miss}(P_1)$, or, if unlucky, both Q_1 and Q_2 miss d-torsion. The probability that both Q_1 and Q_2 miss d-torsion is $\frac{1}{d^2}$. Hence, if d is small, this is unlikely but possible. If d is a large prime, we are almost certain P_1 misses d-torsion. In the former case, we sample a third point Q_3 and repeat the same procedure. In the latter case, we use Q_1 and Q_2 to compute a full-torsion Q. Using Q, we compute f_{rQ} and apply the same procedure to points P_i to create a full-torsion point P (reusing P_1).

Distinguishing between these cases is highly dependent on the value of d, which in turn depends on L_χ and p. We leave these case-dependent details to the reader. See `bigfastfinding.rs` for the implementation of this algorithm.

Remark 6. One can improve on randomly sampling P_1 and Q_1, as we can sample points directly in $E \setminus [2]E$ [14] by ensuring the x-coordinates are not quadratic residues in $\mathbb{F}_p$. Similar techniques from p-descent might also apply for $\ell_i > 2$.

4.4   Concrete Cost for CSIDH-512

We have implemented and evaluated the performance of the algorithms in Sect. 4 for p512, the prime used in CSIDH-512. Table 2 shows the performance in $\mathbb{F}_p$-operations, compared to well-known or state-of-the-art algorithms.

Verifying Torsion Points. We find that Algorithm 3 specifically for p512 takes about 19293 operations, with 12426 operations taken up by the pairing, hence order verification of ζ using Lucas exponentiation requires only 6867 operations, closely matching the predicted cost $C_{\mathrm{Lucas}} \cdot \log n \cdot \log p$. In comparison, the

Table 2. Concrete cost of the algorithms in this section using the prime in CSIDH-512. 'Total' gives the number of $\mathbb{F}_p$-operations, with cost model $1\mathsf{S} = 0.8\mathsf{M}$ and $1\mathsf{A} = 0.01\mathsf{M}$.

	Source	M	S	A	Total
Product-tree torsion verif	[6]	51318	29388	73396	75562
Pairing-based torsion verif	Algorithm 3	13693	6838	18424	19293
Pairing-based (given λ)	Sect. 4.1	10472	3471	11616	13364
CSIDH-Supersingularity verif	[9]	13324	7628	19052	19617
Doliskani's test	[2,18]	13789	2	30642	14097
Approach 1 (pairing-based)	Sect. 4.2	11081	4112	12914	14500
Approach 2 (pairing-based)	Algorithm 4	9589	5801	10434	14334

currently-used method [6] to verify full-torsion points requires 75562 operations, hence we achieve a speed-up of 75%, due to the difference in cost per bit between C_{curve} and C_{Lucas}. If we include a system parameter ζ_0 and a discrete log λ, our cost drops down to 13364 operations, increasing the speedup from 75% to 82%.

Supersingularity Verification. We find that Doliskani's test is still slightly faster, but our algorithms come within 2% of performance. Saving a single M or S in Dbl or Add would push Algorithm 4 below Doliskani's test for p512. When we include λ, as mentioned above, we outperform Doliskani's test by 6%.

Finding Torsion Points. Although the cost of this algorithm depends highly on divisors ℓ_i of $p + 1$, heuristics for p512 show that we usually only require 2 points $P_1, P_2 \in E(\mathbb{F}_p)$ and two points $Q_1, Q_2 \in E^t(\mathbb{F}_p)$, together with pairing computations $e_r(P_1, Q_1)$ and $e_R(P_1, Q_2)$ to find full-torsion points P and Q. We leave out concrete performance numbers, as this varies too much per case.

5 Applications of Pairing-Based Algorithms

The pairing-based algorithms from Sect. 4 are of independent interest, but also find natural applications in (deterministic) variants of CSIDH.

Applying Pairing-Based Algorithms. In all versions of CSIDH, supersingularity verification is required on public keys. We estimate that, depending on the shape and size of the prime p, either Doliskani's test or one of the pairing-based algorithms (Sect. 4.2) is optimal.

For deterministic variants of CSIDH [6,11], including (an Elligator seed for) a torsion basis of E_A in the public key is only natural, and this is exactly what is proposed for the dCSIDH variant of [6]. This requires verification of such a torsion basis. For this verification, Algorithm 3 clearly outperforms curve-based approaches. Furthermore, the verification of such a torsion basis also verifies the supersingularity of E_A, which would otherwise have cost an additional $\mathcal{O}(\log p)$ operations, using either Doliskani's test or one of our pairing-based algorithms.

Including torsion-point information in the public key also requires a party to *find* such a torsion basis in key generation. The pairing-based approach described in Sect. 4.3 heuristically beats current approaches based on random sampling.

Constant-Time Versions. Both Algorithms 3 and 4 are easy to implement in constant-time, given constant-time curve and field arithmetic. However, constant-time verification is usually not required, as both E_A and (P, Q) should be public.

For a constant-time approach to finding full-torsion points, a major roadblock is finding a constant-time version of Gauss's Algorithm. This is both mathematically interesting as well as cryptographically useful, but seems to require a better understanding of the distribution of the x-coordinates of full-torsion points for curves, or the $(p + 1)$-th primitive roots for fields.

Beyond Current Implementations. Current deterministic variants of CSIDH [6,10,11] are limited to exponents $e_i \in \{-1, 0, +1\}$. Going beyond such exponents requires sampling new points during the class group action evaluation on an intermediate curve E'. To not leak any information on E' in a deterministic implementation, therefore, requires a constant-time torsion-basis algorithm as sketched above. This would allow approaches with $e_i \geq 1$ for multiple small ℓ_i to reduce the number of ℓ_i-isogenies for large ℓ_i, which is deemed favorable in constant-time probabilistic approaches [1,12,30].

For ordinary CSIDH and CTIDH, using full-torsion points in every round would have the further improvement that the number of rounds is constant, and we have no trial-and-error approaches in the group action computation, providing a stronger defence against certain side-channel attacks [3]. In particular for CTIDH, we can use full-torsion points to remove the "coin flip" that decides if a batch is performed. This improves performance and design properties. We leave a full analysis for future work.

A final remark should be made about the use of theta functions to compute pairings [27,28]. Such an approach might yield speed-ups in comparison to the methods used in this work and the use of theta functions could provide a more general framework for higher dimensional isogeny-based cryptography.

References

1. Banegas, G., et al.: CTIDH: faster constant-time CSIDH. In: TCHES 2021, pp. 351–387 (2021)
2. Banegas, G., Gilchrist, V., Smith, B.: Efficient supersingularity testing over $\mathbb{F}_p$ and CSIDH key validation. Math. Cryptol. **2**(1), 21–35 (2022)
3. Banegas, G., et al.: Disorientation faults in CSIDH. In: Hazay, C., Stam, M. (eds.) EUROCRYPT 2023. LNCS, vol. 14008, pp. 310–342. Springer, Cham (2023). https://doi.org/10.1007/978-3-031-30589-4_11

4. Barreto, P.S.L.M., Kim, H.Y., Lynn, B., Scott, M.: Efficient algorithms for pairing-based cryptosystems. In: Yung, M. (ed.) CRYPTO 2002. LNCS, vol. 2442, pp. 354–369. Springer, Heidelberg (2002). https://doi.org/10.1007/3-540-45708-9_23
5. Barreto, P., Lynn, B., Scott, M.: Efficient implementation of pairing-based cryptosystems. J. Cryptol. **17**(4), 321–334 (2004)
6. Campos, F., et al.: On the Practicality of Post-Quantum TLS Using Large-Parameter CSIDH. ePrint 2023/793
7. Campos, F., Kannwischer, M.J., Meyer, M., Onuki, H., Stöttinger, M.: Trouble at the CSIDH: protecting CSIDH with dummy-operations against fault injection attacks. In: FDTC 2020, pp. 57–65. IEEE (2020)
8. Campos, F., Meyer, M., Reijnders, K., Stöttinger, M.: Patient zero and patient six. SAC (2022)
9. Castryck, W., Lange, T., Martindale, C., Panny, L., Renes, J.: CSIDH: an efficient post-quantum commutative group action. In: Peyrin, T., Galbraith, S. (eds.) ASIACRYPT 2018. LNCS, vol. 11274, pp. 395–427. Springer, Cham (2018). https://doi.org/10.1007/978-3-030-03332-3_15
10. Cervantes-Vázquez, D., Chenu, M., Chi-Domínguez, J.-J., De Feo, L., Rodríguez-Henríquez, F., Smith, B.: Stronger and faster side-channel protections for CSIDH. In: Schwabe, P., Thériault, N. (eds.) LATINCRYPT 2019. LNCS, vol. 11774, pp. 173–193. Springer, Cham (2019). https://doi.org/10.1007/978-3-030-30530-7_9
11. Chávez-Saab, J., Chi-Domínguez, J.-J., Jaques, S., Rodríguez-Henríquez, F.: The SQALE of CSIDH. J. Cryptogr. Eng. **12**(3), 349–368 (2022)
12. Chi-Domínguez, J.-J., Rodríguez-Henríquez, F.: Optimal strategies for CSIDH. Adv. Math. Commun. **16**(2), 383–411 (2022)
13. Costello, C.: Pairings for beginners (2015). https://www.craigcostello.com.au/
14. Costello, C., Jao, D., Longa, P., Naehrig, M., Renes, J., Urbanik, D.: Efficient compression of SIDH public keys. In: Coron, J.-S., Nielsen, J.B. (eds.) EUROCRYPT 2017. LNCS, vol. 10210, pp. 679–706. Springer, Cham (2017). https://doi.org/10.1007/978-3-319-56620-7_24
15. Costello, C., Longa, P., Naehrig, M.: Efficient algorithms for supersingular isogeny Diffie-Hellman. In: Robshaw, M., Katz, J. (eds.) CRYPTO 2016. LNCS, vol. 9814, pp. 572–601. Springer, Heidelberg (2016). https://doi.org/10.1007/978-3-662-53018-4_21
16. Costello, C., Smith, B.: Montgomery curves and their arithmetic: the case of large characteristic fields. J. Cryptogr. Eng. **8**, 227–240 (2018)
17. De Feo, L., Kohel, D., Leroux, A., Petit, C., Wesolowski, B.: SQISign: compact post-quantum signatures from quaternions and isogenies. In: Moriai, S., Wang, H. (eds.) ASIACRYPT 2020. LNCS, vol. 12491, pp. 64–93. Springer, Cham (2020). https://doi.org/10.1007/978-3-030-64837-4_3
18. Doliskani, J.: On division polynomial pit and supersingularity. Appl. Algebra Eng. Commun. Comput. **29**(5), 393–407 (2018)
19. Galbraith, S.D.: Pairings (2005)
20. Galbraith, S.D., Lin, X.: Computing pairings using x-coordinates only. Des. Codes Crypt. **50**(3), 305–324 (2009)
21. Hutchinson, A., LeGrow, J., Koziel, B., Azarderakhsh, R.: Further optimizations of CSIDH: a systematic approach to efficient strategies, permutations, and bound vectors. In: Conti, M., Zhou, J., Casalicchio, E., Spognardi, A. (eds.) ACNS 2020. LNCS, vol. 12146, pp. 481–501. Springer, Cham (2020). https://doi.org/10.1007/978-3-030-57808-4_24
22. Joye, M., Quisquater, J.-J.: On the importance of securing your bins: The garbage-man-in-the-middle attack. In: CCS 1997, pp. 135–141 (1997)

23. Kiyomura, Y., Takagi, T.: Efficient algorithm for Tate pairing of composite order. IEICE Trans. Fundam. Electron. Commun. Comput. Sci. **97**(10), 2055–2063 (2014)
24. Kobayashi, T., Aoki, K., Imai, H.: Efficient algorithms for Tate pairing. IEICE Trans. Fundam. Electron. Commun. Comput. Sci. **89**(1), 134–143 (2006)
25. LeGrow, J.T., Hutchinson, A.: (Short Paper) analysis of a strong fault attack on static/ephemeral CSIDH. In: Nakanishi, T., Nojima, R. (eds.) IWSEC 2021. LNCS, vol. 12835, pp. 216–226. Springer, Cham (2021). https://doi.org/10.1007/978-3-030-85987-9_12
26. Lin, K., Wang, W., Xu, Z., Zhao, C.: A faster software implementation of sqisign. Cryptology ePrint Archive, Paper 2023/753 (2023)
27. Lubicz, D., Robert, D.: A generalisation of miller's algorithm and applications to pairing computations on abelian varieties. J. Symb. Comput. **67**, 68–92 (2015)
28. Lubicz, D., Robert, D.: Efficient pairing computation with theta functions. In: Hanrot, G., Morain, F., Thomé, E. (eds.) ANTS 2010. LNCS, vol. 6197, pp. 251–269. Springer, Heidelberg (2010). https://doi.org/10.1007/978-3-642-14518-6_21
29. McEliece, R.: Finite Fields for Computer Scientists and Engineers, vol. 23. Springer, New York (2012). https://doi.org/10.1007/978-1-4613-1983-2
30. Meyer, M., Campos, F., Reith, S.: On lions and elligators: an efficient constant-time implementation of CSIDH. In: Ding, J., Steinwandt, R. (eds.) PQCrypto 2019. LNCS, vol. 11505, pp. 307–325. Springer, Cham (2019). https://doi.org/10.1007/978-3-030-25510-7_17
31. Meyer, M., Reith, S.: A faster way to the CSIDH. In: Chakraborty, D., Iwata, T. (eds.) INDOCRYPT 2018. LNCS, vol. 11356, pp. 137–152. Springer, Cham (2018). https://doi.org/10.1007/978-3-030-05378-9_8
32. Miller, V.: The weil pairing, and its efficient calculation. J. Cryptol. **17**(4), 235–261 (2004)
33. Onuki, H., Aikawa, Y., Yamazaki, T., Takagi, T.: A faster constant-time algorithm of CSIDH keeping two points. In: IWSEC 2019 (2019)
34. Reitwiesner, G.: Binary arithmetic. In: Advances in Computers, vol. 1, pp. 231–308. Elsevier (1960)
35. Scott, M.: Pairing implementation revisited. ePrint 2019/077 (2019)
36. Scott, M.: Understanding the Tate pairing (2004). http://www.computing.dcu.ie/~mike/tate.html
37. Scott, M., Barreto, P.S.L.M.: Compressed pairings. In: Franklin, M. (ed.) CRYPTO 2004. LNCS, vol. 3152, pp. 140–156. Springer, Heidelberg (2004). https://doi.org/10.1007/978-3-540-28628-8_9
38. Silverman, J.H.: A Survey of Local and Global Pairings on Elliptic Curves and Abelian Varieties. In: Joye, M., Miyaji, A., Otsuka, A. (eds.) Pairing 2010. LNCS, vol. 6487, pp. 377–396. Springer, Heidelberg (2010). https://doi.org/10.1007/978-3-642-17455-1_24
39. Stange, K.E.: The Tate pairing via elliptic nets. In: Takagi, T., Okamoto, T., Okamoto, E., Okamoto, T. (eds.) Pairing 2007. LNCS, vol. 4575, pp. 329–348. Springer, Heidelberg (2007). https://doi.org/10.1007/978-3-540-73489-5_19
40. Sutherland, A.: Identifying supersingular elliptic curves. LMS J. Comput. Math. **15**, 317–325 (2012)
41. Vélu, J.: Isogénies entre courbes elliptiques. Comptes Rendus de l'Académie des Sciences de Paris, Séries A **273**, 238–241 (1971)
42. Vercauteren, F.: Optimal pairings. IEEE Trans. Inf. Theory **56**(1), 455–461 (2009)

Fast and Frobenius: Rational Isogeny Evaluation over Finite Fields

Gustavo Banegas[1]($\boxtimes$), Valerie Gilchrist[2]($\boxtimes$), Anaëlle Le Dévéhat[3]($\boxtimes$), and Benjamin Smith[3]($\boxtimes$)

[1] Qualcomm France SARL, Valbonne, France
gustavo@cryptme.in
[2] Université Libre de Bruxelles and FRIA, Brussels, Belgium
valerie.gilchrist@ulb.be
[3] Inria and Laboratoire d'Informatique de l'École Polytechnique,
Institut Polytechnique de Paris, Palaiseau, France
anaelle.le-devehat@inria.fr, smith@lix.polytechnique.fr

Abstract. Consider the problem of efficiently evaluating isogenies $\phi :$ $\mathcal{E} \to \mathcal{E}/H$ of elliptic curves over a finite field $\mathbb{F}_q$, where the kernel $H = \langle G \rangle$ is a cyclic group of odd (prime) order: given $\mathcal{E}$, G, and a point (or several points) P on $\mathcal{E}$, we want to compute $\phi(P)$. This problem is at the heart of efficient implementations of group-action- and isogeny-based post-quantum cryptosystems such as CSIDH. Algorithms based on Vélu's formulæ give an efficient solution when the kernel generator G is defined over $\mathbb{F}_q$, but for general isogenies G is only defined over some extension $\mathbb{F}_{q^k}$, even though $\langle G \rangle$ as a whole (and thus ϕ) is defined over the base field $\mathbb{F}_q$; and the performance of Vélu-style algorithms degrades rapidly as k grows. In this article we revisit isogeny evaluation with a special focus on the case where $1 \leq k \leq 12$. We improve Vélu-style evaluation for many cases where $k = 1$ using special addition chains, and combine this with the action of Galois to give greater improvements when $k > 1$.

1 Introduction

Faced with the rising threat of quantum computing, demand for quantum-secure, or post-quantum, cryptographic protocols is increasing. Isogenies have emerged as a useful candidate for post-quantum cryptography thanks to their generally small key sizes, and the possibility of implementing post-quantum group actions which offer many simple post-quantum analogues of classical discrete-log-based algorithms (see e.g. [26]).

A major drawback of isogeny-based cryptosystems is their relatively slow performance compared with many other post-quantum systems. In this paper,

Authors listed in alphabetical order: see https://www.ams.org/profession/ leaders/CultureStatement04.pdf. This work was funded in part by a FRIA grant by the National Fund for Scientfic Research (F.N.R.S.) of Belgium, by the French Agence Nationale de la Recherche through ANR CIAO (ANR-19-CE48-0008), and by a Plan France 2030 grant managed by the Agence Nationale de la Recherche (ANR-22-PETQ-0008). Date of this document: 2023-08-30.

A. Aly and M. Tibouchi (Eds.): LATINCRYPT 2023, LNCS 14168, pp. 129–148, 2023.
https://doi.org/10.1007/978-3-031-44469-2_7

we improve evaluation times for isogenies of many prime degrees $\ell > 3$ given a generator of the kernel; these computations are the fundamental building blocks of most isogeny-based cryptosystems. Specifically, we propose simple alternative differential addition chains to enumerate points of (subsets of) the kernel more efficiently. This speeds up many ℓ-isogeny computations over the base field by a factor depending on ℓ, and also permits a full additional factor-of-k speedup for ℓ-isogenies over $\mathbb{F}_q$ whose kernel generators are defined over an extension $\mathbb{F}_{q^k}$.

Our techniques have constructive and destructive applications. First, accelerating basic isogeny computations can speed up isogeny-based cryptosystems. The methods in Sect. 4 apply for many $\ell > 3$, so they would naturally improve the performance of commutative isogeny-based schemes such as CSIDH [5], and CSI-FiSh [4] and its derivatives (such as [12] and [14]), which require computing many ℓ-isogenies for various primes ℓ. They may also improve the performance of other schemes like SQISign [16], which computes many ℓ-isogenies in its signing process. (We discuss applications further in Sect. 6.)

In Sect. 5 we focus on rational isogenies with irrational kernels; our methods there could further accelerate the improvements of [13] for Couveignes–Rostovtsev–Stolbunov key exchange (CRS) and related protocols of Stolbunov [11,24,27,28]. This is a small step forward on the road to making CRS a practical "ordinary" fallback for CSIDH in the event of new attacks making specific use of the full supersingular isogeny graph (continuing the approach of [6], for example).

Our results also have applications in cryptanalysis: the best classical and quantum attacks on commutative isogeny-based schemes involve computing massive numbers of group actions, each comprised of a large number of ℓ-isogenies (see e.g. [3] and [8]). Any algorithm that reduces the number of basic operations per ℓ-isogeny will improve the effectiveness of these attacks.

Proof-of-concept implementations of our algorithms in SageMath are available at https://github.com/vgilchri/k-velu. The scripts include operation-counting code to verify the counts claimed in this article.

Disclaimer. In this paper, we quantify potential speedups by counting finite field operations. Real-world speed increases depend on many additional variables including parameter sizes; the application context; implementation choices; specificities of the runtime platform (including architecture, vectorization, and hardware acceleration); and the availability of optimized low-level arithmetic.

2   Background

We work over (extensions of) the base field $\mathbb{F}_q$, where q is a power of a prime $p > 3$. The symbol ℓ always denotes a prime $\neq p$. In our applications, $3 < \ell \ll p$.

Elliptic Curves. For simplicity, elliptic curves are supposed to be in a general Weierstrass form $\mathcal{E} : y^2 = f(x)$. Our algorithms focus on *Montgomery models*

$$\mathcal{E} : By^2 = x(x^2 + Ax + 1) \qquad \text{where} \qquad B(A^2 - 4) \neq 0 \,.$$

but our results extend easily to other models such as twisted Edwards and short Weierstrass models. The multiplication-by-m map is denoted by $[m]$. The q-power Frobenius endomorphism is $\pi : (x, y) \mapsto (x^q, y^q)$.

Field Operations. While the curve $\mathcal{E}$ will always be defined over $\mathbb{F}_q$, we will often work with points defined over $\mathbb{F}_{q^k}$ for $k \geq 1$. We write $\mathbf{M}$, $\mathbf{S}$, and $\mathbf{a}$ for the cost of multiplication, squaring, and adding (respectively) in $\mathbb{F}_{q^k}$. We write $\mathbf{C}$ for the cost of multiplying an element of $\mathbb{F}_{q^k}$ by an element of $\mathbb{F}_q$ (typically a curve constant, or an evaluation-point coordinate). Note that $\mathbf{C} \approx (1/k)\mathbf{M}$ (when k is not too large). Later, we will write $\mathbf{F}$ for the cost of evaluating the Frobenius map on $\mathbb{F}_{q^k}$; see §5.1 for discussion on this.

x-only Arithmetic. Montgomery models are designed to optimize x-only arithmetic (see [20] and [10]). The xADD operation is

$$\texttt{xADD} : (x(P), x(Q), x(P - Q)) \longmapsto x(P + Q);$$

it can be computed at a cost of $4\mathbf{M} + 2\mathbf{S} + 6\mathbf{a}$ using the formulæ

$$\begin{cases} X_+ = Z_- \left[(X_P - Z_P)(X_Q + Z_Q) + (X_P + Z_P)(X_Q - Z_Q)\right]^2, \\ Z_+ = X_- \left[(X_P - Z_P)(X_Q + Z_Q) - (X_P + Z_P)(X_Q - Z_Q)\right]^2 \end{cases} \quad (1)$$

where $(X_P : Z_P)$, $(X_Q : Z_Q)$, $(X_+ : Z_+)$, and $(X_- : Z_-)$ are the x-coordinates $x(P)$, $x(Q)$, $x(P + Q)$, and $x(P - Q)$, respectively (so $x(P) = \frac{X_P}{Z_P}$, and so on).

The xDBL operation is

$$\texttt{xDBL} : x(P) \longmapsto x([2]P);$$

it can be computed at a cost of $2\mathbf{M} + 2\mathbf{S} + \mathbf{C} + 4\mathbf{a}$ using the formulæ

$$\begin{cases} X_{[2]P} = (X_P + Z_P)^2(X_P - Z_P)^2, \\ Z_{[2]P} = (4X_P Z_P)((X_P - Z_P)^2 + ((A + 2)/4)(4X_P Z_P)). \end{cases} \quad (2)$$

Isogenies. Let $\mathcal{E}_1, \mathcal{E}_2$ be elliptic curves over a finite field $\mathbb{F}_q$. An isogeny $\phi : \mathcal{E}_1 \to \mathcal{E}_2$ is a non-constant morphism mapping the identity point of $\mathcal{E}_1$ to the identity point of $\mathcal{E}_2$. Such a morphism is automatically a homomorphism. For more details see [25, Chapter 3, Sect. 4]. The kernel of ϕ is a finite subgroup of $\mathcal{E}_1$, and vice versa: every finite subgroup $\mathcal{G}$ of $\mathcal{E}_1$ determines a separable *quotient isogeny* $\mathcal{E}_1 \to \mathcal{E}_1/\mathcal{G}$. The *kernel polynomial* of ϕ is

$$D(X) := \prod_{P \in S} (X - x(P))$$

where $S \subset \mathcal{G}$ is any subset satisfying

$$S \cap -S = \emptyset \quad \text{and} \quad S \cup -S = \mathcal{G} \setminus \{0\}. \quad (3)$$

Every separable isogeny $\phi : \mathcal{E}_1 \to \mathcal{E}_2$ defined over $\mathbb{F}_q$ can be represented by a rational map in the form

$$\phi : (x, y) \longmapsto \left(\phi_x(x), \phi_y(x, y)\right) \quad (4)$$

with

$$\phi_x(x) = \frac{N(x)}{D(x)^2} \quad \text{and} \quad \phi_y(x,y) = c \cdot y \frac{d\phi_x}{dx}(x) \tag{5}$$

where D is the kernel polynomial of ϕ, N is a polynomial derived from D, and c is a normalizing constant in $\mathbb{F}_q$.

Vélu's Formulæ. Given a curve $\mathcal{E}$ and a finite subgroup $\mathcal{G} \subset \mathcal{E}$, Vélu [29] gives explicit formulæ for the rational functions that define a separable isogeny $\phi : \mathcal{E} \to \mathcal{E}' := \mathcal{E}/\mathcal{G}$ with kernel $\mathcal{G}$, as well as the resulting codomain curve $\mathcal{E}'$. Although the quotient curve $\mathcal{E}'$ and the isogeny ϕ are defined up to isomorphism, Vélu's formulæ construct the unique *normalized* isogeny (i.e. with $c = 1$ in (5)). See Kohel's thesis [18, Sect. 2.4] for a modern treatment of Vélu's results.

3   Evaluating Isogenies

Let $\mathcal{E}$ be an elliptic curve over $\mathbb{F}_q$, and let $\langle G \rangle$ be a subgroup of prime order ℓ (where ℓ is not equal to the field characteristic p). We suppose $\langle G \rangle$ is defined over $\mathbb{F}_q$; then, the quotient isogeny $\phi : \mathcal{E} \to \mathcal{E}/\langle G \rangle$ is also defined over $\mathbb{F}_q$.

When we say $\langle G \rangle$ is defined over $\mathbb{F}_q$, this means $\langle G \rangle$ is *Galois stable*: that is, $\pi(\langle G \rangle) = \langle G \rangle$ (where π is the q-power Frobenius endomorphism). We will mostly be concerned with algorithms taking $x(G)$ as an input, so it is worth noting that

$$x(G) \in \mathbb{F}_{q^{k'}} \quad \text{where} \quad k' := \begin{cases} k & \text{if } k \text{ is odd,} \\ k/2 & \text{if } k \text{ is even.} \end{cases}$$

The set of projective x-coordinates of the nonzero kernel points is

$$\mathcal{X}_G := \{(X_P : Z_P) = x(P) : P \in \langle G \rangle \setminus \{0\}\} \subset \mathbb{P}^1(\mathbb{F}_{q^{k'}});$$

each X_P/Z_P corresponds to a root of the kernel polynomial $D(X)$, and vice versa. If $\#\langle G \rangle$ is an odd prime ℓ, then $\#\mathcal{X}_G = (\ell - 1)/2$.

3.1   The Isogeny Evaluation Problem

We want to evaluate the isogeny $\phi : \mathcal{E} \to \mathcal{E}/\langle G \rangle$. More precisely, we want efficient solutions to the problem of Definition 1:

Definition 1 (Isogeny Evaluation). *Given an elliptic curve $\mathcal{E}$ over $\mathbb{F}_q$, a list of points $(P_1, \ldots, P_n)$ in $\mathcal{E}(\mathbb{F}_q)$, and a finite subgroup $\mathcal{G}$ of $\mathcal{E}$ corresponding to the separable isogeny $\phi : \mathcal{E} \to \mathcal{E}/\mathcal{G}$, compute $(\phi(P_1), \ldots, \phi(P_n))$.*

In most cryptographic applications n is relatively small, especially compared to ℓ. We do *not* assume the codomain curve $\mathcal{E}/\mathcal{G}$ is known; if required, an equation for $\mathcal{E}/\mathcal{G}$ can be interpolated through the image of well-chosen evaluation points.

For each separable isogeny ϕ of degree d defined over $\mathbb{F}_q$, there exists a sequence of primes $(\ell_1, \ldots, \ell_n)$ and a sequence of isogenies $(\phi_1, \ldots, \phi_n)$, all defined over $\mathbb{F}_q$, such that $\phi_n \circ \cdots \circ \phi_1$ and

- $\phi_i = [\ell_i]$ (the non-cyclic case) or
- ϕ_i has cyclic kernel of order ℓ_i.

The kernel of ϕ_1 is $\ker \phi \cap \mathcal{E}[\ell_1]$, and so on. The maps $[\ell_i]$ can be computed in $O(\log \ell_i)$ $\mathbb{F}_q$-operations, so we reduce quickly to the case where ϕ has prime degree ℓ, assuming the factorization of d is known (as it is in our applications).

In general, the isogeny evaluation problem can be reduced to evaluating the map $\alpha \mapsto D(\alpha)$, where D is the kernel polynomial and α is in $\mathbb{F}_q$ or some $\mathbb{F}_q$-algebra (see e.g. [2, §4]). The polynomial D need not be explicitly computed.

3.2   The Costello-Hisil Algorithm

The Costello-Hisil algorithm [9], generalized in [23], is the state-of-the-art for evaluating isogenies of Montgomery models. This algorithm is a variation of Vélu's formulæ working entirely on the level of x-coordinates, using the fact that for an ℓ-isogeny ϕ with kernel $\langle G \rangle$, the rational map on x-coordinates is

$$\phi_x(x) = x \cdot \left(\prod_{i=1}^{(\ell-1)/2} \left(\frac{x \cdot x([i]G) - 1}{x - x([i]G)} \right) \right)^2. \tag{6}$$

Moving to projective coordinates $(U : V)$ such that $x = U/V$ and using the fact that $\mathcal{X}_G = \{(x([i]G) : 1) : 1 \leq i \leq (\ell - 1)/2\}$, Eq. (6) becomes

$$\phi_x((U : V)) = (U' : V'), \quad \begin{cases} U' = U\left[\prod_{(X_Q:Z_Q)\in\mathcal{X}_G}(UX_Q - VZ_Q) \right]^2, \\ V' = V\left[\prod_{(X_Q:Z_Q)\in\mathcal{X}_G}(UZ_Q - VX_Q) \right]^2. \end{cases} \tag{7}$$

Algorithm 1 (from [9]) and Algorithm 2 (our space-efficient variant) compute ϕ_x at a series of input points using an efficient evaluation of the expressions in (7). For the moment, we assume that we have subroutines

- `KernelPoints` (see Sect. 4): given $(X_G : Z_G)$, returns $\mathcal{X}_G$ as a list.
- `KernelRange` (see Sect. 4): a *generator* coroutine which, given $(X_G : Z_G)$, constructs and yields the elements of $\mathcal{X}_G$ to the caller one by one.
- `CrissCross` [9, Algorithm 1]: takes $(\alpha, \beta, \gamma, \delta)$ in $\mathbb{F}_{q^k}^4$ and returns $(\alpha\delta + \beta\gamma, \alpha\delta - \beta\gamma)$ in $\mathbb{F}_{q^k}^2$ at a cost of $2\mathbf{M} + 2\mathbf{a}$.

4   Accelerating Vélu: Faster Iteration over the Kernel

Let $\mathcal{E}/\mathbb{F}_q$ be an elliptic curve, and let G be a point of prime order ℓ in $\mathcal{E}$. For simplicity, in this section we will assume that G is defined over $\mathbb{F}_q$, but all of the results here apply when G is defined over an extension $\mathbb{F}_{q^k}$: in that case $\mathbf{M}$, $\mathbf{S}$, and $\mathbf{a}$ represent operations in the extension field $\mathbb{F}_{q^k}$, while $\mathbf{C}$ represents multiplication of an element of $\mathbb{F}_{q^k}$ by a curve constant of the subfield $\mathbb{F}_q$ (which is roughly k times cheaper than $\mathbf{M}$). We return to the case where $k > 1$ in Sect. 5.

Algorithm 1: Combines Algorithms 3 and 4 from [9] to evaluate an ℓ-isogeny of Montgomery models at a list of input points. The total cost is $2n\ell\mathbf{M} + 2n\mathbf{S} + ((n+1)(\ell+1) - 2)\mathbf{a}$, *plus* the cost of `KernelPoints`.

Input: The x-coordinate $(X_G : Z_G)$ of a generator G of the kernel of an ℓ-isogeny ϕ, and a list of evaluation points $((U_i : V_i) : 1 \le i \le n)$

Output: The list of images $((U_i' : V_i') = \phi_x((U_i : V_i)) : 1 \le i \le n)$

1 $((X_1, Z_1), \ldots, (X_{(l-1)/2}, Z_{(l-1)/2})) \leftarrow$ `KernelPoints`$((X_G : Z_G))$ `// See` `Sect. 4`

2 **for** $1 \le i \le (\ell - 1)/2$ **do**

3 $\quad \lfloor\ (\hat{X}_i, \hat{Z}_i) \leftarrow (X_i + Z_i, X_i - Z_i)$ `// 2a`

4 **for** $i = 1$ *to* n **do**

5 $\quad (\hat{U}_i, \hat{V}_i) \leftarrow (U_i + V_i, U_i - V_i)$ `// 2a`

6 $\quad (U_i', V_i') \leftarrow (1, 1)$

7 $\quad$ **for** $j = 1$ *to* $(\ell - 1)/2$ **do**

8 $\quad\quad \lfloor\ (t_0, t_1) \leftarrow$ `CrissCross`$(\hat{X}_j, \hat{Z}_j, \hat{U}_i, \hat{V}_i)$ `// 2M + 2a`

9 $\quad\quad \lfloor\ (U_i', V_i') \leftarrow (t_0 \cdot U_i', t_1 \cdot V_i')$ `// 2M`

10 $\quad \lfloor\ (U_i', V_i') \leftarrow (U_i \cdot (U_i')^2, V_i \cdot (V_i')^2)$ `// 2M + 2S`

11 **return** $((U_1', V_1'), \ldots, (U_n', V_n'))$

Algorithm 2: A generator-based version of Algorithm 1, with much lower space requirements when $\ell \gg n$. The total cost is $2n\ell\mathbf{M} + 2n\mathbf{S} + (2n + (\ell - 1)(n + 1))\mathbf{a}$, *plus* the cost of a full run of `KernelRange`.

Input: The x-coordinate $(X_G : Z_G)$ of a generator G of the kernel of an ℓ-isogeny ϕ, and a list of evaluation points $((U_i : V_i) : 1 \le i \le n)$

Output: The list of images $((U_i' : V_i') = \phi_x((U_i : V_i)) : 1 \le i \le n)$

1 **for** $1 \le i \le n$ **do**

2 $\quad (\hat{U}_i, \hat{V}_i) \leftarrow (U_i + V_i, U_i - V_i)$ `// 2a`

3 $\quad \lfloor\ (U_i', V_i') \leftarrow (1, 1)$

4 **for** $(X : Z)$ *in* `KernelRange`$((X_G : Z_G))$ **do**   `// See Sect. 4`

5 $\quad (\hat{X}, \hat{Z}) \leftarrow (X + Z, X - Z)$ `// 2a`

6 $\quad$ **for** $1 \le i \le n$ **do**

7 $\quad\quad (t_0, t_1) \leftarrow$ `CrissCross`$(\hat{X}, \hat{Z}, \hat{U}_i, \hat{V}_i)$ `// 2M + 2a`

8 $\quad\quad \lfloor\ (U_i', V_i') \leftarrow (t_0 \cdot U_i', t_1 \cdot V_i')$ `// 2M`

9 **for** $1 \le i \le n$ **do**

10 $\quad \lfloor\ (U_i', V_i') \leftarrow (U_i \cdot (U_i')^2, V_i \cdot (V_i')^2)$ `// 2M + 2S`

11 **return** $((U_1', V_1'), \ldots, (U_n', V_n'))$

4.1 Kernel Point Enumeration and Differential Addition Chains

We now turn to the problem of enumerating the set $\mathcal{X}_G$. This process, which we call *kernel point enumeration*, could involve constructing the entire set (as in `KernelPoints`) or constructing its elements one by one (for `KernelRange`).

For $\ell = 2$ and 3, there is nothing to be done because $\mathcal{X}_G = \{(X_G : Z_G)\}$; so from now on we consider the case $\ell > 3$.

We allow ourselves two curve operations for kernel point enumeration: xADD and xDBL. In Sect. 5, where G is assumed to be defined over a nontrivial extension of the base field, we will also allow the Frobenius endomorphism.

Every algorithm constructing a sequence of elements of $\mathcal{X}_G$ using a series of xADD and xDBL instructions corresponds to a *modular differential addition chain*.

Definition 2. *A **Modular Differential Addition Chain (MDAC)** for a set $S \subset \mathbb{Z}/\ell\mathbb{Z}$ is a sequence of integers $(c_0, c_1, c_2, \ldots, c_n)$ such that*

1. *every element of S is represented by some c_i (mod ℓ),*
2. *$c_0 = 0$ and $c_1 = 1$, and*
3. *for each $1 < i \leq n$ there exist $0 \leq j(i), k(i), d(i) < i$ such that $c_i \equiv c_{j(i)} + c_{k(i)}$ (mod ℓ) and $c_{j(i)} - c_{k(i)} \equiv c_{d(i)}$ (mod ℓ).*

Algorithms to enumerate $\mathcal{X}_G$ using xADD and xDBL correspond to MDACs $(c_0, \ldots, c_n)$ for $\{1, \ldots, (\ell - 1)/2\}$: the algorithm starts with $x([c_0]G) = x(0) = (1 : 0)$ and $x([c_1]G) = x(G) = (X_G : Z_G)$, then computes each $x([c_i]G)$ using

$$x([c_i]G) = \begin{cases} \text{xADD}(x([c_{j(i)}]G), x([c_{k(i)}]G), x([c_{d(i)}]G)) & \text{if } d(i) \neq 0, \\ \text{xDBL}([c_{j(i)}]G) & \text{if } d(i) = 0. \end{cases}$$

4.2 Additive Kernel Point Enumeration

The classic approach is to compute $\mathcal{X}_G$ using repeated xADDs. Algorithm 3 is Costello and Hisil's KernelPoints [9, Algorithm 2], corresponding to the MDAC $(0, 1, 2, 3, \ldots, (\ell - 1)/2)$ computed by repeatedly adding 1 (except for 2 which is computed by doubling 1). The simplicity of this MDAC means that Algorithm 3 converts to a KernelRange with a small internal state: to generate the next $(X_{i+1} : Z_{i+1})$, we only need the values of $(X_i : Z_i)$, $(X_{i-1} : Z_{i-1})$, and $(X_1 : Z_1)$.

4.3 Replacing xADDs with xDBLs

Comparing x-only operations on Montgomery curves, replacing an xADD with an xDBL trades 2M and 2a for 1C. We would therefore like to replace as many xADDs as possible in our kernel enumeration with xDBLs.

As a first attempt, we can replace Line 4 of Algorithm 3 with

$$(X_i : Z_i) \leftarrow \begin{cases} \text{xDBL}((X_{i/2} : Z_{i/2})) & \text{if } i \text{ is even,} \\ \text{xADD}((X_{i-1} : Z_{i-1}), (X_G : Z_G), (X_{i-2}, Z_{i-2})) & \text{if } i \text{ is odd.} \end{cases}$$

But applying this trick systematically requires storing many more intermediate values, reducing the efficiency of KernelRange. It also only replaces half of the xADDs with xDBLs, and it turns out that we can generally do much better.

Algorithm 3: Basic kernel point enumeration by repeated addition.
Uses exactly 1 xDBL and $(\ell - 5)/2$ xADD operations (for prime $\ell > 3$).

Input: The x-coordinate $(X_G : Z_G) = x(G)$ of a point G of order ℓ in $\mathcal{E}(\mathbb{F}_q)$
Output: $\mathcal{X}_G$ as a list

1 $(X_1 : Z_1) \leftarrow (X_G : Z_G)$
2 $(X_2 : Z_2) \leftarrow \text{xDBL}((X_G : Z_G))$
3 **for** $i = 3$ **to** $(\ell - 1)/2$ **do**   // Invariant: $(X_i : Z_i) = x([i]G)$
4 $\quad \lfloor \ (X_i : Z_i) \leftarrow \text{xADD}((X_{i-1} : Z_{i-1}), (X_G : Z_G), (X_{i-2}, Z_{i-2}))$
5 **return** $((X_1 : Z_1), \ldots, (X_{(\ell-1)/2} : Z_{(\ell-1)/2}))$

4.4 Multiplicative Kernel Point Enumeration

We can do better for a large class of ℓ by considering the quotient

$$M_\ell := (\mathbb{Z}/\ell\mathbb{Z})^\times / \langle \pm 1 \rangle \,.$$

(note: M_ℓ is a quotient of the *multiplicative* group.) For convenience, we write

$$m_\ell := \#M_\ell = (\ell - 1)/2 \,.$$

We can now reframe the problem of enumerating $\mathcal{X}_G$ as the problem of enumerating a complete set of representatives for M_ℓ. The MDAC of Algorithm 3 computes the set of representatives $\{1, 2, \ldots, m_\ell\}$, but for the purposes of enumerating $\mathcal{X}_G$, *any* set of representatives will do. Example 1 is particularly useful.

Example 1. Suppose 2 generates M_ℓ. This is the case if 2 is a primitive element modulo ℓ—that is, if 2 has order $(\ell-1)$ modulo ℓ—but also if 2 has order $(\ell-1)/2$ modulo ℓ and $\ell \equiv 3 \pmod 4$. In this case

$$M_\ell = \{2^i \bmod \ell : 0 \le i < m_\ell\} \,,$$

so $(0, 1, 2, 4, 8, \ldots, 2^{m_\ell})$ is an MDAC for M_ℓ using *only* doubling, and *no* differential additions. The corresponding KernelPoints replaces *all* of the xADDs in Algorithm 3 with cheaper xDBLs, trading $(\ell-5)\mathbf{M} + (\ell-5)\mathbf{a}$ for $(\ell-5)/2$ $\mathbf{C}$. The corresponding KernelRange is particularly simple: each element depends only on its predecessor, so the state consists of a single $(X_i : Z_i)$.

How often does this trick apply? The quantitative form of Artin's primitive root conjecture (see [30]) says that $M_\ell = \langle 2 \rangle$ for a little over half of all ℓ. Experimentally, 5609420 of the first 10^7 odd primes ℓ satisfy $M_\ell = \langle 2 \rangle$.

One might generalize Example 1 to other generators of M_ℓ: for example, if $M_\ell = \langle 3 \rangle$, then we could find an MDAC for $\{3^i \bmod \ell : 0 \le i < (\ell-1)/2\}$. But this is counterproductive: x-only tripling is *slower* than differential addition.

4.5   Stepping Through Cosets

What can we do when $M_\ell \neq \langle 2 \rangle$? A productive generalization is to let

$$A_\ell := \langle 2 \rangle \subseteq M_\ell \quad \text{and} \quad a_\ell := \#A_\ell,$$

and to try to compute a convenient decomposition of M_ℓ into cosets of A_ℓ. Within each coset, we can compute elements using repeated xDBLs as in Example 1; then, it remains to step from one coset into another using differential additions. This can be done in a particularly simple way for the primes ℓ such that

$$M_\ell = \langle 2, 3 \rangle, \quad \text{so} \quad M_\ell = \bigsqcup_{i=0}^{m_\ell/a_\ell - 1} 3^i A_\ell. \tag{$*$}$$

We can move from the i-th to the $(i+1)$-th coset using the elementary relations

$$\begin{cases} c \cdot 2^{j+1} + c \cdot 2^j = 3c \cdot 2^j \\ c \cdot 2^{j+1} - c \cdot 2^j = c \cdot 2^j \end{cases} \quad \text{for all integers } c \text{ and } j \geq 0. \tag{8}$$

In particular, having enumerated $3^i A_\ell$ by repeated doubling, we can compute an element of $3^{i+1} A_\ell$ by applying a differential addition to any two consecutive elements of $3^i A_\ell$ (and the difference is the first of them). Algorithm 4 minimizes storage overhead by using the last two elements of the previous coset to generate the first element of the next one. The KernelRange of Algorithm 4 therefore has an internal state of only two x-coordinates—so not only is it faster than the KernelRange of Algorithm 3, but it also has a smaller memory footprint.

Algorithm 4: Kernel enumeration for $\ell > 3$ satisfying $(*)$. Cost: $(1 - 1/a_\ell) \cdot m_\ell$ xDBLs and $m_\ell/a_\ell - 1$ xADDs.

Input: Projective x-coordinate $(X_G : Z_G)$ of the generator G of a cyclic subgroup of order ℓ in $\mathcal{E}(\mathbb{F}_q)$, where ℓ satisfies $(*)$.
Output: $\mathcal{X}_G$ as a list

1   $(a, b) \leftarrow (a_\ell, m_\ell/a_\ell)$
2   **for** $i = 0$ *to* $b - 1$ **do**   // Invariant: $(X_{ai+j} : Z_{ai+j}) = x([3^i 2^{i(a-2)+(j-1)}]G)$
3   **if** $i = 0$ **then**
4      $|$ $(X_1 : Z_1) \leftarrow (X_G : Z_G)$
5   **else**   // Compute new coset representative
6      $\lfloor$ $(X_{ai+1} : Z_{ai+1}) \leftarrow \text{xADD}\big((X_{ai} : Z_{ai}), (X_{ai-1} : Z_{ai-1}), (X_{ai-1} : Z_{ai-1})\big)$
7   **for** $j = 2$ *to* a **do**   // Exhaust coset by doubling
8      $\lfloor$ $(X_{ai+j} : Z_{ai+j}) \leftarrow \text{xDBL}\big((X_{ai+j-1} : Z_{ai+j-1})\big)$

9   **return** $\big((X_1 : Z_1), \ldots, (X_{(\ell-1)/2} : Z_{(\ell-1)/2})\big)$

Algorithm 4 performs better the closer a_ℓ is to m_ℓ. In the best case, when $A_\ell = M_\ell$, it uses $m_\ell - 1$ xDBLs and no xADDs at all. The worst case is when the order of 2 in M_ℓ is as small as possible: that is, $\ell = 2^k - 1$. In this case $a_\ell = k$, and compared with Algorithm 3 we still reduce the xADDs by a factor of k.

4.6   The Remaining Primes

While 1878 of the 2261 odd primes $\ell \leq 20000$ satisfy $(*)$, there are still 383 primes that do not. We can, to some extent, adapt Algorithm 4 to handle these primes, but on a case-by-case basis and with somewhat less satisfactory results.

For example, the CSIDH-512 parameter set specifies 74 isogeny-degree primes

$$\ell = 3, 5, 7, 11, 13, \ldots, 367, 373, \text{ and } 587.$$

All but seven of these ℓ satisfy $(*)$: the exceptions are $\ell = 73, 97, 193, 241, 313,$ and 337. Table 1 lists a candidate decomposition of M_ℓ for each of these ℓ. In each case, we need to produce an element of either $5A_\ell$ or $7A_\ell$. This can certainly be done using previously-computed elements, but this requires a larger internal state and a more complicated execution pattern, depending on ℓ.

Table 1. Primes ℓ in the CSIDH-512 parameter set that do not satisfy $(*)$.

Prime ℓ	a_ℓ	$[M_\ell : \langle 2,3\rangle]$	Coset decomposition of M_ℓ	Notes
73	9	2	$M_{73} = A_{73} \sqcup 3A_{73} \sqcup 5A_{73} \sqcup 5 \cdot 3A_{73}$	
97	24	2	$M_{97} = A_{97} \sqcup 5A_{97}$	3 is in A_{97}
193	48	2	$M_{193} = A_{193} \sqcup 5A_{193}$	3 is in A_{193}
241	12	2	$M_{241} = \left(\bigsqcup_{i=0}^4 3^i A_{241}\right) \sqcup \left(\bigsqcup_{i=0}^4 7 \cdot 3^i A_{241}\right)$	
307	51	3	$M_{307} = A_{307} \sqcup 5A_{307} \sqcup 7A_{307}$	3 is in A_{313}
313	78	2	$M_{313} = A_{313} \sqcup 5A_{313}$	3 is in A_{193}
337	21	2	$M_{337} = \left(\bigsqcup_{i=0}^3 3^i A_{337}\right) \sqcup \left(\bigsqcup_{i=0}^3 5 \cdot 3^i A_{337}\right)$	

Example 2. Consider $\ell = 97$. Now $3 \equiv 2^{19} \pmod{97}$, so 3 is in A_{97}, and in fact $M_{97} = A_{97} \sqcup 5A_{97}$. To adapt Algorithm 4 to this case, we can still enumerate A_{97} using repeated doubling. Then, we must construct an element of $5A_{97}$ from elements of A_{97}, using a differential addition like $5 \cdot 2^i = 2^{i+2} + 2^i$ (difference $3 \cdot 2^i$) or $5 \cdot 2^i = 2^{i+1} + 3 \cdot 2^i$ (difference 2^i). Each involves near powers of 2 (modulo 97), but also $3 \cdot 2^i \equiv 2^{i+19} \pmod{97}$, which must be stored while enumerating A_{97}. This gives an algorithm using one xADD and 48 xDBLs, just like Algorithm 4, but with a slightly larger state and a more complicated execution pattern specific to $\ell = 97$. Alternatively, after enumerating A_{97}, we could redundantly recompute $3 = 1 + 2$ (difference 1) to get 5 as $1 + 4$ (difference 3) or $2 + 3$ (difference 1).

Ultimately, there does not seem to be a "one size fits all" generalization of Algorithm 4 for enumerating $\mathcal{X}_G$ without a more complicated state or redundant recomputations. We can get reasonable results for many ℓ not satisfying $(*)$ by finding a good MDAC for $M_\ell / \langle 2, 3\rangle$ and then using Algorithm 4 to exhaust the coset containing each representative but the savings are generally not optimal.

4.7   (In)Compatibility with Vélusqrt

It is natural to ask whether these techniques can be used to further accelerate the Vélusqrt algorithm [2], which evaluates isogenies of large prime degree ℓ in $\widetilde{O}(\sqrt{\ell})$ time (with $O(\sqrt{\ell})$ space). Vélusqrt never explicitly computes all of $\mathcal{X}_G$. Instead, it relies on the existence of a decomposition

$$S := \{1, 3, 5, \ldots, \ell - 2\} = (I + J) \sqcup (I - J) \sqcup K \tag{9}$$

where I, J, and K are sets of integers of size $O(\sqrt{\ell})$ such that the maps $(i, j) \to i + j$ and $(i, j) \to i - j$ are injective with disjoint images. In [2], these sets are

$$
\begin{aligned}
I &:= \{2b(2i + 1) : 0 \leq i < b'\} && \text{(``giant steps''),} \\
J &:= \{2j + 1 : 0 \leq j < b\} && \text{(``baby steps''),} \\
K &:= \{4bb' + 1, \ldots, \ell - 4, \ell - 2\} && \text{(``the rest''),}
\end{aligned}
$$

where $b := \lfloor \sqrt{\ell - 1}/2 \rfloor$ and $b' := \lfloor (\ell - 1)/4b \rfloor$.

The key thing to note here is that this decomposition is essentially additive, and the elements of I, J, and K are in arithmetic progression. Algorithm 4, however, is essentially multiplicative: it works with subsets in geometric progression. We cannot exclude the existence of subsets I, J, and K of size $O(\sqrt{\ell})$ satisfying (9) and which are amenable to enumeration by a variant of Algorithm 4 for some ℓ, but it seems difficult to construct nontrivial and useful examples.

5   Irrational Kernel Points: Exploiting Frobenius

Now suppose G is defined over a nontrivial extension $\mathbb{F}_{q^k}$ of $\mathbb{F}_q$, but $\langle G \rangle$ is defined over the subfield $\mathbb{F}_q$: that is, it is Galois-stable. In particular, the q-power Frobenius endomorphism π of $\mathcal{E}$, which maps points in $\mathcal{E}(\mathbb{F}_{q^k})$ to their conjugates under $\mathrm{Gal}(\mathbb{F}_{q^k}/\mathbb{F}_q)$, maps $\langle G \rangle$ into $\langle G \rangle$, and hence restricts to an endomorphism of $\langle G \rangle$. But since the endomorphisms of $\langle G \rangle$ are $\mathbb{Z}/\ell\mathbb{Z}$, and Frobenius has no kernel (so π is not 0 on $\langle G \rangle$), it must act as multiplication by an eigenvalue $\lambda \neq 0$ on $\langle G \rangle$. The precise value of λ is not important here, but we will use the fact that λ has order k in $(\mathbb{Z}/\ell\mathbb{Z})^\times$ and order k' in $(\mathbb{Z}/\ell\mathbb{Z})^\times/\langle \pm 1 \rangle$.

Now let

$$F_\ell := \langle \lambda \rangle \subseteq M_\ell \qquad \text{and} \qquad c_F := [M_\ell : F_\ell] = m_\ell/k'.$$

Let R_0 be a set of representatives for M_ℓ/F_ℓ; set $S_0 := \{[r]G : r \in R_0\}$, and note

$$\#S_0 = (\ell - 1)/k'.$$

5.1   The Cost of Frobenius

We want to use the Galois action to replace many $\mathbf{M}$ and $\mathbf{S}$ with a few $\mathbf{F}$. For this to be worthwhile, $\mathbf{F}$ must be cheap: and it is, even if this is not obvious given the definition of the Frobenius map on $\mathbb{F}_{q^k}$ as q-th powering. Indeed, we do not compute Frobenius by powering. Instead, we use the fact that Frobenius is $\mathbb{F}_q$-linear, acting as a $k \times k$ matrix (with entries in $\mathbb{F}_q$) on the coefficient vectors of elements in $\mathbb{F}_{q^k}$. The form of this matrix, and the cost of applying it, depends on the basis of $\mathbb{F}_{q^k}/\mathbb{F}_q$. For example:

1. If $k = 2$ and $\mathbb{F}_{q^2} = \mathbb{F}_q(\sqrt{\Delta})$, then Frobenius simply negates $\sqrt{\Delta}$ and the matrix is $\mathrm{diag}(1, -1)$, so $\mathbf{F} \approx 0$.
2. If $\mathbb{F}_{q^k}/\mathbb{F}_q$ is represented with a normal basis, then the matrix represents a cyclic permutation, and again $\mathbf{F} \approx 0$.

Even in the worst case where the basis of $\mathbb{F}_{q^k}/\mathbb{F}_q$ has no special Galois structure, $\mathbf{F}$ is just the cost of multiplying a k-vector by a $k \times k$ matrix over $\mathbb{F}_q$: that is, k^2 multiplications and $k^2 - k$ additions. This is close to the cost of one "schoolbook" $\mathbb{F}_{q^k}$-multiplication; so when $k \leq 12$, we have $\mathbf{F} \approx \mathbf{M}$.

5.2   Galois Orbits

Each point $P \in \mathcal{E}(\mathbb{F}_{q^k})$ is contained in a *Galois orbit* containing all the conjugates of P. The kernel subgroup $\langle G \rangle$ breaks up (as a set) into *Galois orbits*: if we write

$$\mathcal{O}_P := \{P, \pi(P), \ldots, \pi^{k-1}(P)\} \qquad \text{for } P \in \mathcal{E}(\mathbb{F}_{q^k}),$$

then

$$\langle G \rangle = \{0\} \sqcup \begin{cases} \bigsqcup_{P \in S_0} \mathcal{O}_P & \text{if } k \text{ is even,} \\ \left(\bigsqcup_{P \in S_0} \mathcal{O}_P\right) \sqcup \left(\bigsqcup_{P \in S_0} \mathcal{O}_{-P}\right) & \text{if } k \text{ is odd.} \end{cases} \tag{10}$$

To get a picture of where we are going, recall from §3 that in general, isogeny evaluation can be reduced to evaluations of the kernel polynomial

$$D(X) := \prod_{P \in S} (X - x(P)),$$

where $S \subset \langle G \rangle$ is any subset such that $S \cap -S = \emptyset$ and $S \cup -S = \langle G \rangle \setminus \{0\}$. The decomposition of (10) can be seen in the factorization of $D(X)$ over $\mathbb{F}_{q^k}$:

$$D(X) = \prod_{P \in S} (X - x(P)) = \prod_{P \in S_0} \prod_{i=0}^{k'-1} (X - x(\pi^i(P))) = \prod_{P \in S_0} \prod_{i=0}^{k'-1} (X - x(P)^{q^i}),$$

and the factors corresponding to each P in S_0 are the irreducible factors of D over $\mathbb{F}_q$. Transposing the order of the products, if we let

$$D_0(X) := \prod_{P \in S_0} (X - x(P))$$

then for α in the base field $\mathbb{F}_q$, we can compute $D(\alpha)$ using

$$D(\alpha) = \mathrm{Norm}(D_0(\alpha)) \quad \text{for all } \alpha \in \mathbb{F}_q$$

where

$$\text{Norm}(x) := \prod_{i=0}^{k'-1} x^{q^i} = x(x(\cdots(x(x)^q)^q \cdots)^q)^q\,,$$

which can be computed for the cost of $(k-1)\mathbf{F} + (k-1)\mathbf{M}$ (some multiplications can be saved with more storage, but for small k this may not be worthwhile).

Similarly, we can rewrite the rational map ϕ_x from (6) as

$$\phi_x(x) = x \cdot \Big[\prod_{P \in S} \Big(\frac{x \cdot x(P) - 1}{x - x(P)} \Big) \Big]^2 = x \cdot \Big[\prod_{P \in S_0} \prod_{i=0}^{k'-1} \Big(\frac{x \cdot x(P)^{q^i} - 1}{x - x(P)^{q^i}} \Big) \Big]^2\,.$$

Evaluating ϕ_x at α in $\mathbb{F}_q$, rearranging the products gives

$$\phi_x(\alpha) = \alpha \cdot \Big[\prod_{P \in S_0} \prod_{i=0}^{k'-1} \Big(\frac{\alpha \cdot x(P)^{q^i} - 1}{\alpha - x(P)^{q^i}} \Big) \Big]^2 = \alpha \cdot \text{Norm}(\overline{\phi}_x(\alpha))^2\,,$$

where

$$\overline{\phi}_x(X) := \prod_{P \in S_0} \frac{X \cdot x(P) - 1}{X - x(P)}\,.$$

Projectively, from (7) we get $\phi_x : (U : V) \mapsto (U' : V')$ where

$$\begin{cases} U' = U \cdot \big[\prod_{i=0}^{k'-1} \prod_{P \in S_0} (U X_P^{q^i} - Z_P^{q^i} V) \big]^2\,, \\ V' = V \cdot \big[\prod_{i=0}^{k'-1} \prod_{P \in S_0} (U Z_P^{q^i} - X_P^{q^i} V) \big]^2\,, \end{cases}$$

so if we set

$$F(U,V) := \prod_{P \in S_0} (U \cdot X_P - Z_P \cdot V) \quad \text{and} \quad G(U,V) := \prod_{P \in S_0} (U \cdot Z_P - X_P \cdot V)\,,$$

then for α and β in $\mathbb{F}_q$ we get

$$\phi_x((\alpha : \beta)) = (\alpha' : \beta') := \big(\alpha \cdot \text{Norm}(F(\alpha,\beta))^2 : \beta \cdot \text{Norm}(G(\alpha,\beta))^2 \big)\,.$$

5.3   Enumerating Representatives for the Galois Orbits

We now need to enumerate a set S_0 of representatives for the Galois orbits modulo ± 1 or, equivalently, a set of representatives R_0 for the cosets of F_ℓ in M_ℓ. Given an MDAC driving enumeration of the coset representatives, there are obvious adaptations of Algorithms 1 and 2 to this extension field case. Rather than iterating over all of the kernel x-coordinates, we just iterate over a subset representing the cosets of $\mathbb{F}_\ell$, and then compose with the norm.

Concretely, in Algorithm 2, we should

1. Replace `KernelRange` in Line 4 with a generator driven by an efficient MDAC for M_ℓ/F_ℓ;
2. Replace Line 10 with $(U_i', V_i') \leftarrow (U_i \cdot \text{Norm}(U_i')^2, V_i \cdot \text{Norm}(V_i')^2)$.

First, we can consider Algorithm 3: that is, enumerating M_ℓ/F_ℓ by repeated addition. Unfortunately, we do not have a nice bound on the length of this MDAC: the coset representatives may not be conveniently distributed over M_ℓ, so we could end up computing a lot of redundant points.

Example 3. Consider the "naive" S_0 comprised of the minimal elements (up to negation) in each Galois orbit. We computed the percentage of primes $3 \leq \ell < 10^4$ where an optimal MDAC (without redundant values) exists for this S_0:

k	1	2	3	4	5	6	7	8	9	10	11	12
%	100	100	100	100	84	86	76	67	60	56	45	42

For an example of what can go wrong, take $(\ell, k) = (89, 11)$. In this case, we get $R_0 = \{1, 3, 5, 13\}$; the shortest MDAC is $(0, 1, 2, 3, 5, 8, 13)$, which enumerates the kernel using one xDBL operation and six xADD operations, but requires the computation of two intermediate points not used in the final result.

But when we say that the coset representatives are not conveniently distributed over M_ℓ, we mean convenient with respect to addition. If we look at M_ℓ multiplicatively, then the path to efficient MDACs is clearer.

If $M_\ell = \langle 2, \lambda \rangle$ then we can take $R_0 = \{2^i : 0 \leq i < c_F\}$, which brings us to the 2-powering MDAC of Example 1—except that we stop after $c_F - 1$ xDBLs. We thus reduce the number of xDBLs by a factor of $\approx k'$, at the expense of two norm computations. This MDAC actually applies to more primes ℓ here than in Sect. 4, because we no longer need 2 to generate all of M_ℓ; we have λ to help. (In fact, the suitability of this MDAC depends not only on ℓ, but also on k.)

We can go further if we assume

$$M_\ell = \langle 2, 3, \lambda \rangle . \qquad (**)$$

To simplify notation, we define

$$a_{\ell,k} := [\langle 2, \lambda \rangle : F_\ell], \qquad b_{\ell,k} := [\langle 2, 3, \lambda \rangle : \langle 2, \lambda \rangle] = c_F/a_{\ell,k} .$$

Algorithm 5 is a truncated version of Algorithm 4 for computing S_0 instead of $\mathcal{X}_G$ when $(**)$ holds. Algorithm 6 uses Algorithm 5 to evaluate an ℓ-isogeny over $\mathbb{F}_q$ with kernel $\langle G \rangle$ at n points of $\mathcal{E}(\mathbb{F}_q)$, where $x(G)$ is in $\mathbb{F}_{q^{k'}}$ with $k' > 1$.

Table 2 compares the total costs of Algorithms 6 and 5 with Algorithms 1 and 3. In both algorithms, we can take advantage of the fact that many of the multiplications have one operand in the smaller field $\mathbb{F}_q$: notably, the multiplications involving coordinates of the evaluation points. In the context of isogeny-based cryptography (where curve constants look like random elements of $\mathbb{F}_q$), this means that in Algorithm 1, we can replace the $2\mathbf{M} + 2\mathbf{a}$ in Line 8 and the $2\mathbf{M} + 2\mathbf{S}$ in Line 10 with $2\mathbf{C} + 2\mathbf{a}$ and $2\mathbf{C} + 2\mathbf{S}$, respectively. Table 3 gives examples of the resulting costs for various (ℓ, k) with a single evaluation point.

Algorithm 5: Compute S_0 when $(**)$ holds. Cost: $b_{\ell,k} - 1$ xADDs and $(c_F - b_{\ell,k})$ xDBLs, or $(2c_F + 2b_{\ell,k} + 4)\mathbf{M} + (2c_F - 2)\mathbf{S} + (c_F - b_{\ell,k})\mathbf{C} + (4c_F + 4b_{\ell,k} - 6)\mathbf{a}$

Input: Projective x-coordinate $(X_G : Z_G)$ of the generator G of a cyclic subgroup of order ℓ in $\mathcal{E}(\mathbb{F}_{q^k})$, where ℓ satisfies $M_\ell = \langle 2, 3, \lambda \rangle$.
Output: S_0 as a list

1 **Function** SZeroPoints$((X_G : Z_G))$
2    $(a, b) \leftarrow (a_{\ell,k}, b_{\ell,k})$
3   **for** $i = 0$ **to** $b - 1$ **do**   // Invariant: $x_{ai+j} = x([3^i 2^{i(a-2)+(j-1)}]G)$
4   **if** $i = 0$ **then**
5        $\lfloor$ $x_1 \leftarrow (X_G : Z_G)$
6   **else**   // Compute new coset representative
7        $\lfloor$ $x_{ai+1} \leftarrow$ xADD$(x_{ai}, x_{ai-1}, x_{ai-1})$
8   **for** $j = 2$ **to** a **do**   // Exhaust coset by doubling
9        $\lfloor$ $x_{ai+j} \leftarrow$ xDBL(x_{ai+j-1})

10   **return** $(x_1, \ldots, x_{c_F})$

Algorithm 6: Isogeny evaluation using SZeroPoints and Frobenius. Cost: $2(c_F + k - 1)n\mathbf{M} + 2n\mathbf{S} + 2(c_F + 1)n\mathbf{C} + 2c_F(n + 1)\mathbf{a} + 2(k - 1)n\mathbf{F}$ *plus* the cost of SZeroPoints.

Input: The x-coordinate $(X_G : Z_G)$ of a generator G of the kernel of an ℓ-isogeny ϕ, and a list of evaluation points $((U_i : V_i) : 1 \le i \le n)$
Output: The list of images $((U_i' : V_i') = \phi_x((U_i : V_i)) : 1 \le i \le n)$

1 $((X_1, Z_1), \ldots, (X_{c_F}, Z_{c_F})) \leftarrow$ SZeroPoints$((X_G : Z_G))$ // Algorithm 5
2 **for** $1 \le i \le c_F$ **do**
3    $\lfloor$ $(\hat{X}_i, \hat{Z}_i) \leftarrow (X_i + Z_i, X_i - Z_i)$ // 2a

4 **for** $i = 1$ **to** n **do**
5    $(\hat{U}_i, \hat{V}_i) \leftarrow (U_i + V_i, U_i - V_i)$ // 2a
6    $(U_i', V_i') \leftarrow (1, 1)$
7   **for** $j = 1$ **to** c_F **do**
8      $(t_0, t_1) \leftarrow$ CrissCross$(\hat{X}_j, \hat{Z}_j, \hat{U}_i, \hat{V}_i)$ // 2C + 2a
9      $\lfloor$ $(U_i', V_i') \leftarrow (t_0 \cdot U_i', t_1 \cdot V_i')$ // 2M
10    $(U_i', V_i') \leftarrow ($Norm$(U_i'),$ Norm$(V_i'))$ // $2(k' - 1)$M + $2(k' - 1)$F
11    $\lfloor$ $(U_i', V_i') \leftarrow (U_i \cdot (U_i')^2, V_i \cdot (V_i')^2)$ // 2C + 2S
12 **return** $((U_1', V_1'), \ldots, (U_n', V_n'))$

Table 2. ℓ-isogeny evaluation comparison for kernels $\langle G \rangle$ defined over $\mathbb{F}_q$ but with $x(G) \in \mathbb{F}_{q^{k'}}$. Here, **C** denotes multiplications of elements of $\mathbb{F}_{q^{k'}}$ by elements of $\mathbb{F}_q$.

	Costello–Hisil (Algorithms 1 and 3)	This work (Algorithm 6)
M	$(\ell - 1)n + 2\ell - 8$	$2(c_F + k' - 1)n + 2c_F + 2b_{\ell,k} + 4$
S	$2n + \ell - 3$	$2n + 2c_F - 2$
C	$(\ell + 1)n + 1$	$2(c_F + 1)n + c_F - b_{\ell,k}$
a	$(n + 1)(\ell + 1) + 3\ell + 17$	$2c_F(n + 1) + 4c_F + 4b_{\ell,k} - 6$
F	0	$2(k' - 1)n$

Table 3. Examples of costs for evaluating an ℓ-isogeny at a single point over $\mathbb{F}_q$, with $x(G) \in \mathbb{F}_{q^{k'}}$, using Costello–Hisil (Algorithm 1 with 3, in white) and Algorithm 6 (in gray). For these k, it is reasonable to use the approximation $\mathbf{F} \approx \mathbf{M}$ (see Sect. 5.1).

$\ell = 13$						$\ell = 19$						$\ell = 23$					
k'	**M**	**S**	**C**	**a**	**F**	k'	**M**	**S**	**C**	**a**	**F**	k'	**M**	**S**	**C**	**a**	**F**
any	30	12	15	54	0	any	48	18	21	84	0	any	60	22	25	104	0
1	22	12	19	46	0	1	34	18	28	70	0	1	42	22	34	86	0
3	10	4	7	14	4	3	14	6	10	22	4	11	22	2	4	6	20
						9	18	2	4	6	16						

6 Applications to Key Exchange

Our algorithms could be applied in any cryptosystem involving isogenies of prime degree $\ell > 3$. We focus on key exchanges like CSIDH [5] here, but similar remarks apply for other schemes such as SQISign [16,17], SeaSign [15], and CSI-FiSh [4].

6.1 CSIDH and Constant-Time Considerations

CSIDH is a post-quantum non-interactive key exchange based on the action of the class group of the imaginary quadratic order $\mathbb{Z}[\sqrt{-p}]$ on the set of supersingular elliptic curves $\mathcal{E}/\mathbb{F}_p$ with $\text{End}_{\mathbb{F}_p}(\mathcal{E}) \cong \mathbb{Z}[\sqrt{-p}]$. The action is computed via compositions of ℓ_i-isogenies for a range of small primes $(\ell_1, \ldots, \ell_m)$.

CSIDH works over prime fields $\mathbb{F}_p$, so the methods of Sect. 5 do not apply; but Algorithm 4 may speed up implementations at least for the ℓ_i satisfying $(*)$. (We saw in Sect. 4.6 that 67 of the 74 primes ℓ_i in the CSIDH-512 parameter set met $(*)$).

The true speedup depends on two factors. The first is the number of evaluation points. Costello and Hisil evaluate at a 2-torsion point other than $(0, 0)$ in order to interpolate the image curve. The constant-time CSIDH of [19] evaluates at one more point (from which subsequent kernels are derived)—that is, $n = 2$; [21] uses $n = 3$; [7] discusses $n > 3$. For large n, the cost of Algorithm 1 overwhelms kernel enumeration, but our results may still make a simple and interesting improvement when n is relatively small.

Table 4. Costello–Hisil (Algorithms 1 and 3, in white) vs. Algorithm 6 (in gray) for the CRS parameters with $k > 1$ proposed in [13]. We omit $(\ell, k) = (1321, 5)$, since in this case $M_\ell \neq \langle 2, 3, \lambda \rangle$. Here **M**, **S**, **a**, and **F** refer to operations on elements of $\mathbb{F}_{q^{k'}}$, while **C** denotes multiplications of elements of $\mathbb{F}_{q^{k'}}$ by elements of $\mathbb{F}_q$.

k	ℓ	$a_{\ell,k}$	$b_{\ell,k}$	M	S	C	a	F
3	19	3	1	18n + 30	2n + 16	20n + 1	20n + 64	0
				10n + 4	2n + 4	8n + 2	8n + 14	4n
	661	110	1	660n + 1314	2n + 658	662n + 1	662n + 2632	0
				224n + 218	2n + 218	222n + 109	222n + 656	4n
4	1013	23	11	1012n + 2018	2n + 1010	1014n + 1	1014n + 4040	0
				48n + 524	2n + 504	48n + 242	48n + 1074	2n
	1181	59	5	1180n + 2354	2n + 1178	1182n + 1	1182n + 4712	0
				120n + 596	2n + 588	120n + 290	120n + 1302	2n
5	31	1	3	30n + 54	2n + 28	32n + 1	32n + 112	0
				10n + 8	2n + 4	4n	4n + 14	8n
	61	6	1	60n + 114	2n + 58	62n + 1	62n + 232	0
				20n + 10	2n + 10	14n + 5	14n + 32	8n
7	29	2	1	28n + 50	2n + 26	30n + 1	30n + 104	0
				16n + 2	2n + 2	6n + 1	6n + 8	12n
	71	5	1	70n + 134	2n + 68	72n + 1	72n + 272	0
				22n + 8	2n + 8	12n + 4	12n + 26	12n
	547	39	1	546n + 1086	2n + 544	548n + 1	548n + 2176	0
				90n + 76	2n + 76	80n + 38	80n + 230	12n
8	881	55	2	880n + 1754	2n + 878	882n + 1	882n + 3512	0
				116n + 220	2n + 218	112n + 108	112n + 548	6n
9	37	2	1	36n + 66	2n + 34	38n + 1	38n + 136	0
				20n + 2	2n + 2	6n + 1	6n + 8	16n
	1693	94	1	1692n + 3378	2n + 1690	1694n + 1	1694n + 6760	0
				204n + 186	2n + 186	190n + 93	190n + 560	16n

The second factor is the organisation of primes into batches for constant-time CSIDH implementations. CTIDH [1] hides the degree ℓ using the so-called *matryoshka* property: ℓ_i-isogeny evaluation is a sub-computation of ℓ_j-isogeny computation whenever $\ell_i < \ell_j$ using Algorithms 1 and 3. Organising primes into similar-sized batches, we can add dummy operations to disguise smaller-degree isogenies as isogenies of the largest degree in their batch.

Our Algorithm 4 has a limited matryoshka property: ℓ_i-isogenies are sub-computations of ℓ_j-isogenies if $a_{\ell_i} \leq a_{\ell_k}$ and $m_{\ell_i}/a_{\ell_i} \leq m_{\ell_j}/a_{\ell,j}$. For constant-time implementations, it would make more sense to make all primes in a batch satisfying (∗) a sub-computation of an algorithm using the maximum a_ℓ and maximum m_ℓ/a_ℓ over ℓ in the batch. Redistributing batches is a delicate matter with an important impact on efficiency; therefore, while our work improves the running time for a fixed ℓ, its impact on batched computations remains uncertain, and ultimately depends on specific parameter choices.

6.2 CRS Key Exchange

The historical predecessors of CSIDH, due to Couveignes [11] and Rostovtsev and Stolbunov [24,27,28], are collectively known as CRS. Here the class group of an quadratic imaginary order $\mathcal{O}$ acts on an isogeny (sub)class of elliptic curves $\mathcal{E}$ with $\mathrm{End}(\mathcal{E}) \cong \mathcal{O}$. CRS performance was greatly improved in [13] using Vélu-style isogeny evaluation, but this requires finding ordinary isogeny classes over $\mathbb{F}_p$ with rational ℓ_i-torsion points over $\mathbb{F}_{q^{k_i}}$ with k_i as small as possible for as many ℓ_i as possible.

One such isogeny class over a 512-bit prime field is proposed in [13, Sect. 4]. The curves ℓ-isogenies with kernel generators over $\mathbb{F}_p$ for $\ell = 3$, 5, 7, 11, 13, 17, 103, 523, and 821, and over $\mathbb{F}_{p^k}$ for $\ell = 19$, 29, 31, 37, 61, 71, 547, 661, 881, 1013, 1181, 1321, and 1693. These "irrational" ℓ are an interesting basis of comparison for our algorithms: Table 4 shows that there are substantial savings to be had.

References

1. Banegas, G., et al.: CTIDH: faster constant-time CSIDH. IACR Trans. Cryptogr. Hardw. Embed. Syst. **2021**(4), 351–387 (2021)
2. Bernstein, D.J., De Feo, L., Leroux, A., Smith, B.: Faster computation of isogenies of large prime degree. In: Galbraith, S.D. (ed.) Proceedings of the Fourteenth Algorithmic Number Theory Symposium, pp. 39–55. Mathematics Sciences Publishers (2020). https://eprint.iacr.org/2020/341
3. Bernstein, D.J., Lange, T., Martindale, C., Panny, L.: Quantum circuits for the CSIDH: optimizing quantum evaluation of isogenies. In: Ishai, Y., Rijmen, V. (eds.) EUROCRYPT 2019. LNCS, vol. 11477, pp. 409–441. Springer, Cham (2019). https://doi.org/10.1007/978-3-030-17656-3_15
4. Beullens, W., Kleinjung, T., Vercauteren, F.: CSI-FiSh: efficient isogeny based signatures through class group computations. In: Galbraith, S.D., Moriai, S. (eds.) ASIACRYPT 2019. LNCS, vol. 11921, pp. 227–247. Springer, Cham (2019). https://doi.org/10.1007/978-3-030-34578-5_9
5. Castryck, W., Lange, T., Martindale, C., Panny, L., Renes, J.: CSIDH: an efficient post-quantum commutative group action. In: Peyrin and Galbraith [22], pp. 395–427 (2018)
6. Castryck, W., Panny, L., Vercauteren, F.: Rational isogenies from irrational endomorphisms. In: Canteaut, A., Ishai, Y. (eds.) EUROCRYPT 2020. LNCS, vol. 12106, pp. 523–548. Springer, Cham (2020). https://doi.org/10.1007/978-3-030-45724-2_18
7. Chi-Domínguez, J.-J., Rodríguez-Henríquez, F.: Optimal strategies for CSIDH. Adv. Math. Commun. **16**(2), 383–411 (2022)
8. Chi-Domínguez, J.J., Esser, A., Kunzweiler, S., May, A.: Low memory attacks on small key CSIDH. In: Tibouchi, M., Wang, X. (eds.) Applied Cryptography and Network Security, pp. 276–304. Springer, Cham (2023). https://doi.org/10.1007/978-3-031-33491-7_11

9. Costello, C., Hisil, H.: A simple and compact algorithm for SIDH with arbitrary degree isogenies. In: Takagi, T., Peyrin, T. (eds.) ASIACRYPT 2017. LNCS, vol. 10625, pp. 303–329. Springer, Cham (2017). https://doi.org/10.1007/978-3-319-70697-9_11

10. Costello, C., Smith, B.: Montgomery curves and their arithmetic. J. Cryptogr. Eng. 8, 227–240 (2017)

11. Couveignes, J.M.: Hard homogeneous spaces. Cryptology ePrint Archive, Paper 2006/291 (2006). https://eprint.iacr.org/2006/291

12. Cozzo, D., Smart, N.P.: Sashimi: cutting up CSI-FiSh secret keys to produce an actively secure distributed signing protocol. In: Ding, J., Tillich, J.-P. (eds.) PQCrypto 2020. LNCS, vol. 12100, pp. 169–186. Springer, Cham (2020). https://doi.org/10.1007/978-3-030-44223-1_10

13. Feo, L.D., Kieffer, J., Smith, B.: Towards practical key exchange from ordinary isogeny graphs. In: Peyrin and Galbraith [22], pp. 365–394 (2018)

14. Feo, L.D., et al.: SCALLOP: scaling the CSI-FiSh. In: Boldyreva, A., Kolesnikov, V. (eds.) Public-Key Cryptography - PKC 2023, pp. 345–375. Springer, Cham (2023). https://doi.org/10.1007/978-3-031-31368-4_13

15. De Feo, L., Galbraith, S.D.: SeaSign: compact isogeny signatures from class group actions. In: Ishai, Y., Rijmen, V. (eds.) EUROCRYPT 2019. LNCS, vol. 11478, pp. 759–789. Springer, Cham (2019). https://doi.org/10.1007/978-3-030-17659-4_26

16. De Feo, L., Kohel, D., Leroux, A., Petit, C., Wesolowski, B.: SQISign: compact post-quantum signatures from quaternions and isogenies. In: Moriai, S., Wang, H. (eds.) ASIACRYPT 2020. LNCS, vol. 12491, pp. 64–93. Springer, Cham (2020). https://doi.org/10.1007/978-3-030-64837-4_3

17. Feo, L.D., Leroux, A., Longa, P., Wesolowski, B.: New algorithms for the deuring correspondence - towards practical and secure sqisign signatures. In: Hazay, C., Stam, M. (eds.) Advances in Cryptology - EUROCRYPT 2023–42nd Annual International Conference on the Theory and Applications of Cryptographic Techniques, Lyon, France, 23–27 April 2023, Proceedings, Part V, vol. 14008 of Lecture Notes in Computer Science, pp. 659–690. Springer, Heidelberg (2023). https://doi.org/10.1007/978-3-031-30589-4_23

18. Kohel, D.R.: Endomorphism rings of elliptic curves over finite fields. PhD thesis, University of California at Berkeley (1996). https://iml.univ-mrs.fr/~kohel/pub/thesis.pdf

19. Meyer, M., Campos, F., Reith, S.: On lions and elligators: an efficient constant-time implementation of CSIDH. In: Ding, J., Steinwandt, R. (eds.) PQCrypto 2019. LNCS, vol. 11505, pp. 307–325. Springer, Cham (2019). https://doi.org/10.1007/978-3-030-25510-7_17

20. Montgomery, P.L.: Speeding the Pollard and elliptic curve methods of factorization. Math. Comput. 48(177), 243–264 (1987)

21. Onuki, H., Aikawa, Y., Yamazaki, T., Takagi, T.: A constant-time algorithm of CSIDH keeping two points. IEICE Trans. Fundam. Electron. Commun. Comput. Sci. 103-A(10), 1174–1182 (2020)

22. Peyrin, T., Galbraith, S. (eds.): ASIACRYPT 2018. LNCS, vol. 11274. Springer, Cham (2018). https://doi.org/10.1007/978-3-030-03332-3

23. Renes, J.: Computing isogenies between montgomery curves using the action of (0, 0). In: Lange, T., Steinwandt, R. (eds.) PQCrypto 2018. LNCS, vol. 10786, pp. 229–247. Springer, Cham (2018). https://doi.org/10.1007/978-3-319-79063-3_11

24. Rostovtsev, A., Stolbunov, A.: Public-key cryptosystem based on isogenies. Cryptology ePrint Archive, Paper 2006/145 (2006). https://eprint.iacr.org/2006/145

25. Silverman, J.H.: The Arithmetic of Elliptic Curves, 2nd edn. Springer-Verlag, New York (2009)
26. Smith, B.: Pre- and post-quantum diffie–hellman from groups, actions, and isogenies. In: Budaghyan, L., Rodríguez-Henríquez, F. (eds.) WAIFI 2018. LNCS, vol. 11321, pp. 3–40. Springer, Cham (2018). https://doi.org/10.1007/978-3-030-05153-2_1
27. Stolbunov, A.: Reductionist security arguments for public-key cryptographic schemes based on group action. In: Norsk informasjonssikkerhetskonferanse (NISK), pp. 97–109 (2009)
28. Stolbunov, A.: Constructing public-key cryptographic schemes based on class group action on a set of isogenous elliptic curves. Adv. Math. Commun. 4(2), 215–235 (2010)
29. Vélu, J.: Isogénies entre courbes elliptiques. Comptes Rendus Hebdomadaires des Séances de l'Académie des Sciences, Série A **273**, 238–241 (1971)
30. Wagstaff, S.S., Jr.: Pseudoprimes and a generalization of Artin's conjecture. Acta Arithmetica **41**, 141–150 (1982)

Towards a Quantum-Resistant Weak Verifiable Delay Function

Thomas Decru[1], Luciano Maino[2(✉)], and Antonio Sanso[3]

[1] COSIC, KU Leuven, Leuven, Belgium
[2] University of Bristol, Bristol, UK
luciano.maino@bristol.ac.uk
[3] Ethereum Foundation, Zug, Switzerland

Abstract. In this paper, we present a new quantum-resistant weak Verifiable Delay Function based on a purely algebraic construction. Its delay depends on computing a large-degree isogeny between elliptic curves, whereas its verification relies on the computation of isogenies between products of two elliptic curves. One of its major advantages is its expected fast verification time. However, it is important to note that the practical implementation of our theoretical framework poses significant challenges. We examine the strengths and weaknesses of our construction, analyze its security and provide a proof-of-concept implementation. (Author list in alphabetical order; see https://www.ams.org//profession/leaders/CultureStatement04.pdf.)

Keywords: Verifiable Delay Function · Post-Quantum · Isogeny · Abelian Surface · Elliptic Curve Product

1 Introduction

A Verifiable Delay Function (VDF) is a cryptographic primitive designed to take a prescribed amount of time t to compute, regardless of the parallel computing power available, while still being easy to verify once the computation is complete. VDFs are used in various applications, such as random number generation and blockchain consensus algorithms, where a delay is needed to ensure that certain operations cannot be performed too quickly. The seminal paper on VDFs, "Verifiable Delay Functions", was published in 2018 by Boneh, Bonneau, Bünz and Fisch [10]. In the paper, the authors introduce the concept of a VDF and describe its potential uses in various applications including auction protocols, proof-of-work systems, and secure multiparty computation. The first efficient VDFs were the ones proposed by Pietrzak [42] and Wesolowski [50]; both VDFs are based on exponentiation in a group of unknown order. We refer to [9] for a survey about these VDFs. Driven by the open problem of finding a VDF that is also quantum resistant, De Feo, Masson, Petit and Sanso [25] employed chains of supersingular isogenies as "sequential slow" functions in order to build their VDF. However, given the usage of bilinear pairing, this isogeny-based VDF is not

© The Author(s), under exclusive license to Springer Nature Switzerland AG 2023
A. Aly and M. Tibouchi (Eds.): LATINCRYPT 2023, LNCS 14168, pp. 149–168, 2023.
https://doi.org/10.1007/978-3-031-44469-2_8

quantum resistant but only provides some *quantum annoyance*. Proving knowledge of isogenies has a rich history of research (see for instance [7,20]), but none of the techniques seem to allow for a natural instantiation of a VDF.

Boneh, Bonneau, Bünz and Fisch [10], and independently Döttling, Garg, Malavolta, and Vasudevan [28] proposed the usage of SNARGs for constructing a VDF. In [17], Chavez-Saab, Rodríguez-Henríquez and Tibouchi describe an isogeny-based VDF that is quantum resistant based on the SNARG approach. Also, in [47], Tan, Sharma, Li, Szalachowski and Zhou report a VDF built over a sequential variant of the zero-knowledge proof system ZKBoo [33].

Our Contribution. In this paper, we present a quantum-resistant *weak* VDF, which is a VDF where a certain amount of parallelism is needed to give an advantage to the evaluator [10, Definition 5]. Our construction is based upon both isogenies between supersingular elliptic curves and Kani's criterion [34]. Kani's criterion determines whether isogenies originating from elliptic products have split codomain. In our case, this criterion is leveraged in a constructive manner, in contrast to previous attacks [14,37,43] against the Supersingular Isogeny Diffie-Hellman key exchange protocol (SIDH) [24] and its instantiation SIKE [2]. While there have been other attempts to build quantum-resistant VDFs [17,47], to the best of our knowledge, this is the first instance where a quantum-resistant VDF has been constructed without relying on SNARG.

Our VDF is inherently noninteractive and does not have the limitation present in [25], where the time required for setting up public parameters is similar to the time required for evaluating the function.

However, our VDF faces two challenges: its *weakness* and the need of curves with unknown endomorphism ring as input. In our case, being weak means that Eval will require $\mathcal{O}(t)$ parallelism to run in parallel time t.

Sampling random supersingular elliptic curves over finite fields of cryptographic size without giving information about the endomorphism ring is necessary to ensure the security of the elliptic curve used in the Eval operation. Currently, finding a way to do this without relying on a trusted authority is an open problem in supersingular isogeny-based cryptography [11,40]. In [4], Basso, Codogni, Connolly, De Feo, Fouotsa, Lido, Morrison, Panny, Patranabis and Wesolowski suggest methods for creating such curves defined over a finite field $\mathbb{F}_{p^2}$ through a trusted setup. Nevertheless, engaging in a trusted setup for every single input is not a practical solution for us. Trusted setups often involve complex procedures and require the involvement of multiple parties or authorities, making them cumbersome to execute on a regular basis. In summary, the weakness of the VDF is a drawback, while the requirement for curves with unknown endomorphism rings as input is a significant obstacle.

Technical Preview. Let $E_0/\mathbb{F}_p$ be a supersingular elliptic curve and ℓ an odd prime, such that there are two horizontal ℓ-isogenies $\psi : E_0 \rightarrow E_1$ and $\psi' : E_0 \rightarrow E_1'$. If the ℓ-torsion of E_0 is only defined over $\mathbb{F}_{p^{\ell-1}}$, then computing these isogenies is expensive, even with parallelization, and they will determine the delay of our weak VDF. On the other hand, one can rapidly verify this computation in dimension two by asking for the evaluation of ψ and ψ' on $E_0[N]$ for certain smooth $N > \ell$ (e.g. N is some power of two). By choosing ℓ and N appropriately, the gap between evaluation and verification is exponential.

Outline. This paper is organized as follows. In Sect. 2, we give a mathematical foundation for understanding the concepts employed in the manuscript, as well as the definition of a weak VDF. Section 3, the main focus of the paper, provides a detailed description of our weak VDF. Section 4 to Sect. 6 present thorough analysis of correctness, soundness and sequentiality. Finally, we draw conclusions in Sect. 7.

Notation. We will call a prime ℓ a *safe* prime if $k = \frac{\ell-1}{2}$ is also an (odd) prime. The prime k is then necessarily a Sophie-Germain prime. The Legendre symbol $\left(\frac{a}{b}\right)$ is used to denote whether a is a quadratic residue modulo b or not. Two prime-field elements $a, b \in \mathbb{F}_p$ will be compared as $a <_{\mathbb{Z}} b$ if their canonical lifts $\bar{a}, \bar{b} \in \mathbb{Z} \cap [0, p-1]$ satisfy $\bar{a} < \bar{b}$, and analogously for $>_{\mathbb{Z}}$. For a point P on an elliptic curve E, we will denote its x-coordinate (respectively y-coordinate) by $x(P)$ (respectively $y(P)$). We will use the term "taking t time to compute" when referring to the evaluation of a polynomial-sized arithmetic circuit with a maximum depth of t, specifying the breadth of the circuit when needed.

2 Preliminaries

In this section, we will discuss some properties related to isogenies and weak VDFs. In general, we will assume the characteristic of the field we work over to be a prime $p > 3$, although certain results generalize beyond this restriction.

2.1 Elliptic Curves and Their Representation

Elliptic curves are smooth projective algebraic curves of genus one with a fixed given point $\mathcal{O}$. Any such curve can be written in long Weierstraß form and then $\mathcal{O}$ is the (only) point at infinity. Often, the curve is given as an affine equation without explicit mention of $\mathcal{O}$; e.g. the Montgomery form of an elliptic curve E_A is given by

$$E_A/K : y^2 = x^3 + Ax^2 + x,$$

where K is the field we work over and A is an element of this field. An elliptic curve comes equipped with a natural group law and the point at infinity $\mathcal{O}_E$ is the neutral element of this group. The K-rational points of E (which include $\mathcal{O}_E$) are denoted by $E(K)$.

In isogeny-based cryptographic settings, elliptic curves are typically only considered up to isomorphism. Two elliptic curves are isomorphic over $\overline{K}$ if and only if they have the same j-invariant $j \in K$. The j-invariant of an elliptic curve E in Montgomery form is denoted by $j(E_A)$ and given by

$$j(E_A) = \frac{(A^2 - 3)^3}{A^2 - 4}.$$

Given a j-invariant $j \neq 1728$, we will define the Weierstraß form

$$E(j) : y^2 + xy = x^3 - \frac{36}{j - 1728}x - \frac{1}{j - 1728}$$

as *the canonical representation* of E in the isomorphism class of E. The canonical representation isomorphism $\iota_j : E \to E(j)$ is easy to compute for any elliptic curve E. An elliptic curve is in canonical form if $E = E(j(E))$. Other forms of elliptic curves than $E(j)$ are often preferred for computational purposes. For instance, the Montgomery form E_A allows efficient x-only arithmetic in the group by means of the Montgomery ladder [6]. From the expression $j(E_A)$ above though, it is clear that for any given j-invariant there may be up to six distinct Montgomery coefficients A. Additionally, one cannot represent every j-invariant as an elliptic curve in Montgomery form without using field extensions, hence the Montgomery coefficient is less useful from a representational point of view. For more information about elliptic curves in general, the book by Silverman is a staple reference [44].

2.2   Isogenies

An isogeny $\phi : E \to E'$ between elliptic curves is a surjective morphism with finite kernel. In this paper, we will restrict ourselves mostly to separable isogenies. Assuming kernel points are considered over the algebraic closure, it holds that $\deg \phi = \# \ker \phi$ for all separable isogenies. An example of an isogeny is the multiplication-by-n map, given by $[n] : E \to E$, $P \mapsto [n]P$. This isogeny is of degree n^2 and its kernel is denoted by $E[n]$. An endomorphism is a homomorphism from an elliptic curve to itself. The endomorphism ring $\text{End}_K(E)$ of an elliptic curve is the ring of all endomorphisms of E defined over the field K.

There are two options for the group structure of $E[p]$, namely $E[p] \cong \{0\}$ or $E[p] \cong \mathbb{Z}/p\mathbb{Z}$. In the former case, the elliptic curves are called supersingular, whereas in the latter case, they are called ordinary. We will restrict ourselves to supersingular elliptic curves and isogenies between them, since it is significantly easier to generate supersingular elliptic curves with certain given orders. For instance, a supersingular elliptic curve has order $p + 1$ over $\mathbb{F}_p$.

For a supersingular elliptic curve $E/\mathbb{F}_p$, either $\text{End}_{\mathbb{F}_p}(E)$ equals $\mathbb{Z}[\sqrt{-p}]$ or $\mathbb{Z}[(1 + \sqrt{-p})/2]$. In the former case, the elliptic curve E is said to be *on the floor*, whereas in the latter case, the elliptic curve is said to be *on the surface*. An isogeny $\phi : E \to E'$ is said to be *horizontal* in this context if $\text{End}_{\mathbb{F}_p}(E) = \text{End}_{\mathbb{F}_p}(E')$ (i.e. E and E' need to either be both on the floor, or both on the surface). We will make use of the following theorem, where two isogenies are considered distinct if they have different kernel.

Theorem 1. *Let $p > 3$ be a prime such that $p \equiv 3 \bmod 4$, and ℓ an odd prime such that $\left(\frac{-p}{\ell}\right) = 1$. If $E/\mathbb{F}_p$ is a supersingular elliptic curve, then there are exactly two distinct $\mathbb{F}_p$-rational horizontal isogenies of degree ℓ with E as domain.*

Proof. This is part of [26, Theorem 2.7].   □

In CSIDH [16], they choose p such that $\#E(\mathbb{F}_p) = p + 1$ has many small odd prime factors ℓ_i. For each ℓ_i, the two horizontal ℓ_i-isogenies are then not only $\mathbb{F}_p$-rational, but they are cyclic with kernel generators in $\mathbb{F}_p$ and $\mathbb{F}_{p^2}$. With a good choice of representation, both isogenies can be computed from the x-coordinate of their respective kernel generator using arithmetic over $\mathbb{F}_p$ only. Generically, however, these two $\mathbb{F}_p$-rational horizontal isogenies have kernel generators in $E(\mathbb{F}_{p^e})$, for some $e \le \ell - 1$.

In our protocol, we will post-compose $\mathbb{F}_p$-rational horizontal isogenies with an isomorphism onto the canonical form of the image curve. Technically, the resulting isogenies are not $\mathbb{F}_p$-rational anymore because of this isomorphism. However, since we work with curves of unknown endomorphism ring, we can discard the case where the j-invariant of the starting curve is either 0 or 1728. As a result, the two horizontal isogenies are still distinct [1, Lemma 3.11]. For more general background regarding isogenies in a cryptographic setting, we refer the reader to the notes by De Feo [23].

2.3 Isogenies Between Abelian Surfaces

Abelian surfaces are abelian varieties of dimension two, which can be seen as a generalization of (necessarily one-dimensional) elliptic curves. In the context of isogeny-based cryptography, it is necessary to equip them with a principal polarization (abbreviated as p.p. from now on). We will not elaborate on the notion of polarizations, but refer the interested reader to [45, Section 2.2] for more details.

All p.p. abelian surfaces (up to $\overline{K}$-isomorphism) are either products of two elliptic curves or Jacobians of genus-2 curves. Arithmetic on a product of elliptic curves (E_1, E_2) is simply arithmetic on the two curves componentwise; e.g. for $(P_1, P_2) \in (E_1, E_2)$ we can compute the multiplication-by-n map as $([n]P_1, [n]P_2) \in (E_1, E_2)$. A genus-2 curve C is a smooth projective algebraic curve of genus two. Over a field of positive odd characteristic p, such a curve can be given by an affine equation of the form $C : y^2 = F(x)$, where $F(x)$ is a degree-six polynomial, together with two points at infinity (which may only exist over a quadratic field extension). From the points on this curve, one can also construct a group called the Jacobian of the genus-2 curve. Remark that to construct all K-rational elements of this Jacobian, one needs to consider all K'-rational points on C for a quadratic extension $K' \supseteq K$. For an explicit construction of this group law, see for example [19].

Just as in the case of elliptic curves, isogenies between p.p. abelian surfaces are surjective morphisms with finite kernel. In order to ensure that the isogeny is compatible with the chosen polarizations of the domain and codomain, this finite kernel will have to satisfy certain conditions. A sufficient condition is that the kernel of the isogeny has to be maximal isotropic with regards to the Weil pairing. For instance, if $\Psi : A \to A'$ is an isogeny between p.p. abelian surfaces with kernel isomorphic to $\mathbb{Z}/3 \oplus \mathbb{Z}/3$, then for any two elements D_1, D_2 in $\ker \Psi$ it must hold that $e_3(D_1, D_2) = 1$. A group satisfying these conditions is called a $(3,3)$-*subgroup* and the associated isogeny a $(3,3)$-*isogeny*.

A theorem by Kani proves under which specific conditions an isogeny Φ with domain $E_1 \times E_2$ has a codomain which is again a product of elliptic curves. These conditions connect E_1 and E_2 by means of another (one-dimensional) isogeny. This criterion underlies Theorem 2 formulated in Sect. 4, which we use to prove correctness of our protocol. If $F_1 \times F_2$ is the codomain of Φ, then we say that Φ has *product codomain passing through* F_i. For an introductory framework with regards to higher-dimensional isogenies in a cryptographic setting, see for example [15].

2.4 Weak VDFs

For the sake of being self-contained, we briefly recall the notion of *weak VDF* introduced by Boneh, Bonneau, Bünz and Fisch [10]. The main difference between a VDF and a weak VDF lies in the parallelization capabilities given to evaluators: in a weak VDF, an evaluator needs arithmetic circuits of breadth $\mathcal{O}(\boldsymbol{poly}(t))$ to achieve the best strategy, where t indicates the delay expected.

Definition 1. *A weak VDF $V = (\mathsf{Setup}, \mathsf{Eval}, \mathsf{Verify})$ consists of a triple of algorithms as follows:*

- *$(\mathsf{ek}, \mathsf{vk}) \leftarrow \mathsf{Setup}(\lambda, t)$: is a randomized algorithm that takes a security parameter λ and a delay parameter t as input, and outputs an evaluation key ek and a verification key vk. The input (λ, t) also defines a domain $\mathcal{X}$ and a codomain $\mathcal{Z}$. Also, Setup should run in $\mathcal{O}(\boldsymbol{poly}(\lambda))$.*
- *$(z \in \mathcal{Z}, \pi) \leftarrow \mathsf{Eval}(\mathsf{ek}, x \leftarrow \mathcal{X})$: on input the evaluation key ek and $x \in \mathcal{X}$, returns $z \in \mathcal{Z}$ and a proof π. This algorithm must run in time t on an arithmetic circuit of breadth $\mathcal{O}(\boldsymbol{poly}(t, \lambda))$.*
- *$\{\mathsf{True}, \mathsf{False}\} \leftarrow \mathsf{Verify}(\mathsf{vk}, x, z, \pi)$: checks whether the output z corresponds to the input x. This algorithm must run in $\mathcal{O}(\boldsymbol{poly}(\log t, \lambda))$ time.*

Furthermore, V must satisfy the following properties:

- ***Correctness:** A weak VDF is correct if, for all parameters λ, t, an honest evaluation of Eval always passes the check made by Verify.*
- ***Soundness:** A weak VDF is sound if the probability of marking a wrong evaluation as correct is negligible in the security parameter λ.*
- ***Sequentiality:** To define sequentiality, we need to introduce the following game applied to the adversary $\mathcal{A} = (\mathcal{A}_0, \mathcal{A}_1)$:*

$$(\mathsf{ek}, \mathsf{vk}) \leftarrow \mathsf{Setup}(\lambda, t)$$
$$L \leftarrow \mathcal{A}_0(\mathsf{ek}, \mathsf{vk})$$
$$x \leftarrow_\$ \mathcal{X}$$
$$z_\mathcal{A} \leftarrow_\$ \mathcal{A}_1(L, \mathsf{ek}, \mathsf{vk}, x)$$

The adversary $\mathcal{A}$ wins the game if $z_\mathcal{A} = z$, where $(z, \pi) = \mathsf{Eval}(\mathsf{ek}, x)$. Given $\sigma(t)$ and $p(t)$, the weak VDF V is (p, σ)−sequential if no pair of randomized algorithms $\mathcal{A}_0$, which runs in time $\mathcal{O}(\boldsymbol{poly}(\lambda, t))$, and $\mathcal{A}_1$, which runs in time strictly less than $\sigma(t)$ on an arithmetic circuit of breadth $p(t)$, can win the security game above with probability greater than $\mathsf{negl}(\lambda)$.

3   The VDF

In this section, we give a high-level description of our weak VDF. Once the evaluation key ek and verification key vk have been sampled, the input space consists of $\mathcal{E}\ell\ell_p$, the set of all j-invariants corresponding to supersingular elliptic curves over $\mathbb{F}_p$ whose $\mathbb{F}_{p^2}$-endomorphism ring is unknown. Currently, finding a way to sample such curves at random is an open problem in supersingular isogeny-based cryptography [11,40]. We define Gen2b to be a deterministic algorithm that, on input a supersingular elliptic curve and a positive integer b, outputs a basis of the 2^b-torsion.

We recall that λ is a security parameter, t is a delay parameter, z is the output and π is the proof of the output.

$(\mathsf{ek}, \mathsf{vk}) \leftarrow \mathsf{Setup}(\lambda, t)$:
1. Sample a random safe prime $\ell \sim t$ and define $k = (\ell - 1)/2$.
2. Let $b > \lambda$ such that $2^b = c^2\ell + d^2$ for some coprime positive integers $c, d \in \mathbb{N}$.
3. Construct a random $\lambda \log^3(t)/2$-bit prime p such that
    (a) $p \equiv -1 \bmod 2^b cd$;
    (b) $p \equiv 1 \bmod k$ and $2^{\frac{p-1}{k}} \not\equiv 1 \bmod p$.
    (c) the order of $-p$ in $\mathbb{F}_\ell^*$ equals k;
    (d) $\left(\frac{-p}{\ell}\right) = 1$;
4. $\mathsf{ek} = (p, b, \ell)$, $\mathsf{vk} = (p, b, \ell, c, d)$.

$(z, \pi) \leftarrow \mathsf{Eval}(j \leftarrow_\$ \mathcal{E}\ell\ell_p, \mathsf{ek})$:
(1) $E_0 \leftarrow E(j)$, $P_0, Q_0 \leftarrow \mathsf{Gen2b}(E_0, b)$.
(2) Compute the two (distinct) horizontal ℓ-isogenies $\psi : E_0 \to E_1/\mathbb{F}_p$ and $\psi' : E_0 \to E_1'/\mathbb{F}_p$, where E_1 and E_1' are in canonical form, as well as $P_1 = \psi(P_0)$, $Q_1 = \psi(Q_0)$, $P_1' = \psi'(P_0)$ and $Q_1' = \psi'(Q_0)$.
(3) If $j(E_1) >_z j(E_1')$, then swap $(E_1, P_1, Q_1) \leftrightarrow (E_1', P_1', Q_1')$.
(4) $z \leftarrow x(P_1) \parallel x(Q_1) \parallel x(P_1') \parallel x(Q_1')$.
(5) $\pi \leftarrow j(E_1) \parallel j(E_1') \parallel y(P_1) \parallel y(Q_1) \parallel y(P_1') \parallel y(Q_1')$.

$\{\mathsf{True}, \mathsf{False}\} \leftarrow \mathsf{Verify}(j, z, \pi, \mathsf{vk})$:
(1) $E_0 \leftarrow E(j)$, $P_0, Q_0 \leftarrow \mathsf{Gen2b}(E_0, b)$.
(2) Verify that $j(E_1) <_z j(E_1')$.[1]
(3) $E_1 \leftarrow E(j(E_1))$, $E_1' \leftarrow E(j(E_1'))$.
(4) Verify that $P_1, Q_1 \in E_1(\mathbb{F}_{p^2})$, and $P_1', Q_1' \in E_1'(\mathbb{F}_{p^2})$.
5. Verify that the subgroups $\langle([d]P_1, [c\ell]P_0), ([d]Q_1, [c\ell]Q_0)\rangle \subset E_1 \times E_0$ and $\langle([d]P_1', [c\ell]P_0), ([d]Q_1', [c\ell]Q_0)\rangle \subset E_1' \times E_0$ define two kernels of $(2^b, 2^b)$-isogenies Φ and Φ', respectively, having product codomain passing through E_0.

---

[1] Checking if $j(E_1)$ is smaller than $j(E_1')$ implicitly verifies that $j(E_1), j(E_1') \in \mathbb{F}_p$.

(5) Verify that, for all $S \in E_1[c]$, the projections of $\Phi(S, 0)$ and $\Phi'(S, 0)$ onto E_0 are equal to the identity.
(6) Verify that, for all $S \in E_0[d]$, the projections of $\Phi(0, S)$ and $\Phi'(0, S)$ onto E_0 are equal to the identity.

For now, we will assume that the evaluation of an ℓ-isogeny in this setting is expensive, even with access to a large amount of parallel processors. We will elaborate on this in Sect. 6 when discussing sequentiality but will explain the choices in the protocol first.

Remark 1. Remark that $\mathsf{ek}, \mathsf{vk}, z, \pi$ can be noticeably compressed in bitsize; e.g. the y-coordinates of P_1, Q_1, P_1' and Q_1' can be compressed to four bits in the classical way.[2] For the clarity of exposition, we elect to omit these details involving bandwidth requirements.

3.1   The Conditions in Setup

The condition $\left(\frac{-p}{\ell}\right) = 1$ ensures that there exist two horizontal ℓ-isogenies, see Theorem 1. The condition $-p$ having order k in $\mathbb{F}_\ell^*$ implies that the minimal field extension over which an ℓ-torsion point is defined is $\mathbb{F}_{p^k}$. Indeed, if E_0 is a supersingular elliptic curve defined over $\mathbb{F}_p$, then $\#E_0(\mathbb{F}_{p^k}) = p^k + 1$. Since $-p$ has order k in $\mathbb{F}_\ell^*$, we have that $\ell \mid (p^k + 1)$. The field $\mathbb{F}_{p^k}$ is the minimal field extension since it is an extension of prime degree of $\mathbb{F}_p$ and $\ell \nmid (p + 1)$. Finally, the form of p implies that all 2^b-, c- and d-torsion is $\mathbb{F}_{p^2}$-rational, which will allow fast verification.

The conditions $k \mid p - 1$ and $2^{\frac{p-1}{k}} \not\equiv 1 \bmod p$ are needed to ensure that the polynomial $x^k + 2$ is irreducible over $\mathbb{F}_p[x]$. Since $2^{\frac{p-1}{k}} \not\equiv 1 \bmod p$, 2 does not admit a k-th root over $\mathbb{F}_p$, which in turn proves that $x^k + 2$ is irreducible over $\mathbb{F}_p[x]$. The polynomial $x^k + 2$ is then used to define the field $\mathbb{F}_{p^k}$, i.e. $\mathbb{F}_{p^k} = \mathbb{F}_p[x]/(x^k + 2)$. This condition is technically not needed but ensures that we do not need to waste time searching for irreducible polynomials to define $\mathbb{F}_{p^k}$.

3.2   The Size of p

The computation of the horizontal ℓ-isogenies correspond to the action of $\mathfrak{l} = (\ell, \pi^k - 1)$ and $\bar{\mathfrak{l}} = (\ell, \pi^k + 1)$ in the class group $\mathrm{Cl}(\mathcal{O})$ of the $\mathbb{F}_p$-endomorphism ring $\mathcal{O}$ of E_0. We will focus on $\mathfrak{l}$, the other case is completely analogously. Assuming access to a sufficiently large quantum computer, the relation lattice for a given set of generators - say $\mathfrak{l}, \mathfrak{l}_1, \ldots, \mathfrak{l}_{d-1}$ - of $\mathrm{Cl}(\mathcal{O})$ can be computed. This means that an adversary could try to simplify the computation of the ℓ-isogeny by means of finding an equivalent element $\mathfrak{l} = \mathfrak{l}_1^{e_1} \cdot \ldots \cdot \mathfrak{l}_{d-1}^{e_{d-1}}$ when seen as elements in $\mathrm{Cl}(\mathcal{O})$. Each $\mathfrak{l}_i$ in this product corresponds to a prime-degree isogeny, such that ideally the e_i are as small as possible. This is exactly how the CSI-FiSh signature scheme is made efficient [8].

---

[2] Given that they serve as part of kernel generators for verifying a two-dimensional isogeny, they can actually be compressed to a combined two bits.

To combat this, we can choose p to be large enough, such that any of the known lattice reduction algorithms takes time at least 2^λ to find a short vector of L^1-norm less than t. This implies that no reasonable lattice reduction can find an equivalent smooth-norm ideal corresponding to less than t sequential isogenies.

Following the argument of Panny [41], the standard lattice reduction algorithm which gives a trade-off between time spent reducing the lattice and the quality (read: norm) of the output vector is the BKZ algorithm. Assuming p is a μ-bit prime, our lattice has dimension d and covolume $2^{\mu/2}$, since the class group has order $\mathcal{O}(\sqrt{p})$. If we are looking for vectors bounded in L^1-norm by $t = 2^\tau$, we can deduce that the optimal trade-off happens for dimension $d \approx \mu/\tau$. The total runtime of the BKZ algorithm is then $2^{\mathcal{O}(2\mu/\tau^2)} \approx 2^{2\mu/\tau^2}$. Assuming BKZ is fully parallelizable, with access to arithmetic circuits of breadth $t = 2^\tau$, it runs in time $2^{2\mu/\tau^3}$. To ensure that this is still more than 2^λ, we must have that $2\mu/\tau^3 \geq \lambda$, or $\mu \geq \lambda \log(t)^3/2$.

Remark that this approach would lead a dishonest evaluator only to the codomain curve E_1, but this can be extended to also compute the images of P_0 and Q_0 as follows.

Write $R_0 = P_0 + Q_0$, such that $\langle R_0 \rangle$ is a cyclic group defining a descending 2^b-isogeny to a curve $E'/\mathbb{F}_{p^2}$. This curve is oriented by an order $\mathcal{O}'$ of conductor 2^b inside $\mathrm{End}(E_0)$; in particular its group action is compatible with the one at the surface. The class group relations can be obtained as well, and hence $\mathfrak{l}_1^{e_1} \cdot \ldots \cdot \mathfrak{l}_{d-1}^{e_{d-1}} \cap \mathcal{O}'$ can be rewritten as an equivalent ideal of smooth norm, say $\mathfrak{m}$. The image curve $\mathfrak{m}E'$ is then equivalent to $E_1/\langle R_1 \rangle$, with R_1 the image of R_0 under the isogeny ψ defined by $\mathfrak{l}$.

Furthermore, $E_1[2^b]$ contains two distinguished cyclic subgroups corresponding to the two eigenvalues of Frobenius. This means that on the level of subgroups, we can distinguish $\langle \psi(P_0) \rangle$ and $\langle \psi(Q_0) \rangle$ easily. Adding our cyclic subgroup $\langle \psi(R_0) \rangle$ as third piece of information, one can use the Weil-pairing and some linear algebra as in [31] to recover the exact images of P_0 and Q_0.

Remark 2. The aforementioned derivation of the size of p is extremely conservative. Not only does it assume full parallelizability of BKZ with no overhead, but it also assumes a dishonest evaluator can compute ℓ_i-isogenies in time $\mathcal{O}(1)$ for d distinct primes ℓ_i. In practice this will also come with a huge overhead, since our parameters are not set up such that both the ℓ_i and the field extension over which the ℓ_i-torsion is defined are simultaneously small.

3.3   Curves with Unknown Endomorphism Ring

If the endomorphism ring of the curve E given as input is known, there exists a polynomial-time algorithm that allows one to compute ℓ-isogenies without using the arithmetic on extension fields [37]: an attacker could extend $(\ell, \pi^k \pm 1)$ to a fractional ideal $I_\pm$ in the maximal order $\mathrm{End}(E_0)$. Then, computing an isogeny associated with $I_\pm$ has complexity $\mathcal{O}(\mathbf{poly}(\log p + C))$, where C is the bit-size of the representation of $\mathrm{End}(E_0)$ [36, Propositon 5].

To avoid this, it is needed to employ elliptic curves where the endomorphism ring remains unknown. Currently, one strategy is to depend on a "trusted party" to generate a random curve and then eliminate any sensitive information connected to it. Another option is to consider a distributed trusted-setup ceremony, as described in [4], which outlines a procedure for obtaining supersingular elliptic curves with an unknown endomorphism ring.

However, having a trusted setup for every single input is not a practical solution in this context. Indeed performing a trusted setup for each input would introduce significant overhead in terms of time, resources, and complexity. Additionally, frequent trusted setups can become prohibitively expensive, especially in scenarios where a large number of inputs need to be processed. Given these challenges, it becomes crucial to explore alternative methods that do not rely on a trusted setup as in [11,40].

3.4   The Role of the Security Parameter

The condition on b is needed to avoid that an attacker having access to the ℓ-modular polynomial $\Phi_\ell(X,Y)$ can break sequentiality with probability greater than $\mathsf{negl}(\lambda)$. The classical modular polynomial $\Phi_\ell(X,Y) \in \mathbb{Z}[X,Y]$ is a polynomial which vanishes on the j-invariants of every pair of elliptic curves which are ℓ-isogenous. The polynomial can be precomputed and stored in space $\mathcal{O}(\ell \log p)$ since it is a symmetric polynomial with bidegree $\ell + 1$. For any given $j(E)$, the univariate polynomial $\Phi_\ell(X,j(E))$ can be computed in parallel by using the Chinese remainder theorem, see for example [46].

The polynomial $\Phi_\ell(X,j(E))$ splits into linear factors over $\mathbb{F}_{p^2}$, and the $\mathbb{F}_p$-rational roots correspond to the $\mathbb{F}_p$-rational ℓ-isogenous curves. However, having the j-invariants of the two curves is not enough to pass Verify. Starting from $E_0/\mathbb{F}_p$, once an ℓ-isogenous elliptic curve $E_1/\mathbb{F}_p$ has been computed via the evaluation of roots in classical modular polynomials, an attacker has to guess the image of the 2^b-torsion under the $\mathbb{F}_p$-rational isogeny. For instance, the attacker could proceed in the following way.

Let $\langle P_0, Q_0 \rangle = E_0[2^b]$ be a basis of eigenvectors for the p-Frobenious endomorphism π. Since the eigenspaces are preserved by horizontal isogenies ψ, we know $\langle \psi(P_0) \rangle$ and $\langle \psi(Q_0) \rangle$. Since $e_{2^b}(\psi(P_0), \psi(Q_0)) = e_{2^b}(P_0, Q_0)^{\deg \psi}$, each guess of $\psi(P_0)$ corresponds to a unique guess of $\psi(Q_0)$. That is, given a $P_1 \in \langle \psi(P_0) \rangle$ and $Q_1 \in \langle \psi(Q_0) \rangle$, for each $s_p \in [0, 2^b - 1]$, an attacker will compute $s_Q \in [0, 2^b - 1]$ such that $e_{2^b}(P_1, Q_1)^{s_P s_Q} = e_{2^b}(P_0, Q_0)^{\deg \psi}$. Then, for each $([s_P]P_1, [s_Q]Q_1)$, he can check that it is the correct image of the (P_0, Q_0) under ψ running Verify. Since $b > \lambda$, the probability of guessing the right image is negligible in λ. We highlight that even if (P_0, Q_0) is not the basis provided as input, an attacker can perform computations with a basis of eigenvectors and then reconstruct the image of the provided basis via a discrete logarithm computation in $\mathbb{Z}/2^b\mathbb{Z}$, which is extremely efficient.

Remark 3. We stress that it is not clear exactly how well the parallelization of [46] performs in practice compared to the work we let our evaluator do. It may thus seem overly cautious to assume that an attacker has early access to $j(E_1)$. However, from pushing points through an isogeny, one can easily reconstruct the codomain curve as well (see for example [5]), which makes the evaluation of points a problem that is at least as hard as finding the codomain curve. Since the image points are needed to make use of Kani's criterion anyway, we thus see no argument to *not* put $j(E_1)$ as part of the proof, since other algorithms to compute it may be faster by a small constant factor. Additionally, Elkies algorithm to reconstruct the ℓ-isogeny from just $j(E_0)$ and $j(E_1)$ involves a recurrence relation of length $\mathcal{O}(\ell^2)$ (see [29]), which will be outperformed by our approach outlined in Sect. 6.

4   Correctness

The correctness of the scheme depends on the following result.

Theorem 2. *Let* $\varphi_{N_1} \colon E_0 \to E_1$ *and* $\varphi_{N_2} \colon E_0 \to E_2$ *be two isogenies of coprime degrees* $\deg(\varphi_{N_1}) = N_1$ *and* $\deg(\varphi_{N_2}) = N_2$, *and let* $\langle P, Q \rangle$ *be a basis of* $E_0[N_1 + N_2]$. *Then, the subgroup*

$$\langle ([N_2]\varphi_{N_1}(P), [N_1]\varphi_{N_2}(P)), ([N_2]\varphi_{N_1}(Q), [N_1]\varphi_{N_2}(Q)) \rangle \subset E_1 \times E_2,$$

is the kernel of an $(N_1 + N_2, N_1 + N_2)$*-polarized isogeny* Φ *having product codomain endowed with the product polarization. Moreover, the isogeny* Φ *has matrix form*

$$\begin{pmatrix} \widehat{\varphi_{N_1}} & -\widehat{\varphi_{N_2}} \\ f_{N_2} & \widehat{f_{N_1}} \end{pmatrix},$$

where the f_{N_i}'s *are* N_i*-isogenies such that* $\varphi_{N_2} \circ \widehat{\varphi_{N_1}} = f_{N_1} \circ f_{N_2}$.

Proof. This result is a consequence of Kani's criterion [34]. We refer to [37, Theorem 1] for a description of how the result is derived from [34].   □

In Verify, one has to check that the subgroups $\langle ([d]P_1, [c\ell]P_0), ([d]Q_1, [c\ell]Q_0) \rangle$ and $\langle ([d]P_1', [c\ell]P_0), ([d]Q_1', [c\ell]Q_0) \rangle$ define two kernels of $(2^b, 2^b)$-isogenies having product codomains passing through E_0 and that the projections onto E_1 and E_1' contain the scalar multiplication $[c]$. Since the two checks are independent, let us focus uniquely on $\mathcal{K} := \langle ([d]P_1, [c\ell]P_0), ([d]Q_1, [c\ell]Q_0) \rangle$.

Recall that $P_1 = \psi(P_0)$, $Q_1 = \psi(Q_0)$, where $\psi \colon E_0 \to E_1$ is a horizontal ℓ-isogeny. Applying Theorem 2 with $\varphi_{N_1} = [c] \circ \psi$ and $\varphi_{N_2} = [d]$, we have that the $(2^b, 2^b)$-isogeny Φ having kernel $\mathcal{K}$ has matrix form

$$\begin{pmatrix} [c] \circ \widehat{\psi} & -[d] \\ [d] & [c] \circ \psi \end{pmatrix} \colon E_1 \times E_0 \to E_0 \times E_1.$$

The isogeny Φ clearly passes through E_0. Moreover, it is easy to check that, for all $S \in E_1[c]$, $\Phi(S, 0) = (0, [d]S)$, which means that the projection onto E_1 contains the scalar multiplication $[c]$. Similarly, for $S \in E_0[d]$, $\Phi(0, S) = (0, [c]\psi(S))$. Evaluating a $(2^b, 2^b)$-isogeny from a given kernel can be done in $\mathcal{O}(b \log b)$ $\mathbb{F}_p$-operations using the optimal strategies described in [2].

5   Soundness

In this section, we prove soundness assuming that $d^2 > \ell$, where d and ℓ are as in the verification key vk in Sect. 3. In practice, the condition $d^2 > \ell$ is trivially satisfied.

Theorem 3. *Let $d^2 > \ell$. The weak VDF described in Sect. 3 is sound.*

Proof. Let ek, vk be the evaluation and verification keys, respectively, obtained via Setup(λ, t) on input some parameters λ and t. Given $j \in \mathcal{E}\ell\ell_p$, let (z, π) be any data such that Verify$(j, z, \pi, \text{vk}) = \text{True}$. We will prove that z has been honestly generated with overwhelming probability.

In what follows, we abide to notation used in Sect. 3. The first four lines in Verify ensure that any adversary cannot swap the points on E_1 and E_1' around and produce other valid outputs. Also, note that Verify performs two independent checks on the triples (E_1, P_1, Q_1) and (E_1', P_1', Q_1'). Hence, we will uniquely focus on the triple (E_1, P_1, Q_1); the other triple is analogous. Observe that the kernel $\langle ([d]P_1, [c\ell]P_0), ([d]Q_1, [c\ell]Q_0) \rangle$ defines a $(2^b, 2^b)$-polarized isogeny Φ having product codomain $E_0 \times F$ (up to polarized isomorphisms), for some supersingular elliptic curve F. In particular, we can write Φ in its matrix form

$$\begin{pmatrix} \alpha_{1,1} & \alpha_{1,2} \\ \alpha_{2,1} & \alpha_{2,2} \end{pmatrix} : E_1 \times E_0 \to E_0 \times F,$$

where the $\alpha_{i,j}$ are isogenies making the matrix meaningful.

Since $\Phi \circ \hat{\Phi} = [2^b]$, $\deg(\alpha_{1,1}) + \deg(\alpha_{1,2}) = 2^b$. Additionally, $\alpha_{1,1} = [c] \circ \mu_1$ and $\alpha_{1,2} = [d] \circ \mu_2$, which implies $c^2 \deg(\mu_1) + d^2 \deg(\mu_2) = 2^b$. Since $c^2\ell + d^2 = 2^b$, we have $\deg(\mu_1) = \ell \pmod{d^2}$. As a consequence of $d^2 > \ell$, we have that $\deg(\mu_1) = \ell$ and $\deg(\mu_2) = 1$, that is $\alpha_{1,1} = [c] \circ \mu_1$ and $\alpha_{1,2} = [d]$ up to isomorphism.

In particular, the isogeny $\widehat{\mu_1} \colon E_0 \to E_1$ is an ℓ-isogeny between supersingular elliptic curves defined over $\mathbb{F}_p$. The codomains of nonhorizontal ℓ-isogenies are defined over $\mathbb{F}_{p^2} \setminus \mathbb{F}_p$ with overwhelming probability. To be more precise, the amount of supersingular elliptic curves over $\mathbb{F}_p$ is $\mathcal{O}(\sqrt{p})$, while the number of those over $\mathbb{F}_{p^2}$ is $\mathcal{O}(p)$. Therefore, the probability of E_1 being defined over $\mathbb{F}_p$ when $\widehat{\mu_1}$ does not correspond to a horizontal isogeny is $\mathcal{O}(1/\sqrt{p})$, which is negligible in λ. □

6   Sequentiality

The sequentiality of the weak VDF relies on the following assumption.

Assumption 1. *Let ℓ be a prime and p a $\lambda \log(\ell)^3/2$-bit prime, where λ is a security parameter. Let $E_0/\mathbb{F}_p$ be a supersingular elliptic curve with unknown endomorphism ring such that the minimal extension for an ℓ-torsion point of E_0 to be defined over is $\mathbb{F}_{p^k}$, where $k = (\ell - 1)/2$ is a prime. Then, the best technique to evaluate a horizontal ℓ-isogeny with domain E_0 requires $\mathcal{O}(\ell \log \ell)$ $\mathbb{F}_p$-operations, even with access to a quantum computer and arithmetic circuits of breadth $\mathcal{O}(\textbf{poly}(\ell))$.*

Accurately defining wall-clock time in formal terms is a difficult task. For a thorough formal definition of a computational model of real-world time, we refer to [50, Section 3.1]. In what follows, we will argue why Assumption 1 is meaningful providing a strategy that achieves that asymptotic complexity – concretely, we will prove that our weak VDF is $(\mathcal{O}(\mathbf{poly}(\ell)), \mathcal{O}(\ell \log \ell))$−sequential. Throughout this section, we will assume (time) complexity to be the number of arithmetic operations in $\mathbb{F}_p$, unless stated otherwise.

First note that there are many ways to compute an isogeny in this setting. In Subsect. 3.2, we argued that this cannot be done efficiently by means of an equivalent smooth-norm ideal in the class group due to the size of p. Given that we work with a supersingular elliptic curve with unknown endomorphism ring, we can also not use a maximal order in $\mathrm{End}(E_0)$ as discussed in Subsect. 3.3. Using classical modular polynomials is an option, but regardless of their efficiency, they only provide the codomain curve and do not allow us to evaluate the isogeny on points (see Subsect. 3.4).

To the best of our knowledge, all other known ways of evaluating such isogenies require using its kernel polynomial in some way. This polynomial can be constructed from an ℓ-torsion kernel generator by means of Vélu-style formulae, or it can be found as a factor from the ℓ-division polynomial. The latter is a degree-$(\ell^2 - 1)/2$ polynomial which over $\mathbb{F}_p[x]$ factors into two irreducible polynomials of degree $(\ell - 1)/2$ and $(\ell - 1)/2$ irreducible polynomials of degree $\ell - 1$. These two factors of degree $(\ell - 1)/2$ correspond exactly to the kernel polynomials of the horizontal isogenies, so the correct factors are easy to distinguish. Note that the ℓ-division polynomial is of degree $\mathcal{O}(\ell^2)$ however, such that it is infeasible to try to factor this in time $\mathcal{O}(\ell \log \ell)$. For a more elaborate argumentation of this statement, we refer to Appendix A. We will now discuss how to compute this kernel polynomial from a kernel generator, starting with the Fast Fourier Transform (FFT) for arithmetic in $\mathbb{F}_{p^k}$.

6.1   The Parallel FFT

Elements in $\mathbb{F}_{p^k}$ in our setting can be represented as polynomials modulo an irreducible polynomial of degree $k = \mathcal{O}(\ell)$. Hence, multiplying two elements in $\mathbb{F}_{p^k}$ is equivalent to multiplying two polynomials of degree $k - 1$ over $\mathbb{F}_p$. The naive algorithm to multiply such polynomials requires $\mathcal{O}(\ell^2)$ $\mathbb{F}_p$-operations. However, it is possible to lower it down to $\mathcal{O}(\ell \log \ell)$ via the Fast Fourier transform (FFT) [18]. It is worth mentioning that this asymptotic complexity is theoretical and could be difficult to reach in practical applications. In what follows, we will uniquely discuss the best theoretical complexity ignoring engineering challenges. For the sake of designing a VDF, we are only interested in the best case scenario for our delay. In practice, given our choice of k, FFT may perform slightly worse.

One of the main advantages of FFT algorithms is that they can be parallelized. For instance, in [22], Cui-xiang, Guo-qiang and Ming-he describe a parallel FFT algorithm. Assuming one has access to arithmetic circuits of breadth m, this algorithm has complexity $\mathcal{O}((\ell/m) \log \ell)$ with a communication cost of $\mathcal{O}(\log m)$. In particular, for $\ell = m$, the complexity becomes $\mathcal{O}(\log \ell)$ and the communication cost becomes $\mathcal{O}(\log \ell)$. FFT can also be used for multiplying two elements in $\mathbb{F}_p$, but this speed-up is only asymptotic. In practice, even for p thousands of bits, the FFT does not outperform plain Montgomery multiplication. We refer the reader to [18] for further background on FFT.

Other algorithms for multiplying polynomials exist, such as the Toom-Cook multiplication [21,48]. To the best of our knowledge, none of these can be parallelized faster than the FFT. While addition of two polynomials can be done componentwise on all the coefficients with enough separate processors, we do not see how this can happen for multiplication.

6.2 Computing a Point of Order ℓ

An ℓ-torsion point is generated by sampling a random point and multiplying it by its cofactor; i.e. for each $P \in E_0(\mathbb{F}_{p^k})$ and $c = \#E(\mathbb{F}_{p^k})/\ell$ we have that $[c]P \in E_0[\ell]$. In practice, we can restrict ourselves to computing $x([c]P)$ since x-only arithmetic can be used to compute isogenies (see for instance [16]). This may require an isomorphism from $E_0/\mathbb{F}_p$ to a curve in Montgomery form, but this comes at negligible cost. Writing c as $\sum_{i=0}^{k-1} a_i p^i$, we can use the following strategy to obtain $[c]P$.

First, for all $i \in \{0, \ldots, k-1\}$, we compute and store $[a_i]P$. This can be done in parallel in $\mathcal{O}(\log p)$ $\mathbb{F}_{p^k}$-operations, which corresponds to $\mathcal{O}((\ell/m) \log p \log \ell)$ $\mathbb{F}_p$-operations using arithmetic circuits of breadth m for each of the arithmetic circuits of breadth $k = \mathcal{O}(\ell)$ we are using to compute the $[a_i]P$'s. This implies we should use arithmetic circuits of breadth mk just for this step.

We observe that

$$[c]P = [a_0]P + [p]([a_1]P + [p]([a_2]P + \ldots + [p]([a_{k-2}]P + [p][a_{k-1}]P))).$$

Since E is supersingular, $\pi^2 = [-p]$. Hence, to compute $[p]Q$ for any $Q \in E$, we need to apply the p-Frobenius twice. Each Frobenius costs $\mathcal{O}(\ell)$ $\mathbb{F}_p$-operations, which can be reduced to $\mathcal{O}(1)$ $\mathbb{F}_p$-multiplications using arithmetic circuits of breadth k. Summing two points $P_1, P_2 \in E(\mathbb{F}_{p^k})$ requires $\mathcal{O}(1)$ $\mathbb{F}_{p^k}$-operations, which amounts to $\mathcal{O}(\log \ell)$ $\mathbb{F}_p$-operations using parallel FFT with arithmetic circuits of breadth k. Therefore, each sum of the form $[a_{i-1}]P + [p][a_i]Q$ can be done in $\mathcal{O}(\log \ell)$ $\mathbb{F}_p$-operations using parallel FFT.

To compute $[c]P$, we need to perform $\mathcal{O}(\ell)$ operations of the form $[a_{i-1}]P + [p][a_i]Q$, which amounts to $\mathcal{O}(\ell \log \ell)$ $\mathbb{F}_p$-operations. Therefore, having arithmetic circuits of breadth mk, the asymptotic cost of computing a point of order ℓ is

$$\mathcal{O}(\max\{\ell \log \ell, (\ell/m) \log p \log \ell\})$$

$\mathbb{F}_p$-operations. Therefore, taking $m \approx \log p$, computing a point of order ℓ takes $\mathcal{O}(\ell \log \ell)$ $\mathbb{F}_p$-operations with arithmetic circuits of breadth $2k \log p$.

Remark 4. Note that in our weak VDF protocol one needs to sample two ℓ-torsion points corresponding to two horizontal ℓ-isogenies; one is on the curve itself and one is on the twist. In protocols such as CSIDH, this is typically done by using x-only arithmetic as described here, followed by a square check for the y-coordinate to see on which curve the point is. Given that a square check is much more expensive over $\mathbb{F}_{p^k}$ than over $\mathbb{F}_p$ for large k, one can instead opt to use the Elligator point sampling method (see for example [3,38]). Indeed, as our protocol does not need to differentiate between the ℓ-torsion point on the curve and the one on the twist, we can simply compute both simultaneously.

6.3   Computing the Kernel Polynomial

There are several ways of constructing the kernel polynomial given a kernel generator. For instance, in [5], they provide an asymptotic speed-up over the classical Vélu formulae by a square-root factor. In [30], a new algorithm to compute the kernel polynomials from irrational points is also provided. While these works may be of interest, they all assume the knowledge of the x-coordinate of an ℓ-torsion point, which we argued has already complexity $\mathcal{O}(\ell \log \ell)$. So it suffices for us to provide a way of computing the kernel polynomial in this time complexity.

Let $P \in E(\mathbb{F}_{p^{\ell-1}})$ be a point of order ℓ such that $x(P) \in \mathbb{F}_{p^k}$. Our goal is to compute the isogeny having kernel $\langle P \rangle$ only utilising the x-coordinate of P. We will show a strategy to do so having arithmetic circuits of breadth $\mathcal{O}(\ell)$. To obtain the set $\mathcal{P} := \{x([s]P) \mid s = 1, \ldots, k\}$, using arithmetic circuits of breadth $k = (\ell - 1)/2$, each of the arithmetic circuits of breadth k will compute one of the elements in $\mathcal{P}$ at the same time. The most demanding task is to compute $x([k]P)$, which requires $\mathcal{O}(\log \ell)$ $\mathbb{F}_{p^k}$-operations. Equivalently, $\mathcal{O}(\ell/m'(\log \ell)^2)$ $\mathbb{F}_p$-operations employing parallel FFT with arithmetic circuits of breadth m'. As a result, computing $\mathcal{P}$ takes $\mathcal{O}(\ell \log \ell)$ $\mathbb{F}_p$-operations using arithmetic circuits of breadth $m'k$.

The kernel polynomial is given precisely by

$$P(x) = \prod_{x_i \in \mathcal{P}} (x - x_i).$$

This product can be computed pairwise in a (binary) tree of height $\log(k)$, where each step requires some multiplications over $\mathbb{F}_{p^k}$. More precisely, using arithmetic circuits of breadth m', we can use parallel FFT such that it takes $\mathcal{O}((\ell/m') \log \ell)$ $\mathbb{F}_p$-operations. The computation of $P(x)$ will thus take $\mathcal{O}((\ell/m')(\log \ell)^2)$ $\mathbb{F}_p$-operations. Taking arithmetic circuits of breadth $m' = \lceil \log \ell \rceil$, we then have that computing this kernel polynomial requires at most $\mathcal{O}(\ell \log \ell)$ $\mathbb{F}_p$-operations. From this degree-k kernel polynomial $P(x) \in \mathbb{F}_p[x]$, one can evaluate the corresponding isogeny in time $\mathcal{O}(\ell)$ with well-known formulae such as those in [35].

7   Conclusion

In this paper, we have introduced a novel weak Verifiable Delay Function (VDF) that is resistant to quantum attacks. Our construction is based on isogenies, which are mappings between elliptic curves, and leverages the strengths of elliptic curves and elliptic products to enable efficient verification of slow one-dimensional isogenies. The slowness of these isogenies arises from the fact that their kernel generators are defined over large extension fields. This feature contributes to their resistance against quantum attacks. Our weak VDF incorporates two horizontal delay-generating isogenies, and their computation is verified in dimension two through the reconstruction of these isogenies.

We implemented the weak VDF described in Sect. 3 in SageMath. The source code is freely available at https://github.com/pq-vdf-isogeny/pq-vdf-isogeny. The purpose of this implementation is to demonstrate the correctness of the algorithm. It is important to note that this implementation should be considered as a proof-of-concept (the size of p in the default parameters is 256 bits and does not meet the security requirements), and there is room for optimizing several subroutines. Notably, the parallel algorithms outlined in Subsects. 6.3 and 6.2 have not been included in the provided source code.

Additionally, to enhance performance, lower-level languages such as C and leveraging platform-specific instructions such as AVX could be utilized. By adopting these techniques, it is possible to significantly reduce the running time of the implementation. Ideally, when evaluating isogeny-based delay functions, the utilization of specialized hardware or Field-Programmable Gate Arrays (FPGAs) would be beneficial.

Throughout the paper, we have identified and discussed several open problems in this area. One such problem is the requirement for curves with an unknown endomorphism ring as input without the ability to rely on a trusted setup. This issue has been a persistent challenge in various isogeny-based protocols and continues to be an active area of research.

Acknowledgments. We would like to thank the CRYPTO 2023 and LATINCRYPT 2023 anonymous reviewers; in particular the CRYPTO reviewer pointing out the attack described in Subsect. 3.2. We would also like to thank Wouter Castryck, Chloe Martindale and Frederik Vercauteren for fruitful discussions and feedback on a previous version of this manuscript. This work was supported in part by CyberSecurity Research Flanders with reference number VR20192203, by the European Research Council (ERC) under the European Union's Horizon 2020 research and innovation programme (grant agreement ISOCRYPT - No. 101020788) and by the UK Engineering and Physical Sciences Research Council (EPSRC) Centre for Doctoral Training (CDT) in Trust, Identity, Privacy and Security in Large-scale Infrastructures (TIPS-at-Scale) at the Universities of Bristol and Bath.

A   Factoring the ℓ-Division Polynomial

The ℓ-division polynomial in our setting is a degree-$(\ell^2 - 1)/2$ polynomial in $\mathbb{F}_p[x]$. The fastest way to construct this polynomial is by a recurrence relationship taking $\mathcal{O}(\ell^2 \log \ell)$ multiplications. Remark that the ℓ-division polynomial can be precomputed from a specific form of elliptic curves (e.g. based on a Montgomery coefficient A). Both the degree of the ℓ-division polynomial as well as the degree of A in this precomputation are $\mathcal{O}(\ell^2)$. Hence, using arithmetic circuits of breadth $m = \mathcal{O}(\ell^4)$, one can evaluate the expression in A by means of square-and-multiply in time $\mathcal{O}(\log \ell)$.

The ℓ-division polynomial factors in $\ell+1$ factors of degree $(\ell-1)/2$ in $\mathbb{F}_{p^2}[x]$, where each factor determines a kernel polynomial of an ℓ-isogeny. In [49], von zur Gathen and Panario survey some algorithms to factor polynomials over finite field. Even though in our case we could use the more efficient equal-degree factorization algorithms, their complexity is not competitive with the strategy we described in Sect. 6. However, it is worth noting that this survey does not consider parallel versions of these algorithms. In [32], Gathen describes a parallel version of the Cantor-Zassenhaus's algorithm [13]. Adapting the complexity in [32, Theorem 4.1] to our setting, factoring the ℓ-division over $\mathbb{F}_{p^2}$ requires $\mathcal{O}(\log^2 \ell \log p)$ $\mathbb{F}_p$-operations utilising arithmetic circuits of breadth $\mathcal{O}(\mathbf{poly}(\ell^2))$.

Despite being polynomial in ℓ^2, and in turn allowed by the definition of weak VDF, the exponent of $\mathbf{poly}(\ell^2)$ is likely to be huge. For instance, one of the steps of Cantor-Zassenhaus parallel algorithm relies on the computation of the quotient and reminder of two polynomials. As explained in [12, Remark 2], this step itself reaches complexity $\mathcal{O}(\log^2 n)$ when $\mathcal{O}(n^{3.5})$ parallel processors are employed, where n is the degree of the two polynomials.[3] This essential step is required for $\mathbf{poly}(n)$ parallel steps, further increasing the breadth of arithmetic circuits required by Cantor-Zassenhaus parallel algorithm. A brief discussion on the exponent of the polynomial describing the breadth of arithmetic circuits required by this algorithm is contained in [39], where the authors estimate the exponent to be 13. Thus, one would need arithmetic circuits of breadth $\mathcal{O}(\ell^{26})$ to apply this algorithm in our case. For instance, if the delay parameter t provided as input in Setup is as small as 2^5, one already needs arithmetic circuits of breadth $\sim 2^{130}$, which is an unrealistic requirement. On top of this analysis, we shall also mention that the algorithm is theoretical and does not take into account communication costs. A real-world implementation of this algorithm would be a major breakthrough on its own.

Finally, to the best of our knowledge, no known quantum algorithm can help us factor polynomials over finite fields faster. Doliskani gives a quantum algorithm that can factor a degree-n polynomial over $\mathbb{F}_q$ in $\mathcal{O}(n^{1+o(1)} \log^{2+o(1)} q)$ bit operations [27]. In our case however, this reduces to $\mathcal{O}(\ell^{2+o(1)} \log^{2+o(1)} p)$ for factoring the ℓ-division polynomial, and hence provides no speed-up.

References

1. Arpin, S., et al.: Adventures in supersingularland. Exp. Math. (2021). https://doi.org/10.1080/10586458.2021.1926009
2. Azarderakhsh, R., et al.: Supersingular Isogeny Key Encapsulation (2017). http://sike.org

---

[3] It is possible to have complexity $\mathcal{O}(\log n)$ if arithmetic circuits of breadth $\mathcal{O}(n^{15})$ are used.

3. Banegas, G., et al.: Disorientation faults in CSIDH. In: Advances in Cryptology - EUROCRYPT 2023, part II, pp. 310–342. Springer, Heidelberg (2023). https://doi.org/10.1007/978-3-031-30589-4_11

4. Basso, A., et al.: Supersingular curves you can trust. In: EUROCRYPT 2023, Part II, pp. 405–437. Springer, Heidelberg (2023). https://doi.org/10.1007/978-3-031-30617-4_14

5. Bernstein, D.J., De Feo, L., Leroux, A., Smith, B.: Faster computation of isogenies of large prime degree. ANTS-XIV Open Book Series 4(1), 39–55 (2020). https://doi.org/10.2140/obs.2020.4.39

6. Bernstein, D.J., Lange, T.: Montgomery curves and the Montgomery ladder. Cryptology ePrint Archive, Paper 2017/293 (2017). https://eprint.iacr.org/2017/293

7. Beullens, W., De Feo, L., Galbraith, S., Petit, C.: Proving knowledge of isogenies: a survey. Des. Codes Cryptogr. (2023). https://doi.org/10.1007/s10623-023-01243-3

8. Beullens, W., Kleinjung, T., Vercauteren, F.: CSI-FiSh: Efficient isogeny based signatures through class group computations. In: ASIACRYPT 2019, Part I. pp. 227–247. Springer (2019), https://doi.org/10.1007/978-3-030-34578-5_9

9. Boneh, D., Bünz, B., Fisch, B.: A survey of two verifiable delay functions. Cryptology ePrint Archive, Paper 2018/712 (2018). https://eprint.iacr.org/2018/712

10. Boneh, D., Bonneau, J., Bünz, B., Fisch, B.: Verifiable delay functions. In: Shacham, H., Boldyreva, A. (eds.) CRYPTO 2018. LNCS, vol. 10991, pp. 757–788. Springer, Cham (2018). https://doi.org/10.1007/978-3-319-96884-1_25

11. Booher, J., et al.: Failing to hash into supersingular isogeny graphs. Cryptology ePrint Archive, Report 2022/518 (2022). https://eprint.iacr.org/2022/518

12. Borodin, A., von zur Gathen, J., Hopcroft, J.: Fast parallel matrix and GCD computations. Inf. Control 52(3), 241–256 (1982). https://doi.org/10.1016/S0019-9958(82)90766-5

13. Cantor, D.G., Zassenhaus, H.: A new algorithm for factoring polynomials over finite fields. Math. Comput. 36, 587–592 (1981). https://doi.org/10.2307/2007663

14. Castryck, W., Decru, T.: An efficient key recovery attack on SIDH. In: EUROCRYPT 2023, Part II, pp. 423–447. Springer, Heidelberg (2023). https://doi.org/10.1007/978-3-031-30589-4_15

15. Castryck, W., Decru, T., Smith, B.: Hash functions from superspecial genus-2 curves using Richelot isogenies. J. Math. Cryptol. 14(1), 268–292 (2020). https://doi.org/10.1515/jmc-2019-0021

16. Castryck, W., Lange, T., Martindale, C., Panny, L., Renes, J.: CSIDH: an efficient post-quantum commutative group action. In: Peyrin, T., Galbraith, S. (eds.) ASIACRYPT 2018. LNCS, vol. 11274, pp. 395–427. Springer, Cham (2018). https://doi.org/10.1007/978-3-030-03332-3_15

17. Chavez-Saab, J., Rodríguez-Henríquez, F., Tibouchi, M.: Verifiable isogeny walks: towards an isogeny-based postquantum VDF. In: AlTawy, R., Hülsing, A. (eds.) SAC 2021. LNCS, vol. 13203, pp. 441–460. Springer, Cham (2022). https://doi.org/10.1007/978-3-030-99277-4_21

18. Chu, E., George, A.: Inside the FFT Black Box: Serial and Parallel Fast Fourier Transform Algorithms. CRC Press, Boca Raton (1999). https://doi.org/10.1201/9780367802332

19. Cohen, H., et al.: Handbook of Elliptic and Hyperelliptic Curve Cryptography. CRC Press, Boca Raton (2005)

20. Cong, K., Lai, Y.F., Levin, S.: Efficient isogeny proofs using generic techniques. In: Applied Cryptography and Network Security, pp. 248–275. Springer, Heidelberg (2023). https://doi.org/10.1007/978-3-031-33491-7_10

21. Cook, S.A.: On the minimum computation time of functions. Ph.D. thesis, Harvard University (1966)
22. Cui-xiang, Z., Guo-qiang, H., Ming-he, H.: Some new parallel fast Fourier transform algorithms. In: Sixth International Conference on Parallel and Distributed Computing Applications and Technologies (PDCAT 2005), pp. 624–628 (2005). https://doi.org/10.1109/PDCAT.2005.224
23. De Feo, L.: Mathematics of isogeny based cryptography. The Arxive abs/1711.04062 (2017). http://arxiv.org/abs/1711.04062
24. De Feo, L., Jao, D., Plût, J.: Towards quantum-resistant cryptosystems from supersingular elliptic curve isogenies. J. Math. Cryptol. 8(3), 209–247 (2014). https://doi.org/10.1515/jmc-2012-0015
25. De Feo, L., Masson, S., Petit, C., Sanso, A.: Verifiable delay functions from supersingular isogenies and pairings. In: Galbraith, S.D., Moriai, S. (eds.) ASIACRYPT 2019. LNCS, vol. 11921, pp. 248–277. Springer, Cham (2019). https://doi.org/10.1007/978-3-030-34578-5_10
26. Delfs, C., Galbraith, S.D.: Computing isogenies between supersingular elliptic curves over $\mathbb{F}_p$. Des. Codes Cryptogr. 78(2), 425–440 (2016). https://doi.org/10.1007/s10623-014-0010-1
27. Doliskani, J.: Toward an optimal quantum algorithm for polynomial factorization over finite fields. Quant. Info. Comput. 19(1–2), 1–13 (2019)
28. Döttling, N., Garg, S., Malavolta, G., Vasudevan, P.N.: Tight verifiable delay functions. In: Galdi, C., Kolesnikov, V. (eds.) SCN 2020. LNCS, vol. 12238, pp. 65–84. Springer, Cham (2020). https://doi.org/10.1007/978-3-030-57990-6_4
29. Elkies, N.D.: Elliptic and modular curves over finite fields and related computational issues. In: Computational Perspectives on Number Theory, Studies in Advanced Mathematics, vol. 7, pp. 21–76. AMS (1998)
30. Eriksen, J.K., Panny, L., Sotáková, J., Veroni, M.: Deuring for the people: supersingular elliptic curves with prescribed endomorphism ring in general characteristic. Cryptology ePrint Archive, Paper 2023/106 (2023). https://eprint.iacr.org/2023/106
31. Fouotsa, T.B., Petit, C.: A new adaptive attack on SIDH. In: Galbraith, S.D. (ed.) CT-RSA 2022. LNCS, vol. 13161, pp. 322–344. Springer, Cham (2022). https://doi.org/10.1007/978-3-030-95312-6_14
32. von zur Gathen, J.: Parallel algorithms for algebraic problems. In: Symposium on Theory of Computing, STOC 1983, pp. 17–23. Association for Computing Machinery (1983). https://doi.org/10.1145/800061.808728
33. Giacomelli, I., Madsen, J., Orlandi, C.: ZKBoo: faster zero-knowledge for boolean circuits. In: Conference on Security Symposium, SEC 2016, pp. 1069–1083. USENIX Association (2016)
34. Kani, E.: The number of curves of genus two with elliptic differentials. J. für die reine und angewandte Mathematik 1997(485), 93–122 (1997). https://doi.org/10.1515/crll.1997.485.93
35. Kohel, D.R.: Endomorphism rings of elliptic curves over finite fields. Ph.D. thesis, University of California, Berkeley (1996)
36. Leroux, A.: A new isogeny representation and applications to cryptography. In: ASIACRYPT 2022, Part II, pp. 3–35. Springer, Heidelberg (2022). https://doi.org/10.1007/978-3-031-22966-4_1
37. Maino, L., Martindale, C., Panny, L., Pope, G., Wesolowski, B.: A direct key recovery attack on SIDH. In: EUROCRYPT 2023, Part II, pp. 448–471. Springer, Heidelberg (2023). https://doi.org/10.1007/978-3-031-30589-4_16

38. Meyer, M., Campos, F., Reith, S.: On lions and elligators: an efficient constant-time implementation of CSIDH. In: Ding, J., Steinwandt, R. (eds.) PQCrypto 2019. LNCS, vol. 11505, pp. 307–325. Springer, Cham (2019). https://doi.org/10.1007/978-3-030-25510-7_17

39. Morgenstern, M., Shamir, E.: Parallel algorithms for arithmetics, irreducibility and factoring of GFq-polynomials. Technical report, Stanford University (1983). https://dl.acm.org/doi/10.5555/892306

40. Mula, M., Murru, N., Pintore, F.: On Random Sampling of Supersingular Elliptic Curves. Cryptology ePrint Archive, Paper 2022/528 (2022). https://eprint.iacr.org/2022/528

41. Panny, L.: CSI–FiSh really isn't polynomial-time. https://yx7.cc/blah/2023-04-14.html#fn5

42. Pietrzak, K.: Simple verifiable delay functions. In: Innovations in Theoretical Computer Science (ITCS 2019). Leibniz International Proceedings in Informatics (LIPIcs), vol. 124, pp. 60:1–60:15. Schloss Dagstuhl-Leibniz-Zentrum fuer Informatik (2018). https://doi.org/10.4230/LIPIcs.ITCS.2019.60

43. Robert, D.: Breaking SIDH in polynomial time. In: EUROCRYPT 2023, Part II, pp. 472–503. Springer, Heidelberg (2023). https://doi.org/10.1007/978-3-031-30589-4_17

44. Silverman, J.H.: The Arithmetic of Elliptic Curves, vol. 106. Springer, Heidelberg (2009). https://doi.org/10.1007/978-0-387-09494-6

45. Smith, B.: Explicit endomorphisms and correspondences. Ph.D. thesis, University of Sydney (2006)

46. Sutherland, A.: On the evaluation of modular polynomials. Open Book Ser. 1(1), 531–555 (2013). https://dx.doi.org/10.2140/obs.2013.1.531

47. Tan, T.G., Sharma, V., Li, Z., Szalachowski, P., Zhou, J.: ZKBdf: a ZKBoo-based quantum-secure verifiable delay function with prover-secret. Cryptology ePrint Archive, Paper 2022/1373 (2022). https://eprint.iacr.org/2022/1373

48. Toom, A.L.: The complexity of a scheme of functional elements realizing the multiplication of integers. In: Soviet Mathematics Doklady, vol. 3, pp. 714–716 (1963)

49. von zur Gathen, J., Panario, D.: Factoring polynomials over finite fields: a survey. J. Symb. Comput. 31(1), 3–17 (2001). https://doi.org/10.1006/jsco.1999.1002

50. Wesolowski, B.: Efficient verifiable delay functions. J. Cryptol. 33(4), 2113–2147 (2020). https://doi.org/10.1007/s00145-020-09364-x

Discrete Logarithm Problem

Making the Identity-Based Diffie–Hellman Key Exchange Efficiently Revocable

Kohei Nakagawa[1]([⊠]), Atsushi Fujioka[2], Akira Nagai[1], Junichi Tomida[1], Keita Xagawa[3], and Kan Yasuda[1]

[1] NTT Corporation, Tokyo, Japan
kohei.nakagawa@ntt.com
[2] Kanagawa University, Yokohama, Japan
[3] Technology Innovation Institute, Abu Dhabi, UAE

Abstract. We propose an efficient identity-based authenticated-key exchange (IB-AKE) protocol that is equipped with scalable key revocation. Our protocol builds upon the most efficient identity-based Diffie–Hellman key exchange (without revocation mechanisms) presented by Fiore and Gennaro at CT-RSA 2010, which can be constructed from pairing-free groups. The key revocation is essential for IB-AKE protocols in long-term practical operation. Our key revocation mechanism allows the key exchange protocol to remain comparable to the original Fiore–Gennaro identity-based key exchange, unlike other revocable schemes that require major (inefficient) modifications to their original IB-AKE protocols. Moreover, our revocation mechanism is scalable, in the sense that its computational cost is logarithmic, rather than linear, to the number of users. We provide a security proof in the identity-based extended Canetti–Krawczyk security model that is further extended in order to incorporate key revocation. The security of our scheme reduces to the well-established strong Diffie–Hellman assumption. For this proof, we devise a *multi-forking lemma*, an extended version of the general forking lemma.

Keywords: Identity-based authenticated-key exchange · Revocable · Elliptic-curve cryptography · Pairing-free · Protocol implementations · ARM Cortex-M MCU · General forking lemma · Random oracle model

1 Introduction

Secretly and reliably establishing a session key is the initial and vital step of secure communication between parties. This step can be realized by a cryptographic algorithm called an authenticated-key exchange (AKE) protocol. The security of session keys established by an AKE protocol is based on that of static secret keys, each of which must be ensured by each corresponding party prior to beginning their sessions.

© The Author(s), under exclusive license to Springer Nature Switzerland AG 2023
A. Aly and M. Tibouchi (Eds.): LATINCRYPT 2023, LNCS 14168, pp. 171–191, 2023.
https://doi.org/10.1007/978-3-031-44469-2_9

There are two different systems for ensuring static secret keys. Widespread are public-key infrastructures (PKIs), where each party generates a pair of a public key and a private (i.e., static secret) key and requests a certificate authority (CA) to issue a digital certificate that guarantees the identity of the party together with the public key. On the other hand, relatively new (though the idea has been around for approximately four decades [41]) is identity-based cryptography. Here, the private key generator (PKG) who has the master secret key issues static secret keys corresponding to the identifiers (e.g., device serial numbers) of its clients (i.e., parties) and distributes each key to the corresponding client. The clients, having their static secret keys, can communicate with each other using a common identity-based cryptographic algorithm. In reality, several identity-based cryptosystems have been already standardized [10,15,23,39] and put into practical use [14,48,53].

Today, identity-based cryptography has attracted attention again with the spread of the Internet of things (IoT) [44,49]. There are a couple of reasons. One is that a client can initiate its cryptographic algorithm to communicate with another client by just specifying its identifier: there is no need to verify public keys as in PKI. This feature fits a number of IoT scenarios where the identifiers are given systematically [1]. Another is that the certificateless feature reduces communication costs. Smaller data traffic is suitable for wireless sensor networks (WSNs), which have limited bandwidths and are widely adopted by IoT systems [30,33].

In either case of PKI-based or identity-based cryptography, it is crucial to equip the system with a key revocation mechanism if we want to operate the system for an extended period of time. In the case of PKI-based cryptography, basically, a digital certificate is valid until its expiration date, written in a field of the certificate. In order to revoke certificates before their expiration, a CA issues a certificate revocation list or provides service via the Online Certificate Status Protocol . In the case of identity-based cryptography, the basic idea of revocation is that the PKG issues key update information and distributes it to the (still-valid) clients. Then only those clients that remain valid can update their secret keys, whereas revoked clients would not, even if they have somehow received the update information.

It is desirable that such updating by the PKG is efficient. Note that it can be costly when the number of clients becomes large. For example, if the PKG is to generate key update information for each valid client [9], then the computational cost would increase linearly with the number of clients. Clearly, such a mechanism would not be scalable. Hence many of the revocable identity-based cryptographic algorithms are equipped with much more efficient (i.e., scalable) mechanisms [8,37,43].

A significant challenge to the above setting is the computational overhead. Most of the identity-based cryptographic (AKE or encryption) algorithms rely on the use of pairings whose computation is one order of magnitude more expensive than a scalar multiplication [24,35]. Such a high computational cost is not acceptable to resource-restricted IoT devices. Moreover, the use of pairings involves a dedicated (i.e., pairing-friendly) elliptic curve whose size is nearly twice that of an ordinary one when the security levels are the same (e.g., the 461-bit Barreto–Lynn–Scott curve or the 462-bit Barreto–Naehrig curve vs. a 256-bit ordinary curve for 128-bit security) [5]. This incurs extra communication overhead, counteracting the certificateless effect of identity-based cryptography.

Fortunately, for AKE (rather than encryption), there exists an exceptionally efficient protocol: the identity-based authenticated-key exchange (IB-AKE) presented by Fiore and Gennaro (FG IB-AKE) [19]. The FG IB-AKE is based on the Diffie–Hellman (DH) key exchange and does not require pairings. The protocol is secure in the random oracle model (ROM) under the well-established strong DH assumption. There have been some variants proposed [11,36,45,46,57], and they all essentially rely on the FG IB-AKE.

The main theme of this paper is to make this outstanding IB-AKE protocol revocable, in a scalable manner, but the task in hand is challenging. As far as we know, there are two lines of works to date that study IB-AKE with revocation: Okano et al. showed how to generically construct revocable (hierarchical) IB-AKE satisfying the above requirements from CCA-secure revocable (hierarchical) identity-based encryption [37], and Tsai et al. considers IB-AKE scheme with non-scalable revocation (the computational cost of the key update is linear in the total number of parties) [50,51,55,56]. Hence, the techniques used in these works seem not to fit our purpose of equipping the FG IB-AKE protocol with a scalable revocation mechanism. Furthermore, the security requirement for revocable identity-based authenticated-key exchange is much different from that for revocable identity-based *encryption* (RIBE) (cf. Sect. 1.2), and thus we need rather different techniques from those developed in RIBE.

1.1   Our Contribution

Our main contribution is that we construct an efficient revocable identity-based authenticated-key exchange (RIB-AKE) protocol with scalability. Our protocol is based on the FG IB-AKE [19] and can be constructed from pairing-free groups. To the best of our knowledge, our RIB-AKE protocol is the first one without pairings and is estimated to be over 50 times faster than any other existing RIB-AKE protocols depending on the curves [37,50,51,55,56]. Furthermore, our protocol is easy to deploy as it does not use pairings and works with standard elliptic curve libraries, such as the OpenSSL library or the Mbed TLS library. For security, we adopt the rid-eCK model, which is a non-hierarchical version of the rhid-eCK model [37] and based on one of the strongest models for IB-AKE, namely, the identity-based eCK model [26]. The rid-eCK model incorporates a wide range of security notions such as forward secrecy, ephemeral secret key leak resistance, and current secret key exposure resistance (CSKER). Finally, we prove that our RIB-AKE protocol is rid-eCK secure under the strong Diffie–Hellman assumption in the ROM.

1.2   Related Works

There are many studies on how to construct revocable identity-based encryption (RIBE) schemes, unlike RIB-AKE protocols, and we referred to these studies to construct RIB-AKE protocols. Therefore, we briefly recall RIBE here. The first RIBE scheme was proposed by Boneh and Franklin [9] (BF RIBE). The BF RIBE naively achieved the key revocation system by sending key update information to all non-revoked parties. However, the BF RIBE has a problem in which the computational time for key updates increases linearly with the number of parties. From the perspective of large-scale operation, the key update time should be in logarithmic order in the number of parties. When a revocation mechanism satisfies this requirement, it is said to be *scalable*.

The first scalable RIBE scheme was proposed by Boldyreva, Goyal, and Kumar [8]. They achieved scalability by using a binary tree, where each party is assigned to a leaf, and an algorithm called KUNode. KUNode outputs the highest nodes, none of whose descendants are revoked. This approach is similar to the Subset Cover framework which was used for broadcast encryption [4]. Since then, many scalable RIBE schemes using KUNode have been proposed [25,32,58].

Seo and Emura proposed the *decryption key exposure resistance* (DKER) and showed that these RIBE schemes are not secure enough because they do not have DKER which the BF RIBE has. Therefore, in their same paper, they also proposed a scalable RIBE scheme with DKER. Since then, a lot of RIBE schemes with DKER have been proposed [17,27,31,34,47,52,54].

1.3   Technical Overview

Fiore–Gennaro IB-AKE: We first briefly recall the notion of IB-AKE. In an IB-AKE system, the PKG first generates a master public key (MPK) and a master secret key (MSK) to start the system. On the request of static secret key (SSK) generation from a party with identity ID, the PKG generates one for ID using the MSK and gives it to the party. A pair of parties holding their SSKs can run a key exchange protocol based on their identities to securely share a session key. In the protocol, each party sends a message called an ephemeral public key (EPK) to the partner, and the randomness used to generate the EPK is called an ephemeral secret key (ESK).

Our starting point is the FG IB-AKE [19]. Roughly speaking, this IB-AKE mixes the Diffie–Hellman key exchange with Schnorr signatures [42]. The MPK and MSK of FG IB-AKE are the verification and signing keys of the Schnorr signature scheme, respectively. That is, the MSK is a random $\mathbb{Z}_q$ element x and the corresponding MPK is g^x. A static secret key for a party ID is a Schnorr signature for the message ID, namely, $(g^r, s = r + xH(g^r \parallel ID))$. In the key exchange protocol, each party chooses a random exponent w as an ESK and sends (g^r, g^w) to the partner as an EPK. When two parties engage in the key exchange protocol, one has (s, w) as (SSK, ESK), and the other has (s', w'), both parties can compute $Z_1 = g^{(w+s)(w'+s')}$ and $Z_2 = g^{ww'}$ after exchanging EPKs. Then, they use these terms to derive a session key $SK = H'(Z_1, Z_2)$ where H' is a key derivation function modeled as a random oracle.

Making the FG IB-AKE id-eCK-secure: Cheng and Ma [13] pointed out the FG IB-AKE is insecure against an attack compromising an ephemeral secret key: roughly speaking, if the adversary knows an ephemeral secret key of a party A, then it can impersonate any honest party and share a correct session key with the party A. Thus, the original FG IB-AKE does not achieve id-eCK security. Ni et al. [36] proposed two variants of the FG IB-AKE by doubling the static secret key, in which the static secret key consists of *two* Schnorr signatures, and show that both protocols are id-eCK secure.

To make the scheme id-eCK secure more efficiently, we solve the issue in a different manner: we introduce an additional term $Z_3 = g^{ss'}$ computed from the parties' SSK, and make a session key involve the additional term. This technique is inspired by the id-eCK secure IB-AKE protocol by Fujioka et al. [20]. Intuitively, amid the security proof in the id-eCK model there exists a case where the reduction algorithm can extract only $Z = g^{uv+ss'}$ from the queries to the random oracle H' where g^{uv} is the answer of the strong DH problem. Adding Z_3 to the session key derivation allows the reduction algorithm to extract Z_3 and compute $g^{uv} = Z/Z_3$.

Revocable IB-AKE: As well as RIBE, RIB-AKE [37] allows the PKG to revoke parties. More precisely, the PKG maintains a revocation list, which contains revoked parties, and *key-update information*. Each party uses a *current secret key* (CSK) instead of a static secret key to run the RIB-AKE protocol. A legitimate party computes its CSK from its SSK and the key update information published by the PKG in the current time period. However, the revoked parties in the revocation list cannot compute their CSK for the current time period from their SSK and the key update information.

Recap of Previous Revocable IBEs: In order to construct efficient RIB-AKE protocols, we employ the subset cover framework using KUNode [4,25,32,47,58] following previous constructions of RIBE (for KUNode, see Sect. 3.1). In this framework, we can publicly compute a set P_{ID} for any party ID and a set Q for any set of revoked parties such that: 1) the sizes of P_{ID} and Q are logarithmic in the total number of parties; 2) P_{ID} and Q have exactly one shared element (denoted by θ) if party ID is not revoked; and 3) P_{ID} and Q are disjoint if party ID is revoked.

Most previous RIBE schemes based on pairings and the KUNode framework basically use the following blueprint. Informally, the static secret key ssk_{ID} for ID and the key update information ku_T for time period T can be written as

$$ssk_{ID} = (g^{r_i}, g^{\alpha+E(ID,r_i)+F(i)})_{i\in P_{ID}}, \quad ku_T = (g^{t_i}, g^{E'(T,t_i)-F(i)})_{i\in Q}$$

where g is a generator of pairing groups, α is the MSK, r_i, t_i are random exponents, E, E' are IBE encodings, and F is a pseudorandom function. For now considering E, E' as the encoding of Boneh-Boyen IBE [3] suffices where $E(ID, r_i) = r_i(IDu + h)$. In the CSK generation, only non-revoked parties can compute $csk_{ID,T} = (g^{r_\theta}, g^{t_\theta}, g^{\alpha+E(ID,r_\theta)+E'(T,t_\theta)})$ (recall that θ is the intersection of P_{ID} and Q). The point is that $csk_{ID,T}$ works as a secret key of IBE for identity (ID, T) and can be used to decrypt a ciphertext for identity (ID, T), which represents one for identity ID in the time period T.

However, if $csk_{ID,T}$ is revealed, the adversary can compute ssk_{ID} since ku_T is public in the above construction. This is called the CSK exposure attack. To prevent the attack, previous RIBE schemes re-randomize $csk_{ID,T}$ in the CSK generation and outputs $csk'_{ID,T} = (g^{r'}, g^{t'}, g^{\alpha+E(ID,r')+E'(T,t')})$ where r', t' are fresh random exponents. Such re-randomization is possible via linear operations given the MPK.

Our Design: A naive idea to make FG IB-AKE revocable is to apply the above template to it. However, it quickly turns out that a CSK in the candidate FG IB-AKE with revocation using the above idea is *not* re-randomizable: we would have

$$csk_{ID,T} = (g^{r_\theta}, g^{t_\theta}, r_\theta + t_\theta + x(H(g^{r_\theta}||ID) + H(g^{t_\theta}||T)))$$

by the adaptation of the above template, but how to compute the third element that is consistent with the re-randomized first and second elements is unclear. The problem lies in the fact that to re-randomize r_θ, t_θ we need to also change the inputs to the hash function H to compute the third element.

To circumvent this problem, we devise a completely different approach from RIBE. In our scheme, a SSK for party ID is the same as the FG IB-AKE, namely, $ssk_{ID} = (g^r, s = r + xH(g^r||ID))$. The key update information ku_T for time period T consists of a set of Schnorr signatures $(g^{r_i}, s_i = r_i + xH(g^{r_i}||(i, T)))_{i \in Q}$ for the elements in Q and T. In the CSK generation, party ID takes (ssk_{ID}, ku_T), choose a random exponent $\hat{r}$, and computes

$$csk_{ID,T} = (g^r, g^{r_\theta}, g^{\hat{r}}, \hat{s} = \hat{r} + (s + s_\theta)H(g^{\hat{r}}||(ID, T))) \tag{1}$$

which can be seen a variant of the Schnorr signature for (ID, T) with the signing key being $s + s_\theta$. Observe that ssk_{ID} cannot be efficiently computed from ku_T and $csk_{ID,T}$, and thus our scheme is CSK exposure resilient.

The key exchange protocol almost remains the same. That is, each party sends $(g^r, g^{r_\theta}, g^{\hat{r}}, g^w)$ to the partner and computes a shared session key as $SK = H'(g^{(w+\hat{s})(w'+\hat{s}')}, g^{ww'}, g^{\hat{s}\hat{s}'})$ where symbols with a prime denote the corresponding values owned by the partner.

Security Proof: The security proof of our scheme basically follows that of FG IB-AKE, but we need a major modification at some points. As well as the security proof of Schnorr signatures, that of FG IB-AKE scheme uses the forking lemma in a similar manner. In our case, however, CSKs that are used for key exchange protocols are the *variant* of Schnorr signatures described in Eq. (1). Roughly speaking, the reason that we need the major modification in the security proof of our RIB-AKE is basically the same as the reason that we cannot prove the security of the variant using the standard forking lemma. For simplicity, we consider the security proofs of Schnorr signatures and the variant in what follows.

In Schnorr signatures, recall that the forking lemma allows the reduction algorithm to compute two signatures $s = r + xh$ and $s' = r + xh'$ and obtain

$x = \frac{s-s'}{h-h'}$ as the answer to the discrete log problem of g^x where h, h' are independently sampled hash values of (g^r, m). In the case of the variant, however, the corresponding part s is computed as

$$s = r_3 + (r_1 + r_2 + x(h_1 + h_2))h_3$$

where x is the signing key and h_1, h_2, h_3 are hash values involving r_1, r_2, r_3, respectively. A naive application of the forking lemma only allows the reduction algorithm to compute $s = r_3 + (r_1 + r_2 + x(h_1 + h_2))h_3$ and $s' = r_3' + (r_1 + r_2' + x(h_1' + h_2))h_3$ such that $h_1 \neq h_1', r_2 \neq r_2', r_3 \neq r_3'$. Hence, it cannot extract x from s and s'. The problem here is that the r_2 and r_3 can change if the reply of the random oracle is changed from h_1 to h_1'. Changing the hash value h_3 also does not work: even if r_1, r_2, r_3 do not change, the reduction algorithm obtains $s = r_3 + (r_1 + r_2 + x(h_1 + h_2))h_3$ and $s' = r_3 + (r_1 + r_2 + x(h_1 + h_2))h_3'$, from which it cannot extract x.

To solve these problems, we devise an extended version of the general forking lemma [7] called the *multi-forking lemma*. This lemma has two major differences over the general forking lemma. First, it shows that r_1, r_2, r_3 do not change with a large enough probability when the reduction algorithm changes the last hash value $h_i \in \{h_1, h_2, h_3\}$ queried by the adversary. Second, we change the format of input and output of the forking algorithm to allow the lemma to be used repeatedly. Armed with the new lemma, the forking algorithm can extract x as follows. If $h_i \neq h_3$, it can easily obtain $x = \frac{s-s'}{(h_i - h_i')h_3}$ by using the lemma once. Otherwise, it first obtains $\sigma = \frac{s-s'}{h_3 - h_3'} = r_1 + r_2 + x(h_1 + h_2)$. Then, a *meta* forking algorithm can extract $x = \frac{\sigma - \sigma'}{h_j - h_j'}$ by using the new lemma again on the second hash value $h_j \in \{h_1, h_2\}$.

2   Definition of RIB-AKE

In this section, we show the definition of RIB-AKE protocol.

We first briefly overview the definition. In RIB-AKE, the PKG first outputs a master public/secret key pair with a security parameter and the number of parties as input and then releases the master public key to all parties. Next, the PKG uses the master secret key and each party's ID to generate static secret keys associated with the ID and then distributes each key to each party via a secure channel. In addition, the PKG updates the revocation list, generates the key update information, and broadcasts them to all parties via a public channel at regular intervals. Each party can generate their current secret key, valid only in that period, from their static secret key and the key update information given by the PKG only when they are not revoked.

In order to share a session key between two parties, the initiator generates an ephemeral public/secret key pair and sends the ephemeral public key to the responder, who is the other party. The responder also generates an ephemeral public/secret key pair and sends its ephemeral public key to the initiator. Both parties can generate a session key from the master public key of the PKG, their own current secret key and ephemeral secret key, the ephemeral public key of the other party, both IDs, and the time counter. Note that the static secret key and the key update information are not used to generate the session key but are only used to create the current secret key.

2.1 Syntax of RIB-AKE

The RIB-AKE protocol Π consists of the following seven probabilistic polynomial-time (PPT) algorithms:

- **ParGen**$(1^\lambda, N) \to (MSK, MPK, RL, T)$: Parameter generation algorithm to be executed only once by the PKG. With the security parameter λ and the maximum number of parties N as input, it outputs the master secret key MSK, the master public key MPK, the initial revocation list RL, and the time counter T. The master public key is distributed to all parties via a public channel. The master secret key MSK is the secret information of the PKG. The revocation list RL is not secret information but only used by the PKG, so it does not necessarily have to be distributed. Assume $RL = \emptyset$ and $T = 0$ as the initial state. (We assume to include MPK in the input of all algorithms below.)
- **SSKGen**$(MSK, ID) \to ssk_{ID}$: Static secret key generation algorithm performed by the PKG only once for each party. It takes the master secret key MSK and the party's ID as input and outputs the static secret key ssk_{ID} corresponding to ID. Each static secret key is distributed to each party via a secret channel.
- **Revoke**(rl): Algorithm for updating the revocation list executed by the PKG at certain intervals. It receives the list of newly revoked user's IDs rl. Then, it updates $RL \leftarrow RL \cup rl$. In addition, it increments the time counter $T \leftarrow T+1$.
- **KeyUp**$(MSK, T, RL) \to ku_T$: Algorithm for generating key update information executed by the PKG after **Revoke**. It takes the master secret key MSK, the time counter T, and the revocation list RL as input and outputs the key update information ku_T. The key update information with the time counter (ku_T, T) is distributed to all parties via a public channel.
- **CSKGen**$(ID, T, ssk_{ID}, ku_T) \to csk_{ID,T}$: The current secret key generation algorithm executed by each party after receiving (ku_T, T). It takes ID, the time counter T, the static secret key ssk_{ID}, and the key update information ku_T as input and outputs the current secret key $csk_{ID,T}$ or $\bot$. The $\bot$ means that the ID has been revoked.
- **EKGen**$(ID_A, ID_B, T, csk_{A,T}) \to (esk_A, epk_A)$: Ephemeral key generation algorithm executed by each party for each session. It takes as input the identifier ID_A of executor U_A, the identifier ID_B of communication partner U_B, the time counter T, and the current secret key $csk_{A,T}$ of executor U_A. It outputs the ephemeral secret/public key pair (esk_A, epk_A) of executor U_A for the session. The ephemeral public key epk_A is distributed to communication partner U_B via a public channel.

– **SKGen**$(ID_A, ID_B, T, csk_{A,T}, esk_A, epk_B) \rightarrow SK$: Session key generation algorithm executed by each party for each session. It takes as input the identifier ID_A of executor U_A, the identifier ID_B of communication partner U_B, the time counter T, the current secret key $csk_{A,T}$ of executor U_A, the ephemeral secret key esk_A of executor U_A, and the ephemeral public key epk_B of communication partner U_B. It outputs the session key SK.

We show the overall behavior of the RIB-AKE protocol in Table 1.

Table 1. Behavior of the RIB-AKE protocol

Parameter Setting
PKG's computation.
$(MSK, MPK, RL, T) \leftarrow \mathbf{ParGen}(1^\lambda, N)$
PKG's secret key: MSK, PKG's public key: MPK, Revocation list: RL, Time counter: T
Distribute MPK to all users.

Static Secret Key Distribution	
PKG's computation for U_A.	**PKG's computation for U_B.**
$ssk_A \leftarrow \mathbf{SSKGen}(MSK, ID_A)$	$ssk_B \leftarrow \mathbf{SSKGen}(MSK, ID_B)$
Send ssk_A to U_A via a secret channel.	Send ssk_B to U_B via a secret channel.

Update Information Distribution
PKG's computation at certain intervals.
Update RL by $\mathbf{Revoke}(RL)$, $ku_T \leftarrow \mathbf{KeyUp}(MSK, T, RL)$
Distribute (ku_T, T) to all users.

Current Secret Key Generation	
U_A's computation	U_B's computation
when U_A receives ku_T.	**when U_B receives ku_T.**
$csk_{A,T} \leftarrow \mathbf{CSKGen}(ID_A, T, ssk_A, ku_T)$	$csk_{B,T} \leftarrow \mathbf{CSKGen}(ID_B, T, ssk_B, ku_T)$
Current secret key of U_A: $csk_{A,T}$	Current secret key of U_B: $csk_{B,T}$

Session Key Generation	
U_A's computation	U_B's computation
when U_A makes a session with U_B.	**when U_B makes a session with U_A.**
$(esk_A, epk_A) \leftarrow \mathbf{EKGen}(ID_A, ID_B, T, csk_{A,T})$	$(esk_B, epk_B) \leftarrow \mathbf{EKGen}(ID_B, ID_A, T, csk_{B,T})$
Ephemeral secret key of U_A: esk_A	Ephemeral secret key of U_B: esk_B
Ephemeral public key of U_A: epk_A	Ephemeral public key of U_B: epk_B
Send epk_A to U_B via a public channel.	Send epk_B to U_A via a public channel.
U_A's computation	U_B's computation
when U_A receives epk_B.	**when U_B receives epk_A.**
$SK \leftarrow \mathbf{SKGen}(ID_A, ID_B, T, csk_{A,T}, esk_A, epk_B)$	$SK \leftarrow \mathbf{SKGen}(ID_B, ID_A, T, csk_{B,T}, esk_B, epk_A)$
Session key shared by U_A and U_B: SK	

3   Our Construction

In this section, we show our construction of the RIB-AKE protocol.

3.1   Sub-algorithms for Our Construction

Here, we show two sub-algorithms used in our protocol. First, we review the
KUNode algorithm [8]. The notation in the algorithm is summarized as follows:

BT : A binary tree with leaves associated with every ID including IDs not
assigned to a specific party. For example, if we use IPv4 addresses as IDs, the
number of leaves will be $N = 2^{32}$.

RL : List of leaves associated with the ID of the revoked party.

$root$: Root of the binary tree BT.

Path(ID) : Set of $nodes$ on the path from the leaf associated with the ID to
$root$.

x_{left}, x_{right} : Left child and right child of node x.

We show the pseudo-code and example output of **KUNode** in Fig. 1. This algorithm outputs the set of the maximal nodes whose descendants cover all non-
revoked ID and do not contain any revoked ID. It is known that the size of the
output and the computational cost are both logarithmic in the number of leaves,
and this makes our protocol scalable. Note that the binary tree BT is fixed even
when some parties are newly assigned or revoked.

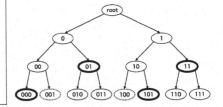

KUNode(BT, RL)

1. $X, Y \leftarrow \emptyset$.
2. $\forall ID \in RL$, $X \leftarrow X \cup$ **Path**(ID).
3. for $\forall x \in X$,
   (a) If $x_{left} \notin X$, add x_{left} to Y.
   (b) If $x_{right} \notin X$, add x_{right} to Y.
4. If $Y = \emptyset$, add $root$ to Y.
5. Output Y.

(a) Pseudo-code of **KUNode**   (b) An example output of **KUNode**

Fig. 1. The pseudo-code of **KUNode** (a) and an example output of **KUNode** for
eight parties (b). Parties with the identifier 001 and 100 are revoked and the bold
nodes are the outputs.

Secondly, let **GenG** be a PPT algorithm that takes 1^{λ} as input, randomly
selects a prime, q, of size λ, a cyclic group, $\mathbb{G}$, of order q, and a generator, g, of
$\mathbb{G}$, and outputs $(\mathbb{G}, q, g)$.

3.2   Our Construction of RIB-AKE

Now, we show our construction of RIB-AKE. Our protocol consists of the PPT algorithm shown below. Note that we use the same notations defined in Sect. 2.1 as the same meaning. The executor and execution timing of each algorithm are also described in Sect. 2.1.

- **ParGen**$(1^\lambda, N) \to (MSK, MPK, RL, T)$:
  1. Generate $(\mathbb{G}, q, g) \leftarrow \mathbf{GenG}(1^\lambda)$.
  2. Take $x \in_U \mathbb{Z}_q$ and set $X = g^x$.
  3. Let BT be a binary tree with N number of leaves.
  4. Take two hash functions $H_1 \colon \{0,1\}^* \times \mathbb{G} \to \mathbb{Z}_q$ and $H_2 \colon \{0,1\}^* \times \mathbb{G}^3 \to \{0,1\}^\lambda$.
  5. Output $MSK = x$, $MPK = (\mathbb{G}, q, g, X, BT, H_1, H_2)$, $RL = \emptyset$, and $T = 0$.
- **SSKGen**$(MSK, ID) \to ssk_{ID}$:
  1. Take $r_{ID} \in_U \mathbb{Z}_q$ and set $R_{ID} = g^{r_{ID}}$.
  2. Set $s_{ID} = r_{ID} + x \cdot H_1(ID, R_{ID})$.
  3. Output $ssk_{ID} = (s_{ID}, R_{ID})$. (Note that $g^{s_{ID}} = R_{ID} \cdot X^{H_1(ID, R_{ID})}$ holds.)
- **Revoke**(rl): The input rl is the list of IDs of the newly revoked parties. Just update $RL \leftarrow RL \cup rl$ and increment time $T \leftarrow T + 1$.
- **KeyUp**$(MSK, T, RL) \to ku_T$:
  1. For each $\theta \in \mathbf{KUNode}(BT, RL)$, calculate $(s_{T\|\theta}, R_{T\|\theta}) \leftarrow \mathbf{SSKGen}(MSK, T \| \theta)$.
  2. Output $ku_T = \{(\theta, s_{T\|\theta}, R_{T\|\theta})\}_{\theta \in \mathbf{KUNode}(BT, RL)}$.
     (Note that $g^{s_{T\|\theta}} = R_{T\|\theta} \cdot X^{H_1(T\|\theta, R_{T\|\theta})}$ holds.)
- **CSKGen**$(ID, T, ssk_{ID}, ku_T) \to csk_{ID,T}$:
  1. Take $\theta \in \mathbf{KUNode}(BT, RL) \cap \mathbf{Path}(ID)$. If it does not exist, output $\perp$.
  2. Parse $ssk_{ID} = (s_{ID}, R_{ID})$.
  3. Take $r_{ID,T} \in_U \mathbb{Z}_q$ and set $R_{ID,T} = g^{r_{ID,T}}$.
  4. Set $s_{ID,T} = r_{ID,T} + (s_{ID} + s_{T\|\theta}) \cdot H_1(ID \| T, R_{ID,T})$.
  5. Output $csk_{ID,T} = (s_{ID,T}, R_{ID}, R_{T\|\theta}, R_{ID,T}, \theta)$.
     (Note that $g^{s_{ID,T}} = R_{ID,T} \cdot Y^{H_1(ID\|T, R_{ID,T})}$ holds for $Y := g^{s_{ID} + s_{T\|\theta}}$.)
- **EKGen**$(-, -, -, csk_{ID,T}) \to (esk_{ID}, epk_{ID})$: (IDs and T can be given as input, but not used anyway in this algorithm.)
  1. Parse $csk_{ID,T} = (s_{ID,T}, R_{ID}, R_{T\|\theta}, R_{ID,T}, \theta)$.
  2. Take $w_{ID} \in_U \mathbb{Z}_q$ and set $W_{ID} = g^{w_{ID}}$.
  3. Output $esk_{ID} = w_{ID}$ and $epk_{ID} = (W_{ID}, R_{ID}, R_{T\|\theta}, R_{ID,T}, \theta)$.
- **SKGen**$(ID_A, ID_B, T, csk_{A,T}, esk_A, epk_B) \to SK$:
  1. Parse $csk_{A,T} = (s_{A,T}, R_A, R_{T\|\theta_A}, R_{A,T}, \theta_A)$, $esk_A = w_A$, and $epk_B = (W_B, R_B, R_{T\|\theta_B}, R_{B,T}, \theta_B)$.
  2. If θ_B is not prefix of ID_B, then abort.
  3. Let $Y = R_B \cdot X^{H_1(ID_B, R_B)} \cdot R_{T\|\theta_B} \cdot X^{H_1(T\|\theta_B, R_{T\|\theta_B})}$.
  4. Let $Z_1 = \left(W_B \cdot R_{B,T} \cdot Y^{H_1(ID_B\|T, R_{B,T})}\right)^{s_{A,T} + w_A}$.
  5. Let $Z_2 = W_B^{w_A}$.
  6. Let $Z_3 = \left(R_{B,T} \cdot Y^{H_1(ID_B\|T, R_{B,T})}\right)^{s_{A,T}}$
  7. Let $m = (ID_A \| ID_B \| T \| epk_A \| epk_B)$.
  8. Output $SK = H_2(m, Z_1, Z_2, Z_3)$.

Table 2 shows how U_A and U_B shares SK by using **EKGen** and **SKGen**.

Table 2. Behavior of our RIB-AKE protocol

Parameter and Update Information
$MPK = (\mathbb{G}, q, g, X, BT, H_1, H_2),\ RL,\ T,\ ku_T = \{(\theta, s_{T\|\theta}, R_{T\|\theta})\}_{\theta \in \mathbf{KUNode}(BT, RL)}$

Static Secret Key	
$U_A:\ ID_A,\ ssk_A = (s_A, R_A)$	$U_B:\ ID_B,\ ssk_B = (s_B, R_B)$

Current Secret Key Generation	
$\{\theta_A\} := \mathbf{KUNode}(BT, RL) \cap \mathbf{Path}(ID_A)$	$\{\theta_B\} := \mathbf{KUNode}(BT, RL) \cap \mathbf{Path}(ID_B)$
$r_{A,T} \in_U \mathbb{Z}_q$	$r_{B,T} \in_U \mathbb{Z}_q$
$R_{A,T} := g^{r_{A,T}}$	$R_{B,T} := g^{r_{B,T}}$
$s_{A,T} := r_{A,T} + (s_A + s_{T\|\theta_A})H_1(ID_A \| T, R_{A,T})$	$s_{B,T} := r_{B,T} + (s_B + s_{T\|\theta_B})H_1(ID_B \| T, R_{B,T})$
$csk_{A,T} := (s_{A,T}, R_A, R_{T\|\theta_A}, R_{A,T}, \theta_A)$	$csk_{B,T} := (s_{B,T}, R_B, R_{T\|\theta_B}, R_{B,T}, \theta_B)$

Ephemeral Key Generation	
$esk_A := w_A \in_U \mathbb{Z}_q$	$esk_B := w_B \in_U \mathbb{Z}_q$
$W_A := g^{w_A}$	$W_B := g^{w_B}$
$epk_A := (W_A, R_A, R_{T\|\theta_A}, R_{A,T}, \theta_A)$	$epk_B := (W_B, R_B, R_{T\|\theta_B}, R_{B,T}, \theta_B)$

Session Key Generation	
$Y_B := R_B \cdot X^{H_1(ID_B, R_B)} \cdot R_{T\|\theta_B} \cdot X^{H_1(T\|\theta_B, R_{T\|\theta_B})}$	$Y_A := R_A \cdot X^{H_1(ID_A, R_A)} \cdot R_{T\|\theta_A} \cdot X^{H_1(T\|\theta_A, R_{T\|\theta_A})}$
$Z_{A,1} := \left(W_B \cdot R_{B,T} \cdot Y_B^{H_1(ID_B\|T, R_{B,T})}\right)^{s_{A,T}+w_A}$	$Z_{B,1} := \left(W_A \cdot R_{A,T} \cdot Y_A^{H_1(ID_A\|T, R_{A,T})}\right)^{s_{B,T}+w_B}$
$Z_{A,2} := W_B^{w_A}$	$Z_{B,2} := W_A^{w_B}$
$Z_{A,3} := \left(R_{B,T} \cdot Y_B^{H_1(ID_B\|T, R_{B,T})}\right)^{s_{A,T}}$	$Z_{B,3} := \left(R_{A,T} \cdot Y_A^{H_1(ID_A\|T, R_{A,T})}\right)^{s_{B,T}}$
$SK_A := H_2(m, Z_{A,1}, Z_{A,2}, Z_{A,3})$	$SK_A := H_2(m, Z_{B,1}, Z_{B,2}, Z_{B,3})$

3.3   Correctness

Definition 1 (Correctness). *If both no-revoked parties U_A and U_B run the protocol honestly, their session key SK_A and SK_B are equal.*

Here, we prove the correctness of our protocol. We consider the session between U_A and U_B. See the transcript in Table 2. Let $Y_B, Z_{A,1}, Z_{A,2}, Z_{A,3}, SK_A$ (resp. $Y_A, Z_{B,1}, Z_{B,2}, Z_{B,3}, SK_B$) be the values Y, Z_1, Z_2, Z_3, SK computed by U_A (resp. U_B) through **SKGen**, respectively. Let the current secret key $csk_{A,T} = (s_{A,T}, R_A, R_{T\|\theta_A}, R_{A,T}, \theta_A)$ and $esk_A = w_A$ be U_A's current and ephemeral secret key. U_B's current and ephemeral secret keys are denoted in the same way. By the definition of our protocol, we have

$$Y_B = R_B \cdot X^{H_1(ID_B, R_B)} \cdot R_{T\|\theta_B} \cdot X^{H_1(T\|\theta_B, R_{T\|\theta_B})} = g^{s_B + s_{T\|\theta_B}}$$

and $R_{B,T} \cdot Y_B^{H_1(ID_B\|T, R_{B,T})} = g^{s_{B,T}}$. (See the definition of **CSKGen**.) Thus, U_A obtains

$$Z_{A,1} = \left(W_B \cdot R_{B,T} \cdot Y_B^{H_1(ID_B\|T, R_{B,T})}\right)^{s_{A,T}+w_A}$$
$$= (g^{w_B} \cdot g^{s_{B,T}})^{s_{A,T}+w_A} = g^{(s_{A,T}+w_A)(s_{B,T}+w_B)},$$
$$Z_{A,2} = W_B^{w_A} = (g^{w_B})^{w_A} = g^{w_A w_B},$$
$$Z_{A,3} = \left(R_{B,T} \cdot Y_B^{H_1(ID_B\|T, R_{B,T})}\right)^{s_{A,T}}$$
$$= (g^{s_{B,T}})^{s_{A,T}} = g^{s_{A,T} s_{B,T}}.$$

Since the values obtained by U_B are the replacement of A and B above, we have $Z_{A,i} = Z_{B,i}$ for $i \in \{1,2,3\}$. Therefore, $SK_A = H_2(m, Z_{A,1}, Z_{A,2}, Z_{A,3}) = H_2(m, Z_{B,1}, Z_{B,2}, Z_{B,3}) = SK_B$ holds and our protocol is correct.

3.4 Efficiency

In this subsection, we show that our protocol is the most efficient among (R)IB-AKE protocols with the (r)id-eCK secure, indicating that our protocol is practical. In other words, our proposed protocol can use the revocation function without performance degradation.

First, we theoretically evaluate the computational costs of (R)IB-AKE protocols. In order to be a fair comparison, we selected efficient protocols [19,36,37,49] from among protocols that can be the (r)id-eCK secure. Since Okano et al.'s construction [37] is a general one of RHIB-AKE, we made comparisons using instantiation by these protocols [12,16,18]. Instantiation by other protocols is possible, but it is not expected to drastically improve performance.

We also use the symbols P, S_i, and E_T to explain the computational cost of paring, scalar multiplication in $\mathbb{G}_i$, and exponentiation over $\mathbb{G}_T$ in each scheme, respectively. For simplicity, only these expensive operations are counted. Moreover, we define $d = \log_2 N$, and $k = r \log_2 \left(\frac{N}{r}\right)$, where N is the number of all parties, and r is the number of revoked parties.

While our protocol, Fiore et al.'s and Ni et al.'s protocol can be constructed with general elliptic curves, Okano et al., Tomida et al., and others' protocols are pairing-based protocols and thus require the use of pairing-friendly curves.

Table 3 shows the computational cost of (R)IB-AKE protocols. Our protocol is the most efficient among protocols with the (r)id-eCK secure because the FG IB-AKE [19] is id-CK secure not id-eCK secure. Note that the cost of **KeyUp** is $O(k) = O(\log N)$ for a fixed r (or a small enough r). Therefore, our protocol is scalable.

Table 3. Computational cost of RIB-AKE and IB-AKE protocols

Function	RIB-AKE		IB-AKE		
	Ours	Okano et al. [37]	Fiore et al. [19]	Ni et al. [36]	Tomida et al. [49]
SSKGen	S	$3S_1$	S	$2S$	S_2
KeyUp	kS	$3(k + r + 1)S_1$	–	–	–
CSKGen	S	$3(k + 1)S_1$	–	–	–
EKGen	S	$(12d + 19)S_1$	S	S	$2S_1$
SKGen	$5S$	$12P + 4S_1 + (2d + 3)E_T$	$3S$	$6S$	$3S_1 + P$

Next, we measure the performance of each operation in Table 3 to show the practicality of not using pairing and describe the results in Table 4. We used the Apache Milagro Crypto Library (AMCL) [2] for this measurement, which supports Edwards, NIST, and BLS curves. The AMCL library is an open-source library provided by the Apache project and is available for download. To select the 128-bit security parameters, we chose Curve25519 (Ed25519) and NIST P-256 (SECP256) for elliptic curves. For pairing friendly curves, we chose the BLS curve with embedding degree 12, a characteristic of 461 bits, called BLS12_461 in [40]. We summarize our environment for the experiments in Table 5. Table 4 contains the number of average clock cycles (kCycles) of 100 iterations.

Pairing is not only a very heavy operation but also requires the use of libraries that support pairing operations. This has made RIB-AKE and IB-AKE difficult to achieve real-world applications, but our scheme has the advantage of not using pairing, and thus contributes greatly to the realization of practical applications. Unlike the pairing-friendly curve, the Edwards curve and the NIST curve are implemented in many popular cryptographic libraries, such as the MbedTLS library, and thus our protocol can be easily implemented. Our protocol makes it possible to apply revocation and authentication functions to microcontrollers with small CPU resources, such as sensor devices.

Table 4. Experimental results

Curve	Operation	kCycles	(msec)
Ed25519	S	4925	(44)
SECP256		16088	(146)
BLS12_461	S_1	25735	(233)
	S_2	67906	(617)
	P	134242	(1220)
	E_T	48887	(444)

Table 5. Execution Environment

Item	Value
CPU	Cortex-M33
Clock	110 MHz
RAM	256 KB
Development Board	STM32L552ZE
Instruction Cache	On
Compiler	IAR C Compiler

4   Security Model of RIB-AKE

In this section, we define the security model of RIB-AKE. This security model is a non-hierarchical version of rhid-eCK model [37] and is based on Huang–Cao's ID-based eCK (id-eCK) model [26]. The differences of our model from the id-eCK model are as follows:

- When the adversary specifies the session, he also specifies not only the ID but also the time T.
- The adversary can query to the oracle that returns a current session key of use ID for the time T (**CSKRev**), which captures each party's current secret key exposure. It can also query to the oracle that returns a key update information for time T (**KeyUp**), which captures the broadcast of the key update information, and the oracle that updates the revoke list (**Revoke**), which captures the revocation list's system-wide update.
- We modify the definition of freshness based on the additional queries above.

Our security model guarantees that "as long as the current secret key for the target ID and time T pair is not exposed, the target session key is secure even if other current secret keys and the ephemeral secret keys are exposed," and that "even if the static secret key for the target ID is exposed, the session key is secure if the ID is revoked at the target time T."

4.1 Session

An invocation of a protocol is called a session. A session is activated via an incoming message of the forms $(\Pi, \mathcal{I}, T, ID_A, ID_B)$ or $(\Pi, \mathcal{R}, T, ID_A, ID_B)$, where Π is the protocol identifier, $\mathcal{I}$ and $\mathcal{R}$ are role identifiers, T is the time period, and ID_A and ID_B are user identifiers. When ID_A is activated with $(\Pi, \mathcal{I}, T, ID_A, ID_B)$, we call ID_A an *initiator*. When ID_A is activated with $(\Pi, \mathcal{R}, T, ID_A, ID_B)$, we call ID_A a *responder*.

On activation, an initiator (resp. responder) ID_A returns epk_A. Receiving an incoming message $(\Pi, \mathcal{I}, T, ID_A, ID_B, epk_B)$ (resp. $(\Pi, \mathcal{R}, T, ID_A, ID_B, epk_B)$) from the responder (resp. initiator) ID_B, ID_A computes the session key SK.

If ID_A is the initiator, the session identifier sid is $(\Pi, \mathcal{I}, T, ID_A, ID_B, epk_A)$ or $(\Pi, \mathcal{I}, T, ID_A, ID_B, epk_A, epk_B)$. If ID_A is the responder, the session is identified by $sid = (\Pi, \mathcal{R}, T, ID_A, ID_B, epk_A)$ or $(\Pi, \mathcal{R}, T, ID_A, ID_B, epk_B, epk_A)$. It is said that ID_A is the *owner* of the session sid when the fourth component of sid is ID_A. Also, ID_B is said to be a *peer* of session sid when the fifth component of sid is ID_B. A session is *completed* when the session key has been computed in that session.

A matching session of $sid = (\Pi, \mathcal{I}, T, ID_A, ID_B, epk_A, epk_B)$ is a session with $(\Pi, \mathcal{R}, T, ID_B, ID_A, epk_A, epk_B)$, and vice versa.

4.2 Adversary

The adversary $\mathcal{A}$ is modeled as a PPT Turing machine that controls all communication between the parties, including session activation. Let T_{cu} and $RL_{T_{cu}}$ be the time counter and the revoke list maintained by the challenger, respectively. We model the adversary's capability by the following queries.

- **ParGen**$(1^\lambda, N)$: The adversary requests the PKG to generate the parameter and obtains the master public key MPK.
- **SSKRev**(ID): The adversary obtains the static secret key ssk_{ID}.
- **KeyUp**(T): If $T \leq T_{cu}$, then the adversary obtains the key update information ku_T, else obtains $\bot$.
- **CSKRev**(ID, T): If $T \leq T_{cu}$, then the adversary obtains the current secret key $csk_{ID,T}$, else obtains $\bot$.
- **ESKRev**(sid): The adversary obtains the ephemeral key esk of the session owner.
- **SKRev**(sid): The adversary obtains the session key if the session is completed.
- **MSKRev**$()$: The adversary obtains the master secret key MSK.

- **EstablishUser**(U, ID): The query allows the adversary to join the party as the user U with the identity ID and obtain the static secret key ssk_{ID}. If this query establishes a party, then we call the party *dishonest*. If not, we call the party *honest*.
- **Send**$(message)$: $message$ is given in the form $(\Pi, \mathcal{I}, T_{cu}, ID_A, ID_B)$, $(\Pi, \mathcal{R}, T_{cu}, ID_A, ID_B)$, $(\Pi, \mathcal{I}, T_{cu}, ID_A, ID_B, epk_B)$, or $(\Pi, \mathcal{R}, T_{cu}, ID_A, ID_B, epk_B)$. The adversary obtains the response from the party according to the protocol specification.
- **Revoke**(RL): If $RL_{T_{cu}} \not\subset RL$, return $\perp$. Otherwise, T_{cu} is incremented as $T_{cu} \leftarrow T_{cu} + 1$, update the revoke list as $RL_{T_{cu}} \leftarrow RL$, and return T_{cu}.

4.3 Freshness

Here, we give the definition of freshness, which is similar to that of the rhid-eCK security model [37].

Definition 2. *Let* $sid^* = (\Pi, \mathcal{I}, T^*, ID_A, ID_B, epk_A, epk_B)$ *or* $(\Pi, \mathcal{R}, T^*, ID_A, ID_B, epk_B, epk_A)$ *be a completed session between the honest party* U_A *with the identifier* ID_A *and the honest party* U_B *with the identifier* ID_B. *When there exists a matching session of* sid^*, *we denote it as* $\overline{sid^*}$. *We say that* sid^* *is* fresh *if none of the following conditions are satisfied.*

1. *The adversary* $\mathcal{A}$ *issues* **SKRev**(sid^*), *or* **SKRev**$(\overline{sid^*})$ *if* $\overline{sid^*}$ *exists.*
2. $\overline{sid^*}$ *exists and adversary* $\mathcal{A}$ *makes either of the following queries:*
   - **ESKRev**(sid^*) *and* **SSKRev**(ID_A) *with* $ID_A \notin RL_{T^*}$.
   - **ESKRev**$(\overline{sid^*})$ *and* **SSKRev**(ID_B) *for the identity* ID_B *with* $ID_B \notin RL_{T^*}$.
   - **ESKRev**(sid^*) *and* **CSKRev**(ID_A, T^*).
   - **ESKRev**$(\overline{sid^*})$ *and* **CSKRev**(ID_B, T^*).
3. $\overline{sid^*}$ *does not exist and adversary* $\mathcal{A}$ *makes either of the following queries:*
   - **ESKRev**(sid^*) *and* **SSKRev**(ID_A) *for the identity* ID_A *with* $ID_A \notin RL_{T^*}$.
   - **SSKRev**(ID_B) *for the identity* ID_B *with* $ID_B \notin RL_{T^*}$.
   - **ESKRev**(sid^*) *and* **CSKRev**(ID_A, T^*).
   - **CSKRev**(ID_B, T^*).

Note that case 3 is essentially the same as **ESKRev**$(\overline{sid^*})$ being executed, since there is no matching session and the adversary $\mathcal{A}$ is free to create esk for $\overline{sid^*}$. Also note that if adversary $\mathcal{A}$ issues **MSKRev**$()$, we regard $\mathcal{A}$ as having issue **CSKRev**(ID_A, T^*) and **CSKRev**(ID_B, T^*).

4.4 Security Experiment

We consider the following security game. First, the adversary $\mathcal{A}$ receives a RIB-AKE protocol Π, a master public key MPK, and a set of honest parties. The adversary $\mathcal{A}$ then arbitrarily executes the query described in Sect. 4.2 multiple times. Along the way, $\mathcal{A}$ executes the following query only once.

- **Test**(sid^*): The session sid^* must be fresh. Randomly select a bit $b \in \{0,1\}$ and return the session key for sid^* if $b = 0$, or a randomly generated key if $b = 1$.

The game continues until the adversary $\mathcal{A}$ outputs a guess b'. The adversary wins the game when the test session sid^* is fresh and the adversary's guess is correct, i.e., $b' = b$. We define the adversary's advantage as $Adv_{\Pi}^{\text{RIB-AKE}}(\mathcal{A}) :=$ $|2 \Pr(\mathcal{A} \text{ wins}) - 1|$. Then, we define the security of RIB-AKE as follows.

Definition 3 (rid-eCK security model). *An RIB-AKE protocol Π is said to be secure in the rid-eCK model if the advantage $Adv_{\Pi}^{\text{RIB-AKE}}(\mathcal{A})$ defined above is negligible for any adversary $\mathcal{A}$.*

5 Security Analysis for Our Protocol

This section proves that our proposed protocol is rid-eCK secure under the Strong Diffie–Hellman (SDH) assumption in the random oracle model (ROM). It is worth to note here that we do not consider the reflection attack in this paper as the security against it is expected to rely on the square version of the assumption. The detailed discussion will be shown in the full version.

First, we prepare the prior knowledge necessary for the security analysis.

Definition 4 (SDH assumption). *Generate $(\mathbb{G}, q, g) \leftarrow \textbf{GenG}(1^{\lambda})$, choose $u, v \in_U \mathbb{Z}_q$, and let $U := g^u$ and $V := g^v$. Now, we consider the oracle $\textbf{DDH}(\cdot, \cdot)$ that on input $V', W' \in \mathbb{G}$, return 1 if $W' = (V')^u$ and 0 otherwise. For any PPT algorithm $\mathcal{A}^{\textbf{DDH}(\cdot, \cdot)}$ that can access this oracle $\textbf{DDH}(\cdot, \cdot)$ in polynomial time, we say that the Strong Diffie–Hellman (SDH) assumption holds if the following probability is negligible: $\Pr\left(\mathcal{A}^{\textbf{DDH}(\cdot, \cdot)}(\mathbb{G}, q, g, U, V) = g^{uv}\right)$.*

Multi-Forking Lemma. In our security proof, we use a new lemma, named *multi-forking lemma*, that is our remake of the general forking lemma stated by Bellare and Neven [7]. $\mathcal{B}$ in our lemma outputs a *set* of indexes J, while that in the general forking lemma outputs an index.

Lemma 1 (Multi-Forking Lemma). *Fix integers n, $Q \geq 1$, set H with $|H| \geq 2$, and set $\Lambda_n := \{(j_1, \ldots, j_n) \in \mathbb{Z}^n : 1 \leq j_1 < \cdots < j_n \leq Q\}$. Let $\mathcal{B}$ be a randomized algorithm that on inputs inp, $h_1, \ldots, h_Q$, returns a pair (J, σ), where $J = (j_1, \ldots, j_n) \in \mathbb{Z}^n$ and σ is referred as side output. Let R be a set of random tapes for the randomized algorithm $\mathcal{B}$. Let*

$$acc_{\mathcal{B}}(inp) := \Pr\left(J \in \Lambda_n \mid h_1, \ldots, h_Q \leftarrow H; (J, \sigma) \leftarrow \mathcal{B}(inp, h_1, \ldots, h_Q)\right)$$

be the acceptance probability of $\mathcal{B}$.

The forking algorithm, $F_{\mathcal{B}}$, associated to $\mathcal{B}$ is the randomized algorithm that takes in input inp and proceeds as follows:

- *Algorithm $F_{\mathcal{B}}(inp, h_1, \ldots, h_Q)$:*

1. *Choose random tape* $\phi \in_U R$ *for* $\mathcal{B}$.
2. *Let* $(J, \sigma) \leftarrow \mathcal{B}(inp, h_1, \ldots, h_Q; \phi)$.
3. *If* $J \notin \Lambda_n$, *return* $(\mathbf{0}, \bot)$.
4. *Choose* $h'_1, \ldots, h'_Q \in_U H$.
5. *Let* $(J', \sigma') \leftarrow \mathcal{B}(inp, h_1, \ldots, h_{j_n-1}, h'_{j_n}, \ldots, h'_Q; \phi)$.
6. *If* $J = J'$ *and* $h_{j_n} \neq h'_{j_n}$, *return* (J, τ),
   where τ *is side output calculated from* $(J, \sigma, \sigma', h_1, \ldots, h_Q, h'_1, \ldots, h'_Q)$.
7. *Else return* $(\mathbf{0}, \bot)$.

Let $fork(inp) := \Pr\left(J \in \Lambda_n \mid h_1, \ldots, h_Q \in_U H; (J, \tau) \leftarrow F_{\mathcal{B}}(inp, h_1 \ldots, h_Q)\right)$.
Then the following inequality holds:

$$fork(inp) \geq acc_{\mathcal{B}}(inp) \cdot \left(acc_{\mathcal{B}}(inp)/\binom{Q}{n} - 1/|H|\right).$$

The essential difference from the general forking lemma is that the algorithm $\mathcal{B}$ and $F_{\mathcal{B}}$ output *multiple* integers with side output. Note that the general forking lemma corresponds to the $n = 1$ case of our lemma since $|\Lambda_1| = Q$. The proof for this lemma is given in the auxiliary materials.

By using this lemma, we proved the following theorem which claims the security of our protocol.

Theorem 1. *Our RIB-AKE protocol is rid-eCK secure in the random oracle model under the SDH assumption.*

The proof for this theorem is given in the full version.

References

1. Anggorojati, B., Prasad, R.: Securing communication in inter domains internet of things using identity-based cryptography. In: IWBIS 2017, pp. 137–142 (2017)
2. The Apache Software Foundation. The Apache Milagro Cryptographic Library (AMCL) (2022). https://github.com/apache/incubator-milagro-crypto. Accessed 26 Dec 2022
3. Boneh, D., Boyen, X.: Efficient selective-ID secure identity-based encryption without random oracles. In: Cachin, C., Camenisch, J.L. (eds.) EUROCRYPT 2004. LNCS, vol. 3027, pp. 223–238. Springer, Heidelberg (2004). https://doi.org/10.1007/978-3-540-24676-3_14
4. Baek, J., Safavi-Naini, R., Susilo, W.: Efficient multi-receiver identity-based encryption and its application to broadcast encryption. In: Vaudenay, S. (ed.) PKC 2005. LNCS, vol. 3386, pp. 380–397. Springer, Heidelberg (2005). https://doi.org/10.1007/978-3-540-30580-4_26
5. Barbulescu, R., Duquesne, S.: Updating key size estimations for pairings. J. Cryptol. **32**, 1298–1336 (2019)
6. Barreto, P.S.L.M., Naehrig, M.: Pairing-friendly elliptic curves of prime order. In: Preneel, B., Tavares, S. (eds.) SAC 2005. LNCS, vol. 3897, pp. 319–331. Springer, Heidelberg (2006). https://doi.org/10.1007/11693383_22
7. Bellare, M., Neven, G.: Multi-signatures in the plain public-key model and a general forking lemma. In: ACM CCS 2006, pp. 390–399 (2006)

8. Boldyreva, A., Goyal, V., Kumar, V.: Identity-based encryption with efficient revocation. In: ACM CCS 2008, pp. 417–426 (2008)
9. Boneh, D., Franklin, M.: Identity-based encryption from the weil pairing. In: Kilian, J. (ed.) CRYPTO 2001. LNCS, vol. 2139, pp. 213–229. Springer, Heidelberg (2001). https://doi.org/10.1007/3-540-44647-8_13
10. Broustis, I., Cakulev, V., Sundaram, G.: IBAKE: identity-based authenticated key exchange. In: RFC 6539 (2012). https://rfc-editor.org/rfc/rfc6539.txt
11. Chakraborty, S., Raghuraman, S., Pandu Rangan, C.: A pairing-free, one round identity based authenticated key exchange protocol secure against memory-scrapers. J. Wirel. Mob. Netw. Ubiq. Comput. Depend. Appl. **7**(1), 1–22 (2016)
12. Chen, J., Wee, H.: Dual system groups and its applications – compact HIBE and more. IACR Cryptology ePrint Archive: Report 2014/265 (2014)
13. Cheng, Q., Ma, C.: Ephemeral key compromise attack on the IB-KA protocol. IACR Cryptology ePrint Archive: Report 2009/568 (2009)
14. Cloudflare Inc: Geo key manager: How it works (2017). https://blog.cloudflare.com/geo-key-manager-how-it-works/
15. Dearlove, C.: Identity-Based Signatures for Mobile Ad Hoc Network (MANET) Routing Protocols. RFC 7859 (2016). https://rfc-editor.org/rfc/rfc7859.txt
16. Dent, A.W.: ECIES-KEM vs. PSEC-KEM. Technical Report NES/DOC/RHU/WP5/028/2, NESSIE (2002)
17. Emura, K., Seo, J.H., Watanabe, Y.: Efficient revocable identity-based encryption with short public parameters. Theor. Comput. Sci. **863**, 127–155 (2021)
18. Emura, K., Takayasu, A., Watanabe, Y.: Generic constructions of revocable hierarchical identity-based encryption. IACR Cryptology ePrint Archive: Report 2021/515 (2021)
19. Fiore, D., Gennaro, R.: Making the Diffie-Hellman protocol identity-based. In: Pieprzyk, J. (ed.) CT-RSA 2010. LNCS, vol. 5985, pp. 165–178. Springer, Heidelberg (2010). https://doi.org/10.1007/978-3-642-11925-5_12
20. Fujioka, A., Suzuki, K., Ustaoğlu, B.: Ephemeral key leakage resilient and efficient ID-AKEs that can share identities, private and master keys. In: Joye, M., Miyaji, A., Otsuka, A. (eds.) Pairing 2010. LNCS, vol. 6487, pp. 187–205. Springer, Heidelberg (2010). https://doi.org/10.1007/978-3-642-17455-1_12
21. Gallant, R.P., Lambert, R.J., Vanstone, S.A.: Faster point multiplication on elliptic curves with efficient endomorphisms. In: Kilian, J. (ed.) CRYPTO 2001. LNCS, vol. 2139, pp. 190–200. Springer, Heidelberg (2001). https://doi.org/10.1007/3-540-44647-8_11
22. Galbraith, S.D., Lin, X., Scott, M.: Endomorphisms for faster elliptic curve cryptography on a large class of curves. J. Cryptol. **24**, 446–469 (2011)
23. Groves, M.: Sakai-Kasahara Key Encryption (SAKKE). RFC 6508 (2012). https://rfc-editor.org/rfc/rfc6508.txt
24. Hajny, J., Dzurenda, P., Ricci, S., Malina, L., Vrba, K.: Performance analysis of pairing-based elliptic curve cryptography on constrained devices. In: ICUMT 2018, pp. 1–5 (2018)
25. Hu, Z., Liu, S., Chen, K., Liu, J.K.: Revocable identity-based encryption from the computational Diffie-Hellman problem. In: Susilo, W., Yang, G. (eds.) ACISP 2018. LNCS, vol. 10946, pp. 265–283. Springer, Cham (2018). https://doi.org/10.1007/978-3-319-93638-3_16
26. Huang, H., Cao, Z.: An ID-based authenticated key exchange protocol based on bilinear Diffie-Hellman problem. In: ASIACCS 2009, pp. 333–342 (2009)

27. Ishida, Y., Watanabe, Y., Shikata, J.: Constructions of CCA-secure revocable identity-based encryption. In: Foo, E., Stebila, D. (eds.) ACISP 2015. LNCS, vol. 9144, pp. 174–191. Springer, Cham (2015). https://doi.org/10.1007/978-3-319-19962-7_11

28. ISO/IEC, ISO/IEC 15946–5:2022 Information security - Cryptographic techniques based on elliptic curves -Part 5: Elliptic curve generation (2022). https://www.iso.org/standard/80241.html

29. Katsumata, S., Matsuda, T., Takayasu, A.: Lattice-based revocable (hierarchical) IBE with decryption key exposure resistance. Theor. Comput. Sci. **809**, 103–136 (2020)

30. Kupwade Patil, H., Szygenda, S.A.: Security for Wireless Sensor Networks using Identity-Based Cryptography. Auerbach Publications, Boca Raton (2012)

31. Lee, K., Lee, D.H., Park, J.H.: Efficient revocable identity-based encryption via subset difference methods. Des. Codes Cryptogr. **85**(1), 39–76 (2017)

32. Libert, B., Vergnaud, D.: Adaptive-ID secure revocable identity-based encryption. In: Fischlin, M. (ed.) CT-RSA 2009. LNCS, vol. 5473, pp. 1–15. Springer, Heidelberg (2009). https://doi.org/10.1007/978-3-642-00862-7_1

33. Lu, H., Li, J., Kameda, H.: A secure routing protocol for cluster-based wireless sensor networks using ID-based digital signature. In: GLOBECOM 2010, pp. 1–5 (2010)

34. Ma, X., Lin, D.: A generic construction of revocable identity-based encryption. In: Inscrypt 2019, pp. 381–396 (2019)

35. S. Mitsunari: mcl - A Portable and Fast Pairing-Based Cryptography Library (2016). https://github.com/herumi/mcl

36. Ni, L., Chen, G., Li, J., Hao, Y.: Strongly secure identity-based authenticated key agreement protocols without bilinear pairings. Inf. Sci. **367**, 176–193 (2016)

37. Okano, Y., Tomida, J., Nagai, A., Yoneyama, K., Fujioka, A., Suzuki, K.: Revocable hierarchical identity-based authenticated key exchange. In: ICISC 2021, pp. 17–40 (2021)

38. Pointcheval, D., Stern, J.: Security arguments for digital signatures and blind signatures. J. Cryptol. **13**(3), 361–396 (2000)

39. Boyen, X., Martin, L.: Identity-Based Cryptography Standard (IBCS) #1: Supersingular Curve Implementations of the BF and BB1 Cryptosystems. RFC5091 (2007). https://rfc-editor.org/rfc/rfc5091.txt

40. Sakemi, Y., Kobayashi, T., Saito, T., Wahby, R.: Pairing-friendly curves. draft-irtf-cfrg-pairing-friendly-curves-10. https://datatracker.ietf.org/doc/html/draft-irtf-cfrg-pairing-friendly-curves-10

41. Shamir, A.: Identity-based cryptosystems and signature schemes. In: Blakley, G.R., Chaum, D. (eds.) CRYPTO 1984. LNCS, vol. 196, pp. 47–53. Springer, Heidelberg (1985). https://doi.org/10.1007/3-540-39568-7_5

42. Schnorr, C.-P.: Efficient Signature Generation by Smart Cards. J. Cryptol. **4**(3), 161–174 (1991)

43. Seo, J.H., Emura, K.: Revocable identity-based encryption revisited: security model and construction. In: Kurosawa, K., Hanaoka, G. (eds.) PKC 2013. LNCS, vol. 7778, pp. 216–234. Springer, Heidelberg (2013). https://doi.org/10.1007/978-3-642-36362-7_14

44. Sankaran, S.: Lightweight security framework for IoTs using identity based cryptography. In: ICACCI 2016, pp. 880–886 (2016)

45. Sun, H., Wen, Q., Zhang, H., Jin, Z.: A strongly secure identity-based authenticated key agreement protocol without pairings under the GDH assumption. Secur. Commun. Netw. **8**(17), 3167–3179 (2015)

46. Sun, H., Wen, Q., Li, W.: A strongly secure pairing-free certificateless authenticated key agreement protocol under the CDH assumption. Sci. China Inf. Sci. **59**(3), 1–16 (2016)
47. Takayasu, A.: Adaptively secure lattice-based revocable IBE in the QROM: compact parameters, tight security, and anonymity. Des. Codes Cryptogr. **89**(8), 1965–1992 (2021)
48. TechTarget: Comparing the Best Email Encryption Software Products (2015). https://searchsecurity.techtarget.com/feature/Comparing-the-best-email-encryption-software-product
49. Tomida, J., Fujioka, A., Nagai, A., Suzuki, K.: Strongly secure identity-based key exchange with single pairing operation. In: Sako, K., Schneider, S., Ryan, P.Y.A. (eds.) ESORICS 2019. LNCS, vol. 11736, pp. 484–503. Springer, Cham (2019). https://doi.org/10.1007/978-3-030-29962-0_23
50. Tsai, T.-T., Chuang, Y.-H., Tseng, Y.-M., Huang, S.-S., Hung, Y.-H.: A leakage-resilient ID-based authenticated key exchange protocol with a revocation mechanism. IEEE Access **9**, 128633–128647 (2021)
51. Tseng, Y.-M., Huang, S.-S., Tsai, T.-T., Ke, J.-H.: List-free ID-based mutual authentication and key agreement protocol for multiserver architectures. IEEE Trans. Emerg. Topics Comput. **4**(1), 102–112 (2015)
52. Wang, C., Li, Y., Xia, X., Zheng, K.: An efficient and provable secure revocable identity-based encryption scheme. PLOS One **9**(9), e106925 (2014)
53. VIBE Cybersecurity International: Verifiable Identity-Based Encryption (VIBE) Eliminates Public-Key Certificates (2021). https://vibecyber.com/
54. Watanabe, Y., Emura, K., Seo, J.H.: New revocable IBE in prime-order groups: adaptively secure, decryption key exposure resistant, and with short public parameters. In: Handschuh, H. (ed.) CT-RSA 2017. LNCS, vol. 10159, pp. 432–449. Springer, Cham (2017). https://doi.org/10.1007/978-3-319-52153-4_25
55. Wu, T.-Y., Tseng, Y.-M., Tsai, T.-T.: A revocable ID-based authenticated group key exchange protocol with resistant to malicious participants. Comput. Netw. **56**(12), 2994–3006 (2012)
56. Wu, T.-Y., Tsai, T.-T., Tseng, Y.-M.: A provably secure revocable id-based authenticated group key exchange protocol with identifying malicious participants. Sci. World J. (2014). ID 367264
57. Yang, G., Tan, C.-H.: Strongly secure certificateless key exchange without pairing. In: ACM CCS 2011, pp. 71–79 (2011)
58. Zhang, R., Tao, Y.: Key dependent message security for revocable identity-based encryption and identity-based encryption. In: Naccache, D., et al. (eds.) ICICS 2018. LNCS, vol. 11149, pp. 426–441. Springer, Cham (2018). https://doi.org/10.1007/978-3-030-01950-1_25

On the Discrete Logarithm Problem
in the Ideal Class Group
of Multiquadratic Fields

S. A. Novoselov[✉]

Immanuel Kant Baltic Federal University, A. Nevskogo str., 14, Kaliningrad 236016,
Russia
snovoselov@kantiana.ru

Abstract. In this work we show that the discrete logarithm problem in
the ideal class group of the multiquadratic field $K = \mathbb{Q}(\sqrt{d_1}, \ldots, \sqrt{d_n})$
of degree $m = 2^n$ can be solved in classical time $e^{\tilde{\mathcal{O}}(\max(\log m, \sqrt{\log D}))}$
using an adaptation of Pohlig-Hellman approach, where $D = d_1 \cdot \ldots \cdot d_n$.
This complexity is for the case when the factorization of the target ideal
norm is not given. Thanks to our implementation, we provide numerical examples of discrete logarithm computation in real and imaginary
number fields.

Keywords: multiquadratic field · ideal class group · norm relation ·
discrete logarithm problem · complexity

1   Introduction

A multiquadratic field is a number field defined as

$$K = \mathbb{Q}(\sqrt{d_1}, \ldots, \sqrt{d_n}),$$

where $d_i \in \mathbb{Z}$ for $i = 1, \ldots, n$ are square-free and nonzero. In the case when
all $d_i > 0$ the field K is called real, otherwise it is called imaginary. Ideal class
group Cl_K of K is a factor group of fractional ideals of K modulo principal ideals.
The ideal class group is a finite Abelian group. In general it is a non-cyclic group.

The *discrete logarithm problem (DLP)* in the ideal class group of K is
defined as follows. Given a target ideal I and the generators of the ideal class
group $\mathfrak{g}_1, \ldots, \mathfrak{g}_k$, find integers $\ell_1, \ldots, \ell_k$ such that $[I] = [\mathfrak{g}_1^{\ell_1} \cdot \ldots \cdot \mathfrak{g}_k^{\ell_k}]$. The
brackets [] here denote the representative of an ideal I in the class group Cl_K.

Multiquadratic fields are remarkable from the algorithmic perspective: some
problems that are known to be hard in general, turn out to have efficient classical
algorithms in case of multiquadratics. Examples include the result of Bauch et

The research was funded by the Russian Science Foundation (project No. 22-41-04411,
https://rscf.ru/en/project/22-41-04411/).

al. in [2] showing an efficient algorithm for the approximate shortest vector problem in principal ideals of multiquadratic fields (alongside with an algorithm for computing the unit group), as well as the work of Biasse-van Vredendaal [7] on computing the class group of multiquadratic number fields. In general number fields however, these tasks are not known to have efficient classical algorithms (in quantum setting there are polynomial time algorithms [6], and there are also efficient algorithms for special number fields [5,17,18]).

With this work we continue this line of work by showing how, a generally hard problem such as the discrete logarithm problem, has an efficient solution in multiquadratic fields. The main motivation of looking at this task is to extend the result of Bauch et al. from [2] to *non-principal* ideals and, therefore, being able to find short vectors in non-principal ideals efficiently. There is an extensive line of work [3,12,13] that considers the problem of finding a short element in non-principal ideals, and there the first step is to solve the discrete logarithm problem.

Prior Work. Thanks to the work Biasse-van Vredendaal [7], we can assume that we know the group structure of the class group Cl_K of a multiquadratic field K, and hence, we can define the DLP properly. Now let us consider the state-of-the-art in DLP computations in K.

Generic algorithms for solving the discrete logarithm problem are certainly applicable to the class group of multiquadratics. In particular, Pohlig-Hellam-Teske algorithm [24] solves this task in time subexponential in the discriminant of K and the size of the largest subgroup of Cl_K. The discrete logarithm problem in quadratic fields was considered in [8,26]. There it was proved that the complexity of solving DLP is $L_{\Delta_K}(1/2)$. For the fields that admit norm relations there is a general algorithm for the discrete logarithm computation [4, §5.1] based on the saturation techniques that can be applied also to multiquadratic fields, but this work does not present a complexity analysis of the algorithm (with exception of cyclotomic fields).

We should also mention here that the discrete logarithm problem in Cl_K becomes "easy", when we know the factorization of the target ideal I over the so-called factor base. In more details, let $S = \{\mathfrak{p}_i\}_{i=1,\dots,d}$ be a set of prime ideals generating Cl_K. If we know the factorization $I = \prod_{i=1}^{d} \mathfrak{p}_i^{e_i}$ of the target ideal I over the factor base S, then the discrete logarithm problem is reduced to the task of computing the class group (we give more details in Sect. 3).

In this work, we consider the general case, when we *do not* have the factorization of the target ideal over a factor base and we cannot just use class group computation algorithm [7].

Our Contributions

1. Inspired by the techniques from [2,7] on using norm relations, we show that the discrete logarithm problem in the ideal class group can be reduced to the corresponding problem in its quadratic subfields. As a result the complexity of

computing the discrete logarithm is reduced from $e^{\widetilde{\mathcal{O}}(\sqrt{\log \Delta_K})} = e^{\widetilde{\mathcal{O}}(\sqrt{m \log D})}$ ideal class group operations to $e^{\widetilde{\mathcal{O}}(\max(\log m, \sqrt{\log D}))}$ field operations where $D = d_1 \cdot \ldots \cdot d_n$ is the largest discriminant of the quadratic subfield of K. The main differences with the general algorithm from [4] for the fields admitting norm relations are the usage of Pohlig-Hellman approach in combination with saturation techniques and providing a complete complexity analysis of the algorithm.

2. One of the computational task we are facing during the discrete logarithm computations is computing square roots in the class group Cl_K. To this end, we provide an algorithm for square root computation, which again can be viewed as a variation of Pohlig-Hellman method [21].

3. We implemented our algorithms for discrete logarithm computation in class groups of both imaginary and real multiquadratic fields and provide examples of computations.

Our Techniques. A particular structure of the Galois group of a multiquadratic field K gives an efficient way of solving norm relations. This in turn allows to reduce some computational tasks from K to its subfields and then lift the solutions back to K. Notably, both works [2] resp. [7] use norm relations to lift the solutions of the unit group resp. class group from the subfields of K to the field K itself. In our work we exploit the norm relations too, but now we extend this approach to non-principal ideals and to the solution of the discrete logarithm problem with Pohlig-Hellman approach.

Another important ingredient of our algorithm is square root computations in the class group Cl_K. We show how to reduce the problem from Cl_K to cyclic subgroups of Cl_K, and then using Pohlig-Hellman method for the latter task.

Organization of the Paper. In Sect. 2 we give all necessary notations. Section 3 contains preliminaries with definitions of general routines used for the class group computation and for solving DLP. In Sect. 4 we describe algorithms for computation of square roots of non-principal ideals of the form $I = h \prod_{i=1}^{d} \mathfrak{p}_i^{e_i}$ for $h \in K$. These algorithms are essential parts of the discrete logarithm computations. Section 5 contains the main part of the work where an algorithm for solving DLP is described. In Sect. 6 we describe our implementation of the algorithm and provide examples of computations.

2 Notation

We use the following notations.

- $K = \mathbb{Q}(\sqrt{d_1}, \ldots, \sqrt{d_n})$ is a n-quadratic field where all d_i are pairwise coprime and square-free, $\mathcal{O}_K$ is its ring of integers. It is known [2, Th. 2.1] that a basis of K (as a $\mathbb{Q}$-vector space) consist of 2^n complex numbers $\prod_{j \in J} \sqrt{d_j}$ for all $J \subseteq \{1, \ldots, n\}$. So the degree of K is 2^n;

- τ is the complex conjugation;
- $\mathrm{Cl}_K := I_K / \mathrm{Princ}_K$ – class group of K, i.e. the factor group of fractional ideals I_K of K modulo principal ideals of $\mathcal{O}_K$;
- h_K is the order of Cl_K;
- $[I]$ is the class of the ideal I in the ideal class group Cl_K;
- $G_K := \mathrm{Gal}(K/\mathbb{Q})$ is the absolute Galois group of K;
- K_σ is a fixed field of an automorphism $\sigma \in G_K$;
- Δ_K is the discriminant of K;
- $L_N(\alpha) := L_N(\alpha, c) = e^{(\log N)^\alpha (\log \log N)^{1-\alpha}(c+o(1))}$;
- $v_{\mathfrak{p}}(I)$ is the valuation of ideal I at a prime ideal $\mathfrak{p}$;
- $N(I)$, $N(a)$ is the absolute norm of an ideal I or $a \in K$;
- $\max \mathbf{v}, \max M$ are the maximums of absolute values of entries in vector $\mathbf{v}$ or a matrix M.

3   Background on Class Group and Discrete Logarithm Computation in Number Fields

3.1   Ideal Class Group Computation

In this section we recall known methods to find the generators of the class group Cl_K. Assume that we have a factor base $S = \{\mathfrak{p}_1, \ldots, \mathfrak{p}_d\}$ – a set of all prime ideals of $\mathcal{O}_K$ that generate the class group Cl_K. For this purpose we can take all prime ideals of norm $\leq 12 \log^2 \Delta_K$, see [1]. In practice this general bound is very pessimistic and a better heuristic bound can be computed "ad-hoc" using Grenié-Molteni algorithm [15] under the Generalized Rieman Hypothesis (GRH). For our purpose of discrete logarithm computation we can take even a smaller bound, but in this case our algorithm can sometimes fail and we may have to run it several times, since we may end up working in a subgroup of the class group.

Let us recall a method of obtaining the generators $\mathfrak{g}_i$'s of Cl_K. For the given factor base $S = \{\mathfrak{p}_1, \ldots, \mathfrak{p}_d\}$, we call $(\alpha, \mathbf{e}) \in K \times \mathbb{Z}^d$ a relation if $\alpha \mathcal{O}_K = \prod_{i=1}^d \mathfrak{p}_i^{e_i}$. One relation is computed by taking a random element $\alpha \in K$ such that it splits over the factor base S. After collecting enough relations we form a matrix of relations A whose rows are vectors $\mathbf{e}$. The Smith Normal Form $A = UBV$ of this matrix gives us the group structure of Cl_K and its generators. In particular, we have $B = \mathrm{diag}(b_1, \ldots, b_k)$ and the ideal class group Cl_K is the following product of cyclic groups

$$\mathrm{Cl}_K \simeq C_{b_1} \times \ldots \times C_{b_k} \simeq \langle \mathfrak{g}_1 \rangle \times \ldots \times \langle \mathfrak{g}_k \rangle,$$

where $\mathfrak{g}_i = \prod_{j=1}^d \mathfrak{p}_j^{v'_{i,j}}$ for $V^{-1} = (v'_{i,j})$. In addition, we have $\mathfrak{p}_i = \prod_{j=1}^k \mathfrak{g}_j^{v_{i,j}}$. Moreover, let $\{(\alpha_i, \mathbf{e}_i) \mid i = 1, \ldots, r\}$ be a full set of relations. Then we have

$$\mathfrak{g}_i^{b_i} = \beta_i \mathcal{O}_K = \prod_{j=1}^r \alpha_j^{u_{i,j}} \mathcal{O}_K, \tag{1}$$

where $U = (u_{i,j})$.

It is well known that the general process of computing the ideal class group takes subexponential time [8, §3] in Δ_K – the discriminant of the field K. However, as it was shown by Biasse and van Vredendaal [7], for multiquadratic fields the problem can be efficiently reduced to finding such relations in certain quadratic subfields of K, which is a much simpler task, and then lifting them to K. It results in an algorithm of complexity subexponential in $D = d_1 \cdot \ldots \cdot d_n$ – the largest discriminant of quadratic subfields, which is always smaller than Δ_K.

3.2   Discrete Logarithm Problem in the Ideal Class Group of Number Fields

The discrete logarithm problem (DLP) for an input ideal I and the generators of the class group $\mathfrak{g}_1, \ldots, \mathfrak{g}_k$ consists of finding integers $\ell_1, \ldots, \ell_k$ such that

$$[I] = [\mathfrak{g}_1^{\ell_1} \cdot \ldots \cdot \mathfrak{g}_k^{\ell_k}].$$

The complexity of solving the discrete logarithm problem in the ideal class group depends on the given ideal I and its representation. In this section we consider two cases: when the given ideal I is smooth relative to a factor-base S, and a general case, when I is not S-smooth. The DLP in the former case can be solved by a straightforward application of linear algebra to the relations described in Sect. 3.1. For the latter case we describe here a general method for solving DLP due to Buchmann-Düllmann [8]. It will be used later for quadratic subfields of multiquadratic fields.

S-Smooth Ideal Case. Let $A = UBV$ be a matrix of class group relations (as in Sect. 3.1) in its Smith Normal Form. If the target ideal I factors over the factor base S (it is S-smooth), i.e. $I = \prod_{i=1}^{d} \mathfrak{p}_i^{e_i}$, then the solution of the discrete logarithm problem can be found in the following way. Using the equality $\mathfrak{p}_i = \prod_{j=1}^{k} \mathfrak{g}_j^{v_{i,j}}$, we can express the target ideal as

$$I = \prod_{i=1}^{d} \mathfrak{p}_i^{e_i} = \prod_{i=1}^{d} \prod_{j=1}^{k} \mathfrak{g}_j^{v_{i,j} e_i}. \tag{2}$$

From this we can compute the desired values of ℓ_j as $\ell_j = \sum_{i=1}^{d} v_{i,j} e_i$. Note that the ideal I is S-smooth only if its norm factors into the product of primes p such that $\mathfrak{p} \mid p\mathcal{O}_K$ for $\mathfrak{p} \in S$. In this case the values e_i can be computed efficiently as $e_i = v_{\mathfrak{p}_i}(I)$ using [11, Alg. 4.8.17]. The computation of $v_{\mathfrak{p}_i}(I)$ requires the knowledge of a basis of $\mathcal{O}_K$. For arbitrary number fields an efficient algorithm for computing such basis is not known. However, for multiquadratic fields there is an efficient algorithm [10].

If we know the factorization $N(I) = q_1^{x_1} \cdot \ldots \cdot q_r^{x_r}$ of the absolute norm $N(I)$ of the input ideal I, then we can add all prime ideals $\mathfrak{q}_i \mid q_i \mathcal{O}_K$ to the factor base S and then run a class group computation algorithm. This process gives us a matrix of relations that include $\mathfrak{q}_i$'s and we can apply Eq. (2) to our ideal

$$I = \prod_{i=1}^{r} \mathfrak{q}_i^{v_{\mathfrak{q}_i}(I)}$$

to obtain a solution to DLP.

Arbitrary Ideal Case (Algorithm 1). In the case when we do not know the factorization of $N(I)$ or the primes in the factorization are too big to run a class group computation algorithm, we can reduce the discrete logarithm problem to the S-smooth case by finding an S-smooth ideal J such that $[I \cdot J] = [1]$. Then $[I] = [J^{-1}]$ and we can apply Eq. (2) to J^{-1} to solve the discrete logarithm problem.

Finding such an ideal J can be achieved by selecting random J, computing the product $I \cdot J$, and applying the LLL-reduction [16] to the matrix of HNF-representation (see [11, §4.7.1]) of this product. The reduced ideal $I \cdot J$ belongs to the same class as $I \cdot J$, but has smaller coefficients in the matrix representation.

We select random ideals J (see steps 1–2 of Algorithm 1) until we obtain a S-smooth reduced ideal that gives us a solution to DLP. The described method for finding S-smooth representation of ideal I is due to Buchmann-Düllmann [8]. The complete version of this method is presented in Algorithm 1. For completeness, we give the analysis of this algorithm.

Algorithm 1: GenCLDL(I, S). Finding a S-smooth representation of the ideal in the ideal class group of a number field.

Input: An ideal I of a number field K, a set $S = \{\mathfrak{p}_1, \ldots, \mathfrak{p}_d\}$ of prime ideals of K s.t. $\mathfrak{p}_1 \mid (p_1), \ldots, \mathfrak{p}_d \mid (p_d)$ for some prime numbers $p_1, \ldots, p_d$ and S generates the class group Cl_K.

Output: an ideal hJ^{-1} represented by a pair $(h, \mathbf{a}) \in K \times \mathbb{Z}^d$ such that $I \cdot J = I \cdot \prod_{i=1}^{d} \mathfrak{p}_i^{a_i} = h\mathcal{O}_K$.

1 Choose random $\mathbf{a} \in [0, \ldots, \Delta_K - 1]^d$;

2 $I' = \mathrm{LLL}(I \cdot \prod_{i=1}^{d} \mathfrak{p}_i^{a_i})$;

3 **if** $N(I') = p_1^{e_1} \cdot \ldots \cdot p_d^{e_d}$ *for* $(e_1, \ldots, e_d) \in \mathbb{Z}^d$ **then**

4      $b_i = v_{\mathfrak{p}_i}(I')$ for $i = 1, \ldots, d$;

5      $J = \prod_{i=1}^{d} \mathfrak{p}_i^{a_i - b_i}$;

6   **return** PrincipalGenerator$(I \cdot J) \cdot J^{-1}$

7 **else**

8   Go to Step 1.

9 **end**

Proposition 1. *The complexity of the finding a S-smooth representation of an ideal I of a number field K of fixed degree in the ideal class [I] using Algorithm 1 is heuristically $L_{\Delta_K}(1/2)$ ideal multiplications and reductions.*

Proof. For quadratic fields the proof is in [8, §3]. It is widely assumed that it is also valid for any number fields, but we did not find such a proof. So, for completeness we include a proof here. Assume heuristically that the norm of the reduced ideal product in Step 2 is bounded by $|\Delta_K|$ and it is uniformly distributed among the integers of such size. The probability that a number bounded by $|\Delta_K|$ is $L_{\Delta_K}(1/2)$-smooth is equal to $1/L_{\Delta_K}(1/2)$ according to results of Canfield, Erdős, Pomerance [9] (we use the formulation from [11, Th. 10.2.1]). Therefore we expect to obtain a smooth representation after $L_{\Delta_K}(1/2)$ trials. Assuming we use fast multiplication algorithms, each trial requires $d \cdot \log \Delta_K$ plus 1 (for the multiplication by I in Step 2 of Algorithm 1) multiplications of ideals with LLL-reduction [11, Alg. 6.5.5] after each multiplication. The complexity of LLL-reduction of ideal product is bounded by $\widetilde{\mathcal{O}}(\text{poly}(\deg K \cdot \log N(I) \cdot \Delta_K))$ field operations. To generate the class group it is enough to take all prime ideals with norms $\leq 12 \ln^2 \Delta_K$ (Bach bound [1]). Then $d = \mathcal{O}(\log \log \Delta_K)$ and each trial requires $\text{poly}(\log \Delta_K)$ ideal multiplications and reductions. The resulting complexity of Algorithm 1 is $L_{\Delta_K}(1/2)$. □

In subsequent sections we describe a more efficient algorithm for multiquadratic fields that reduces the discrete logarithm problem to the corresponding problem in certain quadratic subfields and apply Algorithm 1 only to these quadratic subfields. For lifting solutions from quadratic subfields back to the base field we will need to perform square root computation of non-principal ideal. In the next section we develop efficient tools for this task.

4   Square Root Computation for Decomposed Ideals

Assume that we have an ideal I of the multiquadratic field K given in HNF and we want to find a decomposition of this ideal over a factor base S, i.e. to find $h \in K$ and a vector $\mathbf{e}$ such that $I = h \prod_i \mathfrak{p}_i^{e_i}$ for $\mathfrak{p}_i \in S$. In the following we will see that the norm relation gives us such a decomposition for the ideal I^2. This is achieved by joining solutions of the problem from specially selected subfields of K. In this section we describe a method for restoring decomposition of I from the decomposition of I^2. Our method reduces the problem to the computation of square roots in cyclic subgroups of class group and can be viewed as a variation of Pohlig-Hellman approach. Combining square roots from cyclic subgroups produces exponential (in the degree of the field) number of square roots. So, we use also a saturation technique for efficient selection of a suitable square root.

4.1   Square Root Computation in Cyclic Groups

Since we reduce the discrete logarithm problem to the cyclic subgroups of class group, we consider first the square root computation problem in such subgroups.

In general the problem of computing square roots in Abelian groups is known to be hard [22]. For example, taking square roots in the group $\mathbb{Z}_N^\times$ is equivalent to the factorization of the number N. However, extracting square roots in a cyclic group can be done efficiently whenever we know a generator of the group.

For a cyclic group $\langle \mathfrak{g} \rangle$ of odd order b, the computation of square root reduces to raising the input element of the group to the power of $\frac{b+1}{2}$. For the cyclic group of even order, the problem reduces to the discrete logarithm computation in a power-of-2 order subgroup. The discrete logarithm problem in a group of power-of-2 order can be solved using the Pohlig-Hellman method [21]. In the following we denote by $\mathrm{DLOG}_{\mathfrak{g}}(\mathfrak{h})$ the computation of the discrete logarithm in the cyclic group $\langle \mathfrak{g} \rangle$ for the element $\mathfrak{h} \in \langle \mathfrak{g} \rangle$.

The procedure for computing square roots in cyclic group is standard, we give it in Algorithm 2. For elementary explanation of this algorithm and more details on taking square roots in cyclic groups we refer to [22]. The algorithm returns FAIL when the square root does not exist. This can occur only for cyclic groups of even order, since in such groups half of the elements are squares and half are non-squares, while in the cyclic groups of odd order every element is a square. Note that if the exponent e of the input element $\mathfrak{h} = \mathfrak{g}^e$ is given explicitly, the algorithm does not require operations in the group $\langle \mathfrak{g} \rangle$. In our context of class group computations it is very important, since such operations are slow.

Algorithm 2: CycSqrt$(\mathfrak{g}, e)$. Square root computation in a cyclic subgroup of class group CL_K.

Input: An ideal $\mathfrak{g}$ that generates a cyclic subgroup of class group, $b = \# \langle \mathfrak{g} \rangle$, and an exponent e for an element $\mathfrak{g}^e \in \langle \mathfrak{g} \rangle$.

Output: A pair $(\mathfrak{a}, \mathfrak{b})$ of ideals s.t. $[(\mathfrak{a}\mathfrak{b})^2] = [\mathfrak{b}^2] = [\mathfrak{g}^e]$ or FAIL if there are no square roots.

1 **if** b *is odd* **then**
2 $\quad$ **return** $(\mathfrak{g}^0, \mathfrak{g}^{e(\frac{b+1}{2})})$
3 **end**
4 Find r, s such that $b = 2^r \cdot t$ where t is odd;
5 Compute $\ell = \mathrm{DLOG}_{\mathfrak{g}^t}(\mathfrak{g}^{t \cdot e})$, a discrete logarithm in the group of order 2^r;
6 **if** $\ell \bmod 2 \neq 0$ **then**
7 $\quad$ **return** FAIL
8 **end**
9 **return** $(\mathfrak{g}^{\frac{tb}{2}}, \mathfrak{g}^{e(\frac{t+1}{2}) - \frac{t\ell}{2}})$.

A pair $(\mathfrak{a}, \mathfrak{b})$ of ideals returned by the algorithm represents two square roots (in the class group Cl_K) of input element $\mathfrak{g}^e$, namely $\mathfrak{a}\mathfrak{b}$ and $\mathfrak{b}$. In the following such representation allows us to efficiently store the set of square roots in the product of cyclic groups (when we compute a square root in the product of k cyclic groups, these representation allows us to store k elements instead of 2^k).

Proposition 2. *Assume that $\mathfrak{g}$ is represented as an ideal product $\prod_{i=1}^{d} \mathfrak{p}_i^{f_i}$, where $S = \{\mathfrak{p}_1, \ldots, \mathfrak{p}_d\}$ is a set of primes that generates the class group. Then the computation of square root(s) of $\mathfrak{g}^e$ in the order b cyclic subgroup $\langle \mathfrak{g} \rangle$ of the class group CL_K using Algorithm 2 requires $\mathcal{O}(\log b)$ operations in $\mathbb{Z}/b\mathbb{Z}$. Moreover, these square roots are also represented as ideal products.*

Proof. In the case of odd b the complexity is $\mathcal{O}(1)$ operations in $\mathbb{Z}/b\mathbb{Z}$, if the exponent e is given. In the even case we have to solve the discrete logarithm problem in a cyclic group of power-of-2 order group of size $2^{\mathcal{O}(\log b)}$ in the worst case (i.e., $t = 1$ in the notations of Step 4 on Algorithm 2). This can be done [19, Fact 3.66] in time $\mathcal{O}(\log b)$. $\qquad\square$

4.2   Saturation Technique

The saturation technique described in [2, §4] and [7, §4C] allows us, for a given set $T = \{a_1, \ldots, a_m\} \subset K$ and an element $h \in K$, to find efficiently the set of exponent vectors $\mathbf{e}$ such that $h \cdot a_1^{e_1} \cdot \ldots \cdot a_m^{e_m}$ is a square. The technique uses quadratic characters defined in the following way. Let $\mathfrak{D}_1, \ldots, \mathfrak{D}_k$ be a set of random prime ideals of residue degree 1 that *do not* belong to the factor base and let $Q_i = \mathrm{N}(\mathfrak{D}_i)$ for $i = 1, \ldots, k$. Let

$$\phi_{\mathfrak{D}_i} : \mathbb{Z}[x_1, \ldots, x_n]/(x^2 - d_1, \ldots, x^2 - d_n) \simeq \mathbb{Z}[\sqrt{d_1}, \ldots, \sqrt{d_n}] \to \mathbb{F}_{Q_i},$$

be a map defined by the substitution $x_j \mapsto s_j$ where s_j is a square root of d_j modulo Q_i for $j = 1, \ldots, n$. Then the map

$$\chi_{\mathfrak{D}_i} : x \mapsto \left(\frac{\phi_{\mathfrak{D}_i}(x)}{Q_i} \right)$$

is a quadratic character from K to $\{0, 1, -1\}$. If it occurs that $\chi_{\mathfrak{D}_i}$ is zero on the one of elements $h, a_1, \ldots, a_m$, then choose another $\mathfrak{D}_i$. The key idea used for recognizing the squares in the field K is the fact that for a square $x \in (K^{\times})^2$ we have $\chi_{\mathfrak{D}_i}(x) = 1$, and for a non-square we expect that for at least one character $\chi_{\mathfrak{D}_i}$ holds $\chi_{\mathfrak{D}_i}(x) = -1$. To detect squares with error probability $1/2^t$ it is enough (heuristic from [2, §4.2]) to take $k = m + \sqrt{t}$ characters. Now, we can define a group homomorphism

$$X : x \mapsto \log_{-1} \chi_{\mathfrak{D}_i}(x)$$

from K to $\mathbb{F}_2$. Since we expect that for non squares at least one of the characters will return -1, all squares lie in the kernel of this map with high probability depending on the number of characters. So, we can recognize a square now via solving the matrix equation

$$X(h) = \mathbf{e} A$$

for $A = (X(a_i))$.

In more precise form the procedure is described in Algorithm 3.

Algorithm 3: FindSquare($h, a_1, \ldots, a_m$). Finding a square in the multi-quadratic field.

Input: An element $h \in K$, a subset $\{a_1, \ldots, a_m\}$ of a multiquadratic field $K = \mathbb{Q}(\sqrt{d_1}, \ldots, \sqrt{d_n})$.

Output: A vector $\mathbf{e} \in \{0,1\}^m$ such that $h \cdot a^{e_1} \cdot \ldots \cdot a^{e_m}$ is a square in K or FAIL if it does not exist.

1 Define enough characters $\chi_{\mathfrak{D}_i}$ and the map X;

2 Compute matrix $A = \begin{pmatrix} X(a_1) \\ \ldots \\ X(a_m) \end{pmatrix}$;

3 Compute $v = X(h)$;

4 Solve matrix equation $v = \mathbf{e} \cdot A \pmod 2$;

5 **return** $\mathbf{e}$ or FAIL if there are no solutions.

If we take $a_1, \ldots, a_m$ to be generators of the unit group of $\mathcal{O}_K$ and h as a generator of some a principal ideal, we obtain IdealSqrt procedure from [2, Alg. 6.1] for computing a square root of a principal ideal. The following proposition analyses Algorithm 3.

Proposition 3. *Given elements $h, a_1, \ldots, a_m$ from a multiquadratic field K Algorithm 3 finds a binary vector $\mathbf{e}$ such that $h \cdot a_1^{e_1} \cdot \ldots \cdot a_m^{e_m}$ is a square in $\widetilde{\mathcal{O}}(\max(m^3, m^2 B \deg K))$ bit operations with probability of error $\leq 1/2^{\sqrt{m}}$. Here, B is a bound for bit sizes of coefficients of $h, a_1, \ldots, a_m$.*

Proof. According to the heuristic from [2, §4.2], taking r random characters allows us to detect squares among the elements $a_1, \ldots, a_m$ with success probability at least $1 - 2^{r-m}$. To have error probability $\leq 1/2^{\sqrt{m}}$, we have to take $r = m + \sqrt{m}$ characters. Defining each character takes time $\widetilde{\mathcal{O}}(\deg K)$. Then Step 1 in the algorithm takes time $\widetilde{\mathcal{O}}(m \cdot \deg K)$. Evaluation of each character takes time $\widetilde{\mathcal{O}}(B \cdot \deg K)$ [2, §4.1]. In total we have to evaluate $m + \sqrt{m}$ characters for each element from the set $\{h, a_1, \ldots, a_m\}$. Thus, Steps 2, 3 take time $\widetilde{\mathcal{O}}(B \cdot m^2 \cdot \deg K)$. Step 4 can be done using Gaussian elimination $\pmod 2$ and this takes time $\widetilde{\mathcal{O}}(m^3)$. Combining the complexities of all steps gives us now total complexity of $\widetilde{\mathcal{O}}(\max(m^3, m^2 B \deg K))$ of Algorithm 3. $\qquad\square$

4.3 Square Root of Decomposed Ideal by Reducing to Cyclic Groups

Having now a procedure to compute square roots in a cyclic group and the saturation technique, we are able to define an algorithm for the square root extraction of a given decomposed ideal $I = \alpha \prod_{i=1}^{d} \mathfrak{p}_i^{e_i} = \alpha J$ for $\alpha \in K$. Recall that $S = \{\mathfrak{p}, \ldots, \mathfrak{p}_d\}$ is a set of prime ideals generating the class group $\mathrm{Cl}_K = \langle \mathfrak{g}_1 \rangle \times \ldots \times \langle \mathfrak{g}_k \rangle$. Every ideal of the number field K can be decomposed to the above form for some $\alpha \in K$ and exponent vector **e**. Since the ideal J is S-smooth, we can write it in terms of the class group generators $\mathfrak{g}_1, \ldots, \mathfrak{g}_k$ using the equality

$$\mathfrak{p}_i = \prod_{j=1}^{k} \mathfrak{g}_j^{v_{i,j}},$$

where $v_{i,j}$ are coefficients of the matrix V from the Smith normal form $A = U \cdot B \cdot V$ of a matrix of class group relations A. We consider the matrices A, U, V as the precomputed data available as the result of class group computation.

After computing the above representation of J in terms of $\mathfrak{g}_1, \ldots, \mathfrak{g}_k$, the square roots of $[J]$ can be found by extracting square roots in cyclic groups $\langle \mathfrak{g}_1 \rangle$, $\ldots, \langle \mathfrak{g}_k \rangle$. Extracting square roots in a cyclic group can be done efficiently using Algorithm 2 whenever we know the generator of the group $\langle \mathfrak{g}_i \rangle$ and the corresponding power of J in $\mathfrak{g}_i$ (see Sect. 4.1 for details). Each such a square root extraction in a cyclic group gives us one (if the order of the cyclic group is odd) or two (if the order of the cyclic group is even) square root(s). After taking all possible combinations of these square roots we have 2^s square roots of $[J]$ where s is a number of cyclic groups of even order. In the worst case we have $s = \log_2 h_K = \mathcal{O}(\log \Delta_K)$ and working with such amount of roots will lead us to an exponential algorithm. To avoid this, we use the saturation technique described in [2, §4.1,§4.2] for efficient selection of a suitable square root. Recall that Algorithm 2 for square root computation in cyclic group $\langle \mathfrak{g}_i \rangle$ returns a pair $\mathfrak{a}_i, \mathfrak{b}_i$ of S-smooth ideals such that $[\mathfrak{a}_i]$ is of order 2 if b_i is even and order 1 if b_i is odd. So, we have two square roots $[\mathfrak{a}_i \mathfrak{b}_i]$ and $[\mathfrak{b}_i]$ which coincide when the cyclic group has odd order. After computing all square roots in cyclic groups we have that a square root of $[J]$ is of the form $[\prod_{i=1}^{k} \mathfrak{a}_i^{x_i} \mathfrak{b}_i]$ for

some $x_1, \ldots, x_k \in \{0, 1\}$. This means that ideal $J/\prod_{i=1}^{k} (\mathfrak{a}_i^{x_i} \mathfrak{b}_i)^2$ is principal. Enumerating all of $x_1, \ldots, x_k \in \{0, 1\}$ will give us all square roots of $[J]$. Our goal is to find such a binary vector **x** that

$$\alpha J / \prod_{i=1}^{k} (\mathfrak{a}_i^{x_i} \mathfrak{b}_i)^2 = \alpha'^2 \mathcal{O}_K$$

for some $\alpha' \in K$. If we find such a vector **x**, we have

$$I = \alpha J = \alpha'^2 \left(\prod_{i=1}^{k} \mathfrak{a}_i^{x_i} \mathfrak{b}_i \right)^2$$

and so the square root of the ideal I is equal to $\alpha' \prod_{i=1}^{k} \mathfrak{a}_i^{x_i} \mathfrak{b}_i$. It remains to describe a way to find such a binary vector **x**. Since $\mathfrak{a}_i^2$ is principal (recall that $[\mathfrak{a}_i]$ is of order 2), the ideal $J/\prod_{i=1}^{k} \mathfrak{b}_i^2$ is also principal. Let $\alpha_i \mathcal{O}_K = \mathfrak{a}_i^2$

and $\beta\mathcal{O}_K = J/\prod_{i=1}^{k}\mathfrak{b}_i^2$. Since ideals $J, \mathfrak{a}_1, \ldots, \mathfrak{a}_k, \mathfrak{b}_1, \ldots, \mathfrak{b}_k$ are all S-smooth, we can compute $\alpha_1, \ldots, \alpha_k, \beta$ efficiently by solving matrix equation with the relations matrix A. This computation requires in addition that we have the generators for relations (S-units) in the class group (stored in compact representation of field elements) from class group computation. Since ideals are defined up to units we also use generators of unit group (mod torsion) $\mathcal{O}_K^\times \setminus \mu \simeq \langle u_1, \ldots, u_r \rangle$. For multiquadratic fields the unit group generators can be found efficiently using [2]. Now using the saturation technique (FindSquare procedure from Sect. 4.2) we can find a binary vector $\mathbf{x}$ such that $h = (\alpha \cdot \beta)/(\prod_{i=1}^{k}\alpha_i^{x_i} \prod_{i=1}^{r} u_i^{x_{i+k}})$ is a square. Thus, we have

$$\sqrt{I} = \sqrt{h}\prod_{j=1}^{k}\mathfrak{a}_j^{x_j}\mathfrak{b}_j.$$

The complete procedure for square root extraction for a decomposed ideal is presented in Algorithm 4.

Algorithm 4: IdealSqrt(I, S). Computation of square root for a decomposed ideal of a number field K.

Input:

- An ideal $I = \alpha \prod_{i=1}^{d}\mathfrak{p}_i^{e_i}$ given by a vector $\mathbf{e} = (e_1, \ldots, e_d)$ and $\alpha \in K$,
- $S = \{\mathfrak{p}_1, \ldots, \mathfrak{p}_d\}$ is a set of prime ideals generating the class group Cl_K,
- $\mathrm{Cl}_K = \langle \mathfrak{g}_1 \rangle \times \ldots \times \langle \mathfrak{g}_k \rangle$, a matrix A of class group relations in SNF.

Output: Ideal $J = \alpha' \prod_{i=1}^{d}\mathfrak{p}_i^{f_i}$ s.t. $J^2 = I$ or FAIL.

1 Compute $\mathbf{g}$ s.t. $\prod_{i=1}^{d}\mathfrak{p}_i^{e_i} = \prod_{i=1}^{k}\mathfrak{g}_i^{g_i}$ using Eq. (2);
2 Compute ideals $(\mathfrak{a}_i, \mathfrak{b}_i) = \mathrm{CycSqrt}(\mathfrak{g}_i^{g_i}, b_i)$ for $b_i = \#\langle \mathfrak{g}_i \rangle$ and all $i = 1, \ldots, k$ or return FAIL if any of square roots does not exist;
3 Compute $\beta \in K$, s.t. $\beta\mathcal{O}_K = \prod_{i=1}^{d}\mathfrak{p}_i^{e_i} / \prod_{j=1}^{k}\mathfrak{b}_j^2$;
4 Compute $\alpha_i \in K$, s.t. $\alpha_i\mathcal{O}_K = \mathfrak{a}_i^2$;
5 Compute the generators of the unit group $u_1, \ldots, u_r$ using [2];
6 $\mathbf{x} = \mathrm{FindSquare}(\alpha \cdot \beta, \alpha_1, \ldots, \alpha_k, u_1, \ldots, u_r)$;

7 Return $\sqrt{\dfrac{\alpha\beta}{\prod_{i=1}^{k}\alpha_i^{x_i}\prod_{i=1}^{r}u_i^{x_{i+k}}}}\prod_{j=1}^{k}\mathfrak{a}_j^{x_j}\mathfrak{b}_j$;

The algorithm can be applied to any number field with exception of FindSquare procedure which requires an adaptation from multiquadratic fields to the general case. We prove (classical) polynomial time complexity only for multiquadratic fields. The proof presented in the following proposition.

Proposition 4. *If a square root of a given ideal* $I = \alpha \prod\limits_{i=1}^{d} \mathfrak{p}_i^{e_i}$ *of a multiquadratic number field K exists, then Algorithm 4 computes it in*

$$\widetilde{\mathcal{O}}(\mathrm{poly}(\log \max \mathbf{e}, \mathrm{Size}(\alpha), \log \Delta_K))$$

bit operations. The algorithm fails only when a square root does not exist. Here, $\max \mathbf{e}$ *is the maximum of absolute values of coefficients in* $\mathbf{e}$ *and* $\mathrm{Size}(\alpha)$ *is the bit size of α.*

Proof. We assume that all number field arithmetic is performed in compact representation, i.e. a field element γ is represented as $\gamma = \prod\limits_i \gamma_i{}^{v_i}$ where $\gamma_1, \gamma_2, \ldots$ are small field elements of polynomial size. This allows us to work with field elements of exponential size using polynomial time arithmetic. For details we refer to [7, §4C]. When dealing with multiplication or division of ideals, we assume that all ideals are given in the form $\prod\limits_{i=1}^{d} \mathfrak{p}_i^{v_i}$, i.e. they are represented by a vector $\mathbf{v} \in \mathbb{Z}^d$, and all operations are performed using vectors of exponents only. We do not evaluate such ideal products explicitly. As input we have precomputed a matrix of relations A in SNF with transformation matrices U, V such that $UAV = B = \mathrm{diag}(b_1, \ldots, b_k)$. The coefficients of A are in $e^{\widetilde{\mathcal{O}}(\log \deg K \cdot \sqrt{\log D})}$ if we have computed the class group with the algorithm from [7]. Since the algorithm returns a basis of S-units, the matrix A has $\mathcal{O}(d)$ rows and columns. Due to Bach's bound [1] we have $d = \mathcal{O}(\log \log \Delta_K)$. Since $\#\mathrm{Cl}_K = \mathcal{O}(\sqrt{\Delta_K})$, we have also $k = \mathcal{O}(\log \Delta_K)$ and the maximal size of k is achieved when the class group is a direct product of cyclic groups of order 2. The transformation matrices U, V for SNF of A can be computed using the algorithm from [23, Ch. 8]. In this case we have [23, Lemma 8.9] that $\max V < d \cdot b_k^2 = \widetilde{\mathcal{O}}(\Delta_K)$. So, the bit sizes of elements in V are polynomial in the $\log \Delta_K$.

Given a matrix A of relations in Cl_K in SNF and an ideal I, we can compute each exponent g_i in $J = \prod\limits_{i=1}^{k} \mathfrak{g}_i^{g_i}$ for $i = 1, \ldots, k$ using Eq. (2) in $2d$ operations modulo b_i. Then the complexity of Step 1 is $\mathcal{O}(dk) = \mathcal{O}(\log \Delta_K \log \log \Delta_K)$ operations in $\mathbb{Z}/b\mathbb{Z}$, where $b = \max(b_1, \ldots, b_k)$. Since, $g_j = \sum\limits_{i=1}^{d} v_{i,j} \cdot e_i$ we have $g_j = \widetilde{\mathcal{O}}(\max \mathbf{e} \cdot \Delta_K)$.

Using Proposition 2, we compute k square roots in cyclic groups $\langle \mathfrak{g}_i \rangle$ in time $\mathcal{O}(k \log b) = \mathcal{O}(\log \Delta_K \log \log \Delta_K)$. Thus, Step 2 requires $\mathcal{O}(\log \Delta_K \log \log \Delta_K)$ operations in $\mathbb{Z}/b\mathbb{Z}$ in total. If a square root does not exist, it does not exist in one of the cyclic groups $\langle \mathfrak{g}_i \rangle$. In this case the algorithm returns FAIL.

In the following we will need estimates for the sizes of exponents in S-smooth ideals returned by CycSqrt procedure. At the end of the Step 2 we have $\mathfrak{a}_i = \mathfrak{g}_i^{a_i'}, \mathfrak{b}_i = \mathfrak{g}_i^{b_i'}$, where $a_i' = \widetilde{\mathcal{O}}(\Delta_K)$ and $b_i' = \widetilde{\mathcal{O}}(\max \mathbf{e} \cdot \Delta_K^2)$. We have $\mathfrak{g}_i = \prod\limits_{j=1}^{d} \mathfrak{p}_j^{v_{i,j}'}$ where elements $v_{i,j}'$ are such that $V^{-1} = (v_{i,j}')$. For the matrix V^{-1} we have a bound [23, Lemma 8.9]:

$$\max V^{-1} = d^{2d+1}(\max A)^{2d} = e^{\widetilde{\mathcal{O}}(\log^2(\deg K)\cdot\sqrt{\log D})},$$

since $d = \log\log \Delta_K = \log(\deg K \cdot \log D)$. Then

$$v_{\mathfrak{p}_j}(\mathfrak{a}_i) = \widetilde{\mathcal{O}}(\Delta_K) \cdot e^{\widetilde{\mathcal{O}}(\log^2(\deg K)\cdot\sqrt{\log D})}$$

and

$$v_{\mathfrak{p}_j}(\mathfrak{b}_i) = \widetilde{\mathcal{O}}(\max \mathbf{e} \cdot \Delta_K^2) \cdot e^{\widetilde{\mathcal{O}}(\log^2(\deg K)\cdot\sqrt{\log D})}.$$

Steps 3 and 4 can be performed by solving matrix equations of the form $\mathbf{x}A = \mathbf{v}$, where $\mathbf{v} = \{e_j - 2\sum_{i=1}^{k} v_{\mathfrak{p}_j}(\mathfrak{b}_i)\}_{j=1,\ldots,d}$ when we compute β and $\mathbf{v} = \{2v_{\mathfrak{p}_j}(\mathfrak{a}_i)\}_{j=1,\ldots,d}$ when we compute α_i. After solving the matrix equation we obtain a vector $\mathbf{x}$ and we compute β (and $\alpha_1, \alpha_2, \ldots$ with different $\mathbf{x}$) as $\prod_i s_i^{x_i}$, where s_i's are S-units that corresponds to the rows of the relations matrix A. We assume that S-units are precomputed during class group computation and they are stored in a compact representation (all this data can be computed with algorithm from [7]). Solving matrix equation takes time $\widetilde{\mathcal{O}}(d^3 \log(\max A + \max\mathbf{v}))$ bit operations [14]. The coefficients of A are in $e^{\widetilde{\mathcal{O}}(\log\deg K\cdot\sqrt{\log D})}$, the value of $\max\mathbf{v}$ is in $\widetilde{\mathcal{O}}(\max\mathbf{e}\cdot\Delta_K^2)\cdot e^{\widetilde{\mathcal{O}}(\log^2(\deg K)\cdot\sqrt{\log D})}$ for β and it belongs to $\widetilde{\mathcal{O}}(\Delta_K) \cdot e^{\widetilde{\mathcal{O}}(\log^2(\deg K)\cdot\sqrt{\log D})}$ for each α_i.

Therefore, solving the matrix equations takes time $\widetilde{\mathcal{O}}(\max(\log\max\mathbf{e}, \log\Delta_K))$. To simplify the expressions we used the fact [7, Lemma 2.2] that $\log\Delta_K = \mathcal{O}(\deg K \cdot \log D)$. After solving the matrix equation we obtain [14, p.138] a vector $\mathbf{x}$ of size

$$\max(\max A, \max\mathbf{v})^d \cdot d^{d/2}.$$

Then for β we have $\max\mathbf{x} = \widetilde{\mathcal{O}}(\max\mathbf{e} \cdot \Delta_K^2) \cdot e^{\widetilde{\mathcal{O}}(\log^3(\deg K)\cdot\sqrt{\log D})}$ and for α_i we have $\max\mathbf{x} = \widetilde{\mathcal{O}}(\Delta_K) \cdot e^{\widetilde{\mathcal{O}}(\log^3(\deg K)\cdot\sqrt{\log D})}$. Thus the computation of $\beta, \alpha_1, \alpha_2, \ldots$ in compact representation takes time $\widetilde{\mathcal{O}}(\mathrm{poly}(\log\max\mathbf{e}, \log\Delta_K))$.

Generators of the unit group at Step 5 can be computed [2] for multiquadratic fields in polynomial time in $\deg K$. FindSquare procedure takes time

$$\widetilde{\mathcal{O}}(\max((r+k)^3, (r+k)^2 B \deg K)) = \widetilde{\mathcal{O}}(\mathrm{poly}(\mathrm{Size}(\alpha), \log\Delta_K, \deg K))$$

due to Proposition 3. The square root computation at the final step can be performed in polynomial time [2], [7, §4C] in the degree of the field and the size of the input element. □

5   Discrete Logarithm Computation in the Ideal Class Group of Multiquadratic Fields

In this section we present an algorithm for computing the discrete logarithm in the class group for an ideal I in multiquadratic fields. We assume that the factorization of the norm of I is not known. Otherwise we can solve the discrete logarithm problem by appending primes from this factorization to the factor base and running the ideal class group computation algorithm (see details in Sect. 3.2).

The ideal class group of a multiquadratic field K can be computed using the algorithm of Biasse-van Vredendaal [7]. The idea of this algorithm is to compute relations in the quadratic subfields of K using Algorithm 1 and lift them back to the field K by solving the following equation that is called "norm relation". Let $\sigma, \tau, \sigma\tau$ be three different non-trivial automorphisms from G_K. Then for every $\alpha \in K$ we have

$$\alpha^2 = \frac{\mathrm{N}_{K/K_\sigma}(\alpha) \cdot \mathrm{N}_{K/K_\tau}(\alpha)}{\sigma(\mathrm{N}_{K/K_{\sigma\tau}}(\alpha))}. \tag{3}$$

This equation holds due to the fact that all automorphisms in multiquadratic fields have order 2 (see the proof of [2, Lemma 5.1] or [7, Lemma 4.2]). The key procedure which makes the multiquadratic class group computation algorithm efficient and allows us to lift relations $(\alpha^2, 2e)$ to (α, e), is a square root computation for principal ideals that was proposed in [2]. However, this algorithm does not work with non-principal ideals. We will use our Algorithm 4 for that purpose.

Let us describe now our algorithm for the discrete logarithm computation in the ideal class group of multiquadratic fields based on the reduction of the problem to subfields. Let I be an ideal of K and our goal is to find $\ell_1, \ldots, \ell_k$ such that $[I] = [\mathfrak{g}_1^{\ell_1} \cdot \ldots \cdot \mathfrak{g}_k^{\ell_k}]$ for the class group generators $\mathfrak{g}_1, \ldots, \mathfrak{g}_k$ computed using Biasse-van Vredendaal algorithm. Since all automorphisms have order 2, Eq. (3) can also be extended to arbitrary ideals as

$$\frac{\mathrm{N}_{K/K_\sigma}(I) \cdot \mathrm{N}_{K/K_\tau}(I)}{\sigma(\mathrm{N}_{K/K_{\sigma\tau}}(I))} = \frac{I \cdot \sigma(I) \cdot I \cdot \tau(I)}{\sigma(\sigma\tau(I) \cdot I)} = I^2. \tag{4}$$

Having this equation we can now solve the discrete logarithm problem for the ideal I^2 as follows. Recall that we have $S = \{\mathfrak{p}_1, \ldots, \mathfrak{p}_d\}$ – a generator set of Cl_K.

1. Compute relative norms $I_\gamma = \mathrm{N}_{K/K_\gamma}(I)$ for each $\gamma \in \{\sigma, \tau, \sigma\tau\}$.
2. In each subfield K_γ, find S_γ-smooth ideals J_γ such that $I_\gamma \cdot J_\gamma = h_\gamma \mathcal{O}_{K_\gamma}$ for some $h_\gamma \in K_\gamma$. Here, $S_\gamma = \{\mathfrak{p}_i \cap K_\gamma \mid i = 1, \ldots, d\}$.
3. Compute the ideal $J = \frac{J_\sigma \cdot J_\tau}{\sigma(J_{\sigma\tau})}$ and its lift to the field K by lifting the prime ideals in the factorization of J_γ. Note that the resulting ideal J is S-smooth as the result of the lift. From the Eq. (4) we have $I^2 J = h\mathcal{O}_K$ for $h = \frac{h_\sigma h_\tau}{\sigma(h_{\sigma\tau})}$, since $[\mathrm{N}_{K/K_\gamma}(I)] = [I_\gamma] = [J_\gamma^{-1}]$. Thus, we have obtained $[I^2] = [J^{-1}]$ for the S-smooth ideal J^{-1}.

Now we have a solution to the discrete logarithm problem for the ideal I^2 obtained by solving the problem in the subfields of K. To find a solution for the ideal I we have to extract a square root of $[J^{-1}]$ for the S-smooth ideal J. Such square root always exists due to the equality $[I^2] = [J^{-1}]$. It can be computed efficiently using Algorithm 4.

We have now all necessary components to describe the complete algorithm for the discrete logarithm computation in class groups of multiquadratic fields. We recursively apply the method above to the computation of J_γ for each $\gamma \in \{\sigma, \tau, \sigma\tau\}$ until we reach a quadratic subfield where we use Algorithm 1 to solve the discrete logarithm problem. After that we lift the solution back to the base field K step-by-step by combining information from subfields to obtain at first a solution for I^2 and then the solution for I by the square root computation. The complete procedure is presented in Algorithm 5. The procedure Lift() does the lift from the subfield K_γ to the field K for a S_γ-smooth ideal J_γ using precomputed trees (from class group computation) describing prime ideals splitting over the subfields of K. All these steps are summarized in Algorithm 5.

Algorithm 5: mqCLDL(I, S). Discrete logarithm computation in the ideal class group of the multiquadratic field.

Input: An ideal I of multiquadratic field $K = \mathbb{Q}[\sqrt{d_1}, \ldots, \sqrt{d_n}]$, a set
$S = \{\mathfrak{p}_1, \ldots, \mathfrak{p}_d\}$ of prime ideals of K s.t. $\mathfrak{p}_1 \mid (p_1), \ldots, \mathfrak{p}_d \mid (p_d)$ for some
prime numbers $p_1, \ldots, p_d$.

Output: an ideal $\tilde{J} = h \cdot J^{-1}$ of K represented by a pair $(h, \alpha) \in K \times \mathbb{Z}^d$ such
that $J = \prod\limits_{i=1}^{d} \mathfrak{p}_i^{\alpha_i}$ and $I \cdot J = h\mathcal{O}_K$.

1 **if** $[K : \mathbb{Q}] = 2$ **then**
2 $\quad$ **return** GenCLDL(I, S).
3 **end**
4 Select distinct $\sigma, \tau, \sigma\tau \in G_K$ of order 2;
5 $I_\sigma = N_{K/K_\sigma}(I)$, $I_\tau = N_{K/K_\tau}(I)$, $I_{\sigma\tau} = N_{K/K_{\sigma\tau}}(I)$;
6 $\tilde{J}_\sigma = $ mqCLDL(I_σ, S_σ) for $S_\sigma = \{\mathfrak{p} \cap K_\sigma \mid \mathfrak{p} \in S\}$;
7 $\tilde{J}_\tau = $ mqCLDL(I_τ, S_τ) for $S_\tau = \{\mathfrak{p} \cap K_\tau \mid \mathfrak{p} \in S\}$;
8 $\tilde{J}_{\sigma\tau} = $ mqCLDL$(I_{\sigma\tau}, S_{\sigma\tau})$ for $S_{\sigma\tau} = \{\mathfrak{p} \cap K_{\sigma\tau} \mid \mathfrak{p} \in S\}$;
9 $\tilde{J} = $ Lift$(\tilde{J}_\sigma) \cdot$ Lift$(\tilde{J}_\tau) /$ Lift$(\sigma(\tilde{J}_{\tau\sigma})) = h \cdot \prod\limits_i \mathfrak{p}_i^{-\alpha_i}$;
10 **return** IdealSqrt$(\tilde{J}, S)$.

Theorem 1. *Let $K = \mathbb{Q}(\sqrt{d_1}, \ldots, \sqrt{d_n})$ be a multiquadratic field of degree $m = 2^n$, let I be an ideal of $\mathcal{O}_K$, $D = d_1 \cdot \ldots \cdot d_n$, and $S = \{\mathfrak{p}_1, \ldots, \mathfrak{p}_d\}$ be a set of prime ideals generating the ideal class group Cl_K. Then computing the ideal $J = \prod_i \mathfrak{p}_i^{\alpha_i}$ such that $I \cdot J = h\mathcal{O}_K$ for some $h \in K$ requires $e^{\tilde{\mathcal{O}}(\max(\log m, \sqrt{\log D}))}$ field operations.*

Proof. To prove the theorem we need to prove the correctness of Algorithm 5 and perform its complexity analysis.

Correctness. After computing the relative norms of ideals in Step 5, we call the algorithm recursively up until we reach quadratic fields, where we solve the problem using Algorithm 1. To lift solutions back to the field K, we join the results from three subfields of K fixed by the selected automorphisms σ, τ, $\sigma\tau$. To do so we use Eq. (4):

$$\frac{N_{K/K_\sigma}(I) \cdot N_{K/K_\tau}(I)}{\sigma(N_{K/K_{\sigma\tau}}(I))} = I^2.$$

Note that in the formula above we omitted lifts of norms from subfields to the field K. For $\gamma \in \{\sigma, \tau, \sigma\tau\}$, we have $I_\gamma = h_\gamma \cdot J_\gamma^{-1}$ for some $h_\gamma \in K_\gamma$. Then from the norm relation we obtain:

$$\frac{h_\sigma h_\tau}{\sigma(h_{\sigma\tau})} \cdot \frac{\sigma(J_{\sigma\tau})}{J_\sigma \cdot J_\tau} = I^2$$

and

$$\frac{h_\sigma h_\tau}{\sigma(h_{\sigma\tau})} \mathcal{O}_K = I^2 \cdot \frac{J_\sigma \cdot J_\tau}{\sigma(J_{\sigma\tau})}.$$

Since J^{-1} and I^2 belong to the same ideal class, the square root of J^{-1} always exists if the factor base S generates the class group. The algorithm IdealSqrt (Algorithm 4) returns an ideal I' such that $I'^2 = \tilde{J} = I^2$. Due to uniqueness of ideal factorization in number fields this implies $I' = I$.

Complexity. Class group can be computed using Biasse-van Vredendaal algorithm [7, Prop. 5.1] in time $\text{polylog}(\Delta_K) \cdot e^{\tilde{\mathcal{O}}(\sqrt{\log D})}$. For the factor base S we can take as in [1] all prime ideals $\mathfrak{p}$ such that

$$N(\mathfrak{p}) \leq 12 \ln^2 \Delta_K = \mathcal{O}(m^2 \ln^2 D).$$

In the following by polynomial time we mean $\text{polylog}(\Delta_K) = \mathcal{O}(\text{polylog}(m \cdot D))$.

Step 2. Finding S-smooth representation of an ideal in a quadratic field takes time $e^{\tilde{\mathcal{O}}(\sqrt{\log D})}$ according to [8, §3]. Moreover, we have to repeat this step for every quadratic subfield we encounter during the algorithm. The number of quadratic subfields encountered by the algorithm is m. So, we have to repeat this step m times and in total we have $e^{\tilde{\mathcal{O}}(\max(\log m, \sqrt{\log D}))}$ field operations.

Step 5. Relative norms computation can be done using standard techniques in polynomial time. To simplify norm computation we can use the representation of ideals in K due to [2, §6.1] admitting fast relative norms for subfields.

Step 9. Lifting operation for the ideals $\tilde{J}_\sigma$, $\tilde{J}_\tau$, $\tilde{J}_{\sigma\tau}$ can be done in polynomial time using precomputed (during the class group computation) trees. These trees describe splitting of prime ideals over subfields that are encountered during the recursive algorithm. The trees contain for each prime ideal $\mathfrak{P} \in S_\gamma$ of $\mathcal{O}_{K_\gamma}$ a vector $\mathbf{x} = (x_1, \ldots, x_d)$ such that $\mathfrak{P}\mathcal{O}_K = \prod_{i=1}^{d} \mathfrak{p}_i^{x_i}$. This information allows us to efficiently lift products of prime ideals from the subfield K_γ to the base field K.

Step 10. IdealSqrt procedure performed with Algorithm 4 takes polynomial time according to Proposition 4.

In total, we have to repeat Steps 1–10 for $m^{\mathcal{O}(1)}$ subfields of K. Therefore, the overall complexity is $e^{\tilde{\mathcal{O}}(\max(\log m, \sqrt{\log D}))}$. □

6   Implementation

6.1   Class Group Computation

The algorithm of Biasse-van Vredendaal and its implementation [7] is given for real multiquadratic fields. In [20] the implementation was adopted to imaginary multiquadratic fields with optimizations for both cases. For class group computations we used the code from [20].

6.2   Discrete Logarithm Computation

In this section we give the results of computational experiments to check correctness of the algorithm. We implemented[1] Algorithm 5 in Sage [25] on top of Biasse-van Vredendaal implementation and its adaptation to imaginary fields [20].

The timings (in seconds) of computations are presented in Table 1. They are given for the mutliquadratic fields $K = \mathbb{Q}(\sqrt{d_1}, \ldots, \sqrt{d_n})$ such that $d_1, \ldots, d_n$ are first primes with $d_i \equiv 1 \bmod 4$. In our experiments we took random ideals in the representation of [2] that admit fast relative norms. The results of the computations were checked by testing the equality $v_{\mathfrak{p}_i}(I) = v_{\mathfrak{p}_i}(h \cdot \prod_i \mathfrak{p}_i^{-\alpha_i})$ where $h, \alpha_1, \alpha_2, \ldots$ are the output of Algorithm 5. The timings are given for discrete logarithm computations only and they do not include the time for class group computation that we assume as precomputed (this data can be found in [7] for real fields and in [20] for imaginary fields). For comparison we included in Table 1 the timings for Sage's builtin method ideal_class_log(proof = False).

The experiments were done on one core of Intel Core i7-8700 clocked at 3.20 GHz on computer with 64 GB RAM. Precomputation of the class group and computation of SNF for the relation matrix were done on core of Intel Xeon Silver 4201R clocked at 2.40 GHz on the machine with 629 GB RAM.

Table 1. Discrete logarithm computation for multiquadratic fields.

$[K : \mathbb{Q}]$	Field	Algorithm 5	Sage	Cl_K
16	real	325	0.19	C_4^2
32	real	1607	64	$C_2 \times C_4 \times C_8^4$
64	real	4743	-	$C_2^9 \times C_4^3 \times C_8 \times C_{16}^4 \times C_{48} \times C_{240}$
16	imag.	159	0.41	$C_8 \times C_{48}$
32	imag.	1487	26	$C_2 \times C_4^3 \times C_{24} \times C_{48}^2 \times C_{3360}$
64	imag.	3941	-	$C_2^2 \times C_4^9 \times C_8^3 \times C_{16} \times C_{48} \times C_{96}^2 \times C_{192}^2 \times C_{6720}^2 \times C_{927360}$

* Timings are given in seconds.

As we can see for fields of degrees 16 and 32 our algorithm works much slower than builtin methods of Sage. However, for big degrees Sage's methods do not terminate, while our implementation successfully computed discrete logarithms.

---

[1] Source code is available here: https://github.com/novoselov-sa/mqCLDL.

References

1. Bach, E.: Explicit bounds for primality testing and related problems. Math. Comput. **55**(191), 355–380 (1990)
2. Bauch, J., Bernstein, D.J., de Valence, H., Lange, T., van Vredendaal, C.: Short generators without quantum computers: the case of multiquadratics. In: Coron, J.-S., Nielsen, J.B. (eds.) EUROCRYPT 2017. LNCS, vol. 10210, pp. 27–59. Springer, Cham (2017). https://doi.org/10.1007/978-3-319-56620-7_2
3. Bernard, O., Lesavourey, A., Nguyen, T.H., Roux-Langlois, A.: Log-S-unit lattices using Explicit Stickelberger Generators to solve Approx Ideal-SVP. Cryptology ePrint Archive, Report 2021/1384 (2021). https://ia.cr/2021/1384
4. Biasse, J.F., Erukulangara, M.R., Fieker, C., Hofmann, T., Youmans, W.: Mildly short vectors in ideals of cyclotomic fields without quantum computers. Math. Cryptol. **2**(1), 84–107 (2022)
5. Biasse, J.F., Fieker, C., Hofmann, T., Page, A.: Norm relations and computational problems in number fields. J. Lond. Math. Soc. **105**(4), 2373–2414 (2022)
6. Biasse, J.F., Song, F.: Efficient quantum algorithms for computing class groups and solving the principal ideal problem in arbitrary degree number fields. In: Proceedings of the Twenty-Seventh Annual ACM-SIAM Symposium on Discrete Algorithms, pp. 893–902. SIAM (2016)
7. Biasse, J.F., Van Vredendaal, C.: Fast multiquadratic S-unit computation and application to the calculation of class groups. Open Book Ser. **2**(1), 103–118 (2019). https://scarecryptow.org/publications/multiclass.html
8. Buchmann, J., Düllmann, S.: On the computation of discrete logarithms in class groups. In: Menezes, A.J., Vanstone, S.A. (eds.) CRYPTO 1990. LNCS, vol. 537, pp. 134–139. Springer, Heidelberg (1991). https://doi.org/10.1007/3-540-38424-3_9
9. Canfield, E.R., Erdös, P., Pomerance, C.: On a problem of Oppenheim concerning "factorisatio numerorum". J. Number Theory **17**(1), 1–28 (1983)
10. Chatelain, D.: Bases des entiers des corps composés par des extensions quadratiques de Q. Ann. Sci. Univ. Besançon Math. (3) (6), 38 (1973)
11. Cohen, H.: A Course in Computational Algebraic Number Theory. Springer, Heidelberg (1993). https://doi.org/10.1007/978-3-662-02945-9
12. Cramer, R., Ducas, L., Wesolowski, B.: Short stickelberger class relations and application to ideal-SVP. In: Coron, J.-S., Nielsen, J.B. (eds.) EUROCRYPT 2017. LNCS, vol. 10210, pp. 324–348. Springer, Cham (2017). https://doi.org/10.1007/978-3-319-56620-7_12
13. Cramer, R., Ducas, L., Wesolowski, B.: Mildly short vectors in cyclotomic ideal lattices in quantum polynomial time. J. ACM **68**(2) (2021)
14. Dixon, J.D.: Exact solution of linear equations using P-Adic expansions. Numer. Math. **40**(1), 137–141 (1982)
15. Grenié, L., Molteni, G.: Explicit bounds for generators of the class group. Math. Comput. **87**(313), 2483–2511 (2018)
16. Lenstra, A.K., Lenstra, H.W., Lovász, L.: Factoring polynomials with rational coefficients. Math. Ann. **261**, 515–534 (1982)
17. Lesavourey, A., Plantard, T., Susilo, W.: Short principal ideal problem in multicubic fields. J. Math. Cryptol. **14**(1), 359–392 (2020)
18. Lesavourey, A., Plantard, T., Susilo, W.: On the Short Principal Ideal Problem over some real Kummer fields. Cryptology ePrint Archive, Paper 2021/1623 (2021). https://eprint.iacr.org/2021/1623

19. Menezes, A.J., Katz, J., van Oorschot, P.C., Vanstone, S.A.: Handbook of Applied Cryptography. CRC Press, Boca Raton (1996)
20. Novoselov, S.A.: On ideal class group computation of imaginary multiquadratic fields. Prikl. Diskr. Mat. (58), 22–30 (2022). https://github.com/novoselov-sa/multiclass-im
21. Pohlig, S.C., Hellman, M.E.: An improved algorithm for computing logarithms over GF(p) and its cryptographic significance. IEEE Trans. Inf. Theory **24**, 106–110 (1978)
22. Pomerance, C.: Elementary thoughts on discrete logarithms. In: Algorithmic Number Theory: Lattices, Number Fields, Curves and Cryptography, vol. 44 (2008). https://math.dartmouth.edu/~carlp/PDF/dltalk4.pdf
23. Storjohann, A.: Algorithms for matrix canonical forms. Ph.D. thesis, ETH Zurich (2000)
24. Teske, E.: The Pohlig-Hellman method generalized for group structure computation. J. Symb. Comput. **27**(6), 521–534 (1999)
25. The Sage Developers: Sagemath, the Sage Mathematics Software System (Version 10.0) (2023). https://www.sagemath.org
26. Vollmer, U.: Asymptotically fast discrete logarithms in quadratic number fields. In: Bosma, W. (ed.) ANTS 2000. LNCS, vol. 1838, pp. 581–594. Springer, Heidelberg (2000). https://doi.org/10.1007/10722028_39

Cryptographic Protocols

Stronger Lower Bounds
for Leakage-Resilient Secret Sharing

Charlotte Hoffmann[1]([⊠])[iD] and Mark Simkin[2][iD]

[1] Institute of Science and Technology Austria, Klosterneuburg, Austria
charlotte.hoffmann@ist.ac.at
[2] Ethereum Foundation, Aarhus, Denmark
mark.simkin@ethereum.org

Abstract. Threshold secret sharing allows a dealer to split a secret s into n shares, such that any t shares allow for reconstructing s, but no $t - 1$ shares reveal any information about s. Leakage-resilient secret sharing requires that the secret remains hidden, even when an adversary additionally obtains a limited amount of leakage from every share. Benhamouda et al. (CRYPTO'18) proved that Shamir's secret sharing scheme is one bit leakage-resilient for reconstruction threshold $t \geq 0.85n$ and conjectured that the same holds for $t = c \cdot n$ for any constant $0 \leq c \leq 1$. Nielsen and Simkin (EUROCRYPT'20) showed that this is the best one can hope for by proving that Shamir's scheme is not secure against one-bit leakage when $t = c \cdot n / \log(n)$.

In this work, we strengthen the lower bound of Nielsen and Simkin. We consider noisy leakage-resilience, where a random subset of leakages is replaced by uniformly random noise. We prove a lower bound for Shamir's secret sharing, similar to that of Nielsen and Simkin, which holds even when a constant fraction of leakages is replaced by random noise. To this end, we first prove a lower bound on the share size of any noisy-leakage-resilient sharing scheme. We then use this lower bound to show that there exist universal constants c_1, c_2, such that for sufficiently large n it holds that Shamir's secret sharing scheme is not noisy-leakage-resilient for $t \leq c_1 \cdot n / \log(n)$, even when a c_2 fraction of leakages are replaced by random noise.

Keywords: Threshold secret sharing · Noisy leakage-resilience · Lower bounds · Shamir's secret sharing scheme

1 Introduction

Threshold secret sharing was introduced by Shamir [Sha79] and Blakley [Bla79] and allows a dealer to split a secret s into shares $\mathsf{sh}_1, \ldots, \mathsf{sh}_n$, such that any t shares allow for reconstructing s, but no $t - 1$ shares reveal anything about s at all in the information-theoretic sense. Since its introduction, this primitive

A. Aly and M. Tibouchi (Eds.): LATINCRYPT 2023, LNCS 14168, pp. 215–228, 2023.
https://doi.org/10.1007/978-3-031-44469-2_11

in general, and Shamir's secret sharing scheme in particular, has found count-less applications in various fields of cryptography. Naturally, it is important to understand the precise security it provides.

The security definitions for regular threshold secret sharing schemes and variants like robust [RB89] or verifiable secret sharing [CGMA85] all assume that some shares are fully known and some shares are fully hidden from the adversary. As it turns out, these all-or-nothing type of security models do not always precisely reflect the security we want in practice. Real-world implementations of cryptographic primitives are susceptible to different types of side-channel attacks, which may give the adversary limited access to secrets that should ideally be fully hidden from her. Cryptographic primitives have, for example, been successfully attacked through leakages obtained via timing [Koc96] and power consumption [KJJ99] side-channels.

Motivated by the emergence of such side-channel attacks, the security definitions of secret sharing have been strengthened to account for additional leakages from the shares that were previously assumed to be fully hidden. Such schemes require that the secret that is shared remains hidden, when the adversary not only receives $t-1$ shares, but additionally obtains some limited amount of leakage from *all* other shares. Leakage-resilient secret sharing schemes have received significant interest and many constructions have been proposed over the past few years [DP07, BGK14, GK18b, GK18a, ADN+19, KMS19, SV19, CKOS21, CKOS22]. Realistically, however, it seems unlikely that Shamir's secret sharing scheme will be replaced by a leakage-resilient alternative any time soon. Shamir's scheme is a cornerstone of many cryptographic constructions and has been implemented and deployed as part of many different projects. Replacing a scheme that is so deeply embedded into so many different projects, seems like a insurmountable challenge. For this reason, it is crucially important to understand the leakage-resilience of Shamir's secret sharing scheme itself.

Benhamouda et al. [BDIR18] studied this question in a setting, where the adversary submits arbitrary leakage functions $\text{LEAK}_1, \ldots, \text{LEAK}_n$ and obtains leakages $\text{LEAK}_i(\text{sh}_i)$ for $i \in [n]$. The only restriction imposed on the leakage functions is that they are having a bounded output length. The authors show that Shamir's scheme provides some leakage-resilience, when $t \geq 0.85n$ and they conjecture that Shamir's scheme is leakage-resilient against one bit leakages for any $t = c \cdot n$, where $0 \leq c \leq 1$ is a constant. Subsequently, Nielsen and Simkin [NS20] showed that Shamir's scheme is not secure against one bit leakages when $t = c \cdot n / \log(n)$, thereby showing that their conjecture is the best one can hope for.

1.1 Our Contribution

The works' of Benhamouda et al. [BDIR18] and Nielsen and Simkin [NS20] assume that the adversary is able to obtain the precise outputs of its leakage functions. In practice, however, side-channel attacks are inherently noisy and there are practical techniques that can amplify this noise [CCD00, CK09, MOP07, CJRR99] to counter potential side-channel attacks. One might hope that it is possible to circumvent the lower bound of Nielsen and Simkin by considering a weaker, but more realistic noisy leakage model, where some random subset of the leakages is replaced by uniformly random noise.

In this work we show that this is *not* the case. We prove a lower bound similar to that of Nielsen and Simkin for Shamir's secret sharing scheme, which holds even when a *constant fraction* of leakages is replaced by random noise. To this end, we first prove a lower bound on the share size of any noisy-leakage-resilient secret sharing scheme. We then use this lower bound to obtain the following theorem:

Theorem 1 (Informal). *There exist universal constants[1] c_1, c_2, such that for sufficiently large n, it holds that $(c_1 \cdot n/\log(n))$-out-of-n Shamir secret sharing is not leakage-resilient against one bit leakage, even when a c_2 fraction of the leakage function outputs are replaced by random noise.*

We note that the constants c_1 and c_2 in our lower bound are not too relevant. The main takeaway of our result is that the reconstruction threshold t must be as large as a function of the number of shares n, i.e. it must hold that $t \in \Omega(n/\log(n))$, even if we relax the notion of leakage-resilience that we aim for considerably.

To prove this lower bound, we construct a generic adversary $\mathcal{A}$ that can use the noisy leakage to recover the secret shared value, whenever the shares are too small in size. The main idea of this attack is similar to the one in the proof of [NS20, Theorem 2]. We apply a separate uniformly random leakage function to each share. Given the noisy leakage vector, our adversary $\mathcal{A}$ iterates over all possible secret values and all possible secret sharings thereof.[2] Whenever there is a vector of shares that would produce a leakage vector that is consistent enough with the obtained noisy leakage vector, the adversary remembers the corresponding secret value in an initially empty set S. Finally, the adversary hopes that S contains exactly one element in which case she returns that element as her guess for what was the actual secret shared value.

In contrast to the previous lower bound of Nielsen and Simkin, our adversary needs to account for the noise in the leakage vector and thus it needs to add values s to S, even if there was no secret sharing of s that produced a fully consistent vector of leakages. Relaxing the conditions under which values s are added to S needs to be done carefully, since we would like to ensure that we do not add too many elements to the S. In a nutshell, our lower bound shows that the noisy leakage vector and any other leakage vector belonging to the incorrect secret, will differ in many positions. Making this intuition formal and arguing that our adversary is successful with a sufficiently high probability requires a careful analysis, which is the main contribution of this work.

---

[1] Concretely, we show the statement for $c_1 < 1/3$ and $c_2 = 1/64$, but a more careful analysis can allow for better constants, if desired.

[2] We are only concerned with information-theoretic security in which case the adversary is unbounded.

1.2   Other Related Works

The work by Guruswami and Wootters [GW16] demonstrated that some linear secret sharing schemes, such as Shamir's scheme over certain fields, allow for very communication efficient reconstruction of the secret. More precisely, they show that Shamir's scheme over fields of characteristic two, allows for recovering a multi-bit secret from only one bit of leakage from each share.

Inspired by these results, Benhamouda et al. [BDIR18] investigate to what extend natural secret sharing schemes offer leakage-resilience. They prove that Shamir's secret sharing scheme is leakage-resilient against one bit leakages, when the reconstruction thresholds is at least 0.92 times the number of parties. This constant was then improved to 0.8675 [MPSW21], then to 0.85 [BDIR21] and later to 0.78 [MNPCW22].

The currently best known constant is 0.69, which was recently proven by Klein and Komargodski [KK23]. The authors additionally show that whenever the leakage functions are guaranteed to be *balanced*, i.e. approximately half of the domain gives output 1 and the other half gives output −1, then the constant can be reduced to 0.58. Similarly, whenever the leakage functions are guaranteed to be sufficiently *unbalanced*, then Shamir's scheme is leakage resilient as long as the reconstruction threshold is at least 0.01 times the number of parties. This result is the first one that breaks the barrier of 0.5, which was known to be inherent in the proof techniques used in the previous works.

Maji et al. [MNP+21] consider much weaker *physical-bit leakages*, which only allows for a fixed number of bits to be leaked from the binary representation of each secret share. They prove that Shamir's secret sharing scheme with random evaluation points is physical-bit leakage resilient if the order of the field is sufficiently large. Adams et al. [AMN+21] consider *noisy* physical-bit leakage, where each physical-bit leakage is replaced by noise with some fixed probability. They prove a lower bound for the reconstruction threshold of $\log(\lambda)/\log\log(\lambda)$ for Shamir's secret sharing scheme, when the size of the field is 2^λ and the evaluation points can be chosen adversarially. In [MNPC+22] Maji et al. improve their lower bound to $\log(\lambda)$. This bound is interesting in the setting where the size of the field is much larger than the number of parties. In the setting we consider, we have $\lambda \approx \log(n)$, in which case their lower says that the reconstruction threshold needs to be larger than $\log\log(n)$.

In another work, Maji et al. [MNP+22] consider *global leakage* functions with bounded output length that can compute arbitrary functions over all shares simultaneously. Generally, this would allow the leakage functions to just reconstruct the secret, which is an attack that cannot be prevented. For this reason, the authors artificially restrict their leakage functions to not depend on some of the random choices made by the secret sharing scheme. For the case of Shamir secret sharing with random evaluation points, the authors show that one obtains some leakage-resilience properties, if the leakage functions are not allowed to depend on the evaluation points.

2 Preliminaries

Notation. We write $[n]$ to denote the set $\{1, \ldots, n\}$. For a set X, we write $x \leftarrow X$ to denote the process of sampling a uniformly random element x from the set X. For a vector $v = (v_1, \ldots, v_n)$ and a vector $w = (w_1, \ldots, w_t) \in [n]^t$, we define $v_w := (v_{w_1}, \ldots, v_{w_t})$. We will sometimes abuse notation and write v_w, where w is a set, rather than a vector. In this case the elements can be ordered arbitrarily in the vector. We denote by $\text{NOISE}(v, \ell, p)$ the algorithm that takes vector $v = (v_1, \ldots, v_n) \in (\{0,1\}^\ell)^n$, $\ell \in \mathbb{N}$, and $0 \le p \le 1$ as input and returns a new vector $(\tilde{v}_1, \ldots, \tilde{v}_n)$, where for $i \in [n]$ each $\tilde{v}_i = v_i$ with probability $1 - p$ and $\tilde{v}_i \leftarrow \{0,1\}^\ell$ with probability p. That means that $\text{NOISE}(v, \ell, 1)$ returns a uniformly random vector and $\text{NOISE}(v, \ell, 0)$ returns v.

2.1 Leakage-Resilient Secret Sharing

We define threshold secret sharing schemes similarly to how it was done by Nielsen and Simkin [NS20]. The full reconstruction parameter $\hat{t}$ defines how many shares are needed to reconstruct all shares of a particular secret sharing. Intuitively, $\hat{t}$ corresponds to a crude measure of how much entropy the vector of shares contains.

Definition 1 (Threshold Secret Sharing Scheme). *A t-out-of-n threshold secret sharing scheme is a pair* $(\text{SHARE}, \text{REC})$ *of efficient algorithms. The randomized sharing algorithm* $\text{SHARE} : \{0,1\}^k \to (\{0,1\}^p)^n$ *takes a k-bit secret as input and returns a vector of n secret shares, each p-bits long. The deterministic reconstruction algorithm* $\text{REC} : (\{0,1\}^p)^t \to \{0,1\}^k$ *takes t of the shares as input and returns a k-bit string. We require a secret sharing scheme to satisfy the following properties:*

Perfect Correctness: *For $t, n \in \mathbb{N}$ with $t \le n$, any $T \subseteq [n]$ with $|T| = t$ and any $x \in \{0,1\}^k$, it holds that*

$$\Pr[\text{REC}(\text{SHARE}(x)_T) = x] = 1,$$

where the probability is taken over the random coins of SHARE.

Full Reconstruction: $(\text{SHARE}, \text{REC})$ *has $\hat{t}$-full-reconstruction, if for any x, the vector* $\text{SHARE}(x)$ *can be computed from any subvector* $\text{SHARE}(x)_T$ *with $|T| \ge \hat{t}$.*

We assume for simplicity that all shares are of the same size p but the proof of our lower bound can easily be adapted to schemes with shares of different sizes.

Definition 2 (Leakage Functions). *Let* $(\text{SHARE}, \text{REC})$ *with* $\text{SHARE} : \{0,1\}^k \to \times_{i=1}^n \{0,1\}^p$ *be a secret sharing scheme and for $i \in [n]$, let* $\text{LEAK}_i : \{0,1\}^p \to \{0,1\}^\ell$. *We call* $\text{LEAK} = (\text{LEAK}_1, \ldots, \text{LEAK}_n)$ *an ℓ-leakage function for* $(\text{SHARE}, \text{REC})$. *We define* $\text{LEAK}(\text{sh}_1, \ldots, \text{sh}_n) := (\text{LEAK}_1(\text{sh}_1), \ldots, \text{LEAK}_n(\text{sh}_n))$.

We now define the privacy notion, which is a direct extension of the (noise-less) weak one-way local leakage resilience notion of Nielsen and Simkin [NS20, Definition 5], for which we will prove our lower bounds. The adversary $\mathcal{A}$ obtains a noisy leakage vector and it knows the probability η with which each leakage is replaced by noise. She does, however, not know *which* leakage outputs are replaced by random noise. Our privacy notion requires that $\mathcal{A}$ is not able to learn the secret with probability greater than $1/2$.

Definition 3 (Weak One-Way Noisy Local Leakage-Resilience). *We say a secret sharing scheme* (SHARE, REC) *is* (ℓ, η)-*weakly one-way noisy local leakage-resilient* $((\ell, \eta) - \text{WOW-NLLR})$, *if for any ℓ-leakage function* LEAK *and any adversary* $\mathcal{A}$, *it holds that*

$$\Pr\left[\begin{array}{c} x \leftarrow \{0,1\}^k \\ (\mathsf{sh}_1, \ldots, \mathsf{sh}_n) \leftarrow \text{SHARE}(x) \\ (\text{LEAK}_1, \ldots, \text{LEAK}_n) \leftarrow \mathcal{A}(n) \\ (\tilde{b}_1, \ldots, \tilde{b}_n) \leftarrow \text{LEAK}(\mathsf{sh}_1, \ldots, \mathsf{sh}_n) \\ (b_1, \ldots, b_n) \leftarrow \text{NOISE}((\tilde{b}_1, \ldots, \tilde{b}_n), \ell, \eta) \\ x' \leftarrow \mathcal{A}(b_1, \ldots, b_n) \end{array} : x' = x \right] \leq \frac{1}{2},$$

where the probability is taken over the random coins of SHARE, NOISE *and* $\mathcal{A}$.

We note that this is a very weak privacy notion. We only require a form of one-wayness that prevents the adversary from fully recovering the secret shared value and we only require the adversary to be successful with a probability less than $1/2$. Notably, this notion is even weaker than a standard indistinguishability type of notion. Since we are proving a *lower bound*, working with a weaker privacy notion only *strengthens* our lower bounds.

3 Lower Bound

In this section we prove our lower bound on the share size of any threshold secret sharing scheme that satisfies $(\ell, \eta) - \text{WOW-NLLR}$.

Theorem 2. *Let* $\mathcal{S} = $ (SHARE, REC) *be a t-out-of-n secret sharing scheme with* $\hat{t}$-*full-reconstruction and shares consisting of p bits each. Let $\ell \geq 1$ and let $0 < \eta \leq (n-t)/4n$. If $\mathcal{S}$ is $(\ell, \eta) - \text{WOW-NLLR}$, then*

$$p \geq \frac{\ell(n-t)}{\hat{t}} - \frac{4n\eta(\ell + \log(1/\eta)) + 1}{\hat{t}}.$$

Remark 1. We note that the theorem requires $\eta \leq (n-t)/4n$. In principle, our lower bound could be tightened to only require, for instance, $\eta \leq (n-t)/1.1n$ by replacing a single Markov inequality in the proofs with a stronger tail bound. We opted for clarity instead of optimizing the constants in our exposition. Next, we note that $\eta \leq (n-t)/n$ is a sensible restriction. If $\eta > (n-t)/n$ would hold, then with high probability $n - t + 1$ leakages would be replaced by random noise. In this case, our adversary could not hope to recover the secret, even if the leakage functions would leak the full shares.

Remark 2. It can be interesting to compare our lower bound to the one of Nielsen and Simkin [NS20]. Their work shows that any secret sharing scheme that satisfies $(\ell, 0) - \mathsf{WOW\text{-}NLLR}$, needs to satisfy

$$p \geq \frac{\ell(n - t)}{\hat{t}}.$$

As η approaches 0, our work effectively proves the same lower bound.

Proof (of Theorem 2). Towards proving the theorem statement, we provide a generic attacker that successfully wins the $(\ell, \eta) - \mathsf{WOW\text{-}NLLR}$ game against any secret sharing scheme that does not satisfy the constraints on the share size p that are stated in the theorem statement. This adversary works as follows. It picks $\mathrm{LEAK} = (\mathrm{LEAK}_1, \ldots, \mathrm{LEAK}_n)$ by picking each $\mathrm{LEAK}_i : \{0,1\}^p \to \{0,1\}^\ell$ for $i \in [n]$ uniformly and independently at random. The challenger picks a uniformly random secret s and computes $(\mathsf{sh}_1, \ldots, \mathsf{sh}_n) \leftarrow \mathrm{SHARE}(s)$. Adversary $\mathcal{A}$ submits the ℓ-leakage function LEAK to the challenger, who responds with $(b_1, \ldots, b_n)$, where each b_i is either $\mathrm{LEAK}_i(\mathsf{sh}_i)$ with probability $1 - \eta$ or a uniformly random value from $\{0,1\}^\ell$ with probability η. Let N be the number of components that were replaced by uniformly random noise values by the challenger and let $S = \emptyset$. The adversary now iterates over all possible secrets s' and random coins r' to compute

$$(\mathsf{sh}'_1, \ldots, \mathsf{sh}'_n) \leftarrow \mathrm{SHARE}(s'; r')$$

and

$$(b'_1, \ldots, b'_n) \leftarrow \mathrm{LEAK}(\mathsf{sh}'_1, \ldots, \mathsf{sh}'_n).$$

If $|\{i \in [n] \mid b'_i = b_i\}| \geq n(1 - 4\eta)$ for some r', then add s' to S. Finally, once $\mathcal{A}$ iterated over all possible secret sharings, if $|S| = 1$, then it outputs that one element in S and in any other case it returns $\perp$.

Let us now analyze the success probability of $\mathcal{A}$. We observe that if the challenger replaced at most $4n\eta$ coordinates by uniformly random noise, i.e. if $N \leq 4n\eta$, then $s \in S$. Since in expectation N is equal to $n\eta$, it holds by Markov's inequality that

$$\begin{aligned}
\Pr[s \in S] &= \Pr[s \in S \mid N \leq 4n\eta] \cdot \Pr[N \leq 4n\eta] \\
&\quad + \Pr[s \in S \mid N > 4n\eta] \cdot \Pr[N > 4n\eta] \\
&= \Pr[N \leq 4n\eta] + \Pr[s \in S \mid N > 4n\eta] \cdot \Pr[N > 4n\eta] \\
&\geq \Pr[N \leq 4n\eta] \geq 3/4.
\end{aligned}$$

Our adversary is successful, if and only if s is the *only* element in S. Let $E_{s'}$ be the event that $s' \in S$. Then

$$\Pr\left[S = \{s\}\right] = \Pr\left[\left(\bigwedge_{s' \neq s} \neg E_{s'}\right) \wedge E_s\right] \geq \Pr\left[\left(\bigwedge_{s' \neq s} \neg E_{s'}\right) \wedge N \leq 4n\eta\right]$$

$$\geq \Pr\left[\left(\bigwedge_{s' \neq s} \neg E_{s'}\right) \mid N \leq 4n\eta\right] \cdot 3/4$$

$$= \left(1 - \Pr\left[\bigvee_{s' \neq s} E_{s'} \mid N \leq 4n\eta\right]\right) \cdot 3/4.$$

To prove the theorem statement, we need to show that the adversary's attack is successful with a sufficiently high probability, i.e. we need to show that $\Pr\left[S = \{s\}\right] \geq 1/2$ and thus by the above it suffices to show that

$$\Pr\left[\bigvee_{s' \neq s} E_{s'} \mid N \leq 4n\eta\right] \leq 1/3.$$

By the union bound[3] we have that

$$\Pr\left[\bigvee_{s' \neq s} E_{s'} \mid N \leq 4n\eta\right] \leq \sum_{s' \neq s} \Pr\left[E_{s'} \mid N \leq 4n\eta\right].$$

Let us now fix an arbitrary $s' \neq s$, fix random coins r', and let $(\mathsf{sh}'_1, \ldots, \mathsf{sh}'_n) \leftarrow \textsc{Share}(s'; r')$. Let $E_{s',r'}$ be the event that the adversary includes s' into S based on the leakage from $(\mathsf{sh}'_1, \ldots, \mathsf{sh}'_n)$, i.e. the event that $|\{i \in [n] \mid b'_i = b_i\}| \geq n(1 - 4\eta)$, where $b'_i \leftarrow \textsc{Leak}_i(\mathsf{sh}'_i)$. Let us bound the probability of $E_{s',r'}$ conditioned on $N \leq 4n\eta$. From the perfect correctness of the secret sharing scheme and since $s \neq s'$, we know that there exists a set of indices $I \subseteq [n]$ with $|I| \geq n - t + 1$, such that for all $i \in I$, it holds that $\mathsf{sh}_i \neq \mathsf{sh}'_i$. For each $i \in I$, there are two cases. Either the leakage b_i is the real leakage or it is a uniformly random element from $\{0,1\}^\ell$. In either case, it holds that $b_i = b'_i$ with probability $2^{-\ell}$, since the corresponding shares are different and the leakage function $\textsc{Leak}_i$ is chosen uniformly random and independently of its inputs.

Let $\mathcal{T}$ be the set of subsets of I of size $n - t + 1 - 4n\eta$. Note that $n - t + 1 - 4n\eta > 0$, since $\eta \leq (n - t)/4n$ by assumption. For $T \in \mathcal{T}$, let $E_{s',r',T}$ be the event that the noisy leakage vector $(b_1, \ldots, b_n)$ and the noiseless vector $(b'_1, \ldots, b'_n)$ agree on all coordinates in T. Note that by the union bound

$$\Pr\left[E_{s',r'} \mid N \leq 4n\eta\right] \leq \sum_{T \in \mathcal{T}} \Pr\left[E_{s',r',T} \mid N \leq 4n\eta\right].$$

---

[3] The union bound also holds for conditional probabilities, meaning that $\Pr[A \vee B \mid C] = \Pr[(A \vee B) \wedge C]/\Pr[C] \leq (\Pr[A \wedge C] + \Pr[B \wedge C])/\Pr[C] = \Pr[A \mid C] + \Pr[B \mid C]$.

To see this, observe that even if $(\mathsf{sh}_1, \ldots, \mathsf{sh}_n)$ and $(\mathsf{sh}'_1, \ldots, \mathsf{sh}'_n)$ agree on $t-1$ coordinates, then there must still exist at least $n-t+1-4n\eta$ distinct indices $i \in I$ for which it holds that $b_i = b'_i$ to satisfy the condition $|\{j \in [n] \mid b'_j = b_j\}| \geq n(1-4\eta)$. It is easy to see that

$$\Pr\left[E_{s',r',T} \mid N \leq 4n\eta\right] \leq 2^{-(n-t+1-4n\eta)\ell}$$

and thus, it holds that

$$\Pr\left[E_{s',r'} \mid N \leq 4n\eta\right] \leq |T| \cdot 2^{-(n-t+1-4n\eta)\ell}$$

$$= \binom{n-t+1}{n-t+1-4n\eta} \cdot 2^{-(n-t+1-4n\eta)\ell}$$

$$= \binom{n-t+1}{4n\eta} \cdot 2^{-(n-t+1-4n\eta)\ell}$$

$$\leq \left(\frac{e(n-t+1)}{4n\eta}\right)^{4n\eta} \cdot 2^{-(n-t+1-4n\eta)\ell}$$

$$\leq \left(\frac{n-t+1}{n\eta}\right)^{4n\eta} \cdot 2^{-(n-t+1-4n\eta)\ell}$$

$$\leq \left(\frac{1}{\eta}\right)^{4n\eta} \cdot 2^{-(n-t+1-4n\eta)\ell}$$

At this point, recall that each share is p-bits long and that $\hat{t}$ is the full reconstruction threshold, i.e. that any $\hat{t}$ shares are enough to uniquely determine all remaining shares of a specific secret sharing. Thus there are at most $2^{p\hat{t}}$ different secret sharings in total and therefore

$$\sum_{s' \neq s} \Pr\left[E_{s'} \mid N \leq 4n\eta\right] \leq \left(\frac{1}{\eta}\right)^{4n\eta} \cdot 2^{p\hat{t}-(n-t+1-4n\eta)\ell}.$$

As discussed before, the adversary we constructed is successful, if

$$\left(\frac{1}{\eta}\right)^{4n\eta} \cdot 2^{p\hat{t}-(n-t+1-4n\eta)\ell} \leq 1/3$$

$$\iff \log(1/\eta)4n\eta + p\hat{t} - (n-t+1-4n\eta)\ell \leq -\log 3$$

$$\iff p\hat{t} \leq (n-t+1-4n\eta)\ell - \log(1/\eta)4n\eta - \log 3$$

$$\iff p\hat{t} \leq (n-t+1)\ell - \log 3 - 4n\eta(\ell + \log(1/\eta)).$$

From here it follows that

$$p \geq \frac{(n-t)\ell - 1 - 4n\eta(\ell + \log(1/\eta))}{\hat{t}}$$

must hold, if the secret sharing scheme wants to prevent the attack described above. □

The bound in Theorem 2 can be a little unwieldy and for this reason we also provide a slightly weaker, but simpler to state lower bound in the following corollary.

Corollary 3. *Let $t \leq n/2$. Let $\mathcal{S} = (\mathrm{SHARE}, \mathrm{REC})$ be a t-out-of-n secret sharing scheme with $\hat{t}$-full-reconstruction and shares consisting of p bits each. Let $\ell \geq 1$ and let $0 < \eta \leq 1/64$. If $\mathcal{S}$ is $(\ell, \eta) - \mathrm{WOW\text{-}NLLR}$, then*

$$p \geq \frac{\ell(n - 2t)}{2\hat{t}} - 1.$$

Proof. For Theorem 2 to be applicable, it must hold that $0 < \eta \leq (n - t)/4n$, which is always satisfied, when $0 \leq \eta \leq 1/64$, since $t \leq n/2$. Furthermore, it holds that

$$\frac{4n\eta(\ell + \log(1/\eta)) + 1}{\hat{t}} \leq \frac{n\ell}{16\hat{t}} + \frac{4n\eta \log(1/\eta)}{\hat{t}} + 1$$

$$\leq \frac{n\ell}{16\hat{t}} + \frac{3n}{8\hat{t}} + 1 \leq \frac{7n\ell}{16\hat{t}} + 1 \leq \frac{n\ell}{2\hat{t}} + 1$$

From Theorem 2, we know that it must hold that

$$p \geq \frac{\ell(n - t)}{\hat{t}} - \frac{4n\eta(\ell + \log(1/\eta)) + 1}{\hat{t}}.$$

Thus it must at least hold that

$$p \geq \frac{\ell(n - t)}{\hat{t}} - \frac{n\ell}{2\hat{t}} - 1$$

$$\iff p \geq \frac{\ell(n - 2t)}{2\hat{t}} - 1.$$

$\square$

4   Leakage-Resilience of Shamir's Secret Sharing

In this section we apply our result to Shamir's secret sharing scheme.

4.1   Shamir's Secret Sharing Scheme

In t-out-of-n Shamir secret sharing [Sha79], the secrets are elements of a field $\mathbb{F}_q$ for some prime q, which is chosen as the smallest prime larger than n. To distribute a secret s, the dealer picks a uniformly random polynomial f of degree $t - 1$ from $\mathbb{F}_q[X]$ and defines $\mathrm{sh}_i = f(i)$ for $i \in [n]$. Reconstruction of the secret from a subset of t shares is performed via polynomial interpolation, as any polynomial of degree $t - 1$ is uniquely defined by t evaluation points.

4.2   Noisy Leakage-Resilience

Benhamouda et al. [BDIR18] conjecture that Shamir's scheme is leakage-resilient against one-bit leakage for any $t = c \cdot n$, where $0 \leq c \leq 1$ is a constant. Nielsen and Simkin [NS20] showed that this is the best one can hope for by proving that the scheme is not secure against one-bit leakage when $t = cn/\log(n)$. In Theorem 4 we show that this lower bound holds even if a constant fraction of leakages is replaced by noise.

Theorem 4. *There exist universal constants c_1, c_2, such that for sufficiently large n, it holds that $(c_1 \cdot n/\log(n))$-out-of-n Shamir secret sharing is not $(1, c_2)-$* WOW-NLLR.

Remark 3. We note again that the precise values of the constants c_1 and c_2 are not too important. As we will see below, setting them to $c_1 < 1/3$ and $c_2 = 1/64$ suffices. There are multiple ways in which one could optimize these values. As already noted in Remark 1, one could use a tighter tail bound in the proof of Theorem 4. Another way could be to strengthen the notion of WOW-NLLR, i.e. slightly weaken the lower bound, to require the adversary to win with some probability smaller than half. These changes would, however, not change the main takeaway of our result, which is that Shamir secret sharing can not be leakage-resilient, unless $t \in \Omega(n/\log(n))$.

Proof. Let $c_1 < 1/3$ be arbitrary but fixed and let $c_2 = 1/64$. By Corollary 3, we know that
$$p \geq \frac{n - 2t}{2\hat{t}} - 1$$
has to hold for the secret sharing scheme to be $(1, c_2) -$ WOW-NLLR. We note that the full reconstruction threshold $\hat{t} = t$ for Shamir secret sharing, since any t shares allow interpolating any other share. Now plugging in the concrete parameters, we get that
$$p \geq \frac{n - 2c_1 n/\log(n)}{2c_1 n/\log(n)} - 1$$
$$\Longleftrightarrow p \geq \frac{\log(n)}{2c_1} - 2$$
$$\Longleftrightarrow p \geq \frac{3\log(n)}{2} - 2$$
has to hold.

Let q be the first prime larger than n and note that $p = \log(q)$. By the Bertrand-Chebyshev Theorem, we know that $n < q \leq 2n$ and thus it must hold that
$$\log(2n) \geq \frac{3\log(n)}{2} - 2$$
$$\Longleftrightarrow 4 \geq 3\log(n) - 2\log(2n)$$
$$\Longleftrightarrow 4 \geq \log\left(\frac{n^3}{4n^2}\right),$$
which is clearly not true once n is large enough. $\square$

Conclusion. In this work, we strengthened the lower bounds on the share size of leakage-resilient secret sharing schemes of Nielsen and Simkin [NS20] by showing that similar bounds hold, even if we considerably weaken the security notion we aim for. We show that Shamir secret sharing is not noisy leakage-resilient, if $t \leq c_1 \cdot n/\log(n)$, where c_1 and c_2 are constants, where t is the reconstruction threshold and n is the number of shares. We leave the reader with an interesting open question. Our lower bound crucially relies on an adversary running in exponential time in n. A natural question to consider is whether one can either improve the running time of the adversary to make the attacks more practical or whether one can prove a form of computational leakage-resilience for Shamir secret sharing under an appropriate computational assumption.

References

[ADN+19] Aggarwal, D., et al.: Stronger leakage-resilient and non-malleable secret sharing schemes for general access structures. In: Boldyreva, A., Micciancio, D. (eds.) CRYPTO 2019. LNCS, vol. 11693, pp. 510–539. Springer, Cham (2019). https://doi.org/10.1007/978-3-030-26951-7_18

[AMN+21] Adams, D.Q., et al.: Lower bounds for leakage-resilient secret-sharing schemes against probing attacks. In: 2021 IEEE International Symposium on Information Theory (ISIT), pp. 976–981. IEEE (2021)

[BDIR18] Benhamouda, F., Degwekar, A., Ishai, Y., Rabin, T.: On the local leakage resilience of linear secret sharing schemes. In: Shacham, H., Boldyreva, A. (eds.) CRYPTO 2018. LNCS, vol. 10991, pp. 531–561. Springer, Cham (2018). https://doi.org/10.1007/978-3-319-96884-1_18

[BDIR21] Benhamouda, F., Degwekar, A., Ishai, Y., Rabin, T.: On the local leakage resilience of linear secret sharing schemes. J. Cryptol. 34(2), 10 (2021)

[BGK14] Boyle, E., Goldwasser, S., Kalai, Y.T.: Leakage-resilient coin tossing. Distrib. Comput. 27, 147–164 (2014)

[Bla79] Blakley, G.R.: Safeguarding cryptographic keys. In: Proceedings of AFIPS 1979 National Computer Conference, vol. 48, pp. 313–317 (1979)

[CCD00] Clavier, C., Coron, J.-S., Dabbous, N.: Differential power analysis in the presence of hardware countermeasures. In: Koç, Ç.K., Paar, C. (eds.) CHES 2000. LNCS, vol. 1965, pp. 252–263. Springer, Heidelberg (2000). https://doi.org/10.1007/3-540-44499-8_20

[CGMA85] Chor, B., Goldwasser, S., Micali, S., Awerbuch, B.: Verifiable secret sharing and achieving simultaneity in the presence of faults (extended abstract). In: 26th Annual Symposium on Foundations of Computer Science, Portland, Oregon, 21–23 October 1985, pp. 383–395. IEEE Computer Society Press (1985)

[CJRR99] Chari, S., Jutla, C.S., Rao, J.R., Rohatgi, P.: Towards sound approaches to counteract power-analysis attacks. In: Wiener, M. (ed.) CRYPTO 1999. LNCS, vol. 1666, pp. 398–412. Springer, Heidelberg (1999). https://doi.org/10.1007/3-540-48405-1_26

[CK09] Coron, J.-S., Kizhvatov, I.: An efficient method for random delay generation in embedded software. In: Clavier, C., Gaj, K. (eds.) CHES 2009. LNCS, vol. 5747, pp. 156–170. Springer, Heidelberg (2009). https://doi.org/10.1007/978-3-642-04138-9_12

[CKOS21] Chandran, N., Kanukurthi, B., Obbattu, S.L.B., Sekar, S.: Adaptive extractors and their application to leakage resilient secret sharing. In: Malkin, T., Peikert, C. (eds.) CRYPTO 2021. LNCS, vol. 12827, pp. 595–624. Springer, Cham (2021). https://doi.org/10.1007/978-3-030-84252-9_20

[CKOS22] Chandran, N., Kanukurthi, B., Obbattu, S.L.B., Sekar, S.: Short leakage resilient and non-malleable secret sharing schemes. In: Dodis, Y., Shrimpton, T. (eds.) CRYPTO 2022. LNCS, vol. 13507, pp. 178–207. Springer, Heidelberg (2022). https://doi.org/10.1007/978-3-031-15802-5_7

[DP07] Dziembowski, S., Pietrzak, K.: Intrusion-resilient secret sharing. In: 48th Annual Symposium on Foundations of Computer Science, Providence, RI, USA, 20–23 October 2007, pp. 227–237. IEEE Computer Society Press (2007)

[GK18a] Goyal, V., Kumar, A.: Non-malleable secret sharing. In: Diakonikolas, I., Kempe, D., Henzinger, M. (eds.) 50th Annual ACM Symposium on Theory of Computing, Los Angeles, CA, USA, 25–29 June 2018, pp. 685–698. ACM Press (2018)

[GK18b] Goyal, V., Kumar, A.: Non-malleable secret sharing for general access structures. In: Shacham, H., Boldyreva, A. (eds.) CRYPTO 2018. LNCS, vol. 10991, pp. 501–530. Springer, Cham (2018). https://doi.org/10.1007/978-3-319-96884-1_17

[GW16] Guruswami, V., Wootters, M.: Repairing reed-solomon codes. In: Proceedings of the Forty-Eighth Annual ACM Symposium on Theory of Computing, STOC 2016, New York, NY, USA, pp. 216–226. Association for Computing Machinery (2016)

[KJJ99] Kocher, P.C., Jaffe, J., Jun, B.: Differential power analysis. In: Wiener, M. (ed.) CRYPTO 1999. LNCS, vol. 1666, pp. 388–397. Springer, Heidelberg (1999). https://doi.org/10.1007/3-540-48405-1_25

[KK23] Klein, O., Komargodski, I.: New bounds on the local leakage resilience of shamir's secret sharing scheme. Cryptology ePrint Archive, Paper 2023/805 (2023). https://www.eprint.iacr.org/2023/805

[KMS19] Kumar, A., Meka, R., Sahai, A.: Leakage-resilient secret sharing against colluding parties. In: Zuckerman, D. (ed.) 60th Annual Symposium on Foundations of Computer Science, Baltimore, MD, USA, 9–12 November 2019, pp. 636–660. IEEE Computer Society Press (2019)

[Koc96] Kocher, P.C.: Timing attacks on implementations of Diffie-Hellman, RSA, DSS, and other systems. In: Koblitz, N. (ed.) CRYPTO 1996. LNCS, vol. 1109, pp. 104–113. Springer, Heidelberg (1996). https://doi.org/10.1007/3-540-68697-5_9

[MNP+21] Maji, H.K., Nguyen, H.H., Paskin-Cherniavsky, A., Suad, T., Wang, M.: Leakage-resilience of the shamir secret-sharing scheme against physical-bit leakages. In: Canteaut, A., Standaert, F.-X. (eds.) EUROCRYPT 2021. LNCS, vol. 12697, pp. 344–374. Springer, Cham (2021). https://doi.org/10.1007/978-3-030-77886-6_12

[MNP+22] Maji, H.K., et al.: Leakage-resilient linear secret-sharing against arbitrary bounded-size leakage family. In: Kiltz, E., Vaikuntanathan, V. (eds.) TCC 2022. LNCS, vol. 13747, pp. 355–383. Springer, Heidelberg (2022). https://doi.org/10.1007/978-3-031-22318-1_13

[MNPC+22] Maji, H.K., et al.: Tight estimate of the local leakage resilience of the additive secret-sharing scheme & its consequences. In: Dachman-Soled, D. (ed.) 3rd Conference on Information-Theoretic Cryptography (ITC 2022). Leibniz International Proceedings in Informatics (LIPIcs), vol. 230, pp. 16:1–16:19, Dagstuhl, Germany. Schloss Dagstuhl - Leibniz-Zentrum für Informatik (2022)

[MNPCW22] Maji, H.K., Nguyen, H.H., Paskin-Cherniavsky, A., Wang, M.: Improved bound on the local leakage-resilience of Shamir's secret sharing. In: 2022 IEEE International Symposium on Information Theory (ISIT), pp. 2678–2683. IEEE (2022)

[MOP07] Mangard, S., Oswald, E., Popp, T.: Power Analysis Attacks: Revealing the Secrets of Smart Cards. Springer, New York (2007). https://doi.org/10.1007/978-0-387-38162-6

[MPSW21] Maji, H.K., Paskin-Cherniavsky, A., Suad, T., Wang, M.: Constructing locally leakage-resilient linear secret-sharing schemes. In: Malkin, T., Peikert, C. (eds.) CRYPTO 2021. LNCS, vol. 12827, pp. 779–808. Springer, Cham (2021). https://doi.org/10.1007/978-3-030-84252-9_26

[NS20] Nielsen, J.B., Simkin, M.: Lower bounds for leakage-resilient secret sharing. In: Canteaut, A., Ishai, Y. (eds.) EUROCRYPT 2020. LNCS, vol. 12105, pp. 556–577. Springer, Cham (2020). https://doi.org/10.1007/978-3-030-45721-1_20

[RB89] Rabin, T., Ben-Or, M.: Verifiable secret sharing and multiparty protocols with honest majority (extended abstract). In: 21st Annual ACM Symposium on Theory of Computing, Seattle, WA, USA, 15–17 May 1989, pp. 73–85. ACM Press (1989)

[Sha79] Shamir, A.: How to share a secret. Commun. ACM 22(11), 612–613 (1979)

[SV19] Srinivasan, A., Vasudevan, P.N.: Leakage resilient secret sharing and applications. In: Boldyreva, A., Micciancio, D. (eds.) CRYPTO 2019. LNCS, vol. 11693, pp. 480–509. Springer, Cham (2019). https://doi.org/10.1007/978-3-030-26951-7_17

Folding Schemes with Selective Verification

Carla Ráfols[1]([✉]) [ID] and Alexandros Zacharakis[2] [ID]

[1] Pompeu Fabra University, Barcelona, Spain
`carla.rafols@upf.edu`
[2] Toposware Inc., Tokyo, Japan
`alexandros.zacharakis@toposware.com`

Abstract. In settings such as delegation of computation where a prover is doing computation as a service for many verifiers, it is important to amortize the prover's costs without increasing those of the verifier. We introduce *folding schemes with selective verification*. Such a scheme allows a prover to aggregate m NP statements $x_i \in \mathcal{L}$ in a single statement $x \in \mathcal{L}$. Knowledge of a witness for x implies knowledge of witnesses for all m statements. Furthermore, each statement can be individually verified by asserting the validity of the aggregated statement and an individual proof π_i with size *sublinear in the number of aggregated statements*. In particular, verification of statement x_i does not require reading (or even knowing) all the statements aggregated. We demonstrate natural folding schemes for various languages: inner product relations, vector and polynomial commitment openings and relaxed R1CS of NOVA. All these constructions incur a minimal overhead for the prover, comparable to simply reading the statements.

Keywords: Folding · Aggregation · Delegation of computation · SNARKs · Vector commitments · Verifiable databases

1 Introduction

Succinct non-interactive arguments of knowledge (SNARKs) have been proven an invaluable tool in the last decade, both in theoretical as well as practical terms. Such constructions allow a prover to convince a verifier that some NP relation is satisfied in a way such that communication and (in some cases) verification time are sublinear in the size of the NP witness. They can also be adapted to satisfy the zero-knowledge property, guaranteeing that no information about the NP witness leaks through the proof.

While the first real-world application of SNARKs [2] aimed at preserving the privacy of the prover, the potential of this primitive for improving scalability in many applications is increasingly recognized, for example, roll-up architectures or the Filecoin network. In these applications, where the size of the computations is really large, the efficiency of the prover is the main bottleneck. Therefore, improving prover's efficiency is an active area of research, trying to reduce prover

---

The research leading to this work was funded by Protocol Labs under grant agreement PL-RGP1-2021-048.

A. Aly and M. Tibouchi (Eds.): LATINCRYPT 2023, LNCS 14168, pp. 229–248, 2023.
https://doi.org/10.1007/978-3-031-44469-2_12

overhead [5, 6, 23] or memory requirements [8] or building hardware accelerators for the provers, to name a few approaches.

Despite the many improvements achieved and those that will come after the considerable research effort we have seen in reducing this cost, SNARK proofs remain expensive for the prover. Also, it is natural to envisage a scenario where these proofs are outsourced to some powerful entity, in the spirit of secure delegation of computation [17], where an untrusted prover performs computations as a service to several "muggles", or computationally weak verifiers. In this scenario, the prover is providing a service to many verifiers and has their data (i.e., there are no privacy requirements). The efficiency of the prover is essential in this scenario, as it will seriously hinder scalability. Also, the prover's cost directly affects the service's cost. On the other hand, using some batching or recursive proof composition in this setting seems unsatisfactory, as each verifier does not necessarily want to know all the other statements that are being verified and incur the additional costs that this represents.

1.1   Our Contributions

This work aims to mitigate the necessity of considerable computational resources for the prover in applications where he provides services to many clients. Instead of improving SNARK constructions' efficiency, we take a different approach: we amortize the proving cost across multiple proofs of independent and unrelated statements. When having to make M computations of different statements, instead of producing M separate SNARK proofs for each, the prover "collapses" all these statements into a single statement in a verifiable way and only produces a proof for the latter using a SNARK. This is a novel application of *folding schemes* [20], introduced initially to improve recursive proof composition. The guarantee we get is that if the proof for the aggregated statement verifies, then all statements are correct.

Additionally, since the ultimate goal is to prove unrelated statements, possibly coming from different parties, we augment aggregation with a local property we call *selective verification*. This property captures that a small proof π_i - which, notably, is sublinear in the number of aggregated statements- is evidence that a statement x_i was included in the construction of the final aggregated statement and, thus, a proof for the latter along with π_i stands as a proof for the validity of x_i. Note that it is not necessary to even know the statements used in aggregation to assert the validity of x_i.

A crucial requirement for efficiency is that aggregation of M statements is more efficient than producing M SNARK proofs. We demonstrate this in the full version [22] of this paper by considering natural aggregation schemes for various relations through simple public coin protocols and the Fiat-Shamir transform. Specifically, we consider (1) inner product relations of committed values, (2) vector commitment openings, (3) knowledge of openings of polynomial commitments at the same point, and (4) the relaxed R1CS relation of NOVA [20]. Our construction is generic enough and applies in any folding scheme, for example the recent constructions [19, 21].

All the constructions are highly efficient for the prover, who, during folding does work comparable to reading the statements/witnesses (modulo a linear number of hash function computations needed to derive the non-interactive challenge of the Fiat-Shamir transform). Verification incurs a small overhead since now the verifier also needs to check, apart from the SNARK proof, that the statement in question is indeed "contained" in the aggregated statement. This is dominated by $\log M$ hash function computations where M is the number of aggregated statements. This seems a reasonable compromise since the verifier also benefits from the reduced service costs.

Nevertheless, there are several other advantages in the construction for the verifier. First, the same techniques used for folding can be used "locally" by the verifier to aggregate many statements into a single statement x_i, which will then be aggregated with independent queries from other verifiers. Therefore, the additional cost of each verifier can be amortized when the verifier makes multiple queries. Second, since all verifiers need to assert the validity of the same folded statement, one could explore the possibility of distributing this task, incentivizing a few randomly chosen verifiers to check the aggregated statement. As long as one is honest, a cheating prover will be identified. If a verifier does not validate the proof himself, it can still query it in the future to the prover (along with other statements of interest that it locally aggregates) instead of simply relying on other parties. Thus, the verification cost can be fine-tuned on large-scale systems without compromising security.

Our techniques are pretty general. In particular, (1) we show a generic way to augment every non-interactive 2-folding scheme to a non-interactive M-scheme using combinatorial techniques, (2) show that this construction achieves selective verification, and (3) we do not rely on some specific SNARK construction.

1.2   Applications

As we have discussed, selective verification can improve efficiency on applications with a single server serving multiple clients in a trustless way. It allows us to amortize the server's costs across multiple queries from clients while only incurring a small overhead for the clients. We discuss two applications in more detail.

Delegation of Computation as a Service. For delegation of computation in a trustless setting, one would normally resort to a SNARK, especially in cases where interaction is prohibitive. We discuss how to use folding schemes to mitigate the problem of the prover's costs.

We will consider two cases: (1) each party needs to perform arbitrary computations, and (2) all parties are interested in doing the same computation on different inputs. Especially in the latter case, we can significantly reduce the costs of the prover through folding schemes with selective verification.

For case (1), many SNARKs are constructed by separately considering some information-theoretic part and a cryptographic primitive. Two main approaches are known: (i) using interactive oracle proofs [1] and vector commitments [14] and (ii) using algebraic [15] or polynomial [13] holographic proofs and polynomial commitments [18]. In the former, the prover and verifier, after interacting, reduce the validity of the claim to the opening of some vector commitments at a few random indices. In contrast, in the latter, the statement's truth reduces to opening some polynomial commitments at random values. Interaction can be removed through the Fiat-Shamir transform.

In either case, we can use the folding constructions of the previous section to amortize the cost of the latter step: inner product arguments for the former and polynomial commitment for the latter[1]. Specifically, with each computational query, the prover computes all the commitments that are part of the SNARK, but it refrains for the time from computing the opening of (the vector or polynomial) commitment. After multiple interactions with different verifiers, it folds all the (vector or polynomial) commitments to a single one and opens the latter at some random indices or points, respectively. The randomness is derived by hashing the folded statement. Each verifier can now assert the folding proof as well as some evidence sent by the server asserting the inclusion of her statement. To be concrete, for example in Plonk [16], the prover will compute until round 3 for each different statement. Then, it will wait to open the polynomial commitments until it has the transcripts of many other protocols until round 3. Using a technique presented by Turel et al. in [25], the prover will then create a Merkle tree of hashes of the transcript, to derive an opening point that is a hash of all involved transcripts. Then, the prover will send all the openings that each verifier needs to verify its statement (including an opening of the linearization polynomial $r(X)$), together with a proof that all the commitments corresponding to these openings have been folded into a single commitment value, and a proof of correct opening of this commitment[2].

In case (2), where all parties are interested in performing the same computation on different inputs, one could use the NOVA approach. Specifically, the computation is encoded as a relaxed R1CS statement, and the various instances of this statement are aggregated using the NOVA folding scheme compiled to support selective verification. As we discussed, a folding of this type of statements is very efficient. This is in contrast to the previous case since the SNARK information theoretic part (which needs to be executed for each query to the proving server) is, in fact, costly for the prover. Considering the case of a single

---

[1] In fact, both inner product arguments and polynomial commitment folding can be used for either approach but the presentation becomes more natural by using one approach for each.

[2] We note that it is also possible to use a different strategy if one changes the statement about the polynomial commitments slightly: the prover can fold statements of the form "I know a polynomial that is a valid opening of a commitment" and fold such statements for each verifier resulting in a claim about a single polynomial commitment. Then, it can prove this statement at a single point which will be the same for all verifiers. The point is derived by hashing the final folded statement. During folding, the transcript of the first protocol rounds is included in the hashing part of the folding. Thus, each verifier can check that its transcript indeed contributed in the sampling of the FS challenge point.

computation allows us to completely remove the need for this part and directly fold statements, which is not much costlier than simply reading the statements.

Verifiable Databases. In a verifiable database, a client outsources the storage of a database to a server in a trustless way. Specifically, the client only holds a small digest of the database and can query/modify the database in a verifiable way through communication with the prover. Such a construction can be built using vector commitments. The database is encoded as a vector, and the client only needs to hold the (constant size) commitment to the database. A query to the database can be answered verifiably by asking the server to open the commitment to the desired locations. Furthermore, if the underlying commitment scheme is homomorphic (for example, the Pedersen commitment), updating the database is efficient since one just needs to homomorphically update the digest by removing the old values and adding the new ones.

Consider the case where a server outsources storage to various clients. Naively implementing this would require that it sends an (expensive to produce) proof of opening for every query of every client to its database. Using a folding scheme with selective verification (for example, the inner product language construction) can naturally minimize this cost.

In particular, each query to the server is answered without any verifiability guarantee; the clients simply get their responses and perform their updates acting in good faith. However, periodically, the server folds all the claims from all the clients using the folding scheme and publishes a single statement and individualized proofs for each client to convince them about the validity of all statements of one period. Due to the efficiency of the folding scheme, the amortized cost for this is much less than proving each claim individually.

An interesting feature of the described mechanism is that it can be used for any algebraic commitment (i.e., any Pedersen type) commitment in particular, it can be used in DLOG groups without pairings. In this setting, to open a vector to many positions, the cost of the verifier is linear in the size of the commitment. Our solution allows amortizing the prover cost in this setting without much overhead to the verifier, which is critical in this setting where individual verification is already quite expensive.

1.3   Related Work

The techniques in this work are inspired by a recent line of work on *proof composition techniques*, namely [4,9,11,12]. In general, these techniques consider the notion of proof aggregation, namely, how to derive a single proof π that asserts the validity of two or more proofs. The motivation for this line of work is twofold. First, amortizing the cost of the (inefficient) verification of folding technique based constructions [7,10] and second, to construct proof carrying data [3] and incrementally verifiable computation [24].

Our work differs in that (1) the main goal is to amortize the proving cost and (2) we consider the notion of aggregating unrelated statements, that is, one should assert the validity of statement without even knowing the other statements considered during aggregation. NOVA [20] is closer to our work in that it directly considers aggregating statements instead of proofs, in an attempt to minimize the proving cost.

Perhaps closest to our work is [25]. There, they use a tree like structure similar to ours in order to derive the same Fiat-Shamir challenge across multiple parallel executions of an inner product argument protocol [10] with different parties. In particular, the protocol transcripts are committed in a Merkle tree so that each party can assert that its transcript was considered in the production of the challenge. We consider statement aggregation instead of executing multiple proofs in parallel which is conceptually different and more efficient.

2   Definitions

In this section, we recall the definition of *folding schemes* for NP relations introduced in NOVA [20]. On a high level, given an NP language $\mathcal{L}$ and the corresponding NP relation $\mathcal{R}$, a folding scheme allows a prover and a verifier to reduce the validity of 2 or more statements of the form $x_i \in \mathcal{L}$ to a single one $x \in \mathcal{L}$. The resulting statement is of the same form, so it can be further aggregated. A prover knowing witnesses w_i s.t. $(x_i, w_i) \in \mathcal{R}$ for all the statements also obtains a witness w for the folded statement x.

A folding scheme takes to the extreme *proof composition techniques* used to construct PCD [3] and IVC [24]. The core idea of these techniques is to incrementally prove statements that assert that (1) a computation step is performed correctly and (2) there exists a proof that asserts that the input of the computation in this step is correct. Using generic constructions, however, is extremely inefficient.

To alleviate this, a recent line of work [4,9,11,12] follows a different approach: they defer an expensive part of proof verification of the proof mentioned above and aggregate it with deferred parts from other steps. At any point, the verifier can perform this expensive part and assert that all computation steps are correct. Notably, the aggregation part is cheap, and the deferred part does not grow with the number of computational steps proven. Therefore, the expensive part is performed once for an arbitrarily large number of steps.

NOVA takes this approach to the extreme in the following sense: *it defers the verification of the statement itself.* More concretely, the statement asserting the correctness of the first $i-1$ steps is encoded as a statement $X \in \mathcal{L}$ for some language and the correctness of the i-th step as $x \in \mathcal{L}$ for the *same* language. The two statements are then "folded" to a new one $X^* \in \mathcal{L}$, and the truth of the folded statement implies the truth of both statements. Since all statements are of the same form, the process can be repeated for an arbitrary number of steps, and it is enough to prove the final statement to assert the correctness of all steps.

Assuming the existence of such a mechanism to fold statements, one can then encode in a circuit the verification process of this folding and construct an IVC scheme. Importantly, the folding verification is cheap, achieving very low recursion overheads.

In our work, we consider using similar techniques, albeit for a different goal: aggregating statements to reduce the amortized proving cost of proving many different statements. Instead of encoding the folding verification as a circuit and building IVC, we directly use the folding scheme to allow a prover to prove the validity of a bunch of M different statements using only a single proof by means of aggregation. Additionally, we present a mechanism, *selective verification*, that allows a verifier to assert the correctness of one of the M statements efficiently: it does not need to know neither all the M aggregated statements nor the entire proof of aggregation (which grows linearly in M). It simply needs the proof of the final statement and a proof that is sublinear in M.

Taking into account that producing proofs is a computationally intense task, this allows much better amortized proving time with little overhead for verification. Indeed, [20] introduces a folding scheme construction that captures all NP computations and allows very fast statement aggregation.

2.1   Folding Schemes

We next present the formal definition of a folding scheme. The notion is essentially the same as presented in [20] with two modifications: we only consider a non-interactive definition, namely the prover simply presents a proof of correct folding to the verifier, and we consider a definition that allows aggregating M statements instead of 2 as it is discussed in NOVA. Looking ahead, our concrete instantiations will be folding schemes for 2 statements that are then bootstrapped to folding schemes of M statements using a generic bootstrapping compiler.

The formalization of a folding scheme is quite natural. Given a number of instance/witness pairs (x_i, w_i) that satisfy some NP relation, there exists a folding algorithm that outputs a new instance/witness pair (x, w) that also satisfies the NP relation, along with some evidence π that the new instance x is indeed a "folded" statement derived from the statements x_i. One can think of the folded statement as encoding all statements of interest. The properties required are:

1. *completeness*, stating that if we aggregate instance-witness pairs (x_i, w_i) satisfying the NP relation, then (1) folding results in an instance-witness pair also satisfying the relation and (2) the folding proof is accepted;
2. *knowledge soundness*, stating that if after correct aggregation the proving party knows a witness for the resulting statement, then it should also know witnesses for all statements (x_i, w_i) that were considered during aggregation.

Definition 1 (Folding scheme). *Let $\lambda \in \mathbb{N}$ be a security parameter and $\mathcal{L}_{pp}$ be an NP language parametrized by some parameters $pp(\lambda)$ depending on λ and $\mathcal{R}_{pp}$ the corresponding relation. Finally, let $M = poly(\lambda)$. An M-folding scheme FS for the language family $\mathcal{L} = \{\mathcal{L}_{pp}\}_{pp \in \{0,1\}^*}$ is a tuple of an algorithms FS = (Fold, FoldVrfy) such that for all $pp = pp(\lambda)$ and $m \leq M$*

- $(x, w, \pi) \leftarrow \mathsf{Fold}\,(pp, x_1, w_1, \ldots, x_m, w_m)$: *takes as input the parameters pp, and m instance-witness pairs $(x_i, w_i) \in \mathcal{L}_{pp}$ and outputs a new instance-witness pair $(x, w) \in \mathcal{R}_{pp}$ and a proof of correct folding π,*

- $0/1 \leftarrow \mathsf{FoldVrfy}\,(\mathsf{pp}, x_1, \ldots, x_m, x, \pi)$: *takes as input the parameters* pp, m *instances* x_i, *an aggregated statement* x *and a proof of correct folding* π *and outputs a bit indicating whether folding was done correctly or not,*

that satisfies the following properties:

1. **Completeness:** *for all* $m \leq M$, *all* $\mathsf{pp} = \mathsf{pp}(\lambda)$ *and all (even computationally unbounded) algorithms* $\mathcal{A}$,

$$\Pr\left[\begin{array}{c} \{q_1, \ldots, q_m\} \subseteq \mathcal{R}_{\mathsf{pp}} \wedge \\ ((x, w) \notin \mathcal{R}_{\mathsf{pp}} \vee b = 0) \end{array} \middle| \begin{array}{c} (x_1, w_1), \ldots, (x_m, w_m) \leftarrow \mathcal{A}(\mathsf{pp}) \\ q_1 = (x_1, w_1), \ldots, q_m = (x_m, w_m) \\ (x, w, \pi) \leftarrow \mathsf{Fold}\,(\mathsf{pp}, \mathbf{q}) \\ b \leftarrow \mathsf{FoldVrfy}\,(\mathsf{pp}, \mathbf{x}, x, \pi) \end{array} \right] \leq \mathsf{negl}(\lambda)$$

2. **Knowledge soundness:** *for all* $m \leq M$ *and all* $\mathsf{pp} = \mathsf{pp}(\lambda)$ *there exists a PPT extractor* $\mathcal{E}$ *such that for all PPT algorithms* $\mathcal{A}$

$$\Pr\left[\begin{array}{c} (x, w) \in \mathcal{R}_{\mathsf{pp}} \wedge \\ b = 1 \wedge \\ \exists 1 \leq i \leq m \ s.t. \ (x_i, w_i) \notin \mathcal{R}_{\mathsf{pp}} \end{array} \middle| \begin{array}{c} (\mathbf{x}, x, w, \pi) \leftarrow \mathcal{A}(\mathsf{pp}) \\ w \leftarrow \mathcal{E}^{\mathcal{A}}(\mathsf{pp}) \\ b \leftarrow \mathsf{FoldVrfy}\,(\mathsf{pp}, \mathbf{x}, x, \pi) \end{array} \right] \leq \mathsf{negl}(\lambda)$$

In Sect. 4 we present 2-folding schemes for various relations: inner product relations of committed values, vector and polynomial commitment openings and the relaxed R1CS relation of [20]. We derive the constructions by means of public coin protocols that we compile to a non-interactive variant through the Fiat-Shamir heuristic.

Remark 1. We emphasize that after folding the statements, the corresponding witnesses are not needed. In particular, the witnesses are only used to construct the witness for the final folded statement and then they can be safely deleted. Indeed, to assert the validity of all statements, it is enough to (1) present the proof of correct folding and (2) convince about the validity of the folded statement. The latter can be done using only the folded statement/witness pair, for example with a SNARK. Put it differently, while the folded statements "encodes" all the aggregated statements by means of a folding proof, it is also -in some sense- independent of them after the folding has taken place.

2.2   Folding Schemes with Selective Verification

As we discuss in the introduction, the main goal of this work to allow to reduce the resources used in "as a service" scenarios: a prover needs to serve multiple verifiers in a trustless way. A characteristic example is a prover that verifiably outsources its computational resources to verifiers who need to perform arbitrary computations.

We emphasize that this is a different goal from NOVA [20] and related works, which aim to achieve proof composition and construct IVC schemes. In our case, there are natural additional properties one would want to achieve. Perhaps the most natural is to allow verifying single statements that are "encoded" in the folded statements without the need to know or even care about the validity of the rest of the statements. Let us elaborate on this.

Consider the case where a prover wants to serve m statements for m different parties. Simple folding is indeed a means to that goal: the prover needs to convince for the validity of a single statement to convince all verifiers about the validity of all m statements. Nevertheless, it is still inefficient in terms of verification. The inefficiency stems from the fact that in order to verify correct folding, all the statements need to be considered as part of the proof of correct aggregation.

While this is natural in cases where a single verifier is interested in many statements, it can be prohibitive in scenarios where multiple verifiers are interested in the validity of different statements: first, the verifiers need to know each others' queries to the prover to assert validity of the folded statement, and second, the verification cost scales linearly with the total number of statements considered.

In this section, we mitigate this issue by considering a stronger notion of folding schemes that allows to assert that a single statement was considered during aggregation of multiple statements -and hence knowledge of a witness of the latter implies knowledge of the witness of the former, without the need to know all the statements involved. Importantly, verification of inclusion of a single statement to the folded statement is *sublinear* in the total number of statements involved. We call this stronger notion folding with *selective verification*.

We require (and later achieve) a strong version of this notion: one can derive a proof of inclusion of a single statement to a folded statement *only by knowing the aggregated statements and the proof of correct folding*. In particular, creation of such a proof does not require any witness information on the statements and can be performed by parties different than the prover. Looking ahead, our bootstrapping construction achieves this property by simply handing *parts* of the folding proof corresponding to each statement, each being sublinear (logarithmic) in the total size of the folding proof.

We next define the stronger notion of a folding scheme that supports *selective verification*.

Definition 2 (Folding scheme with selective verification). *Let $\lambda \in \mathbb{N}$ be a security parameter and $\mathcal{L}_{pp}$ be an NP language parametrized by some parameters $pp(\lambda)$ depending on λ and $\mathcal{R}_{pp}$ the corresponding relation. Finally, let $M = poly(\lambda)$ and let $FS = (Fold, FoldVrfy)$ be an M-folding scheme for $\mathcal{L} = \{\mathcal{L}_{pp}\}_{pp \in \{0,1\}^*}$. FS has selective verification if there exists a pair of algorithms $(SelPrv, SelVrfy)$ such that for all $m \le M$,*

- $(\pi_1, \ldots, \pi_m) \leftarrow SelPrv(pp, x_1, \ldots, x_m, x, \pi)$*: takes as input the parameters pp, m instances $x_1, \ldots, x_m$, a folded instance x and a folding proof π and outputs m proofs $\pi_1, \ldots, \pi_m$,*

- $0/1 \leftarrow \mathsf{SelVrfy}(\mathsf{pp}, x, i, x_i, \pi_i)$: *takes as input the parameters* pp, *a folded state-ment* x, *a position* $i \in \{1, \ldots, m\}$, *a statement* x_i *and a proof* π_i *and outputs a bit indicating if* x_i *was aggregated (among other statements) to* x,

that satisfies the following properties:

1. **Selective completeness:** *for all* $m \leq M$, *all* $\mathsf{pp} = \mathsf{pp}(\lambda)$ *and all (even computationally unbounded) algorithms* $\mathcal{A}$,

$$\mathrm{Pr}\left[\begin{array}{c} \{q_1, \ldots, q_m\} \subseteq \mathcal{R}_{\mathsf{pp}} \wedge \\ \exists i \in \{1, \ldots, m\} : \\ b_i = 0 \end{array} \middle| \begin{array}{c} x_1, w_1, \ldots, x_m, w_m \leftarrow \mathcal{A}(\mathsf{pp}) \\ q_1 = (x_1, w_1), \ldots, q_m = (x_m, w_m) \\ (x, w, \pi) \leftarrow \mathsf{Fold}\,(\mathsf{pp}, \mathbf{q}) \\ (\pi_1, \ldots, \pi_m) \leftarrow \mathsf{SelPrv}(\mathsf{pp}, \mathbf{x}, x, \pi) \\ b_i \leftarrow \mathsf{SelVrfy}(\mathsf{pp}, x, i, x_i, \pi_i) \end{array} \right] \leq \mathsf{negl}(\lambda)$$

2. **Selective knowledge soundness:** *for all* $m \leq M = \mathsf{poly}(\lambda)$ *and all* $\mathsf{pp} = \mathsf{pp}(\lambda)$ *there exists a PPT extractor* $\mathcal{E}$ *such that for all PPT algorithms* $\mathcal{A}$

$$\mathrm{Pr}\left[\begin{array}{c} \mathsf{SelVrfy}(\mathsf{pp}, x, i, x_i, \pi_i) = 1 \wedge \\ (x, w) \in \mathcal{R}_{\mathsf{pp}} \wedge (x_i, w_i) \notin \mathcal{R}_{\mathsf{pp}} \end{array} \middle| \begin{array}{c} (i, x_i, \pi_i, x, w) \leftarrow \mathcal{A}(\mathsf{pp}) \\ w_i \leftarrow \mathcal{E}^{\mathcal{A}}(\mathsf{pp}) \end{array} \right] \leq \mathsf{negl}(\lambda)$$

3. **Efficiency:** $|\pi_i| = o(m \cdot |x|)$, *namely, the proof size should be asymptotically smaller than the total size of folded statements.*

The definition captures that if (1) the prover knows a valid witness w for the folded statement x and (2) the i-th proof verifies, then it should be the case that the prover knows witness w_i such that $(x_i, w_i) \in \mathcal{R}_{\mathsf{pp}}$. Note that from the perspective of a party asserting the validity of x_i, it is not necessary to know the other statements considered in the construction of x. Furthermore, the other statements need not be honestly generated; even if the adversary samples them, knowledge of the witness of the i-th statement is still guaranteed.

The efficiency condition rules out trivial constructions. Without it, one could set the proof of statement i to be simply the set of all aggregated statements along with a proof of correct folding. The verifier would then simply need to check that one of the statements corresponds to the one that is of interest to her. The interesting part of the definition is to achieve the same goal with *sublinear communication*.

Finally, note that we do not require the extractor to be able to extract all m statements that would "explain" the folded statement x; rather, we ask that given a witness for the folded statement and a valid proof, we can extract a witness only for the i-th statement. This is exactly what one would want for selective verification since ultimately, this is a *local property*: we want to ensure that some statement is correct without caring how we end up with the folded statement; the latter is simply a means to verify correctness of the statement of interest.

3   Bootstrapping Construction for Folding Schemes

In this section, we show how to bootstrap any 2-folding scheme to an M-folding scheme for any polynomial M. Additionally, the bootstrapped construction satisfies the stronger notion of selective verifiability. Thus, to construct a selectively verifiable folding scheme, it is enough to construct a simple 2-folding scheme – which as we shall see is a relatively simple task using Σ-protocol techniques– and simply applying the bootstrapping compiler.

The crucial observation to bootstrapping is that statement aggregation is by definition "incremental". The fact that the folded statement is of the same form as the folded ones directly implies that we can further fold the former with a new statement. A simple argument shows the final statement "encodes" all three statements and a single proof for it along with the two folding proofs is convincing for the validity of all. The process can be repeated an arbitrary amount of times.

To achieve the additional property of selective verifiability we only rely on combinatorial properties: instead of incrementally aggregating statements, we arrange them in a *statement tree*. Thus, the fact that a single statement is "encoded" in the final folded statement only depends on a small amount of statements: the ones that consist the path from the leaf (statement we want a proof for) to the root (folded statement). Thus, the corresponding proof is sublinear in the number of statements, consisting of the folding proofs for the statements in this path.

We next present the bootstrapping construction and then we show that it also achieves the stronger notion of selective verifiability.

3.1   Construction

Our construction allows to derive an M-folding scheme from any 2-folding scheme[3].

Roughly, to aggregate $M = 2^k$ (w.l.o.g.) statements, we create a *statement aggregation tree* as follows. We build a tree by putting the statements on the leaves of the tree and we fold each pair of them resulting in 2^{k-1} statements of the same form. Then we proceed recursively until we are left with a single statement.

To prove that the folded statement encodes all the statements, we give a proof π consisting of all the 2-folding proofs we made along the way to derive the root of the tree.

It is easy to see that the construction satisfies knowledge soundness. Consider the final 2-folding proving that the root is the folded statement of its two children. Given a valid witness for the folded statement and a proof of correct aggregation,

---

[3] The bootstrapping construction can in fact bootstrap any m-folding scheme for $m \geq 2$. We only present the $m = 2$ case for ease of presentation. All constructions in this work are derived from 2-folding schemes but one could in fact consider $m > 2$ to improve concrete efficiency.

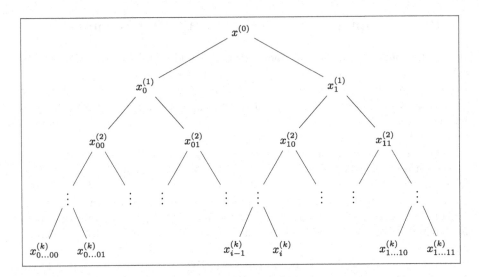

Fig. 1. Demonstration of the process of deriving the folding tree. We assume we fold 2^k statements (the leaves of the tree). We index with the position of the node in the tree in binary and we use superscript for the level of the node in the tree. A node $x_{\mathsf{b}}^{(l)}$ is computed as the (non-interactive) folding of $x_{\mathsf{b}0}^{(l-1)}$ and $x_{\mathsf{b}1}^{(l-1)}$ using the underlying scheme FS. The aggregation proof consists of all the folding proof performed.

we can extract witnesses for its two children –guaranteed by the knowledge soundness of the base 2-folding scheme.

We emphasize that our construction is incremental as well: the final statement –having the same form as the folded statement– can be furthered aggregated if needed.

We give a pictorial representation of the construction in Fig. 1 and present the bootstrapping construction in Fig. 2. Next we show that the resulting construction is an M-folding scheme for any polynomial size m.

Theorem 1. *Let* FS *be a 2-folding scheme for a language family* $\mathcal{L}$ *with corresponding relations* $\mathcal{R}$. *Then, for any constant constant* $k \in \mathbb{N}$, *construction* BootstrapFS *of Fig. 2 is a* 2^k-*folding scheme for the same language family.*

Proof. Completeness follows directly by straightforward calculations and the completeness of BootstrapFS. We next show that BootstrapFS satisfies knowledge soundness.

Let $m = 2^k$, $x_1, \ldots, x_m$ be statements and w a witness for the folded statement x output by an adversary $\mathcal{A}$. We construct an extractor $\mathcal{E}$ that extracts the witnesses $w_1, \ldots, w_m$ given a witness for the folded statement w and a valid folding proof π, that uses as a black box the extractor $\mathcal{E}'$ for FS guaranteed to exist by knowledge soundness of FS.

Consider the binary tree defined by the honest BootstrapFS.FoldVrfy algorithm: the leaves are defined in the first level by the statements, that is, we label each leaf with $(x_1^{(k)}, \bot), (x_2^{(k)}, \bot), \ldots, (x_m^{(k)}, \bot)$ where $x_j^{(k)} = x_j$ and for each pair

---

BootstrapFS.Fold(pp, $q_1 = (x_1, w_1), \ldots, q_m = (x_m, w_m)$):
- Denote $m = 2^k$
- if $k = 0$ then output $q_1, \pi_1 = \bot$, otherwise group the 2^k statements to 2 groups of 2^{k-1} elements each and denote them $\mathbf{q}_1, \mathbf{q}_2$
- Recursively compute:
  $(\tilde{q}_1 = (\tilde{x}_1, \tilde{w}_1), \tilde{\pi}_1) \leftarrow$ BootstrapFS.Fold(pp, $\mathbf{q}_1$)
  $(\tilde{q}_2 = (\tilde{x}_2, \tilde{w}_2), \tilde{\pi}_2) \leftarrow$ BootstrapFS.Fold(pp, $\mathbf{q}_2$)
- $(q = (x, w), \pi^*) \leftarrow$ FS.Fold(pp, $\tilde{q}_1, \tilde{q}_2$)
- output $q, \pi = (\pi_1, \pi_2, \tilde{x}_1, \tilde{x}_2, \pi^*)$

BootstrapFS.FoldVrfy(pp, $x_1, \ldots, x_m, x, \pi$):
- Denote $m = 2^k$
- if $k = 0$ then output 1 iff $x = x_1$, otherwise
  1. group the 2^k statements to 2 groups of 2^{k-1} elements each and denote them $\mathbf{x}_1, \mathbf{x}_2$
  2. parse the proof as $\pi = (\pi_1, \pi_2, \tilde{x}_1, \tilde{x}_2, \pi^*)$
- recursively compute
  $b_1 \leftarrow$ BootstrapFS.FoldVrfy(pp, $\mathbf{x}_1, \tilde{x}_1, \tilde{\pi}_1$)
  $b_2 \leftarrow$ BootstrapFS.FoldVrfy(pp, $\mathbf{x}_2, \tilde{x}_2, \tilde{\pi}_2$)
- $b \leftarrow$ FS.FoldVrfy(pp, $\tilde{x}_1, \tilde{x}_2, x, \pi^*$)
- output $b \wedge b_1 \wedge b_2$

Fig. 2. Bootstrapping construction BootstrapFS for deriving an m-folding scheme from a 2-folding scheme FS. We assume (w.l.o.g.) that the number of initial statements is 2^k.

of statements folded, we define a parent node connected to each of them labeled by the folded statement and the proof of correct folding. Note that verification passes, if

1. for any node labeled $(x_j^{(i-1)}, \pi_j^{(i-1)})$ with child nodes $(x_{2j-1}^{(i)}, \cdot), (x_{2j}^{(i)}, \cdot)$ verification passes, namely, FS.FoldVrfy(pp, $x_{2j-1}^{(i)}, x_{2j}^{(i)}, x_j^{(i-1)}, \pi_j^{(i-1)}$) = 1
2. the root node is labeled with $(x, \cdot)$

We next show that for all such adversaries $\mathcal{A}$, there exists a family of extractors $\mathcal{E}_j^i$ for $0 \leq i \leq k - 1$, $1 \leq j \leq 2^i$ such that given as input a derived tree for some statements $x_1, \ldots, x_m$, $\mathcal{E}_j^{(i)}$ extracts valid witnesses $w_{2j-1}^{(i+1)}, w_{2j}^{(i+1)}$ for the statements $x_{2j-1}^{(i+1)}, x_{2j}^{(i+1)}$ that are the children nodes of $x_j^{(i)}$ in the derived tree. The construction is recursive. We denote $\mathcal{E}^{(*)}$ the trivial extractor that given the witness for the root node (output by the adversary $\mathcal{A}$), it simply outputs it.

Base Case: $\mathcal{E}_1^{(0)}$ runs $\mathcal{E}^{(*)}$ to get the witness $w_1^{(0)}$ for the root. It then queries the derived tree and constructs the adversary $\mathcal{A}_1^{(0)}$ that outputs $x_1^{(1)}, x_2^{(1)}$, folded statement-witness pair $x_1^{(0)}, w_1^{(0)}$ and proof $\pi_1^{(0)}$ which is part of the label of the root node. Finally, it invokes $\mathcal{E}'$ with access to $\mathcal{A}_1^{(0)}$ to derive witnesses $w_1^{(1)}, w_2^{(1)}$ for the statements $x_1^{(1)}, x_2^{(1)}$.

Recursive Case: Now, let $i \geq 1$ and consider any j with $1 \leq j \leq 2^i$. We construct an extractor $\mathcal{E}_j^{(i)}$ assuming the existence of an extractor for a level closer to the root node. Let $(x_{p(j)}^{(i-1)}, \cdot)$ denote the label of the parent node of the node labeled with $(x_j^{(i)}, \pi_j^{(i)})$ and let $(x_{2j-1}^{(i+1)}, \cdot), (x_{2j}^{(i+1)}, \cdot)$ be the labels of the children of $x_j^{(i)}$. Now, we construct $\mathcal{A}_j^{(i)}$ that has hardcoded the binary tree and works as follows:

- It invokes the extractor $\mathcal{E}_{p(j)}^{(i-1)}$ corresponding to statement $x_{p(j)}^{(i-1)}$ to get a witness $w_j^{(i)}$ for $x_j^{(i)}$ (and all its siblings which it ignores).
- It then constructs an adversary $\mathcal{A}_j^{(i)}$ that outputs $x_{2j-1}^{(i+1)}, x_{2j}^{(i+1)}$, the folded statement-witness pair $x_j^{(i)}, w_j^{(i)}$ and the proof of correct folding $\pi_j^{(i)}$ contained in the node label.
- Finally, it invokes the extractor $\mathcal{E}'$ of FS with access to $\mathcal{A}_j^{(i)}$ and gets witnesses $w_{2j-1}^{(i+1)}, w_{2j}^{(i+1)}$.
- It outputs witnesses $w_{2j-1}^{(i+1)}, w_{2j}^{(i+1)}$.

We are now ready to construct the extractor $\mathcal{E}$. $\mathcal{E}$ queries $\mathcal{A}$ to get statements $x_1, \ldots, x_m$, a folded statement-witness pair $(x_1^{(0)}, w_1^{(0)})$ and a proof of correct folding π. It then uses the proof and the statements to construct the tree, queries the extractors $\mathcal{E}_1^{(k-1)}, \ldots, \mathcal{E}_{m/2}^{(k-1)}$ -each of which outputs 2 witnesses for 2 leaf nodes- and concatenates their outputs.

Let's now consider the running time and the probability of success of the extractor $\mathcal{E}$.

For the running time, let $t(\lambda)$ be the running time of $\mathcal{E}'$ and denote $t_i(\lambda)$ the running time of an extractor on level i (note that all these extractors are identical). By construction, we have that $t_i(\lambda) = t_{i-1}(\lambda) + t(\lambda)$ and $t_0(\lambda) = |w|$, namely the time to output the folded witness w. This recurrence relation corresponds to $t_i(\lambda) = i \cdot t(\lambda) + |w|$. Finally, the running time of the extractor $\mathcal{E}$ is

$$t_{\mathcal{E}}(\lambda, k) = t_{\mathsf{BootstrapFS}}(\lambda, k) + 2^{k-1} t_{k-1}(\lambda) =$$
$$= t_{\mathsf{BootstrapFS}}(\lambda, k) + 2^{k-1}(k-1) \cdot t(\lambda) + |w|$$

where $t_{\mathsf{BootstrapFS}}(k)$ is the time of BootstrapFS.FoldVrfy algorithm for folding $m = 2^k$ statements (equivalently the time needed to construct the statement tree). This corresponds to a quasilinear overhead $m \log m$ for the time of the extractor $\mathcal{E}$, which is polynomial for any number of polynomial statements.

We next show that the advantage of $\mathcal{E}$ is polynomially related to that of $\mathcal{E}'$. We denote with p' the probability that extractor $\mathcal{E}'$ succeeds in outputting the witnesses in FS conditioned on $\mathcal{A}$ outputting a valid witness for the folded statement and a verifying proof, namely,

$$p' = \Pr \left[\{(x_1, w_1), (x_2, w_2)\} \subseteq \mathcal{R}_{\mathsf{pp}} \left| \begin{array}{l} (x_1, x_2, x, w, \pi) \leftarrow \mathcal{A}(\mathsf{pp}) \\ (w_1, w_2) \leftarrow \mathcal{E}'^{\mathcal{A}}(\mathsf{pp}) \\ \mathsf{FoldVrfy}\,(\mathsf{pp}, x_1, x_2, x, \pi) = 1 \\ (x, w) \in \mathcal{R}_{\mathsf{pp}} \end{array} \right. \right]$$

Claim. Consider any adversary $\mathcal{A}$ against BootstrapFS and the folding tree derived by its output. Fix i, j such that $0 \leq i \leq k - 1$ and $1 \leq j \leq 2^i$ and consider the tree node $(x_j^{(i)}, \pi_j^{(i)})$ and let $(x_{2j-1}^{(i+1)}, \cdot), (x_{2j}^{(i+1)}, \cdot)$ be its children. Let W_i be the event that the extractor $\mathcal{E}_j^{(i)}$ outputs a valid witness for all the children nodes of $x_j^{(i)}$, that is

$$W_i = \left\{ \left\{ (x_{2j-1}^{(i+1)}, w_{2j-1}^{(i+1)}), (x_{2j}^{(i+1)}, w_{2j}^{(i+1)}) \right\} \subseteq \mathcal{R}_{pp} \left| \begin{matrix} (x_1, \ldots, x_m, x, w, \pi) \leftarrow \mathcal{A}(pp) \\ (w_{2j-1}^{(i+1)}, w_{2j}^{(i+1)}) \leftarrow \mathcal{E}_j^{(i)\,\mathcal{A}}(pp) \end{matrix} \right. \right\}$$

Then $\Pr[W_i] \geq p' \Pr[W_{i-1}]$.

Proof. We have $\Pr[W_i] \geq \Pr[W_i \mid W_{i-1}] \Pr[W_{i-1}]$. Now, the probability of W_i conditioned on W_{i-1} is the probability that an extractor on the i-th level succeeds conditioned on the probability that the extractor on level $i - 1$ succeeds. If the extractor of the parent node succeeds, then its output contains a valid statement/witness $x_j^{(i)}, w_j^{(i)}$ and therefore $\mathcal{A}_j^{(i)}$ outputs a valid folded witness by construction. Thus, the probability of this event is exactly p'. ∎

Solving the recurrence relation gives that $\Pr[W_{k-1}] \geq p'^{k-2} \Pr[W_1]$. Now, $\Pr[W_1]$ is the probability that the extractor associated with the root node outputs valid witnesses assuming that $\mathcal{A}$ outputs a valid witness for the (final) folded statement. This means that, conditioned on $\mathcal{A}$ outputting a valid witness, $\Pr[W_{k-1}] \geq p'^{k-1}$.

Finally, consider the probability that $\mathcal{E}$ succeeds conditioned on $\mathcal{A}$ outputting a valid witness. This events happens if all extractors in level $k - 1$ succeed. So, the probability that $\mathcal{E}$ fails is bounded by $\frac{m}{2}(1 - p'^{k-1}) = 2^{k-1}(1 - p'^{k-1})$. Noting that $1 - p'^{k-1} = (1 - p')(p'^{k-2} + \cdots + 1) \leq (1 - p')(k - 1)$ we get for any adversaries $\mathcal{A}, \mathcal{A}'$ against knowledge soundness of BootstrapFS and FS respectively, $\mathsf{Adv}_{\mathcal{A}}(\lambda, k) \leq (k - 1)2^{k-1}\mathsf{Adv}_{\mathcal{A}'}(\lambda)$ □

Remark 2. As noted in Remark 1, after performing a folding and computing a witness for the folded statement, there is no need to store the witnesses for the initial statements any more. We note that this is the case for the compiled construction as well. In particular, in applications where the statements to be aggregated are "streamed" the prover can be implemented to perform the folding by storing only three witness at any time. This can drastically reduce the memory requirements for aggregation.

Remark 3. NOVA and similar related work inherently rely on heuristic arguments for security. In particular, to construct IVC schemes, it is inherent in the techniques used in these works that one needs to encode the folding/proof aggregation in a circuit and prove statements about it. Since aggregation relies on the random oracle, one needs to instantiate it using a hash function and prove statements about it. Thus, we need to make the heuristic argument that the proving system is secure even when treating the RO in a non-black box way. In contrast,

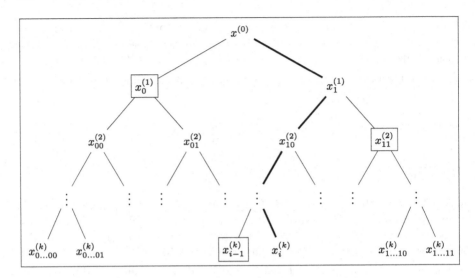

Fig. 3. Demonstration of the process of deriving the folding tree. We assume we fold 2^k statements (the leaves of the tree). We index with the position of the node in the tree in binary and we use superscript for the level of the node in the tree. A node $x_{\mathrm{b}}^{(l)}$ is computed as the (non-interactive) folding of $x_{\mathrm{b}0}^{(l-1)}$ and $x_{\mathrm{b}1}^{(l-1)}$ using the underlying scheme FS. Bold edges denote the path the verification follows and rectangles the statements the prover presents to the verifier of statement i.

our application does not involve encoding the folding argument in a circuit and proving statements about it. Therefore, our construction is provably secure in the random oracle model.

3.2   Selective Verifiability of the Bootstrapped Construction

Our bootstrapping construction also satisfies the stronger notion of selective verifiability without further modifications. This follows by the tree structure employed: proving inclusion of a single statement needs only to consider the foldings occurring from the root node (final statement) to the leaf corresponding to the statement in consideration. This is similar to how tree-based vector commitment schemes (e.g. Merkle trees) work.

A crucial observation is that if we have a statement of the form $x_1 \in \mathcal{L}$ and we are presented with a different statement $x_2 \in \mathcal{L}$, after folding these to a third statement $x \in \mathcal{L}$, knowledge of a witness for the latter ensures knowledge for both statements (in particular the first which is of interest to us) *even if the second is selected adversarially*. This means that from the perspective of a verifier interested in a specific statement, it is not important what other statements are considered or how they are sampled as long as they correctly end up to the claimed aggregated statement.

We first demonstrate how a statement "inclusion" proof works in Fig. 3. Next, we formally present the algorithms that lead to selective verifiability of the bootstrapped construction in Fig. 4. The resulting protocol achieves selective verifiability with proof size $|\pi_i| = \mathcal{O}(|x| \cdot k)$ when folding $m = 2^k$ statements. This means we can aggregate polynomially many statements while each statement can be verified with a proof that is logarithmic in the number of statements.

An important observation, as far as efficiency is concerned, is that the proofs themselves are folded statements with their corresponding proofs, and thus yield little overhead to produce/verify –assuming the underlying folding scheme is concretely efficient. Essentially, the prover has to perform $\mathcal{O}(2^k)$ number of foldings and simply save the intermediate results in the process to be able to present as evidence later. As we will see in the next section, folding itself can be extremely efficient for many languages of interest. In some cases, the overhead induced by folding for the prover is comparable to the time needed to simply read the statements. This can lead to significant improvements compared to -for example- producing a SNARK proof for each statement.

We next show that the bootstrapped construction equipped with the additional algorithms presented in Fig. 4 achieves the stronger notion of selective verifiability. The proof is essentially identical to that of Theorem 1; the only difference is that we simply focus on a small part of the implicit tree which we construct using the elements contained in the proof for a single statement. We refer the reader to the full version [22] for the proof.

Theorem 2. *Let* FS *be a 2-aggregation scheme for a language family* $\mathcal{L}$ *with corresponding relations* $\mathcal{R}$ *Then, for any constant* k *construction* BootstrapFS *of Fig. 2 satisfies selective verification through the algorithms of Fig. 4*

4   Folding Schemes from Interactive Public Coin Protocols

In the full version [22] we present folding schemes for various relations to demonstrate (1) the prover efficiency as far as folding is concerned, and (2) their simplicity. We present four constructions:

1. a folding scheme for the language of inner product relations of committed values under algebraic commitments,
2. a folding scheme for the language of openings of algebraic vector commitments,
3. a folding scheme for the language of openings of polynomial commitments at the same point.

We also recall the 2-folding scheme construction of NOVA [20] that allows to fold arbitrary (variants of) R1CS relations that capture general computation.

All the constructions are derived through simple public coin protocols. Thus, they can be compiled to non-interactive folding schemes through the Fiat-Shamir transform. Selective verification can then be achieved by means of the bootstrapping construction of Fig. 2 and 4. In all constructions we assume a base folding scheme for folding $m = 2$ statements.

BootstrapFS.SelPrv(pp, $x_1, \ldots, x_m, x, \pi$):
- Parse the input $(\mathbf{x}, x, \pi)$ as a tree where
  - $(x_1^{(k)}, \perp), \ldots, (x_m^{(k)}, \perp)$ are the leaves
  - For each pair of nodes $x_L = (x_{2j-1}^{(\ell)}, \perp)$, $x_R = (x_{2j}^{(\ell)}, \perp)$ add the node $(x_F, \pi_F) = (x_j^{(\ell-1)}, \pi_j^{(\ell-1)})$ where π_F is a proof of correctness of the folding of x_L, x_R to x_F, namely: FS.FoldVrfy(pp, $x_L, x_R, x_F, \pi_F) = 1$
- For $1 \leq j \leq m$:
  - set $\pi_j := ()$
  - Let $j = b_k \cdots b_1$ in binary notation
  - For $1 \leq \ell \leq k$:
    $$\pi_j := \left(\pi_j, \left(x_{b_k \cdots b_{k-\ell+2}0}^{(\ell)}, x_{b_k \cdots b_{k-\ell+2}1}^{(\ell)}, \pi_{b_k \cdots b_{k-\ell+2}}^{(\ell-1)} \right) \right)$$
- Output $\pi_1, \ldots, \pi_m$

BootstrapFS.SelVrfy(pp, x, j, x_j, π_j):
- Let $j = b_k \cdots b_1$ in binary notation.
- Set $x_1^{(0)} = x$
- Parse $\pi_j = \left((x_0^{(1)}, x_1^{(1)}, \pi_1^{(0)}), \ldots, (x_{b_k \cdots b_2 0}^{(k)}, x_{b_k \cdots b_2 1}^{(k)}, \pi_{b_k \cdots b_2}^{(k-1)}) \right)$
- For $1 \leq \ell \leq k$
  Set $x_L = x_{b_k \cdots b_{k-\ell+2}0}^{(\ell)}$, $x_R = x_{b_k \cdots b_{k-\ell+2}1}^{(\ell)}$,
  Set $x_F = x_{b_k \cdots b_{k-\ell+2}}^{(\ell-1)}$, $\pi_F = \pi_{b_k \cdots b_{k-\ell+2}}^{(\ell-1)}$
  $b_\ell := $ FS.FoldVrfy(pp, x_L, x_R, x_F, π_F)
- Output $b_1 \wedge \cdots \wedge b_\ell \wedge (x_j = x_{b_k \cdots b_1}^{(k)})$

Fig. 4. The SelPrv, SelVrfy that make construction BootstrapFS achieve selective verification. We again assume (w.l.o.g.) that the number of initial statements is $m = 2^k$ for some fixed constant k.

We emphasize that the folding overhead for all constructions is low. The prover is dominated by field operations and the verifier by group operations (constant for each 2-folding). Both need to also perform hash computations in the non-interactive version of the protocols. Nevertheless, since we do not need to encode the folding as a circuit and prove statements about it –as is done by previous works– we can instantiate the construction with any hash function instead of "SNARK friendly" ones. Thus, the overhead for hashing is insignificant.

References

1. Ben-Sasson, E., Chiesa, A., Spooner, N.: Interactive oracle proofs. In: Hirt, M., Smith, A. (eds.) TCC 2016, Part II. LNCS, vol. 9986, pp. 31–60. Springer, Heidelberg (2016). https://doi.org/10.1007/978-3-662-53644-5_2
2. Ben-Sasson, E., et al.: Zerocash: decentralized anonymous payments from bitcoin. In: 2014 IEEE Symposium on Security and Privacy, pp. 459–474. IEEE Computer Society Press (2014). https://doi.org/10.1109/SP.2014.36

3. Bitansky, N., et al.: Recursive composition and bootstrapping for SNARKS and proof-carrying data. In: Boneh, D., Roughgarden, T., Feigenbaum, J. (eds.) 45th ACM STOC, pp. 111–120. ACM Press (2013). https://doi.org/10.1145/2488608.2488623

4. Boneh, D., Drake, J., Fisch, B., Gabizon, A.: Halo Infinite: proof-carrying data from additive polynomial commitments. In: Malkin, T., Peikert, C. (eds.) CRYPTO 2021, Part I. LNCS, vol. 12825, pp. 649–680. Springer, Cham (2021). https://doi.org/10.1007/978-3-030-84242-0_23

5. Bootle, J., Chiesa, A., Groth, J.: Linear-time arguments with sublinear verification from tensor codes. In: Pass, R., Pietrzak, K. (eds.) TCC 2020, Part II. LNCS, vol. 12551, pp. 19–46. Springer, Cham (2020). https://doi.org/10.1007/978-3-030-64378-2_2

6. Bootle, J., Chiesa, A., Liu, S.: Zero-Knowledge Succinct Arguments with a Linear-Time Prover. In: IACR Cryptology ePrint Archive, p. 1527 (2020). https://eprint.iacr.org/2020/1527

7. Bootle, J., Cerulli, A., Chaidos, P., Groth, J., Petit, C.: Efficient zero-knowledge arguments for arithmetic circuits in the discrete log setting. In: Fischlin, M., Coron, J.-S. (eds.) EUROCRYPT 2016, Part II. LNCS, vol. 9666, pp. 327–357. Springer, Heidelberg (2016). https://doi.org/10.1007/978-3-662-49896-5_12

8. Bootle, J., et al.: Gemini: Elastic SNARKs for Diverse Environments. In: IACR Cryptology ePrint Archive, p. 420 (2022). https://eprint.iacr.org/2022/420

9. Bowe, S., Grigg, J., Hopwood, D.: Halo: Recursive Proof Composition without a Trusted Setup. Cryptology ePrint Archive, Report 2019/1021 (2019). https://eprint.iacr.org/2019/1021

10. Bünz, B., et al.: Bulletproofs: short proofs for confidential transactions and more. In: 2018 IEEE Symposium on Security and Privacy, pp. 315–334. IEEE Computer Society Press (2018). https://doi.org/10.1109/SP.2018.00020

11. Bünz, B., Chiesa, A., Lin, W., Mishra, P., Spooner, N.: Proof-carrying data without succinct arguments. In: Malkin, T., Peikert, C. (eds.) CRYPTO 2021, Part I. LNCS, vol. 12825, pp. 681–710. Springer, Cham (2021). https://doi.org/10.1007/978-3-030-84242-0_24

12. Bünz, B., Chiesa, A., Mishra, P., Spooner, N.: Recursive proof composition from accumulation schemes. In: Pass, R., Pietrzak, K. (eds.) TCC 2020, Part II. LNCS, vol. 12551, pp. 1–18. Springer, Cham (2020). https://doi.org/10.1007/978-3-030-64378-2_1

13. Campanelli, M., et al.: Lunar: a Toolbox for More Efficient Universal and Updatable zkSNARKs and Commit-and-Prove Extensions. Cryptology ePrint Archive, Report 2020/1069 (2020). https://eprint.iacr.org/2020/1069

14. Catalano, D., Fiore, D.: Vector commitments and their applications. In: Kurosawa, K., Hanaoka, G. (eds.) PKC 2013. LNCS, vol. 7778, pp. 55–72. Springer, Heidelberg (2013). https://doi.org/10.1007/978-3-642-36362-7_5

15. Chiesa, A., Hu, Y., Maller, M., Mishra, P., Vesely, N., Ward, N.: Marlin: preprocessing zkSNARKs with universal and updatable SRS. In: Canteaut, A., Ishai, Y. (eds.) EUROCRYPT 2020, Part I. LNCS, vol. 12105, pp. 738–768. Springer, Cham (2020). https://doi.org/10.1007/978-3-030-45721-1_26

16. Gabizon, A., Williamson, Z.J., Ciobotaru, O.: PLONK: Permutations over Lagrange-bases for Oecumenical Noninteractive arguments of Knowledge. Cryptology ePrint Archive, Report 2019/953 (2019). https://eprint.iacr.org/2019/953

17. Goldwasser, S., Kalai, Y.T., Rothblum, G.N.: Delegating computation: interactive proofs for muggles. In: Ladner, R.E., Dwork, C. (eds.) 40th ACM STOC, pp. 113–122. ACM Press (2008). https://doi.org/10.1145/1374376.1374396

18. Kate, A., Zaverucha, G.M., Goldberg, I.: Constant-size commitments to polynomials and their applications. In: Abe, M. (ed.) ASIACRYPT 2010. LNCS, vol. 6477, pp. 177–194. Springer, Heidelberg (2010). https://doi.org/10.1007/978-3-642-17373-8_11

19. Kothapalli, A., Setty, S.: HyperNova: recursive arguments for customizable constraint systems. In: IACR Cryptology ePrint Archive, p. 573 (2023). https://eprint.iacr.org/2023/573

20. Kothapalli, A., Setty, S., Tzialla, I.: Nova: recursive zero-knowledge arguments from folding schemes. In: Dodis, Y., Shrimpton, T. (eds.) CRYPTO 2022. LNCS, vol. 13510, pp. 359–388. Springer, Cham (2022). https://doi.org/10.1007/978-3-031-15985-5_13

21. Mohnblatt, N.: Sangria: A Folding Scheme for PLONK. https://github.com/geometryresearch/technical_notes/blob/main/sangria_folding_plonk.pdf. Accessed 07 Aug 2023

22. Ràfols, C., Zacharakis, A.: Folding Schemes with Selective Verification. In: IACR Cryptology ePrint Archive, p. 1576 (2022). https://eprint.iacr.org/2022/1576

23. Ron-Zewi, N., Rothblum, R.: Proving as fast as computing: succinct arguments with constant prover overhead. In: Electronic Colloquium on Computational Complexity, p. 180 (2021). https://eccc.weizmann.ac.il/report/2021/180

24. Valiant, P.: Incrementally verifiable computation or proofs of knowledge imply time/space efficiency. In: Canetti, R. (ed.) TCC 2008. LNCS, vol. 4948, pp. 1–18. Springer, Heidelberg (2008). https://doi.org/10.1007/978-3-540-78524-8_1

25. Yurek, T., et al.: hbACSS: How to Robustly Share Many Secrets. Cryptology ePrint Archive, Report 2021/159 (2021). https://eprint.iacr.org/2021/159

Composable Oblivious Pseudo-random Functions via Garbled Circuits

Sebastian Faller[1,2]([✉]) [iD], Astrid Ottenhues[3,4] [iD], and Johannes Ottenhues[5] [iD]

[1] IBM Research Europe, Zurich, Switzerland
sebastian.faller@ibm.com
[2] ETH Zurich, Zurich, Switzerland
[3] KASTEL Security Research Labs, Karlsruhe, Germany
astrid.ottenhues@kit.edu
[4] Karlsruhe Institute of Technology, Karlsruhe, Germany
[5] University of St. Gallen, St. Gallen, Switzerland
johannes.ottenhues@posteo.org

Abstract. Oblivious Pseudo-Random Functions (OPRFs) are a central tool for building modern protocols for authentication and distributed computation. For example, OPRFs enable simple login protocols that do not reveal the password to the provider, which helps to mitigate known shortcomings of password-based authentication such as password reuse or mix-up. Reliable treatment of passwords becomes more and more important as we login to a multitude of services with different passwords in our daily life.

To ensure the security and privacy of such services in the long term, modern protocols should always consider the possibility of attackers with quantum computers. Therefore, recent research has focused on constructing post-quantum-secure OPRFs. Unfortunately, existing constructions either lack efficiency, or they are based on complex and relatively new cryptographic assumptions, some of which have lately been disproved.

In this paper, we revisit the security and the efficiency of the well-known "OPRFs via Garbled Circuits" approach. Such an OPRF is presumably post-quantum-secure and built from well-understood primitives, namely symmetric cryptography and oblivious transfer. We investigate security in the strong Universal Composability model, which guarantees security even when multiple instances are executed in parallel and in conjunction with arbitrary other protocols, which is a realistic scenario in today's internet. At the same time, it is faster than other current post-quantum-secure OPRFs. Our implementation and benchmarks demonstrate that our proposed OPRF is currently among the best choices if the privacy of the data has to be guaranteed for a long time.

Keywords: Oblivious Pseudo-Random Function · Garbled Circuits · Post-Quantum Cryptography · Universal Composability

1 Introduction

An Oblivious Pseudo-Random Function (OPRF) is a two-party protocol for obliviously evaluating a Pseudo-Random Function (PRF), which is a function

A. Aly and M. Tibouchi (Eds.): LATINCRYPT 2023, LNCS 14168, pp. 249–270, 2023.
https://doi.org/10.1007/978-3-031-44469-2_13

that outputs a pseudorandom value. One party (the server) holds the key k and the other party (the user) has the input p. The goal is that the user does not learn anything about the server's key k while the server does neither learn anything about the user's input nor the output. This interaction is shown in Fig. 1.

Fig. 1. Sketch of the Oblivious Pseudo-Random Function (OPRF) functionality.

OPRFs lie at the heart of many privacy-preserving protocols. To illustrate the importance of secure OPRF protocols we elaborate on some examples: Private set intersection [34] for instance allows two users to find out which contacts they both have in common, without revealing the full list of their contacts to each other or a service provider. The OPRF allows one party to hide its input while still computing some fingerprints of its elements for the other party. PrivacyPass [23] allows users to bypass subsequent Captchas (after solving the first one), while preventing tracking of the users. In this use-case, the OPRF is used for letting a user retrieve unlinkable tokens after solving a Captcha. OPAQUE [33] enables password-based authentication while hiding the password from the server, which alleviates many of the known problems of passwords. In OPAQUE, the OPRF is used to turn a low entropy password into a high entropy secret while completely hiding the password from the server. At the time of writing, OPAQUE is in the process of being standardized by the IETF[1]. One can see that all these protocols crucially rely on an OPRF as a cryptographic building block.

The above-mentioned protocols are designed to run in today's Internet, where many protocols run concurrently and are used as building blocks for other protocols. In these complex environments, attackers may be able to gain information by maliciously relaying messages from different sessions, or by otherwise making different protocol executions interfere. One of the most common approaches to construct *composable* protocols that keep their security guarantees in these complex situations was proposed in [16], called *universal composability*. Subsequently, this concept has also been applied to formalize and construct *composable* OPRFs [31–33]. Formally proving the security of an OPRF protocol in a model that guarantees composability is an important aspect of ensuring the security of a protocol in reality.

The security of most existing OPRF constructions is based on concrete hardness assumptions. A disadvantage of this is that any concrete assumption may be broken, which would then break the corresponding OPRF. On the other hand, if

---

[1] https://www.ietf.org/archive/id/draft-irtf-cfrg-opaque-09.html.

a protocol relies on more general assumptions such as secure symmetric encryption, one can easily switch from one symmetric encryption scheme to another in case new attacks render the former one insecure. This makes generic, versatile OPRFs an important goal.

OPRFs were intensively studied in the literature and by now, classical, i.e., Discrete Logarithm (DLog) based protocols are amazingly efficient and enjoy a rich set of additional properties. Nonetheless, it still remains a challenge to construct similarly efficient and versatile OPRFs in the presence of adversaries with quantum computers. In their vision paper, Kampanakis et al. [35] identify the research on post-quantum (pq) OPRFs as a highly relevant research area for post-quantum migration, in particular because of the importance of OPRFs for pq anonymous authentication protocols. In this work, we focus on *presumably pq-secure* protocols, i.e., protocols that can be instantiated from pq-assumptions. This does not necessarily mean that the security proof considers quantum attackers.

When OPRFs are used in practice efficiency is a major concern. Therefore, it is important that OPRF proposals are accompanied by an implementation to analyze their efficiency and compare them to related results. A too slow OPRF in PrivacyPass [23] or OPAQUE [33] can significantly disturb user experience during web-browsing or authentication. Thus, improving the efficiency of pq OPRFs is a decisive objective, as the current (presumably) pq-secure OPRFs still do not match the classical constructions in terms of efficiency.

All together these motivations raise the following question:

Can we obtain an efficient, composable, and presumably post-quantum secure oblivious pseudo-random function constructed from generic techniques?

We answer this question in the affirmative. We show how to adapt an OPRF protocol from [40] based on Yao's garbled circuits such that this adapted version can be proven to be secure in the universal composability model of [16]. Because both garbled circuits and oblivious transfer can be instantiated from pq-secure primitives, our protocol is presumably pq-secure. We demonstrate its concrete efficiency via detailed benchmarks of our implementations.

1.1   Contribution

Our work on answering the above question is based on different areas, wherefore our contribution is threefold. We give a brief technical overview for each part. It can be summarized as follows:

1. We use the Multi-Party Computation (MPC) technique of Garbled Circuits to construct an OPRF protocol and prove its security in the Universal Composability (UC) framework against malicious users and semi-honest servers.
2. We implemented two versions of our protocol and compare it to other state-of-the-art protocols in extensive performance tests.
3. We compare two different approaches from the literature of defining OPRF security in the UC framework and show that one of them is strictly stronger and that it cannot be achieved by a large class of protocols.

(1) *Construction and Proof of OPRFs via Garbled Circuits.* By now multiple presumably post-quantum OPRF protocols have been proposed [1, 2, 11, 12, 28, 29]. Some are based on new cryptographic assumptions and some have been broken. Therefore, an OPRF protocol that relies on generic and well studied building blocks is very desirable. The idea of using generic MPC techniques such as Garbled Circuits (GCs) to construct OPRFs has first been described in [40]. As we will argue, the protocol described in [40] does not satisfy the strong OPRF security definition of [32,33]. Our first contribution is that we show how a modification of the protocol from [40] can be proven secure in the model of [32,33] assuming semi-honest corruption of the server and malicious users. GCs have been optimized intensively [7,37,44], such that they have become efficient for computing functions that have a small representation as a boolean circuit. Furthermore, [13] shows that GCs can be proven secure against quantum attackers in a certain model [10], if instantiated with appropriate building blocks. As Oblivious Transfer (OT) and symmetric primitives can be instantiated in many different ways, the security of GCs does not depend just on a single hardness assumption—that might or might not be broken in the future. Because of these advantages of GCs, we followed an idea from [40] to construct OPRFs via GCs that can be sketched as follows: If a server and a user participate in a secure two-party computation, where the jointly evaluated circuit is a PRF, the resulting protocol is an OPRF. However, this construction does not yet achieve composability which is one of our main goals. To get security in the UC framework, we additionally introduce two hash functions, wich will be modeled as Random Oracles (ROs), following a general idea from [33]. The ROs are crucial for the security proof in the UC framework. We prove security assuming semi-honest servers and malicious users. We will elaborate further on this in Sect. 3.2. Because we prove security in the UC framework, the protocol can be securely used—even in parallel or concurrently—with itself or with other protocols.

(2) *Implementation and Benchmarks of our OPRF Protocol.* We implemented our protocol twice to compare its performance to the current state-of-the-art protocol, *2HashDH*, by [31–33], the lattice-based protocol by [2], and the isogeny-based protocol by [29]. The first implementation is in a C++ framework, called *EMP-Toolkit*[2], which offers most known optimizations for GCs. We also implemented the protocol with PQ-MPC[3]. This framework builds upon EMP-Toolkit and implements a garbling scheme that was proven secure by [13] in a model that considers powerful quantum adversaries [10]. We chose the Advanced Encryption Standard (AES) as the concrete instantiation of the PRF. We compared our implementations to an implementation of 2HashDH [33] building upon OPENSSL[4] and to a simplified implementation of the lattice-based protocol of [2]. We assess the efficiency of the implementations in terms of running time and network traffic. We performed our experiments on a conventional consumer laptop and measured the running time over the local network interface as well

---

[2] https://github.com/emp-toolkit/emp-tool.

[3] https://github.com/encryptogroup/PQ-MPC.

[4] https://www.openssl.org/.

as over a simulated Wide Area Network (WAN). The experiments show that our protocol is much faster than the lattice-based construction of [2] and the isogeny-based protocols of [29]. Further, the experiments show that 2HashDH by [31–33] is still about 50 times faster than our construction and requires less than 100 B of communication. However, with a running time of about 22 ms and traffic of about 250 kB our protocol is still in a reasonable efficiency range. Considering the benchmark results, we see GC-based OPRFs as promising candidates for practically efficient OPRFs that are secure in the presence of adversaries with quantum computers.

(3) *Comparison of Different OPRF Functionalities.* In the literature on composable OPRFs, one can find two different approaches defining OPRFs in the UC framework. We compare a definition from [31–33] and an approach from [14]. We are the first to show that the first one is strictly stronger. This justifies our use of the stronger definition from [31–33] throughout this paper. We show that the plain protocol from [40] does not satisfy the stronger definition from [31–33] and we further show that it is impossible to prove a huge class of protocols secure under the stronger definition from [31–33] in the Non-Programmable Random Oracle Model (NPROM). The impossibility justifies our approach to achieving UC-security for the OPRF from [40] and it rules out the UC-security of a variety of constructions, including [12, Sec. 8] and [29].

1.2   Related Work

Started by [27], there is an ongoing research-line on OPRF protocols in which most protocols are based on the DLog or the integer factorization problem. This renders them vulnerable to potential quantum attacks. However, recent works focused on OPRFs based on presumably pq-secure assumptions. The first lattice-based construction was proposed by [2]. However, prohibitively large parameters must be chosen and expensive lattice-based zero-knowledge proofs are used. Additionally, the security analysis does not consider composition as our analysis does. A more efficient lattice-based OPRF was proposed in [1]. It uses FHE to evaluate the *Dark Matter weak PRF* proposed by [11]. Boneh at al. [11] also proposed an OPRF using the same weak PRF but instead of FHE they used MPC with preprocessing. This line of work was continued by Dinur et al. [24] who use secret-sharing-based MPC to evaluate a PRF that also builds on the modulus-switching idea from [11]. All those works have in common that they rely on the relatively new Dark Matter weak PRF. Although it is a very promising weak PRF candidate that currently receives a lot of attention from the research community, it is arguably not as thoroughly understood as well-established symmetric primitives like AES. Further, none of these works considers security in the UC framework which is crucial to applications like OPAQUE [33]. Two isogeny-based constructions were proposed by [12]. The authors estimate 424 kB of communication for the other protocol. However, it is not clear if the chosen parameters are sufficient or if bigger parameters are necessary to achieve a secure protocol, see [4,18,19]. Also there is no UC proof for this OPRF. A second isogeny-based OPRF is proposed in the same work [12]. However, the construction was broken by [5], even before the underlying SIDH assumption was recently broken by [18]. Further, there is ongoing work on how to fix the shortcomings of the broken construction [4,29]. Another approach is to combine the PRF based on the Decisional Shifted Legendre Symbol Problem (DSLS) [22], which is presumably pq-secure, with a protocol allowing secure function evaluation over $\mathbb{F}_p$ for $p > 2$. The construction is proposed in [42] but no proof of security is given. A second drawback is that the pseudo-randomness of the Legendre symbol with hidden shift is not a standard assumption. There has been some work on the cryptanalysis of the assumption [9]. But one might be more confident in generic assumptions, e.g. OT or the existence of PRFs—like we use in our construction—because they are well-studied and there are several concrete instantiations.

To the best of our knowledge, the authors of [40] were the first proposing an OPRF construction from generic building blocks. They suggest realizing an OPRF by using GCs to evaluate the circuit of a PRF. The privacy requirement for the OPRF is satisfied as the GC protocol guarantees the privacy of inputs. A formal proof of security is not given in [40]. However, the work refers to the general proof for garbled circuit security in the presence of active adversaries of [38]. However, this proof analyzes very costly cut-and-choose techniques that make the garbling scheme rather impractical. The simulation-based proof uses the framework of [15] that even considers a weak form of composition. Note that the provided guarantees are not as strong as in the UC definition from [33]. In [36] a different approach is chosen. The authors use efficient OT extensions, introduced in [30], to instantiate something close to an OPRF protocol. The defined security notion is called batched related-key OPRF (BaRK-OPRF). This notion is related to usual OPRFs but it is not equivalent. BaRK-OPRF has the drawback that each PRF value is computed under a different key. While this limitation is not problematic for their use case of private set-intersection, it is not clear how to instantiate e.g. asymmetric Password Authenticated Key Exchange (aPAKE) [33], Password-Protected Secret Sharing (PPSS) [32], or distributed Single Sign On (SSO) [6] with BaRK-OPRF as these protocols require that the PRF is evaluated under the same key. The security is analyzed in a stand-alone simulation-based model, assuming server *and* client to be semi-honest, while our protocol only assumes semi-honest servers but allows malicious clients. A similarity between our protocols is that both rely only on the security of OT and symmetric cryptography. We summarized the above discussion in Table 1. For a more thorough discussion of OPRFs, we refer to [17].

2   Preliminaries

Pseudo-Random Functions. A Pseudo-Random Function (PRF) is a function that produces "random looking" output values. More precisely, the function is indexed by a key k and takes inputs x. If the key is chosen uniformly at random, the output $\mathsf{F}_k(x)$ is indistinguishable from a random value. The security is defined via a Probabilistic Polynomial Time (PPT) distinguisher $\mathcal{D}$ that either gets oracle access to $\mathsf{F}_k(\cdot)$ for randomly chosen $k \in \{0,1\}^m$ or to a truly random function RF. The goal of $\mathcal{D}$ is to tell those situations apart.

Table 1. Overview of related protocols. We write ($\checkmark$) if we have not implemented the protocol in this work but an implementation will likely be efficient. We write $\checkmark$ (OT) if a protocol is presumably pq-secure, as long as a pq-secure OT is used. We write M if the protocol is secure against malicious adversaries and SH if it is secure against semi-honest adversaries.

Protocol	UC Secure	(presum.) pq Secure	Pract. Efficient	Adv. Model	Assumption
Our work	$\checkmark$	$\checkmark$ (OT)	$\checkmark$	SH	OT, symm. crypto
2HashDH [33]	$\checkmark$	$\times$	$\checkmark$	M	om-DH
Plain Garbled Circuits [40]	$\times$	$\checkmark$ (OT)	$\checkmark$	SH	OT, symm. crypto
BaRK-OPRF [36]	$\times$	$\checkmark$ (OT)	$\checkmark$	SH	OT, symm. crypto
Lattice-based [2]	$\times$	$\checkmark$	$\times$	M	RLWE, 1D-SIS
TFHE-based [1]	$\times$	$\checkmark$	$\times$	SH	Dark-Matter wPRF
NR Isogeny-based [12]	$\times$	$\checkmark$	($\checkmark$)	SH	CSIDH
OPUS [29]	$\times$	$\checkmark$	$\times$	SH	CSIDH,CSI-FiSh
Legendre-based [22, 28]	$\times$	$\checkmark$	?	?	DSLS
MPC w. preprocessing [11, 24]	$\times$	$\checkmark$	($\checkmark$)	SH	Dark-Matter wPRF

Definition 1 (PRF & PRP). Let $\mathsf{F} : \{0,1\}^m \times \{0,1\}^n \to \{0,1\}^l$ be a function family such that there is a polynomial-time algorithm that takes $k \in \{0,1\}^m$ and $p \in \{0,1\}^n$ and outputs $\mathsf{F}_k(p) \in \{0,1\}^l$. Let $p_0 := \Pr{*}\mathcal{D}^{\mathsf{F}_k(\cdot)}(1^n) = 1$ and $p_1 := \Pr[\mathcal{D}^{\mathsf{RF}(\cdot)}(1^n) = 1]$, where the probabilities are taken over random choices of $k \in \{0,1\}^m$ and $\mathsf{RF} \in \{f : \{0,1\}^n \to \{0,1\}^l\}$. We say F is a *pseudo-random function* if the advantage $\mathrm{Adv}_{\mathsf{F}}^{\mathsf{PRF}}(\mathcal{D}, n) := |p_0 - p_1|$ is negligible for every PPT distinguisher $\mathcal{D}$. If F_k is indistinguishable from a random permutation $\mathsf{RF} \xleftarrow{\$} \mathcal{S}_n$ then we say F is a *pseudo-random permutation.*

Oblivious Pseudo-random Functions. A conventional PRF must be evaluated by a single party, which knows k as well as p. An OPRF for a certain PRF consists of two parties that interact to jointly compute an output of the PRF. One party—the server—holds the key k of the PRF and the other party—the user—holds the input value p. In the end, the user learns the output value $y = \mathsf{F}_k(p)$, but nothing about the key k. The server obtains no additional information from the interaction. In particular, it learns nothing about the user's input p.

The ROM and NPROM for UC. A random oracle $H: A \to B$ maps elements from a set A to elements of a set B. If H receives an input query $x \in A$ for the first time, it outputs a uniformly random drawn value $y \in B$ and stores the tuple $\langle x, y \rangle$. If H receives the query x again, it outputs y. To not clutter notation too much, we will notate the random oracle in our work like a "conventional hash function" instead of an ideal functionality.

In [39], the NPROM is defined as a variant of the UC framework of [16]. In contrast to the original UC framework, each machine—including the environment machine—gets access to an oracle $\mathcal{O}$. The oracle is a random oracle in the sense that it answers queries of the form $x \in \{0,1\}^*$ with a uniformly random $y \in$

$\{0,1\}^l$, where $l \in \mathbb{N}$ is fixed, and it records the tuple $\langle x, y \rangle$. If x is queried again, $\mathcal{O}$ answers again with y. The difference to a normal random oracle described before is that $\mathcal{O}$ is *not* a hybrid functionality. In particular, a simulator in the UC experiment has no way of influencing the output of $\mathcal{O}$. More precisely, we write $M^{\mathcal{O}}$ to denote that a machine M gets an oracle input tape, where M can write queries to x and an oracle output tape, where M receives the answers from $\mathcal{O}$. We say a protocol π UC-emulates a protocol ϕ in the NPROM if $\text{EXEC}_{\pi^{\mathcal{O}}, \mathcal{A}^{\mathcal{O}}, \mathcal{E}^{\mathcal{O}}} \overset{c}{\approx} \text{EXEC}_{\phi^{\mathcal{O}}, \mathcal{S}^{\mathcal{O}}, \mathcal{E}^{\mathcal{O}}}$.

Oblivious Transfer. In its simplest form, OT [41] allows a sender to transfer one of two messages to a receiver (1-out-of-2 OT). The receiver can choose which message it wants. The security guarantee for the receiver is that the sender does not learn anything about the choice of the receiver. The security guarantee for the sender is that the receiver does not learn anything about the message that was not chosen. Looking ahead, OT allows the evaluator of a Garbled Circuit (GC) to get the wire labels for their input, without leaking the input to the GC creator.

Garbled Circuits. Garbled circuits are a technique for secure two-party computation, which allows two parties to jointly evaluate any boolean circuit in a secure way. GCs ensure that the input of each party remains hidden from the other party. The original construction offers only security against a semi-honest garbler. The garbler could for example garble a different circuit, even one that leaks information about the evaluator's input. Several works improved the efficiency of GCs, most notably the techniques called *free-xor* [37] and *half-gates* [44]. The authors of [8] defined an abstraction of the above-described technique.

Definition 2 ('Garbling Scheme [8, Sec. 3.1]). A *garbling scheme* is a tuple of a probabilistic garble algorithm Gb and deterministic algorithms En for encoding, De for decoding, Ev for garbled evaluation, and ev for "plain" evaluation, i.e., $\mathcal{G} = (\text{Gb}, \text{En}, \text{De}, \text{Ev}, \text{ev})$. Let $f \in \{0,1\}^*$ be a description of the function that shall be garbled. The function $\text{ev}(f, \cdot) : \{0,1\}^n \to \{0,1\}^m$ denotes the actual function, we want to garble, where $n \in \mathbb{N}$ and $m \in \mathbb{N}$ must be efficiently computable from f. On input f and a security parameter $n \in \mathbb{N}$, the algorithm Gb returns a triple of strings $(F, e, d) \leftarrow \text{Gb}(1^n, f)$. String e describes an encoding function, $\text{En}(e, \cdot)$, that maps an initial input $x \in \{0,1\}^n$ to a garbled input $X = \text{En}(e, x)$. String F describes a garbled function, $\text{Ev}(F, \cdot)$, that maps each garbled input X to an encoded output $Z = \text{Ev}(F, X)$. String d describes a decoding function, $\text{De}(d, \cdot)$, that maps an encoded output Z to a final output $z = \text{De}(d, Z)$.

When we talk about the encoded input (sometimes we say *labels*) generated by Gb, we will write $X[0]$ (or $X[1]$, rsp.) to denote that the label is an encoding of 0 (or 1, rsp.). When $b \in \{0,1\}^n$ we will write $X[b]$ to denote the concatenation of the encodings of all bits in b.

We require a garbling scheme to have *privacy* as defined in [8]. Intuitively, privacy means that anything that can be learned from the garbled circuit F, the input labels X, and the decoding information d, can also be learned from the output value y and the public circuit f alone. In particular, no efficient adversary can "break" the scheme to get the input value of one of the parties.

3   Construction

In this section we present a protocol that UC-realizes $\mathcal{F}_{\mathrm{OPRF}}$—the ideal OPRF functionality—under static malicious corruptions of users and static semi-honest corruptions of servers.

Adversarial Model. We formulate the assumptions about our adversaries: We will implement an OPRF with garbled circuits. As "textbook versions" of garbled circuits offer only security against a passive, i.e., semi-honest garbler, we will restrict our construction to these adversaries. This means that a corrupted garbler (in our case the server) follows the protocol honestly but tries to learn additional information from its view of the protocol execution. In Sect. 3.2 we discuss more reasons why evaluating a PRF with MPC is not sufficient to realize $\mathcal{F}_{\mathrm{OPRF}}$ in the presence of a malicious server. However, we do allow malicious corruption of the evaluator (the user). Further, we assume static corruption. This means the adversary can only corrupt parties at the start of the protocol. If a party is corrupted, we assume that the adversary learns the party's input, the content of the party's random tape, and all messages received by the party. The adversary can send messages in the name of a corrupted party.

Security Notion. We will not use the same formulation of the ideal OPRF functionality $\mathcal{F}_{\mathrm{OPRF}}^*$ from [33], but rather a slightly simplified version described in Fig. 2. Note that $\mathcal{F}_{\mathrm{OPRF}}$ does not capture the adaptive compromise of the server, as we only assume static corruption of servers. For the sake of simplicity, we also omit the prefixes used in $\mathcal{F}_{\mathrm{OPRF}}^*$.

3.1   The Main Construction

Let $m, n \in \Omega(n)$ and $F \colon \{0,1\}^m \times \{0,1\}^n \to \{0,1\}^n$ be a Pseudo-Random Permutation (PRP). In our implementation in Sect. 4, we instantiate the PRP with AES. We will garble the circuit C that describes F to construct our OPRF.

The user runs with $p \in \{0,1\}^*$ as input. This input is hashed to an n bit value, so we can use it as input to $\mathcal{C}$. Our construction involves two hash functions $H_1 \colon \{0,1\}^* \to \{0,1\}^n$ and $H_2 \colon \{0,1\}^* \times \{0,1\}^m \to \{0,1\}^l$, where $l \in \Omega(n)$. We will model these hash functions as random oracles. The server takes no input. Initially, for each session, it chooses a key $k \in \{0,1\}^m$ uniformly at random. The PRF, that is computed by the OPRF protocol is $\mathsf{F}_k(p) := H_2(p, \mathcal{C}_k(H_1(p)))$.

In our description of the protocol depicted in Fig. 3, the server garbles the circuit and the user evaluates the circuit. The user starts the execution of the protocol by hashing its input p. The obtained value $x = H_1(p)$ will be used as the user's input to the circuit. The user then requests a garbled circuit by sending $(\textsc{Garble}, sid, ssid)$ to the server. The server proceeds by generating the garbled circuit. In particular, it encodes its key as input for the circuit. It sends the garbled circuit, the input labels of the key, and the decoding information to the user. The user and the server perform n parallel 1-out-of-2-OTs to equip the user with the wire labels for its input $x = H_1(p)$. Next, the user can evaluate

---

Functionality $\mathcal{F}_{\mathrm{OPRF}}$

Initialization: For each value i and each session sid, an empty table $T_{sid}(i, \cdot)$ is initially undefined. Whenever $T_{sid}(i, p)$ is referenced below while it is undefined, draw $T_{sid}(i, p) \xleftarrow{\$} \{0,1\}^l$.

On (INIT, sid) from S, if this is the first INIT message for sid, set $\mathsf{tx}(sid) = 0$ and send (INIT, sid, S) to $\mathcal{A}$. From now on, use "S" to denote the unique entity which sent the INIT message for sid. Ignore all subsequent INIT messages for sid.

Offline Evaluation: On (OFFLINEEVAL, sid, i, p) from P $\in \{S, \mathcal{A}\}$, send (OFFLINEEVAL, sid, $T_{sid}(i, p)$) to P if any of the following hold: (i) S is corrupted and $i = S$, (ii) P = S and $i = S$, (iii) P = $\mathcal{A}$ and $i \neq S$.

Online Evaluation:
- On (EVAL, sid, $ssid$, S, p) from P $\in \{U, \mathcal{A}\}$, record $\langle ssid, S, P, p \rangle$ and send (EVAL, sid, $ssid$, P, S) to $\mathcal{A}$.
- On (SNDRCMPLT, sid, $ssid$) from S, increment $\mathsf{tx}(sid)$ or set to 1 if previously undefined, send (SNDRCMPLT, sid, $ssid$, S) to $\mathcal{A}$. On OK from $\mathcal{A}$, send (SNDRCMPLTED, sid, $ssid$) to S.
- On (RCVCMPLT, sid, $ssid$, P, i) from $\mathcal{A}$, retrieve $\langle ssid, S, P, p \rangle$, where P $\in \{U, \mathcal{A}\}$. Ignore this message if at least one of the following holds: (i) There is no record $\langle ssid, S, P, p \rangle$, (ii) $i = S$ but $\mathsf{tx}(sid) = 0$, (iii) S is honest but $i \neq S$. Send (EVALOUT, sid, $T_{sid}(i, p)$) to P. If $i = S$ decrement $\mathsf{tx}(sid)$.

Fig. 2. The ideal functionality $\mathcal{F}_{\mathrm{OPRF}}$ like in [33].

the garbled circuit on the encoded inputs X and K and receives an output label Y. This label can be decoded to obtain the output value of the circuit y. Finally, the user hashes its input and the output of the circuit again to obtain the output $\rho = H_2(p, y)$. We describe the OPRF more precisely in Fig. 4.

Theorem 1. *Let the garbling scheme* $\mathcal{G} = (\mathsf{Gb}, \mathsf{En}, \mathsf{De}, \mathsf{Ev}, \mathsf{ev})$ *have privacy. Let* $\mathcal{C}$ *denote the boolean circuit of a PRP. Then* GC-OPRF *UC-realizes* $\mathcal{F}_{\mathrm{OPRF}}$ *in the* $\mathcal{F}_{\mathrm{OT}}, \mathcal{F}_{\mathrm{AUTH}}, \mathcal{F}_{\mathrm{RO}}$*-hybrid model.*

Proof Sketch: The general strategy of the proof is as follows: First consider the case where both parties are honest. The simulator chooses a uniformly random key k and runs the protocol like the real server would. The simulator does not get the user's input. But as it plays the role of $\mathcal{F}_{\mathrm{OT}}$ it can report messages to the environment as if the user had given input to $\mathcal{F}_{\mathrm{OT}}$. The simulator requests user output from $\mathcal{F}_{\mathrm{OPRF}}$. We must argue why $\mathcal{F}_{\mathrm{OPRF}}$ provides this output, i.e., why the counter is not exceeded. As both parties are honest, this is ensured by the simulator receiving a SNDRCMPLT message for the honest server. The OPRF output comes from $\mathcal{F}_{\mathrm{OPRF}}$ and thus is a random value. The environment $\mathcal{E}$ can only distinguish it from the real output if it queries $H_2(p, \mathcal{C}_k(H_1(p))$. We use the PRP property of $\mathcal{C}$ to argue that without any information about k, $\mathcal{E}$ sends this query with negligible probability. Next we consider the case where the user is maliciously corrupted. In contrast to the first case, $\mathcal{E}$ obtains the labels K of the key. Thus, $\mathcal{E}$ can query H_2 on p and $\mathsf{De}(d, \mathsf{Ev}(F, X[H_1(p)] \| K))$. Hence, the

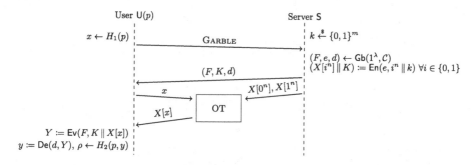

Fig. 3. Overview of GC-OPRF.

simulator must program H_2 accordingly on that input. To that end, Sim uses the RCVCMPLT interface. However, that means the counter is decreased. We argue that $\mathcal{E}$ can only query $\mathsf{De}(d, \mathsf{Ev}(F, X[H_1(p)]\|K))$ if it received a garbling (F, K, d) and labels $X[H_1(p)]$ before. Sim produces this garbling if the counter was increased once. By the privacy of the garbling scheme, $\mathcal{E}$ gets only enough information to query H_2 on one such critical point for every garbling with labels that it obtains. Finally we consider the case where the server is passively corrupted. In this case, $\mathcal{E}$ learns the key $k_{\hat{S}}$ of the server and can thus query $H_2(p, \mathcal{C}_{k_{\hat{S}}}(H_1(p)))$. The simulator must detect these queries and use its OFFLINEEVAL interface to receive an output value ρ to program $H_2(p, \mathcal{C}_{k_{\hat{S}}}(H_1(p))) := \rho$. It is crucial that OFFLINEEVAL does not change $\mathcal{F}_{\mathrm{OPRF}}$'s counter. Sim knows the key $k_{\hat{S}}$, as we assume passive corruption of the server, i.e., the server does not maliciously choose some other key. Note that we used H_1 as a non-programmable but observable RO and H_2 as a programmable RO. We present the complete proof in the full version of this paper [26].

3.2 Some Remarks on the Construction

In the following, we give some remarks on the construction and explain the decisions on the protocol design.

Who Garbles? We believe that the above-described approach could easily be adapted to feature switched roles of garbler and evaluator. More precisely, we believe that it is also possible to construct a similar OPRF protocol where the user garbles the circuit and the server evaluates the circuit. However, we decided to let the server garble the circuit because our construction only is secure against a semi-honest garbler. If the protocol would be implemented in a real-world scenario, it is a more realistic assumption that a server behaves in a semi-honest way than to assume that a user behaves that way. A server might be maintained by a company that would fear economic damage if malicious behavior of their servers is uncovered, while arbitrary users on the internet are likely to behave maliciously. Nonetheless, we are aware that malicious security is more desirable. However, techniques from the literature to achieve this are expensive in terms

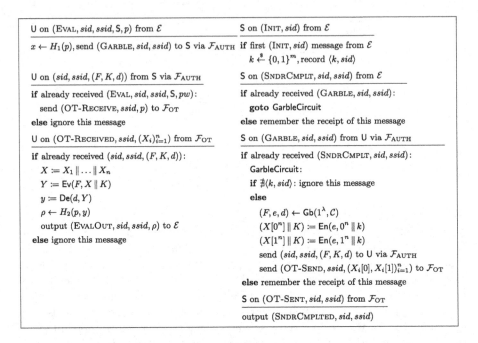

Fig. 4. The GC-OPRF construction in the $\mathcal{F}_{\text{OT}}, \mathcal{F}_{\text{RO}}, \mathcal{F}_{\text{AUTH}}$-hybrid model.

of running time and network traffic [38,43]. If actively secure garbled circuits would be used, it might even be beneficial to switch roles. Then the user has to "invest" computation time on the creation of a garbled circuit, which decreases the threat of Denial of Service (DOS) attacks on the server. Note that actively secure garbling is still not enough to make our construction UC-realize $\mathcal{F}_{\text{OPRF}}$ in the presence of malicious servers, as we will detail below.

On the Need for Authenticated Channels. In the proof of security, we assume authenticated channels. This is necessary, as otherwise, we could not rely on the semi-honest nature of messages sent to the simulator. Assuming that the server behaves semi-honest, does not explicitly include the adversary. Thus, the adversary could still replace the honestly generated circuit from the server with a malformed circuit. To avoid this problem, we assume authenticated channels, which prevent the adversary from replacing or injecting messages.

One could argue that the need for authenticated channels renders our construction impractical for many settings. For instance, if the OPRF is used for password-based authentication, one might not necessarily accept to already have an authenticated channel. But in fact, authenticated channels are already established in many practical scenarios! Typically, a user would connect to a server over a Transport Layer Security (TLS) channel, and thus, at least the server is authenticated via digital certificates. We expect the security of our construction to hold even if only the server is authenticated. This does guarantee that the garbled circuit was generated by the party with which the user intends to communicate. Applications that build on top of TLS can thus make use of our OPRF protocol.

On Security Against Semi-honest Servers. Because our construction only provides security against semi-honest servers, let us discuss the implications of this in various use cases. When our OPRF protocol is used for secure password-based authentication as in OPAQUE, then a malicious server could learn the user's password. Note, however, that the main problem in practice is usually not that the service provider itself (e.g. email provider) is actively malicious, but rather that the server gets hacked and the data stolen. Multiple big tech companies[5] did log cleartext passwords. So if we trust the service provider not to be actively malicious, then our OPRF can be used to protect against such problems as inadvertent logging of cleartext passwords. Also, note that our protocol is secure against malicious users and, thus, one user cannot impersonate another user in an authentication setting like OPAQUE. In Privacy Pass[6] a malicious server may be able to learn the user-chosen token, which would allow them to track the user. This is probably an unacceptable risk for dissident Tor users, but for many others, it may be an acceptable risk. In Private Set Intersection (PSI) a malicious OPRF sender could learn all set elements of the other party, which clearly violates the security goals. The practical impact of this again depends on the trust relation between the two parties. If the OPRF sender is a somewhat trusted service provider then semi-honest security may be sufficient. Of course, it is better to choose a maliciously secure OPRF, if an efficient pq secure protocol is available, even though the semi-honest version provides sufficient security guarantees in many settings.

Challenges Towards Full Malicious Security. We like to highlight that for securing our construction against malicious servers it is likely necessary to employ actively secure garbled circuits (e.g. using cut-and-choose [38] or authenticated garbling [43]) but it is not sufficient, as the definition of $\mathcal{F}_{OPRF}$ has very strict security requirements. It guarantees that the output is uniformly random even if the server is malicious, in particular, the server cannot force the output to be a specific value. For some protocols such as [33] this guarantee is necessary to prevent a Man-in-the-Middle attacker from impersonating an honest server. The first reason why evaluating a PRF with MPC is not enough to realize $\mathcal{F}_{OPRF}$ in the presence of a malicious server is that a PRF F can have *weak keys* (such as a key k, where $F(k, x) = 0$, regardless of x). The function F can still be a secure PRF because the definition of a PRF only requires the output to look random if the key was chosen uniformly at random. However, the malicious server is not bound to choose the key randomly, but can deliberately choose a weak key, thereby violating the security guarantees of $\mathcal{F}_{OPRF}$. The second reason is more

---

[5] https://www.zdnet.com/article/twitter-says-bug-exposed-passwords-in-plaintext, https://about.fb.com/news/2019/03/keeping-passwords-secure.

[6] Privacy Pass requires a *verifiable* OPRF. One can follow the idea of [2] to achieve this using garbled circuits. We leave a proof of security of that to future work.

specific to the proof and the simulator. When the PRF key is the same in two sessions, then the same inputs must yield the same outputs. In the ideal world, the simulator determines a table via the RCVCMPLT message, from which $\mathcal{F}_{\text{OPRF}}$ chooses the output value. To choose the correct table, the simulator has to be able to determine a value that uniquely identifies the key that the server used. In [32] this is achieved by letting the simulator include a DLOG trapdoor in the simulated messages of the honest user to the malicious server. In our case, as well as in other general MPC protocols, it is unclear how this unique identifier can be derived. The first reason shows that one would need to make stronger assumptions about the PRF to use it to build a maliciously secure OPRF. The second reason is an obstacle to the proof that may be solvable but would need new insights. Using covert security, which lies in between semi-honest and malicious security, also does not help, because a server choosing a different PRF key cannot be caught and, thus, has no incentive to be honest.

4   Comparison of Concrete Efficiency

As we were interested in the concrete efficiency of GC based OPRFs, we implemented the protocol from Sect. 3 in two versions and compared it to other OPRF protocols. We used AES-128 and AES-256 as instantiations for the circuit $\mathcal{C}$. For the first implementation, we leveraged a C++ framework, called EMP-Toolkit[7]. Because the available OT implementations from the EMP-Toolkit (and PQ-MPC) do not provide UC-security we opted for the most efficient OT protocol available in that library. We employed the Chou-Orlandi OT [20] protocol. Note that this is not a UC-secure OT protocol, as explained in the full-version of their paper [21]. It is also not post-quantum (PQ) secure as it relies on the GapDH assumption. If one wants to instantiate the OT using a protocol that is UC secure and plausible pq secure, one can use e.g. the OT proposed in [25]. The protocol from [25] is UC secure and can be instantiated under Learning Parity With Noise (LPN) in the CRS model. The protocol only requires two messages. Alternatively, one can employ the protocol proposed in [3]. It can also be instantiated under LPN and is secure in the Random Oracle Model (ROM). However, it is a four-message protocol, which might result in worse performance than [25]. We leave it to future work to implement a pq and UC secure OT protocol. We also used the pq-secure adaptation of the EMP-Toolkit, called PQ-MPC[8]. The security of this instantiation of garbled circuits against quantum adversaries is proven in [13] in the Quantum-accessible Random Oracle Model (QROM) [10]. Our resulting OPRF implementation is presumably secure against quantum adversaries. As we are garbling a 128-bit-key AES circuit, we reach the same level of quantum security as defined in the NIST post-quantum competition as Security Strength Category 1[7]. Further, we implemented a version of the state-of-the-art OPRF protocol, 2HashDH, by [31–33]. Finally, we also compared the two former protocols to the lattice-based protocols of [2] and the isogeny-based protocol from [29]. We used the implementations that were provided by the respective works

---

[7] https://csrc.nist.gov/CSRC/media/Projects/Post-Quantum-Cryptography/documents/call-for-proposals-final-dec-2016.pdf.

and run them on our machine. The main goal was to compare the concrete efficiency of different OPRFs on the same hardware. All source code described below can be found in the repository https://github.com/SebastianFaller/Composable-OPRF-via-Garbled-Circuits[8]. We also tried to run the provided implementation of [1]. But one OPRF evaluation did not finish within several hours on a normal laptop and therefore we did not benchmark the protocol extensively. This is not surprising as the benchmarks of [1] were performed on a server with 96 cores and over 700 GB RAM.

Benchmarks. We tested the implementations on a machine with an 11th Gen Intel®Core™ i7-1165G7 @ 2.80 GHz × 8 CPU. We made measurements on the local network interface, as well as a simulated WAN with limited bandwidth of 50 Mbit and a delay of 100 ms. We used the Linux tool `tc` for the latter. The WAN measurement simulates the situation where the server and user operate on machines in different countries or even continents. We measured the running time in milliseconds that each implementation needs from the invocation of a single OPRF session until the user calculated the output. The server used the same PRF key for all executions. We also measured the amount of data that the protocols exchange over the network, meaning data sent from the user to the server and vice-versa. We summarized the results in Table 2.

Table 2. Overview of the benchmark results. The protocol from [2] is a simplified version that does not include any Zero-Knowledge (ZK) proofs. The column UC marks if the implementation with their concrete building blocks is UC secure. Similarly, the column PQ indicates the same for plausible PQ security.

Protocol	Avg. Runtime (Local) [ms]	Avg. Runtime (WAN) [ms]	Network Traffic [kB]	UC	PQ
Our work (AES-128, EMP-Tool)	19.92 ± 0.77	268.19 ± 19.42	232.71	×	×
Our work (AES-256, EMP-Tool)	26.53 ± 0.99	282.48 ± 26.04	299.78	×	×
Our work (AES-128, PQ-MPC)	47.12 ± 3.22	1696.91 ± 53.62	4746.13	×	✓
Our work (AES-256, PQ-MPC)	72.63 ± 4.51	2074.42 ± 22.98	6787.48	×	✓
2HashDH [33]	0.36 ± 0.13	201.88 ± 0.21	0.07	✓	×
Lattice VOPRF [2]	88512.92 ± 2079.35	95418.25 ± 989.30	513.25 ± 0.17	×	✓
OPUS [29]	11218.45 ± 61.98	35285.26 ± 36.50	24.70	×	✓

Running Time. We measured an average running time of 19.92 ms and 26.53 ms for our GC-OPRF implementation with EMP-Toolkit for AES-128 and AES-256, respectively. We measured an average running time of 47.12 ms and 72.63 ms for our GC-OPRF implementation with PQ-MPC for AES-128 and AES256, respectively. The performance of the PQ-MPC version of the protocol is still reasonable, as it is about twice as high as the running time for the classical circuit. The difference is a bit higher in the simulated WAN. This is most likely due to the

---

[8] The benchmark results refer to the version of commit `ece1921`.

bandwidth limitation, as the PQ-MPC version sends about 20 times as much data over the network as the EMP-Toolkit version.

Comparing with the other protocols in Table 2, we can see that our protocol is orders of magnitude more efficient than the competing pq-secure protocols. However, the elliptic curve protocol 2HashDH [33] is still more efficient than our protocol. Note that the comparison to [2] has to be taken with a grain of salt. On the one hand, their implementation omits all ZK proofs, which are necessary to make the protocol secure. These proofs would make the protocol even more impractical. On the other hand, the implementation was done with SageMath , while the implementations of our work, [33] and [29] were written in C++ and C, respectively. Further, the OPRF protocol from [2] is verifiable, which means that a server cannot arbitrarily choose new keys for each query. The other implementations do not have this property.

Network Traffic. Our EMP-Toolkit implementation with AES-128 sends 232.71 kB of data over the network, while the PQ-MPC version of our construction with AES-128 sends 4.746 MB. This huge difference comes from the fact that PQ-MPC uses a pq secure OT protocol based on FHE and does not use optimizations for garbled circuits, as e.g. free-xor [37] or half-gates [44]. While the Chou-Orlandi OT from the EMP-Toolkit implementation is based on GapDH, and thus, is certainly not pq secure, it is still plausible that all implemented garbled-circuit-optimizations from EMP-Toolkit are pq secure, as they do not involve DLog- or RSA-type assumptions. Also, note that the network traffic of all implementations except of [2] are constant values, while there are slight variations in the measurement for the protocol of [2]. This is because the transmitted value in the protocol is a random element in a cyclotomic ring. SageMath seems to automatically compress those elements if possible which leads to a varying size.

5   On the Ideal OPRF Functionality

In this section, we discuss two different UC-definitions of OPRFs and their relation. We show that the definition that we use is strictly stronger than the alternative formulation. It is important to note that security in the UC framework is always defined relative to an ideal functionality. Broadly speaking, a protocol UC-realizes a functionality if every attack that is possible against the real protocol is also possible against the ideal functionality. Thus, the security of the protocol highly depends on the definition of the ideal functionality.

5.1   Existing OPRF Functionalities

There exist several descriptions of ideal OPRF functionalities in the literature [14, 31–33]. What most of them have in common is that the ideal functionality internally holds a truly random table of outputs from which the functionality delivers outputs to the user, when a protocol execution takes place. This ensures

---

Functionality $\mathcal{F}_{\text{OPRF}}^{\text{F}}$

Initialization: For each value i and each session sid, an empty table $\boxed{F_{sid,i}(p), \text{ for all inputs } p \in \{0,1\}^n}$ keys(sid, i) is initially undefined. Whenever $\boxed{F_{sid,i}(p)}$ keys(sid, i) is referenced below while it is undefined, draw $\boxed{F_{sid,i}(p) \overset{\$}{\leftarrow} \{0,1\}^l}$ keys(sid, i) $\overset{\$}{\leftarrow} \{0,1\}^m$.

On (INIT, sid) from S, if this is the first INIT message for sid, set tx(sid) = 0 and send (INIT, sid, S) to $\mathcal{A}$. From now on, use "S" to denote the unique entity which sent the INIT message for sid. Ignore all subsequent INIT messages for sid.

Offline Evaluation: On (OFFLINEEVAL, sid, i, p) from P $\in$ {S, $\mathcal{A}$}, send (OFFLINEEVAL, $sid,$ $\boxed{F_{sid,i}(p)}$ keys(sid, i)) to P if any of the following hold: (i) S is corrupted and $i = $ S, (ii) P = S and $i = $ S, (iii) P = $\mathcal{A}$ and $i \neq$ S.

Online Evaluation:

- On (EVAL, $sid, ssid,$ S, p) from P $\in$ {U, $\mathcal{A}$}, record $\langle ssid, \text{S}, \text{P}, p \rangle$ and send (EVAL, $sid, ssid,$ P, S) to $\mathcal{A}$.
- On (SNDRCMPLT, $sid, ssid$) from S, increment tx(sid) or set to 1 if previously undefined, send (SNDRCMPLT, $sid, ssid,$ S) to $\mathcal{A}$. On OK from $\mathcal{A}$, send (SNDRCMPLTED, $sid, ssid$) to S.
- On (RCVCMPLT, $sid, ssid,$ P, i) from $\mathcal{A}$, retrieve $\langle ssid, \text{S}, \text{P}, p \rangle$, where P $\in$ {U, $\mathcal{A}$}. Ignore this message if at least one of the following holds: (i) There is no record $\langle ssid, \text{S}, \text{P}, p \rangle$, (ii) $i = $ S but tx(sid) = 0, (iii) S is honest but $i \neq$ S. Send (EVALOUT, $sid,$ $\boxed{F_{sid,i}(p)}$ $\mathsf{F}_{\text{keys}(sid,i)}(p)$) to P. If $i = $ S set tx(sid)$--$.

Fig. 5. Comparison between the ideal functionality $\mathcal{F}_{\text{OPRF}}$ inspired by [33] and the one inspired by [14]. Text in $\boxed{\text{boxes}}$ is as in $\mathcal{F}_{\text{OPRF}}$, text in grey is inspired by [14]. Normal text is shared between both functionalities.

pseudo-randomness, as the output of the real-world protocol must be computationally indistinguishable from those random values. However, we are aware of one OPRF functionality that works differently. In [14] an ideal functionality is proposed that internally chooses a PRF key and delivers output values from one specific PRF to the user. We depict the differences in Fig. 5. We will denote the first functionality that chooses the output values randomly by $\mathcal{F}_{\text{OPRF}}$ and the second functionality that is parameterized by a PRF F: $\{0,1\}^m \times \{0,1\}^n \to \{0,1\}^l$ as $\mathcal{F}_{\text{OPRF}}^{\text{F}}$. As a first step, we will show that the two definitions are indeed not equal in the sense that $\mathcal{F}_{\text{OPRF}}$ UC-realizes $\mathcal{F}_{\text{OPRF}}^{\text{F}}$ but not vice-versa. We will also argue on a high level why a protocol using the weaker functionality $\mathcal{F}_{\text{OPRF}}^{\text{F}}$ cannot e.g. control the number of password guesses after a server is compromised. This shows that password-based protocols such as aPAKE or PPSS must rely on the stronger functionality $\mathcal{F}_{\text{OPRF}}$. As a next step, we argue that a natural class of protocols cannot UC-realize $\mathcal{F}_{\text{OPRF}}$ in the NPROM from [39]. Finally, we argue that the garbled circuit-based OPRF proposed by [40] does not UC-realize $\mathcal{F}_{\text{OPRF}}$. This suggests the need to introduce a random oracle to our construction Sect. 3.1 and to program it in our proof of security.

5.2   Relation Between $\mathcal{F}_{OPRF}$ and $\mathcal{F}^{F}_{OPRF}$

First, we establish that $\mathcal{F}_{OPRF}$ is stronger than $\mathcal{F}^{F}_{OPRF}$. Second, we show that $\mathcal{F}_{OPRF}$ can not be realized in the NPROM by a natural class of protocols. Lastly, we show that computing a PRF with garbled circuits alone cannot realize $\mathcal{F}_{OPRF}$. This gives a theoretical foundation for our proposed changes from Sect. 3, as we added a *programmable* random oracle to the construction from [40] to achieve the strong security notion of $\mathcal{F}_{OPRF}$. We defer the complete proofs to the full version of this paper [26] and give only an intuition for each claim.

Claim 1. $\mathcal{F}_{OPRF}$ *UC-emulates* $\mathcal{F}^{F}_{OPRF}$.

Proof Sketch. The simulator just forwards all messages between $\mathcal{E}$ and the functionality. On corruption of the server, the simulator gets the key from $\mathcal{F}^{F}_{OPRF}$, which makes answering OFFLINEEVAL queries trivial.

Claim 2. $\mathcal{F}^{F}_{OPRF}$ *does not UC-emulate* $\mathcal{F}_{OPRF}$.

Proof Sketch. The second claim can be shown by contradiction. Assume there is a simulator. An environment can query arbitrarily many PRF values. If $\mathcal{E}$ corrupts the server after sufficiently many PRF queries, a simulator can find a key that matches all previously produced PRF outputs only with negligible probability. Thus, there cannot be such a simulator.

Note that we make use of $\mathcal{F}^{F}_{OPRF}$'s (COMPROMISE, sid, S) interface that allows an adversary to get the key of the underlying PRF. Once the adversary has this key it can evaluate the PRF as often as it likes. Typically in password-based protocols, a user and a server execute the OPRF with the user's password as input. Now, if an adversary gets unlimited PRF evaluations it can mount offline dictionary attacks against the password. This is also possible when using $\mathcal{F}_{OPRF}$ but the difference is that $\mathcal{F}_{OPRF}$ outputs one PRF-output per (OFFLINEEVAL, sid, p) message. Therefore, a protocol that uses $\mathcal{F}_{OPRF}$ as hybrid functionality can keep track of all password-guessing attempts of the adversary. The same is not possible with $\mathcal{F}^{F}_{OPRF}$, as the adversary can guess "locally" after it received the key.

Next, we formalize a natural class of protocols that cannot realize $\mathcal{F}_{OPRF}$.

Definition 3. We say a protocol has *reproducible output* if the following holds: In an execution with a passive, (i.e., semi-honest) adversary $\mathcal{A}$, every user U outputs—with overwhelming probability—the same output y when executing the protocol π on input p with a server S with fixed state k. In other words, the output of a protocol execution depends only on the user's input and on the server's internal state (and *not* e.g. on the user's internal state).

One can think of the server's state as the key of the server. But we cannot assume how this state may look for arbitrary protocol.

Claim 3. *Let π be a protocol that does not use any additional hybrid functionality and that has reproducible output. Then π does not UC-realize $\mathcal{F}_{OPRF}$ in the NPROM.*

Proof Sketch. The environment can execute a protocol run between a server and a user *internally* without the simulator being able to detect this. Then $\mathcal{E}$ can instruct two actual parties, i.e., parties that are not just internally run by $\mathcal{E}$, to let them execute the protocol. As the protocol π has reproducible output the output of the internal execution will be the same as the output of the external execution in the real-world experiment. By the definition of $\mathcal{F}_{OPRF}$ the output of the user in the external execution will be drawn uniformly random in the ideal-world experiment. Therefore, both outputs will not match with high probability.

We can use a very similar argument to prove a statement about the protocol proposed in [40]. We assume that the employed garbling scheme is correct and has privacy. Because it makes no difference to our argument, we can even assume that the employed garbling scheme from [40] uses a programmable random oracle.

Claim 4. *Executing garbled circuits to jointly compute a PRF F between a user and a server is not sufficient to UC-realize $\mathcal{F}_{OPRF}$ in the NPROM.*

Claim 3 and Claim 4 justify our method to achieve a UC-secure protocol from the protocol of [40]. Loosely speaking, they say that without exploiting the programmability of a random oracle, one cannot realize the strong OPRF notion of [33] that is used e.g. in OPAQUE or the PPSS scheme [32]. To overcome this, we added two random oracles and carefully programmed them in the UC-proof.

6   Conclusion

In this work, we investigated the security of a garbled-circuit-based OPRF in the UC-framework [16]. To realize an ideal OPRF functionality in the style of [31–33], we augmented the construction of [40] with two hash functions, of which the second was modeled as a programmable random oracle. The resulting protocol is secure assuming static passive corruptions of servers and malicious users. We implemented two prototypes of our protocol—one using the optimized garbling scheme from EMP-Toolkit and one using the post-quantum garbling scheme from PQ-MPC. Although both implementations use building blocks that are not proven to be UC secure, to the best of our knowledge, our implementation is the only presumably pq secure implementation that can be made UC secure by plugging in UC secure building blocks. We also implemented the state-of-the-art OPRF protocol 2HashDH by [31–33]. We compared the implementations to a simplified implementation of the lattice-based OPRF by [2] and the isogeny-based protocol from [29]. The experiments showed that our construction is significantly faster than the lattice-based and isogeny-based protocol. We also found that our construction is not as efficient as the DLog-based 2HashDH protocol. Nonetheless, the efficiency is still in a reasonable range with a running time of around 22 ms and around 250 kB network traffic. This indicates, that garbled-circuit-based OPRF protocols are very promising candidates for pq secure OPRFs. Finally, we investigated the theoretical differences between definitions of OPRFs in the UC framework. We compared the ideal functionalities in the style of [31–33] and a functionality in the style of [14] and showed that the functionality from [31–33] is strictly stronger. We show that a natural class of protocols cannot realize this strong functionality in the NPROM. We further show that the OPRF protocol from [40], cannot realize the strong functionality. The last two claims justify our approach of augmenting the protocol from [40] by a random oracle and programming it in the security proof.

Acknowledgements. We thank the LATINCRYPT 2023 anonymous reviewers for their valuable feedback, and especially Octavio Pérez Kempner for the constructive and helpful support during the shepherding process. Astrid Ottenhues: This work was supported by funding by the German Federal Ministry of Education and Research (BMBF) under the projects "PQC4MED" (ID 16KIS1044) and "Sec4IoMT" (ID 16KIS1692), and by KASTEL Security Research Labs.

References

1. Albrecht, M.R., Davidson, A., Deo, A., Gardham, D.: Crypto dark matter on the torus: oblivious PRFs from shallow PRFs and FHE. Cryptology ePrint Archive, Report 2023/232 (2023)
2. Albrecht, M.R., Davidson, A., Deo, A., Smart, N.P.: Round-optimal verifiable oblivious pseudorandom functions from ideal lattices. In: Garay, J.A. (ed.) PKC 2021. LNCS, vol. 12711, pp. 261–289. Springer, Cham (2021). https://doi.org/10.1007/978-3-030-75248-4_10
3. Barreto, P.S.L.M., David, B., Dowsley, R., Morozov, K., Nascimento, A.C.A.: A framework for efficient adaptively secure composable oblivious transfer in the ROM. Cryptology ePrint Archive, Report 2017/993 (2017)
4. Basso, A.: A post-quantum round-optimal oblivious PRF from isogenies. Cryptology ePrint Archive, Report 2023/225 (2023)
5. Basso, A., Kutas, P., Merz, S.-P., Petit, C., Sanso, A.: Cryptanalysis of an oblivious PRF from supersingular isogenies. In: Tibouchi, M., Wang, H. (eds.) ASIACRYPT 2021. LNCS, vol. 13090, pp. 160–184. Springer, Cham (2021). https://doi.org/10.1007/978-3-030-92062-3_6
6. Baum, C., Frederiksen, T.K., Hesse, J., Lehmann, A., Yanai, A.: Proactively secure distributed single sign-on, or how to trust a hacked server. Cryptology ePrint Archive, Report 2019/1470 (2019)
7. Bellare, M., Hoang, V.T., Keelveedhi, S., Rogaway, P.: Efficient garbling from a fixed-key blockcipher. In: IEEE Symposium on Security and Privacy, Berkeley, CA, USA. IEEE Computer Society Press (2013)
8. Bellare, M., Hoang, V.T., Rogaway, P.: Foundations of garbled circuits. In: ACM CCS 2012, Raleigh, NC, USA. ACM Press (2012)
9. Beullens, W., Beyne, T., Udovenko, A., Vitto, G.: Cryptanalysis of the legendre PRF and generalizations. IACR Trans. Symm. Cryptol. **2020**(1) (2020)
10. Boneh, D., Dagdelen, Ö., Fischlin, M., Lehmann, A., Schaffner, C., Zhandry, M.: Random oracles in a quantum world. In: Lee, D.H., Wang, X. (eds.) ASIACRYPT 2011. LNCS, vol. 7073, pp. 41–69. Springer, Heidelberg (2011). https://doi.org/10.1007/978-3-642-25385-0_3
11. Boneh, D., Ishai, Y., Passelègue, A., Sahai, A., Wu, D.J.: Exploring crypto dark matter: new simple PRF candidates and their applications. In: Beimel, A., Dziembowski, S. (eds.) TCC 2018. LNCS, vol. 11240, pp. 699–729. Springer, Cham (2018). https://doi.org/10.1007/978-3-030-03810-6_25

12. Boneh, D., Kogan, D., Woo, K.: Oblivious pseudorandom functions from isogenies. In: Moriai, S., Wang, H. (eds.) ASIACRYPT 2020. LNCS, vol. 12492, pp. 520–550. Springer, Cham (2020). https://doi.org/10.1007/978-3-030-64834-3_18
13. Büscher, N., et al.: Secure two-party computation in a quantum world. In: Conti, M., Zhou, J., Casalicchio, E., Spognardi, A. (eds.) ACNS 2020. LNCS, vol. 12146, pp. 461–480. Springer, Cham (2020). https://doi.org/10.1007/978-3-030-57808-4_23
14. Camenisch, J., Lehmann, A.: Privacy-preserving user-auditable pseudonym systems. In: 2017 IEEE European Symposium on Security and Privacy (EuroSP) (2017)
15. Canetti, R.: Security and composition of multi-party cryptographic protocols. Cryptology ePrint Archive, Report 1998/018 (1998)
16. Canetti, R.: Universally composable security: a new paradigm for cryptographic protocols. In: 42nd FOCS, Las Vegas, NV, USA. IEEE Computer Society Press (2001)
17. Casacuberta, S., Hesse, J., Lehmann, A.: SoK: oblivious pseudorandom functions. Cryptology ePrint Archive, Report 2022/302 (2022)
18. Castryck, W., Decru, T.: An efficient key recovery attack on SIDH. In: Hazay, C., Stam, M. (eds.) EUROCRYPT 2023. LNCS, vol. 14008, pp. 423–447. Springer, Heidelberg (2023). https://doi.org/10.1007/978-3-031-30589-4_15
19. Chávez-Saab, J., Chi-Domínguez, J.J., Jaques, S., Rodríguez-Henríquez, F.: The SQALE of CSIDH: Sublinear Vélu quantum-resistant isogeny action with low exponents. Cryptology ePrint Archive, Report 2020/1520 (2020)
20. Chou, T., Orlandi, C.: The simplest protocol for oblivious transfer. In: Lauter, K., Rodríguez-Henríquez, F. (eds.) LATINCRYPT 2015. LNCS, vol. 9230, pp. 40–58. Springer, Cham (2015). https://doi.org/10.1007/978-3-319-22174-8_3
21. Chou, T., Orlandi, C.: The simplest protocol for oblivious transfer. Cryptology ePrint Archive, Report 2015/267 (2015)
22. Damgård, I.B.: On the randomness of Legendre and Jacobi sequences. In: Goldwasser, S. (ed.) CRYPTO 1988. LNCS, vol. 403, pp. 163–172. Springer, New York (1990). https://doi.org/10.1007/0-387-34799-2_13
23. Davidson, A., Goldberg, I., Sullivan, N., Tankersley, G., Valsorda, F.: Privacy pass: bypassing internet challenges anonymously. PoPETs **2018**(3), 164–180 (2018)
24. Dinur, I., et al.: MPC-friendly symmetric cryptography from alternating moduli: candidates, protocols, and applications. In: Malkin, T., Peikert, C. (eds.) CRYPTO 2021. LNCS, vol. 12828, pp. 517–547. Springer, Cham (2021). https://doi.org/10.1007/978-3-030-84259-8_18
25. Döttling, N., Garg, S., Hajiabadi, M., Masny, D., Wichs, D.: Two-round oblivious transfer from CDH or LPN. In: Canteaut, A., Ishai, Y. (eds.) EUROCRYPT 2020. LNCS, vol. 12106, pp. 768–797. Springer, Cham (2020). https://doi.org/10.1007/978-3-030-45724-2_26
26. Faller, S., Ottenhues, A., Ernst, J.: Composable oblivious pseudo-random functions via garbled circuits. Cryptology ePrint Archive, Paper 2023/1176 (2023)
27. Freedman, M.J., Ishai, Y., Pinkas, B., Reingold, O.: Keyword search and oblivious pseudorandom functions. In: Kilian, J. (ed.) TCC 2005. LNCS, vol. 3378, pp. 303–324. Springer, Heidelberg (2005). https://doi.org/10.1007/978-3-540-30576-7_17
28. Grassi, L., Rechberger, C., Rotaru, D., Scholl, P., Smart, N.P.: MPC-friendly symmetric key primitives. In: ACM CCS 2016, Vienna, Austria. ACM Press (2016)
29. Heimberger, L., Meisingseth, F., Rechberger, C.: OPRFs from isogenies: designs and analysis. Cryptology ePrint Archive, Paper 2023/639 (2023)

30. Ishai, Y., Kilian, J., Nissim, K., Petrank, E.: Extending oblivious transfers efficiently. In: Boneh, D. (ed.) CRYPTO 2003. LNCS, vol. 2729, pp. 145–161. Springer, Heidelberg (2003). https://doi.org/10.1007/978-3-540-45146-4_9

31. Jarecki, S., Kiayias, A., Krawczyk, H.: Round-optimal password-protected secret sharing and T-PAKE in the password-only model. In: Sarkar, P., Iwata, T. (eds.) ASIACRYPT 2014. LNCS, vol. 8874, pp. 233–253. Springer, Heidelberg (2014). https://doi.org/10.1007/978-3-662-45608-8_13

32. Jarecki, S., Kiayias, A., Krawczyk, H., Xu, J.: Highly-efficient and composable password-protected secret sharing (or: How to protect your bitcoin wallet online). Cryptology ePrint Archive, Report 2016/144 (2016)

33. Jarecki, S., Krawczyk, H., Xu, J.: OPAQUE: an asymmetric PAKE protocol secure against pre-computation attacks. In: Nielsen, J.B., Rijmen, V. (eds.) EUROCRYPT 2018. LNCS, vol. 10822, pp. 456–486. Springer, Cham (2018). https://doi.org/10.1007/978-3-319-78372-7_15

34. Jarecki, S., Liu, X.: Efficient oblivious pseudorandom function with applications to adaptive OT and secure computation of set intersection. In: Reingold, O. (ed.) TCC 2009. LNCS, vol. 5444, pp. 577–594. Springer, Heidelberg (2009). https://doi.org/10.1007/978-3-642-00457-5_34

35. Kampanakis, P., Lepoint, T.: Vision paper: do we need to change some things? In: Günther, F., Hesse, J. (eds.) SSR 2023. LNCS, vol. 13895, pp. 78–102. Springer, Cham (2023). https://doi.org/10.1007/978-3-031-30731-7_4

36. Kolesnikov, V., Kumaresan, R., Rosulek, M., Trieu, N.: Efficient batched oblivious PRF with applications to private set intersection. In: ACM CCS 2016, Vienna, Austria. ACM Press (2016)

37. Kolesnikov, V., Schneider, T.: Improved garbled circuit: free XOR gates and applications. In: Aceto, L., Damgård, I., Goldberg, L.A., Halldórsson, M.M., Ingólfsdóttir, A., Walukiewicz, I. (eds.) ICALP 2008. LNCS, vol. 5126, pp. 486–498. Springer, Heidelberg (2008). https://doi.org/10.1007/978-3-540-70583-3_40

38. Lindell, Y., Pinkas, B.: An efficient protocol for secure two-party computation in the presence of malicious adversaries. In: Naor, M. (ed.) EUROCRYPT 2007. LNCS, vol. 4515, pp. 52–78. Springer, Heidelberg (2007). https://doi.org/10.1007/978-3-540-72540-4_4

39. Nielsen, J.B.: Separating random oracle proofs from complexity theoretic proofs: the non-committing encryption case. In: Yung, M. (ed.) CRYPTO 2002. LNCS, vol. 2442, pp. 111–126. Springer, Heidelberg (2002). https://doi.org/10.1007/3-540-45708-9_8

40. Pinkas, B., Schneider, T., Smart, N.P., Williams, S.C.: Secure two-party computation is practical. In: Matsui, M. (ed.) ASIACRYPT 2009. LNCS, vol. 5912, pp. 250–267. Springer, Heidelberg (2009). https://doi.org/10.1007/978-3-642-10366-7_15

41. Rabin, M.O.: How to exchange secrets with oblivious transfer. Cryptology ePrint Archive, Report 2005/187 (2005)

42. Seres, I.A., Horváth, M., Burcsi, P.: The legendre pseudorandom function as a multivariate quadratic cryptosystem: Security and applications. Cryptology ePrint Archive, Report 2021/182 (2021)

43. Wang, X., Ranellucci, S., Katz, J.: Authenticated garbling and efficient maliciously secure two-party computation. In: ACM CCS 2017, Dallas, TX, USA. ACM Press (2017)

44. Zahur, S., Rosulek, M., Evans, D.: Two halves make a whole. In: Oswald, E., Fischlin, M. (eds.) EUROCRYPT 2015. LNCS, vol. 9057, pp. 220–250. Springer, Heidelberg (2015). https://doi.org/10.1007/978-3-662-46803-6_8

Real-World Cryptography

Quotable Signatures for Authenticating Shared Quotes

Joan Boyar[1] , Simon Erfurth[1] , Kim S. Larsen[1]([⊠]) ,
and Ruben Niederhagen[1,2]

[1] University of Southern Denmark, Odense, Denmark
`joan@imada.sdu.dk`, `simon@serfurth.dk`, `kslarsen@imada.sdu.dk`
[2] Academia Sinica, Taipei, Taiwan
`ruben@polycephaly.org`

Abstract. Quotable signature schemes are digital signature schemes with the additional property that from the signature for a message, any party can extract signatures for (allowable) quotes from the message, without knowing the secret key or interacting with the signer of the original message. Crucially, the extracted signatures are still signed with the original secret key. We define a notion of security for quotable signature schemes and construct a concrete example of a quotable signature scheme, using Merkle trees and classical digital signature schemes. The scheme is shown to be secure, with respect to the aforementioned notion of security. Additionally, we prove bounds on the complexity of the constructed scheme. Finally, concrete use cases of quotable signatures are considered, using them to combat misinformation by bolstering authentic content on social media. We consider both how quotable signatures can be used, and why using them could help mitigate the effects of fake news.

Keywords: quotable signatures · digital signatures · Merkle trees · authenticity · fake news

1 Introduction

Digital signature schemes are a classical and widely used tool in modern cryptography (the canonical reference is [11], and [6] contains some current standards). A somewhat newer concept is *quotable signature schemes* [18], which are digital signature schemes with the additional property that signatures are *quotable* in the following sense. The *Signer* of a message m generates a quotable signature s for m using a private key sk. Given a message m and the quotable signature s, a

The first and third authors were supported in part by the Independent Research Fund Denmark, Natural Sciences, grant DFF-0135-00018B. All authors are currently associated with DDC – the Digital Democracy Center at the University of Southern Denmark.

A. Aly and M. Tibouchi (Eds.): LATINCRYPT 2023, LNCS 14168, pp. 273–292, 2023.
https://doi.org/10.1007/978-3-031-44469-2_14

Quoter (any third party) can extract a second quotable signature s' for a quote q from m without knowing sk or interacting with the original *Signer*. A quote can be any "allowable subsequence" of m. We write $q \preceq m$ to indicate that q is a quote from m. This quotable signature s' is still signed with the private key sk of the *Signer* and hence authenticates the original *Signer* as the author of the quote. These signatures for quotes have the same required properties with respect to verification and security as a standard digital signature, in addition to allowing one to derive where content has been removed, relative to the quote. A signature for a quote is again a quotable signature with respect to sub-quotes of the quote, and neither authenticating a quote nor sub-quoting require access to the original message.

Quotable signatures can be used to mitigate the effects of fake news and disinformation. These are not new problems, and it is becoming increasingly apparent that they are posing a threat for democracy and for society. There is not one single reason for this, but one reason among many is a fundamental change in how news is consumed: a transition is happening, where explicit news products such as printed newspapers and evening news programs are still consumed, but are increasingly giving way for shorter formats and snippets of news on social media platforms [25]. However, people tend to be unable to recall from which news brand a story originated when they were exposed to it on social media [17]. This is problematic since the news media's image is an important heuristic when people evaluate the quality of a news story [34]. In addition, according to the Reuters Institute Digital News Report 2022 [26], across markets, 54% of those surveyed say they worry about identifying the difference between what is real and fake on the Internet when it comes to news, but people who say they mainly use social media as a source of news are more worried (61%).

In recent years, a common approach to fighting back against fake news has been flagging (potentially) fake news, using either manual or automatic detection systems. While this might be a natural approach, research has shown repeatedly that flagging problematic content tends to have the opposite result, i.e., it increases the negative effects of fake news [13,21,29]. This indicates that flagging problematic content is not sufficient and alternative approaches need to be developed.

We present a method that complements flagging problematic content with the goal of mitigating the effect of fake news. Our idea builds on the observation that *which* news media published a news article is an important heuristic people use to evaluate the quality of the article [34]. However, since people get their news increasingly via social media, it is becoming more likely that they are not aware of who published the news they are consuming. To address this, we propose using quotable signatures to allow people on social media to find out and be certain of where the text they are reading originates from, and to verify that any modifications to the text were all allowed. Specifically for news, the proposed idea is that a news media publishing an article also publishes a quotable signature for the article signed with their private key. When someone shares a quote from the article, they then also include the signature for the quote that is derived from the initial signature (without access to the private key), which we emphasize is signed with the same key. Finally, when one reads the quote, the signature can be checked, and it can be verified from where the quote originates.

The idea of mitigating the effects of fake news and misinformation, by using digital signatures to verify the source of media content, is one that has been addressed by others. One example is C2PA [9], which involves many companies, including Adobe, the BBC, Microsoft, and Twitter. C2PA focuses on providing a history of a published item, i.e., which device was used to capture it, how it has been edited and by whom, etc. Thus, quotable signatures could be of interest to their approach.

Another issue involving fake news is that news articles are perceived as more credible if they contain attributed quotes [32]. This is misused by fake news to appear more credible by providing attributions for their content [2,12,19,27,30], but can in turn be used to automatically detect fake news by considering the existence and quality of attributions [1,24,33] (among other things). Quotable signatures, in contrast, could be used to sign quotes to make a strong and verifiable connection between the original source and the quote. On the other hand, fake news would generally not be able to link their quotes to reputable sources, thereby providing another heuristic helping users to distinguish between authentic and fake content.

Without major changes to the system, it could be extended to further use cases such as signing Facebook and Twitter posts, official governmental rules and regulations, scientific publications, etc. For all of these instances, an important feature of our system that we have not used explicitly so far is that signing also binds the Signer, meaning that the signing party cannot later deny having signed the signed document.

We provide an overview over related work in Sect. 2. In Sect. 3, we give a more thorough introduction to and definition of quotable signatures, and we show how we can realize quotable signatures using Merkle trees [22,23]. We define a notion of security for quotable signature schemes, and prove that the notion is satisfied by our construction. Additionally, we prove a number of bounds on the size and computational costs of quotable signatures obtained using Merkle trees. We revisit the application of quotable signatures to counter fake news in more detail in Sect. 4 and we conclude the paper with an outlook to future work in Sect. 5. In the full version of this paper we also describe concrete algorithms for our construction of quotable signatures from Merkle trees.

2 Related Work

Quotable signatures have been introduced in [18], which suggests constructing quotable signatures using Merkle trees and provides a rudimentary complexity analysis. The authors also suggest using quotable signatures to mitigate the effects of fake news. Compared to [18], we define a security model, and prove that our construction is secure in this security model. Additionally, we also provide proofs of our claims about the cost of using Merkle trees for quotable signatures, and provide more in-depth considerations for why one could expect this to be a good approach.

A concept closely related to quotable signature schemes is *redactable signature schemes* (RSSs). Simultaneously introduced in [31] (as *Content Extraction Signatures*) and [16], RSSs essentially allow an untrusted redactor to remove ("redact") parts of a signed message, without invalidating the signature. Often this requires modifying the signature, but crucially, it is still signed with the original key, despite the redactor not having access to the private key. Thus, quotable signatures share many similarities with RSSs; if one considers a quotation as a redaction of all parts of a text except for the quote, they are conceptually identical. Where quotable signatures and RSSs differ is in the security they must provide. Both signature schemes require a similar notion of unforgeability, but an RSS must also guarantee that the redacted parts remain private. A standard formulation is that an outsider not holding any private keys should "not be able to derive any information about redacted parts of a message", and even stronger requirements, such as transparency or unlinkability, are not uncommon [7]. Quotable signatures have no such privacy requirements, allowing quotable signatures to be faster. In fact, it is worth noting that there are scenarios where RSSs' notion of privacy would be directly harmful to a quotable signature. For instance, RSS would specifically make it impossible to tell if a quote is contiguous or not, something that we consider essential for a quotable signature scheme. To see the value of dropping the privacy requirement, we observe that some RSSs with $O(n)$ performance may have $O(n)$ expensive public key cryptography operations [8,28], whereas quotable signatures can be obtained with $O(n)$ (cheap) symmetric cryptographic operations (hashing), and only one expensive public key operation. There are approaches obtaining RSSs using only one expensive operation, but they either require many more cheap operations than quotable signatures do, or they result in considerably larger signatures, for example [14]. Early examples of RSSs had a weaker notion of privacy, but still stronger than what we require. They require only hiding of the redacted elements, not their location and number. Examples can be found in [16,31]. Their approaches are similar to ours, also using Merkle trees, but we provide rigorous proofs of the claimed performance, and our lack of privacy requirements allows our scheme to be both more efficient and conceptually simpler. One consideration that is very relevant for quotable signatures, is how a quote (redaction) being contiguous will affect the complexity results. In a different setting [10] considers this question for Merkle trees, but provides no rigorous proof.

Considering the motivating example again, approaches to mitigate the impact of fake news, using either digital signatures or directly rating the source of the content, have been proposed and tried before. One approach, serving as inspiration for our approach, is [3]. They use digital signatures to verify the authenticity of images and other forms of multimedia. One drawback of their implementation is that it requires the media to be bit-for-bit identical to the version that was signed. Hence, the image can for instance not be compressed or resized, and thus their solution is not compatible with many platforms, e.g., Facebook compresses uploaded images, and many news websites resize images for different screen sizes. An example of directly rating the source of content, and flagging trustworthy sources, can be found in "NewsGuard Ratings" (NG), which provides a rating of trustworthiness for news sources. NG adds a flag that indicates if a news source is generally trustworthy (green) or not (red) to websites and outgoing links on websites. This approach has not been widely successful. For example, the study in [4] shows that NG's labels have "limited average effects on news diet quality and fail to reduce misperceptions". While this is somewhat related to our approach, there are two major differences. (1) NG only flags content that directly links to the source of the content with a URL. In contrast, our digital signature can be attached to any text quote. Hence, NG only adds additional information when it is already straightforward to figure out from where the content originates. Our approach also provides this information where there might otherwise be no clear context. (2) NG focuses on providing a rating for how trustworthy a news source is. This approach is similar to the typical approach of telling people when something might be problematic, which tends to have the opposite result. In contrast, we focus solely on providing and authenticating the source of a quote.

Summing up, the contributions of this paper is as follows. (1) We rigorously define the notion of security that quotable signature schemes must satisfy. (2) We rigorously prove the security of and analyze the complexity of, a quotable signature scheme constructed using Merkle trees. (3) This provides a scheme for quotable signatures that is more efficient than using an RSS for the same purpose.

3 Quotable Signatures

To construct a quotable signature scheme, we follow the approach suggested in [18] and use a combination of a classical digital signature scheme [11] and Merkle trees [22,23].

Before getting into the construction, we summarize the setting of quotable signatures. In Sect. 3.1, we define the security notion that quotable signature schemes should satisfy. Then, in Sect. 3.2, we introduce Merkle trees, in Sect. 3.3 we construct a quotable signature scheme and show it is secure, and finally we analyze the complexity of the scheme in Sect. 3.4.

General Setting for Quotable Signatures. A quotable signature scheme consists of four efficient algorithms, $\mathsf{QS} = (\mathsf{KeyGen}, \mathsf{Sign}, \mathsf{Quo}, \mathsf{Ver})$. These four algorithms are essentially the standard three algorithms from a classical digital signature scheme for key generation, signing, and verification, with the added quoting algorithm Quo. To quote from a message, Quo allows extracting a valid signature for the quote from the signature of the message in such a way that it is still signed with the public key used to sign the original message. Additionally, it should be possible to derive from the signature of a quote where tokens from the original message have been removed relative to the quote.

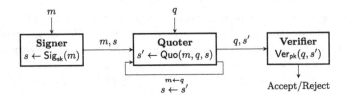

Fig. 1. The general setting for a quotable signature.

We refer to the involved parties as the *Signer*, the *Quoter*, and the *Verifier*. We use λ to denote the security parameter. To summarize:

- $(\mathsf{sk}, \mathsf{pk}) \leftarrow \mathsf{KeyGen}(1^\lambda)$ takes as input the security parameter 1^λ. It outputs a public key pair. This is typically done by the Signer once, offline as part of the initial setup.
- $s \leftarrow \mathsf{Sig}_{\mathsf{sk}}(m)$ takes as input a secret key sk and a message m. It outputs a quotable signature for m. This is done by the Signer.
- $s' \leftarrow \mathsf{Quo}(m, q, s)$ takes as input a message m, a quote q from m, and a quotable signature s for m. It outputs a quotable signature s' for q, that is still signed with the secret key used to generate s. Verifying s' does not require knowing m. Note that m and s could have been obtained via an earlier quote operation. This is done by the Quoter.
- $\top/\bot \leftarrow \mathsf{Ver}_{\mathsf{pk}}(q, s')$ takes as input a public key pk, a quote (message) q, and a signature s' for q. It outputs $\top$ if s' is a valid signature for q with respect to pk, and $\bot$ otherwise. This is done by the Verifier.

Figure 1 illustrates the typical interactions between the parties.

3.1 Security Model

Taking inspiration from the RSS notion of unforgeability, we define the security notion of quotable signatures schemes in Definition 1. At its core, this is the standard notion of unforgeability for digital signature schemes, with the additional requirement that the adversary's chosen message cannot be a quote from any of the messages that the adversary sent to the signing oracle.

Definition 1 (Unforgeability). *Let* $\mathsf{QS} = (\mathsf{KeyGen}, \mathsf{Sign}, \mathsf{Quo}, \mathsf{Ver})$ *be a quotable signature scheme. We say that* QS *is existentially unforgeable, if for every probabilistic polynomial time adversary* $\mathcal{A}$, *the probability of the following experiment returning 1 is negligible:*

$(\mathsf{pk}, \mathsf{sk}) \leftarrow \mathsf{KeyGen}(1^\lambda)$

$(m^*, s^*) \leftarrow \mathcal{A}^{\mathsf{Sign}_{\mathsf{sk}}(\cdot)}(\mathsf{pk})$

// *denote the queries that* $\mathcal{A}$ *make to the signing oracle by* $m_1, m_2, \ldots, m_Q$.

if $(\mathsf{Ver}_{\mathsf{pk}}(m^*, s^*) = \top) \wedge (\forall k \in \{1, 2, \ldots, Q\} : m^* \not\preceq m_k)$

   return *1*

3.2   Merkle Trees

A Merkle tree (also known as a *hash tree*) allows one to efficiently and securely verify that one or more *tokens* are contained in a longer sequence of tokens, without having to store the entire sequence [22,23]. Examples of this could be words forming a sentence, sentences forming an article, or data blocks making up a file.

Since our scheme will rely on hash functions, we assume that the tokens are binary strings. Equivalently, one could assume an implicitly used, well defined injective mapping from the token space to the space of binary strings. For data blocks, the identity mapping suffices and for words one such mapping could be the mapping of words to their UTF-8 representations.

The structure of a Merkle tree for a sequence of tokens is a binary tree, where each leaf corresponds to a token from the sequence, with the leftmost leaf corresponding to the first token, its sibling corresponding to the second token, and so on. Each leaf is labeled with the hash of its token and each internal node is labeled with the hash of the concatenation of the labels of its children. Hence, the i'th internal node on the j'th level will be labeled as

$$u_{j,i} = H(u_{j+1,2i} \parallel u_{j+1,2i+1}).$$

This way, one can show that any specific token is in the sequence by providing the "missing" hashes needed to calculate the hashes on the path from the leaf corresponding to the token to the root of the tree. Following established terminology, we call this the *verification path* for the token.[1]

Figure 2 shows the Merkle tree for a sequence of words forming the sentence "The quick brown fox jumps over the dog". The verification path for the word "jumps" consisting of nodes $u_{3,5}$, $u_{2,3}$, and $u_{1,0}$ is highlighted in red. Similarly, one can obtain the verification path for a subsequence of more than just one token. In Fig. 2, we also indicate the verification path for the contiguous subsequence "the quick" in blue. Note that the size of the verification path depends not only on how many tokens are chosen, but also on where in the sequence they are placed. In Sect. 3.4, we analyze how large the verification path can become, i.e., how many nodes need to be provided in the signature in the worst case.

In these examples, we have chosen a sequence of tokens where the length of the sequence, i.e., the number of tokens, is a power of two. If the sequence length is not a power of two, we require that the tree is *heap-shaped*, i.e., all levels are filled, except for possibly the lowest level, which is filled from the left up to some point, after which the lowest level is empty.

Remark 1. Observe that from the structure of the Merkle tree, one can see where in the sequence the quoted tokens are placed, and if they are sequential or discontinuous.

---

[1] This use of "path" is slightly counter intuitive, since it refers to the hashes needed to calculate the hashes on the path from the leaf to the root, and hence not the nodes on this path but their siblings.

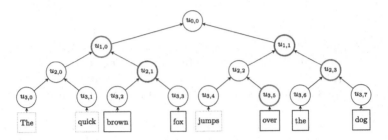

Fig. 2. An example of a Merkle tree where the tokens are words and the sequence is a sentence. The verification path for the token "jumps" is highlighted in red $(u_{1,0}, u_{2,3}, u_{3,5})$, and the verification path for the subsequence "The quick" is highlighted in blue $(u_{1,1}, u_{2,1})$. (Color figure online)

3.3 A Quotable Signature Scheme

Using a Merkle tree, we can now devise a scheme by which the Quoter can convince the Verifier that some quote is contained in a larger text, if the Verifier is already in possession of the root hash. The Quoter simply shares the verification path together with the quote, and the Verifier verifies that this indeed leads to the original root hash. In order to turn this into a quotable signature scheme, we include a classical digital signature for the root hash, signed by the Signer, with the verification path. Thus, letting $DS = (KeyGen^{DS}, Sign^{DS}, Ver^{DS})$ be a classical digital signature scheme, our quotable signature scheme can be described as follows:

- KeyGen: Identical to $KeyGen^{DS}$.
- Sign: Find the root hash of the Merkle tree and sign it with $Sign^{DS}$.
- Quo: Find the verification path of the quote. Together with the signature of the root hash, this forms the signature for the quote.
- Find the root hash of the Merkle tree using the quote and its verification path. Use Ver^{DS} to verify the authenticity of the root hash.

Proof of Security. We will show that the construction of the previous section is secure with respect to the notion of security introduced in Definition 1, when instantiated with a secure hash function and a secure classical signature scheme. Before doing so, we observe that currently, our scheme is trivially vulnerable to a forgery attack, as follows. An adversary obtains a quotable signature for a message from a signing oracle and then simply replaces the last two tokens on the lowest level with a single token, which is the concatenation of the tokens' hashes. For example, using this attack on the message used in Fig. 2, would give the message "The quick brown fox jumps over $H(\text{the}) \| H(\text{dog})$". However, there is an easy fix to this vulnerability. Noting that the problem is that an adversary can claim that an internal node is a leaf, we can prevent this by applying domain separation in the form of adding one value to the leaves before hashing, and another value to the internal nodes before hashing. Taking inspiration from RFC

6962 [20], the Merkle trees are modified by prepending 00 to the leaves before hashing and 01 to the internal nodes before hashing. From now on, we implicitly assume that this is done.

We can now argue that the construction is secure.

Theorem 1. *Under the assumption that*

- *H comes from a family of cryptographic hash functions,*
- *$DS = (KeyGen^{DS}, Sign^{DS}, Ver^{DS})$ is an existentially unforgeable classical signature scheme,*

$QS = (KeyGen, Sign, Quo, Ver)$ *constructed as described above, is an existentially unforgeable quotable signature scheme.*

We have to show that no probabilistic polynomial time adversary can win the unforgeability experiment in Definition 1 with non-negligible probability.

Proof. Assume that $\mathcal{A}$ is a probabilistic polynomial time adversary against the unforgeability of QS. We show that the probability of $\mathcal{A}$ being successful is negligible. Let (m^*, s^*) be the output of $\mathcal{A}$, where $s^* = (Sig_{sk}^{DS}(u_{0,0}^*), \{u_{i,j}^*\})$, i.e., the classical digital signature of the root hash and a (possibly empty) verification path.

Consider first the case where the root hash $u_{0,0}^*$ of m^* (found using $\{u_{i,j}^*\}$) is different from the root hashes of the queries $\mathcal{A}$ made to the signing oracle. In this case, $(u_{0,0}^*, Sig_{sk}^{DS}(u_{0,0}^*))$ is a forgery against DS, and since DS is assumed to be existentially unforgeable, this can only happen with negligible probability. Denote this probability as ϵ_{DS}.

If this is not the case, there must be an m_k, such that the root hash of m_k is $u_{0,0} = u_{0,0}^*$, but $m^* \not\preceq m_k$. Denote by T^* the tree for m^* (constructed using the verification path, if one is included) and by T the tree for m_k.

Consider first the case where all leaves, corresponding to tokens, in T^* are at a location in the tree, where there is also a leaf, corresponding to a token, in T. Since $m^* \not\preceq m_k$ there must be tokens a^*, a such that $a^* \in m^*$ and $a \in m_k$ are at the same positions in their respective trees, and $a^* \neq a$. Observe that if $H(00\,\|\,a^*) = H(00\,\|\,a)$, we have found a collision to H. If $H(00\,\|\,a^*) \neq H(00\,\|\,a)$, let the nodes on the path between the leaf corresponding to a^* and the root of T^* be denoted by $u_{i,j_i}^*, u_{i-1,j_{i-1}}^*, \ldots, u_{1,j_1}^*, u_{o,o}^*$ and the nodes on the path between the leaf corresponding to a and the root of T by $u_{i,j_i}, u_{i-1,j_{i-1}}, \ldots, u_{1,j_1}, u_{o,o}$. Since $u_{i,j_i}^* \neq u_{i,j_i}$ and $u_{o,o}^* = u_{o,o}$, there exists a $0 \leq \ell < j$ such that $u_{\ell,j_\ell}^* = u_{\ell,j_\ell}$ and $u_{\ell+1,j_{\ell+1}}^* \neq u_{\ell,j_{\ell+1}}$. Thus, $u_{\ell+1,j_{\ell+1}}^*$ and $u_{\ell,j_{\ell+1}}$ (together with their siblings and 01) form a collision.

Consider now the case where there is a leaf, corresponding to a token, in T^* that is not at a location in the tree, where there is a leaf, corresponding to a token, in T. In this case there must be nodes $u_{i,j}^* \in T^*$ and $u_{i,j} \in T$ at the same position in their respective trees such that one of them is internal and the other corresponds to a token. If $u_{i,j}^*$ and $u_{i,j}$ do not have the same label, we can apply the method from the precious paragraph to find a collision. If they

Table 1. Theoretical bounds on the performance of our version of a quotable signature. For the Quoter, we consider both if we allow quoting arbitrary tokens from the sequence, and when we require that the quoted tokens must be consecutive.

	Computation Time	Signature Size
The Signer	$2n - 1$ hashes and 1 classical signature	1 classical signature
The Quoter		
Arbitrary	$2n - 1$ hashes	1 classical signature, at most $t(\lceil \log n \rceil - \lceil \log t \rceil - 1) + 2^{\lceil \log t \rceil}$ hashes
Consecutive	$2n - 1$ hashes	1 classical signature, at most $2\lceil \log n \rceil - 2$ hashes
The Verifier	1 classical verification and up to $2n - 1$ hashes	–

have the same label, we must have two nodes $u_{i+1,2j}, u_{i+1,2j+1}$ in T or T^*, and a token a in m^* or m_k such that $H(01 \parallel u_{i,j} \parallel u_{i,j+1}) = H(00 \parallel a)$, and we have found a collision.

We observe that in all cases, we have found a collision for H. Since H is assumed to be secure, and hence collision resistant, this can happen only negligible probability. Denote this probability as ϵ_H.

Hence, $\mathcal{A}$'s advantage of at most $\epsilon_{DS} + \epsilon_H$ is negligible.

3.4 Performance

Table 1 shows the cost of our quotable signature scheme for each of the three parties. This is measured in terms of computation due to the number of required hash operations and classical signature operations as well as in terms of the size of the generated signature due to the required hash values and classical signatures, presumably the dominant operations. In all cases, we assume that the message m has length n, i.e., m consists of n tokens. For the Quoter and the Verifier, we additionally assume that the quote has length $t \leq n$.

To put the results into context, running the command `openssl speed` on a modern laptop shows that it is capable of computing hundreds of thousands or even millions of hashes every second (depending on the size of the data being hashed and the hash algorithm being used). Additionally, a classical digital signature only takes a fraction of a second create or verify. Thus, it is nearly instantaneous to generate/quote/verify a quotable signature, even for sequences and quotes that are thousands of tokens long.

The cost for the Signer, the Quoter, and the Verifier is derived as follows.

The Signer. To generate the Merkle tree, the Signer needs to compute $2n - 1$ hashes. To create the quotable digital signature for m, she creates a classical digital signature for the root hash. This classical digital signature is the Signer's signature for her message m.

The Quoter. The Quoter also has to generate the entire Merkle tree, from which he can extract the verification path for the quote he wishes to make. However, the size of the verification path (and hence the signature for the quote) depends on the size of the quote, and where in the text the quote is located. The most simple case is when just one token is quoted, in which case the size of the verification path is at most $\lceil \log n \rceil$, which, together with the classical signature for the root hash, forms the signature for the quote. Similarly, as shown in the following, the worst case can be obtained by quoting every second token, in which case the Quoter would need $\lceil \frac{n}{2} \rceil$ hashes on the verification path.[2]

In Proposition 1 we quantify the worst-case size of the verification path (and hence the signature) for the quote in terms of message and quote lengths. In Proposition 2, we consider the special case where we require that the quote be contiguous.

Proposition 1. *For a message m of size n tokens and a quote of size t tokens, the worst-case size of the verification path of the quote is at most*

$$t(\lceil \log n \rceil - \lceil \log t \rceil - 1) + 2^{\lceil \log t \rceil}.$$

Proof. In Lemma 2, we consider the case where n is a power of two. In this case, we identify a worst-case set of t leaves of the Merkle tree on n tokens. In Lemma 3, we establish that it is sufficient to consider n a power of two.

To argue about the size of the signature, we consider what we call the *forest of independent trees* for a quote. To find the forest of independent trees for a quote, we do the following. For each token in the quote, consider the path between the node corresponding to that quote and the root (the root-token path). Define the *independent tree corresponding to that token* to be the subtree rooted in the highest node on the root-token path, which is not on the root-token path for any other token in the quote. The forest of independent trees for the quote is now the collection of the independent trees of all the tokens in the quote. In Fig. 3, we consider a message of size $n = 8$ and a quote of size $t = 3$, quoting the first, third, and fifth token. The red line indicates a separation between the independent trees and the nodes that are on multiple root-token paths. The forest of independent trees consists of the trees rooted in $u_{2,0}, u_{2,1}$, and $u_{1,1}$.

Lemma 1. *If n is a power of two, the heights of the trees in the independent forest for a quote that maximizes the size of the signature can differ by at most 1.*

Proof. Assume towards a contradiction that Q is a quote that maximizes the size of the signature for Q such that the difference between the heights of the smallest and largest trees in the forest of independent trees for Q is at least 2. Let A be the root of a tree of minimal height in the forest of independent trees, and let B be its sibling. Note that B is also the root of a tree in the forest

---

[2] Of course, algorithms can be adapted to include the entire text instead in such (rare) cases where that might require less space.

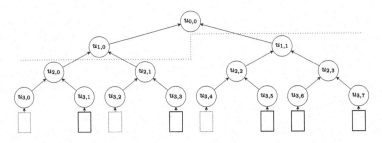

Fig. 3. A Merkle tree for a sequence of size $n = 8$ and a quote of size $t = 3$. (Color figure online)

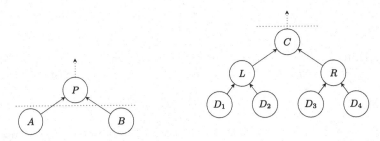

Fig. 4. Note that there might be trees rooted at A, B, D_1, D_2, D_3, and D_4, which we have omitted drawing, but by our assumption, the trees rooted at D_1, D_2, D_3, and D_4 must be at least as high as the ones rooted at A and B. (Color figure online)

of independent trees (otherwise the tree rooted at A would not be of minimal height). Additionally, let C be the root of a tree of maximal height in the forest of independent trees. We illustrate this in Fig. 4.

Observe that we can now create a quote Q' requiring more hashes than Q, by changing Q in the following ways:

- Instead of quoting one token from the tree rooted at A and one token from the tree rooted at B, Q' quotes only one token from the tree rooted at P.
- Instead of quoting just one token from the tree rooted at C, Q' quotes one token from the tree rooted at L and one token from the tree rooted at R.

It is clear that Q and Q' quote equally many tokens and that the forest of independent trees for Q' is only changed from the forest for Q in the trees that involves A, B, and C. The new situation is illustrated in Fig. 5.

If each of the trees rooted at A and B contributed with k hashes to Q, then the tree rooted at C contributed with $k' + 2$ hashes, where $k' \geq k$. In total, A, B, and C contributed $2k + k' + 2$ hashes. However, in Q' we see that the tree rooted at P contributes $k + 1$ hashes, and each of the trees rooted at L and R contributes $k' + 1$ hashes, for a total of $k + 2k' + 3$ hashes. But since $k' \geq k$, we have that $k + 2k' + 3 \geq 2k + k' + 3 > 2k + k' + 2$, contradicting that Q maximizes the size of the signature.

Lemma 2. *When n is a power of two, we can assume that the quote generating the largest signature has the properties that*

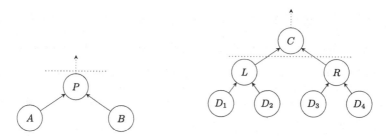

Fig. 5. Note that there might be trees rooted at A, B, D_1, D_2, D_3, and D_4, which we have omitted drawing, but by our assumption, the trees rooted at D_1, D_2, D_3, and D_4 must be at least as high as the ones rooted at A and B. (Color figure online)

1. *the heights of the trees in the independent forest for the quote differ by at most 1,*
2. *for each tree in the forest of independent trees, the left-most leaf corresponds to the token that is quoted, and*
3. *the trees in the forest of independent trees are arranged with the smallest trees first.*

Proof. Claim 2.1 follows immediately from Lemma 1. Further, Claim 2.2 follows from observing that we can bring any tree to this form simply by swapping the children of some of the nodes on the path to the leaf corresponding to a quoted token (hereby changing which token is quoted, but not how many are quoted), and that these swaps do not affect the size of the signature. Finally, Claim 2.3 follows from observing that if two nodes are on the same level of the Merkle tree, and the labels of both are known, then we can "swap" the subtrees that they are roots of without affecting the size of the signature. By "swapping", we mean that if the i'th leaf in the first node's subtree corresponds to a quote before the swap, then the i'th leaf in the second node's subtree corresponds to a quote after the swap, and so on. To see that this does not affect the size of the quote, note that outside of the two subtrees, nothing has changed; the hash of both nodes is still known. Additionally, from the first subtree we now get as many hashes as we got from the second subtree before the swap, and vice versa.

Lemma 2 implies that for any n a power of two and $t \leq n$, we need only consider one choice of which tokens are quoted. For example, Fig. 3 shows the only quote of size $t = 3$ in a tree of size $n = 8$ that we need to consider.

Lemma 3. *For any message m of length n and quote Q of length t, there is a quote Q' of length t from a message m' of length $2^{\lceil \log n \rceil}$ such that the signature for Q' is no smaller than the signature for Q.*

Proof. For fixed m and Q, we create m' by adding tokens to m until $|m'| = 2^{\lceil \log n \rceil}$. We now create Q' from Q by going over each quote q in Q.

1. If the leaf corresponding to q in the Merkle tree for m is on the deepest level, we quote the same token in m'.

2. If the leaf corresponding to q in the Merkle tree for m is not on the deepest level, there is an internal node in the Merkle tree for m' at the location of the leaf in m. We quote the token corresponding to its left child, which is a leaf.

Clearly, the tokens in Q' from case 1 contribute with the same number of hashes to the signature for Q' as the corresponding ones did to the signature for Q, and the tokens from case 2 contribute with exactly one more hash. Hence, the signature for Q' is at least as large as the signature for Q.

We are now ready to derive the claim in Proposition 1. For any message m and quote Q we can assume that $|m| = n$ is a power of two, i.e., $n = 2^{\lceil \log n \rceil}$ (otherwise Lemma 3 allows us to instead consider an m' that is a power of two), and that Q has size $|Q| = t$ and exactly the structure described in Lemma 2.

There are t trees in the forest of independent trees for the quote, and all the way up to (but not including) their roots, each of these trees provides one hash per level. The roots of the trees in the forest are on the deepest level with less than t nodes and the first level with more than t nodes (if t is a power of two, all roots are instead on the level with exactly t nodes). Hence, all levels that are at depth more than $\lceil \log t \rceil$ contributes with 1 hash per tree, for a total of $t(\lceil \log n \rceil - \lceil \log t \rceil)$ hashes. Additionally, we need to count how many hashes we get from the level at depth $\lceil \log t \rceil$. On this level, every node is either a root of an independent tree or a child of a root of an independent tree. In the first case, the hash of the node is calculable from information from lower levels. In the second case, for every pair of siblings, one of the nodes' hash is calculable from information from lower levels (the one on a root-token path for a token corresponding to a quoted token) and the other nodes' hash must be provided by the signature. Since there are $2^{\lceil \log t \rceil}$ nodes on this level, and t independent trees, the signature must provide $2^{\lceil \log t \rceil} - t$ hashes on this level.

In total, this shows that an upper bound on the number of hashes provided by the signature for a quote of t tokens from an n tokens sequence is

$$t(\lceil \log n \rceil - \lceil \log t \rceil) + 2^{\lceil \log t \rceil} - t$$
$$= t(\lceil \log n \rceil - \lceil \log t \rceil - 1) + 2^{\lceil \log t \rceil},$$

which finishes the proof of Proposition 1.

Corollary 1. *For a message of size n tokens and any quote, the worst-case size of the verification path of the quote is $\lceil \frac{n}{2} \rceil$.*

Another easy corollary to the proof of Proposition 1—and Lemma 3 in particular—we can bound the error when n is not a power of two (when n *is* a power of two, the bound is, of course, exact).

Corollary 2. *When n is not a power of two, the bound of Proposition 1 over-counts by at most t hashes.*

Proof. At each level of the Merkle tree, the signature needs to provide at most one hash for each quoted token. In the construction used in the proof of Proposition 1 when n is not a power of two, no levels are added to the Merkle tree, and hence the signature becomes no more than t hashes larger.

Proposition 2. *For a message of size $n > 2$ tokens and a contiguous quote of t tokens, the worst-case size of the verification path of the quote is $2\lceil \log n \rceil - 2$ hashes.*

Proof. We prove this proposition by induction on the height of the Merkle tree.

As the base case, we consider trees of height 2. Either picking just one token or picking one token among the first two tokens and one token among the last one or two tokens, gives a verification path of worst-case size $2 \cdot 2 - 2 = 2$.

Assume now that in a tree of height k, the largest possible size of the verification path for a contiguous quote is $2k - 2$. As our inductive step, we show that if the height of the Merkle tree of a message is $k + 1$, then the largest possible size of the verification path for a contiguous quote from the message is $2(k + 1) - 2$. For any contiguous quote Q, we consider two cases: (1) Q is either contained in the first 2^k tokens or contains none of the first 2^k tokens, and (2) Q contains both the 2^k'th and the $(2^k + 1)$'st token.

Case 1: If Q corresponds to leaves that are completely contained in one of the subtrees of the root, it follows from the induction hypothesis that the verification path consists of at most $2k - 2$ hashes from that subtree. The verification path contains only one additional hash, that of the root of the other subtree. Thus, the total number of hashes is at most $2k - 2 + 1 < 2(k + 1) - 2$.

Case 2: We make a few observations. Considering a level of the Merkle tree from left to right, the nodes with hashes that the Verifier calculates are consecutive. In Fig. 6, we have illustrated this by highlighting in green all the nodes with labels that the Verifier calculates.

Additionally, observe that for any level of depth $j \geq 2$, the only nodes of depth $j - 1$ with a label that the Verifier has to calculate and that, at the same time, (potentially) has a child outside the consecutive sequence of nodes that the Verifier calculated the labels for at depth j, are the parents of the leftmost and rightmost nodes in that consecutive sequence at depth j. All the nodes that might be characterized like this are on the two paths of black arrows in Fig. 6. Hence, it follows that on each level, the verification path needs to provide at most 2 hashes. Clearly, the root's label will not need to be provided by the verification path, and the root's children will also not need to have their labels provided since the quote contains a token from each child's subtree. Finally, observing that there are a total of $k + 2$ levels in a tree of height $k + 1$, allows us to conclude that the verification path needs to provide at most $2 \cdot (k + 2 - 2) = 2 \cdot (k + 1) - 2$ hashes, completing the case and the proof.

The Verifier. The Verifier has to verify one classical digital signature and to reconstruct the Merkle tree using the quote together with the verification path. Once again, the cost of this depends on where in the message the quote is located,

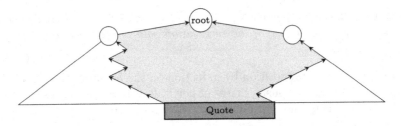

Fig. 6. Merkle tree with a contiguous quote divided between the left- and right subtree. The labels of all the nodes in the green area are calculated from the labels of their children and do not need to be part of the signature. (Color figure online)

with the number of hashes generally going towards $2n-1$ as the quote gets closer to being the full message. For example, if all but one token has been quoted, the Verifier needs to compute $2n - 2$ hashes, and if only one token has been quoted, the Verifier only needs to compute $\lceil \log n \rceil + 1$ hashes.

4   Quotable Signatures and Fake News

In the introduction, we argued that the current approach to mitigating the effects of fake news, focusing on flagging problematic content, is not sufficient. As mentioned, one supplementary approach could be to bolster authentic content by authenticating the source of quotes, for example on social media, and the literature gives reason to believe this could have an impact. This approach could be implemented using a quotable signature scheme. Here, the message that is the original source of a quote would be an article and the creator or distributor of the article (a news agency, for instance) would act as the Signer, the one sharing the quote as the Quoter, and the one verifying the quote as the Verifier. For this approach to be effective, it would need to be widely adopted, both by news media and by users sharing and reading quotes from articles. We make the following observations on these problems.

Regarding the news media, there is wide interest in supporting initiatives to combat fake news, see for example [9]. Additionally, from our discussions with a news media company,[3] it is apparent that the current workflow employed by modern media companies is already highly automated, and it appears that it should be quite simple to integrate a process by which, when an article is published (or updated), it is automatically signed with the media company's public key. Regarding user adoption, there is the challenge of getting a sufficiently large proportion of users using the tool, but one would also have to teach users what a quote being authenticated means, i.e., that the source and integrity of

---

[3] Specifically, we talked with the editor in charge of the platforms and the editor in charge of the digital editorial office at a large media company that produces multiple newspapers for different regional areas, in both paper and digital versions.

the quote has been assessed, but not its truthfulness or the quality of its source, for example.

If news media and social media integrate this approach into their websites, our methods can be employed without any explicit user awareness. With such an integration, when a user copies a quote from a signed article, a signature for the quote is automatically generated, and an element including both quote and text is put into the clipboard, together with the plain text quote (in practise, this would be a `text/html` element and a `text/plain` element). When the user then pastes the quote, a website supporting signatures will use the clipboard element with a signature [35]. One challenge with this approach is that the verification is now performed by the websites, rather than a browser extension, for example. Thus, the user has to trust the website to perform the authentication correctly.

An essential choice is how to divide text into tokens, since any subsequence of the tokens is an allowable quote. Natural choices could be by word, sentence, or paragraph. As a more involved choice, one could also define the tokens at a per-token basis, and simply mark the tokens in the HTML code. A variation of this would be to have a default setting, but to allow the Signer to decide how to split the article into tokens when signing. As a variant, one could also consider using content extraction policies, as in [31], so the Signer can specify which subsequences of tokens are allowable quotes. A media company might want to disallow quotes of noncontiguous segments, for example, or disallow including only parts of a sentence containing a negative, such as "not", "neither", or "never". Such restrictions could be handled efficiently using regular expressions.

We are implementing a prototype,[4] separated into two parts: a library that can be used by media companies to sign their articles and a browser extension that allows users to quote with signatures and to verify signatures for quotes. The library contains implementations of the proposed methods that each media companies can integrate into their publishing workflow. The browser extension modifies websites such that text (both full articles and quotes) with verified signatures is shown to be signed, and allows the user to make quotes from the signed text that include a signature for the quote. The browser extension also allows the user to get more information from the signature for a quote, e.g., who signed it, when it was signed, an indication of where text was removed, and a link to the original article.

One could further extend the system with different labels, depending on the quality of the source of a quote. For example, many countries have press councils enforcing press ethics, which includes providing correct information, e.g., by researching sufficiently and publishing errata when needed. Hence, it may make sense to mark quotes from articles written by news media certified as following press ethics and rulings of a national press council. One could even go so far as to authenticate only signatures signed by such sources.

To make a difference in the future, media companies and users on social media need to adopt these quotable signatures. To have the best effect, social

---

[4] To be made available at https://serfurth.dk/research/archive/.

media platforms should directly support quotable signatures and the required extension should be natively integrated into browsers.

5   Future Work

With this paper, we have extended the theory on quotable signatures and presented an application of quotable signatures as a supplementary approach to mitigating the effect of fake news.

Further work on quotable signatures could include using methods similar to the ones employed in [15] and [5] to remove the requirement that the used hash function be collision-resistant, and thereby remedy a vulnerability against multi-target attacks against hash functions. Additionally, variants of quotable signatures optimized for different types of media should be developed and compared. Our current variant is in some sense optimized for cases where one will often wish to quote something contiguous in one dimension, such as text. If, instead, the goal is to crop an image, one would end up with a "quote" that is contiguous in two dimensions. We have not yet explored how to handle this case effectively. Finally, as discussed in Sect. 4, different policies for dividing text into tokens could be studied.

A natural next step towards using quotable signatures to combat misinformation would be to verify the effectiveness of the proposed method experimentally. In particular, the effects of using quotable signatures for verifying news shared on social media and elsewhere need to be investigated. A suggestion for a first study could be to investigate if the use of quotable signatures improves participants' ability to recall from which news brand a story originated, which was an issue identified in [17]. Additional studies along the lines of [4], investigating the effects on the quality of the news diet of participants, would also be of interest.

References

1. Abu Salem, F.K., Al Feel, R., Elbassuoni, S., Ghannam, H., Jaber, M., Farah, M.: Meta-learning for fake news detection surrounding the Syrian war. Patterns **2**(11) (2021)
2. ADDO. How hate speech trolls targeted Kenya's 2022 elections (2023). https://disinfo.africa/early-detection-and-countering-hate-speech-during-the-2022-kenyan-elections-e0f183b7bdd1
3. Amoruso, E.L., Johnson, S.P., Avula, R.N., Zou, C.C.: A web infrastructure for certifying multimedia news content for fake news defense. In: Symposium on Computers and Communications (ISCC), pp. 1–7. IEEE Computer Society (2022)
4. Aslett, K., Guess, A.M., Bonneau, R., Nagler, J., Tucker, J.A.: News credibility labels have limited average effects on news diet quality and fail to reduce misperceptions. Sci. Adv. **8**(18) (2022)
5. Aumasson, J.-P., et al.: SPHINCS+. Submission to the NIST post-quantum project, v.3.1 (2022). https://sphincs.org/data/sphincs+-r3.1-specification.pdf
6. Barker, E.: Digital Signature Standard (DSS). Federal Information Processing Standards(NIST FIPS). National Institute of Standards and Technology, Gaithersburg (2013)

7. Bilzhause, A., Pöhls, H.C., Samelin, K.: Position paper: the past, present, and future of sanitizable and redactable signatures. In: Availability, Reliability and Security - ARES 2017. ACM (2017)
8. Brzuska, C., et al.: Redactable signatures for tree-structured data: definitions and constructions. In: Zhou, J., Yung, M. (eds.) ACNS 2010. LNCS, vol. 6123, pp. 87–104. Springer, Heidelberg (2010). https://doi.org/10.1007/978-3-642-13708-2_6
9. C2PA. Coalition for Content Provenance and Authenticity (C2PA) (2023). https://c2pa.org/
10. Devanbu, P.T., Gertz, M., Martel, C.U., Stubblebine, S.G.: Authentic third-party data publication. In: Data and Application Security - IFIP 2000. IFIP Conference Proceedings, vol. 201, pp. 101–112. Kluwer (2000)
11. Diffie, W., Hellman, M.: New directions in cryptography. IEEE Trans. Inf. **22**(6), 644–654 (1976)
12. Domingos, R.: É fake que g1 publicou reportagem afirmando que Lula disse que, se eleito, irá revogar o PIX (2023). https://g1.globo.com/fato-ou-fake/eleicoes/noticia/2022/10/06/e-fake-que-g1-publicou-reportagem-afirmando-que-lula-disse-que-se-eleito-ira-revogar-o-pix.ghtml
13. Drummond, C., Siegrist, M., Árvai, J.: Limited effects of exposure to fake news about climate change. Environ. Res. Commun. **2**(8) (2020). Article 081003
14. Hirose, S., Kuwakado, H.: Redactable signature scheme for tree-structured data based on Merkle tree. In: Conference on Security and Cryptography - SECRYPT 2013, pp. 313–320. IEEE (2013)
15. Hülsing, A., Rijneveld, J., Song, F.: Mitigating multi-target attacks in hash-based signatures. In: Cheng, C.-M., Chung, K.-M., Persiano, G., Yang, B.-Y. (eds.) PKC 2016. LNCS, vol. 9614, pp. 387–416. Springer, Heidelberg (2016). https://doi.org/10.1007/978-3-662-49384-7_15
16. Johnson, R., Molnar, D., Song, D., Wagner, D.: Homomorphic signature schemes. In: Preneel, B. (ed.) CT-RSA 2002. LNCS, vol. 2271, pp. 244–262. Springer, Heidelberg (2002). https://doi.org/10.1007/3-540-45760-7_17
17. Kalogeropoulos, A., Fletcher, R., Nielsen, R.K.: News brand attribution in distributed environments: do people know where they get their news? New Media Soc. **21**(3), 583–601 (2018)
18. Kreutzer, M., Niederhagen, R., Shrishak, K., Simo Fhom, H.: Quotable signatures using merkle trees. In: INFORMATIK 2019. Lecture Notes in Informatik, vol. P-294, pp. 473–477 (2019)
19. Kristensen, N.R.: Schmeichel om fabrikeret, mavesur udtalelse: "Det er noget sludder" (2023). https://www.tjekdet.dk/faktatjek/schmeichel-om-fabrikeret-mavesur-udtalelse-det-er-noget-sludder
20. Laurie, B., Langley, A., Käsper, E.: Certificate transparency. RFC **6962**, 1–27 (2013)
21. Lewandowsky, S., Ecker, U.K.H., Seifert, C.M., Schwarz, N., Cook, J.: Misinformation and its correction: continued influence and successful debiasing. Psychol. Sci. Public Interest **13**(3), 106–131 (2012)
22. Merkle, R.C.: Protocols for public key cryptosystems. In: IEEE Symposium on Security and Privacy 1980, pp. 122–134. IEEE Computer Society (1980)
23. Merkle, R.C.: A certified digital signature. In: Brassard, G. (ed.) CRYPTO 1989. LNCS, vol. 435, pp. 218–238. Springer, New York (1990). https://doi.org/10.1007/0-387-34805-0_21
24. Molina, M.D., Sundar, S.S., Le, T., Lee, D.: "Fake news" is not simply false information: a concept explication and taxonomy of online content. Am. Behav. Sci. **65**(2), 180–212 (2021)

25. Newman, N., Fletcher, R., Kalogeropoulos, A., Nielsen, R.K.: Reuters institute digital news report 2019. Technical report, Reuters Institute for the Study of Journalism (2019)

26. Newman, N. Fletcher, R., Robertson, C.T., Eddy, K., Nielsen, R.K.: Reuters institute digital news report 2022 (2022). https://reutersinstitute.politics.ox.ac.uk/sites/default/files/2022-06/DigitalNews-Report2022.pdf

27. Reuters Fact Check. Fact Check-Screenshot of BBC News report on Russia is fake (2023). https://www.reuters.com/article/factcheck-bbc-screenshotfalse-idUSL2N2VL1D4

28. Samelin, K., Pöhls, H.C., Bilzhause, A., Posegga, J., de Meer, H.: On structural signatures for tree data structures. In: Bao, F., Samarati, P., Zhou, J. (eds.) ACNS 2012. LNCS, vol. 7341, pp. 171–187. Springer, Heidelberg (2012). https://doi.org/10.1007/978-3-642-31284-7_11

29. Schaewitz, L., Krämer, N.C.: Combating disinformation: effects of timing and correction format on factual knowledge and personal beliefs. In: van Duijn, M., Preuss, M., Spaiser, V., Takes, F., Verberne, S. (eds.) MISDOOM 2020. LNCS, vol. 12259, pp. 233–245. Springer, Cham (2020). https://doi.org/10.1007/978-3-030-61841-4_16

30. Schiochet, A.H.: É falso que instituto alemão apontou fraude nas eleições do Brasil (2023). https://lupa.uol.com.br/jornalismo/2022/11/17/e-falso-que-instituto-alemao-apontou-fraude-nas-eleicoes-do-brasil

31. Steinfeld, R., Bull, L., Zheng, Y.: Content extraction signatures. In: Kim, K. (ed.) ICISC 2001. LNCS, vol. 2288, pp. 285–304. Springer, Heidelberg (2002). https://doi.org/10.1007/3-540-45861-1_22

32. Sundar, S.S.: Effect of source attribution on perception of online news stories. Journal. Mass Commun. Q. **75**(1), 55–68 (1998)

33. Traylor, T. Straub, J., Gurmeet, Snell, N.: Classifying fake news articles using natural language processing to identify in-article attribution as a supervised learning estimator. In: IEEE International Conference on Semantic Computing - ICSC 2019, pp. 445–449. IEEE (2019)

34. Urban, J., Schweiger, W.: News quality from the recipients' perspective. Journal. Stud. **15**(6), 821–840 (2014)

35. W3C. Clipboard API and events, W3C Working Draft, 6 August 2021 (2021). https://www.w3.org/TR/2021/WD-clipboard-apis-20210806/

Post-quantum Hybrid KEMTLS Performance in Simulated and Real Network Environments

Alexandre Augusto Giron[1,2(✉)] 🆔, João Pedro Adami do Nascimento[1],
Ricardo Custódio[1], Lucas Pandolfo Perin[3] 🆔, and Víctor Mateu[3] 🆔

[1] Graduate Program on Computer Science, Department of Informatics and Statistics,
Federal University of Santa Catarina (UFSC), Florianópolis, SC, Brazil
[2] Federal University of Technology-Parana (UTFPR), Toledo, PR, Brazil
alexandregiron@utfpr.edu.br
[3] Cryptography Research Center, Technology Innovation Institute (TII),
Abu Dhabi, UAE

Abstract. Integrating Post-Quantum Cryptography (PQC) in network protocols presents a significant challenge. The efficiency of the Transport Layer Security (TLS) protocol can be significantly impacted by adopting larger PQC public keys and signatures. In this context, the KEMTLS approach has emerged as a promising solution, leveraging PQC Key Encapsulation Mechanisms (KEMs) with smaller sizes to replace handshakes and signatures. Besides efficiency, security and reliability are also at risk when adopting new cryptographic primitives. Hybrid PQC methodologies minimize these risks by adding classical cryptographic schemes into the post-quantum protocols. This work introduces the incorporation of hybrid PQC into the KEMTLS and KEMTLS-PDK protocols, integrating elliptic curve-based KEMs. We perform a comprehensive benchmarking analysis across diverse network conditions, KEM types, and security parameters to evaluate the effectiveness of hybrid models. Moreover, we conduct a comparative assessment between our hybrid KEMTLS and a hybrid PQTLS variant, which uses handshake signatures. Our results demonstrate that the performance penalty incurred by hybrid KEMTLS, compared to PQC-only KEMTLS, remains negligible within specific security thresholds. Overall, our findings highlight the advantages of adopting hybrid protocols, outweighing the marginal performance trade-offs observed at higher security parameters. These results underscore the practical feasibility of employing hybrid PQC protocols, enhancing network security in an interconnected environment.

Keywords: Hybrid Post-Quantum Cryptography · KEMTLS · Network Security

1 Introduction

Network protocols such as TLS 1.3 rely on Public-Key Cryptography (PKC) to provide secure communications. However, most of the PKC schemes in use

A. Aly and M. Tibouchi (Eds.): LATINCRYPT 2023, LNCS 14168, pp. 293–312, 2023.
https://doi.org/10.1007/978-3-031-44469-2_15

today are known to be insecure against attackers with access to a Cryptographically Relevant Quantum Computer (CRQC) [16] due to Shor's algorithm [25]. Standardization entities worldwide have initiated movements towards new PKC algorithms based on mathematical problems that are assumed to be hard to solve even for quantum computers. This field is known as Post-Quantum Cryptography (PQC). One of the driving motivations is to be prepared early enough to transition all the PKC algorithms before a CRQC becomes a real threat.

One of the most relevant applications of PKC in our current communications is within cryptographic protocols such as TLS. Recent research suggests that replacing and transitioning TLS to PQC is challenging due to the associated high cost, mainly caused by the increased size of the cryptographic artifacts [19,31]. In anticipation of the required transition to quantum-safe primitives, researchers have begun evaluating PQC in various scenarios and network protocols. Several alternatives have been proposed for TLS, one of which is PQTLS [18,26], which replaces the current PKC primitives with PQC components. PQTLS utilizes two PQC components: a Key Encapsulation Mechanism (KEM) for establishing symmetric keys between peers and Digital Signatures (DS) for end-entity authentication. Currently, TLS performs key agreement using Diffie-Hellman key exchange, which has different properties than KEMs. Consequently, PQTLS introduces modifications to the original TLS besides just replacing the primitives.

Another approach for adopting PQC in TLS, aimed at improving protocol performance, is called KEMTLS [23]. KEMTLS employs KEMs for end-entity authentication since encapsulations are usually smaller than PQC signatures. KEMTLS has been evaluated with different PQC algorithms and compared with existing alternatives such as RSA and ECDSA. One variant of KEMTLS is KEMTLS-PDK, which involves pre-distributed public keys. KEMTLS-PDK targets scenarios where the client already possesses the server's long-term KEM public key, enabling the client to perform protocol operations in advance and reduce the time required for a complete handshake.

In this paper, we refer to schemes that derive their security from both classical and post-quantum cryptographic primitives as PQC hybrids. For instance, in the context of Key Exchange (KEX), one can combine the output of classical and post-quantum algorithms by concatenating them, followed by a key-derivation method that generates the desired symmetric keys for communication. Therefore, both outputs contribute to the derivation process [23,28].

PQC schemes have received less scrutiny compared to classical ones, especially considering the lack of real-world deployment of these primitives. PQC hybrid modes are recommended for adoption because they maintain the existing confidence in the security of traditional cryptography while preventing store-now-decrypt-later attacks by future CRQCs. Thus, PQC hybrids can be used until confidence in PQC is fully established. The Open Quantum Safe project (OQS) [20] recommends PQC hybrids, and NIST acknowledges hybrid modes using the concatenation-prior-derivation approach as compliant with their standards [1]. Standard drafts for using PQC hybrids in TLS have started to emerge, such as the proposal for "Hybrid key exchange in TLS 1.3" [27].

PQTLS has been evaluated by several authors [11,18,26] using the "Hybrid Penalty" metric, which measures the additional costs of using the hybrid mode compared to the PQC-only approach. Although the penalty of using the hybrid mode depends on several factors, it can be minor for the selected algorithms. However, the hybrid mode of KEMTLS has not yet been analyzed. It is crucial to evaluate KEMTLS with hybrids since they are the expected method for migrating real-world applications to PQC. Therefore, this paper aims to fill this gap. Our main contributions are described below.

- A design and implementation of Hybrid KEMTLS, incorporating classical cryptography into all of NIST's Round 3 finalist KEM schemes.
- An extensive evaluation of our approach for Hybrid KEMTLS, considering simulated networks and geographically-distant servers.
- A comparison of hybrids between KEMTLS, KEMTLS-PDK, and PQTLS under the same network conditions and security levels.

This paper is structured as follows. Section 2 provides the necessary background on KEMTLS and its variants. Section 3 presents our design for Hybrid KEMTLS. All configurations and evaluation metrics are described in Sect. 4. Section 5 presents the results of the experiments, and Sect. 6 concludes the study.

2   Background

2.1   Transport Layer Security

Transport Layer Security (TLS) is a network protocol that provides a confidential and authenticated communication channel. TLS is widely used for securing Internet connections and finds applications in microservice architectures [30], VPN connections [23], and is recommended for standardization in SDN and 5G networks [32].

An Authenticated Key Exchange (AKE) occurs in every TLS 1.3 full handshake, which is typically the initial interaction between a client and a server. The handshake protocol [22] begins with an ephemeral Key Exchange (KEX), where secret data is shared between the peers. Each peer derives secrets into a set of traffic keys, which are used for protecting the communication using symmetric cryptography. During the handshake, the TLS server authenticates itself to the TLS client using an x509 digital certificate or a Pre-Shared Key. Optionally, the server may request client authentication, referred to as mutual authentication.

A TLS 1.3 handshake is designed to complete within one Round-Trip-Time (RTT). However, there is a 0-RTT mode for resumptions, and when the client authenticates, it adds another RTT to the protocol. The first handshake message (`ClientHello`) includes a random nonce, protocol versions, a list of supported symmetric cipher/HKDF hash pairs by the client, and other relevant information. The *key_share* consists of an ephemeral public key for the KEX. While optional, at least a keyshare or a Pre-Shared Key (PSK) message must be sent. The server responds with its corresponding information (`ServerHello` message), which may include additional optional messages such as `Certificate` and `CertificateVerify`. These two messages are part of the TLS authentication process using digital signatures. Alternatively, server authentication through

PSK is possible, such as in a session resumption, where the server does not send the certificate. The authentication process concludes with the `Finished` message, where an HMAC is computed from the transcript of the handshake context. All the necessary keys for encryption in TLS 1.3 are derived based on the HKDF function [14].

2.2 Post-quantum Cryptography

One of the primary concerns in TLS is that the cryptographic computations in TLS 1.3 AKE are not resistant to attacks from quantum computers. Cryptography based on the Integer Factorization Problem (IFP), Discrete Logarithm Problem (DLP), and Elliptic Curve Discrete Logarithm Problem (ECDLP) are all vulnerable to Shor's algorithm [25]. Although practical quantum computers do not yet exist, the threat of quantum adversaries capturing TLS packets for future decryption is a cause for concern. To address this issue, researchers have begun studying and developing Post-Quantum Cryptography (PQC) and its integration into TLS and other protocols [9,18,26]. PQC includes schemes based on mathematical problems for which there is no known efficient solution by both classical and quantum computers [3].

Public-key cryptography is often employed for KEX and peer authentication in network protocols. To protect network communications from quantum adversaries, PQC schemes must be incorporated. Post-Quantum Key Encapsulation Mechanisms (KEMs) and Digital Signatures are required, or at least one PQC KEM [23]. However, one of the main challenges in selecting PQC schemes is their increased size compared to classical schemes [28]. Table 1 allows for a comparison of sizes between some PQC and classical algorithms used for KEX (for a comparison of PQC signature sizes, please refer to [31]). The sizes vary for each NIST security level, with each level indicating that the scheme is as difficult to break (using exhaustive key search) as symmetric AES-128 (level one), AES-192 (level three), and AES-256 (level five) [15]. In this work, we adopt a naming convention where the algorithm name is followed by a number corresponding to the security level (e.g., "KyberL5" refers to the `Kyber1024` parameter).

Currently, the most notorious PQC standardization effort is being conducted by the US National Institute of Standards and Technology (NIST) [17]. The PQC proposals submitted to the process can be classified in the following groups [3]: *lattice-based cryptography*, which uses linear algebra constructions; *code-based cryptography*, which uses error-correcting codes; *multivariate-based cryptography*, using systems of multivariate equations; *isogeny-based cryptography*, based on Supersingular elliptic curve isogenies; and *hash-based cryptography*, using cryptographic hash functions.

The third round of the NIST process identified four finalists for Key Encapsulation Mechanisms (KEMs): Classic McEliece, Kyber, Saber, and NTRU. Additionally, three finalists were selected for digital signatures: Dilithium, Falcon, and Rainbow. Subsequently, the fourth round of the process determined the algorithms to be standardized. The chosen algorithms include **Kyber**, based on lattice-based cryptography, for KEM; and for signatures **Dilithium** (primary

Table 1. Classical and PQC schemes comparison

Algorithm Name	Parameter Set Name	Public Key size (bytes)	Claimed NIST Security Level	Quantum-safe?
NIST P256	secp256r1 (L1)	64	1	✗
NIST P384	secp384r1 (L3)	96	3	✗
NIST P521	secp521r1 (L5)	132	5	✗
Kyber	Kyber512 (KyberL1)	800	1	✓
	Kyber768 (KyberL3)	1184	3	✓
	Kyber1024 (KyberL5)	1568	5	✓
Saber	LightSaber (Saber L1)	672	1	✓
	Saber (Saber L3)	992	3	✓
	FireSaber (Saber L5)	1312	5	✓
NTRU	NTRU-HPS-2048-509 (NTRU L1)	699	1	✓
	NTRU-HPS-2048-677 (NTRU L3)	930	3	✓
	NTRU-HPS-4096-821 (NTRU L5)	1230	5	✓

choice), also based on lattice-based cryptography; **Falcon**, based on lattice-based cryptography; and **Sphincs+**, based on hash functions.

Numerous international agencies are closely following the NIST process, and a fourth round is currently underway, where additional algorithms will undergo scrutiny. The KEMs selected for the fourth round are BIKE, Classic McEliece, HQC, and SIKE [29]. However, it should be noted that both Rainbow and SIKE are now broken [4,6]. Furthermore, NIST has issued a call for new digital signature schemes, with a particular interest in those with small signature sizes compared to other PQC schemes.

2.3 Hybrid PQC

As mentioned above, the process of standardization of post-quantum schemes has not finished yet. The current round considers schemes such as SIKE which has been recently broken efficiently with a classical computer. The situation is a bit contradictory, on one side the community is pushing for a transition to PQC as soon as possible to prevent store-now-decrypt-later attacks. On the other side, the schemes have been recently proposed and, even though their security problems are usually existing mathematical problems, the reality is that the research community lacked a proper motivation to perform thorough cryptanalysis on problems that previously had limited real world application.

In this specific situation, a solution that mitigates classical and the quantum threats is to use both classical and post-quantum cryptography together. Proposals following this line are called hybrids and they are designed with the idea of relying on both security problems so that if one problem is easily solved, the other maintains the whole primitive secure. One important consideration regarding the Hybrid PQC design is the *cryptographic combiner* in use [5]. The combiner is responsible for keeping security if one of the combined schemes is not secure anymore. This security property comes with a performance drawback because both primitives need to be computed, and the size of the communications is now the sum of both signatures, ciphertexts, and public keys in some cases. As a consequence, Hybrid PQC is not meant to be a final solution, but a low risk intermediate step. Once the confidence in PQC is fully established it is recommended to abandon the classical cryptographic primitives.

As mentioned before, one of the challenges of adopting PQC for TLS is that the most prominent PQC algorithms substantially increase the size of cryptographic objects, consequently increasing the protocol's communication sizes. Some PQC algorithms cannot be deployed in the TLS protocol "as-is", a change in the protocol might required to fit the algorithm. Moreover, network control mechanisms on the Internet, such as the TCP Congestion Control, can impose a performance slowdown when message sizes surpass a pre-determined threshold. Due to the use of PQC, all these issues are inherited by the Hybrid schemes too.

Literature shows a few examples of PQTLS evaluated with hybrid modes [18,26], but KEMTLS has not yet been evaluated with hybrids. For a practical adoption, hybrid designs accompanied by their performance and security analysis are essential. Understanding the penalties when transitioning to hybrid modes contributes to the PQC adoption.

2.4   KEMTLS

KEMTLS is a post-quantum size-optimized alternative for TLS, as described in the paper by Schwabe, Stebila, and Wiggers [23]. It utilizes post-quantum key encapsulation mechanisms (KEMs) which generally have smaller sizes compared to post-quantum digital signatures. The design of KEMTLS involves the use of an ephemeral KEM for key exchange and another KEM for long-term usage. This approach replaces the digital signature found in a standard TLS 1.3 handshake with KEMs. To further enhance KEMTLS, the authors introduced KEMTLS-PDK [24], which is a variant of KEMTLS that incorporates pre-distributed keys. This makes it suitable for scenarios where the client possesses the server's long-term public key prior to communication. By performing key encapsulation against the server's long-term public key in the initial round of messages, the client can improve performance.

The KEMTLS protocol consists of three phases: ephemeral key exchange using KEMs, implicitly authenticated key exchange using KEMs, and confirmation/explicit authentication. During the second phase, when the server is implicitly authenticated, the client has the option to send application data after just one round. However, the handshake is fully completed in two rounds, only after the third phase when the server is explicitly authenticated. On the other hand, KEMTLS-PDK improves on this by achieving explicit authentication of the server after just one round. This earlier authentication of the server in the protocol flow ensures that the handshake is fully completed simultaneously with the client's ability to send application data. The one-round-trip time (1-RTT) of

KEMTLS-PDK makes it more competitive with standard TLS in terms of the time required to complete a full handshake.

Celi et al. [7] provided an evaluation of KEMTLS, KEMTLS-PDK, and PQTLS using a fork of the Go Standard Library. In their implementation, the server's certificate contains a delegated credential that uses a post-quantum signature algorithm for PQTLS or a post-quantum KEM algorithm for KEMTLS and KEMTLS-PDK. This approach decouples the handshake authentication algorithm from the authentication algorithms used in the certificate chain, enhancing the cryptographic agility principle in the protocol's design. The results of their study demonstrate the promise of KEMTLS, but an investigation of the impact of a hybrid post-quantum design has not yet been proposed for KEMTLS.

3   Hybrid KEMTLS Proposed Design

Our proposal incorporates classical cryptography computations to create a hybrid protocol while preserving the original KEMTLS properties, such as offline deniability and a smaller trusted codebase. The design of Hybrid KEMTLS is depicted in Fig. 1, which focuses on a handshake configuration involving server-only authentication. For the mutual authentication design, please refer to the full version of the paper [12]). The cryptographic computations performed by the client and server are described on their respective sides. The modifications made to the original KEMTLS are highlighted using square dotted boxes. It is important to note that while signatures are not utilized in the handshake process, signature algorithms are still required in the certificate chain to establish a root of trust.

The Hybrid KEMTLS protocol operates similarly to KEMTLS, but now each cryptographic operation has a corresponding classic counterpart, as indicated by the square dotted boxes. The first step in the protocol, in terms of cryptographic operations, is generating key pairs for both the PQC and classic ephemeral KEMs. The resulting public keys pk_e and pk_{ec} are concatenated and transmitted to the server via the key_share extension in the ClientHello TLS message. Upon receiving these keys, the server performs encapsulation for each one, generating the ephemeral shared secrets K_e (post-quantum) and K_{ec} (classic), as well as the ciphertexts ct_e (post-quantum) and ct_{ec} (classic). Subsequently, both ciphertexts are sent back to the client through the key_share extension of the ServerHello message. During the same exchange, the EncryptedExtensions and Certificate messages are also sent. The Certificate message contains an X.509 Certificate consisting of two concatenated static KEM public keys (classic and PQC).

Upon receiving the server's reply messages, the client decapsulates both the post-quantum ciphertext and the classic ciphertext, obtaining the same two ephemeral shared secrets as the server: K_e and K_s. Then, the client performs encapsulation against the server's static KEM public keys, resulting in the static shared secrets K_s and K_{sc}, as well as the ciphertexts ct_s and ct_{sc}. These values are concatenated and sent to the server through the ClientKEMCipher text

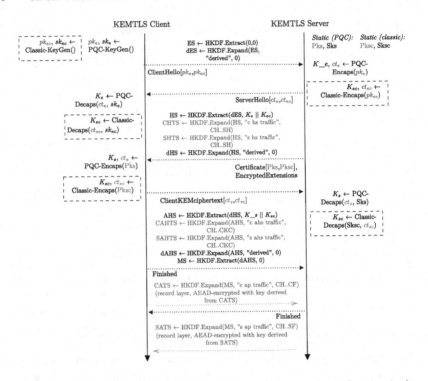

Fig. 1. Proposed Hybrid KEMTLS Handshake (Server-only authentication)

message in KEMTLS, along with the Finished message. The server then decapsulates the received ciphertexts, obtaining the same static shared secrets K_s and K_{sc} as the client. After that, the server can send the Finished message back to the client, thereby completing the Hybrid KEMTLS Handshake.

The proposed Key Schedule for Hybrid KEMTLS follows the KEMTLS Key Schedule, which is inspired by the TLS 1.3 Key Schedule [22]. The TLS 1.3 Key Schedule is based on a series of calls to HKDF extract-and-expand functions. HKDF-Extract takes Input Keying Material (IKM) and a Salt, generating an output secret. On the other hand, the HKDF-Expand function takes a secret, a label, and a transcript hash, as described in RFC 8446 [22] - Section 4.4.1. The output secret from HKDF-Extract serves as the input secret for HKDF-Expand, which generates a protocol traffic secret that is then derived into a TLS 1.3 traffic key, following RFC 8446 [22] Section 7.3.

KEMTLS slightly modifies this Key Schedule by partially removing TLS 1.3's Early Secret stage and adding a new stage between TLS 1.3's Handshake Secret (HS) and Master Secret. This additional stage produces the Authenticated Handshake Secret (AHS). In KEMTLS, the HS is obtained through an HKDF-Extract operation using the ephemeral KEM shared secret, while the AHS is derived from the static KEM shared secret. Thus, both types of shared secrets contribute to generating the application traffic keys.

In this work, our Hybrid KEMTLS Key Schedule follows the same structure as the KEMTLS Key Schedule, with the only difference being the data used as Input Keying Material for the Handshake Secret and Authenticated Handshake Secret. Additionally, we employ a cryptographic combiner that maintains security even if one of the KEMs is compromised. First, the IKM used to generate the Handshake Secret is the concatenation of the shared secrets K_e and K_{ec}. The second IKM is used to derive the Authenticated Handshake Secret, also achieved by concatenating the shared secrets K_s and K_{sc}. It should be noted that both concatenations are further combined using HKDF calls. In this manner, we incorporate the dualPRF combiner, proposed by Bindel et al. [5], into our hybrid design. The main distinction is that we combine shared secrets from both the ephemeral (K_e, K_{ec}) and static (K_s, K_{sc}) components.

Regarding the concatenation (prior to KDF), we justify this choice based on the NIST standards for key derivation that allow such a construction [1]. Besides, modeling our combiner with dualPRF [5] ensures the security properties required for hybrid KEMs. Since all shared secrets are used, if a hybrid mode is selected, each K contributes to the generation of the traffic keys, requiring both parties (i.e., client and server) to support all the algorithms of the selected hybrid mode. However, this should not be a significant issue since we add one algorithm (pre-quantum) cryptography to KEMTLS, which is commonly used nowadays. As KEMTLS, our design allows us to select the same algorithm for KEX and authentication, which can simplify the negotiation procedure of the protocol.

The KEMTLS protocol is based on two KEM key pairs: one ephemeral and one static. To "hybridize" it, we introduced classic KEM key pairs to the protocol. We instantiated Hybrid KEMTLS with the following classic KEMs: KEM_P256_HKDF_SHA256, which utilizes the P256 curve and the HKDF SHA-256; KEM_P384_HKDF_SHA384, and KEM_P521_HKDF_SHA512 which use the curves P384 and P521, and HKDFs SHA-384 and SHA-512 respectively. All the classical KEMs we employ are obtained from the CIRCL library [8].

In the following lines we will refer to the hybrid proposals as KyberL1 H., SaberL1 H., and NTRUL1 H. to denote the instantiation of a KEMTLS hybrid using Kyber, Saber, or NTRU with NIST security level 1, paired with the corresponding classic KEM, in this case KEM_P256_HKDF_SHA256. Moreover, we also target NIST security levels 3 and 5. All the instances are listed in Table 2.

3.1 Inherited Security Analysis

Our proposal preserves the cryptographic primitives and the message flows from the original KEMTLS scheme [23]. For the specific case of hybrid modes, the security is based on two parts, the protocol covered in [23], and the cryptographic combiner [5,10]. In our case, we rely on the following assumptions: PRF and Dual-PRF [2], which corresponds to the assumptions present in Bindel's et al. dualPRF combiner [5]. The security properties of the construction have already been demonstrated for dualPRF for our specific instantiation.

3.2 Modelling Cost of the Instantiations

Depending on the algorithms selected for instantiating Hybrid KEMTLS, an associated cost will be added to the protocol in terms of size. The algorithm parameters define the sizes, and then we can model an estimate of the impact in the protocol. In our design, the protocol cost C_{size} can be defined as:

$$C_{size} = \text{KEX}_{size} + \text{Auth}_{size} + \text{Certificates}_{size} + \text{Metadata}_{size},$$

where KEX_{size} refers to the size of the protocol's Key Exchange messages, including ClientHello and ServerHello; Auth_{size} is the size of KEMTLS server-only or mutual authentication ciphertexts; $\text{Certificates}_{size}$ is the sum of sizes of the server certificate plus Intermediate CA certificate; and Metadata_{size} is the sum of other protocol-related data sizes. If mutual authentication is required, two additional messages must be considered: Server KEM Ciphertext and the client's Certificate. Section 4 describes additional certificate chain configurations used in this work.

Table 2 shows the protocol-level cost of hybrid KEMTLS instances in terms of size (in bytes). It considers cryptographic object sizes and additional protocol data (e.g., ECDHE group numbers) compared to a baseline TLS 1.3 configuration. The last two columns show the total size for Server-only authentication (the letter 'S') and Mutual authentication (the letter 'M'). We omitted the metadata column, but it adds approximately 320 bytes to C_{size}, or 540 for mutual authentication. We kept X509 metadata inside the Certificates column. Mutual authentication shows similar result but adds 540 as metadata value, and it approximately doubles the columns 'Auth' and 'Certificates'. Using this table, one can see the cost of using the Hybrid KEMTLS instance we proposed. Besides, it allows estimating impact in networks. For example, all P521 instances are close to (default) TCP congestion window size (cwnd), measured by the number of segments. Typically, the Maximum Segment Size (MSS) is close to MTU size (e.g., 1460, 1500 bytes), and the cwnd defaults to 10 MSS. Due to the TCP congestion control, hybrids with greater size will incur additional round-trips.

Table 2. Expected cost (bytes) of hybrid KEMTLS instances

Hybrid Instance	Security Level	KEX	Auth	Certificates	C_{size} S	M
P256 (Baseline)	1	484	74	839	1715	2847
P256_Kyber512 (KyberL1 H.)	1	2052	833	7807	11012	19872
P384_Kyber768 (KyberL3 H.)	3	2820	1185	10708	15033	27141
P521_Kyber1024 (KyberL5 H.)	5	3756	1701	14475	20252	36650
P256_LightSaber (SaberL1 H.)	1	1892	801	7679	10692	19390
P384_Saber (SaberL3 H.)	3	2628	1185	10514	14647	26564
P521_FireSaber (SaberL5 H.)	5	3404	1605	14220	19549	35595
P256_NTRU_HPS_2048_509 (NTRU L1 H.)	1	1882	764	7707	10673	19363
P384_NTRU_HPS_2048_677 (NTRU L3 H.)	3	2408	1027	10454	14209	25909
P521_NTRU_HPS_4096_821 (NTRU L5 H.)	5	3080	1363	14138	18901	34623

We also model computational cost our hybrid KEMTLS design. The focus of this model is on the cost of cryptographic computations since they are only modified part in our proposal. In this case, we can define the client's computational cost when using hybrid KEMTLS as $C_{clientops}$:

$$C_{clientops} = \text{HKeyGen}_{time} + \text{HDecaps}_{time} + \text{HEncaps}_{time} + 2 * \text{HVerify}_{time},$$

where HKeyGen_{time} and HDecaps_{time} are KEM operations and HEncaps_{time} and $2 * \text{HVerify}_{time}$ are authentication operations (with long-term keys). Although a KEM is used, two signatures must be verified to complete the authentication (server and Intermediate CA certificates), for each algorithm (PQC and Classical). For the server-side, the cost $C_{serverops}$ has the main difference: it does not have HVerify_{time} involved, nor signing operation, only: HEncaps_{time} for KEX, HDecaps_{time} for authentication. Lastly, the 'H' letter represents the hybrid mode, requiring two operations: one for the PQC and the other for the classical algorithm. Note, however, that are other costs when using the hybrid protocol in practice (e.g., network latency time).

4 Evaluation Methodology

We conducted our experiments using two environments: geographical-distant servers and simulated network experiments. For the first experiment, we utilized two Google N2 VMs, each configured with an Intel(R) Xeon(R) 2.80 GHz CPU and 8 GiB RAM. These VMs were located in different geographical regions: europe-central2-a (Warsaw, Poland) and southamerica-east1-a (São Paulo, Brazil), resulting in an average latency of 108 ms.

In the simulated experiment, we employed NetEm [13] with two parameters: latencies (2 ms, 10 ms, 100 ms, 300 ms) and packet loss probabilities (1%, 2%, 3%, 5%). The simulations were executed on an Intel i5-8250U 1.60GHz machine with turbo boost technology disabled. In both experiments, we evaluated 1000 handshakes, one at a time.

Unlike the TLS 1.3 handshake, the KEMTLS protocol requires an additional round-trip to authenticate the server and complete the handshake. While comparing the two protocols, it's important to note that the handshake completion time occurs when a peer receives a Finished message. Therefore, the Finished message concludes the handshake at different points in the two protocols. Due to the added round-trip, the KEMTLS handshake completion time is longer than that of PQTLS. However, from a practical perspective, the client can send application data at the exact moment the handshake completes in both protocols. It's worth mentioning that the client is typically the party that initiates communication, such as with an HTTPS request.

Our tests are based on the NIST Round 3 Finalists in terms of algorithm selection for the experiments. We evaluated scenarios using Kyber, Saber, and NTRU variants in the three security levels, always in hybrid mode with NIST curves. In KEMTLS, we utilize a KEM-based ECDH and a PQC KEM to compose our hybrid scheme. A similar configuration is used in PQTLS, but for authentication, we employ `Falcon` and `Dilithium`, also in hybrid mode. Both protocols use a fixed certificate chain, which is hybrid and contains only one hybrid algorithm, chosen to be Dilithium. This choice of a fixed certificate chain allows for a comparison between KEMTLS and PQTLS at the protocol level in terms of handshake operations. Other options could include a classical certificate chain, mixed-chains [19], or PQC-only chains. However, our work focuses on the transition with Hybrid PQC. Furthermore, RFC 8446 allows peers to avoid sending Root CAs certificates, minimizing the impact of PQC adoption. Hence, the `Certificate` message in the protocol includes two certificates: the server (or client) certificate and the Intermediate CA certificate.

We use the same NIST security level for all algorithms involved in the handshake protocol. This means that the KEX, authentication, and certificate chain are all set at the same security level. Consequently, we anticipate better performance for the minimum security level and the most significant performance impact for the maximum (NIST) security level. By employing this approach, the experiments provide indicators for both the minimum and maximum scenarios.

For our experiments, we adapted an implementation from Celi et al. [7] in Golang. We "hybridized" their KEMTLS and PQTLS implementation using NIST curves `p256`, `p384`, or `p521`, depending on the security level of each algorithm version. Additionally, we developed a new testbed to support different PQC algorithms and ensure the reproducibility of our experiments. To integrate all algorithms in KEMTLS, we utilized the liboqs-go wrapper [21] from the OQS project. Our implementation is publicly available[1].

In the context of hybrid adoption and aiming for a fair comparison, our evaluation considers the following metrics: Handshake Completion Time, which measures the time from the start of the protocol at the client until it receives the `Finished` message; Time-to-Send-App-Data, which indicates the required time for the client to send application data to the server; and the Hybrid Penalty, calculated as $H - P$, where H is the measured time in a hybrid instantiation and P is the PQC-only time. This metric quantifies the performance impact of the hybrid approach. In the full version of the paper, we also present additional load test metrics, including HTTPS/TLS request successes and failures, as well as server-side memory load.

5   Hybrid KEMTLS Evaluation

5.1   Hybrid Penalty in Geographical-Distant Servers

This experiment evaluates Hybrid KEMTLS (and KEMTLS-PDK) using geographically separated peers, considering handshake completion times. Figures 2 and 3 present the box plots for the KEMTLS and KEMTLS-PDK timings, considering server-only authentication. Figure 4 corresponds to the instantiations using security level 5. Note that we present results focusing on the Kyber

---

[1] https://github.com/AAGiron/hybrid-kemtls-tests

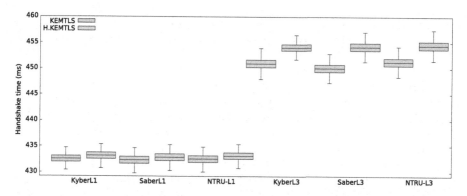

Fig. 2. KEMTLS and Hybrid KEMTLS (L1-L3)

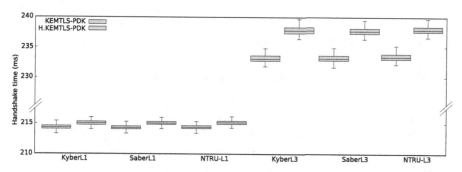

Fig. 3. KEMTLS-PDK and Hybrid KEMTLS-PDK (L1-L3)

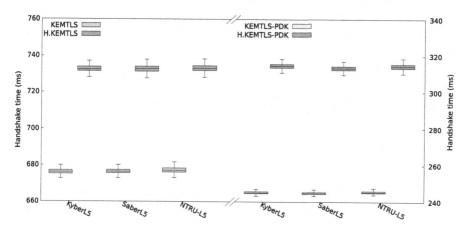

Fig. 4. KEMTLS, KEMTLS-PDK and Hybrids (L5)

instance. We observed similar results for NTRU and Saber, which are accessible in the full version of the paper [12].

In the geographical-distant scenario, we do not control network variations or load variations that might occur in the Google VMs. On the other hand, such a test environment better reflects a realistic scenario. In this scenario, we observed different results regarding the hybrid penalties (i.e., the cost of adopting our hybrid). The box plots for security level 1 show overlapping timings, which means that the penalties are minor, regardless of the tested algorithms. However, increasing the security level, the boxes no longer overlap, increasing the penalty. As seen in Fig. 4, with level 5, the hybrid penalties are much more significant than the other levels caused by the classical algorithm.

Due to design differences, KEMTLS-PDK obtained better timings because of its reduced number of RTTs. The RTT conceals most cryptographic operation timings in such a geographical-distant connection. When analyzing the hybrid penalties, KEMTLS and KEMTLS-PDK have similar results. These results favor hybrid versions but not much at higher security levels. Please refer to the supplementary material for results when using mutual authentication, where the penalties have similar behavior, corroborating these findings.

5.2 Hybrid Penalty in Simulated Environment

Unlike the geographical-distant experiment, the simulated environment allows controlling the effect of parameter variations such as network latency. Table 3 highlights the hybrid penalties in KEMTLS using the average handshake time (HS) as the metric and increasing the simulated latency. The network latency plays a significant role in the handshake completion time. By configuring 1 ms of link latency, the client and the server will be delayed by 2 ms, and since KEMTLS requires two round trips to complete the handshake, it doubles this number, reaching 4 ms. The same behavior happens in KEMTLS mutual authentication, requiring three instead of two round trips. However, in practice, KEMTLS allows the client to send application data before handshake completion, removing one (additional) round trip and its performance impact.

Table 3 shows that the hybrid penalty is negligible at lower security levels and significant at level 5. For instance, the largest penalty in security level 1 is 1.0 ms (e.g., KyberL1 H.), for security level 3 is 8.3 ms from KyberL3 H., and for security level 5 is 133 ms from KyberL5 H. The latency variation did not impact the hybrid penalty significantly since they are more affected when changing to different security levels. Similar behavior was observed in NTRU and Saber (available in the full version [12]).

We also simulated different packet loss probabilities looking for hybrid penalties. Table 4 shows the results of using the time-to-send-app-data metric for PQC-Only and hybrid versions of KEMTLS, focusing again on Kyber. We do not use handshake completion time here because it would double the actual packet loss employed (due to the additional RTT). When analyzing columns from Table 4, we observed significant changes in the penalties in medians. When reaching 5% loss probabilities, some connections can slow down significantly, which can be seen at the 95% percentile. This slowdown happens because with increasing size the likelihood of losing packets increases. However, this increase

Table 3. Average Handshake time (HS, in ms) for PQC-Only and Hybrid KEMTLS under different simulated latencies ('L' means security level and 'H' if in hybrid mode).

Algorithm and Security Level	Latency: 1 ms			Latency: 5 ms			Latency: 50 ms			Latency: 150 ms		
	HS Time	Penalty	St. Dev.	HS Time	Penalty	St. Dev.	HS Time	Penalty	St. Dev.	HS Time	Penalty	St. Dev.
KyberL1	6.0	–	0.4	22.3	–	0.3	202.8	–	0.2	602.9	–	0.2
KyberL1 H	7.0	**1.0**	0.4	23.2	**0.9**	0.3	203.6	**0.9**	0.3	603.7	**0.8**	0.4
KyberL3	38.5	–	0.8	54.8	–	0.8	236.3	–	1.0	636.6	–	1.0
KyberL3 H	46.8	**8.3**	0.9	62.9	**8.1**	2.3	243.2	**6.9**	1.2	643.9	**7.3**	1.6
KyberL5	63.0	–	0.8	78.4	–	0.8	261.1	–	6.0	659.9	–	1.0
KyberL5 H	194.6	**131.6**	2.4	211.4	**133.0**	3.7	393.0	**132.0**	4.5	791.6	**131.7**	3.2

Table 4. Time-to-send-app-data (in ms) considering different packet loss probabilities.

Algorithm and Security Level	Packet Loss: 1%		Packet Loss: 2%		Packet Loss: 3%		Packet Loss: 5%	
	Median	95% percentile	Median	95% percentile	Median	95% percentile	Median	95% percentile
KyberL1	1.6	2.9	1.6	3.3	1.6	207.5	1.7	208.3
KyberL1 H	2.3	3.4	2.3	7.9	2.3	207.3	2.4	209.4
KyberL3	34.0	36.1	34.3	39.2	34.8	239.6	34.9	242.0
KyberL3 H	39.9	42.1	39.8	43.4	40.3	246.1	40.7	247.2
KyberL5	58.4	60.9	58.5	63.6	57.6	263.1	58.9	266.3
KyberL5 H	162.6	166.8	162.0	167.2	161.0	359.2	162.1	368.0

happens with PQC-only and hybrids, with a larger increase in security level 5 (for example, KyberL5 H. differs near 100 ms to PQC-only, for all packet loss probabilities). Overall, using level 1 hybrid instantiations, we do not anticipate a large penalty if a wireless connection experiences packet loss.

5.3   Hybrid KEMTLS Compared to Hybrid PQTLS

This section analyzes the performance of different hybrids (H. KEMTLS and H. PQTLS). We selected the time-to-send-app-data metric, measured in the client, since it is the first to send application data in practice. For applications dependent on the handshake completion time, one can compare hybrid PQTLS timings with the KEMTLS timings provided in Figs. 2 and 4. In such a case, KEMTLS additional round-trip imposes a delay which is often worse than PQTLS timings.

Figures 5 and 6 compare hybrids using the time-to-send-app-data metric and each NIST security level. At level 1, the hybrid's boxes overlap, meaning similar timings. The main difference is that hybrid PQTLS has a dual-signature operation for the handshake transcript data. Hybrid KEMTLS replaces it with two KEM encapsulations (using a classical and a PQC algorithm).

The hybrid approaches achieved similar performance at security level 1. At security level 3, however, we observed an interesting result when comparing them. The hybrid KEMTLS is significantly faster than PQTLS in the time-to-send-app-data metric. Hybrid PQTLS sizes, usually larger than KEMTLS sizes, can easily surpass network thresholds such as TCP Maximum Segment Size. For example, considering the TCP window standard size (10 MSS), if we compare hybrids C_{size}: KEMTLS using KyberL3 H. has 15033 bytes, and it is 16.57%

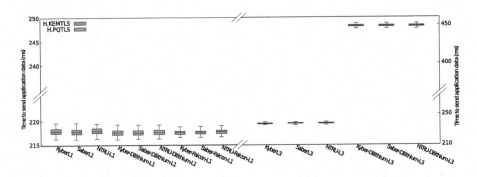

Fig. 5. Hybrids Comparison (L1-L3)

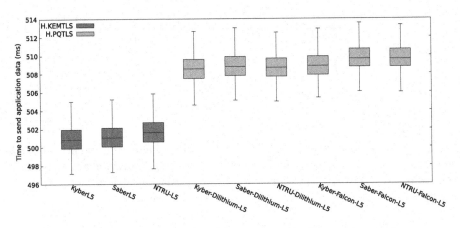

Fig. 6. Hybrids Comparison (L5)

smaller than hybrid PQTLS using KyberL3 and DilithiumL3, both in hybrid mode (18019 bytes). This difference incurs an additional round-trip at the TCP level. If we increase MSS size, the performance can be equated, but such a change can affect network performance negatively, as discussed by Sikeridis et al. [26]. We could not test Falcon in security level 3 (no parameter set available). Lastly, level 5 instantiations also exhibit a performance difference that favors the deployment of hybrid KEMTLS rather than PQTLS.

5.4 Summarizing Results

Figure 7 provides a summary of the experiments conducted in this work, including the load testing metrics (discussed in detail in the full version). The figure presents an aggregation of average handshake time, average time-to-send-appdata (from the simulated environment), handshake sizes, number of successful requests, and peak memory usage by the server, all considering hybrid implementations at security level 1. Initially, we compared hybrid to PQC-only implementations, but now all the data is normalized to the baseline configuration, which utilizes classical cryptography.

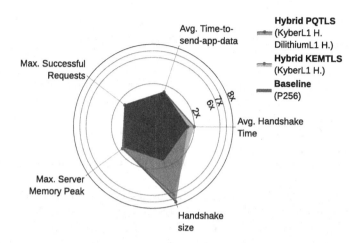

Fig. 7. Summary of performance of hybrids at level 1

The main finding for security level 1, as depicted in Fig. 7, is that the performance penalties incurred by the hybrid approach (when compared to the baseline) are small. The handshake sizes increased by approximately 7x in our hybrid implementation at level 1, and the average handshake time nearly doubled due to the additional round-trip time (introduced by KEMTLS' original design). However, there is no significant penalty observed for the time-to-send-application-data at this level. Nevertheless, as we increased the security parameters, we observed a change in behavior. The penalties started to grow when comparing hybrids to PQC-only alternatives, which was observed both in simulated and geographically-distant scenario.

In terms of the number of requests, it may not be evident in the scale of Fig. 7, but the maximum number of successful requests decreased by 3% and 6% for hybrids (PQTLS and KEMTLS, respectively, at level 1). In absolute terms, this decrease ranged between 2485 and 5604 requests, which could be significant depending on the application transitioning to hybrids. Finally, the memory requirements increased by approximately 64 MB (for KEMTLS) and 43 MB (for PQTLS) when using hybrid alternatives, which is not significant in current server configurations.

6   Conclusions

Hybrid modes represent an initial step towards the transition to post-quantum cryptography. This study is the first to explore hybrids using the KEMTLS and KEMTLS-PDK approaches. While KEMTLS offers the advantage of smaller TLS configurations, the inclusion of hybrids in KEMTLS ensures a more secure transition by incorporating classical algorithms. Classical algorithms have undergone extensive security analysis over time compared to PQC algorithms.

Overall, the performance penalties associated with the addition of classical algorithms in the KEMTLS design are minimal, particularly when considering instantiations with lower security parameters. This holds true for both simulated and geographically-distant connections. Hence, hybrids are well-suited for KEMTLS (including its PDK variant) as they provide the confidence of classical algorithms with small performance penalties. Our evaluation covers algorithms from the NIST PQC standardization process. Notably, the average timings of Kyber, Saber, and NTRU in KEMTLS, as well as Dilithium and Falcon in PQTLS, are closely matched, making it difficult to identify the optimal algorithm configuration for hybrid instantiations. This was expected given that all these algorithms are lattice-based among the NIST's Round 3 finalists, including the chosen candidate Kyber.

We also compared different hybrid approaches using various metrics, specifically hybrid modes for KEMTLS and PQTLS. At security level 3, the importance of byte conservation becomes evident as hybrid KEMTLS outperformed hybrid PQTLS. The former was better suited for fitting within the TCP congestion window. Additionally, a load test was conducted on a hybrid HTTPS web server, where it was observed that hybrid PQTLS performs better than hybrid KEMTLS as the number of client threads increases. However, both hybrids show drawbacks in performance compared to classical cryptography configuration. This load test experiment allowed us to assess the impact on the server when providing HTTP content while adopting hybrid PQC.

In conclusion, there are additional scenarios that warrant exploration when considering PQC adoption in TLS. We leave for future work the investigation of hybrid KEMTLS applied in contexts involving Internet of Things (IoT) and 5G networks, where energy consumption may serve as a critical evaluation metric.

Acknowledgment. We would like to thank Sofía Celi and Thom Wiggers for their valuable comments about KEMTLS and hybrid modes. We also acknowledge the Federal University of Technology - Parana (UTFPR) for its support.

References

1. Barker, E., Chen, L., Davis, R.: Recommendation for key-derivation methods in key-establishment schemes revision 2. NIST Special Publication **800**, 56C (2020). https://doi.org/10.6028/NIST.SP.800-56Cr2
2. Bellare, M., Lysyanskaya, A.: Symmetric and dual PRFs from standard assumptions: a generic validation of an HMAC assumption. Cryptology ePrint Archive, Report 2015/1198 (2015). https://ia.cr/2015/1198
3. Bernstein, D.J., Lange, T.: Post-quantum cryptography. Nature **549**(7671), 188–194 (2017). https://doi.org/10.1038/nature23461
4. Beullens, W.: Breaking rainbow takes a weekend on a laptop. Cryptology ePrint Archive, Paper 2022/214 (2022). https://eprint.iacr.org/2022/214

5. Bindel, N., Brendel, J., Fischlin, M., Goncalves, B., Stebila, D.: Hybrid key encapsulation mechanisms and authenticated key exchange. In: Ding, J., Steinwandt, R. (eds.) PQCrypto 2019. LNCS, vol. 11505, pp. 206–226. Springer, Cham (2019). https://doi.org/10.1007/978-3-030-25510-7_12

6. Castryck, W., Decru, T.: An efficient key recovery attack on SIDH (preliminary version). Cryptology ePrint Archive, Paper 2022/975 (2022). https://eprint.iacr.org/2022/975

7. Celi, S., et al.: Implementing and measuring KEMTLS. In: Longa, P., Ràfols, C. (eds.) LATINCRYPT 2021. LNCS, vol. 12912, pp. 88–107. Springer, Cham (2021). https://doi.org/10.1007/978-3-030-88238-9_5

8. Cloudflare: Circl (cloudflare interoperable, reusable cryptographic library). Online (2021). https://github.com/cloudflare/circl

9. Crockett, E., Paquin, C., Stebila, D.: Prototyping post-quantum and hybrid key exchange and authentication in TLS and SSH. Cryptology ePrint Archive, Report 2019/858 (2019)

10. Giacon, F., Heuer, F., Poettering, B.: KEM combiners. In: Abdalla, M., Dahab, R. (eds.) PKC 2018. LNCS, vol. 10769, pp. 190–218. Springer, Cham (2018). https://doi.org/10.1007/978-3-319-76578-5_7

11. Giron, A.A., Custódio, R., Rodríguez-Henríquez, F.: Post-quantum hybrid key exchange: a systematic mapping study. J. Cryptogr. Eng. **13**(1), 71–88 (2023). https://doi.org/10.1007/s13389-022-00288-9

12. Giron, A.A., do Nascimento, J.P.A., Custódio, R., Perin, L.P.: Post-quantum hybrid KEMTLS performance in simulated and real network environments. Cryptology ePrint Archive, Paper 2022/1639 (2022). https://eprint.iacr.org/2022/1639

13. Hemminger, S.: Linux network emulator. Online (2011). https://www.linux.org/docs/man8/tc-netem.html

14. Krawczyk, H.: Cryptographic extraction and key derivation: the HKDF scheme. In: Rabin, T. (ed.) CRYPTO 2010. LNCS, vol. 6223, pp. 631–648. Springer, Heidelberg (2010). https://doi.org/10.1007/978-3-642-14623-7_34

15. Moody, D.: Let's get ready to rumble- the NIST PQC competition (2018). https://csrc.nist.gov/CSRC/media/Presentations/Let-s-Get-Ready-to-Rumble-The-NIST-PQC-Competiti/images-media/PQCrypto-April2018_Moody.pdf

16. Mosca, M., Piani, M.: Quantum threat timeline report 2020 (2020). https://globalriskinstitute.org/publications/quantum-threat-timeline-report-2020/. Accessed 20 July 2021

17. NIST: Post-quantum cryptography (2016). https://csrc.nist.gov/Projects/Post-Quantum-Cryptography. Accessed 26 June 2021

18. Paquin, C., Stebila, D., Tamvada, G.: Benchmarking post-quantum cryptography in TLS. In: Ding, J., Tillich, J.-P. (eds.) PQCrypto 2020. LNCS, vol. 12100, pp. 72–91. Springer, Cham (2020). https://doi.org/10.1007/978-3-030-44223-1_5

19. Paul, S., Kuzovkova, Y., Lahr, N., Niederhagen, R.: Mixed certificate chains for the transition to post-quantum authentication in TLS 1.3. Cryptology ePrint Archive, Report 2021/1447 (2021). https://ia.cr/2021/1447

20. Open Quantum Safe Project: OQS-OpenSSL github repository (2022). https://github.com/open-quantum-safe/openssl. Accessed 10 Mar 2022

21. Open Quantum Safe Project: liboqs-go: Go bindings for liboqs (2022). https://github.com/open-quantum-safe/liboqs-go. Accessed 25 Jan 2022

22. Rescorla, E.: The transport layer security (TLS) protocol version 1.3. RFC 8446, RFC Editor (2018)

23. Schwabe, P., Stebila, D., Wiggers, T.: Post-quantum TLS without handshake signatures, pp. 1461–1480. Association for Computing Machinery, New York (2020). https://doi.org/10.1145/3372297.3423350
24. Schwabe, P., Stebila, D., Wiggers, T.: More efficient post-quantum KEMTLS with pre-distributed public keys. In: Bertino, E., Shulman, H., Waidner, M. (eds.) ESORICS 2021. LNCS, vol. 12972, pp. 3–22. Springer, Cham (2021). https://doi.org/10.1007/978-3-030-88418-5_1
25. Shor, P.W.: Algorithms for quantum computation: discrete logarithms and factoring. In: Proceedings 35th Annual Symposium on Foundations of Computer Science, Santa Fe, NM, USA, pp. 124–134. IEEE (1994)
26. Sikeridis, D., Kampanakis, P., Devetsikiotis, M.: Assessing the overhead of post-quantum cryptography in TLS 1.3 and SSH. In: Proceedings of the 16th International Conference on emerging Networking EXperiments and Technologies, pp. 149–156. Association for Computing Machinery, New York (2020)
27. Stebila, D., Fluhrer, S., Gueron, S.: Hybrid key exchange in TLS 1.3 (2022). http://tools.ietf.org/html/draft-ietf-tls-hybrid-design-05. Internet-Draft
28. Stebila, D., Mosca, M.: Post-quantum key exchange for the internet and the open quantum safe project. In: Avanzi, R., Heys, H. (eds.) SAC 2016. LNCS, vol. 10532, pp. 14–37. Springer, Cham (2017). https://doi.org/10.1007/978-3-319-69453-5_2
29. Team NP: PQC standardization process: announcing four candidates to be standardized, plus fourth round candidates (2022). https://csrc.nist.gov/News/2022/pqc-candidates-to-be-standardized-and-round-4
30. Weller, D., van der Gaag, R.: Incorporating post-quantum cryptography in a microservice environment. Technical report, Security and Network Engineering - University of Amsterdam (2020)
31. Westerbaan, B.: Sizing up post-quantum signatures (2021). https://blog.cloudflare.com/sizing-up-post-quantum-signatures/
32. Zhang, S., Wang, Y., Zhou, W.: Towards secure 5G networks: a survey. Comput. Netw. **162**, 106871 (2019). https://doi.org/10.1016/j.comnet.2019.106871. http://www.sciencedirect.com/science/article/pii/S138912861830817X

Zero-Knowledge Proofs

Physical Zero-Knowledge Proofs for Five Cells

Suthee Ruangwises[✉][iD]

Department of Informatics, The University of Electro-Communications, Tokyo,
Japan
ruangwises@gmail.com

Abstract. Five Cells is a logic puzzle consisting of a rectangular grid,
with some cells containing a number. The player has to partition the grid
into pentominoes such that the number in each cell must be equal to the
number of edges of that cell that are borders of pentominoes. In this
paper, we propose two physical zero-knowledge proof protocols for Five
Cells using a deck of playing cards, which allow a prover to physically
show that he/she knows a solution of the puzzle without revealing it.
In the optimization of our first protocol, we also develop a technique to
reduce the number of required cards from quadratic to linear in the number of cells, which can be used in other zero-knowledge proof protocols
related to graph coloring as well.

Keywords: zero-knowledge proof · card-based cryptography · Five
Cells · puzzle

1 Introduction

Five Cells is a logic puzzle developed by Nikoli, a Japanese company that pub-
lished many popular puzzles including Sudoku, Kakuro, and Numberlink. A Five
Cells puzzle consists of a rectangular grid, with some cells containing a number.
The objective of the puzzle is to partition the grid into pentominoes called *blocks*.
The number in each cell must be equal to the number of edges of that cell that
are borders of pentominoes (including the outer boundary of the grid) [14]. See
Fig. 1.

Determining whether a given Five Cells puzzle has a solution has been proved
to be NP-complete [9].

1.1 Zero-Knowledge Proof

We are interested in constructing a *zero-knowledge proof (ZKP)* for Five Cells,
which allows a prover P to convince a verifier V that P knows a solution of the
puzzle without revealing any information about it. Formally, a ZKP is an interactive protocol between P and V, where both of them are given a computational
problem x, but only P knows its solution w. A ZKP has to satisfy the following
three properties.

© The Author(s), under exclusive license to Springer Nature Switzerland AG 2023
A. Aly and M. Tibouchi (Eds.): LATINCRYPT 2023, LNCS 14168, pp. 315–330, 2023.
https://doi.org/10.1007/978-3-031-44469-2_16

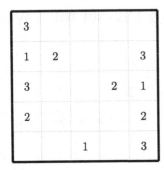 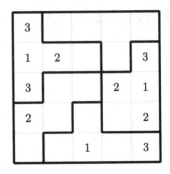

Fig. 1. An example of a Five Cells puzzle (left) and its solution (right)

1. **Completeness:** If P knows w, then V accepts with high probability. (Here, we consider the *perfect completeness* property where V always accepts.)
2. **Soundness:** If P does not know w, then V rejects with high probability. (Here, we consider the *perfect soundness* property where V always rejects.)
3. **Zero-knowledge:** V obtains no information about w, i.e. there exists a probabilistic polynomial time algorithm S (called a *simulator*) that does not know w but has an access to V, and the outputs of S follow the same probability distribution as the ones of the real protocol.

The concept of a ZKP was introduced by Goldwasser et al. [7] in 1989. In the past decade, many researchers have been focusing on constructing physical ZKPs using portable objects such as a deck of cards and envelopes. These protocols have benefits that they require only objects easily found in everyday life and do not require computers. They also allow external observers to verify that the prover truthfully executes the protocol (which is a challenging task for digital protocols). Moreover, these protocols have didactic values and can be used to teach the concept of a ZKP to non-experts.

1.2   Related Work

Physical card-based ZKP protocols for many logic puzzles have been developed in the recent years, including Sudoku [8,23,29], Nonogram [4,20], Akari [1], Takuzu [1,12], Kakuro [1,13], KenKen [1], Makaro [2,28], Norinori [5], Slitherlink [11], Juosan [12], Numberlink [25], Suguru [15], Ripple Effect [26], Nurikabe [16], Hitori [16], Bridges [27], Masyu [11], Heyawake [16], Shikaku [24], Usowan [18], Nurimisaki [17], ABC End View [6,22], Ball sort puzzle [21], and Goishi Hiroi [22].

1.3   Our Contribution

In this paper, we propose two physical ZKP protocols for Five Cells with perfect completeness and soundness using a deck of cards.

Most of the paper will cover our first protocol, which combines many existing protocols to construct each block on the grid in a straightforward way. The most important part is the optimization of the protocol. We develop a *color shifting protocol*, which enables P to gradually color a graph while maintaining that no two adjacent vertices have the same color without revealing any information about the coloring. This technique reduces the number of required cards in the protocol from quadratic to linear in the number of cells, and it can also be used in other ZKP protocols related to graph coloring.

In Appendix A, we describe our second protocol, which takes a completely different approach from the first one. It uses a newly developed *printing protocol* to directly put each block on the grid. The number of required cards in the second protocol is also linear in the number of cells, but is asymptotically lower than that of the first one.

2 Verifying Connected Area

First, P needs to convince V that each block is a pentomino, i.e. consists of exactly five cells connected to each other horizontally or vertically. The following tools and subprotocols are necessary for this phase.

2.1 Cards

Each card used in our protocol has a non-negative integer on the front side. All cards have indistinguishable back sides denoted by $\boxed{?}$.

For $1 \leq y \leq q$, define $E_q(y)$ to be a sequence of q cards, all of them being $\boxed{0}$ s except the y-th leftmost card being a $\boxed{1}$, e.g. $E_4(2)$ is $\boxed{0}\boxed{1}\boxed{0}\boxed{0}$. Also, define $E_q(0)$ to be a sequence of q $\boxed{0}$ s, e.g. $E_4(0)$ is $\boxed{0}\boxed{0}\boxed{0}\boxed{0}$. We may sometimes stack the cards in $E_q(y)$ into a single stack.

2.2 Pile-Shifting Shuffle

A *pile-shifting shuffle* [30] shifts the columns of a matrix of cards by a uniformly random cyclic shift (see Fig. 2). It can be implemented in real world by putting the cards in each column into an envelope and then applying several *Hindu cuts* (taking some envelopes from the bottom and putting them on the top) to the pile of envelopes [32].

Note that each card in the matrix may be replaced by a stack of cards, as long as each stack in the same row has the same number of cards.

2.3 Chosen Pile Cut Protocol

Suppose there is a sequence of q face-down stacks $A = (a_1, a_2, ..., a_q)$, where each stack has the same number of cards. A *chosen pile cut protocol* [10] allows P to select a desired stack a_i (to use in other protocols) without revealing the index

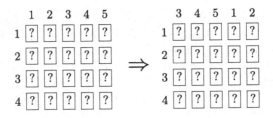

Fig. 2. A pile-shifting shuffle on a 4×5 matrix

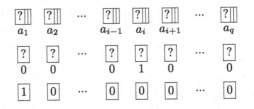

Fig. 3. A $3 \times n$ matrix M constructed in Step 1 of the chosen pile cut protocol

i to V. The protocol also reverts the sequence A back to its original state after P finishes using a_i.

In the chosen pile cut protocol, P performs the following steps.

1. Construct the following $3 \times q$ matrix M (see Fig. 3).
   (a) In Row 1, publicly place the sequence A.
   (b) In Row 2, secretly place a face-down sequence $E_q(i)$.
   (c) In Row 3, publicly place a sequence $E_q(1)$.
2. Turn over all face-up cards and apply the pile-shifting shuffle to M.
3. Turn over all cards in Row 2. Locate the position of the only $\boxed{1}$. A stack in Row 1 directly above this $\boxed{1}$ will be the desired stack a_i.
4. After finishing using a_i, place a_i back in M at the same position.
5. Turn over all face-up cards and apply the pile-shifting shuffle to M again.
6. Turn over all cards in Row 3. Locate the position of the only $\boxed{1}$. Shift the columns of M cyclically such that this $\boxed{1}$ moves to Column 1. The sequence A is now reverted back to its original state.

2.4   Sea Formation Protocol

A *sea formation protocol* [16] allows P to convince V that an area in an $m \times n$ grid consists of t cells that are connected to each other horizontally or vertically, without revealing any other information about the area. A technique similar to the one in this protocol will be implicitly used in our main protocol.

The idea of this protocol is that P first colors all cells with color 1. Then, for each of the t cells in the given area, P will change its color from color 1 to color 2 one cell at a time, each time selecting a cell adjacent to some cell selected earlier.

A cell with color c is represented by a sequence $E_k(c)$ for a fixed $k \geq 2$. First, P publicly places an $E_k(1)$ on every cell in the grid. To handle edge cases where the selected cell is on the grid boundary, P also publicly appends a row and a column of "dummy stacks" $E_k(0)$s to the bottom and to the right of the grid. Then, turn all cards face-down. We now have an $(m + 1) \times (n + 1)$ matrix of stacks (see Fig. 4).

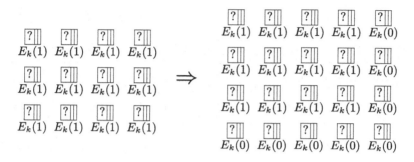

Fig. 4. The way P appends dummy stacks to a 3×4 grid

If we arrange all $(m + 1)(n + 1)$ stacks in the matrix into a single sequence $A = (a_1, a_2, ..., a_{(m+1)(n+1)})$, starting at the top-left corner and going from left to right in Row 1, then from left to right in Row 2, and so on, we can locate exactly where the four neighbors of any given stack are. Namely, the stacks on the neighbor to the left, right, top, and bottom of a cell containing a_i are a_{i-1}, a_{i+1}, a_{i-n-1}, and a_{i+n+1}, respectively. Hence, P can apply the chosen pile cut protocol to select a desired neighbor without revealing which one (since the chosen pile cut protocol preserves the cyclic order of the input sequence).

In the sea formation protocol to verify an area of size t, P performs the following steps.

1. Apply the chosen pile cut protocol (for $(m + 1)(n + 1)$ stacks) to select a desired $E_k(1)$.
2. Reveal the selected stack that it is an $E_k(1)$ (otherwise V rejects) and replace it with an $E_k(2)$.
3. Perform the following steps for $t - 1$ iterations.
   (a) Apply the chosen pile cut protocol (for $(m + 1)(n + 1)$ stacks) to select a desired $E_k(2)$.
   (b) Reveal the selected stack that it is an $E_k(2)$ (otherwise V rejects).
   (c) Pick the four neighbors of the selected stack and apply the chosen pile cut protocol (for four stacks) to select a desired neighbor.
   (d) Reveal the selected neighbor that it is an $E_k(1)$ (otherwise V rejects) and replace it with an $E_k(2)$.

Observe that in each iteration, the "sea" of cells with color 2 expands by one cell, while all cells with color 2 remain connected to each other horizontally or vertically. Therefore, after $t - 1$ iterations, V is convinced that there is an area of t cells with color 2 in the grid that are connected to each other.

3   Verifying Border Condition

Also, P needs to convince V that the number in each cell is equal to the number of edges of that cell that are borders of blocks. Note that this condition means if a cell contains a number x, then exactly $4 - x$ of its four neighbors (including the "dummy neighbors" outside the grid) must be in the same block as that cell. The following tools and subprotocols are necessary for this phase.

3.1   Enhanced Matrix

Starting from a $p \times q$ matrix of cards, publicly place cards $\boxed{1}$, $\boxed{2}$, ..., $\boxed{q}$ from left to right on top of Row 1; this new row is called Row 0. Then, place cards $\boxed{2}$, $\boxed{3}$, ..., $\boxed{p}$ from top to bottom (starting at Row 2) to the left of Column 1; this new column is called Column 0. This modified matrix is called a $p \times q$ *enhanced matrix* (see Fig. 5).

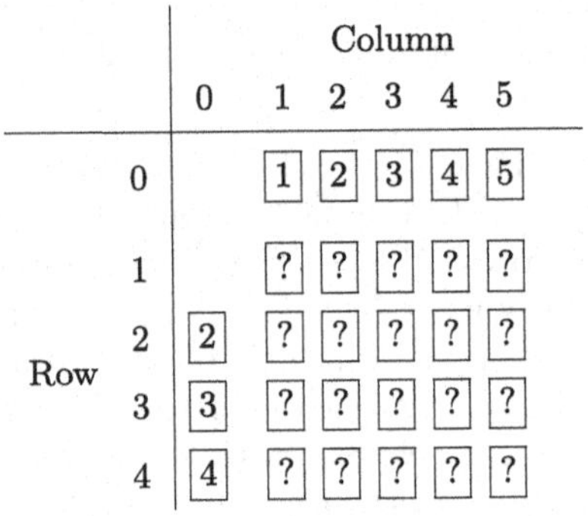

Fig. 5. A 4×5 enhanced matrix

3.2   Double-Scramble Shuffle

To perform a *double-scramble shuffle* [25] on a $p \times q$ enhanced matrix, first turn all cards face-down. Then, rearrange Columns $1, 2, ..., q$ (including Row 0) by a uniformly random permutation (which can be implemented in real world by putting the cards in each column into an envelope and scrambling all envelopes together). After that, leave Row 1 as it is and rearrange Rows $2, 3, ..., p$ (including Column 0) by a uniformly random permutation unknown to all parties.

3.3   Rearrangement Protocol

A *rearrangement protocol* [25] reverts an enhanced matrix back to its original state. To perform the rearrangement protocol on a $p \times q$ enhanced matrix, first apply the double-scramble shuffle to the matrix. Then, turn over all cards in Row 0 and rearrange the columns such that each card with number i will be in Column i. Analogously, turn over all cards in Column 0 and rearrange Rows $2, 3, ..., p$ accordingly.

3.4 Neighbor Counting Protocol

Suppose there are p sequences $E_q(y_1), E_q(y_2), ..., E_q(y_p)$ of cards, with $1 \leq y_1 \leq q$ and $0 \leq y_i \leq q$ for each $i = 2, 3, ..., p$. A *neighbor counting protocol* [25] allows P to show to V the number of indices $i \geq 2$ such that $y_i = y_1$ without revealing any other information about the sequences.

In the neighbor counting protocol, P performs the following steps.

1. Construct a $p \times q$ matrix with each Row i $(i = 1, 2, ..., p)$ consisting of the sequence $E_q(y_i)$.
2. Place cards in Row 0 and Column 0 to make the matrix become a $p \times q$ enhanced matrix M.
3. Apply the double-scramble shuffle to M.
4. Turn over all cards in Row 1. Locate the position of the only $\boxed{1}$. Suppose it is at Column j.
5. Turn over all cards in Column j (except Row 0). Count the number of $\boxed{1}$s besides the one in Row 1. This is the number of indices as desired.
6. Turn over all face-up cards and apply the rearrangement protocol to M.

4 Putting Together

Let $b = mn/5$ be the number of blocks in the Five Cells grid. Let $B_2, B_3, ..., B_{b+1}$ be the blocks in the grid.[1] The idea of our protocol is that P initially colors all cells with color 1. Then, for each $i = 2, 3, ..., b+1$, P will apply the sea formation protocol to change the color of each cell in B_i from color 1 to color i.

After that, for each cell with a number x written on it, P will apply the neighbor counting protocol to verify that exactly $4 - x$ of its neighbors have the same color as that cell.

The formal steps of our protocols are as follows.

Initially, P publicly places an $E_{b+1}(1)$ on every cell in the grid. P also publicly appends a row and a column of dummy stacks $E_k(0)$s to the bottom and to the right of the grid. Then, P turns all card face-down. We now have an $(m + 1) \times (n + 1)$ matrix of stacks.

In the first phase (to verify the connected area), for each $i = 2, 3, ..., b+1$, P performs the following steps.

1. Apply the chosen pile cut protocol (for $(m + 1)(n + 1)$ stacks) to select a desired $E_{b+1}(1)$ in block B_i.

---

[1] We intentionally start the indices at 2 so that our protocol will be more intuitive.

2. Reveal the selected stack that it is an $E_{b+1}(1)$ (otherwise V rejects) and replace it with an $E_{b+1}(i)$.
3. Perform the following steps for four iterations.
   (a) Apply the chosen pile cut protocol (for $(m+1)(n+1)$ stacks) to select a desired $E_{b+1}(i)$ in block B_i.
   (b) Reveal the selected stack that it is an $E_{b+1}(i)$ (otherwise V rejects).
   (c) Pick the four neighbors of the selected stack and apply the chosen pile cut protocol (for four stacks) to select a desired neighbor in block B_i.
   (d) Reveal the selected neighbor that it is an $E_{b+1}(1)$ (otherwise V rejects) and replace it with an $E_{b+1}(i)$.

Now V is convinced that the grid is partitioned into b disjoint blocks, each consisting of exactly five cells.

In the second phase (to verify the border condition), for each cell with a number x written on it, P performs the following steps.

1. Pick a sequence of cards on that cell. Call this sequence $E_{b+1}(y_1)$.
2. Pick the four neighbors of that cell (including dummy neighbors if that cell is on the grid boundary). Call these sequences $E_{b+1}(y_2)$, $E_{b+1}(y_3)$, $E_{b+1}(y_4)$, and $E_{b+1}(y_5)$.
3. Apply the neighbor counting protocol on the sequences $E_{b+1}(y_1)$, $E_{b+1}(y_2)$, ..., $E_{b+1}(y_5)$ to show that the number of indices $i \geq 2$ such that $y_i = y_1$ is $4 - x$ (otherwise V rejects).

Now V is convinced that each number satisfies the border condition of the puzzle. If both verification phases pass, then V accepts.

Our protocol uses $(b+3)(m+1)(n+1) + b + 13 = \Theta(bmn) = \Theta(m^2 n^2)$ cards.

5   Optimization

Our protocol in Sect. 4 requires $\Theta(m^2 n^2)$ cards, which is quadratic in the number of cells, making it impractical to implement in real world. Therefore, we will modify our protocol to reduce the number of required cards to linear in the number of cells.

The key idea is that P does not need to color the blocks with as many as b colors. If we view each block as a vertex and two vertices have en edge if the corresponding blocks touch each other horizontally or vertically, then the resulting graph is a planar graph. Using an appropriate algorithm such as the ones in [3,31], P can color this graph with five colors in linear time such that no two adjacent vertices have the same color.[2] Note that this coloring is known to only P but not V (as V must not know the structure of the graph).

An extra step to add is that, during the sea formation protocol, when coloring a block B_i with color c, P has to show that none of the cells in B_i is adjacent

---

[2] Although there is a polynomial time algorithm to 4-color any planar graph [19], the algorithm is very complicated and runs in quadratic time, making it impractical.

to a cell in another block with the same color c. To accommodate this, let the five colors used in P's 5-coloring be colors 3, 4, 5, 6, and 7. When coloring a block B_i, P first changes color of each cell in B_i from color 1 to color 2, and at the same time applies the neighbor counting protocol to show that none of its neighbor has color c. After all cells in B_i become color 2, P applies the chosen pile cut protocol five times, each time changing color of a cell with color 2 to color c. Note that a cell with color j is represented by a sequence $E_7(j)$.

However, this modified protocol has a major problem: it is not zero-knowledge. Since P reveals the color of each block, V will know the number of blocks having each color and thus will gain some information about the structure of the graph. For example, if P colors the blocks with only three colors, then V will gain information that the graph is 3-colorable.

We can prevent this by making the colors dynamic in a cyclic order: $7 \rightarrow 6 \rightarrow 5 \rightarrow 4 \rightarrow 3 \rightarrow 7$. Before P starts coloring each new block, the colors of all blocks will be shifted by a random cyclic shift known only to P. By doing this, V will gain no information about the number of blocks with each color, while the property that adjacent blocks must have different colors is still preserved.

We introduce the following subprotocol to shift the colors cyclically.

5.1   Color Shifting Protocol

A *color shifting protocol* shifts the colors of all cells in a cyclic order $7 \rightarrow 6 \rightarrow 5 \rightarrow 4 \rightarrow 3 \rightarrow 7$ by r steps for a uniformly random $r \in \{0, 1, 2, 3, 4\}$ known only to P. For instance, if $r = 1$, then all cells with color 7 will become color 6, all cells with color 6 will become color 5, and so on.

In the color shifting protocol, P performs the following steps.

1. Secretly choose a uniformly random integer $r \in \{0, 1, 2, 3, 4\}$.
2. Construct the following $5 \times (m+1)(n+1) + 1$ matrix M.
   (a) In Row 1, secretly place a sequence $E_5(r+1)$.
   (b) In each Row i ($i = 2, 3, ..., (m+1)(n+1) + 1$), publicly place a sequence consisting of five rightmost cards taken from from a sequence on each cell in the Five Cells grid.
3. Apply the pile-shifting shuffle to M.
4. Turn over all cards in Row 1. Locate the position of the only $\boxed{1}$. Shift the columns of M cyclically such that this $\boxed{1}$ moves to Column 1.
5. Place cards in Row $2, 3, ..., (m+1)(n+1) + 1$ back to their corresponding cells.

Note that this protocol shifts the color of each cell by r steps if it has color 3, 4, 5, 6, or 7; on the other hand, if a cell has color 0, 1, or 2, its color will not change.

5.2   Optimized Protocol

The formal steps of the optimized protocol are as follows.

Initially, P publicly places an $E_7(1)$ on every cell in the grid. P also publicly appends a row and a column of dummy stacks $E_7(0)$s to the bottom and to the right of the grid. Then, P turns all card face-down. We now have an $(m+1) \times (n+1)$ matrix of stacks.

In the first phase, for $i = 2, 3, ..., b+1$, P performs the following steps.

1. Apply the color shifting protocol and announce that P will color a block B_i with color $c \in \{3, 4, 5, 6, 7\}$.
2. Apply the chosen pile cut protocol (for $(m+1)(n+1)$ stacks) to select a desired $E_7(1)$ in block B_i.
3. Reveal the selected stack that it is an $E_7(1)$ (otherwise V rejects) and replace it with an $E_7(2)$.
4. Pick the four neighbors of the cell in Step 3 (including dummy neighbors if that cell is on the grid boundary). Apply the neighbor counting protocol on a sequence $E_7(c)$ and the four selected sequences to show that none of these four sequences is $E_7(c)$ (otherwise V rejects).
5. Perform the following steps for four iterations.
   (a) Apply the chosen pile cut protocol (for $(m+1)(n+1)$ stacks) to select a desired $E_7(2)$ in block B_i.
   (b) Reveal the selected stack that it is an $E_7(2)$ (otherwise V rejects).
   (c) Pick the four neighbors of the selected stack and apply the chosen pile cut protocol (for four stacks) to select a desired neighbor in block B_i.
   (d) Reveal the selected neighbor that it is an $E_7(1)$ (otherwise V rejects) and replace it with an $E_7(2)$.
   (e) Pick the four neighbors of the cell in Step 5(d) (including dummy neighbors if that cell is on the grid boundary). Apply the neighbor counting protocol on a sequence $E_7(c)$ and the four selected sequences to show that none of these four sequences is $E_7(c)$ (otherwise V rejects).
6. Perform the following steps for five iterations.
   (a) Apply the chosen pile cut protocol (for $(m+1)(n+1)$ stacks) to select a desired $E_7(2)$ in block B_i.
   (b) Reveal the selected stack that it is an $E_7(2)$ (otherwise V rejects) and replace it with an $E_7(c)$.

Note that in Steps 2 to 5, P changes the color of all cells in B_i from color 1 to color 2, while also verifying that none of them is adjacent to a cell with color c. Then, in Step 6, P changes the color of all cells in B_i from color 2 to color c.

In the second phase, the optimized protocol works exactly the same way as in the original protocol in Sect. 4 (except the size of the matrix). If both verification phases pass, then V accepts.

The optimized protocol uses $9(m+1)(n+1) + 26 = \Theta(mn)$ cards, which is linear in the number of cells.

6   Proof of Correctness and Security

We will prove the perfect completeness, perfect soundness, and zero-knowledge properties of the optimized protocol.

Lemma 1 (Perfect Completeness). *If P knows a solution of the Five Cells puzzle, then V always accepts.*

Proof. Suppose P knows a solution of the puzzle. In P's solution, P picks a 5-coloring of the blocks such that adjacent blocks always have different colors.

Consider the first phase for each block B_i. After applying the color shifting protocol, suppose that the color of B_i according to P's 5-coloring becomes color c. Since the color shifting protocol only shifts the colors in a cyclic order $7 \rightarrow 6 \rightarrow 5 \rightarrow 4 \rightarrow 3 \rightarrow 7$, the property that adjacent blocks must have different colors is still preserved. Therefore, none of the cell in B_i is adjacent to a cell with color c, so the first phase will pass.

Now consider the second phase for each cell α with color c and with a number x. Since P's solution is correct, exactly x edges of α are borders of blocks, meaning that exactly x of α's neighbors are in adjacent blocks (or are dummy cells) and thus cannot have color c. Therefore, exactly $4 - x$ of α's neighbors are in the same block and thus have color c, so the second phase will pass.

Hence, we can conclude that V always accepts.   □

Lemma 2 (Perfect Soundness). *If P does not know a solution of the Five Cells puzzle, then V always rejects.*

Proof. We will prove the contrapositive of this statement. Suppose that V accepts, meaning that the coloring phase passes for every iteration, and the verification of the border condition passes for every numbered cell.

Consider each iteration of the first phase. In Steps 2 to 5, P selects five cells with color 1 that are connected horizontally or vertically, and changes them to color 2. P also shows that none of these cells is adjacent to a cell with color c. After that, in Step 6, P selects five cells with color 2 and changes them to color c. As the cells that have been colored in previous iterations must have color 3, 4, 5, 6, or 7, and the cells that have not been colored must have color 1, the only cells with color 2 are the exact five cells P selected in this iteration. Therefore, at the end of this iteration, a new block of five connected cells with color c that is not adjacent to any other block with color c is formed.

After b iterations, the grid is now partitioned into b blocks, each consisting of five cells. Since the color shifting protocol only shifts the colors in a cyclic order $7 \rightarrow 6 \rightarrow 5 \rightarrow 4 \rightarrow 3 \rightarrow 7$, the property that adjacent blocks must have different colors is still preserved.

Now consider the second phase for each cell α with color c and with a number x. Since the verification passes, exactly $4 - x$ of α's neighbors must have color c. However, cells in adjacent blocks (or dummy cells) cannot have color c, which means these $4 - x$ cells must be in the same block as α. Therefore, exactly x edges of α are borders of blocks. Since the verification passes for every numbered cell, the border condition must hold for every numbered cell.

Hence, we can conclude that P knows a correct solution of the puzzle.   □

Lemma 3 (Zero-Knowledge). *During the verification, V obtains no information about P's solution.*

Proof. We will prove that the interaction between P and V can be simulated by a simulator S that does not know P's solution.

First, we will prove the zero-knowledge property of the three subprotocols used in our main protocol: the chosen pile cut protocol in Sect. 2.3, the neighbor counting protocol in Sect. 3.4, and the color shifting protocol in Sect. 5.1. In these subprotocols, it is sufficient to show that all distributions of cards that are turned face-up can be simulated by S.

- In Steps 3 and 6 of the chosen pile cut protocol, the $\boxed{1}$ has an equal probability to be at any of the q columns (due to the pile-shifting shuffles), so these two steps can be simulated by S.
- In Step 4 of the neighbor counting protocol, the $\boxed{1}$ has an equal probability to be at any of the q columns (due to the double-scramble shuffle), so this step can be simulated by S.
- In Step 5 of the neighbor counting protocol, suppose there are t $\boxed{1}$s besides the one in Row 1 (t is public information). The order of Rows $2, 3, ..., p$ is uniformly distributed among all possible permutations (due to the double-scramble shuffle). Hence, all t $\boxed{1}$s have an equal probability to be at any of the $\binom{p-1}{t}$ combinations of rows, so this step can be simulated by S.
- In Step 4 of the color shifting protocol, the $\boxed{1}$ has an equal probability to be at any of the five columns (as r is uniformly selected from $\{0,1,2,3,4\}$ at random), so this step can be simulated by S.

Now consider our main (optimized) protocol.

- In Step 1, 5(e) and 6(b), the information V receives solely depends on the value of c. However, c has an equal probability to be any element of $\{3,4,5,6,7\}$ (due to the color shifting protocol), so this step can be simulated by S.
- In Steps 3, 5(b), 5(d), and 6(b), there is only one deterministic pattern of the cards that are turned face-up, so these steps can be simulated by S.

Hence, we can conclude that V obtains no information about P's solution.

□

7   Future Work

We constructed a card-based ZKP protocol for Five Cells, and also developed an optimization technique to reduce the number of required cards in our protocol from quadratic to linear in the number of cells.

Some existing card-based ZKP protocols for other logic puzzles, such as the one for Numberlink [25], require the number of cards quadratic in the number of cells. These protocols have a common theme that it involves partitioning a grid into several parts (where the number of parts can be linear in the number of cells) and coloring each part with a color different from each other. Therefore, the number of cards on each cell is also linear in the number of cells (due to the encoding rule in Sect. 2.1), resulting in the total number of cards quadratic. A future work is to apply our optimization technique to reduce the total number of cards in these protocols from quadratic to linear.

A   Alternative ZKP Protocol for Five Cells

For the sake of completeness, we also provide an alternative ZKP protocol for Five Cells. This protocol takes a completely different approach from our first protocol. It is based on the fact that there are only $\Theta(1)$ different types of pentomino. Namely, there are 63 of them.[3] Furthermore, inside each pentomino, a number in each cell according to the border condition of Five Cells is fixed, which is exactly the number of edges of that cell that are borders of the pentomino.

In this protocol, P first creates 63 *templates*, one for each type of pentomino. A template consists of a 5×5 matrix of card. In each template, a cell inside the pentomino is represented by a card with a number equal to the number of edges of that cell that are borders of the pentomino, while a cell outside the pentomino is represented by a $\boxed{5}$ (see Fig. 6).

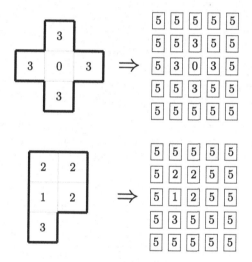

Fig. 6. Templates of the X-shaped pentomino and the P-shaped pentomino

The idea of this protocol is that P initially places a $\boxed{5}$ on each cell in the Five Cells grid. Then, P applies the following *printing protocol* to "print" each pentomino from a template onto the grid one by one for b times.

---

[3] A pentomino obtained by rotating or reflecting another pentomino is considered a different one.

A.1   Printing Protocol

Suppose we have a template of a pentomino, and another 5×5 matrix of cards from the Five Cells grid. A *printing protocol* verifies that an area from the grid corresponding to the pentomino is initially empty, then prints the numbers inside the pentomino from the template onto that area.

In the printing protocol, P performs the following steps.

1. Place each card from the template on top of each corresponding card from the grid, creating 25 stacks of two cards.
2. Perform the following steps for five iterations.
   (a) Apply the chosen pile cut protocol (for 25 stacks) to select a desired stack.
   (b) Reveal the bottom card of the stack that it is a $\boxed{5}$ (otherwise V rejects).
   (c) Swap the top card and bottom card of that stack.
3. Remove the top cards of all stacks and reveal that they are all $\boxed{5}$s (otherwise V rejects).

A.2   Main Protocol

The formal steps of the protocol are as follows.

Initially, P publicly places a $\boxed{5}$ on every cell in the grid. To handle edge cases, P also publicly appends four rows and four columns of "dummy cards" $\boxed{6}$ s to the bottom and to the right of the grid. Then, P turns all card face-down. We now have an $(m + 4) \times (n + 4)$ matrix of cards.

In addition, P prepares 63 templates of all 63 types of pentomino and lets V verify that the templates are correct (otherwise V rejects).

For $i = 2, 3, ..., b + 1$, P performs the following steps.

1. Apply the chosen pile cut protocol (for $(m+4)(n+4)$ stacks) to select a 5×5 area containing block B_i. (To be precise, P actually selects just the top-left corner cell of the area, and the rest will follow as the chosen pile cut protocol preserves the cyclic order).
2. Apply the chosen pile cut protocol (for 63 stacks) to select a template of a pentomino with the same type as block B_i. Apply the printing protocol on the selected template and the selected area to print numbers onto block B_i.
3. Reconstruct a template that has been used and replenish the pile of templates with it. Let V verify again that all 63 templates are correct (otherwise V rejects). Note that V does not know which template has been used.

Finally, P reveals all cards on the cells that contain a number (in the original Five Cell puzzle). V verifies that the numbers on the cards match the numbers on the cells (otherwise V rejects). If all verification steps pass, then V accepts.

While this protocol also uses $\Theta(mn)$ cards, the number of required cards is only $4mn + \Theta(m + n)$, which is asymptotically better than that of our first protocol.

Acknowledgement. The author would like to thank the anonymous reviewers who kindly suggested the idea of the alternative protocol in Appendix A.

References

1. Bultel, X., Dreier, J., Dumas, J.G., Lafourcade, P.: Physical zero-knowledge proofs for Akari, Takuzu, Kakuro and KenKen. In: Proceedings of the 8th International Conference on Fun with Algorithms (FUN), pp. 8:1–8:20 (2016)
2. Bultel, X., et al.: Physical zero-knowledge proof for Makaro. In: Proceedings of the 20th International Symposium on Stabilization, Safety, and Security of Distributed Systems (SSS), pp. 111–125 (2018)
3. Chiba, N., Nishizeki, T., Saito, N.: A linear 5-coloring algorithm of planar graphs. J. Algorithms 2(4), 317–327 (1981)
4. Chien, Y.-F., Hon, W.-K.: Cryptographic and physical zero-knowledge proof: from Sudoku to Nonogram. In: Proceedings of the 5th International Conference on Fun with Algorithms (FUN), pp. 102–112 (2010)
5. Dumas, J.-G., Lafourcade, P., Miyahara, D., Mizuki, T., Sasaki, T., Sone, H.: Interactive physical zero-knowledge proof for Norinori. In: Du, D.-Z., Duan, Z., Tian, C. (eds.) COCOON 2019. LNCS, vol. 11653, pp. 166–177. Springer, Cham (2019). https://doi.org/10.1007/978-3-030-26176-4_14
6. Fukusawa, T., Manabe, Y.: Card-based zero-knowledge proof for the nearest neighbor property: zero-knowledge proof of ABC end view. In: Proceedings of the 12th International Conference on Security, Privacy and Applied Cryptographic Engineering (SPACE), pp. 147–161 (2022)
7. Goldwasser, S., Micali, S., Rackoff, C.: The knowledge complexity of interactive proof systems. SIAM J. Comput. 18(1), 186–208 (1989)
8. Gradwohl, R., Naor, M., Pinkas, B., Rothblum, G.N.: Cryptographic and physical zero-knowledge proof systems for solutions of sudoku puzzles. Theory Comput. Syst. 44(2), 245–268 (2009)
9. Iwamoto, C., Ide, T.: Five cells and tilepaint are NP-complete. IEICE Trans. Inf. Syst. 105-D(3), 508–516 (2022)
10. Koch, A., Walzer, S.: Foundations for actively secure card-based cryptography. In: Proceedings of the 10th International Conference on Fun with Algorithms (FUN), pp. 17:1–17:23 (2020)
11. Lafourcade, P., Miyahara, D., Mizuki, T., Robert, L., Sasaki, T., Sone, H.: How to construct physical zero-knowledge proofs for puzzles with a "single loop" condition. Theoret. Comput. Sci. 888, 41–55 (2021)
12. Miyahara, D., et al.: Card-based ZKP protocols for Takuzu and Juosan. In: Proceedings of the 10th International Conference on Fun with Algorithms (FUN), pp. 20:1–20:21 (2020)
13. Miyahara, D., Sasaki, T., Mizuki, T., Sone, H.: Card-based physical zero-knowledge proof for kakuro. IEICE Trans. Fundam. Electron. Commun. Comput. Sci. E102.A(9), 1072–1078 (2019)
14. Nikoli: Five Cells. www.nikoli.co.jp/en/puzzles/five_cells/
15. Robert, L., Miyahara, D., Lafourcade, P., Libralesso, L., Mizuki, T.: Physical zero-knowledge proof and NP-completeness proof of Suguru puzzle. Inf. Comput. 285(B), 104858 (2022)
16. Robert, L., Miyahara, D., Lafourcade, P., Mizuki, T.: Card-based ZKP for connectivity: applications to nurikabe, Hitori, and Heyawake. N. Gener. Comput. 40(1), 149–171 (2022)
17. Robert, L., Miyahara, D., Lafourcade, P., Mizuki, T.: Card-based ZKP protocol for Nurimisaki. In: Devismes, S., Petit, F., Altisen, K., Di Luna, G.A., Fernandez Anta, A. (eds.) SSS 2022. LNCS, vol. 13751, pp. 285–298. Springer, Cham (2022). https://doi.org/10.1007/978-3-031-21017-4_19

18. Robert, L., Miyahara, D., Lafourcade, P., Mizuki, T.: Hide a liar: card-based ZKP protocol for Usowan. In: Du, D.Z., Du, D., Wu, C., Xu, D. (eds.) Theory and Applications of Models of Computation (TAMC). LNCS, vol. 13571, pp. 201–217. Springer, Cham (2022). https://doi.org/10.1007/978-3-031-20350-3_17

19. Robertson, N., Sanders, D.P., Seymour, P., Thomas, R.: Efficiently four-coloring planar graphs. In: Proceedings of the 28th Annual ACM Symposium on Theory of Computing (STOC), pp. 571–575 (1996)

20. Ruangwises, S.: An improved physical ZKP for Nonogram and Nonogram color. J. Comb. Optim. **45**(5), 122 (2023)

21. Ruangwises, S.: Physical zero-knowledge proof for ball sort puzzle. In: Proceedings of the 19th Conference on Computability in Europe (CiE), pp. 246–257 (2023)

22. Ruangwises, S.: Physically verifying the first nonzero term in a sequence: physical ZKPs for ABC end view and Goishi Hiroi. In: Proceedings of the 17th Conference on Frontiers of Algorithmic Wisdom (FAW), pp. 171–183 (2023)

23. Ruangwises, S.: Two standard decks of playing cards are sufficient for a ZKP for Sudoku. N. Gener. Comput. **40**(1), 49–65 (2022)

24. Ruangwises, S., Itoh, T.: How to physically verify a rectangle in a grid: a physical ZKP for Shikaku. In: Proceedings of the 11th International Conference on Fun with Algorithms (FUN), pp. 24:1–24:12 (2022)

25. Ruangwises, S., Itoh, T.: Physical zero-knowledge proof for Numberlink puzzle and k vertex-disjoint paths problem. N. Gener. Comput. **39**(1), 3–17 (2021)

26. Ruangwises, S., Itoh, T.: Physical zero-knowledge proof for ripple effect. Theoret. Comput. Sci. **895**, 115–123 (2021)

27. Ruangwises, S., Itoh, T.: Physical ZKP for connected spanning subgraph: applications to bridges puzzle and other problems. In: Proceedings of the 19th International Conference on Unconventional Computation and Natural Computation (UCNC), pp. 149–163 (2021)

28. Ruangwises, S., Itoh, T.: Physical ZKP for Makaro using a standard deck of cards. In: Proceedings of the 17th Annual Conference on Theory and Applications of Models of Computation (TAMC), pp. 43–54 (2022)

29. Sasaki, T., Miyahara, D., Mizuki, T., Sone, H.: Efficient card-based zero-knowledge proof for Sudoku. Theoret. Comput. Sci. **839**, 135–142 (2020)

30. Shinagawa, K., et al.: Card-based protocols using regular polygon cards. IEICE Trans. Fundam. Electron. Commun. Comput. Sci. **E100.A**(9), 1900–1909 (2017)

31. Thomassen, C.: Every planar graph is 5-choosable. J. Comb. Theory Ser. B **62**(1), 180–181 (1994)

32. Ueda, I., Miyahara, D., Nishimura, A., Hayashi, Y., Mizuki, T., Sone, H.: Secure implementations of a random bisection cut. Int. J. Inf. Secur. **19**(4), 445–452 (2020)

Testudo: Linear Time Prover SNARKs with Constant Size Proofs and Square Root Size Universal Setup

Matteo Campanelli[1(✉)], Nicolas Gailly[2], Rosario Gennaro[3], Philipp Jovanovic[4], Mara Mihali[5], and Justin Thaler[6]

[1] Protocol Labs, Aarhus, Denmark
matteo@protocol.ai
[2] Aarhus, Denmark
[3] Protocol Labs & CCNY, Aarhus, Denmark
rosario.gennaro@protocol.ai
[4] UCL, London, UK
p.jovanovic@ucl.ac.uk
[5] Aztec Labs, Johannesburg, South Africa
mara@aztecprotocol.com
[6] Georgetown & a16z Crypto Research, Washington, D.C., USA
justin.thaler@georgetown.edu

Abstract. We present Testudo, a new FFT-less SNARK with a near linear-time prover, constant-time verifier, constant-size proofs and a square-root-size universal setup. Testudo is based on a variant of Spartan [28]–and hence does not require FFTs–as well as a new, fast multivariate polynomial commitment scheme (PCS) with a square-root-sized trusted setup that is derived from PST [25] and IPPs [9]. To achieve constant-size SNARK proofs in Testudo we then combine our PCS openings proofs recursively with a Groth16 SNARK. We also evaluate Testudo and its building blocks: to compute a PCS opening proof for a polynomial of size 2^{25}, our new scheme opening procedure achieves a 110x speed-up compared to PST and 3x compared to Gemini [6], since opening computations are heavily parallelizable and operate on smaller polynomials. Furthermore, a Testudo proof for a witness of size $2^{30} (\approx 1\,\text{GB})$ requires a setup of size only 2^{15} ($\approx$tens of kilobytes). Finally, we show that a Testudo variant for proving data-parallel computations is almost 10x faster at verifying 2^{10} Poseidon-based Merkle tree opening proofs than the regular version.

1 Introduction

Succinct Non-Interactive Arguments of Knowledge (SNARKs) have been a prolific area of research in the last decade: a SNARK allows a prover to prove to a verifier that a certain (non-deterministic) computation F has been performed correctly, or more specifically that there exists a *witness w* such that $y =' F(x, w)$

N. Gailly—Work done mainly while the author was affiliated with Protocol Labs.
M. Mihali—Work done mainly while the author was affiliated with UCL and Protocol Labs.

where x is a public input. The crucial property of SNARKs is that the size of the proof and the verification time should be *short*, i.e., sublinear in the size of the computation F and of the witness w. Otherwise a simple proof would be to send w and have the verifier recompute $F(x, w)$. Additionally, SNARKs can be zero-knowledge, i.e., they do not reveal any information about w.

SNARKs are evaluated according to various performance metrics where the three most important ones are (1) the time it takes the prover to generate a proof, (2) the size of the proof, and (3) the time it takes the verifier to validate a proof. There are various design trade-offs that can be explored to optimize those metrics and an essential distinguishing factor that impacts performance are the preprocessing phases of SNARK systems.

On the one end of the spectrum, there is, for example, the Groth16 SNARK [18] which produces proofs consisting of only 3 group elements and which has a verification that is independent of the complexity of F, only requiring the evaluation of a few pairings. This makes Groth16 essentially optimal in terms of proof size and verifier time but it comes at the expense of a super-linear overhead in prover time and a function-specific trusted setup, the latter of which is a serious drawback in practice. On the other end are (*transparent*) SNARKs that do not require a trusted setup [5,8,32] at all but they tend to have larger proofs and verifier times, e.g., at least logarithmic in the size of the witness. Finally, there are (*universal*) SNARKS which offer a compromise, as they permit smaller proofs in comparison to transparent systems at the cost of a single setup that is universal enabling them to prove any circuit up to a certain size [19]. However, these schemes are still suboptimal as they have slower provers than Groth16 [12], which becomes particularly evident for large circuits [34], and they do not have constant size proofs or verification times. Finally, all of the schemes with a trusted setup produce a linear-size common reference string (CRS) which is particularly problematic for large circuits (again), as the CRS has to be downloaded, stored, and moved into RAM at proving time. For example, Filecoin [21] uses Groth16 for circuits of size $\approx 2^{30}$ but producing a trusted setup for this size was practically infeasible. As a workaround, provers work with (sub-)circuits of size $\approx 2^{27}$ and generate ≈ 10 proofs per (large) circuit.

In summary, all of these observations led us to the following research question:

Can we design a SNARK with a small universal trusted setup, constant size proofs and verification time, and a fast prover?[1]

1.1   Contributions

In this section we present our main contributions together with an informal overview of the techniques used to achieve them.

Testudo: Near-Linear Time Prover with Succinct Verification. To achieve this goal, we start our design from Spartan [28] a sumcheck-based argument requiring only field arithmetic (e.g. much faster that its point counterpart) and

---

[1] To maximize backward compatibility to already deployed systems, we require that our SNARK system works with R1CS-based circuits.

a single multilinear polynomial opening. The original Spartan is a transparent scheme which relies only on discrete based log curves and transparent polynomial commitment schemes, giving substantially larger proof sizes and verification times ($\approx \sqrt{N}$). To improve on those, the main idea is to have a Groth16 prover verifying the Spartan proof. Below we describe the technical challenges of this approach, but one important thing to note here is that in order to obtain a ZK-SNARK it is sufficient to run the (much simpler and more efficient) non-ZK version of Spartan since the outer Groth16 proof will hide any information possibly leaked by the non-ZK inner Spartan proof.

Embedding the verification of a Spartan-based SNARK in a Groth16 circuit presents various implementation challenges. The sumcheck component of the proof operates only on field elements and requires the use of a hash function to make it non-interactive via Fiat Shamir. Field operations can be natively encoded in R1CS constraints and we adapted our codebase to use Poseidon, a SNARK friendly hash function, having the advantage of a more efficient representation in a circuit. However, things get more complicated for writing the R1CS constraints for the verification of the polynomial commitment opening, since it requires point arithmetic which, if naively encoded in the circuit, would massively increase the number of constraints by multiple orders of magnitude. This issue would be amplified by the relative large size of Spartan's original commitment's proof size and verification – $O(\sqrt{N})$ – which can potentially be reduced if we leverage using a different PCS with a trusted setup.

WHY THE NAME TESTUDO? Testudo was a type of battle formation that ancient Rome adopted, where its soldiers operated "under the hood" of their shields. Testudo, the proof scheme, is similar: a Spartan prover working under the hood of Groth16.

Testudo-Comm: New Multivariate Polynomial Commitment Scheme.

To reduce the size of the PCS opening, we devise a new polynomial commitment scheme based on PST [25] and inner pairing product [9] that avoids the use of FFTs. Testudo, as Spartan, considers circuits of size $N = 2^n$ where the polynomial representation of the circuit has n variables, n is logarithmic and so N will be linear in the size of the circuit. The high level idea is to express the coefficients of the witness multivariate polynomial from Spartan as a square matrix of size $\sqrt{N} \times \sqrt{N}$. To commit to this polynomial, the prover commits to each row of the matrix using PST, leading to a vector $\vec{A}$ of size $\sqrt{N}$. Then the prover commits to $\vec{A}$ using the MIPP commitment in [9] (e.g., a pairing product between commitments and random base) to create the final commitment T - a single group element. To open, the prover carefully performs PST and MIPP opening on $\sqrt{N}$ sized polynomials with many operations in parallel. Both the MIPP and PST part operate on $\sqrt{N}$ sized polynomials.

Since the 2 opening operations can be done in parallel we obtain a considerable speedup in practice (about 2 orders of magnitude faster) than PST, even though it requires heavier operations like $\log N$ pairings to create the combined commitment. Moreover, when comparing with Gemini [6], we estimate our opening procedure to be 3x faster for large N such as 2^{25}, where [6] is likely faster for small sizes, with the additional cost that it requires to perform FFTs for practical deployment.

Usage of 2-Chain Curves for Efficient Verification. To enable verifying group operations in a circuit, we use the standard approach of running Spartan over a 2-chain curve (such as BLS12-377) where group elements can be encoded as field elements in a companion curve over which the Groth16 prover is then implemented. For backwards compatibility reason, we also explored the possibility to run Testudo on curves without a companion curve (such as BLS12-381, which is currently used by Filecoin proofs).

Aggregation. Additionally, we show how Testudo proofs can be aggregated. Since the outer layer is a Groth16 proof, we can use standard aggregation tools such as SnarkPack [16] to aggregate several Groth16 proofs together. Another option is to aggregate proofs at the inner level and then run a single Groth16 proof on top of the aggregated inner proofs.

Note that an interesting point of this design is that the Groth16 prover can be outsourced to more powerful machines or a "prover-as-a-service" infrastructure. Indeed, if the "Spartan" prover ran the sumcheck and the commitment opening, then resulting proof already hides the witness thanks to the zero knowledge property of Spartan. As a consequence, more powerful machine can aggregate many of these "semi" proofs inside one Groth16 proof, without ever seeing the witness, similar to how Snarkpack works. This settings has practical implications in terms of deployment that we believe are worth exploring.

Analysis and Experimental Results. As explained in the body of the paper, our SNARK avoids the use of FFT altogether and obtains a nearly linear-time prover[2]. In practice, we show that:

- Our polynomial commitment scheme has a commitment time comparable to PST while producing opening proofs at two order of magnitude faster (at the cost of larger proof sizes).
- Our experimental results show that for data parallel circuits, we can estimate Testudo to run more than $\approx$5x to $\approx$10x faster than the fastest Groth16 implementation (i.e., Bellperson [4]), depending on the size of the small subcircuit. For example, if the sub-circuit is of size 2^{15}, as an upper bound to a circuit verifying a Poseidon based Merkle Tree opening proofs with 32 layers, then Testudo can verify 2^{10} such proofs $\approx$9.7x faster than the Groth16 equivalent.

1.2   Related Work

The literature on SNARKs is very large and we refer the reader to Thaler's monograph [30] for a comprehensive survey. In this section we focus on a few works that are relevant to Testudo.

---

[2] Our prover runs N multi-exponentiations of size N, which is roughly $O(N\frac{\lambda}{\log N})$ group operations with $\lambda > \log N$ for security reason.

We were inspired to use a 1-level recursion with Groth16 verifying a faster inner SNARK by the work of Belling et al. [3] where the verification of a GKR proof [17] for hash computations is outsourced to a Groth16 prover. Concurrently to our efforts, a similar approach was also taken in the ZKBridge paper [31], where the verification of a Virgo [32] proof is outsourced to a Groth16 prover. Because Virgo is also GKR-based, the underlying SNARK in either case is known to be efficient for large "parallel" computations. We believe we are the first to apply this approach to a general purpose SNARK like Spartan.

When it comes to universal trusted setup proofs, many systems today do not use R1CS but rather "custom gates" (sometimes also called Plonkish arithmetization), and apply SNARKs such as Plonk [15] (or alternatives such as Hyperplonk [11]) to the resulting constraint systems. The use of "custom gates" makes a comparison to pure R1CS-based schemes not immediate. We are still working on achieving meaningful comparisons but we estimate that Testudo is competitive with approaches that do use custom gates. We point out that many applications (including our main motivating one – Filecoin proofs) are already encoded as R1CS systems, and therefore it is very useful to have an efficient SNARK with universal trusted setup that can be used off-the-shelves.

Our new PCS Testudo-Comm leverages ideas from [16] and [9] to reduce the size of the trusted setup for the KZG univariate polynomial commitment [20] to square-root size from linear. We adapted them to achieve the same reduction for the PST commitment. We note that, as far as we know, we are the first to implement these techniques. We also point out that the reduction of the trusted setup size comes at the expense of larger opening proofs: however in our case that drawback is "absorbed" by the outer Groth16 proof, which compresses the final proof down to constant.

The work in [6] presents a generic transformation to turn a univariate polynomial commitment into a multilinear one. In Sect. 4 we discuss why we believe using Testudo-Comm is a better choice for us.

2 Preliminaries

We assume the reader is familiar with the definitions of R1CS, Polynomial Commitment Schemes and SNARKs.

2.1 Notation

We assume we have cyclic groups $\mathbb{G}_1, \mathbb{G}_2, \mathbb{G}_T$ of order q generated by g and equipped with a bilinear pairing $e : \mathbb{G}_1 \times \mathbb{G}_2 \to \mathbb{G}_T$. We denote by $p(x_1, \ldots, x_n)$ a multilinear polynomial with n variables. For $s_1, \ldots, s_n \in \mathbb{Z}_q$ we write $\vec{s} = (s_1, \ldots, s_n) \in \mathbb{Z}_q^n$. Let $i \in \{0, 1\}^n$, we can denote $i = (i_1 \ldots i_n)$ as $i_j \in \{0, 1\}$. We denote the value $\prod_j s_j^{i_j}$ by $\vec{s}^{\,i}$

2.2 Cryptographic Assumptions

The security of our constructions holds in the Generic Group Model (GGM) [29]. In Sect. 4 and Sect. 5 we rely on the security of the underlying building to claim that of our protocols. The security of these building blocks can be argued from assumptions implied by the GGM. In more detail: • for PST we require the $(\mu + 1)\delta$-Strong Diffie-Hellman and the (δ, μ)-Extended Power Knowledge of Exponent assumption (see [33] and discussion in [10, E.1]). • for MIPP we require a variant of the (q, m)-Auxiliary Structured Single Group Pairing (see [9]).

2.3 PST Polynomial Commitments

We refer the reader to Sect. 2.1 for the notation we use in this section. In Fig. 1 we describe the PST polynomial commitment modified to work over the Lagrange basis [25].

Trusted setup: Let $t_1, \ldots, t_n$ be random values in $\mathbb{Z}_q$. The CRS consists of the N values $g_1^{\chi_i(t)}$ where $\chi_i(X_1, \ldots, X_n) = [\Pi_{j:i_j=1} X_j][\Pi_{j:i_j=0}(1 - X_j)]$ for $i \in \{0,1\}^n$ the multilinear Lagrange polynomial. The CRS also includes the values $g_2^{t_j}$ for $j = 1, 2, \ldots, n$.

Commitment: $Com(p) = g_1^{p(t)} = C$ which can be evaluated given the values of p on the Boolean hypercube and the CRS.

Opening: To prove that $y = p(\vec{a})$ where $\vec{a} = (a_1, \ldots, a_n)$ the prover computes the polynomials $q_i(\vec{x})$ such that

$$p(\vec{x}) - y = \Sigma_i (x_i - a_i) q_i(\vec{x})$$

by repeated polynomial division (note that in reality $q_i(\vec{x}) = q_i(x_i, \ldots, x_n)$, i.e., only of the last $n - i$ variables). The proof is then the vector $\vec{w} = (w_1, \ldots, w_n)$ where $w_i = g_1^{q_i(t)}$ which can be computed given the polynomials q_i and the CRS.

Verification: To verify that $y = p(\vec{w})$ given $\vec{w}$, the verifier checks that

$$e(Cg^{-y}, g) = \Pi_i e(w_i, g_2^{t_i - a_i}) .$$

Fig. 1. The PST commitment scheme in the Lagrange basis.

Note that if $n = \log N$ where N is the size of the R1CS, then the trusted setup is linear in the size of the circuit, and that verification of the opening requires $O(n)$ (i.e., logarithmic in the size of the circuit) work.

P sends the polynomial $p_1(x) = \sum_{i \in \{0,1\}^{n-1}} p(x, i)$.
V checks that $p_1(0) + p_1(1) = a$ and sends back $r_1 \in_R \mathbb{F}$.
P sends the polynomial $p_2(x) = \sum_{i \in \{0,1\}^{n-2}} p(r_1, x, i)$.
V checks that $p_2(0) + p_2(1) = p_1(r_1)$ and sends back $r_2 \in_R \mathbb{F}$.
...

At round j P sends the polynomial $p_j(x) = \sum_{i \in \{0,1\}^{n-j}} p(r_1, \ldots, r_{j-1}, x, i)$.
V checks that $p_j(0) + p_j(1) = p_{j-1}(r_{j-1})$ and sends back $r_j \in_R \mathbb{F}$.
...

At the last round P sends the polynomial $p_{n-1}(x) = p(r_1, \ldots, r_{n-1}, x)$.
V checks that $p_{n-1}(0) + p_{n-1}(1) = p_{n-2}(r_{n-2})$, selects $r_n \in_R \mathbb{F}$ and checks that $p_{n-1}(r_n) = p(r_1, \ldots, r_n)$ via a single query to p.

Fig. 2. The Sumcheck Protocol

2.4 Sumcheck

Let $p(x_1 \ldots, x_n)$ be a multilinear[3] polynomial in n variables defined over a field $\mathbb{F}$. Consider the value $a = \sum_{i \in \{0,1\}^n} p(i)$, i.e., the sum of the value of p on all the vertices of the Boolean hypercube. This computation takes $N = 2^n$ time and the sumcheck protocol [22] described in Fig. 2, is a way for a Prover to convince a Verifier that a is correct in $O(n)$ time, plus a *single* query to the polynomial p on a random point in $\mathbb{F}^n$.

2.5 Spartan Overview

In this section we review Spartan [28], a transparent SNARK for R1CS. For space reasons, ours is a very high level review and the reader is referred to [28] for details.

Recall that a R1CS instance $(\mathbb{F}, A, B, C, x, N, m)$ is satisfiable if there exists a witness $w \in \mathbb{F}^{N-|x|-1}$ such that

$$(A \cdot z) \circ (B \cdot z) = (C \cdot z)$$

where $z = (x, 1, w)$, $\cdot$ is the matrix-vector product, and $\circ$ is the Hadamard (entry-wise) product.

The first step in Spartan is to encode the matrices A, B, C and the vector z via their multilinear polynomial extensions. Let $n = \log N$. For the matrix A consider the unique multilinear polynomial in $2n$ variable $\tilde{A}(t_1, \ldots, t_n, u_1, \ldots, u_n)$ such that $\tilde{A}(i_1, \ldots, i_n, j_1, \ldots, j_n) = A(i, j)$ where $(i_1, \ldots, i_n)$ is the binary expansion of i and $(j_1, \ldots, j_n)$ is the binary expansion of j. The polynomials $\tilde{B}, \tilde{C}$ are defined similarly, as well as the polynomial $\tilde{Z}(u_1, \ldots, u_n)$ where $Z(i_1, \ldots, i_n) = z(i)$.

---

[3] We only care about multilinear polynomials for Testudo but the sumcheck protocol can be run on any multivariate polynomial.

The satisfiability condition is then equivalent to the following polynomial $F(t_1, \ldots, t_n)$ being zero on all the points of the Boolean hypercube

$$F(\vec{t}) = \left(\sum_{\vec{u} \in \{0,1\}^n} \tilde{A}(\vec{t}, \vec{u}) \tilde{Z}(\vec{u}) \right) \cdot \left(\sum_{\vec{u} \in \{0,1\}^n} \tilde{B}(\vec{t}, \vec{u}) \tilde{Z}(\vec{u}) \right) - \sum_{\vec{u} \in \{0,1\}^n} \tilde{C}(\vec{t}, \vec{u}) \tilde{Z}(\vec{u})$$

Consider now the *multilinear extension*[4] of $F(\cdot)$, that is the polynomial $Q(\vec{s}) = \sum_{\vec{t} \in \{0,1\}^n} F(\vec{t}) eq(\vec{t}, \vec{s})$ where $eq(\vec{t}, \vec{s}) = \prod_{i=1}^{n} s_i t_i + (1 - s_i)(1 - t_i)$ is the multilinear polynomial which is equal to 1 if and only if $\vec{t} = \vec{s}$ and otherwise is equal to 0.

Since $F(\vec{t})$ is zero on the Boolean hypercube, $Q(\vec{s})$ is then identical to the zero polynomial by Schwartz-Zippel lemma. This condition can be verified by testing $Q(\vec{s})$ on a random point. Spartan is a way to check this evaluation in an efficient way. More precisely, to verify the satisfiability of the original R1CS Spartan performs the following steps:

1. Proves that $Q(\vec{r}) = 0$ for a random point $\vec{r} \in \mathbb{F}^n$. Note that due to the definition of $Q(\cdot)$ this can be done via a sumcheck protocol.
2. The above sumcheck protocol reduces to proving that $\sigma = F(\vec{\rho})$ for a random $\vec{\rho} \in \mathbb{F}^n$. Due to the definition of F this reduces to proving the value of three summations $\sum_{\vec{u} \in \{0,1\}^n} \tilde{A}(\vec{\rho}, \vec{u}) \tilde{Z}(\vec{u})$, $\sum_{\vec{u} \in \{0,1\}^n} \tilde{B}(\vec{t}, \vec{u}) \tilde{Z}(\vec{u})$, and $\sum_{\vec{u} \in \{0,1\}^n} \tilde{C}(\vec{t}, \vec{u}) \tilde{Z}(\vec{u})$. Each one of them can also be proven via a sumcheck, and in Spartan these 3 sumchecks are aggregated into a single one.
3. Finally the above sumchecks reduce to proving the values of the multilinear extensions on random points, i.e., the values of $\tilde{A}(\vec{r_x}, \vec{r_y})$, $\tilde{B}(\vec{r_x}, \vec{r_y})$, $\tilde{C}(\vec{r_x}, \vec{r_y})$, and $\tilde{Z}(\vec{r_y})$.

The final point is achieved via the use of *polynomial commitments*. The prover commits to the polynomials $\tilde{A}, \tilde{B}, \tilde{C}$ (these are called *computation commitments* since they encode the computation), and $\tilde{Z}$ (*witness commitment*, since it encodes the witness).

A major contribution of Spartan is to show how to efficiently commit to $\tilde{A}, \tilde{B}, \tilde{C}$ to leverage their sparseness (recall that in R1CS matrices have N^2 entries but only m are non-zero). This requires a non-trivial use of memory checking techniques, and introduces a substantial overhead which can be avoided in practice for uniform circuits where the Verifier can evaluate $\tilde{A}, \tilde{B}, \tilde{C}$ on their own.

Spartan's focus was to obtain a transparent SNARK, and therefore it uses a multidimensional Pedersen's commitment together with an inner product proof to implement the polynomial commitment. Because we are already using a trusted setup for the Groth16 layer, we changed the polynomial commitment to a different one which also has a trusted setup.

---

[4] Such a polynomial of degree at most 1 in each variable always exists for any function f mapping $\{0, 1\} \to \mathbb{F}$ [30].

3   A Generalized MIPP Protocol

In order to obtain a multilinear PCS with $O(\sqrt{N})$ trusted setup, in this section we show how to adapt ideas from Section 6 of [9] which were applied to the KZG univariate PCS. We generalize it to work with multivariate polynomials and the PST commitment.

Changes from Original MIPP. The protocol in this section has two changes when compared to the one in [9](we are referring specifically to MIPP_k). First, we generalize MIPP to work on multivariate rather than univariate polynomials. Second, we show that the techniques also work when the polynomial is represented in the Lagrangian basis.

The Generalized MIPP Protocol: Given a vector $\vec{A} = [A_1, \ldots, A_M]$ of group elements in $\mathbb{G}_1$, the IPP commitment to $\vec{A}$ with a CRS $\vec{h} = [h_1, \ldots, h_M]$ of group elements in $\mathbb{G}_2$ is

$$T = CM(\vec{A}, \vec{h}) = \prod_{i=1}^{M} e(A_i, h_i).$$

Let $m = \log M$. In our case, $h_i = h^{\chi_i(\vec{t})}$ for $i \in \{0,1\}^m$, where $\vec{t} = [t_1, \ldots, t_m]$ is a random *secret* vector of field elements and h is a generator of $\mathbb{G}_2$.

Our generalized MIPP protocol allows a prover to prove that given a public vector of field elements $\vec{b} = [b_1, \ldots, b_m]$, we have that

$$U = \langle \vec{A}, \vec{y} \rangle = \vec{A}^{\vec{y}} = \prod_{i=1}^{M} A_i^{y_i},$$

where the vector $\vec{y}$ is defined as $\vec{y} = [y_1, \ldots, y_M]$ with $y_i = \chi_i(\vec{b})$ for $i \in \{0,1\}^m$, where $\chi_i(X)$ is the ith Lagrange polynomial defined as

$$\chi_i(X_1, \ldots, X_m) = \prod_{j:i_j=1} X_j \cdot \prod_{j:i_j=0} (1 - X_j).$$

This proof has size and verification time $O(m)$, which means that the verifier needs only to read the vector $\vec{b}$ and not construct the entire vector $\vec{y}$, which is only implicitly defined.

The protocol is described in Fig. 3.

Note that there will be m levels of recursion. Also note that the Verifier cannot compute the vectors $\vec{A}', \vec{y}', \vec{h}'$ since they are too big. Only the prover will compute those and provide the final value at the end of the recursion to the Verifier. We show later how the Verifier can check that they are correct. The Verifier can compute T', U'.

Properties of the Construction. We make the following claims about the construction above which are easily proven by induction.

   Claim: $T' = CM(\vec{A}', \vec{h}')$

- If $M = 1$, the Prover sends A_1, y_1, and the verifier checks that $T = e(A_1, h_1)$ and $U = A_1^{y_1}$.
- Assume now that $M \geq 2$ and is a power of 2. Let $M' = M/2$.
  - The prover sets the following:
    - $\vec{A_L} = [A_1 \ldots A_{M'}]$ and $\vec{A_R} = [A_{M'+1} \ldots A_M]$
    - $\vec{y_L} = [y_1 \ldots y_{M'}]$ and $\vec{y_R} = [y_{M'+1} \ldots y_M]$
    - $\vec{h_L} = [h_1 \ldots h_{M'}]$ and $\vec{h_R} = [h_{M'+1} \ldots h_M]$
  - The Prover computes and sends to the Verifier the following values $U_L = \langle \vec{A_L}, \vec{y_R} \rangle$; $U_R = \langle \vec{A_R}, \vec{y_L} \rangle$; $T_L = CM(\vec{A_L}, \vec{h_R})$; $T_R = CM(\vec{A_R}, \vec{h_L})$
  - The Verifier chooses a random field element x and sends it to the prover
  - They recurse on the following values (note that the vectors have now size $M' = M/2$):
    $\vec{A}' = \vec{A_L} * \vec{A_R}^x$; $\vec{y}' = \vec{y_L} * \vec{y_R}^{x^{-1}}$; $\vec{h}' = \vec{h_L} * \vec{h_R}^{x^{-1}}$; $T' = T * T_L^{x^{-1}} * T_R^x$; $U' = U * U_L^{x^{-1}} * U_R^x$

Fig. 3. Generalized MIPP Protocol.

Claim: $U' = \langle \vec{A}', \vec{y}' \rangle$

Claim: The Verifier will work only in $O(m) = O(\log M)$ time

How can the verifier compute the vectors $\vec{y}', \vec{h}'$ without reading them? The trick is that they are "structured". It is easy to see by induction that at the end of the recursion the value $\hat{y}$ (the collapsed version of $\vec{y}'$ at the end of the recursion) is equal to $(1 - b_1 + x_1^{-1} b_1), \ldots, (1 - b_m + x_m^{-1} b_m)$ which the verifier can compute in $O(m)$ time on their own.

Similarly the value $\hat{h}$ (the collapsed version of $\vec{h}'$ at the end of the recursion) can be seen to be equal to $\hat{h} = h^{\prod_i (1 - t_i + x_i^{-1} t_i)}$.

Note that $\hat{h}$ is a PST commitment of a multilinear polynomial in m variables. The Verifier does not compute it itself (it would be too expensive) but receives it at the end of the recursion from the Prover. To check that it is correct, the verifier computes the polynomial in a random point and it asks the prover to open this PST commitment. The verification time of this construction is $O(m)$.

4   Testudo-Comm: **Our PCS with Square Root Trusted Setup**

Now we show how to reduce the size of the PST trusted setup to $O(\sqrt{N})$ using the generalized MIPP in Sect. 3. See Fig. 4.

Theorem 1. Testudo-Comm *(Fig. 4) is secure in the GGM.*

Efficiency. Our commitment scheme improves in proving time trading against proof size and verification time. The key observation for proving efficiency is that, even though prover has to do more expensive operations (pairings, $\mathbb{G}_t$ multiplications etc.), it does them on a $\sqrt{N}$ sized polynomial, which makes a large difference in practice for large N. For example, in Gemini [6], for 2^{25}, it takes *at least* 36 s to create an opening proof [23] while we evaluate it takes only 11 s using Testudo's commitment (see Sect. 7.1). However, on smaller N, the Gemini transformation is

Trusted Setup We perform the PST trusted setup for $m = n/2$ variables. Let $t_1, \ldots, t_m$ be random values in $\mathbb{Z}_q$. The CRS consists of the $M = \sqrt{N}$ values $g_1^{\chi_i(t)}$.
There is also the trusted setup to generate the vector $\vec{h}$ for the MIPP proof also of size $M = \sqrt{N}$.

Commitment Let $p(x_1, \ldots, x_n)$ be a multilinear polynomial with n variables. We split the variables in two sets X and Y each of size $m = n/2$, and denote $p(X, Y)$ accordingly. Let $p_i(X) = \left(\sum_{j \in \{0,1\}^m} p(j, i) \cdot \chi_j(X) \right)$, so that

$$p(X, Y) = \sum_{i \in \{0,1\}^m} \left(\sum_{j \in \{0,1\}^m} p(j, i) \cdot \chi_j(X) \right) \chi_i(Y)$$

The prover "in its own head" PST-commits to each $p_i(X)$ (it can do this because each p_i is multilinear and in $m = n/2$ variables). This yields a vector of M group elements in G_1, say $A = (A_1, \ldots, A_M)$, one commitment A_i for each p_i.
The actual commitment the prover sends to the verifier is a MIPP commitment T to the vector A, defined as above i.e. $T = CM(\vec{A}, \vec{h}) = \Pi_i e(A_i, h_i)$

Opening Now suppose the verifier asks for $p(\vec{a}, \vec{b})$ where $\vec{a}, \vec{b} \in \mathbb{F}^m$. This can be written as:

$$p(\vec{a}, \vec{b}) = \sum_{i \in \{0,1\}^m} p_i(\vec{a}) * \chi_i(\vec{b})$$

Let us define the m-variate multilinear polynomial

$$q(X) := \sum_{i \in \{0,1\}^m} p_i(X) \chi_i(\vec{b})$$

Note that q is multilinear, and $p(\vec{a}, \vec{b}) = q(\vec{a})$.
Let $\vec{y}$ denote the length $\sqrt{N}$ vector consisting of $y_i = \chi_i(\vec{a}) \in \mathbb{F}_r$ as i ranges over $\{0, 1\}^m$.
To prove that $v = p(\vec{a}, \vec{b})$ the prover proceeds in three steps as in Section 6 of the IPP paper [9]:
1. P sends U a PST-commitment to q using the same SRS as that used to commit to each p_i. Note that U is the inner product of $\vec{A}$ and $\vec{y}$ i.e., $U = \Pi_i A_i^{y_i}$.
2. Second, P proves using the generalized MIPP protocol that U is indeed the inner product of the vector $\vec{A}$ and the vector $\vec{y}$, where $\vec{A}$ is the opening vector to T.
3. Third, P uses the PST-evaluation protocol to prove that given the commitment U the opening polynomial q evaluated at $\vec{a}$ yields v (i.e. $q(\vec{a}) = v$).

Verification The verifier receives v claimed to be $v = p(\vec{a}, \vec{b})$, the value U, the generalized MIPP proof π_1 and the PST proof π_2 and it performs the MIPP and PST verifications. Note that all verification steps are $O(m) = O(\log N)$.

Fig. 4. Testudo-Comm

likely to outperform Testudo's commitment because of the time required to perform the pairings and $\mathbb{G}_t$ commutations in our case.

We summarize the efficiency properties of the prover in Table 1 assuming a circuit of size $N = 2^n$ and security parameter λ. We then compare the efficiency for the verifier in Table 2.

- **PST:** To open, the prover computes for each of the n rounds, a polynomial division of size 2^{n-1} leading to a $O(2^{n-1})$-sized polynomial division complexity. While this operates on field elements, we found out that this division, because it doesn't use FFTs, is actually a bottleneck on large sizes (such as 2^{25}).
- **Gemini:** To open, the prover computes for each of the n rounds, 1 KZG openings of size 2^{n-i} and 2 of size 2^{n-i-1}, leading to a complexity of

Table 1. Comparison of Prover Efficiency

Scheme	Setup Size	Committing	Opening
Testudo	$O(\sqrt{N})$, $\mathbb{G}_1$, $O(\sqrt{N})\mathbb{G}_2$	$O(\sqrt{N})\mathbb{G}_1$, $O(\sqrt{N})$ pairings, $O(\sqrt{N})\mathbb{G}_t$	$6\sqrt{N}\mathbb{G}_1$, $O(\sqrt{N})\mathbb{G}_2$, $4\sqrt{N}$ pairings, $4\sqrt{N}\mathbb{G}_t$
PST	$O(N)\mathbb{G}_1$	$O(N)\mathbb{G}_1$	$2N\mathbb{G}_1$, $O(N)$ poly division
Gemini	$O(N)\mathbb{G}_1$	$O(N)\mathbb{G}_1$	$4N\mathbb{G}_1$

Table 2. Comparison of Verifier Efficiency

Scheme	Proof Size	Verification Time
Testudo	$\approx \log(N)/2(\mathbb{G}_t + \mathbb{G}_1 + \mathbb{G}_2)$	$\approx \log(N)/2(\mathbb{G}_t + \mathbb{G}_1 + \mathbb{G}_2)$
PST	$O(\log N)\mathbb{G}_2$	$O(\log N)$
Gemini	$3n\mathbb{G}_2$	$8n$pairings, $3n\mathbb{G}_2, 3n\mathbb{G}_1$

$O(2N + N + N) = O(4N)\mathbb{G}_1$ scalar multiplications. For verification, it therefore requires performing $O(8n)$ pairings (or $4n$ pairing checks).

- **Testudo:** To open, the prover must compute:
  - A PST commitment to the $q(X)$ polynomial, so $O(\sqrt{N})\mathbb{G}_1$
  - A MIPP opening proof, consisting of n rounds where prover computes (a) $O(2\sqrt{N}/2^i)\mathbb{G}_1$ scalar multiplication to compute the reduced vectors, and (b) $O(2\sqrt{N}/2^i)\mathbb{G}_t$ and pairings operations to compute the commitment to each reduced vectors. This leads to $O(4\sqrt{N})\mathbb{G}_1$ and $O(4\sqrt{N})\mathbb{G}_t$ + pairings.
  - Two PST opening proofs, each of size $O(\sqrt{N})$, one on $\mathbb{G}_1$ and one on $\mathbb{G}_2$

Remark 1 (Distributed trusted setup). Our construction requires a trusted setup for the polynomial commitment of a specific form. It needs to encode in particular a secret tuple of points and their (multivariate) monomial evaluation. We can obtain an MPC for such a setup by straightforwardly adapting the techniques from [7]. We will detail these techniques in the full version of the paper.

Remark 2 (Proof Size). The proof size for our commitment scheme are 8x bigger at 2^{25} than PST. To reduce the size, we can compress the G_t elements on the torus as in [24]. This could potentially reduce by half the proof size, bringing it to the same order of magnitude as a PST opening proof. Note however, that proof sizes do not matter much in the Testudo SNARK as they are verified by another Groth16 proof on top.

5   Testudo: Our Construction

At this point we recap the general structure of Testudo. Let A, B, C be the input R1CS of size N.

Trusted Setup. We assume that a trusted party (or a distributed multiparty computation protocol, aka ceremony) generates the trusted setup for Testudo-Comm (which is of size $\sqrt{N}$) and the Groth16 trusted setup for an R1CS corresponding to the verification algorithm of the Spartan sumchecks and the Testudo-Comm opening proofs (this R1CS has size $O(\log N)$. This trusted setup is independent of A, B, C and therefore universal.

Computation Commitments. As in Spartan, in a preprocessing stage, the prover encodes A, B, C as sparse polynomials $\tilde{A}, \tilde{B}, \tilde{C}$ and commits to them via polynomial commitments (*computational commitments*). We note that for uniform circuits (e.g., data-parallel, with many sub-circuits repeating in regular patterns), this step is not necessary or much reduced in complexity, since the verifier can efficiently compute $\tilde{A}, \tilde{B}, \tilde{C}$ on their own or is only required to compute the computational commitment for the subcircuit.

Witness Commitments. In the online phase, the prover computes $\tilde{w}$, a multilinear extension of the witness w and commits to it using Testudo-Comm. Note that the polynomials are of size $O(N)$ here, corresponding to the number of R1CS constraints.

Prover. The Testudo prover:

– Executes the Spartan prover to prove the satisfiability of A, B, C (see Sect. 2.5), with the only difference that it uses Testudo-Comm as the underlying polynomial commitment.
– Produces the appropriate openings of the Testudo-Comm PCS.
– Produces and outputs a Groth16 proof that it knows the above modified Spartan proof.

Verifier. The verifier checks the output Groth16 proof and accept/rejects accordingly.

Theorem 2. *Assuming that* Testudo-Comm *is an extractable PCS, and Groth16 is a SNARK, then* Testudo *is a SNARK.*

Informally the proof follows from the fact that if Groth16 is a SNARK we can extract a "modified Spartan" proof – modified to use Testudo-Comm ass the underlying PCS. But if Testudo-Comm is extractable, then we know that we can extract the witness (Spartan is a SNARK as long as the underlying PCS is extractable).

As with all recursive SNARKs we have to heuristically assume that we can instantiate the random oracle in Spartan to a very specific hash function (in our case Poseidon) and not lose security. This is because the code of the hash function has to be embedded in the outer Groth16 proof.

6   Practical Considerations

Choice of Curves. The original version of Spartan (the starting point for the Testudo) uses a custom version of `curve25519-dalek`, which provides an efficient implementation of a prime-order Ristretto group [26], an abstraction that facilitates implementations of prime-order groups with strong security guarantees. However, as this elliptic curve does not support pairings, composing the original Spartan with Groth16 is not possible and, thus, we had to find a pairing-friendly alternative. We opted for BLS12-377 combined with BW6-761 because they represent the most efficient pair that further supports *2-chaining of pairing-equipped elliptic curves* [1,13,14] which is required for our design. See appendix in the full version for more details.

Testudo for Data-Parallel Computation. We can make Testudo particularly efficient for data-parallel computation. Consider a relation R^* composed of several repetitions of the same relation $R(\vec{x}^{(1)}, \vec{w}^{(1)}) \wedge \cdots \wedge R(\vec{x}^{(K)}, \vec{w}^{(K)})$ $(\vec{x}^{(1)}, \ldots, \vec{x}^{(K)})$ We are able to amortize the proving costs related to the wiring of the circuit whenever the circuit is of this form.

In the Spartan lingo the building block for proving the wiring of the circuit refers to a *computation commitment*. A computation commitment is a polynomial commitment opening to polynomials encoding the structure of the circuit. If we apply Testudo naively to such a relation we would need to open a computation commitment of size roughly $K|w|$. Instead, we modify our building blocks appropriately to leverage the structure of the circuit and we require computation commitments whose opening grows only linearly in the size of the small subrelation R. We expand on this construction in the full version.

6.1   Parallelization and Aggregation of Testudo Proofs

We observe that this framework enables aggregation of proofs at different levels, each with their pros and cons, but all being compatible with each other, resulting in a system that can scale to large instances in practice because it enables *parallelization* of the proof generation.

Aggregation at Spartan Level: Assume a prover is running different sumchecks + PCS openings in parallel using different witnesses, *on different machines* (otherwise, the prover should use the data parallel version that requires the whole witness to be present). In this setting, aggregating the verification of the sumcheck can be done either via (a) aggregating the different Groth16 sumcheck-verifier proofs together using Snarkpack-like constructions, or (b) having one Groth16 proof that verifies multiple instances of the sumcheck. Aggregation for the polynomial commitment scheme could be done by the prover (a) at the beginning, by committing to a random linear combination of the different multilinear extensions of the witnesses and (b) by opening at a random point this combined polynomial. This would require communication between the machines to aggregate the polynomials together; given it's a single round of communication, we believe it can still be a useful for a practical deployement inside a cluster of machines.

Aggregation at the Groth16 Level: Instead of verifying a single sumcheck instance Groth16 proof and a single PCS opening proof, the outer proof can verify *multiple of those*. We need further work to estimate the complexity of the final outer circuit but our current estimation (4M constraints for the outer circuit) seem to indicate that it is possible to verify in the order of 5–10 proofs together in a reasonable timeframe, depending on the application.

Note that this aggregation *does not require knowledge of the witness* and therefore can be done by more expensive prover machines.

Aggregation on Top: Because Testudo's final proof is a Groth16 proof, one can use Snarkpack to efficiently pack thousands of such proofs together. Similar to previous category, this aggregation level *does not require knowledge of the witness* and therefore can be done by more expensive prover machines.

7 Implementation and Evaluation

7.1 Implementation

We have a working Testudo implementation[5] that features the sumcheck verifier proof and our Testudo commitment scheme. We based our work on the Spartan [28] codebase, which has been adapted to use the Arkworks [2] framework to enable support for any pairing based curves. We also have started an effort on parallelizing the Spartan codebase, although there are still many low hanging fruits to optimize for. On top of this, we implemented a wrapper around a BLS12-381 library that supports GPU operations and released it open source on Github (we do not provide a link in order to keep anonymity of submission).

7.2 Testudo Commitment

We first evaluate our new multivariate commitment scheme compared to the standard PST algorithm. This has been run over a c5a.12xlarge AWS instance, i.e., 48 cores with 96 threads. We note that the structure of the commitment allows for heavy use of parallelism, which we exploited in our implementation.

Figure 5 shows that the Testudo commitment maintains the performance of the PST commitment and, for large circuit instances, **it is 2 orders of magnitude faster** for opening by significantly reducing the size of the MSM required. Indeed, it operates on $\sqrt{N}$ size MSM. However, verification is slower, due to the logarithmic number of pairings required to verify the inner pairing product argument proof. There are still many low-hanging fruits in the codebase to speed up verification such as batching the pairing operations in MIPP and PST.

---

[5] The current version of the repository is available at https://github.com/cryptonetlab/testudo.

Moreover, we continue to avoid the use of FFT due to the usage of multilinear polynomials

Verification Speed: As mentioned above, there are many low hanging fruits for optimizing the codebase. For example, to speed up verification, one can bundle the MIPP and the PST part together (e.g. run the pairings check all at once). Currently both MIPP and PST codebase are quite separate.

Proof Size: The Testudo Commitment brings an increase to the proof size in comparison to the simple PST by a factor of 3 but we ensure this is not an issue for the communication cost through recursion. Using the BLS12-377, we are able to efficiently verify commitment openings inside a Groth16 circuit as outlined in Sect. 6.1.

7.3 Testudo Groth16 Constraints

In this section, we estimate the number of R1CS constraints necessary to verify the core of Testudo (the sumchecks, the PCS opening and the computation commitment). Figure 6 shows the number of constraints for each parts according to the user circuit size (e.g. the circuit that the user writes on Testudo). In this estimation, we:

- Use Testudo Commitment as the multilinear PCS scheme for the computation commitment part of Spartan. In the original design, it uses Hyrax.
- Thanks to the previous point, we can now do a random linear combination of all the polynomials the prover must perform and having the prover only compute a single Testudo Commitment opening proof
- We verify the core Spartan sumchecks (steps 2 and 3 in Sect. 2.5) and the grand product sumchecks ([27, bottom of pg. 27]) from the computation commitment inside the same Groth16 verifier that checks the sumcheck in the satisfiability proof. This is possible since both are operating on the same fields.
- Note that we need to verify a PST opening both on $\mathbb{G}_1$ and $\mathbb{G}_2$ during the Testudo commitment (for the PST part and for the MIPP part respectively).

The biggest contributor of the R1CS constraints number is the MIPP part, because it requires to compute $log(N)$ $\mathbb{G}_t$ operations (exponentiation is almost 40k in the library we used). We expect this number to drastically go down by roughly 30–50% with optimizations on $\mathbb{G}_t$ computations, such as using the torus arithmetic version and endomorphisms optimizations [24].

7.4 Testudo on Data-Parallel Circuits

We have the necessary building blocks to estimate accurately the proving time of data-parallel circuits (even though the implementation does not yet offer that feature). Specifically, to estimate the time of proving for uniform circuits, we need to add the time for

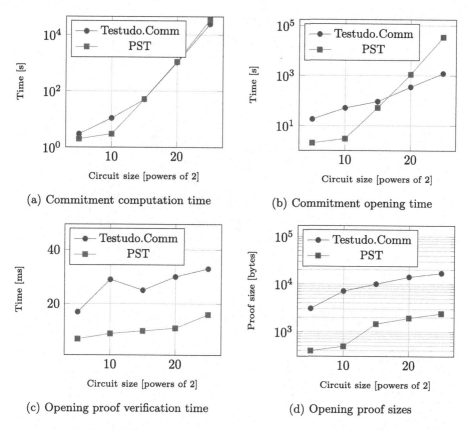

(a) Commitment computation time

(b) Commitment opening time

(c) Opening proof verification time

(d) Opening proof sizes

Fig. 5. Comparison between the Testudo and PST commitment schemes. While the time to compute a commitment is similar for Testudo and PST, see (a), we can see in (b) that Testudo outperforms PST when opening a commitment for large circuit sizes by almost two orders of magnitude. On the other hand, graph (c) shows that PST is faster than Testudo by a factor of 2x which, however, can likely be addressed as there are various straightforward ways to further optimize the Testudo code. Finally, graph (d) shows that Testudo opening proofs are about one order of magnitude larger than PST proofs, which, however, will not have any practical impact on the overall sizes of Testudo SNARK proofs, as the opening proof will be ultimately verified by a constant-size Groth16 proof.

- The first sumcheck on the full R1CS matrix (SC1)
- The second sumcheck on the small subcircuit (SC2)
- The Testudo commitment (TC) times on the full witness size - commitment and opening combined
- The computation commitment time on the small subcircuit (CC)

We have benchmarked these data for two different subcircuit of size (a) 2^{15} and (b) 2^{20}. The subcircuit corresponds roughly to the size of a Merkle Tree proof verification circuit for 32 layers using either (a) Poseidon for 2^{15} or (b) SHA256

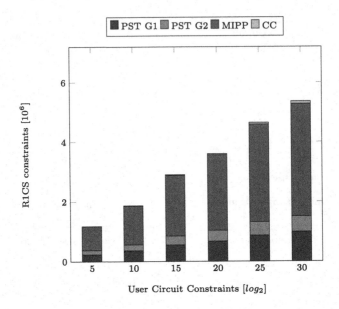

Fig. 6. Constraints for Groth16 verifier of Testudo Proof

Constraints	2^{15}	2^{20}	2^{25}
Commit (s)	0.072	0.723	11
Sumcheck 1 (s)	0.04	0.903	28
Sumcheck 2 (s)	0.036	0.941	29
TC Opening (s)	0.134	0.471	1.5
CC Opening (s)	2	32	939

Fig. 7. Individual cost of data parallel version of Testudo

Subcircuit Size	Proving Time	Speed up vs Groth16
2^{15} constraints (1024 reps)	33s	9.7x
2^{20} constraints (32 reps)	73s	4.3x
Groth16 Proving (2^{25})	322s	—

Fig. 8. Cost of the data parallel version of Testudo vs Groth16

for 2^{20} as the hash function. We're estimating the proving time to repeat these circuits to achieve overall a circuit of 2^{25} constraints: subcircuit (a) is repeated 1024 times (i.e. verify 1024 Merkle Tree proofs), and subcircuit (b) is repeated 32 times. For these parameters, we show that our data parallel Testudo version can be **9.7x faster** for (a) and **4.3x faster** for (b) than their Groth16 equivalent. The improvement is expected to be even larger as the gap of constraints between the subcircuit and the bigger circuit grows. As further work, we will compare these improvement to SNARKs based on plonkish arithmetization, although we are not aware of such speedups for other proof systems at this time (Figs. 7 and 8).

References

1. Aranha, D.F., El Housni, Y., Guillevic, A.: A survey of elliptic curves for proof systems. Cryptology ePrint Archive, Report 2022/586 (2022). https://eprint.iacr.org/2022/586
2. Arkworks contributors (2023). arkworks zksnark ecosystem
3. Belling, A., Soleimanian, A., Bégassat, O.: Recursion over public-coin interactive proof systems; faster hash verification. Cryptology ePrint Archive, Report 2022/1072 (2022). https://eprint.iacr.org/2022/1072
4. Bellperson contributors (2023). The bellperson zk-SNARK library
5. Ben-Sasson, E., Bentov, I., Horesh, Y., Riabzev, M.: Scalable, transparent, and post-quantum secure computational integrity. Cryptology ePrint Archive, Report 2018/046 (2018). https://eprint.iacr.org/2018/046
6. Bootle, J., Chiesa, A., Hu, Y., Orrù, M.: Gemini: elastic SNARKs for diverse environments. In: Dunkelman, O., Dziembowski, S. (eds.) EUROCRYPT 2022. LNCS, vol. 13276, pp. 427–457. Springer, Cham (2022). https://doi.org/10.1007/978-3-031-07085-3_15
7. Bowe, S., Gabizon, A., Miers, I.: Scalable multi-party computation for zk-SNARK parameters in the random beacon model. Cryptology ePrint Archive, Report 2017/1050 (2017). https://eprint.iacr.org/2017/1050
8. Bünz, B., Bootle, J., Boneh, D., Poelstra, A., Wuille, P., Maxwell, G.: Bulletproofs: short proofs for confidential transactions and more. In: 2018 IEEE Symposium on Security and Privacy. IEEE Computer Society Press (2018)
9. Bünz, B., Maller, M., Mishra, P., Tyagi, N., Vesely, P.: Proofs for inner pairing products and applications. In: Tibouchi, M., Wang, H. (eds.) ASIACRYPT 2021. LNCS, vol. 13092, pp. 65–97. Springer, Cham (2021). https://doi.org/10.1007/978-3-030-92078-4_3
10. Campanelli, M., Fiore, D., Querol, A.: LegoSNARK: modular design and composition of succinct zero-knowledge proofs. In: ACM CCS 2019. ACM Press (2019)
11. Chen, B., Bünz, B., Boneh, D., Zhang, Z.: HyperPlonk: plonk with linear-time prover and high-degree custom gates. Cryptology ePrint Archive, Report 2022/1355 (2022). https://eprint.iacr.org/2022/1355
12. Chiesa, A., Hu, Y., Maller, M., Mishra, P., Vesely, N., Ward, N.: Marlin: preprocessing zkSNARKs with universal and updatable SRS. In: Canteaut, A., Ishai, Y. (eds.) EUROCRYPT 2020. LNCS, vol. 12105, pp. 738–768. Springer, Cham (2020). https://doi.org/10.1007/978-3-030-45721-1_26
13. El Housni, Y., Guillevic, A.: Optimized and secure pairing-friendly elliptic curves suitable for one layer proof composition. In: Krenn, S., Shulman, H., Vaudenay, S. (eds.) CANS 2020. LNCS, vol. 12579, pp. 259–279. Springer, Cham (2020). https://doi.org/10.1007/978-3-030-65411-5_13
14. El Housni, Y., Guillevic, A.: Families of SNARK-friendly 2-chains of elliptic curves. In: Dunkelman, O., Dziembowski, S. (eds.) EUROCRYPT 2022. LNCS, vol. 13276, pp. 367–396. Springer, Cham (2022). https://doi.org/10.1007/978-3-031-07085-3_13
15. Gabizon, A., Williamson, Z.J., Ciobotaru, O.: PLONK: permutations over lagrange-bases for oecumenical noninteractive arguments of knowledge. Cryptology ePrint Archive, Report 2019/953 (2019). https://eprint.iacr.org/2019/953

16. Gailly, N., Maller, M., Nitulescu, A.: SnarkPack: practical SNARK aggregation. In: Eyal, I., Garay, J. (eds.) FC 2022. LNCS, vol. 13411, pp. 203–229. Springer, Cham (2022). https://doi.org/10.1007/978-3-031-18283-9_10

17. Goldwasser, S., Kalai, Y.T., Rothblum, G.N.: Delegating computation: interactive proofs for muggles. In: 40th ACM STOC. ACM Press (2008)

18. Groth, J.: On the size of pairing-based non-interactive arguments. In: Fischlin, M., Coron, J.-S. (eds.) EUROCRYPT 2016. LNCS, vol. 9666, pp. 305–326. Springer, Heidelberg (2016). https://doi.org/10.1007/978-3-662-49896-5_11

19. Groth, J., Kohlweiss, M., Maller, M., Meiklejohn, S., Miers, I.: Updatable and universal common reference strings with applications to zk-SNARKs. In: Shacham, H., Boldyreva, A. (eds.) CRYPTO 2018. LNCS, vol. 10993, pp. 698–728. Springer, Cham (2018). https://doi.org/10.1007/978-3-319-96878-0_24

20. Kate, A., Zaverucha, G.M., Goldberg, I.: Constant-size commitments to polynomials and their applications. In: Abe, M. (ed.) ASIACRYPT 2010. LNCS, vol. 6477, pp. 177–194. Springer, Heidelberg (2010). https://doi.org/10.1007/978-3-642-17373-8_11

21. P Labs (2023). Filecoin: A Decentralized Storage Network

22. Lund, C., Fortnow, L., Karloff, H.J., Nisan, N.: Algebraic methods for interactive proof systems. In: 31st FOCS. IEEE Computer Society Press (1990)

23. Michele Orrù, G.K.: (2023). zka.lc

24. Naehrig, M., Barreto, P.S.L.M., Schwabe, P.: On compressible pairings and their computation. In: Vaudenay, S. (ed.) AFRICACRYPT 2008. LNCS, vol. 5023, pp. 371–388. Springer, Heidelberg (2008). https://doi.org/10.1007/978-3-540-68164-9_25

25. Papamanthou, C., Shi, E., Tamassia, R.: Signatures of correct computation. In: Sahai, A. (ed.) TCC 2013. LNCS, vol. 7785, pp. 222–242. Springer, Heidelberg (2013). https://doi.org/10.1007/978-3-642-36594-2_13

26. Ristretto contributors (2023). The Ristretto Group

27. Setty, S.: Spartan: efficient and general-purpose zkSNARKs without trusted setup. Cryptology ePrint Archive, Report 2019/550 (2019). https://eprint.iacr.org/2019/550

28. Setty, S.: Spartan: efficient and general-purpose zkSNARKs without trusted setup. In: Micciancio, D., Ristenpart, T. (eds.) CRYPTO 2020. LNCS, vol. 12172, pp. 704–737. Springer, Cham (2020). https://doi.org/10.1007/978-3-030-56877-1_25

29. Shoup, V.: Lower bounds for discrete logarithms and related problems. In: Fumy, W. (ed.) EUROCRYPT 1997. LNCS, vol. 1233, pp. 256–266. Springer, Heidelberg (1997). https://doi.org/10.1007/3-540-69053-0_18

30. Thaler, J.: (2015–2023). Proofs, Arguments, and Zero-Knowledge

31. Xie, T., et al.: zkBridge: trustless cross-chain bridges made practical. In: ACM CCS 2022. ACM Press (2022)

32. Zhang, J., Xie, T., Zhang, Y., Song, D.: Transparent polynomial delegation and its applications to zero knowledge proof. In: 2020 IEEE Symposium on Security and Privacy. IEEE Computer Society Press (2020)

33. Zhang, Y., Genkin, D., Katz, J., Papadopoulos, D., Papamanthou, C.: A zero-knowledge version of vSQL. Cryptology ePrint Archive, Report 2017/1146 (2017). https://eprint.iacr.org/2017/1146
34. zk Harness contributors (2023). zk-Harness

Set (Non-)Membership NIZKs
from Determinantal Accumulators

Helger Lipmaa and Roberto Parisella[✉]

Simula UiB, Bergen, Norway
robertoparisella@hotmail.it

Abstract. We construct a falsifiable set (non-)membership NIZK Π^* that is considerably more efficient than known falsifiable set (non-)membership NIZKs. It also has a universal CRS. Π^* is based on the novel concept of determinantal accumulators. Determinantal primitives have a similar relation to recent pairing-based (non-succinct) NIZKs of Couteau and Hartmann (Crypto 2020) and Couteau et al. (CLPØ, Asiacrypt 2021) that structure-preserving primitives have to the Groth-Sahai NIZK. We also extend CLPØ by proposing efficient (non-succinct) set *non*-membership arguments for a large class of languages.

Keywords: Commit-and-prove · non-interactive zero-knowledge · set (non-)membership argument · universal accumulator

1 Introduction

In a set (non-)membership NIZK, the prover aims to convince the verifier that an encrypted element χ belongs (does not belong) to a public set $\mathcal{S}$. Fully succinct (constant size and constant-time verifiable) set (non-)membership NIZKs have many applications. Classical applications include anonymous credentials (one has to prove that one has a valid credit card), governmental safelist (to prevent money laundering), and e-voting (one has to prove that one is an eligible voter). A non-membership NIZK can be used to prove that a key is *not* blocklisted. Set membership NIZKs are instrumental in ring signatures. Recently, set (non-)membership NIZKs have gained popularity in cryptocurrencies. For example, in Zcash, to validate a transaction that intends to spend a coin χ requires one to check that χ is in the set UTXO (unspent transaction outputs).

When χ is public, one can use an efficient (universal) accumulator [5,7]. A universal accumulator [11,12,15,18] can be reframed as a set (non-)membership *non-zk* non-interactive argument system. Accumulator's completeness and collision-resistance (see Sect. 2) correspond directly to the completeness and soundness of the set (non-)membership argument system but with public input. To construct a set (non-)membership NIZK, one only needs to add a zero-knowledge (ZK) compiler to the accumulator. Unfortunately, the ZK compiler is quite complicated in existing constructions, resulting in set (non-)membership NIZKs that are either not falsifiable or not sufficiently efficient.

A. Aly and M. Tibouchi (Eds.): LATINCRYPT 2023, LNCS 14168, pp. 352–374, 2023.
https://doi.org/10.1007/978-3-031-44469-2_18

While the random oracle model, other idealized models (like the algebraic group model), and non-falsifiable knowledge assumptions have been used successfully in many practical schemes, they have also drawn severe criticism. See the full version [20] for a longer discussion. Because of this, there has been an enormous focus in the literature on constructing efficient non-falsifiable NIZKs. The most famous such NIZK is GS (Groth-Sahai, [17]) which has been used since then in many different applications, including (non-)membership NIZKs.

On the other hand, there is less of a qualitative distinction between different *falsifiable* assumptions—as long as such assumptions have reasonably tight security reductions in the AGM. All previous "falsifiable" accumulators are based on relatively strong falsifiable q-type assumptions. *Hence, we aim to construct maximally efficient (non-)membership NIZKs under (possibly novel) falsifiable computational assumptions.* There are many non-falsifiable or random-oracle-based set (non-)membership NIZKs; we do not compete with them, and thus we omit almost any discussion.

Related Work. Many set membership NIZKs use either signature schemes or accumulators. In a signature-based set membership NIZKs, the CRS includes signatures of all set elements. The prover proves it knows an (encrypted) signature on the (encrypted) χ. Such NIZKs have several undesirable properties. First, their CRS is non-universal[1] (i.e., it depends on the set). A universal CRS is important in practice since it allows one to rely on a single CRS to construct set (non-)membership NIZKs for different sets. Second, assuming that $|\mathcal{S}|$ is polynomial (and the complement of $\mathcal{S}$ has exponential size), it seems to explicitly disallow the construction of set non-membership arguments.

We will concentrate on accumulator-based constructions since they do not have these two problems. Recall briefly that a (CRS-model) universal accumulator enables one, given a CRS crs, to construct a succinct (non-hiding) commitment $C_{\mathcal{S}}$ of the set $\mathcal{S}$, such that one can efficiently verify whether $\chi \in \mathcal{S}$, given crs, $C_{\mathcal{S}}$, χ, and a succinct accumulator argument ψ of (non-)membership.

In a typical accumulator-based set membership NIZK, the CRS contains *set-independent* elements that are sufficient to compute the accumulator arguments of (non-)membership. (This depends on the underlying accumulator, but importantly, the Nguyen accumulator [21] allows for that.) Thus, their CRS is universal. Since there is no need to add all accumulator arguments to the CRS, one can hope to construct efficient accumulator-based set *non-membership* NIZKs.

Next, we will summarize the published falsifiable set-membership NIZKs. In all cases $\mathcal{S} \subset \mathbb{Z}_p$ and hence $\chi \in \mathbb{Z}_p$. Since the cited papers did not write down all efficiency numbers, our efficiency comparison (see Table 1) is not 100% precise.

Belenkiy et al. (BCKL, [6]) construct a set-membership NIZK by first building a P-signature scheme [6]. They prove that a commitment opens to an element whose signature the prover knows, using a Groth-Sahai NIZK [17]. Daza et al. (DGPRS-GS, [16]) use the more efficient weak Boneh-Boyen (WBB) signature

---

[1] We follow the literature by using "universal" both in *universal accumulators* (have a non-membership argument) and *universal CRS* (does not depend on the language).

scheme instead of the P-signature scheme. Since the WBB signature scheme is not F-unforgeable [6,16] modifies it slightly. Using signature schemes means that the CRS of BCKL and DGPRS-GS is non-universal. Daza et al. [16] also propose a succinct set membership QA-NIZK (DGPRS-QA). However, their verifier's computation is $O_\lambda(|\mathcal{S}|)$; thus, it is unsuitable for our applications. In particular, all solutions in Table 1 have verifier's computation $O_\lambda(1)$. Hence, we omit DGPRS-QA in the comparison.

Acar and Nguyen (AN, [3]) replace the signature scheme with the Nguyen accumulator [21] and then use Groth-Sahai to prove that the prover knows an accumulator argument. Due to the use of an accumulator, the AN NIZK has a universal CRS; they also propose a set non-membership argument.

BCKL, AN, and DGPRS-GS rely on new (though falsifiable) q-type security assumptions. The intuition is that the underlying signature schemes and accumulators are proven to be only secure when the adversary returns χ as an integer. In these NIZKs, χ is essentially encrypted, and the soundness reduction can only recover a group version (say[2], $[\chi]_1$) of χ. BCKL, AN, and DGPRS-GS all modified underlying primitives to stay secure against adversaries that output $[\chi]_1$. In each construction, this resulted in a new but falsifiable assumption. Moreover, such a modification often introduces a noticeable loss of efficiency. We describe all assumptions in the full version [20] for completeness.

Another drawback of the signature-based solutions is that it is unclear how to define a universal argument that efficiently allows for non-membership proofs. From the above solutions, only [3] (that does not rely on signatures) proposes a set non-membership NIZK.

According to [6], BCKL's prover executes 34 multi-scalar-multiplications ([6] does not give separately the number of scalar-multiplications in $\mathbb{G}_1$ and $\mathbb{G}_2$) and the verifer 68 pairings. Neither AN [3] nor Daza et al. [16] give any efficiency numbers. The corresponding entries (marked with an asterisk) in Table 1 are based on our estimations.

Most prior falsifiable set membership NIZKs are based on the Groth-Sahai NIZK [17]. Recently, Couteau and Hartmann (CH, [13]) proposed a methodology to transform a specific class of Σ-protocols to NIZKs. Intuitively, starting with a Σ-protocol with transcript (a, e, z), CH puts $[e]_2$ to the CRS and then modifies the computation of z and the verifier's algorithm to work on $[e]_2$ instead of e. The resulting NIZKs have a CRS consisting of a single group element.

Couteau et al. (CLPØ [14]) significantly extended the CH methodology. They constructed efficient commit-and-prove NIZKs for many languages, including (Boolean and arithmetic) Circuit-SAT. Importantly, [14] constructed efficient NIZKs for languages that can be described by small algebraic branching programs. The CLPØ NIZK is secure under a new but natural assumption CED (*Computational Extended Determinant*). Depending on the parameters, CED can be either falsifiable or non-falsifiable. For many natural problems like Boolean Circuit-SAT and set membership for poly-sized sets, CED is falsifiable.

---

[2] We use the standard additive bracket notation for pairing-based setting. For example, $[\chi]_1 = \chi[1]_1$, where $[1]_1$ is a generator of $\mathbb{G}_1$.

Table 1. Comparison of known fully succinct falsifiable set (non-)membership arguments for univariate sets of size $|\mathcal{S}| \leq q$. Here, $\mathfrak{g}_\iota$ denotes the bit-length of an element of $\mathbb{G}_\iota$, $\mathfrak{m}_\iota$ denotes the cost of a scalar multiplication in $\mathbb{G}_\iota$, $\mathfrak{m}$ denotes the cost of a scalar multiplication in either $\mathbb{G}_1$ or $\mathbb{G}_2$, and $\mathfrak{p}$ denotes the costs of a pairing. The numbers with $*$ are based on our estimation when the original paper did not give enough data. We give online computation, i.e., assuming precomputation. We only mention non-standard assumptions; this excludes say SXDH.

Paper	Belenkiy et al. [6]	Acar-Nguyen [3]	Daza et al. [16]	This work (Fig. 7)
Building blocks				
Primitive	P-signature	Nguyen acc.	WBB signature	determinantal acc
NIZK	Groth-Sahai	Groth-Sahai	Groth-Sahai	CLPØ
Assumptions	TDH, HSDH	EDSH	GSDH	DETACM, DETACNM
Structural properties				
Universal CRS?	✗	✓	✗	✓
Updatable CRS?	✗	✗	✗	✓
Non-membership?	✗	✓	✗	✓
Membership argument efficiency				
|crs|	$(2q+1)\mathfrak{g}_1 + (q+1)\mathfrak{g}_2$	$(q+5)\mathfrak{g}_1 + 4\mathfrak{g}_2*$	$5\mathfrak{g}_1 + (q+5)\mathfrak{g}_2*$	$(q+1)\mathfrak{g}_1 + 4\mathfrak{g}_2$
|π|	$18\mathfrak{g}_1 + 16\mathfrak{g}_2$	$8\mathfrak{g}_1 + 10\mathfrak{g}_2*$	$10\mathfrak{g}_1 + 8\mathfrak{g}_2*$	$6\mathfrak{g}_1 + 3\mathfrak{g}_2$
P computation	$34\mathfrak{m}$	$16\mathfrak{m}_1 + 16\mathfrak{m}_2*$	$17\mathfrak{m}_1 + 18\mathfrak{m}_2*$	$8\mathfrak{m}_1 + 6\mathfrak{m}_2$
V computation	$68\mathfrak{p}$	$30\mathfrak{p}*$	$30\mathfrak{p}*$	$4\mathfrak{p}$
Non-membership argument efficiency				
|crs|	✗	$(q+5)\mathfrak{g}_1 + 4\mathfrak{g}_2*$	✗	$(q+1)\mathfrak{g}_1 + 4\mathfrak{g}_2$
|π|	✗	$11\mathfrak{g}_1 + 16\mathfrak{g}_2*$	✗	$10\mathfrak{g}_1 + 5\mathfrak{g}_2$
P computation	✗	$26\mathfrak{m}_1 + 28\mathfrak{m}_2*$	✗	$14\mathfrak{m}_1 + 10\mathfrak{m}_2$
V computation	✗	$46\mathfrak{p}*$	✗	$5\mathfrak{p}$

[13,14] compare their work to the Groth-Sahai NIZK, showing that in several important use cases, their (falsifiable) NIZKs are more efficient than the Groth-Sahai NIZK. In particular, an important difference between Groth-Sahai and CH/CLPØ is that in the latter, all secret values are only encrypted in $\mathbb{G}_1$. Because of this, the encrypted witness is often three times shorter in CLPØ than in Groth-Sahai; see [13,14] for examples.

Our first main question is whether one can construct CLPØ-based set (non-)membership NIZKs that are more efficient than the known falsifiable NIZKs [3,6,16]. Moreover, Groth-Sahai-based NIZKs use specialized primitives (structure-preserving signatures [2]) that are designed to allow for efficient Groth-Sahai NIZKs. Our second main question is whether one can define a similar class of primitives that allow for efficient CLPØ NIZKs.

Our Contributions. Since a universal accumulator is a non-zk (non-)membership non-interactive argument system, one can construct efficient set (non-)membership NIZKs by creating an efficient universal accumulator and then using an efficient ZK compiler to build a NIZK. Our approach is to make the latter part (ZK compiler) as efficient as possible without sacrificing the former part (accumulator) too much.

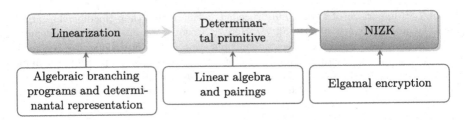

Fig. 1. Our general blueprint for constructing efficient falsifiable NIZKs.

Differently from the previous work, we will ZK-compile the accumulator to a CLPØ NIZK. We define a *determinantal accumulator* as a universal accumulator with a structure that supports efficient ZK compilation to CLPØ. Determinantal accumulators are related to but different from structure-preserving signatures [2] that support efficient Groth-Sahai NIZKs. After that, we construct AC*, an updatable determinantal accumulator with efficient (non-)membership arguments. For this, we follow CLPØ's technique of using algebraic branching programs. Based on AC*, we then construct Π^*, a commit-and-prove, updatable set (non-)membership NIZK with a universal CRS.

We emphasize that this results in a clear, modular framework for constructing efficient falsifiable NIZKs: first, construct an efficient algebraic branching program for the task at hand. Second, construct a determinantal accumulator (or, in general, a non-zk non-interactive argument system). Third, use the efficient CLPØ-inspired ZK compiler to achieve zero knowledge. See Fig. 1 for a high-level diagram of the new approach.

We develop a general efficient technique that allows one to construct non-membership NIZKs for a large class of languages where CLPØ only supported membership NIZKs. We use this technique for AC* and Π^*, but it potentially has many more applications. We show that CLPØ, in general, is amenable to a batching technique that allows decreasing the verifier's computation significantly.

The pairing-based setting is ubiquitous in contemporary public-key cryptography. Any advancement in concrete efficiency in simple problems like set-membership proofs is challenging. Our work demonstrates that the CH/CLPØ framework gives concretely better results than the seminal Groth-Sahai framework in this case. Importantly, this is the only known falsifiable framework that improves on the Groth-Sahai. Because of that, we argue that it is important to study different aspects of the CH/CLPØ framework.

Finally, in Sect. 7, we discuss using CLPØ to handle group elements.

Efficiency. In Table 1, we provide an efficiency comparison with some previously proposed set (non-)membership NIZKs. In the common case when $\mathbb{G}_2$ elements are twice longer than $\mathbb{G}_1$, the communication of Π^* is $\approx 42\%$ of the communication of [3]. Most impressively, the verifier has to execute $7 \ldots 10$ times fewer pairings than in [3]. As a related contribution, we show that CLPØ is (extremely) batching-friendly. Such an efficiency improvement over the best-known Groth-

Sahai-based solution is quite remarkable. In the case of prover's computation, we have taken the standard approach and assumed that the accumulator argument ($[q]_1$ in our case) is precomputed. This always makes sense if S is small (then all accumulator arguments can be precomputed), but it is also common in case S can be large. For example, in an anonymous credential system, one only needs to compute the accumulator argument for its own credential. Moreover, all signature-based solutions have precomputation built-in since the signatures are in the CRS. We hence assume precomputation in all cases.

Notably, AC* and $\mathbf{\Pi}^*$ have an updatable CRS. That is, it is possible to update the CRS sequentially so that the soundness relies only on the honesty of at least one of the updaters (or the original CRS creator). This partially eliminates the undesirable need to trust the CRS creator. None of the previous falsifiable set membership NIZKs (see Table 1) is updatable: this is caused by the use of (non-updatable) signature schemes and Groth-Sahai NIZK. See [11,19] for work on "transparent" accumulators that do not need a trusted CRS at all. We leave it as another open problem to construct a transparent, efficient, falsifiable set (non-)membership NIZK.

One can build more efficient set-membership arguments using (non-falsifiable) zk-SNARKs, but the most efficient zk-SNARKs are not updatable. While $\mathbf{\Pi}^*$'s efficiency is comparable to that of most efficient updatable and universal zk-SNARKs, the latter are only known to be secure in the ROM.

Due to the lack of space, we postpone additional preliminaries, all proofs and many details to the final version [20].

2   Preliminaries

An algebraic branching program (ABP) over a finite field $\mathbb{F}_p$ is defined by a directed acyclic graph (V, E), two special vertices $s, t \in V$, and a labeling function ϕ. It computes a function $F : \mathbb{F}_p^\nu \to \mathbb{F}_p$. Here, ϕ assigns to each edge in E a fixed affine function in input variables, and $F(\boldsymbol{X})$ is the sum over all $s - t$ paths (that is, paths from s to t) of the product of all the values along the path.

Ishai and Kushilevitz related ABPs to matrix determinants. Given an ABP $\mathsf{abp} = (V, E, s, t, \phi)$ computing $F : \mathbb{F}_p^\nu \to \mathbb{F}_p$, we can efficiently (and deterministically) compute a function $\mathsf{IK}_F(\boldsymbol{\chi})$ mapping an input $\boldsymbol{\chi} \in \mathbb{F}_p^\nu$ to a matrix from $\mathbb{F}_p^{\ell \times \ell}$, where $\ell = |V| - 1$, such that: (1) $\det \mathsf{IK}_F(\boldsymbol{\chi}) = F(\boldsymbol{\chi})$, (2) each entry of $\mathsf{IK}_F(\boldsymbol{\chi})$ is an affine map in a single variable χ_i, (3) $\mathsf{IK}_F(\boldsymbol{\chi})$ contains only -1's in the upper 1-diagonal (the diagonal above the main diagonal) and 0's above the upper 1-diagonal.

IK_F is obtained by transposing the matrix you get by removing the column corresponding to s and the row corresponding to t in the matrix $\mathsf{adj}(\boldsymbol{X}) - \boldsymbol{I}$. Here, $\mathsf{adj}(\boldsymbol{X})$ is the adjacency matrix for abp with $\mathsf{adj}(\boldsymbol{X})_{ij} = x$ iff $\phi(i \to j) = x$ and $\mathsf{adj}(\boldsymbol{X})_{ij} = 0$ if there is no edge $i \to j$. For example, assuming $F(X) = X^2 - X$, one can define an ABP with $\mathsf{adj}(X) = \left(\begin{smallmatrix} 0 & X & 0 \\ 0 & 0 & X-1 \\ 0 & 0 & 0 \end{smallmatrix} \right)$ and $\mathsf{IK}_F(X) = \left(\begin{smallmatrix} X & -1 \\ 0 & X-1 \end{smallmatrix} \right)$.

A bilinear group generator $\mathsf{Pgen}(1^\lambda)$ returns $\mathsf{p} = (p, \mathbb{G}_1, \mathbb{G}_2, \mathbb{G}_T, \hat{e}, [1]_1, [1]_2)$, where $\mathbb{G}_1$, $\mathbb{G}_2$, and $\mathbb{G}_T$ are three additive cyclic (thus, abelian) groups of prime order p, $\mathcal{P}_\iota = [1]_\iota$ is a generator of $\mathbb{G}_\iota$ for $\iota \in \{1, 2, T\}$ with $\mathcal{P}_T = [1]_T :=$ $\hat{e}([1]_1, [1]_2)$, and $\hat{e} : \mathbb{G}_1 \times \mathbb{G}_2 \to \mathbb{G}_T$ is a non-degenerate efficiently computable bilinear pairing. We require the bilinear pairing to be Type-3; that is, we assume that there is no efficient isomorphism between $\mathbb{G}_1$ and $\mathbb{G}_2$. We use the standard additive "bracket" notation, writing $[a]_\iota$ to denote $a\mathcal{P}_\iota = a[1]_\iota$ for $\iota \in \{1, 2, T\}$. We denote $\hat{e}([a]_1, [b]_2)$ by $[a]_1 \bullet [b]_2$. Thus, $[a]_1 \bullet [b]_2 = [ab]_T$. We freely use the bracket notation together with matrix notation; for example, if $AB = C$ then $[A]_1 \bullet [B]_2 = [C]_T$. We also define $[A]_2 \bullet [B]_1 := ([B]_1^\top \bullet [A]_2^\top)^\top = [AB]_T$.

We write $A \approx_\lambda B$ if the distributions A and B are computationally indistinguishable. Let $\ell, \mathsf{k} \in \mathbb{N}$, with $\ell \geq \mathsf{k}$, be small constants. In the case of asymmetric pairings, usually $\mathsf{k} = 1$. Let p be a large prime. A PPT-sampleable distribution $\mathcal{D}_{\ell, \mathsf{k}}$ is a *matrix distribution* if it samples matrices $A \in \mathbb{Z}_p^{\ell \times \mathsf{k}}$ of full rank k. $\mathcal{L}_1$ is the matrix distribution over matrices $\binom{1}{a}$, where $a \leftarrow_\$ \mathbb{Z}_p$.

The *XDH assumption in* $\mathbb{G}_\iota$ holds relative to Pgen if for every PPT $\mathcal{A}$,

$$\Pr\left[b' = b \,\middle|\, \begin{array}{l} \mathsf{p} \leftarrow \mathsf{Pgen}(1^\lambda); \sigma, \tau, \zeta \leftarrow_\$ \mathbb{Z}_p; b \leftarrow_\$ \{0,1\}; \\ b' \leftarrow \mathcal{A}([1, \sigma, \tau, \sigma\tau + b\zeta]_\iota) \end{array} \right] \approx_\lambda 0 \ .$$

Let $\ell, \mathsf{k} \in \mathbb{N}$, and $\mathcal{D}_\mathsf{k}$ be a matrix distribution. The $\mathcal{D}_\mathsf{k}$-$(\ell - 1)$-CED *assumption* [14] holds in $\mathbb{G}_\iota$ relative to Pgen, if for all PPT $\mathcal{A}$,

$$\Pr\left[\begin{array}{l} \boldsymbol{\delta} \in \mathbb{Z}_p^{(\ell-1) \times \mathsf{k}} \wedge \boldsymbol{\gamma} \in \mathbb{Z}_p^{\ell \times \mathsf{k}} \wedge \\ C \in \mathbb{Z}_p^{\ell \times \ell} \wedge (\boldsymbol{\gamma} \| C)\binom{D}{\delta} = \mathbf{0} \wedge \\ \mathrm{rk}(C) = \ell \end{array} \,\middle|\, \begin{array}{l} \mathsf{p} \leftarrow \mathsf{Pgen}(1^\lambda), [D]_\iota \leftarrow_\$ \mathcal{D}_\mathsf{k}, \\ ([\boldsymbol{\gamma}, C]_{3-\iota}, [\boldsymbol{\delta}]_\iota) \leftarrow \mathcal{A}(\mathsf{p}, [D]_\iota) \end{array} \right] \approx_\lambda 0 \ .$$

CED may or may not be falsifiable, see [14] for a discussion.

Following [13, 14], we will be only concerned with the case $\mathsf{k} = 1$ and $\mathcal{D}_\mathsf{k} = \mathcal{L}_1$. Then, $(\boldsymbol{\gamma} \| C)\binom{D}{\delta} = \mathbf{0}$ iff, after changing the sign of $\boldsymbol{\gamma}$, $C\binom{e}{\delta} = \boldsymbol{\gamma}$.

In Elgamal, the public key is $\mathsf{pk} = [1 \| \mathsf{sk}]_1$, and $\mathsf{Enc}_{\mathsf{pk}}(\chi; \varrho) \leftarrow (\varrho[1]_1 \| \chi[1]_1 + \varrho[\mathsf{sk}]_1)$, where $\varrho \leftarrow_\$ \mathbb{Z}_p$. We denote the encryption of $[\chi]_1$ by $\mathsf{Enc}_{\mathsf{pk}}([\chi]_1; \varrho) = (\varrho[1]_1 \| [\chi]_1 + \varrho[\mathsf{sk}]_1)$. To decrypt, one computes $[\chi]_1 = \mathsf{Dec}_{\mathsf{sk}}([l]_1) \leftarrow -\mathsf{sk}[c_1]_1 + [c_2]_1$; the result $[\chi]_1$ of the decryption is a group element and not an integer. Note that $\mathsf{pk} = \mathsf{Enc}_{\mathsf{pk}}(0; 1)$ and $[0 \| \chi]_1 = \mathsf{Enc}_{\mathsf{pk}}(\chi; 0)$. As always, we denote $\mathsf{Enc}_{\mathsf{pk}}([a]_1; \varrho) := (\mathsf{Enc}_{\mathsf{pk}}([a_i]_1; \varrho_i))_i$. Elgamal is IND-CPA secure under the XDH assumption.

2.1   Universal NIZK Arguments

Let $\{\mathcal{D}_\mathsf{p}\}_\mathsf{p}$ be a family of distributions, s.t. each $\mathtt{lp} \in \mathcal{D}_\mathsf{p}$ defines a language $\mathcal{L}_{\mathtt{lp}}$. A universal NIZK Π for $\{\mathcal{D}_\mathsf{p}\}_\mathsf{p}$ consists of six probabilistic algorithms:

$\mathsf{Pgen}(1^\lambda)$: generates public parameters p that fix a distribution $\mathcal{D}_\mathsf{p}$.

$\mathsf{Kgen}(\mathsf{p}, q)$: generates a CRS $\mathtt{crs}$ and a trapdoor $\mathtt{td}$. Here, q is a public size parameter (an upper bound of $|\mathcal{S}|$ in our case); we assume q is implicitly in the CRS. We omit q if the CRS does not depend on it. We assume that any group parameters are implicitly included in the CRS. We denote the sequence "$\mathsf{p} \leftarrow \mathsf{Pgen}(1^\lambda); (\mathtt{crs}, \mathtt{td}) \leftarrow \mathsf{Kgen}(\mathsf{p}, q)$" by $(\mathsf{p}, \mathtt{crs}, \mathtt{td}) \leftarrow \mathsf{Kgen}(1^\lambda, q)$.

Com(crs, lp): Given a CRS crs and a language description lp $\in \mathcal{D}_p$, outputs a specialized CRS crs_{lp}. We assume that crs_{lp} implicitly contains lp. Com is a deterministic algorithm that can be run by both the prover and the verifier. (Com is also known as CRS specialization algorithm, indexer, or derive.)

P(crs_{lp}, x, w): Given a specialized CRS crs_{lp} and a statement x with witness w, outputs an argument π for x $\in \mathcal{L}_{lp}$.

V(crs_{lp}, x, π): Given a specialized CRS crs_{lp}, a statement, and an argument, either accepts or rejects the argument.

Sim(crs_{lp}, td, x): Given a specialized CRS crs_{lp}, a trapdoor td, and a statement x, outputs a simulated argument for x $\in \mathcal{L}_{lp}$.

The CRS does not depend on the language distribution or language parameters. However, Com (applied on public arguments) allows one to derive a specialized CRS such that the verifier's operation is efficient given crs_{lp}.

Π for $\{\mathcal{D}_p\}_p$ is *perfectly complete*, if

$$\Pr\left[V(crs_{lp}, x, \pi) = 1 \middle| \begin{array}{l} (p, crs, td) \leftarrow_\$ K_{crs}(1^\lambda); lp \in \mathrm{Supp}(\mathcal{D}_p); \\ crs_{lp} \leftarrow \mathsf{Com}(crs, lp); \\ (x, w) \in \mathcal{R}_{lp}; \pi \leftarrow_\$ P(crs_{lp}, x, w) \end{array}\right] = 1 .$$

Π for $\{\mathcal{D}_p\}_p$ is *computationally sound*, if for every efficient $\mathcal{A}$,

$$\Pr\left[\begin{array}{l} V(crs_{lp}, x, \pi) = 1 \wedge \\ x \notin \mathcal{L}_{lp} \end{array} \middle| \begin{array}{l} (p, crs, td) \leftarrow_\$ K_{crs}(1^\lambda); lp \in \mathrm{Supp}(\mathcal{D}_p); \\ crs_{lp} \leftarrow \mathsf{Com}(crs, lp); (x, \pi) \leftarrow \mathcal{A}(crs, lp) \end{array}\right] \approx 0 .$$

Π for $\{\mathcal{D}_p\}_p$ is *perfectly zero-knowledge*, if for all λ, all $(p, crs, td) \in$ $\mathrm{Supp}(K_{crs}(1^\lambda))$, all lp $\in \mathrm{Supp}(\mathcal{D}_p)$ and all $(x, w) \in \mathcal{R}_{lp}$, the distributions P($crs_{lp}$, x, w) and Sim($crs_{lp}$, td, x) are identical.

Let $\mathcal{D}$ be some finite domain; next, $\mathcal{D} = \mathbb{Z}_p$. Let pk be an Elgamal public key and $\mathcal{S}$ be a set of size $\mathcal{S} \in \mathcal{D}^{\leq q}$ for fixed $q = \mathrm{poly}(\lambda)$. Let lp $= (\mathsf{pk}, \mathcal{S})$. In the case of NIZKs for set membership and non-membership, we are interested in the following complementary (commit-and-prove) languages:

$$\mathcal{L}_{lp}^{sm} = \{ [ct_\chi]_1 \mid \exists \chi, \varrho_\chi \text{ such that } \mathsf{Enc}_{pk}([\chi]_1; \varrho_\chi) = [ct_\chi]_1 \wedge \chi \in \mathcal{S} \} ,$$

$$\bar{\mathcal{L}}_{lp}^{sm} = \{ [ct_\chi]_1 \mid \exists \chi, \varrho_\chi \text{ such that } \mathsf{Enc}_{pk}([\chi]_1; \varrho_\chi) = [ct_\chi]_1 \wedge \chi \notin \mathcal{S} \} .$$

Benaloh and de Mare defined accumulators in [7]. Universal accumulators [11, 12, 18] allow non-membership arguments.

We define accumulators in the CRS model only. Thus, universal accumulators are set (non-)membership NIZKs in the case the input χ is public. That is, for lp $= \mathcal{S}$, a universal (CRS-model) accumulator is a (non-zk) set (non-)membership non-interactive argument system for the complementary languages $\mathcal{L}_{lp}^{acc} = \mathcal{S}$ and $\bar{\mathcal{L}}_{lp}^{acc} = \mathcal{D} \setminus \mathcal{S}$. The computation commitment algorithm Com corresponds to the accumulator's commitment algorithm that inputs a set $\mathcal{S}$ and outputs its short commitment. A CRS-model accumulator can have a trapdoor. However, since χ is public (and no zero-knowledge is required) then the trapdoor is not used.

$\mathsf{Pgen}(1^\lambda)$: the same as the bilinear group generator; returns p.

$\mathsf{Kgen}(\mathsf{p}, q)$: $\sigma \leftarrow_\$ \mathbb{Z}_p$; $\mathsf{crs} \leftarrow (\mathsf{p}, [(\sigma^i)_{i=0}^q]_1, [1, \sigma]_2)$; return $(\mathsf{crs}, \mathsf{td} = \sigma)$;

$\mathsf{Com}(\mathsf{crs}, \mathcal{S})$: given $|\mathcal{S}| = q$: output $[C_{\mathcal{S}}]_1 \leftarrow [\mathbf{Z}_{\mathcal{S}}(\sigma)]_1$;

$\mathsf{P}(\mathsf{crs}, \mathcal{S}, \chi)$: $r \leftarrow \mathbf{Z}_{\mathcal{S}}(\chi)$; $[\mathsf{q}]_1 \leftarrow [(\mathbf{Z}_{\mathcal{S}}(\sigma) - r)/(\sigma - \chi)]_1$;
  If $\chi \in \mathcal{S}$ then $\psi \leftarrow [\mathsf{q}]_1$ else $\psi \leftarrow ([\mathsf{q}]_1, r)$; return ψ;

$\mathsf{V}(\mathsf{crs}, C_{\mathcal{S}}, \chi, \psi)$: If ψ parses as $\psi = ([\mathsf{q}]_1, r)$ and $r = 0$ then return Error;
  If ψ parses as $\psi = [\mathsf{q}]_1$ then $r \leftarrow 0$;
  If $[\mathsf{q}]_1 \bullet ([\sigma]_2 - \chi[1]_2) + (r[1]_1 - [C_{\mathcal{S}}]_1) \bullet [1]_2 \neq [0]_T$ then return Error;
  If $r = 0$ then return Member else return NotMember;

Fig. 2. Nguyen's universal accumulator $\mathsf{ACC}_{\mathsf{Nguyen}}$.

As all argument systems, a universal accumulator must satisfy completeness and soundness properties. Because of the historical reasons, the latter is usually known as *collision-resistance*.

A universal accumulator ACC must be *perfectly complete*: for $(\mathsf{crs}, \mathsf{td}) \in \mathsf{Kgen}(1^\lambda)$, $\chi \in \mathcal{D}$, and $\mathcal{S} \in \mathcal{D}^{\leq q}$, $\mathsf{V}(\mathsf{crs}, \mathsf{Com}(\mathsf{crs}, \mathcal{S}), \chi, \mathsf{P}(\mathsf{crs}, \mathcal{S}, \chi))$ outputs Member if $\chi \in \mathcal{S}$ and NotMember if $\chi \notin \mathcal{S}$.

Definition 1. *Let* ACC *be a universal accumulator.* ACC *is* collision-resistant *[5] if for all* $q = \mathsf{poly}(\lambda)$ *and PPT adversaries* $\mathcal{A}$,

$$\Pr\left[\begin{array}{c} \mathcal{S} \in \mathcal{D}^{\leq q} \wedge \\ \left(\begin{array}{c} (\chi \notin \mathcal{S} \wedge v = \mathsf{Member}) \vee \\ (\chi \in \mathcal{S} \wedge v = \mathsf{NotMember}) \end{array}\right) \end{array} \middle| \begin{array}{l} \mathsf{p} \leftarrow \mathsf{Pgen}(1^\lambda); (\mathsf{crs}, \mathsf{td}) \leftarrow \mathsf{Kgen}(\mathsf{p}, q); \\ (\mathcal{S}, \chi, \psi) \leftarrow \mathcal{A}(\mathsf{crs}); \\ v \leftarrow \mathsf{V}(\mathsf{crs}, \mathsf{Com}(\mathsf{crs}, \mathcal{S}), \chi, \psi) \end{array}\right] \approx_\lambda 0 .$$

Nguyen [21] proposed a pairing-based CRS-model accumulator with $\mathcal{D} = \mathbb{Z}_p$. Damgård and Triandopoulos [15] and Au et al. [4] showed independently how to make it universal by adding a non-membership argument.

In Fig. 2, we depict the resulting CRS-model universal accumulator, assuming that $\mathcal{S} \in \mathcal{D}^{\leq q}$. Here, and in what follows, $\mathbf{Z}_{\mathcal{S}}(\Sigma) := \prod_{s \in \mathcal{S}}(\Sigma - s)$ is the vanishing polynomial of $\mathcal{S}$.

2.2 CLPØ NIZK

Since we build on CLPØ [14], we will give a lengthier description of their results. Fix $\mathsf{p} \leftarrow \mathsf{Pgen}(1^\lambda)$ and define $\mathcal{D}_\mathsf{p} := \{\mathsf{lp} = (\mathsf{pk}, F)\}$, where (1) pk is a randomly chosen Elgamal public key for encrypting in $\mathbb{G}_1$, and (2) F is a polynomial. The simplest version of CLPØ is a set membership NIZK for the set being defined as the set $\mathcal{Z}(F)$ of zeros of the fixed polynomial F.

More precisely, let $\mathcal{S} = \mathcal{Z}(F) := \{x : F(X) = 0\}$ for a polynomial F. Fix $\mathsf{p} \leftarrow \mathsf{Pgen}(1^\lambda)$. For a fixed Elgamal public key pk, let $\mathsf{lp} := (\mathsf{pk}, F)$. (Implicitly, lp also contains p.) Let $[\mathbf{ct}_\chi]_1 := \mathsf{Enc}_\mathsf{pk}([\chi]_1; \varrho) = (\mathsf{Enc}_\mathsf{pk}([\chi_i]_1; \varrho_i))_i$. Define

$$\mathcal{L}_\mathsf{lp} = \{[\mathbf{ct}_\chi]_1 : \exists \chi \text{ such that } \mathsf{Dec}_\mathsf{sk}([\mathbf{ct}_\chi]_1) = [\chi]_1 \wedge \chi \in \mathcal{Z}(F)\} . \tag{1}$$

$\mathsf{Pgen}(1^\lambda)$: returns the system parameters p, as always.

$\mathsf{Kgen}(\mathsf{p})$: $e \leftarrow_\$ \mathbb{Z}_p$; return $(\mathsf{crs}, \mathsf{td}) \leftarrow ([e]_2, e)$;

$\mathsf{Com}(\mathsf{crs}, \mathsf{lp})$: return $\mathsf{crs}_{\mathsf{lp}} \leftarrow (\mathsf{crs}, \mathsf{lp})$;

$\mathsf{P}(\mathsf{crs}_{\mathsf{lp}}, \mathbb{x} = [\mathbf{ct}_\chi]_1, \mathbb{w} = (\chi, \varrho))$: Write $\mathbf{C}(\chi) = (\mathbf{h}\|\mathbf{T})(\chi)$;
   $\varrho_\delta \leftarrow_\$ \mathbb{Z}_p^{\ell-1}$; $\gamma \leftarrow -\mathbf{T}(\chi)\varrho_\delta$;
   Compute $\mathbf{w}$ such that $\mathbf{T}(\chi)\mathbf{w} = \mathbf{h}(\chi)$;
   $[\delta]_2 \leftarrow -(\mathbf{w}[e]_2 + \varrho_\delta[1]_2)$;
   $\varrho_\gamma \leftarrow_\$ \mathbb{Z}_p^\ell$; $[\mathbf{ct}_\gamma]_1 \leftarrow \mathsf{Enc}_{\mathsf{pk}}([\gamma]_1; \varrho_\gamma) \in \mathbb{G}_1^{\ell \times 2}$;
   $[\mathbf{z}]_2 \leftarrow \left(\sum_{k=1}^\nu \varrho_k \mathbf{P}_k\right) \begin{bmatrix} e \\ \delta \end{bmatrix}_2 - \varrho_\gamma[1]_2 \in \mathbb{G}_2^\ell$;
   Return $\pi \leftarrow ([\mathbf{ct}_\gamma]_1, [\delta, \mathbf{z}]_2) \in \mathbb{G}_1^{\ell \times 2} \times \mathbb{G}_2^{2\ell-1}$;

$\mathsf{V}(\mathsf{crs}_{\mathsf{lp}}, \mathbb{x} = [\mathbf{ct}_\chi]_1, \pi)$: check $\sum_{k=1}^\nu \left(\mathbf{P}_k \begin{bmatrix} e \\ \delta \end{bmatrix}_2 \bullet [\mathbf{ct}_{\chi_k}]_1\right) + \mathbf{Q} \begin{bmatrix} e \\ \delta \end{bmatrix}_2 \bullet [0\|1]_1 = [\mathbf{I}_\ell]_2 \bullet [\mathbf{ct}_\gamma]_1 + [\mathbf{z}]_2 \bullet \mathsf{pk}$;

$\mathsf{Sim}(\mathsf{crs}_{\mathsf{lp}}, \mathsf{td}, \mathbb{x} = [\mathbf{ct}_\chi]_1)$: $\delta \leftarrow_\$ \mathbb{Z}_p^{\ell-1}$;
   $\mathbf{z} \leftarrow_\$ \mathbb{Z}_p^\ell$; $[\mathbf{ct}_\gamma]_1 \leftarrow \sum_{k=1}^\nu \mathbf{P}_k(\begin{smallmatrix} e \\ \delta \end{smallmatrix})[\mathbf{ct}_{\chi_k}]_1 + \mathsf{Enc}_{\mathsf{pk}}(\mathbf{Q}(\begin{smallmatrix} e \\ \delta \end{smallmatrix})[1]_1; -\mathbf{z})$;
   Return $\pi \leftarrow ([\mathbf{ct}_\gamma]_1, [\delta, \mathbf{z}]_2) \in \mathbb{G}_1^{\ell \times 2} \times \mathbb{G}_2^{2\ell-1}$;

Fig. 3. The commit-and-prove CLPØ NIZK $\Pi_{\mathsf{clpø}}$ for $\mathcal{L}_{\mathsf{pk}, F}$.

Hence, $\mathcal{L}_{\mathsf{lp}}$ is a commit-and-prove language. For example, if $F(X) = X^2 - X$, then $\mathcal{L}_{\mathsf{pk}, F}$ corresponds to the language of all Elgamal encryptions of Boolean values under the fixed public key pk.

Let $F(\mathbf{X}) \in \mathbb{Z}_p[\mathbf{X}]$ be a ν-variate polynomial. Let $\ell \geq 1$ be an integer. A matrix $\mathbf{C}(\mathbf{X}) = (C_{ij}(\mathbf{X})) \in \mathbb{Z}_p[\mathbf{X}]^{\ell \times \ell}$ is *a quasideterminantal representation* (QDR, [14]) of F, if the following requirements hold. Here, $\mathbf{C}(\mathbf{X}) = (\mathbf{h}(\mathbf{X})\|\mathbf{T}(\mathbf{X}))$, where $\mathbf{h}(\mathbf{X})$ is a column vector.

Affine map: $\mathbf{C}(\mathbf{X}) = \sum_{k=1}^\nu \mathbf{P}_k X_k + \mathbf{Q}$, where $\mathbf{P}_k, \mathbf{Q} \in \mathbb{Z}_p^{\ell \times \ell}$.
F-rank: $\det \mathbf{C}(\mathbf{X}) = F(\mathbf{X})$.
First column dependence: For any $\chi \in \mathcal{Z}(F)$, $\mathbf{h}(\chi) \in \mathrm{colspace}(\mathbf{T}(\chi))$. That is, $\mathbf{h}(\chi) = \mathbf{T}(\chi)\mathbf{w}$ for some $\mathbf{w}$.

The quasideterminantal complexity $\mathsf{qdc}(F)$ of F is the smallest QDR size of F. (Clearly, $\mathsf{qdc}(F) \geq \deg(F)$.) We always assume that the polynomial F in lp satisfies $\mathsf{qdc}(F) = \mathsf{poly}(\lambda)$, that is, there exists a $\mathsf{poly}(\lambda)$-size QDR $\mathbf{C}(\mathbf{X})$ of F. [14] showed that such QDRs exist for many F-s.

In Fig. 3, we depict the commit-and-prove updatable universal CLPØ NIZK $\Pi_{\mathsf{clpø}}$. Intuitively, the verifier checks that $\begin{bmatrix} e \\ \delta \end{bmatrix}_2 \bullet [\mathbf{C}(\mathbf{ct}_\chi)]_1 = [\mathbf{I}_\ell]_2 \bullet [\mathbf{ct}_\gamma]_1 + [\mathbf{z}]_2 \bullet \mathsf{pk}$, where $[\mathbf{C}(\mathbf{ct}_\chi)]_1 := \sum_{k=1}^\nu \mathbf{P}_k \cdot [\mathbf{ct}_{\chi_k}]_1 + \mathbf{Q} \cdot \mathsf{Enc}_{\mathsf{pk}}(1; 0)$ encrypts $\mathbf{C}(\chi)$. Couteau et al. [14] did not use the terminology of commit-and-prove, universal, and updatable NIZKs. Still, $\Pi_{\mathsf{clpø}}$ satisfies these properties.

CLPØ is perfectly complete and perfectly zero-knowledge. It is computationally (adaptive) sound under the $\mathcal{L}_1$-$(\ell - 1)$-CED assumption in $\mathbb{G}_2$ relative to Pgen. See [14].

Couteau et al. [14] constructed a QDR $\mathsf{IK}_F(\mathbf{X})$ for any polynomial F that can be efficiently computed by an algebraic branching program (ABP). As proven

Fig. 4. ABP $\overline{\mathsf{abp}}$ for the $\bar{F}(\boldsymbol{X}, X_{\nu+1}) = F(\boldsymbol{X})X_{\nu+1} - 1$ and the matrix $\mathsf{IK}_{\bar{F}}(\boldsymbol{X}, X_{\nu+1})$.

in [14], if $\mathsf{abp} = (V, E, s, t, \phi)$ is an ABP that computes a ν-variate polynomial $F(\boldsymbol{X})$, then $\mathsf{IK}_F(\boldsymbol{X})$ is a QDR of F with $\ell = |V| - 1$. In particular, $\mathsf{qdc}(F) \leq |V| - 1$. This results in NIZKs for $\mathcal{L}_{\mathsf{pk},F}$ whenever F has a small ABP.

Optimized Verifier. As an independent contribution, we observe that the verifier can be batched by sampling $\eta \leftarrow_s \mathbb{F}$ and then batching together all pairings with the same $\mathbb{G}_2$ argument. It is evident from Fig. 3 that in this case, the verifier needs to perform pairings (at most) with e, each coefficient of $\boldsymbol{\delta}$, $[1]_2$, and each coefficient of $\boldsymbol{z}$. Moreover, pairings with different z_i can also be batched together since they will have related $\mathbb{G}_1$ elements. This results in at most $\ell + 2$ pairings. On the other hand, a non-batched verifier may have to execute $\Theta(\ell^2)$ pairings.

3   General Non-membership NIZK Argument System

For a set $\mathcal{F}$ of polynomials, let $\mathsf{Z}(\mathcal{F})$ be the set of common zeros of all $F_i \in \mathcal{F}$. Next, we construct efficient (commit-and-prove, updatable, universal) non-membership NIZKs for $\mathcal{S} = \mathsf{Z}(\mathcal{F})$, given that for each $F_i \in \mathcal{F}$, there exists a small ABP that computes F_i. The modifications are at the level of ABP and thus do not depend on the details of $\Pi_{\mathsf{clp\o}}$. Since non-membership NIZKs have their own applications [4,8–10], the current section has independent importance.

Assume $\mathcal{F} = \{F\}$, where $F(\boldsymbol{X}) : \mathbb{F}_p^\nu \mapsto \mathbb{F}_p$ is a polynomial that can be computed by a small ABP $\mathsf{abp} = (V, E, s, t, \phi)$. We construct a new ABP $\overline{\mathsf{abp}}$ as follows (see Fig. 4): we add to abp a new target vertex $\bar{t}$ and two edges, $s \to \bar{t}$ and $t \to \bar{t}$. We naturally extend ϕ to a new labeling function $\bar{\phi}$, such that $\bar{\phi}(s \to \bar{t}) = -1$ and $\bar{\phi}(t \to \bar{t}) = X_{\nu+1}$, where $X_{\nu+1}$ is a new indeterminate. Let $\bar{F}(\boldsymbol{X}, X_{\nu+1}) : \mathbb{F}_p^{\nu+1} \mapsto \mathbb{F}_p$, with $\bar{F}(\boldsymbol{X}, X_{\nu+1}) = F(\boldsymbol{X})X_{\nu+1} - 1$, be the polynomial computed by $\overline{\mathsf{abp}}$. Clearly, if $F(\boldsymbol{\chi}) = 0$ for a concrete input assignment $\boldsymbol{\chi}$, then $\bar{F}(\boldsymbol{\chi}, \chi_{\nu+1}) = -1 \neq 0$ for all values of $\chi_{\nu+1}$. On the other hand, if $F(\boldsymbol{\chi}) \neq 0$, then there exists $\chi_{\nu+1} = F(\boldsymbol{\chi})^{-1}$, such that $\bar{F}(\boldsymbol{\chi}, \chi_{\nu+1}) = 0$.

Thus, to obtain a non-membership NIZK for the algebraic set $\mathcal{S} = \mathsf{Z}(F)$, it suffices to construct a membership NIZK for the algebraic set $\bar{\mathcal{S}} = \mathsf{Z}(\bar{F})$. For this, one can use $\Pi_{\mathsf{clp\o}}$ from Fig. 4 for the QDR $\mathsf{IK}_{\bar{F}}$. The resulting NIZK is again secure under a CED assumption. Moreover, if the NIZK for F relies on a falsifiable version of CED, then so does the NIZK for $\bar{F}$.

To show that $\chi \neq 0$, we can run $\Pi_{\mathsf{clp\o}}$ with the QDR $\bar{C}(\mathsf{X}, \mathsf{S}) := \left(\begin{smallmatrix} \mathsf{X} & -1 \\ -1 & \mathsf{S} \end{smallmatrix} \right)$ where in the honest case, $\mathsf{S} = 1/\mathsf{X}$. One can easily extend it to the proof that two plaintexts χ_1 and χ_2 are unequal, by using the QDR $\bar{C}(\mathsf{X}_1, \mathsf{X}_2, \mathsf{S}) := \left(\begin{smallmatrix} \mathsf{X}_1 - \mathsf{X}_2 & -1 \\ -1 & \mathsf{S} \end{smallmatrix} \right)$, where in the honest case, $\mathsf{S} = 1/(\mathsf{X}_1 - \mathsf{X}_2)$.

The argument length of the resulting NIZKs (including encryption of s but not of χ or χ_i) is $6\mathfrak{g}_1 + 3\mathfrak{g}_2$. They are based on a less standard and non-falsifiable assumption (CED instead of SXDH) but are significantly more efficient than Groth-Sahai-based constructions of [9,10]. In particular, the communication of the NIZK of plaintext inequality of [9] consists of 15 elements of $\mathbb{G}_1$, 4 elements of $\mathbb{G}_2$, and 2 elements of $\mathbb{Z}_p$. (The more efficient construction [8] works in the random oracle model.)

Finally, consider the task of proving that an encrypted integer χ is non-Boolean. In this case, one can define the QDR $C_{\{0,1\}}(X, S) := \begin{pmatrix} X & -1 & 0 \\ 0 & X-1 & -1 \\ -1 & 0 & S \end{pmatrix}$.

Let $\mathcal{F} = \{F_1, \ldots, F_\nu\}$ for $\nu > 1$. To obtain a set non-membership NIZK for $\mathcal{S} = \mathcal{Z}(\mathcal{F})$, we first construct an ABP that computes each $\bar{F}_i$ (see the previous subsubsection). Then, we construct an ABP that computes a polynomial $\bar{F}(\boldsymbol{X})$, s.t. $\bar{F}(\chi) = 0$ iff $\bar{F}_i(\chi) = 0$ for some i. Define $\bar{F}(\boldsymbol{X}) = \prod \bar{F}_i(\boldsymbol{X})$, and define its ABP as the concatenation of the ABPs for individual polynomials $\bar{F}_i$:

$$s \longrightarrow \boxed{\text{ABP for } \bar{F}_1(X)} \rightarrow \circ \longrightarrow \boxed{\text{ABP for } \bar{F}_2(X)} \rightarrow \circ \cdots\cdots\cdots \rightarrow \circ \longrightarrow \boxed{\text{ABP for } \bar{F}_n(X)} \rightarrow t$$

We then use $\boldsymbol{\Pi}_{\mathsf{clp\o}}$ for the QDR $\mathsf{IK}_{\bar{F}}$ from Fig. 4. The resulting NIZK is secure under the CED assumption.

4   Determinantal Accumulators

Clearly, universal accumulator is a *non-zk* set (non-)membership non-interactive argument system that possesses both membership and non-membership arguments. It makes sense to construct a set (non-)membership NIZK by constructing an accumulator and then adding a zero-knowledge layer to obtain privacy.

Both steps of the described blueprint can be expensive per se. We are interested in constructing a CLPØ-style set (non-)membership NIZK where the second step is as simple as possible. To achieve this, we first reinterpret $\boldsymbol{\Pi}_{\mathsf{clp\o}}$. We then use the obtained understanding to define and construct *determinantal accumulators* that allow for a lightweight zero-knowledge layer. For the latter, a determinantal accumulator must have a specific structure consistent with $\boldsymbol{\Pi}_{\mathsf{clp\o}}$'s design.

Recall that in $\boldsymbol{\Pi}_{\mathsf{clp\o}}$ [14], one rewrites the condition $\chi \in \mathcal{S}$ as the condition $F_i(\chi) = 0$ for a set of polynomials $\{F_i\}$.[3] After that, one constructs QDRs $C_i(\boldsymbol{X})$ for each F_i, such that $\det C_i(\boldsymbol{X}) = F_i(\boldsymbol{X})$. This step can be seen as linearization: while F_i can be a high-degree polynomial, each entry of C_i is an affine map. As typical in group-based cryptography, it is easier to solve linearized tasks. After that, [14] proposes a technique of constructing QDRs (i.e., linearization algorithm) by using algebraic branching programs.

Given the QDRs, $\boldsymbol{\Pi}_{\mathsf{clp\o}}$'s prover P aims to convince the verifier V that each $\det C_i(\chi)$ is zero. Crucially, V has access only to encrypted $[\chi]_1$ but not to

---

[3] In our new primitives, the set consists of only one polyomial. However, the framework is valid in the more general case.

χ or even $[\chi]_1$. Since each entry of C_i is affine and the cryptosystem is additively homomorphic, V can compute an encryption of $[C_i(\chi)]_1$ given an encryption of $[\chi]_1$. Knowing sk, the soundness reduction decrypts ciphertexts, obtains $[C_i(\chi)]_1$, and uses it to break CED. To preserve privacy, the verifier cannot know $[C_i(\chi)]_1$ and thus also not $\det C_i(\chi)$.

In a *non-zk* CLPØ-style non-interactive argument system, we proceed as in CLPØ, except that we do not encrypt any of the values. In particular, similarly to the soundness reduction in $\boldsymbol{\Pi}_{\mathsf{clpø}}$, V has access to $[\chi]_1$ and thus also to $[C_i(\chi)]_1$. To be compatible with CLPØ, the verifier is not however given access to $\det C_i(\chi)$ or even χ as integers. Given this, we must take additional care to ensure the accumulator's security.

4.1   Determinant Verification

The verifier needs to check efficiently that the determinant of a given matrix $C_i(\chi)$ is zero. The main problem is that since the verifier sees $[C_i(\chi)]_1$ but not $C_i(\chi)$, the verifier's task is intractable. Next, we outline a straightforward but non-satisfactory solution to this problem together with three modifications.

First, without any additional hints given to the verifier, we have an accumulator with inefficient verification, where the verifier computes the discrete logarithm of $[C_i(\chi)]_1$ to obtain $C_i(\chi)$. This might be fine in the NIZK since the NIZK verifier does not have to perform the accumulator verification; instead, the NIZK verifier checks (efficiently) the NIZK argument showing that the accumulator verifier accepts. However, since also the soundness reduction does not get any hints about $C_i(\chi)$, it will not be able to verify whether this results in a non-falsifiable NIZK, as explained in [13,14].

Second, following [1], we can allow the prover to output as hints all partial multiplications needed in the Leibniz formula for the determinant. In that case, one can obtain a PPT verifiable accumulator and thus a NIZK based on falsifiable assumptions. However, while PPT, it is concretely very expensive: if the dimension of the matrix is large, the hint is potentially huge [1].

Moreover, since in the NIZK, one has to encrypt the matrix elements in both groups, and use the less efficient DLIN encryption, see [14].

Third, we can use the undergraduate linear-algebraic fact that $\det C = 0$ iff there exists a non-zero vector x such that $Cx = 0$. We can utilize this fact by outputting $[x]_2$ as a hint to the verifier/soundness reduction. However, $[x]_2$ can reveal secret information and thus must be hidden. We do not want to encrypt $[x]_2$: since $[x]_2$ is given in $\mathbb{G}_2$, this means that one again needs to use DLIN.

Fourth, we rely on CED. Recall that CED states that $\det C = 0$ iff one can compute vectors γ and δ such that $C\left(\begin{smallmatrix}e\\\delta\end{smallmatrix}\right) = \gamma$, where $e \leftarrow_s \mathbb{Z}_p$. (The first coordinate of $x = \left(\begin{smallmatrix}e\\\delta\end{smallmatrix}\right)$ is non-zero w.p. $1 - 1/p$ since C is a QDR.) For the security of CED, γ must not depend on e. Here, as in [13,14], δ is masked by uniformly random addend ϱ_δ and γ is needed to balance ϱ_δ. Thus, the prover gives $([\gamma]_1, [\delta]_2)$ as a hint to the verifier/soundness reduction. In the NIZK, $[\gamma]_1$ is encrypted but $[\delta]_2$ (that looks uniformly random after adding ϱ_δ) is not.

While the resulting accumulator is less efficient than Nguyen's, the new NIZK (see Sect. 6) is very efficient since it reuses the hints $([\gamma]_1, [\delta]_2)$.

The reasoning from Sect. 4.1 shows that one can construct an efficient accumulator (and NIZK) even if χ is only given to the verifier in $\mathbb{G}_1$. This motivates the new definition of determinantal accumulators. The relation between determinantal accumulators and CLPØ is similar to that between structure-preserving signatures and Groth-Sahai. For comparison purposes only, in the final version [20], we will define structure-preserving signature schemes [2].

Our definition of determinantal accumulators is very close in spirit. For clarity, we highlight the differences between "structure preserving" and "determinantal" primitives. Other differences are caused by having an accumulator instead of a signature scheme.

Definition 2 (Determinantal accumulator). *An accumulator is determinantal relative to bilinear group generator* Pgen *if (a) the common parameters* p *and the CRS consist of group description generated by* Pgen, *some constants, and some source group elements in* $\mathbb{G}_1$ *and* $\mathbb{G}_2$, *(b) the verification algorithm* V *consists only of evaluating membership in* $\mathbb{G}_1$ *and* $\mathbb{G}_2$ *and relations described by checking that* $C_i(\chi) = 0$, *where each* $C_i(X)$ *is a QDR, (c) the CRS* crs, *messages* χ, *commitments* C_S, *and membership arguments* ψ *solely consist of group elements in* $\mathbb{G}_1$ *and* $\mathbb{G}_2$, *(d) messages* χ *are given to the verifier as elements of* $\mathbb{G}_1$, *(e) the set of* $\mathbb{G}_2$ *elements in* ψ *is independent of* χ.

Items d and e help creating efficient NIZKs, where one only has to encrypt elements of $\mathbb{G}_1$. We assume that all determinantal accumulators use the fourth method from Sect. 4.1. Since in that case, the only $\mathbb{G}_2$ element in ψ is δ and the latter is chosen uniformly from $\mathbb{G}_2$ in [14], Item e follows automatically.

Clearly, this approach is not restricted to accumulators.

Determinantal primitives are quite different from SPPs. First, compared to SPPs, we restrict the inputs to be from a single source group. While this is a restriction, it potentially boosts efficiency: since all inputs have to be encrypted in one source group, one can use Elgamal instead of less efficient DLIN or Groth-Sahai commitments. Because $\mathbb{G}_2$ elements are often twice longer than $\mathbb{G}_1$ elements, this can make the statement of the NIZK (commitment to χ) three times shorter.

Second, the verifier is not restricted to quadratic equations: the QDRs C_i can be polynomially large. In the new non-membership accumulator, the determinant of the used C_i is a cubic polynomial. This means that some of the known lower-bounds for SPPs (e.g., [2]) *might* not apply.

Third, and crucially, determinantal accumulators are (efficient) CLPØ-style non-zk non-interactive argument systems. On the other hand, structure-preserving signatures are independent primitives with the property that one can construct (efficient) Groth-Sahai NIZKs for tasks like signature possession. It is not known how to construct structure-preserving accumulators.

5   The New Determinantal Accumulator AC^*

In the new set (non-)membership NIZK, χ is Elgamal-encrypted. In the soundness reduction, the reduction decrypts it to obtain $[\chi]_1$ but does not obtain χ. Because of that, the collision-resistance property must hold against adversaries who return $[\chi]_1$ but not χ. Definition 3 is inspired by the definition of F-unforgeable signature schemes, [6], where F is an efficiently computable one-way bijection. Since F is a bijection, $\chi \in \mathcal{S}$ iff $F(\chi) \in F(\mathcal{S})$ iff $\exists s \in \mathcal{S}.F(\chi) = F(s)$.

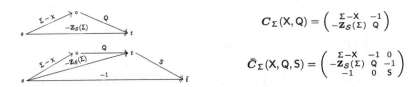

$$C_\Sigma(\mathsf{X},\mathsf{Q}) = \begin{pmatrix} \Sigma - \mathsf{X} & -1 \\ -\mathbf{Z}_S(\Sigma) & \mathsf{Q} \end{pmatrix}$$

$$\bar{C}_\Sigma(\mathsf{X},\mathsf{Q},\mathsf{S}) = \begin{pmatrix} \Sigma - \mathsf{X} & -1 & 0 \\ -\mathbf{Z}_S(\Sigma) & \mathsf{Q} & -1 \\ -1 & 0 & \mathsf{S} \end{pmatrix}$$

Fig. 5. Above: ABP for $F_\Sigma(\mathsf{X},\mathsf{Q})$ and the QDR $C_\Sigma(\mathsf{X},\mathsf{Q})$. Below: ABP for $\bar{F}_\Sigma(\mathsf{X},\mathsf{Q},\mathsf{S})$ and the QDR $\bar{C}_\Sigma(\mathsf{X},\mathsf{Q},\mathsf{S})$.

Definition 3. *Let $\mathcal{D}$ be a domain and F be an efficiently computable (one-way) bijection. A universal accumulator ACC is F-collision resistant if for any $q = \mathsf{poly}(\lambda)$ and PPT adversaries $\mathcal{A}$,* $\mathsf{Adv}_{\mathsf{Pgen},F,\mathsf{ACC},\mathcal{A}}^{\mathsf{f-cr}}(\lambda) :=$

$$\Pr\left[\begin{array}{l} \mathcal{S} \in \mathcal{D}^{\leq q} \wedge \\ \left(\begin{array}{l} (\chi \notin \mathcal{S} \wedge v = \mathsf{Member}) \vee \\ (\chi \in \mathcal{S} \wedge v = \mathsf{NotMember}) \end{array} \right) \end{array} \middle| \begin{array}{l} \mathsf{p} \leftarrow \mathsf{Pgen}(1^\lambda); \\ (\mathsf{crs},\sigma) \leftarrow \mathsf{Kgen}(\mathsf{p},q); \\ (\mathcal{S}, F(\chi),\psi) \leftarrow \mathcal{A}(\mathsf{crs}); \\ v \leftarrow \mathsf{V}(\mathsf{crs},\mathsf{Com}(\mathsf{crs},\mathcal{S}), F(\chi),\psi) \end{array} \right] \approx_\lambda 0 .$$

In what follows, $F = [\cdot]_1$.

In Fig. 6, we propose a new F-collision-resistant determinantal (CRS-model, universal) accumulator AC^*. Next, we give the intuition behind its construction. The first task constructing AC^* is to fix suitable verification equation that defines a polynomial $F(\boldsymbol{X})$, such that the verifier accepts iff $F(\chi) = 0$. Given F, we use an ABP to define a QDR $C(\boldsymbol{X})$ for F.

In the membership argument, we start with the verification equation of $\mathsf{ACC}_{\mathsf{Nguyen}}$ which defines the bivariate polynomial $F_\Sigma(\mathsf{X},\mathsf{Q}) := (\Sigma - \mathsf{X})\mathsf{Q} - \mathbf{Z}_S(\Sigma)$. Here, say, Q is the indeterminate corresponding to $\mathsf{q} \in \psi$ (see Fig. 2. Clearly, the membership argument verifier of $\mathsf{ACC}_{\mathsf{Nguyen}}$ accepts iff $[F_\sigma(\chi,\mathsf{q})]_1 = [0]_1$.

In the non-membership argument, we need to prove that $F_\Sigma(\mathsf{X},\mathsf{Q}) \neq 0$. We use the method of Sect. 3 by defining the polynomial $\bar{F}_\Sigma(\mathsf{X},\mathsf{Q},\mathsf{S}) := ((\Sigma - \mathsf{X})\mathsf{Q} - \mathbf{Z}_S(\Sigma))\mathsf{S} - 1$.

We index F and $\tilde{F}$ with Σ instead of giving Σ as a formal argument. We do it because Σ (a trapdoor indeterminate, with various powers like $[\sigma^i]_1$ being present in the CRS) has a different semantics compared to indeterminates X,

Q, and S that correspond to the argument elements. In particular, $[\sigma^i]_1$ do not have to stay hidden in the set (non-)membership NIZK. Crucially, this allows to think of F_Σ and $\tilde{F}_\Sigma$ as low-degree polynomials with coefficients from $\mathcal{R} = \mathbb{Z}_p[\Sigma]$.

Since F_Σ and $\tilde{F}_\Sigma$ have degrees ≤ 2 and ≤ 3, they have respectively 2×2 and 3×3 QDRs $C_\Sigma(X, Q)$ and $\bar{C}_\Sigma(X, Q, S)$. We construct these QDRs from algebraic branching programs for F_Σ and $\bar{F}_\Sigma$. See Fig. 5 for the description of the resulting ABP and QDR for F_Σ and $\bar{F}_\Sigma$. The membership (resp., non-membership) argument verifier needs to check that $\det C(\chi, q) = 0$ (resp., $\det \bar{C}(\chi, q, s) = 0$).

Since we construct a determinantal accumulator, in the membership argument, we check $\det C(\chi, q) = 0$ by using the hints $[\gamma]_1$ and $[\delta]_2$. The verifier checks that $[C(\chi)]_1 \bullet [{}^e_\delta]_2 = [\gamma]_1 \bullet [1]_2$, which can be rewritten as checking

$$
\begin{aligned}
([\sigma]_1 - [\chi]_1) \bullet [e]_2 - [1]_1 \bullet [\delta]_2 &= [\gamma_1]_1 \bullet [1]_2 \ , \\
-[\mathbf{Z}_\mathcal{S}(\sigma)]_1 \bullet [e]_2 + [q]_1 \bullet [\delta]_2 &= [\gamma_2]_1 \bullet [1]_2 \ .
\end{aligned} \tag{2}
$$

Here, $[\chi]_1$ is the input, $([q, \gamma]_1, [\delta]_2)$ are parts of the (non-)membership argument, and $[\sigma, \mathbf{Z}_\mathcal{S}(\sigma)]_1$ can be computed from crs.

Unfortunately, this is not sufficient. Maliciously chosen $\chi = \chi(\Sigma)$, $q = q(\Sigma)$, and $\delta = \delta(\Sigma)$ can depend non-trivially on σ. Intuitively, Eq. (2) guarantees that $\mathbf{Z}_\mathcal{S}(\Sigma) = (\Sigma - \chi(\Sigma))q(\Sigma)$ and thus $(\Sigma - \chi(\Sigma)) \mid \mathbf{Z}_\mathcal{S}(\Sigma)$. If χ is an integer, we get $\mathbf{Z}_\mathcal{S}(\chi) = 0$. However, if χ depends on σ, then $\mathbf{Z}_\mathcal{S}(\chi) = 0$ does not follow. E.g., to break the membership argument, the adversary can fix any $\delta_1, \delta_2 \in \mathbb{Z}_p$ and set $[\chi]_1 \leftarrow [\sigma]_1 - \delta_2[1]_1$, $[\delta]_2 \leftarrow \delta_1[1]_2 + \delta_2[e]_2$, $[q]_1 \leftarrow [\mathbf{Z}_\mathcal{S}(\sigma)]_1/\delta_2$, $[\gamma_1]_1 \leftarrow -[\delta_1]_1$, $[\gamma_2]_1 \leftarrow \delta_1/\delta_2 \cdot [\mathbf{Z}_\mathcal{S}(\sigma)]_1$. This results in Eq. (2) holding and thus breaks the F-collision-resistance of the version of AC* that only uses Eq. (2) as verification equations. Breaking F-collision-resistance of $\mathsf{ACC}_{\mathsf{Nguyen}}$ is even more trivial.[4]

To counteract this problem, we must guarantee that χ does not depend on σ. We do this by introducing an additional trapdoor τ. We then slightly modify Eq. (2), making the checks explicitly dependent on τ. The resulting modified checks result in b_1 and b_2 in the final construction of AC* in Fig. 6.

Since now crs depends on τ, the adversary can make its outputs depend on τ; this opens a new cheating avenue. Hence, our use of τ is non-trivial, especially since we achieve F-collision-resistance without hampering the efficiency of AC*. We explicitly multiply each term of type $[\alpha]_1 \bullet [\beta]_2$ in b_1 and b_2 by τ, except the terms $[q]_1 \bullet [\delta]_2$ and $[\gamma]_1 \bullet [1]_2$. In the AGM security proof of the underlying assumption, we get that values like χ, which are multiplied by τ, are in the span of 1 (that is, integers). However, q must be a polynomial (it depends on σ), that is, in the span of $\{\sigma^i\tau\}$; thus we do not multiply $[q]_1 \bullet [\delta]_2$ by τ. The same holds for γ_2. Finally, it is not essential whether γ_1 depends on σ or not; not multiplying it by τ simplifies the AGM proof slightly since then we do not need to add $[\tau]_2$ to the CRS. Nevertheless, the AGM proof is very delicate.

Note that the verification equations ($b_1 = b_2 = \mathsf{true}$) are mathematically (but not computationally) equivalent to checking that $C'(\chi, q) \left({}^e_\delta\right) = \gamma$, where

---

[4] In the collision-resistance proof of $\mathsf{ACC}_{\mathsf{Nguyen}}$, χ and r are given as integers and thus do not depend on σ. Such a problem did also not exist in [13,14] since there the CRS only contained a single element $[e]_2$ and thus did not depend on σ.

$$C'(X, Q) := \begin{pmatrix} (\Sigma - X)T & -T \\ -Z_S(\Sigma)T & Q \end{pmatrix}.$$ Here, $\det C'(X, Q) = ((\Sigma - X)Q - Z_S(\Sigma)T)\, T$. That is, we really use the QDR framework of [14]. The description of V in Fig. 6 just spells out how to do this verification in PPT.

Kgen(p, q): $\sigma, \tau, e \leftarrow_\$ \mathbb{Z}_p$; $crs \leftarrow ([1, (\sigma^i \tau)_{i=0}^q]_1, [1, e, \sigma e, \tau e]_2)$; $td \leftarrow (e, \tau)$;
  return (crs, td).

Com(crs, S): $[C_S]_1 \leftarrow [Z_S(\sigma)\tau]_1$; return $crs_{1p} \leftarrow (crs, [C_S]_1, S)$;

P(crs_{1p}, χ): $r \leftarrow Z_S(\chi)$; $f(X) \leftarrow (Z_S(X) - r)/(X - \chi)$; $[q]_1 \leftarrow [f(\sigma)\tau]_1$;
  if $\chi \in S$ then
    1. $\varrho_\delta \leftarrow_\$ \mathbb{Z}_p$; $[\gamma]_1 \leftarrow -\left[\begin{smallmatrix} -\tau \\ q \end{smallmatrix}\right]_1 \varrho_\delta$; $[\delta]_2 \leftarrow [\sigma e]_2 - \chi[e]_2 - \varrho_\delta[1]_2$;
    2. $\psi \leftarrow ([q, \gamma]_1, [\delta]_2)$;   // $3g_1 + g_2$
  else
    1. $s \leftarrow \frac{1}{r}$; $\varrho_\delta \leftarrow_\$ \mathbb{Z}_p^2$; $[\gamma]_1 \leftarrow -\left[\begin{smallmatrix} -\tau & 0 \\ q & -\tau \\ 0 & s \end{smallmatrix}\right]_1 \varrho_\delta$; $[\delta]_2 \leftarrow \left(\begin{smallmatrix} [\sigma e]_2 - \chi[e]_2 \\ r \cdot [e]_2 \end{smallmatrix}\right) - \varrho_\delta[1]_2$;
    2. $\psi \leftarrow ([q, s, \gamma]_1, [\delta]_2)$;   // $5g_1 + 2g_2$
  return ψ;

V($crs_{1p}, [\chi]_1, \psi$): $mem \leftarrow$ NotMember;
  If ψ parses as $\psi = ([q, \gamma]_1, [\delta]_2)$ then $mem \leftarrow$ Member;
  If $mem =$ Member then
    1. $b_1 \leftarrow [\sigma\tau]_1 \bullet [e]_2 - [\chi]_1 \bullet [\tau e]_2 - [\tau]_1 \bullet [\delta]_2 =^? [\gamma_1]_1 \bullet [1]_2$;
    2. $b_2 \leftarrow -[C_S]_1 \bullet [e]_2 + [q]_1 \bullet [\delta]_2 =^? [\gamma_2]_1 \bullet [1]_2$;
    3. if b_1 and b_2 then return Member else return Error;
  else
    1. $\bar{b}_1 \leftarrow ([\sigma]_1 - [\chi]_1) \bullet [\tau e]_2 - [\tau]_1 \bullet [\delta_1]_2 =^? [\gamma_1]_1 \bullet [1]_2$;
    2. $\bar{b}_2 \leftarrow -[C_S]_1 \bullet [e]_2 + [q]_1 \bullet [\delta_1]_2 - [\tau]_1 \bullet [\delta_2]_2 =^? [\gamma_2]_1 \bullet [1]_2$;
    3. $\bar{b}_3 \leftarrow -[1]_1 \bullet [e]_2 + [s]_1 \bullet [\delta_2]_2 =^? [\gamma_3]_1 \bullet [1]_2$;
    4. if $\bar{b}_1$ and $\bar{b}_2$ and $\bar{b}_3$ then return NotMember else return Error;

Fig. 6. The new $[\cdot]_1$-collision-resistant determinantal universal accumulator AC^*.

The non-membership argument verifier checks that $[\bar{C}(\chi)]_1 \bullet [\begin{smallmatrix} e \\ \delta \end{smallmatrix}]_2 = [\gamma]_1 \bullet [1]_2$ (where now $\delta \in \mathbb{Z}_p^2$ and $\gamma \in \mathbb{Z}_p^3$; see Fig. 5), which can be rewritten as checking

$$([\sigma]_1 - [\chi]_1) \bullet [e]_2 - [1]_1 \bullet [\delta_1]_2 = [\gamma_1]_1 \bullet [1]_2 \ ,$$
$$-[Z_S(\sigma)]_1 \bullet [e]_2 + [q]_1 \bullet [\delta_1]_2 - [1]_1 \bullet [\delta_2]_2 = [\gamma_2]_1 \bullet [1]_2 \ , \tag{3}$$
$$-[1]_1 \bullet [e]_2 + [s]_1 \bullet [\delta_2]_2 = [\gamma_3]_1 \bullet [1]_2 \ .$$

As in the case of the membership argument, we need to modify the first two equations by using τ. However, since we require s to be an integer, we do not have to modify the third verification equation.

The verification equations (that is, $\bar{b}_1 = \bar{b}_2 = \bar{b}_3 =$ true, see Fig. 6) are equivalent to checking that $\bar{C}'(\chi, q, s) \left(\begin{smallmatrix} e \\ \delta \end{smallmatrix}\right) = \gamma$, where $\bar{C}'(X, Q, S) := \begin{pmatrix} (\Sigma - X)T & -T & 0 \\ -Z_S(\Sigma)T & Q & -T \\ -1 & 0 & S \end{pmatrix}$, with $\det \bar{C}'(X, Q) = ((\Sigma - \chi)Q - Z_S(\Sigma)T)\, sT - T^2$.

We depict AC^* in Fig. 6. As explained before, the membership verifier checks (on pairings) that $C'(\chi, q) \cdot \left(\begin{smallmatrix} e \\ \delta \end{smallmatrix}\right) = \gamma$, and the non-membership verifier checks that $\bar{C}'(\chi, q, s) \cdot \left(\begin{smallmatrix} e \\ \delta \end{smallmatrix}\right) = \gamma$. Figure 6 does it in PPT. A batched membership verifier has to execute four pairings, while a batched non-membership verifier has to execute five pairings. For example, the membership verifier samples a random $\eta \leftarrow_\$ \mathbb{F}$, and then checks whether $([\sigma\tau]_1 - \eta[\mathsf{C}_\mathcal{S}]_1) \bullet [\mathsf{e}]_2 - [\chi]_1 \bullet [\tau\mathsf{e}]_2 + (\eta[\mathsf{q}]_1 - [\tau]_1) \bullet [\delta]_2 \overset{?}{=} ([\gamma_1]_1 + \eta[\gamma_2]_1) \bullet [1]_2$.

Lemma 1. AC^* *is perfectly complete.*

On Semantics of Non-membership. Recall that AC^* must be F-collision-resistant. Since the CRS contains trapdoor-dependent elements, one must make it precise how to define non-membership. As a motivating example, if $\mathcal{S} = \{0,1\}$, then $[\chi]_1 \leftarrow [\sigma]_1$ satisfies $\chi \in \mathcal{S}$ iff $\sigma \in \{0,1\}$. The AGM security proof handles σ as an indeterminate, and thus it cannot decide whether σ (or, more generally, some known affine map of σ) belongs to $\mathcal{S}$. To avoid such artefacts, we constructed AC^* so that the verifier returns Error when the prover makes $[\chi]_1$ to depend on $[\sigma]_1$ (see the proof of Theorems 1 and 2). While we do not do it here, it allows one to define the extractability of the accumulator naturally; from the proof of Theorems 1 and 2, it is easy to see that AC^* is extractable.

F-Collision-Resistance. We define two tautological assumptions q-DETACM and q-DETACNM that essentially state that AC^* is F-collision-resistant. Then, we prove in AGM that DETACM and DETACNM reduce to PDL.

The most efficient structure-preserving signatures are proven to be secure in the AGM (or in the generic group model), though the assumption of their security by itself is a falsifiable assumption. We can similarly prove the security of AC^* in AGM. However, the collision-resistance of an accumulator is a much simpler (in particular, it is non-interactive) assumption than the unforgeability of a signature scheme and thus the tautological assumption looks less intimidating.

Definition 4. *Let* $\mathcal{A}$ *be a PPT adversary. Let* $q = \mathsf{poly}(\lambda)$. q-DETACM *holds relative to* Pgen, *if for every PPT* $\mathcal{A}$,

$$
\Pr\left[
\begin{array}{l}
\mathcal{S} \in \mathcal{D}^{\leq q} \wedge \\
\chi \notin \mathcal{S} \wedge \\
\boldsymbol{C}'(\chi,\mathsf{q})\left(\begin{smallmatrix} \mathsf{e} \\ \delta \end{smallmatrix}\right) = \gamma
\end{array}
\left|
\begin{array}{l}
\mathsf{p} \leftarrow \mathsf{Pgen}(1^\lambda); \sigma,\tau,\mathsf{e} \leftarrow_\$ \mathbb{Z}_p; \\
\mathsf{crs} \leftarrow (\mathsf{p},[1,(\sigma^i\tau)^q_{i=0}]_1,[1,\mathsf{e},\sigma\mathsf{e},\tau\mathsf{e}]_2); \\
(\mathcal{S},[\chi,\mathsf{q},\gamma]_1,[\delta]_2) \leftarrow \mathcal{A}(\mathsf{crs}); \\
\boldsymbol{C}'(\chi,\mathsf{q}) \leftarrow \left(\begin{smallmatrix} (\sigma-\chi)\tau & -\tau \\ -\mathbf{z}_\mathcal{S}(\sigma)\tau & \mathsf{q} \end{smallmatrix}\right)
\end{array}
\right.
\right] \approx_\lambda 0 \ .
$$

q-DETACNM *holds relative to* Pgen, *if for every PPT* $\mathcal{A}$,

$$
\Pr\left[
\begin{array}{l}
\mathcal{S} \in \mathcal{D}^{\leq q} \wedge \\
\chi \in \mathcal{S} \wedge \\
\bar{\boldsymbol{C}}'(\chi,\mathsf{q},\mathsf{s})\left(\begin{smallmatrix} \mathsf{e} \\ \delta \end{smallmatrix}\right) = \gamma
\end{array}
\left|
\begin{array}{l}
\mathsf{p} \leftarrow \mathsf{Pgen}(1^\lambda); \sigma,\tau,\mathsf{e} \leftarrow_\$ \mathbb{Z}_p; \\
\mathsf{crs} \leftarrow (\mathsf{p},[1,(\sigma^i\tau)^q_{i=0}]_1,[1,\mathsf{e},\sigma\mathsf{e},\tau\mathsf{e}]_2); \\
(\mathcal{S},[\chi,\mathsf{q},\mathsf{s},\gamma]_1,[\delta]_2) \leftarrow \mathcal{A}(\mathsf{crs}); \\
\bar{\boldsymbol{C}}'(\chi,\mathsf{q},\mathsf{s}) \leftarrow \left(\begin{smallmatrix} (\sigma-\chi)\tau & -\tau & 0 \\ -\mathbf{z}_\mathcal{S}(\sigma)\tau & \mathsf{q} & -\tau \\ -1 & 0 & \mathsf{s} \end{smallmatrix}\right)
\end{array}
\right.
\right] \approx_\lambda 0 \ .
$$

Compared to CED, DETACM and DETACNM do not rely on the (possibly, inefficiently verifiable) condition that $\boldsymbol{C}(\chi)$ has a full rank. Thus, importantly, DETACM and DETACNM are efficiently verifiable and thus falsifiable.

For example, as explained above, the verification $\bar{C}'(\chi, \mathsf{q}, \mathsf{s})\left(\begin{smallmatrix} \mathsf{e} \\ \delta \end{smallmatrix}\right) = \gamma$ is equivalent to checking that $\bar{b}_1$, $\bar{b}_2$, and $\bar{b}_3$ hold. Thus, it can be checked efficiently and publicly.

Lemma 2 is trivial since DETACM and DETACNM are tautological assumptions for the F-collision-resistance of AC^*.

The complicated step (see Theorem 1) is establishing that DETACM and DETACNM are secure in the AGM.

Lemma 2. *Let $F = [\cdot]_1$ and $q = \mathsf{poly}(\lambda)$. AC^* is F-collision-resistant under q-DETACM and q-DETACNM.*

Theorem 1. *If $(q+1, 2)$-PDL holds, then q-DETACM is secure in the AGM.*

Theorem 2. *If $(q+1, 2)$-PDL holds, then q-DETACNM is secure in the AGM.*

6 New Set (Non-)Membership NIZK

Next, we use AC^* to construct a succinct set (non-)membership NIZK $\mathbf{\Pi}^*$. First, $\mathbf{\Pi}^*$'s CRS is equal to AC^*'s CRS. Second, the NIZK prover proves that AC^*'s honest verifier accepts the encrypted χ and the encrypted accumulator argument $\psi = \mathsf{AC}^*.\mathsf{P}(\mathsf{crs}, \mathcal{S}, \chi)$. That is, the prover encrypts χ and ψ, and then proves that the verification equation is satisfied.

Following the described blueprint, we construct the new set (non-)membership NIZK $\mathbf{\Pi}^*$ (see Fig. 7). $\mathbf{\Pi}^*$ handles both $\mathcal{L}_{1p}^{sm}$ (set membership arguments, $mem = \mathsf{Member}$) and $\overline{\mathcal{L}}_{1p}$ (set non-membership arguments, $mem = \mathsf{NotMember}$). The prover of $\mathbf{\Pi}^*$ implements the prover of AC^* but it also additionally encrypts all $\mathbb{G}_1$. To make the verification on ciphertexts possible, the prover outputs additional randomizer hints $[z]_2$. The verifier performs AC^* verification on ciphertexts (this relies on the homomorphic properties of Elgamal), taking $[z]_2$ into account. $\mathbf{\Pi}^*$ also defines the simulator algorithm.

Alternatively, $\mathbf{\Pi}^*$ is a version of $\mathbf{\Pi}_{clp\emptyset}$ for the concrete choice of the QDRs (and different CRS). To see the connection between Fig. 7 and Fig. 3, note that $C'(\mathsf{X}, \mathsf{Q}) = \mathsf{Q} + P_1 \mathsf{X} + P_2 \mathsf{Q}$, where $Q = \left(\begin{smallmatrix} \Sigma\mathsf{T} & -1 \\ -z_{\mathcal{S}}(\Sigma)\mathsf{T} & 0 \end{smallmatrix}\right)$, $P_1 = \left(\begin{smallmatrix} -\mathsf{T} & 0 \\ 0 & 0 \end{smallmatrix}\right)$, $P_2 = \left(\begin{smallmatrix} 0 & 0 \\ 0 & 1 \end{smallmatrix}\right)$. For example, starting with Fig. 3, $[z]_2 = \sum_{k=1}^{\nu} \varrho_k P_k \left[\begin{smallmatrix} \mathsf{e} \\ \delta \end{smallmatrix}\right]_2 - \varrho_\gamma [1]_2 = \varrho_\chi \left(\begin{smallmatrix} -\mathsf{T} & 0 \\ 0 & 0 \end{smallmatrix}\right) \left[\begin{smallmatrix} \mathsf{e} \\ \delta \end{smallmatrix}\right]_2 + \varrho_\mathsf{q} \left(\begin{smallmatrix} 0 & 0 \\ 0 & 1 \end{smallmatrix}\right) \left[\begin{smallmatrix} \mathsf{e} \\ \delta \end{smallmatrix}\right]_2 - \varrho_\gamma [1]_2 = \varrho_\chi \left[\begin{smallmatrix} -\mathsf{T}\mathsf{e} \\ 0 \end{smallmatrix}\right]_2 + \varrho_\mathsf{q} \left[\begin{smallmatrix} 0 \\ \delta \end{smallmatrix}\right]_2 - \varrho_\gamma [1]_2 = \left(\begin{smallmatrix} -\varrho_\chi [\mathsf{T}\mathsf{e}]_2 \\ \varrho_\mathsf{q} [\delta]_2 \end{smallmatrix}\right) - \varrho_\gamma [1]_2$. One can represent $\bar{C}'(\mathsf{X}, \mathsf{Q}, \mathsf{R})$ similarly.

Clearly, $\mathbf{\Pi}^*$ is commit-and-prove, updatable, and universal.

Theorem 3. *The set membership argument $\mathbf{\Pi}^*$ in Fig. 7 is perfectly complete. Assuming Elgamal is IND-CPA secure, it is computationally zero-knowledge.*

Theorem 4. *Let $\ell = 2$ and $\mathsf{k} = 1$. Let $\mathcal{D}_\mathsf{k}$ be the distribution of $\left[\begin{smallmatrix} 1 \\ \mathsf{e} \end{smallmatrix}\right]_2$ for $\mathsf{e} \leftarrow_\$ \mathbb{Z}_p$. Let $q = \mathsf{poly}(\lambda)$ be an upper bound on $|\mathcal{S}|$. The set membership NIZK $\mathbf{\Pi}^*$ in Fig. 7 is sound, assuming AC^* is $[\cdot]_1$-collision-resistant.*

$\mathsf{Pgen}(1^\lambda)$: $\mathsf{p} = (p, \mathbb{G}_1, \mathbb{G}_2, \mathbb{G}_T, \hat{e}, [1]_1, [1]_2) \leftarrow \mathsf{Pgen}(1^\lambda)$.

$\mathsf{Kgen}(\mathsf{p})$: $(\mathsf{crs}, \mathsf{td}) \leftarrow \mathsf{AC}^*.\mathsf{Kgen}(\mathsf{p})$;

$\mathsf{Com}(\mathsf{crs}, \mathsf{lp} = (\mathsf{pk}, \mathcal{S}))$: $\mathsf{AC}^*.\mathsf{lp} \leftarrow \mathcal{S}$; $\mathsf{AC}^*.\mathsf{crs}_{\mathsf{lp}} \leftarrow \mathsf{AC}^*.\mathsf{Com}(\mathsf{crs}, \mathsf{AC}^*.\mathsf{lp})$; return $\mathsf{crs}_{\mathsf{lp}} \leftarrow (\mathsf{AC}^*.\mathsf{crs}_{\mathsf{lp}}, \mathsf{pk})$;

$\mathsf{P}(\mathsf{crs}_{\mathsf{lp}}, \mathbb{x} = [\mathsf{ct}_\chi]_1, \mathbb{w} = (\chi, \varrho_\chi))$:
  $\mathsf{AC}^*.\psi \leftarrow \mathsf{AC}^*.\mathsf{P}(\mathsf{AC}^*.\mathsf{crs}_{\mathsf{lp}}, \chi)$;   // $\psi = ([\mathsf{q}, \gamma]_1, [\delta]_2)$ or $\psi = ([\mathsf{q}, \mathsf{s}, \gamma]_1, [\delta]_2)$
  $\varrho_\mathsf{q} \leftarrow_\$ \mathbb{Z}_p$; $[\mathsf{ct}_\mathsf{q}]_1 \leftarrow \mathsf{Enc}_{\mathsf{pk}}([\mathsf{q}]_1; \varrho_\mathsf{q})$;
  If $\chi \in \mathcal{S}$ then
    1. $\varrho_\gamma \leftarrow_\$ \mathbb{Z}_p^2$; $[\mathsf{ct}_\gamma]_1 \leftarrow \mathsf{Enc}_{\mathsf{pk}}([\gamma]_1; \varrho_\gamma) \in \mathbb{G}_1^{2 \times 2}$; $[z]_2 \leftarrow \begin{pmatrix} -\varrho_\chi[\tau e]_2 \\ \varrho_\mathsf{q}[\delta]_2 \end{pmatrix} - \varrho_\gamma[1]_2 \in \mathbb{G}_2^2$;
    2. $\pi \leftarrow ([\mathsf{ct}_\mathsf{q}, \mathsf{ct}_\gamma]_1, [\delta, z]_2)$
  else
    1. $\varrho_\mathsf{s} \leftarrow_\$ \mathbb{Z}_p$; $[\mathsf{ct}_\mathsf{s}]_1 \leftarrow \mathsf{Enc}_{\mathsf{pk}}([\mathsf{s}]_1; \varrho_\mathsf{s}) \in \mathbb{G}_1^{1 \times 2}$;
    2. $\varrho_\gamma \leftarrow_\$ \mathbb{Z}_p^3$; $[\mathsf{ct}_\gamma]_1 \leftarrow \mathsf{Enc}_{\mathsf{pk}}([\gamma]_1; \varrho_\gamma) \in \mathbb{G}_1^{3 \times 2}$; $[z]_2 \leftarrow \begin{pmatrix} -\varrho_\chi[\tau e]_2 \\ \varrho_\mathsf{q}[\delta_1]_2 \\ \varrho_\mathsf{s}[\delta_2]_2 \end{pmatrix} - \varrho_\gamma[1]_2 \in \mathbb{G}_2^3$;
    3. $\pi \leftarrow ([\mathsf{ct}_\mathsf{q}, \mathsf{ct}_\mathsf{s}, \mathsf{ct}_\gamma]_1, [\delta, z]_2)$;
  return π;   // membership: $6\mathfrak{g}_1 + 3\mathfrak{g}_2$; non-membership: $10\mathfrak{g}_1 + 5\mathfrak{g}_2$

$\mathsf{Sim}(\mathsf{crs}_{\mathsf{lp}}, \mathsf{td} = (e, \tau), \mathbb{x} = [\mathsf{ct}_\chi]_1, mem \in \{\mathsf{Member}, \mathsf{NotMember}\})$:
  If $mem = \mathsf{Member}$ then
    1. $\delta \leftarrow_\$ \mathbb{Z}_p$; $z \leftarrow_\$ \mathbb{Z}_p^2$; $\varrho_\mathsf{q} \leftarrow_\$ \mathbb{Z}_p$; $[\mathsf{ct}_\mathsf{q}]_1 \leftarrow \mathsf{Enc}_{\mathsf{pk}}(0; \varrho_\mathsf{q})$;
    2. $[\mathsf{ct}_\gamma]_1 \leftarrow \begin{pmatrix} \mathsf{Enc}_{\mathsf{pk}}([\sigma\tau]_1; 0) - [\mathsf{ct}_\chi]_1 \cdot \tau & -\mathsf{Enc}_{\mathsf{pk}}([\tau]_1; 0) \\ -\mathsf{Enc}_{\mathsf{pk}}([C_\mathcal{S}]_1; 0) & [\mathsf{ct}_\mathsf{q}]_1 \end{pmatrix}\begin{pmatrix} e \\ \delta \end{pmatrix} - \mathsf{Enc}_{\mathsf{pk}}(0; z)$;
    3. $\pi \leftarrow ([\mathsf{ct}_\mathsf{q}, \mathsf{ct}_\gamma]_1, [\delta, z]_2)$
  else
    1. $\delta \leftarrow_\$ \mathbb{Z}_p^2$; $z \leftarrow_\$ \mathbb{Z}_p^3$;
    2. $\varrho_\mathsf{q}, \varrho_\mathsf{s} \leftarrow_\$ \mathbb{Z}_p$; $[\mathsf{ct}_\mathsf{q}]_1 \leftarrow \mathsf{Enc}_{\mathsf{pk}}(0; \varrho_\mathsf{q})$; $[\mathsf{ct}_\mathsf{s}]_1 \leftarrow \mathsf{Enc}_{\mathsf{pk}}(0; \varrho_\mathsf{s})$;
    3. $[\mathsf{ct}_\gamma]_1 \leftarrow -\begin{pmatrix} \mathsf{Enc}_{\mathsf{pk}}([\sigma\tau]_1; 0) - [\mathsf{ct}_\chi]_1 \cdot \tau & -\mathsf{Enc}_{\mathsf{pk}}([\tau]_1; 0) & \mathsf{Enc}_{\mathsf{pk}}(0; 0) \\ -\mathsf{Enc}_{\mathsf{pk}}([C_\mathcal{S}]_1; 0) & [\mathsf{ct}_\mathsf{q}]_1 & -\mathsf{Enc}_{\mathsf{pk}}([\tau]_1; 0) \\ -\mathsf{Enc}_{\mathsf{pk}}(1; 0) & \mathsf{Enc}_{\mathsf{pk}}(0; 0) & [\mathsf{ct}_\mathsf{s}]_1 \end{pmatrix}\begin{pmatrix} e \\ \delta \end{pmatrix} - \mathsf{Enc}_{\mathsf{pk}}(0; z)$;
    4. $\pi \leftarrow ([\mathsf{ct}_\mathsf{q}, \mathsf{ct}_\mathsf{s}, \mathsf{ct}_\gamma]_1, [\delta, z]_2)$;
  return π;

$\mathsf{V}(\mathsf{crs}_{\mathsf{lp}}, \mathbb{x} = [\mathsf{ct}_\chi]_1, \pi)$: $mem \leftarrow \mathsf{NotMember}$;
  if π parses as $\pi = ([\mathsf{ct}_\mathsf{q}, \mathsf{ct}_\gamma]_1, [\delta, z]_2)$ then $mem \leftarrow \mathsf{Member}$;
  If $mem = \mathsf{Member}$ then check
    1. $b_1 \leftarrow \mathsf{Enc}_{\mathsf{pk}}([\sigma\tau]_1; 0) \bullet [e]_2 - [\mathsf{ct}_\chi]_1 \bullet [\tau e]_2 - \mathsf{Enc}_{\mathsf{pk}}([\tau]_1; 0) \bullet [\delta]_2 =^? [\mathsf{ct}_{\gamma 1}]_1 \bullet [1]_2 + [z_1]_2 \bullet \mathsf{pk}$;
    2. $b_2 \leftarrow -\mathsf{Enc}_{\mathsf{pk}}([C_\mathcal{S}]_1; 0) \bullet [e]_2 + [\mathsf{ct}_\mathsf{q}]_1 \bullet [\delta]_2 =^? [\mathsf{ct}_{\gamma 2}]_1 \bullet [1]_2 + [z_2]_2 \bullet \mathsf{pk}$;
    3. if b_1 and b_2 then return Member else return Error;
  else check
    1. $\bar{b}_1 \leftarrow \mathsf{Enc}_{\mathsf{pk}}([\sigma\tau]_1; 0) \bullet [e]_2 - [\mathsf{ct}_\chi]_1 \bullet [\tau e]_2 - \mathsf{Enc}_{\mathsf{pk}}([\tau]_1; 0) \bullet [\delta_1]_2 =^? [\mathsf{ct}_{\gamma 1}]_1 \bullet [1]_2 + [z_1]_2 \bullet \mathsf{pk}$;
    2. $\bar{b}_2 \leftarrow -\mathsf{Enc}_{\mathsf{pk}}([C_\mathcal{S}]_1; 0) \bullet [e]_2 + [\mathsf{ct}_\mathsf{q}]_1 \bullet [\delta_1]_2 - \mathsf{Enc}_{\mathsf{pk}}([\tau]_1; 0) \bullet [\delta_2]_2 =^? [\mathsf{ct}_{\gamma 2}]_1 \bullet [1]_2 + [z_2]_2 \bullet \mathsf{pk}$;
    3. $\bar{b}_3 \leftarrow -\mathsf{Enc}(1; 0) \bullet [e]_2 + [\mathsf{ct}_\mathsf{s}]_1 \bullet [\delta_2]_2 =^? [\mathsf{ct}_{\gamma 3}]_1 \bullet [1]_2 + [z_3]_2 \bullet \mathsf{pk}$;
    4. if $\bar{b}_1$ and $\bar{b}_2$ and $\bar{b}_3$ then return $\mathsf{NotMember}$ else return Error;

Fig. 7. The new set (non-)membership NIZK $\mathbf{\Pi}^*$.

Efficiency. $\mathbf{\Pi}^*$'s CRS length is $q + 1$ elements of $\mathbb{G}_1$ and 4 elements of $\mathbb{G}_2$. The set membership argument length is $6\mathfrak{g}_1 + 3\mathfrak{g}_2$, which comes close to the $\mathbf{\Pi}_{\mathsf{clp\emptyset}}$ argument length $4\mathfrak{g}_1 + 3\mathfrak{g}_2$ for the simple OR language (this corresponds to $\ell = 2$). The difference comes from the fact that here we also encrypt AC^*'s argument ψ. On the other hand, the set non-membership argument length is ten elements of $\mathbb{G}_1$ and five elements of $\mathbb{G}_2$.

The prover's computation can be divided into precomputation and online computation. P precomputes $f(X)$ ($\Theta(|\mathcal{S}|)$ field operations) and $[q]_1$ ($|\mathcal{S}|$ scalar multiplications in $\mathbb{G}_1$). In online computation, (1) the membership prover computes 8 scalar multiplications in $\mathbb{G}_1$ and 6 in $\mathbb{G}_2$ ($2m_1 + 2m_2$ to compute $AC^*.\psi$ and $6m_1 + 4m_2$ in the rest of Π^*), and (2) the non-membership prover computes 14 scalar multiplications in $\mathbb{G}_1$ and 10 in $\mathbb{G}_2$ ($4m_1 + 4m_2$ to compute $AC^*.\psi$ and $10m_1 + 6m_2$ in the rest of Π^*). (The online computation includes the computation of $[ct_q]_1$ and other ciphertexts.) The batched membership (resp., non-membership) verifier's computation is dominated by five (resp., six) pairings. Pairings with $[e]_2$ can be precomputed. (This is replaced with some $\mathbb{G}_T$ exponentiations, so the benefit depends on the implementation.) Online, the verify has to compute four and five pairings, respectively. See the full version [20] for the batched verifier. We refer to Table 1 for an efficiency comparison. In the full version [20], we compare our construction to the most efficient random-oracle based solution.

7   On Handling Group Elements with CLPØ

The CLPØ NIZK [14] works assuming the prover knows all the DR elements as integers. This seems to exclude applications where one needs to prove statements about group elements. In Π^*, we overcome this issue by making the following observation. Consider the case of a single DR $C(X) = (h(X) \| T(X))$, where $h(X)$ is a column vector. Then, for CLPØ to work, it suffices that the prover (1) knows $[C(\chi)]_1$, and (2) can compute $[\delta]_2$; for this, it suffices to compute $[we]_2$, where w is such that $h(X) = T(X)w$ (this follows from CLPØ's construction).

In the case of Π^*, (1) means that the prover must be able to compute $[q, Z_{\mathcal{S}}(\sigma), s]_1$ (and thus χ, but not σ, must be available as an integer, and one must include to the CRS information needed to recompute $[Z_{\mathcal{S}}(\sigma)]_1$), and (2) means that $[\sigma e, e]_2$ must be given as part of the CRS. We leave the grand generalization of this observation for future work.

References

1. Abdolmaleki, B., Lipmaa, H., Siim, J., Zając, M.: On QA-NIZK in the BPK model. In: Kiayias, A., Kohlweiss, M., Wallden, P., Zikas, V. (eds.) PKC 2020, Part I. LNCS, vol. 12110, pp. 590–620. Springer, Cham (2020). https://doi.org/10.1007/978-3-030-45374-9_20

2. Abe, M., Fuchsbauer, G., Groth, J., Haralambiev, K., Ohkubo, M.: Structure-preserving signatures and commitments to group elements. J. Cryptol. **29**(2), 363–421 (2015). https://doi.org/10.1007/s00145-014-9196-7

3. Acar, T., Nguyen, L.: Revocation for delegatable anonymous credentials. In: Catalano, D., Fazio, N., Gennaro, R., Nicolosi, A. (eds.) PKC 2011. LNCS, vol. 6571, pp. 423–440. Springer, Heidelberg (2011). https://doi.org/10.1007/978-3-642-19379-8_26

4. Au, M.H., Tsang, P.P., Susilo, W., Mu, Y.: Dynamic universal accumulators for DDH groups and their application to attribute-based anonymous credential systems. In: Fischlin, M. (ed.) CT-RSA 2009. LNCS, vol. 5473, pp. 295–308. Springer, Heidelberg (2009). https://doi.org/10.1007/978-3-642-00862-7_20
5. Barić, N., Pfitzmann, B.: Collision-free accumulators and fail-stop signature schemes without trees. In: Fumy, W. (ed.) EUROCRYPT 1997. LNCS, vol. 1233, pp. 480–494. Springer, Heidelberg (1997). https://doi.org/10.1007/3-540-69053-0_33
6. Belenkiy, M., Chase, M., Kohlweiss, M., Lysyanskaya, A.: P-signatures and non-interactive anonymous credentials. In: Canetti, R. (ed.) TCC 2008. LNCS, vol. 4948, pp. 356–374. Springer, Heidelberg (2008). https://doi.org/10.1007/978-3-540-78524-8_20
7. Benaloh, J., de Mare, M.: One-way accumulators: a decentralized alternative to digital signatures. In: Helleseth, T. (ed.) EUROCRYPT 1993. LNCS, vol. 765, pp. 274–285. Springer, Heidelberg (1994). https://doi.org/10.1007/3-540-48285-7_24
8. Blazy, O., Bultel, X., Lafourcade, P., Kempner, O.P.: Generic plaintext equality and inequality proofs. In: Borisov, N., Diaz, C. (eds.) FC 2021. LNCS, vol. 12674, pp. 415–435. Springer, Heidelberg (2021). https://doi.org/10.1007/978-3-662-64322-8_20
9. Blazy, O., Chevalier, C., Vergnaud, D.: Non-interactive zero-knowledge proofs of non-membership. In: Nyberg, K. (ed.) CT-RSA 2015. LNCS, vol. 9048, pp. 145–164. Springer, Cham (2015). https://doi.org/10.1007/978-3-319-16715-2_8
10. Blazy, O., Derler, D., Slamanig, D., Spreitzer, R.: Non-interactive plaintext (in-)equality proofs and group signatures with verifiable controllable linkability. In: Sako, K. (ed.) CT-RSA 2016. LNCS, vol. 9610, pp. 127–143. Springer, Cham (2016). https://doi.org/10.1007/978-3-319-29485-8_8
11. Buldas, A., Laud, P., Lipmaa, H.: Accountable certificate management using undeniable attestations. In: Gritzalis, D., Jajodia, S., Samarati, P. (eds.) ACM CCS 2000, pp. 9–17. ACM Press (2000). https://doi.org/10.1145/352600.352604
12. Buldas, A., Laud, P., Lipmaa, H.: Eliminating counterevidence with applications to accountable certificate management. J. Comput. Secur. **10**(3), 273–296 (2002)
13. Couteau, G., Hartmann, D.: Shorter non-interactive zero-knowledge arguments and ZAPs for algebraic languages. In: Micciancio, D., Ristenpart, T. (eds.) CRYPTO 2020, Part III. LNCS, vol. 12172, pp. 768–798. Springer, Cham (2020). https://doi.org/10.1007/978-3-030-56877-1_27
14. Couteau, G., Lipmaa, H., Parisella, R., Ødegaard, A.T.: Efficient NIZKs for algebraic sets. In: Tibouchi, M., Wang, H. (eds.) ASIACRYPT 2021, Part III. LNCS, vol. 13092, pp. 128–158. Springer, Cham (2021). https://doi.org/10.1007/978-3-030-92078-4_5
15. Damgård, I., Triandopoulos, N.: Supporting non-membership proofs with bilinear-map accumulators. Cryptology ePrint Archive, Report 2008/538 (2008). https://eprint.iacr.org/2008/538
16. Daza, V., González, A., Pindado, Z., Ràfols, C., Silva, J.: Shorter quadratic QA-NIZK proofs. In: Lin, D., Sako, K. (eds.) PKC 2019, Part I. LNCS, vol. 11442, pp. 314–343. Springer, Cham (2019). https://doi.org/10.1007/978-3-030-17253-4_11
17. Groth, J., Sahai, A.: Efficient non-interactive proof systems for bilinear groups. In: Smart, N. (ed.) EUROCRYPT 2008. LNCS, vol. 4965, pp. 415–432. Springer, Heidelberg (2008). https://doi.org/10.1007/978-3-540-78967-3_24
18. Li, J., Li, N., Xue, R.: Universal accumulators with efficient nonmembership proofs. In: Katz, J., Yung, M. (eds.) ACNS 2007. LNCS, vol. 4521, pp. 253–269. Springer, Heidelberg (2007). https://doi.org/10.1007/978-3-540-72738-5_17

19. Lipmaa, H.: Secure accumulators from euclidean rings without trusted setup. In: Bao, F., Samarati, P., Zhou, J. (eds.) ACNS 2012. LNCS, vol. 7341, pp. 224–240. Springer, Heidelberg (2012). https://doi.org/10.1007/978-3-642-31284-7_14
20. Lipmaa, H., Parisella, R.: Set (non-)membership NIZKs from determinantal accumulators. Cryptology ePrint Archive, Report 2022/1570 (2022). https://eprint.iacr.org/2022/1570
21. Nguyen, L.: Accumulators from bilinear pairings and applications. In: Menezes, A. (ed.) CT-RSA 2005. LNCS, vol. 3376, pp. 275–292. Springer, Heidelberg (2005). https://doi.org/10.1007/978-3-540-30574-3_19

Benchmarking the Setup of Updatable Zk-SNARKs

Karim Baghery$^{(\boxtimes)}$ ⓘ, Axel Mertensⓘ, and Mahdi Sedaghatⓘ

COSIC, KU Leuven, Leuven, Belgium
{karim.baghery,axel.mertens}@kuleuven.be, ssedagha@esat.kuleuven.be

Abstract. Subversion-resistant zk-SNARKs allow the provers to verify the Structured Reference String (SRS), via an SRS Verification (SV) algorithm and bypass the need for a Trusted Third Party (TTP). Pairing-based zk-SNARKs with *updatable* and *universal* SRS are an extension of subversion-resistant ones which additionally allow the verifiers to update the SRS, via an SRS Updating (SU) algorithm, and similarly bypass the need for a TTP. In this paper, we examine the setup of these zk-SNARKs by benchmarking the efficiency of the SV and SU algorithms within the Arkworks library. The benchmarking covers a range of updatable zk-SNARKs, including Sonic, Plonk, Marlin, Lunar, and Basilisk. Our analysis reveals that relying solely on the standard Algebraic Group Model (AGM) may not be sufficient in practice, and we may need a model with weaker assumptions. Specifically, we find that while Marlin is secure in the AGM, additional elements need to be added to its SRS to formally prove certain security properties in the updatable CRS model. We demonstrate that the SV algorithms become inefficient for mid-sized circuits with over 20,000 multiplication gates and 100 updates. To address this, we introduce Batched SV algorithms (BSV) that leverage standard batching techniques and offer significantly improved performance. As a tool, we propose an efficient verification approach that allows the parties to identify a malicious SRS updater with logarithmic verification in the number of updates. In the case of Basilisk, for a circuit with 2^{20} multiplication gates, a 1000-time updated SRS can be verified in less than 30 s, a malicious updater can be identified in less than 4 min (improvable by pre-computation), and each update takes less than 6 min.

Keywords: Updatable SRS Model · AGM with Hashing · Subversion ZK

1 Introduction

Let **R** be an NP relation which defines the language **L** of all statements, x, for which there exists a witness, w, s.t. $(x, w) \in$ **R**. A Non-Interactive Zero-Knowledge (NIZK) argument [12,25] for **R** allows an untrusted prover P, knowing w, to non-interactively convince a sceptical verifier V about the truth of a statement x, without leaking extra information about the witness w. Due to a wide range of applications, there has been a growing interest in recent years

A. Aly and M. Tibouchi (Eds.): LATINCRYPT 2023, LNCS 14168, pp. 375–396, 2023.
https://doi.org/10.1007/978-3-031-44469-2_19

to develop NIZK proof systems, particularly those allowing for *succinct* proofs and efficient verifications, so-called zk-SNARKs (zero-knowledge Succinct Non-interactive Arguments of Knowledge) [26,35].

A zk-SNARK is expected to satisfy Zero-Knowledge (ZK) and Knowledge Soundness (KS). ZK ensures that V learns nothing beyond the truth of statement, x, from the proof. KS ensures that no malicious P can convince honest V of a false statement, unless he knows the witness. To achieve ZK and KS at the same time, zk-SNARKs rely on a Structured Reference String (SRS), which is supposed to be sampled by a Trusted Third Party (TTP), using the SRS generation algorithm SG [12]. Therefore, in the SRS model a zk-SNARK consists of three algorithms (SG, P, V). In practice, finding a mutually TTP for executing the SG algorithm to generate the SRS can be challenging.

Mitigating the Trust on the Setup of zk-SNARKs. To relax the imposed trust on the setup of zk-SNARK, a line of research distributes the SG algorithm and constructed Multi-Party Computation (MPC) protocols to sample the SRS [11, 13,30]. In such protocols, both P and V need to trust only 1 out of $i > 1$ participants.

In a different research direction, in 2016, Bellare et al. [9] built the first NIZK argument that can achieve ZK, even if its SRS was subverted, so-called Subversion ZK (Sub-ZK). In a Sub-ZK NIZK argument, the prover does not need to trust the SRS generator, instead, it needs to run an algorithm, so-called SRS Verification (SV), and verify the validity of SRS before using it. The SV algorithm uses some pairing equations to verify the well-formedness of SRS elements. Two subsequent works of [2,19] presented subversion-resistant zk-SNARKs that similarly come with an SV algorithm and can achieve Sub-ZK. In a Sub-ZK SNARK, consisting of four algorithms (SG, SV, P, V), the provers can verify the validity of SRS, by one-time executing the SV algorithm, and then bypass the need for a TTP. On the other side, the verifiers either need a TTP to generate the SRS, or they need to run an MPC protocol (e.g. [11,13]) to sample the SRS elements, which will relax the level of trust to 1 out of i (participants).

As an extension to the MPC approach and subversion-resistant zk-SNARKs, in 2018, Groth et al. [27] proposed a new model, so-called updatable SRS model, which allows the verifiers to also bypass the trust on a TTP. To this end, a V needs to update the SRS one time, using an SRS Updating (SU) algorithm, and also verify the validity of previous updates and the final SRS, using the SV algorithm. Roughly speaking, in a zk-SNARK with updatable SRS, which consists of five algorithms (SG, SU, SV, P, V), to bypass the trust on a third party, a P needs to run the SV algorithm, and a V needs to run both SU and SV. In this model, the SRS is universal and can be used for various circuits within a bounded size. Then, Groth et al. [27] built the first zk-SNARK with universal and updatable SRS, but comes with $O(n^2)$ SRS size, where n is the number of multiplication gates in the circuit. In practice, this results in a huge SRS size, and impractical SU and SV algorithms.

Recently, there has been an impressive progress on designing Random Oracle-based zk-SNARKs with linear-size updatable SRS, shorter proofs, and more efficient provers and verifiers. Some of the known schemes that consecutively improve the initial scheme of [27] and the subsequent works are called, Sonic [33], Plonk [22], Marlin [15], Lunar [14], Basilisk [36], and Counting Vampires [32]. In the full version [7], we compare their efficiency in terms of computational costs of (SG, P, V) and the SRS size. Currently, Counting Vampires [32] has the shortest proofs, i.e., two group elements less than Basilisk, but its SRS is 17× larger than the SRS of Basilisk, and this can result in a considerably slower setup phase. The SU and SV algorithms are two essential algorithms for achieving Sub-ZK and Updatable Knowledge Soundness (Upd-KS, KS in the updatable SRS model) and the employment of updatable zk-SNARKs. In order to achieve Sub-ZK and Upd-KS in the updatable SRS model, the underlying SRS *must be publicly verifiable* and *trapdoor extractable* [2,9,19,27]. Meaning that, the consistency of SRS elements should be publicly verifiable, and one should be able to extract the SRS trapdoors from the setup phase (e.g., by relying on a knowledge assumption). The initial scheme [27], and some follow-up generic constructions [3,6,8] come with SU and SV algorithms, under Bilinear Diffie-Hellman Knowledge of Exponent (BDH-KE) assumption. But their SV algorithm is identical for both P and V, which in case of verifying an i-time updated SRS, it brings $O(i)$ pairing operations as an overload for the P. In [32], authors have proposed an SV algorithm to achieve Sub-ZK in their construction. However, their SV algorithm can only be used by P (to achieve Sub-ZK), and it does not consider the verification of an i-time updated SRS, needed by V.

Our Contributions. The main objective of the current paper is to examine the efficiency of the setup phase in updatable zk-SNARKs, and evaluate their empirical performance, particularly in large-scale applications.

To this end, we first present a pair of (SU, SV) algorithms for each of the updatable zk-SNARKs including: Sonic [33], Plonk [22], Marlin [15], LunarLite [14] and Basilisk [36]. Similar to the earlier works [2,9,19,27], the proposed algorithms use pairing products and are tailored to each specific updatable zk-SNARK. As all the aforementioned zk-SNARKs can be instantiated in various ways, we focus on the pairing-based version of them with the shortest proof, which is commonly used for comparison in the literature. During the construction of the SU and SV algorithms, we noticed that relying only on the standard Algebraic Group Model (AGM) may not be enough in practice. In some cases, we may require a model with weaker assumptions, such as the AGM with *hashing* [31]. In fact, there might be a case that a zk-SNARK with monomial SRS is proven to achieve ZK and KS in the AGM model, but their SRS needs to be modified to achieve Sub-ZK and U-KS. The reason is that, to achieve Sub-ZK and Upd-KS the SRS needs to be publicly verifiable and trapdoor extractable [2,27]. In the rest, we show that the SRS of Marlin [15] is not *trapdoor extractable* as it is, but it can be made trapdoor extractable under the BDH-KE assumption, by adding a single group element to its SRS.

In the rest, we show that using the presented SU and SV algorithms, Sonic, Plonk, LunarLite and Basilisk also can achieve trapdoor extractability, under a subverted/maliciously updated SRS. Since all of them already are proven that satisfy ZK and KS, this implies that they also satisfy Sub-ZK and Upd-KS. Similar to the earlier works [2,9,15,19], our SV algorithms use pairing product

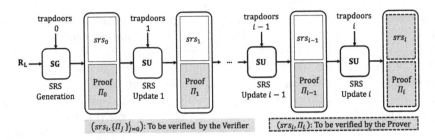

Fig. 1. Setup in the updatable zk-SNARKs: SG, SU, and SV by P or V.

equations to verify the SRS. But, differently our SV algorithms get an additional input, denoted by party, which allows us to determine whether a P or V runs the algorithm. Due to achieving Sub-ZK and Upd-KS in the updatable zk-SNARKs, P only needs to verify the final (srs_i, Π_i), while V additionally needs to verify the intermediate proofs $\{\Pi_j\}_{j=0}^{i-1}$. Figure 1 depicts a graphical representation of the setup phase in the pairing-based updatable zk-SNARKs, and highlights the parts that need to be verified by P or V. By running an SV algorithm, P needs to compute $O(n)$ pairings, where n is the number of multiplication gates in the circuit, and V requires to compute at least $O(n + i)$ pairings, where i is the number of updates done on the SRS. In practice, even for mid-size circuits (e.g. $n \geq 10^4$) with 100 updates, the SV algorithms can be very slow.

Next, we use the standard batching techniques [10] and propose a batched version of the SV algorithms, so-called BSV, for each of the studied updatable zk-SNARKs. Using the BSV algorithms, to verify an i-time updated SRS, P needs $O(n)$ exponentiations (with short exponents) and constant number of pairings, which is independent of the number of updates. A V needs to compute $O(n + i)$ exponentiations (with short exponents) and $O(i)$ pairings. Table 1, compares the efficiency of our proposed SU, SV and BSV algorithms for both P and V.

The schemes built in the updatable SRS model [27] can achieve security only with abort, if the parties do not verify the updated SRS after each update. Namely, by verifying the final SRS srs_i and the intermediate proofs $\{\Pi_j\}_{j=0}^{i}$ [27] the parties will abort the final SRS srs_i and would not be able to identify a malicious SRS generator/updater. To identify a malicious SRS generator/updater, if

Table 1. An efficiency comparison of our proposed SU, SV and BSV algorithms. SV_P: SV run by P, BSV_V: BSV run by V, E_l: Exponentiations in $\mathbb{G}_l$, $\bullet$: Pairing, m: #total (multiplication and addition) gates, n: #multiplication gates, k: #matrix elements with non-zero values describing the circuit, i: # SRS updates

Scheme	SG/SU E_1	E_2	SV_P $\bullet$	SV_V $\bullet$	BSV_P E_1	E_2	$\bullet$	BSV_V E_1	E_2	$\bullet$
Sonic	$4n$	$4n$	$12n$	$12n + 10i$	$8n$	$4n$	7	$8n + 8i$	$6n + 2i$	$4i + 14$
Marlin	k	$\log k$	$2k + 12$	$2k + 9i + 12$	$2k$	$\log k$	4	$2k + 5i$	$2i + \log k$	$2i + 9$
Plonk	$3m$	2	$6m$	$6m + 4i$	$6m$	—	2	$6m + 3i$	i	$i + 3$
LunarLite	n	n	$3n$	$3n + 4i + 2$	$2n$	n	3	$2n + 3i$	$n + i$	$i + 3$
Basilisk	n	2	$2n$	$2n + 4i$	$2n$	—	2	$2n + 3i$	i	$i + 3$

the parties (or a third party) verify each updated SRS $\{\mathsf{srs}_j\}_{j=0}^i$ (instead of only srs_i), then the verification of whole setup phase will be impractical. To deal with that, we introduce an efficient verification approach for identifying the malicious updater. For an i-time updated SRS, it allows the parties to identify the (first) malicious SRS updater with $\log i$ times running the BSV (or SV) algorithm. We discuss different optimizations that can speed up the proposed recursive SRS verification considerably, at the cost of some pre-computations and storage.

Finally, we present a comprehensive benchmark on the efficiency of our proposed SU, SV and BSV algorithms in the Arkworks library , which is written in Rust and currently is one of the most popular libraries programming zk-SNARKs. Full details of the benchmarking are reported in Sect. 4. In summary, for a particular circuit, by comparing the performance of BSV and SV algorithms, we observed that BSV can achieve up to 110–150 × better efficiency. In the case of Basilisk which has the most efficient setup phase, for a circuit with $n = 2^{20}$ multiplication gates, a 1000-time updated SRS can be verified in less than 30 s. In the case that the verification of final SRS fails, using our proposed recursive verification approach, a malicious SRS updater can be identified in less than 4 min (or in less than 1 min by some pre-computations), and each party equipped with a multi-core CPU can update the SRS in less than 6 min. Our BSV_P algorithms are considerably faster than BSV_V ones, in case of a short SRS (e.g. $n \leq 30K$) and a large number of updates (e.g. $i \geq 200$).

Related Works. To mitigate the trust in the setup phase of zk-SNARKs, there are two key research directions. Either, by using an MPC protocol to sample the SRS [1,11,13,30] or by directly constructing subversion-resistant [2,4,9,19] and updatable zk-SNARKs [3,6,8,27,33]. Our work is focused on the latter approach.

A bottleneck with the initial MPC protocols [11], is that the number of parties has to be known in advance. Bowe et al. [13] presented an MPC protocol for Groth16 [26] setup, which has two phases. The first phase is known as "Powers of Tau", which can be used to sample a universal SRS for all circuits up to a given size. In the second phase, given the universal SRS generated in the previous phase, parties generate a circuit-dependent SRS. In the Powers of Tau protocol, a coordinator is used to manage messages between the participants, however the output of the protocol is verifiable. Compared with the case one uses the Powers of Tau protocol [13], 1) our proposed algorithms do not need a random beacon, 2) our SV and BSV algorithms are constructed in the updatable SRS model which allows one to verify an i-time updated SRS considerably more efficient than i-time running their SRS verification algorithm. For verifying even one-time updated SRS, our proposed BSV algorithms can be more than 100× faster than their verification algorithm, 3) our SV and BSV algorithms for the provers and verifiers are different, which allows the provers to verify a large-time updated SRS more efficient than verifiers. 4) our protocols can achieve identifiable security more efficiently (using a new recursive SRS verification approach).

In [30], Kohlweiss et al. presented a more efficient version of the Powers of Tau [13]. Their ceremony protocol [30] uses an RO-based proof system, and comes with a BSV algorithm. Similar to previous SG, SU, SV and BSV algorithms, our algorithms do not use a random beacon or a random oracle. Similar to the earlier works on subversion-resistant or updatable NIZK arguments [2–4,6,8,19, 27],we rely on particular knowledge assumptions. In comparison with the case that one uses the protocol proposed in [30], 1) our proposed algorithms (i.e., SG, SU, SV, and BSV) do not rely on RO, 2) we have different SV (and BSV) algorithms for the provers and verifiers, which allow the provers to verify an updated SRS more efficient than the verifiers, 3) our constructions can achieve identifiable security.

In another related research direction, some studies have defined subversion-resistant and updatable commitments [5,17,23], and have proposed SV and SU algorithms for their studied (knowledge, vector, and polynomial) commitment schemes. Our proposed SV algorithm for Sonic can be considered as an extension of the one proposed in [5], which checks some extra terms and also allows the verifiers to verify an i-time updated SRS. Our SV algorithm for the verifiers in Basilisk is similar to the one proposed in [23], but our SV algorithm for the provers is more efficient. We also propose a batched version of SV algorithms that make them considerably more efficient in practice.

2   Preliminaries

Throughout, we suppose the security parameter of the scheme and its unary representation to be denoted by λ and 1^λ, respectively. We use $x \leftarrow\!\!\$\, X$ to denote x sampled uniformly according to the distribution X.

We use additive and the bracket notation, i.e., in group $\mathbb{G}_\zeta$, $[a]_\zeta = a\,[1]_\zeta$, where $[1]_\zeta$ is the generator of $\mathbb{G}_\zeta$ for $\zeta \in \{1, 2, T\}$. A *bilinear group generator* $\mathsf{BGgen}(1^\lambda)$ returns $(p, \mathbb{G}_1, \mathbb{G}_2, \mathbb{G}_T, \hat{e}, [1]_1, [1]_2)$, where p (a large prime) is the order of cyclic abelian groups $\mathbb{G}_1$, $\mathbb{G}_2$, and $\mathbb{G}_T$. Finally, $\hat{e} : \mathbb{G}_1 \times \mathbb{G}_2 \to \mathbb{G}_T$ is an efficient non-degenerate bilinear pairing, s.t. $\hat{e}([a]_1, [b]_2) = [ab]_T$. Denote $[a]_1 \bullet [b]_2 = \hat{e}([a]_1, [b]_2)$.

2.1   Updatable, Universal and Subversion-Resistant Zk-SNARKs

We adopt the definition of subversion-resistant and updatable zk-SNARKs from [2,27]. Let $\mathcal{R}$ be a relation generator, such that $\mathcal{R}(1^\lambda)$ returns a polynomial-time decidable binary relation $\mathbf{R} = \{(\mathsf{x}, \mathsf{w})\}$, where x is the statement and w is the witness. We assume one can deduce λ from the description of $\mathbf{R}$. Let $\mathbf{L} = \{\mathsf{x} : \exists \mathsf{w} \mid (\mathsf{x}, \mathsf{w}) \in \mathbf{R}\}$ be an **NP**-language including all the statements which there exist corresponding witnesses in relation $\mathbf{R}$. A NIZK argument Ψ_{NIZK} in the updatable SRS model for $\mathcal{R}$ consists of the following PPT algorithms:

- $(\mathsf{srs}_0, \Pi_0) \leftarrow \mathsf{SG}(\mathbf{R})$: Given $\mathbf{R}$, the SRS generator SG first deduces the upper bound N on the relation size. Next, sample the trapdoor ts and then use it to generate srs_0 along with Π_0 as a proof of its well-formedness. Finally, return (srs_0, Π_0) as the output.
- $(\mathsf{srs}_i, \Pi_i) \leftarrow \mathsf{SU}(\mathsf{srs}_{i-1}, \{\Pi_j\}_{j=0}^{i-1})$: Given $(\mathsf{srs}_{i-1}, \{\Pi_j\}_{j=0}^{i-1})$, an SRS updater SU returns the pair of (srs_i, Π_i), where srs_i is the updated SRS and Π_i is a proof for correct updating.

- $(\perp/1) \leftarrow \mathsf{SV}(\mathsf{srs}_i, \{\Pi_j\}_{j=0}^i, \mathsf{party})$: Given a potentially updated srs_i, $\{\Pi_j\}_{j=0}^i$, SV, and party $\in \{\mathsf{P}, \mathsf{V}\}$, return either $\perp$ (if srs_i is incorrectly formed or updated) or 1 (if srs_i is correctly formed or updated).
- $(\pi/\perp) \leftarrow \mathsf{P}(\mathbf{R}, \mathsf{srs}_i, \mathsf{x}, \mathsf{w})$: Given the tuple of $(\mathbf{R}, \mathsf{srs}_i, \mathsf{x}, \mathsf{w})$, such that $(\mathsf{x}, \mathsf{w}) \in \mathbf{R}$, P output an argument π. Otherwise, it returns $\perp$.
- $(0/1) \leftarrow \mathsf{V}(\mathbf{R}, \mathsf{srs}_i, \mathsf{x}, \pi)$: Given $(\mathbf{R}, \mathsf{srs}_i, \mathsf{x}, \pi)$, V verify the proof π and return either 0 (reject) or 1 (accept).

In the standard SRS model, a zk-SNARK for $\mathcal{R}$ has a tuple of algorithms $(\mathsf{SG}, \mathsf{P}, \mathsf{V})$ (and SG does not return the Π_0), while subversion-resistant constructions [2,9] additionally have an SV algorithm which is used to verify the well-formedness of the SRS elements to achieve Sub-ZK [9]. But as listed above, in the *updatable* SRS model, a NIZK argument additionally has an SU algorithm that allows the parties (more precisely, the verifiers) to update the SRS and add their own private shares to the SRS generation. Note that in the latest case, the algorithm SG does not necessarily need $\mathbf{R}$, and it only deduces security parameter 1^λ and the upper bound N from it. We highlight that, in comparison with previous definitions [27], our SV algorithm gets an additional input party $\in \{\mathsf{P}, \mathsf{V}\}$. We later show that this allows us to build a more efficient SV algorithm for the prover. It is worth mentioning that in the updatable SRS model, there also exists a publicly computable deterministic algorithm Derive which given $(\mathbf{R}, \mathsf{srs}_i)$ outputs a specialized SRS for relation $\mathbf{R}$. The output elements of Derive all are in the span of the universal SRS, but they allow to build more efficient proof generation and verification algorithms.

In the subversion-resistant and updatable SRS model, a zk-SNARK is expected to satisfy *updatable completeness*, *Subversion-Zero-Knowledge* (Sub-ZK) and *Updatable Knowledge Soundness* (Upd-KS), of which their definitions are given in the full version of paper [7].

2.2 Assumptions

Definition 1 (Bilinear Diffie-Hellman Knowledge of Exponent (BDH-KE) Assumption [2]). *We say* BGgen *is BDH-KE secure for relation set $\mathcal{R}$ if for any λ, $\mathbf{R} \in \mathrm{im}(\mathcal{R}(1^\lambda))$, and PPT adversary $\mathcal{A}$, there exists a PPT extractor* $\mathsf{Ext}_\mathcal{A}$, *such that, the following probability is* $\mathsf{negl}(\lambda)$,

$$\Pr\left[\begin{array}{l}(p, \mathbb{G}_1, \mathbb{G}_2, \mathbb{G}_T, \hat{e}, [1]_1, [1]_2) \leftarrow \mathsf{BGgen}(1^\lambda), r \leftarrow_\$ \mathsf{RND}(\mathcal{A}), \\ ([\alpha_1]_1, [\alpha_2]_2 \parallel a) \leftarrow (\mathcal{A} \parallel \mathsf{Ext}_\mathcal{A})(\mathbf{R}, r) : [\alpha_1]_1 \bullet [1]_2 = [1]_1 \bullet [\alpha_2]_2 \wedge a \neq \alpha_1 \end{array}\right].$$

The BDH-KE assumption [2] is an asymmetric-pairing version of the original knowledge assumption [16]. We refer to the full version of paper [7] for some preliminaries on polynomial commitments that are used in the rest of paper.

3   SU and SV Algorithms for Updatable Zk-SNARKs

In this section, we present a pair of SRS updating and SRS verification algorithms for each of the studied updatable zk-SNARKs, Sonic [33], Plonk [22], Marlin [15], LunarLite [14] and Basilisk [36].

The General Strategy. Our proposed SV and SU algorithms use pairing checks for SRS verification and the SRS elements are updated in a round-robin multiplicative manner. In comparison with the earlier works, we have a subtle change in the construction of SV algorithms, which allows the provers to verify an updated SRS more efficiently, especially in case of small circuits with a large number of updates. Recall that, a pairing-based zk-SNARK satisfies Sub-ZK if it can achieve ZK, even if its SRS is subverted (i.e., is generated by the adversary). In Sub-ZK zk-SNARKs [2,4,9,19], this is formalized and achieved by building an SV algorithm that verifies the *well-formedness* and *trapdoor extractability* of the SRS. The former guarantees that the whole SRS elements are consistent with each other, and the latter ensures that the (simulation) trapdoors of SRS can be extracted from an SRS subverter. Given the simulation trapdoors of SRS, the proofs are simulated as in the standard ZK. On the other side, a universal zk-SNARK is updatable [27] if its SRS can be sequentially updated by the parties, such that Upd-KS holds if at least one of the updates with SU or the initial SRS generation with SG is done honestly. To ensure that SRS generation/updating is done correctly, parties should return a knowledge assumption-based proof Π when running SG or SU algorithms. This proof is also known as the well-formedness proof of the SRS. In the presented SV algorithms, we use the fact that to achieve Sub-ZK, a P only needs to verify the final SRS. Without loss of generality, one can assume that the initial SRS generation and all the follow-up updates are done with a single adversary who can control all the updaters who run SU and the initial party who runs SG. However, to achieve Upd-KS without a TTP, a V needs to one-time run the SU and update the SRS, and also verify the final SRS and the correctness of all intermediate proofs, generated by all the updaters (See Fig. 1).

Next, in each subsection, we present an overview of a particular updatable zk-SNARK, and then describe its SRS Generation (SG) algorithm. Different from the original papers, in the description of SG algorithms, we also determine what constitutes a well-formedness proof that can be used to extract individual shares from the SRS generator/updaters, and more importantly, can be used to verify the final SRS. The well-formedness proof is shown with Π which consists of two sets of elements ($\Pi^{\mathsf{Agg}}, \Pi^{\mathsf{Ind}}$), where Π^{Agg} can be interpreted as the aggregated elements necessary for verifying the well-formedness of final SRS, and Π^{Ind} can be interpreted as an individual proof for the correctness of updating using the secret shares, e.g. $\bar{x}$. The latter, also enables extracting the individual shares from a malicious SRS generator/updater in the proof of Upd-KS. Finally, we present SU and SV algorithms.

3.1   SU and SV Algorithms for Sonic

Sonic and its SG Algorithm. The first proposed updatable zk-SNARK, presented by Groth et al. [27], came with explicit SU and SV algorithms, but its SRS size scales quadratically in the number of multiplication gates in the circuit that encodes the relation, which made the algorithms very slow. In a follow-up work, Maller et al. [33] proposed Sonic as the first updatable zk-SNARK with linear size SRS. The authors mostly focused on achieving a linear size SRS and more efficient P and V algorithms, and omitted the descriptions of SU and SV algorithms (and even SG which should determine the well-formedness proof) and mentioned that they can built as in [27]. For further details, we refer to the main paper [33]. We describe the SG algorithm of Sonic in Fig. 2.

SU *and* SV *Algorithms and Their Efficiency.* Figure 3 describes the SU and SV algorithms for Sonic. As briefly mentioned before, the SRS update is done in a multiplicative manner, such that the updater multiplies a proper power of its secret shares $\bar{x}_i$ and $\bar{a}_i$ to the SRS elements. Similar to the SG algorithm, we also determine the elements of the well-formedness proof separately. Note that $[a]_T$ is omitted from updating, as due to the fact that $[a]_T := [1]_1 \bullet [a]_2$, it can finally be computed from the other SRS elements. The pairing checks inside SV chase two main goals. First, they check if all the individual proofs generated by the SRS generator and by all the follow-up SRS updaters are correct. If so, then it uses the elements of Π_i and verifies the final SRS, srs_i.

Efficiency. As it can be seen in Figs. 2 and 3, given the SU algorithm, similar to the SG algorithm, to update the SRS of size n in Sonic, one needs to compute $4n + 2$ exponentiations in $\mathbb{G}_1$ and $4n + 2$ exponentiations in $\mathbb{G}_2$. Using the SV algorithm described in Fig. 3, to verify an i-time updated SRS, $i \geq 1$, a prover needs to compute $12n - 1$ pairing operations (importantly, independent of the number of updates), while a verifier needs to compute $12n + 10i + 4$ pairings.

Security Proofs. In [33, Theorem 6.1, 6.2], authors proved that assuming the ability to extract a trapdoor for the subverted/updated SRS (without proving it), Sonic satisfies Sub-ZK and KS. The following lemmas prove that using the SG, SU and SV algorithms (given in Figs. 2 and 3), under the BDH-KE assumption, one can extract the simulation trapdoors from a subverted/updated SRS.

Lemma 1 (Trapdoor Extraction from a Subverted SRS). *Given the algorithm in Figs. 2 and 3, suppose that there exists a PPT adversary $\mathcal{A}$ that outputs a (srs_i, Π_i) such that $\mathsf{SV}(\mathsf{srs}_i, \Pi_i, \mathsf{P}) = 1$ with non-negligible probability. Then, by the BDH-KE assumption (given in Definition 1) there exists a PPT extractor $\mathsf{Ext}_{\mathcal{A}}$ given the random tape of $\mathcal{A}$ as input, outputs (x_i, a_i) such that running SG with (x_i, a_i) results in (srs_i, Π_i).*

SRS Generation, $(\mathsf{srs}_0, \Pi_0) \leftarrow \mathsf{SG}(\mathbf{R})$: Given $\mathbf{R}$, first deduce the security parameter 1^λ and k, then obtain $(p, \mathbb{G}_1, \mathbb{G}_2, \mathbb{G}_T, \hat{e}, [1]_1, [1]_2) \leftarrow \mathsf{BGgen}(1^\lambda)$; after that act as follows:

- Sample $\bar{x}_0, \bar{a}_0 \leftarrow \mathbb{Z}_p^*$, and set $x_0 := \bar{x}_0$ and $a_0 := \bar{a}_0$ which are the simulation trapdoor associated with srs_0;
- For $k = -n, \cdots, n$: compute $\left[x_0^k\right]_1, \left[x_0^k\right]_2, \left[a_0 x_0^k\right]_2$;
- For $k = -n, \cdots, -1, 1, \cdots, n$: compute $\left[a_0 x_0^k\right]_1$; Compute $[a_0]_T$;
- Set $\mathsf{srs}_0 := ((\left[x_0^k\right]_1, \left[x_0^k\right]_2, \left[a_0 x_0^k\right]_2)_{k=-n}^n, \left(\left[a_0 x_0^k\right]_1\right)_{k=-n, k\neq 0}^n, [a_0]_T)$, and the well-formedness proof $\Pi_0 := (\Pi_0^{\mathsf{Agg}}, \Pi_0^{\mathsf{Ind}}) := (([x_0]_1, [a_0 x_0]_1, [a_0]_2), ([x_0]_1, [x_0]_2, [a_0 x_0]_1, [a_0 x_0]_2, [a_0]_2))$;
- Return (srs_0, Π_0);

Fig. 2. SG algorithm for SONIC.

SRS Update, $(\mathsf{srs}_i, \Pi_i) \leftarrow \mathsf{SU}(\mathsf{srs}_{i-1}, \{\Pi_{j-1}\}_{j=0}^{i-1})$: Given $(\mathsf{srs}_{i-1}, \{\Pi_{j-1}\}_{j=0}^{i-1})$,

- Parse $\mathsf{srs}_{i-1} := ((\left[x_{i-1}^k\right]_1, \left[x_{i-1}^k\right]_2, \left[a_{i-1}x_{i-1}^k\right]_2)_{k=-n}^n, (\left[a_{i-1}x_{i-1}^k\right]_1)_{k=-n, k\neq 0}^n)$;
- Sample $\bar{x}_i, \bar{a}_i \leftarrow\!\!\$\, \mathbb{Z}_p^\star$, as the secret shares to be used for updating srs_{i-1}.
- For $k = -n, \cdots, n$: set $\left[x_i^k\right]_1 := \bar{x}_i^k \cdot \left[x_{i-1}^k\right]_1$; set $\left[x_i^k\right]_2 := \bar{x}_i^k \cdot \left[x_{i-1}^k\right]_2$; set $\left[a_ix_i^k\right]_2 := \bar{a}_i\bar{x}_i^k \cdot \left[a_{i-1}x_{i-1}^k\right]_2$;
- For $k = -n, \cdots, -1, 1, \cdots, n$: set $\left[a_ix_i^k\right]_1 := \bar{a}_i\bar{x}_i^k \cdot \left[a_{i-1}x_{i-1}^k\right]_1$;
- Set $\quad \mathsf{srs}_i \quad := \quad ((\left[x_i^k\right]_1, \left[x_i^k\right]_2, \left[a_ix_i^k\right]_2)_{k=-n}^n, (\left[a_ix_i^k\right]_1)_{k=-n, k\neq 0}^n, [a_i]_T)$, and the well-formedness proof $\Pi_i := (\Pi_i^{\mathsf{Agg}}, \Pi_i^{\mathsf{Ind}}) := (([x_i]_1, [a_ix_i]_1, [a_i]_2), ([\bar{x}_i]_1, [\bar{x}_i]_2, [\bar{a}_i\bar{x}_i]_1, [\bar{a}_i\bar{x}_i]_2, [\bar{a}_i]_2))$;
- Return (srs_i, Π_i);

SRS Verify, $(\perp/1) \leftarrow \mathsf{SV}(\mathsf{srs}_i, (\Pi_j)_{j=0}^i, \mathsf{party})$: To verify (an i-time updated) $\mathsf{srs}_i := ((\left[x_i^k\right]_1, \left[x_i^k\right]_2, \left[a_ix_i^k\right]_2)_{k=-n}^n, (\left[a_ix_i^k\right]_1)_{k=-n, k\neq 0}^n, [a_i]_T)$, and $\Pi_j := (\Pi_j^{\mathsf{Agg}}, \Pi_j^{\mathsf{Ind}}) := (([x_j]_1, [a_jx_j]_1, [a_j]_2), ([\bar{x}_j]_1, [\bar{x}_j]_2, [\bar{a}_j\bar{x}_j]_1, [\bar{a}_j\bar{x}_j]_2, [\bar{a}_j]_2))$ for $j = 0, 1, \cdots, i$:
If party = P:
  1. For $k = -n, \cdots, n$: check if $\left[x_i^k\right]_1 \bullet [1]_2 = [1]_1 \bullet \left[x_i^k\right]_2$;
  2. For $k = -n+1, \cdots, n$: check if $\left[x_i^k\right]_1 \bullet [1]_2 = \left[x_i^{k-1}\right]_1 \bullet [x_i]_2$;
  3. For $k = -n, \cdots, -1, 1, \cdots n$: check if $\left[a_ix_i^k\right]_1 \bullet [1]_2 = [1]_1 \bullet \left[a_ix_i^k\right]_2 = \left[x_i^k\right]_1 \bullet [a_i]_2$;
If party = V:
  - If $i = 0$: srs_0 is sampled by verifier, and it does not need to be verified.
  - If $i \geq 1$:
    1. Check that $[x_0]_1 = [\bar{x}_0]_1$, $[a_0x_0]_1 = [\bar{a}_0\bar{x}_0]_1$, and $[a_0]_2 = [\bar{a}_0]_2$;
    2. For $j = 0, 1, \cdots, i$: check if $[\bar{x}_j]_1 \bullet [1]_2 = [1]_1 \bullet [\bar{x}_j]_2$
    3. For $j = 0, 1, \cdots, i$: check if $[\bar{a}_j\bar{x}_j]_1 \bullet [1]_2 = [1]_1 \bullet [\bar{a}_j\bar{x}_j]_2 = [\bar{x}_j]_1 \bullet [\bar{a}_j]_2$;
    4. For $j = 1, 2, \cdots, i$: check if $[x_j]_1 \bullet [1]_2 = [x_{j-1}]_1 \bullet [\bar{x}_j]_2$;
    5. For $j = 1, 2, \cdots, i$: check if $[a_jx_j]_1 \bullet [1]_2 = [x_j]_1 \bullet [a_j]_2 = [a_{j-1}x_{j-1}]_1 \bullet [\bar{a}_j\bar{x}_j]_2$;
    6. For $k = -n, \cdots, n$: check if $\left[x_i^k\right]_1 \bullet [1]_2 = [1]_1 \bullet \left[x_i^k\right]_2$;
    7. For $k = -n+1, \cdots, n$: check if $\left[x_i^k\right]_1 \bullet [1]_2 = \left[x_i^{k-1}\right]_1 \bullet [x_i]_2$;
    8. For $k = -n, \cdots, -1, 1, \cdots n$: check if $\left[a_ix_i^k\right]_1 \bullet [1]_2 = [1]_1 \bullet \left[a_ix_i^k\right]_2 = \left[x_i^k\right]_1 \bullet [a_i]_2$;
  Return 1 if all the checks passed, otherwise return $\perp$.

Fig. 3. SU and SV algorithms for SONIC.

Proof. The proof is given in the full version of paper [7]. □

The following lemma shows that SRS trapdoors can be extracted from an updated SRS. To this end, we first recall a corollary from [24].

Corollary 1. *In the updatable SRS model, single adversarial updates imply full updatable security [24, Lemma 6].*

Lemma 2 (Trapdoor Extraction from an Updated SRS). *Given the algorithm in Figs. 2 and 3, suppose that there exists a PPT $\mathcal{A}$ such that given $(\mathsf{srs}_0, \pi_0) \leftarrow \mathsf{SG}(\mathbf{R})$, $\mathcal{A}$ returns an updated SRS (srs_1, π_1), where $\mathsf{SV}(\mathsf{srs}_1, \Pi_1, \mathsf{V}) = 1$ with a non-negligible probability. Then, the BDH-KE assumption implies that there exists a PPT extractor $\mathsf{Ext}_\mathcal{A}$ that, given the randomness of $\mathcal{A}$ as input, outputs $(\bar{x}_1, \bar{a}_1)$ that are used to update srs_0 and generate (srs_1, Π_1).*

Proof. The proof is given in the full version of paper [7]. □

3.2   SU and SV Algorithms for Marlin

Marlin. As a follow-up work to Sonic and a concurrent work to Plonk, Chiesa et al. proposed Marlin [15], which is comparable to Plonk in performance and outperforms Sonic. Compared to Sonic, Marlin reduces P's computational cost by a factor of $10\times$ and improves V's time by a factor of $4\times$ without compromising the constant-size property of proofs. To this end, the authors first propose an information-theoretic model called Algebraic Holographic Proof (AHP), which is an interactive protocol between algebraic P and V. The verifier performs a small number of queries on an encoding of the circuit instead of receiving the entire circuit description. At the end, the verifier makes a number of queries to the proofs provided by the prover and then performs low-degree tests to be convinced about the validity of proof and the encoding of the circuit. Then, they proposed a transformation that uses PCs with Fiat-Shamir transformation [18] and compiles any public coin AHP for sparse Rank 1 Constraint System (R1CS) instances into a preprocessing zk-SNARK with universal and updatable SRS. To build Marlin, authors first proposed two PC schemes, which one is proven to be secure under a concrete knowledge assumption, and the other one is built in the Algebraic Group Model (AGM) [15, Appendix B]. The scheme built in the AGM model achieves a better efficiency and requires a single group element to commit to a polynomial (instead of two in the initial construction). Marlin is a zk-SNARK which is obtained by instantiating their transformation by the AGM-based PC scheme. Both their PC schemes are proven to be secure (complete, hiding, extractable, as defined in the full version of paper [7]) under a *trusted setup* [15, Lemmas B.5-B.15], and later, the AGM-based one is used to obtain updatable zk-SNARK Marlin.

Achieving Sub-ZK and Upd-KS in Marlin. Marlin uses a universal SRS and assuming that the simulation trapdoors are provided to the ZK simulator, it is proven to achieve ZK and KS in the AGM. In [15, Remark 7.1], authors argue that their constructions have updatable SRS because of using monomial terms in the SRS, and thus fall within the framework of [27]. The SRS of Marlin, which is equivalent to the SRS of their AGM-based PC scheme, consists of $\mathsf{srs} := \left(\left(\left[x^k \right]_1, \left[\gamma x^k \right]_1 \right)_{k=0}^{n}, [1]_2, [x]_2 \right)$ group elements. This SRS is shown to be sufficient for their PC scheme. Note that a standard PC scheme, is constructed under a trusted setup, and there is no guarantee that it will remain secure under a subverted SRS or a maliciously updated SRS. Therefore, once we use the SRS of a PC scheme (with a trusted setup) to build a Sub-ZK zk-SNARK with updatable SRS, we need to ensure that the SRS of resulting zk-SNARK is well-formed and trapdoor-extractable [24]. Since Marlin is proven to satisfy KS under the above SRS srs, therefore, to prove that it also achieves Upd-KS, we need to show that the SRS trapdoors can be extracted from a subverted or a (maliciously) updated SRS. However, one may notice that in practice an adversary, capable of hashing to an elliptic curve, can produce the SRS $([x]_1, [\gamma x]_1, [1]_2, [x]_2)$ without knowing γ. For instance, it can sample a group element from $\mathbb{G}_1$, without knowing its exponent, and then use a known x to compute $([x]_1, [\gamma x]_1, [1]_2, [x]_2)$ for an unknown γ. A malicious SRS updater can perform a similar attack.

One may argue that Marlin (and some follow-up schemes) is proven in the original AGM [20], which adversaries are purely algebraic and do not have the capability to create random group elements without knowing their discrete logarithms. This argument is valid, but the problem still exists in practice and such constructions may not achieve Sub-ZK be default, as an adversary can use elliptic curve hashing [28] to sample random group elements without knowing the exponents. To deal with such concerns, earlier Sub-ZK SNARKs [2,31] used and are proven in more realistic models, namely the Generic Group Model (GGM) with *hashing* [2] and the AGM with *hashing* [31]. The "with hashing" parts mean that the adversary is allowed to sample random group elements without knowing the exponents, say using the elliptic curve hashing [28]. Considering the discussed issue, one can see that to achieve Sub-ZK/Upd-KS in updatable zk-SANRKs, including Marlin, a more realistic option is to prove them in the more realistic variant of AGM, namely AGM with hashing [31], and also explicitly construct the extraction algorithms requited in the games of Sub-ZK/Upd-KS. It is worth to mention that, by chance, the SRS of Kate et al.'s polynomial commitment scheme [29] is well-formed and without further modification, its SRS can achieve trapdoor extractability under BDH-KE assumption. This is the reason that the updatable zk-SNARKs that directly use Kate et al.'s PC scheme [29], e.g., Lunar or Basilisk, do not face with the mentioned issue. In the rest, we focus on constructing a concrete extraction algorithm which is necessary to prove the Sub-ZK and Upd-KS of Marlin. As we argued above, γ cannot be extracted from the original SRS of Marlin, and we need to slightly modify its SRS to achieve trapdoor extractability and prove Sub-ZK and Upd-KS.

Marlin with a Trapdoor Extractable SRS. To deal with the discussed issue, the solution is to force the adversary to add a proof of knowledge of γ to the SRS, such that the simulator would be able to extract γ from a maliciously generated SRS. In earlier works [2,9,24], this is simply achieved by forcing the SRS generator to return γ in two different groups. Then, relying on the BDH-KE assumption one can extract γ from a maliciously generated SRS. Consequently, we slightly modify the SRS of Marlin and add a single group element $[\gamma x]_2$ to it. Then, we show that in the modified version, the SRS trapdoors can be extracted from a subverted/updated SRS, which would allow to prove Sub-ZK/Upd-KS.

SRS Generation, $(\text{srs}_0, \Pi_0) \leftarrow \text{SG}(\mathbf{R})$: Given $\mathbf{R}$, first deduce the security parameter 1^λ and obtain $(p, \mathbb{G}_1, \mathbb{G}_2, \mathbb{G}_T, \hat{e}, [1]_1, [1]_2) \leftarrow \text{BGgen}(1^\lambda)$; then act as follows:

- Sample $\bar{x}_0, \bar{\gamma}_0 \leftarrow \mathbb{Z}_p^*$, and set $x_0 := \bar{x}_0$, and $\gamma_0 := \bar{\gamma}_0$ which are the trapdoors of srs_0;
- For $k = 0, \cdots, n$: compute $\left[x_0^k\right]_1$, $\left[\gamma_0 x_0^k\right]_1$;
- Compute $[x_0]_2$, and $[x_0\gamma_0]_2$;
- Set $\text{srs}_0 := ((\left[x_0^k\right]_1, \left[\gamma_0 x_0^k\right]_1)_{k=0}^n, [x_0]_2, [x_0\gamma_0]_2)$, and the well-formedness proof $\Pi_0 := (\Pi_0^{\text{Agg}}, \Pi_0^{\text{Ind}}) := (([\gamma_0]_1, [x_0\gamma_0]_1, [x_0]_2), ([\bar{x}_0]_1, [\bar{\gamma}_0]_1, [x_0]_2, [\bar{x}_0\bar{\gamma}_0]_2))$;
- Return (srs_0, Π_0);

Fig. 4. Slightly modified SG algorithm of Marlin. The term $[x_0\gamma_0]_2$ is added to SRS and proof to make the SRS well-formed and achieve trapdoor extractability.

SRS Update, $(\text{srs}_i, \Pi_i) \leftarrow \text{SU}(\text{srs}_{i-1}, \{\Pi_{j-1}\}_{j=0}^{i-1})$: Given $(\text{srs}_{i-1}, \{\Pi_{j-1}\}_{j=0}^{i-1})$,

- Parse $\text{srs}_{i-1} := (([x_{i-1}^k]_1, [\gamma_{i-1} x_{i-1}^k]_1)_{k=0}^n, [x_{i-1}]_2, [x_{i-1}\gamma_{i-1}]_2)$;
- Sample $\bar{x}_i, \bar{\gamma}_i \leftarrow \mathbb{Z}_p^*$ as the secret shares to use for updating srs_{i-1}.
- For $k = 0, \cdots, n$: set $[x_i^k]_1 := \bar{x}_i^k \cdot [x_{i-1}^k]_1$, $[\gamma_i x_i^k]_1 := \bar{\gamma}_i \bar{x}_i^k \cdot [\gamma_{i-1} x_{i-1}^k]_1$;
- set $[x_i]_2 := \bar{x}_i \cdot [x_{i-1}]_2$ and $[x_i \gamma_i]_2 := \bar{x}_i \bar{\gamma}_i \cdot [x_i \gamma_i]_2$;
- Set $\text{srs}_i := (([x_i^k]_1, [\gamma_i x_i^k]_1)_{k=0}^n, [x_i]_2, [x_i \gamma_i]_2)$, and the well-formedness proof $\Pi_i :=$ $(\Pi_i^{\text{Agg}}, \Pi_i^{\text{Ind}}) := (([\gamma_i]_1, [x_i \gamma_i]_1, [x_i]_2), ([\bar{x}_i]_1, [\bar{\gamma}_i]_1, [\bar{x}_i]_2, [\bar{x}_i \bar{\gamma}_i]_2))$;
- Return (srs_i, Π_i);

SRS Verify, $(\perp/1) \leftarrow \text{SV}(\text{srs}_i, (\Pi_j)_{j=0}^i, \text{party})$: To verify (an i-time updated) $\text{srs}_i :=$ $(([x_i^k]_1, [\gamma_i x_i^k]_1)_{k=0}^n, [x_i]_2, [x_i \gamma_i]_2)$, and $\Pi_j := (\Pi_j^{\text{Agg}}, \Pi_j^{\text{Ind}}) := (([\gamma_j]_1, [x_j \gamma_j]_1, [x_j]_2), ([\bar{x}_j]_1, [\bar{\gamma}_j]_1, [\bar{x}_j]_2, [\bar{x}_j \bar{\gamma}_j]_2))$; for $j = 0, 1, \cdots, i$: If party = P:

1. For $k = 1, \cdots, n$: check if $[x_i^k]_1 \bullet [1]_2 = [x_i^{k-1}]_1 \bullet [x_i]_2$;
2. For $k = 1, \cdots, n$: check if $[\gamma_i x_i^k]_1 \bullet [1]_2 = [\gamma_i x_i^{k-1}]_1 \bullet [x_i]_2$;
3. Check if $[x_i \gamma_i]_1 \bullet [1]_2 = [1]_1 \bullet [\gamma_i x_i]_2$;

If party = V:
- If $i = 0$: srs_0 is sampled by verifier, and it does not need to be verified.
- If $i \geq 1$:
   1. Check if $[\gamma_0]_1 = [\bar{\gamma}_0]_1$ and $[x_0]_2 = [\bar{x}_0]_2$;
   2. For $j = 0, 1, \cdots, i$: check if $[\bar{x}_j]_1 \bullet [1]_2 = [1]_1 \bullet [\bar{x}_j]_2$ and $[1]_1 \bullet [\bar{x}_j \bar{\gamma}_j]_2 = [\bar{\gamma}_j]_1 \bullet [\bar{x}_j]_2$.
   3. For $j = 1, 2, \cdots, i$: check if $[1]_1 \bullet [x_j]_2 = [\bar{x}_j]_1 \bullet [x_{j-1}]_2$, $[x_j \gamma_j]_1 \bullet [1]_2 = [x_{j-1}\gamma_{j-1}]_1 \bullet [\bar{x}_j \bar{\gamma}_j]_2 = [\gamma_j]_1 \bullet [x_j]_2$;
   4. For $k = 1, \cdots, n$: check if $[x_i^k]_1 \bullet [1]_2 = [x_i^{k-1}]_1 \bullet [x_i]_2$;
   5. For $k = 1, \cdots, n$: check if $[\gamma_i x_i^k]_1 \bullet [1]_2 = [\gamma_i x_i^{k-1}]_1 \bullet [x_i]_2$;
   6. Check if $[x_i \gamma_i]_1 \bullet [1]_2 = [1]_1 \bullet [\gamma_i x_i]_2$;

Return 1 if all the checks passed, otherwise return $\perp$.

Fig. 5. SV and SU algorithms for Marlin with the slightly modified SRS.

We describe the modified SG algorithm of Marlin in Fig. 4, and the new added element is shown with gray background.

SU and SV Algorithms and Their Efficiency. In Fig. 5, we describe our constructed SU and SV algorithms for Marlin with the modified SRS. As the other cases, the SRS update is multiplicative, and at the end, the updater also gives a well-formedness proof which includes the new element $[\bar{x}_i \bar{\gamma}_i]_2$. The new element allows one to verify the well-formedness of the final SRS as well as the validity of intermediate proofs. The SV algorithm verifies if $\{\Pi_j\}_{j=0}^i$ are valid and the final SRS, srs_i, is well-formed.

Using the SU algorithm in Fig. 5, similar to the SG algorithm (in Fig. 4), to update the SRS of size n in Marlin, one needs to compute 2 exponentiations in $\mathbb{G}_2$ and $2n + 1$ exponentiations in $\mathbb{G}_1$. Using the SV algorithm described in Fig. 5, to verify an i-time updated SRS, $i \geq 1$, a prover needs to compute $4n + 2$ pairing operations, while a verifier needs to compute $4n + 2 + 9i + 4$ pairings.

Security Proofs. Relying on the fact that the underlying PC scheme is secure, Marlin, is proven to achieve ZK and KS in the AGM model [15, Theorem 8.1, 8.3 and 8.4]. Our evaluations show that our minimal modification to their PC scheme does not compromise the security of the original scheme (see the full version of paper [7] for further details). Moreover, in the rest, we show that using the presented SG, SU and SV algorithms (given in Figs. 4 and 5), under the BDH-KE assumption (as in [31]), it is also possible to extract the simulation trapdoors from a subverted/updated SRS and achieve Sub-ZK and Upd-KS in the AGM.

Lemma 3 (Trapdoor Extraction from a Subverted SRS). *Given the algorithms in Figs. 4 and 5, suppose that there exists a PPT adversary $\mathcal{A}$ that outputs (srs_i, Π_i) such that $\mathsf{SV}(\mathsf{srs}_i, \Pi_i, \mathsf{P}) = 1$ with a non-negligible probability. Then, by the BDH-KE assumption (given in Definition 1) there exists a PPT extractor $\mathsf{Ext}_{\mathcal{A}}$ that, given the random tape of $\mathcal{A}$ as input, outputs (x_i, γ_i) such that running SG with (x_i, γ_i) results in (srs_i, Π_i).*

Proof. The proof is analogue to the proof of Lemma 1.   □

Lemma 4 (Trapdoor Extraction from an Updated SRS). *Given the algorithms in Figs. 4 and 5, suppose that there exists a PPT $\mathcal{A}$ such that given $(\mathsf{srs}_0, \Pi_0) \leftarrow \mathsf{SG}(\mathbf{R})$, $\mathcal{A}$ returns an updated SRS (srs_1, Π_1) s.t. $\mathsf{SV}(\mathsf{srs}_1, \Pi_1, \mathsf{V}) = 1$, with a non-negligible probability. Then, the BDH-KE assumption implies that there exists a PPT extractor $\mathsf{Ext}_{\mathcal{A}}$ that, given the randomness of $\mathcal{A}$ as input, outputs $(\bar{x}_1, \bar{\gamma}_1)$ that are used to update srs_0 and generate (srs_1, Π_1).*

Proof. The proof is analogue to the proof of Lemma 2.   □

The SU and SV algorithms for Plonk [22], LunarLite [14] and Basilisk [36], are built similar to the previous two cases and are described in the full version of paper [7].

3.3   Batched SRS Verification Algorithms

By now, we presented an SU and SV algorithms for Sonic, Marlin, Plonk, LunarLite and Basilisk, that allow the parties to update/verify the SRS and bypass the need for a TTP. However, when running an SV algorithm, the prover needs to compute at least $O(n)$ pairing operations, where n denotes the number of multiplication gates in the circuit. On the other hand, the verifier needs to compute $O(n + i)$ pairings, where i represents the number of updates done on the SRS. Consequently, even for circuits of moderate size (e.g., $n \geq 10^4$) with a considerable number of updates (e.g., $i = 100$), the efficiency of these algorithms can be severely impacted. In Sect. 4, we will provide concrete numerical examples to further illustrate this inefficiency.

To make them practical, we use batching techniques from [10] and construct a Batched version of the SV algorithms, BSV in short, which allow the provers to verify the SRS by $O(n)$ exponentiations (mostly, short-exponent) and constant pairings, and the verifiers by $O(n + i)$ exponentiations (mostly, short-exponent) and $O(i)$ pairings. To build the BSV algorithms, we use a corollary of the Schwartz-Zippel lemma stating that if $\sum_{i=1}^{s-1} t_i X_i + X_s = 0$ is a polynomial in $\mathbb{Z}_q[t_i]$ with coefficients $X_1, \ldots, X_s, t_i \leftarrow_r \{1, \ldots, 2^\kappa\}$ for $i < s$, then $X_i = 0$ for each i, with probability $1 - 1/2^\kappa$. Namely, if $\sum_{i=1}^{s-1} t_i([a_i]_1 \bullet [b_i]_2) = \sum_{i=1}^{s-1} t_i [c]_T$ for uniformly random t_i, then w.h.p., $[a_i]_1 \bullet [b_i]_2 = [c]_T$ for each individual $i = 1, 2, \cdots, s - 1$.

In Sect. 4, we show that the BSV algorithms can be considerably faster than SV algorithms (at the soundness error rate 2^{-80}, where 80 is a statistical security parameter) and even faster at the soundness error rate 2^{-40}. The detailed description of BSV algorithms is given in the full version of paper [7].

4   Performance Analysis and Identifiable Security

4.1   Implementation Results

Next, we evaluate the efficiency of the presented algorithms using a prototype implementation in Arkworks library[1], which is a Rust library for developing and programming with zk-SNARKs. We have made the source code of our benchmarks publicly available to the research community for reproducibility and further experimentation [2]. For benchmarking Sonic, Plonk, LunarLite, and Basilisk we use the algorithms constructed in Sect. 3 and Sect. 3.3. But in case of Marlin, we use a variant of it, which is implemented in Arkworks[3]. The original paper does not explain this variant, which uses a different PC scheme to reduce proof size, which is a variant of the scheme proposed in [21]. We built the associated $(\mathsf{SG}, \mathsf{SU}, \mathsf{SV}, \mathsf{BSV})$ algorithms for that version in the full version of paper [7].

Our empirical analysis are done with the elliptic curves BLS12-381 that is estimated to achieve between 117 and 120 bits security [34]. All experiments are done on a desktop machine with Ubuntu 20.4.2 LTS, an Intel Core i9-9900 processor at base frequency 3.1 GHz, and 128 GB of memory. All algorithms first are executed in the single-thread mode, while later we show that they all can be parallelized and executed in the multi-thread mode. We also report the benchmarks for Basilisk in the multi-thread mode, with 16 threads. For the benchmarks, we report the running times of all the proposed algorithms, for an arithmetic circuit with different circuit sizes, and by circuit size we mean sum of the multiplication and the addition gates. For Plonk, whose constraint system encodes both multiplication and addition gates, we set the number of addition gates $2\times$ the number of multiplication gates. This choice was based on the evaluation done in the original paper [22]. Motivated by the blockchains and large-scale applications, we also report the SRS verification/updating times for a big number of users and large circuits. All times are expressed in seconds or minutes. In the execution of the BSV algorithms, we first sample some vectors t_i of random numbers from the range $[1 .. 2^{80}]$, the time of sampling randomnesses are not included in the run times of BSV algorithm, as they can be pre-computed. Based on earlier results, one can re-use the same randomness for different verification equations, and zk-SNARKs.

The graphs in Fig. 6 summarize our implementation results based on different criteria for all our studied zk-SNARKs. In the rest, we go through them sequentially and explain the key points. The plot A compares the run times of SG and SU in the single-thread mode, for all the studied zk-SNARKs. Naturally,

---

[1] Available on https://github.com/arkworks-rs.

[2] Our open-source implementations can be accessed on the Git page at https://github.com/Baghery/BMS23.

[3] Available on https://github.com/arkworks-rs/marlin.

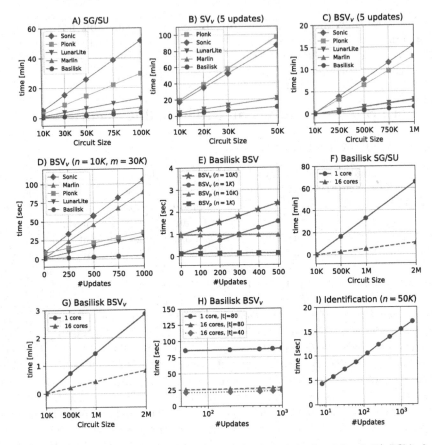

Fig. 6. A) SG or SU, B) SV$_V$ for a fixed $i = 5$, C) BSV$_V$ for a fixed $i = 5$, D) BSV$_V$ for a fixed circuit size ($n = 10K, m = 30K$), E) Comparison of Basilisk's BSV$_P$ and BSV$_V$ for a fixed $n = 10K$, F) Basilisk's SG/SU with multi-threading, G) Basilisk's BSV$_V$ with multi-threading, H) Basilisk's BSV$_V$ with $n = 10^6$, and different security parameters in batching, I) Identifying a malicious SRS updater with recursive verification in Basilisk.

the shorter SRS, the faster SG and SU algorithms. The plot B presents the run times of SV algorithm executed by V, for a 5-time updated SRS and various circuit sizes. As it can be seen, standard SV algorithms can be very slow for even small circuits, e.g. circuits of sizes $< 50K$ (this is why we are not giving its timings for $n > 50K$). In this case, since the size of SRS ($n = 50K$), is considerably larger than the number of updates ($i = 5$), then the run times of SV$_P$ and SV$_V$ are almost the same, therefore SV$_P$ is omitted from the plot.

The plot C illustrates the efficiency of BSV algorithm run by V, for $i = 5$ (5-time updated SRS) and different circuit sizes. One can see that they are considerably faster than standard SV algorithms, and in some cases they are very efficient even for large circuits. e.g. circuits of sizes $> 1M$. Similar to the last plot, in this setting again the run times of SV$_P$ and SV$_V$ are very close. In plot D, we set the circuit size fixed ($n = 10K$ multiplication gates, $m = 30K$

total gates) and plot the run times of BSV_V algorithms for different number of updates. Similar to the previous plots, we observe that the setup phase of Basilisk can be considerably faster than other schemes. Therefore, in the rest of benchmarks, we mainly used Basilisk's algorithms. In plot E, we compare the run times of Basilisk's BSV algorithm executed by the prover (BSV_P) and verifier (BSV_V), for a circuit with $n = 1K$ or $10K$ multiplication gates, and different numbers of updates. As it can be seen, for the cases that a small circuit is updated many times, BSV_P can be significantly faster, independent of the number of updates. The plot shows that BSV_P for $n = 10K$, is as efficient as BSV_V for $n = 1K$ and $i \approx 300$.

By now all evaluations are done in the single-thread mode. In the rest, in both plots F and G, we execute the algorithms of Basilisk in the multi-thread mode and re-evaluate the efficiency of SU (or SG) and BSV_V, for various circuits and different number of updates. We observed that, the SRS of Basilisk for a particular circuit with 2M multiplication gates, can be generated/updated in about 11 min, and verified in less than 1 min. As mentioned before, within the BSV algorithms, the randomness vector t_i are sampled from $[1 .. 2^{80}]$ which assures that the batching causes security gap not bigger than 2^{-80}. This is a conservative approach. In plot H, we compare the run times of BSV_V for Basilisk in the case that the coordinates of t_i were chosen from $[1 .. 2^{40}]$. This makes the SRS verification even faster, but at the cost of a bigger error rate, i.e., 2^{-40}.

4.2 Identifiable Security in the Updatable SRS Model

In the updatable SRS model [27], the initial SRS generator and the follow-up SRS updaters attach a proof to each updated SRS, and the parties do not store every updated SRS but only update proofs. At the end, each party runs the SV (or BSV) algorithm once to verify the validity of proofs in a chain and then uses the final proof to check the well-formedness of the final SRS (see Fig. 1). We also observed that after the final update on SRS, it is sufficient that all the participants in the SRS generation/updating phases run the SV (or BSV) algorithm only once. In the rest, this case is referred to as the *optimistic case* or *optimistic verification*. As we observed in Fig. 6, in this case the setup phase of updatable zk-SNARKs can be significantly fast, and can easily be scaled for a large number of users (e.g. thousands of parties), without the need for a third party. However, then the parties would only abort a maliciously updated SRS at the end, without identifying a malicious party. This can lead to repeat the SRS generation and updates all over again. Note that, the SV (and BSV) algorithm verifies the proofs Π_0 till Π_i, and the final SRS srs_i. If a malicious SRS generator/updater generates a valid proof but an invalid SRS, it cannot be detected by just verifying the proofs. To deal with this concern, a naive solution is to verify the SRS after each update (by either all the participants or a TTP) and identify the malicious party. In practice, the above approach would be impractical for large scale applications.

$\mathrm{BSV}_0^{(16)}$	srs_0 Π_0	srs_1 Π_1	srs_2 Π_2	srs_3 Π_3	srs_4 Π_4	srs_5 Π_5	srs_6 Π_6	srs_7 Π_7	srs_8 $\mathbf{\Pi_8}$	srs_9 Π_9	srs_{10} Π_{10}	srs_{11} Π_{11}	srs_{12} Π_{12}	srs_{13} Π_{13}	srs_{14} Π_{14}	$\mathbf{srs_{15}}$ Π_{15}
↓ $\mathrm{BSV}_1^{(8)}$	srs_0 Π_0	srs_1 Π_1	srs_2 Π_2	srs_3 Π_3	srs_4 Π_4	srs_5 Π_5	srs_6 Π_6	$\mathbf{srs_7}$ Π_7	srs_8 Π_8	srs_9 Π_9	srs_{10} Π_{10}	srs_{11} Π_{11}	srs_{12} Π_{12}	srs_{13} Π_{13}	srs_{14} Π_{14}	srs_{15} Π_{15}
↓ $\mathrm{BSV}_2^{(12)}$	srs_0 Π_0	srs_1 Π_1	srs_2 Π_2	srs_3 Π_3	srs_4 Π_4	srs_5 Π_5	srs_6 Π_6	srs_7 Π_7	srs_8 Π_8	srs_9 Π_9	srs_{10} Π_{10}	$\mathbf{srs_{11}}$ $\mathbf{\Pi_{11}}$	srs_{12} Π_{12}	srs_{13} Π_{13}	srs_{14} Π_{14}	srs_{15} Π_{15}
↓ $\mathrm{BSV}_3^{(10)}$	srs_0 Π_0	srs_1 Π_1	srs_2 Π_2	srs_3 Π_3	srs_4 Π_4	srs_5 Π_5	srs_6 Π_6	srs_7 Π_7	srs_8 Π_8	$\mathbf{srs_9}$ Π_9	srs_{10} Π_{10}	srs_{11} Π_{11}	srs_{12} Π_{12}	srs_{13} Π_{13}	srs_{14} Π_{14}	srs_{15} Π_{15}
↓ $\mathrm{BSV}_4^{(11)}$	srs_0 Π_0	srs_1 Π_1	srs_2 Π_2	srs_3 Π_3	srs_4 Π_4	srs_5 Π_5	srs_6 Π_6	srs_7 Π_7	srs_8 Π_8	srs_9 Π_9	$\mathbf{srs_{10}}$ Π_{10}	srs_{11} Π_{11}	srs_{12} Π_{12}	srs_{13} Π_{13}	srs_{14} Π_{14}	srs_{15} Π_{15}

Fig. 7. Recursive execution of BSV to identify a malicious SRS updater.

Identifying a Malicious Updater with Logarithmic Verification. Next, we describe an efficient approach to identify a malicious party in the updatable SRS model. To this end, the parties need to store all the transcripts, as in current ceremonies, and then recursively run the BSV (or SV) algorithm for one SRS and a smaller set of proofs. More precisely, parties would run the BSV (or SV) algorithm of the target zk-SANRK, with a single SRS and $\frac{i}{2^1}, \frac{i}{2^2}, \cdots, \frac{i}{2^{\log i}}$ proofs, respectively. Note that with this approach, only $\lceil \log i \rceil + 1$ of SRSs are verified (e.g., boldface SRSs $srs_{15}, srs_7, srs_{11}, srs_9, srs_{10}$ in Fig. 7), instead of i. As in practice, the circuit size is considerably higher than the number of SRS updates, e.g. 2^{22} vs. 100 in current ceremonies, therefore the run time of SV (and BSV) is dominated by the size of SRS, rather than the number of updates. Due to this fact, in practice, the proposed verification approach can be considerably faster than the naive solution. Figure 7, presents an example of such recursive execution of BSV algorithms for $i = 15$. We also evaluate the performance of this approach with a sample implementation. The plot I in Fig. 6, illustrates the required time to identify a malicious updater in Basilisk's setup for different number of updates with the SRS of a circuit with $n = 50K$ multiplication gates. As it can be seen, for 2000-time updated SRS of length $50K$, the first malicious updater can be identified in less than 20 s. In similar settings, where $n >> i$, the identification time would be independent of the precise position of the malicious updater, and it will take an approximate run time of $\log i$ times that of a single BSV.

As an optimization, one may notice that once a verifier runs the BSV algorithm on the final SRS, e.g. $\mathrm{BSV}_0^{(16)}$ in the mentioned example, we already compute the batched form of the proof elements required in all the follow-up steps of the recursive search, as e.g. $\sum_{i=0}^{15} t_i [x_i]_1 = \sum_{i=0}^{7} t_i [x_i]_1 + \sum_{i=8}^{15} t_i [x_i]_1 = \sum_{i=0}^{3} t_i [x_i]_1 + \sum_{i=4}^{7} t_i [x_i]_1 + \sum_{i=8}^{11} t_i [x_i]_1 + \sum_{i=12}^{15} t_i [x_i]_1$. By storing a proper set of batched proofs, one can speed up the follow-up executions of BSV. This optimization is more effective in cases that the circuit size is small but the SRS is updated many times. As another optimization, one can precompute the batched version of the checks on some intermediate SRSs, e.g. srs_{11}, srs_7, srs_3, and speed-up the run times of BSV algorithms in the follow-up steps. Note that our BSV and SV algorithms, by default verifies all the proofs for $j = 0$ till the final SRS srs_i, i.e. $j = i$. In the recursive execution, we need to run the BSV (or SV) algorithm for a particular set of SRSs and proofs. In those cases, one can feed proper starting and finishing indexes to the BSV (or SV) algorithms. For instance, to check the SRS srs_{11} and the set of proofs $\{\Pi_8, \Pi_9, \Pi_{10}, \Pi_{11}\}$ one needs to run the algorithms for $j = 8$ till $j = 11$, which will verify a batched variant of $(\Pi_8, \Pi_9, \Pi_{10}, \Pi_{11})$ and the final SRS srs_{11}.

In practice, if the values of i and n will be huge, it might happen that the setup phase would take a long time, especially if a malicious update occurs during the earlier updates. To minimize the run time, as well as to gain the benefits of the optimistic verification, an effective solution would be to verify the updated SRS after a particular number of updates, i.e. one would need to verify the updated SRS every k updates, where $1 < k < i$. Basically, the idea is rather than verifying every update (the slowest case), or all i updates once (the fastest case), the parties will verify the SRS after each k updates. If the verification of srs_k was successful, then the parties will continue with updating the SRS. If not, they would use the recursive search approach (given in Fig. 7) to find the first malicious updater and then will continue the SRS update from there (without the malicious updater).

Since the entire described procedure is accountable, in practice one can minimize the risk of a malicious SRS update significantly by enforcing a high penalty for a malicious SRS updater.

5   Conclusion

In this study, we examined the setup phase of updatable zk-SNARKs. We constructed the necessary algorithms, namely $(\mathsf{SG}, \mathsf{SU}, \mathsf{SV})$, for the setup phase of various updatable zk-SANRKs, including Sonic, Plonk, Marlin, Lunar, and Basilisk. To make SV algorithms practical, we also presented a batched version of them, called BSV. We constructed the algorithms for the most efficient version of each zk-SNARK, in terms of proof size. However, the proposed algorithm can be adapted to their different versions. Our results show that in a few cases, to achieve better efficiency in the setup phase, one option would be to use a version of the studied schemes, with a shorter SRS but slightly larger proofs and slower provers. For instance, Lunar [14] has a version, so-called LunarLite2x, which has the same SRS as Basilisk, therefore can be as efficient as Basilisk in the setup phase, but in cost of slightly longer proofs and slower prover. In another example, we observed that Counting Vampires [32] has only two fewer group elements than Basilisk in the proof, but its SRS size is 17× larger and such an SRS can result in a prolonged setup.

Meanwhile, we observed that to achieve Sub-ZK/Upd-KS in updatable zk-SANRKs, a more realistic model for security proofs could be the AGM with hashing [31], rather than the original AGM [20].

Moreover, we showed that pairing-based updatable zk-SNARKs, or other primitives constructed in the updatable SRS model, by default achieve security with abort, and the parties cannot identify a malicious SRS generator/updater. A naive solution to deal with this concern is verifying the SRS after each update (either by the parties or a third party), but it can be impractical in a large-scale application. To make it practical, we proposed an efficient recursive verification approach, that allows the parties to identify a malicious SRS updater by a logarithmic number of SRS verification (instead of linear) in the number of updates. We believe our proposed approach to achieve identifiable security, can also be used in the MPC SRS generation protocols [30], as well as in other cryptographic primitives (like commitments, signatures, encryptions) constructed in the updatable SRS model [3,6,8,17,23].

Finally, our empirical analysis showed that the algorithms are practical for large-scale applications, and among the current updatable zk-SNARKs, Basilisk (and the Lunarlite2x variant of Lunar) can have the fastest setup phase. Counting Vampires, Sonic and Plonk can have a very slow setup phase, which is mainly because of having a very long SRS or using a specific constraint system (i.e., Plonk) that encodes both addition and multiplication gates.

Acknowledgement. This work has been supported in part by the Defense Advanced ResearchProjects Agency (DARPA) under contract No. HR001120C0085, by the FWO underan Odysseus project GOH9718N, by the Research Council KU Leuven C1 on Security and Privacy for Cyber-Physical Systems and the Internet of Things with contract number C16/15/058, and by CyberSecurity Research Flanders with reference number VR20192203.

References

1. Abdolmaleki, B., Baghery, K., Lipmaa, H., Siim, J., Zając, M.: UC-secure CRS generation for SNARKs. In: Buchmann, J., Nitaj, A., Rachidi, T. (eds.) AFRICACRYPT 2019. LNCS, vol. 11627, pp. 99–117. Springer, Cham (2019). https://doi.org/10.1007/978-3-030-23696-0_6

2. Abdolmaleki, B., Baghery, K., Lipmaa, H., Zając, M.: A subversion-resistant SNARK. In: Takagi, T., Peyrin, T. (eds.) ASIACRYPT 2017 Part III. LNCS, vol. 10626, pp. 3–33. Springer, Cham (2017). https://doi.org/10.1007/978-3-319-70700-6_1

3. Abdolmaleki, B., Ramacher, S., Slamanig, D.: Lift-and-shift: obtaining simulation extractable subversion and updatable SNARKs generically. In Ligatti, J., Ou, X., Katz, J., Vigna, G (eds.) ACM CCS 2020, pp. 1987–2005. ACM Press (2020)

4. Baghery, K.: Subversion-resistant simulation (knowledge) sound NIZKs. In: Albrecht, M. (ed.) IMACC 2019. LNCS, vol. 11929, pp. 42–63. Springer, Cham (2019). https://doi.org/10.1007/978-3-030-35199-1_3

5. Baghery, K.: Subversion-resistant commitment schemes: definitions and constructions. In: Markantonakis, K., Petrocchi, M. (eds.) STM 2020. LNCS, vol. 12386, pp. 106–122. Springer, Cham (2020). https://doi.org/10.1007/978-3-030-59817-4_7

6. Baghery, K., Bardeh, N.G.: Updatable NIZKs from non-interactive zaps. In: Beresford, A.R., Patra, A., Bellini, E. (eds.) CANS 22. LNCS, vol. 13641, pp. 23–43. Springer, Heidelberg (2022). https://doi.org/10.1007/978-3-031-20974-1_2

7. Baghery, K., Mertens, A., Sedaghat, M.: Benchmarking the setup of updatable zk-SNARKs. Cryptology ePrint Archive, Paper 2023/1161 (2023). https://eprint.iacr.org/2023/1161

8. Baghery, K., Sedaghat, M.: Tiramisu: Black-box simulation extractable NIZKs in the updatable CRS model. In: Conti, M., Stevens, M., Krenn, S. (eds.) CANS 2021. LNCS, vol. 13099, pp. 531–551. Springer, Heidelberg (2021). https://doi.org/10.1007/978-3-030-92548-2_28

9. Bellare, M., Fuchsbauer, G., Scafuro, A.: NIZKs with an untrusted CRS: security in the face of parameter subversion. In: Cheon, J.H., Takagi, T. (eds.) ASIACRYPT 2016 Part II. LNCS, vol. 10032, pp. 777–804. Springer, Heidelberg (2016). https://doi.org/10.1007/978-3-662-53890-6_26

10. Bellare, M., Garay, J.A., Rabin, T.: Batch verification with applications to cryptography and checking. In: Lucchesi, C.L., Moura, A.V. (eds.) LATIN 1998. LNCS, vol. 1380, pp. 170–191. Springer, Heidelberg (1998). https://doi.org/10.1007/BFb0054320

11. Ben-Sasson, E., Chiesa, A., Green, M., Tromer, E., Virza, M.: Secure sampling of public parameters for succinct zero knowledge proofs. In 2015 IEEE Symposium on Security and Privacy, pp. 287–304. IEEE Computer Society Press (2015)

12. Blum, M., Feldman, P., Micali, S.: Non-interactive zero-knowledge and its applications. In Proceedings of the Twentieth Annual ACM Symposium on Theory of Computing, pp. 103–112. ACM (1988)

13. Bowe, S., Gabizon, A., Miers, I.: Scalable multi-party computation for zk-SNARK parameters in the random beacon model. Cryptology ePrint Archive, Report 2017/1050 (2017). https://eprint.iacr.org/2017/1050

14. Campanelli, M., Faonio, A., Fiore, D., Querol, A., Rodríguez, H.: Lunar: a toolbox for more efficient universal and updatable zkSNARKs and commit-and-prove extensions. In: Tibouchi, M., Wang, H. (eds.) ASIACRYPT 2021 Part III. LNCS, vol. 13092, pp. 3–33. Springer, Cham (2021). https://doi.org/10.1007/978-3-030-92078-4_1

15. Chiesa, A., Hu, Y., Maller, M., Mishra, P., Vesely, N., Ward, N.: Marlin: preprocessing zkSNARKs with universal and updatable SRS. Cryptology ePrint Archive, Report 2019/1047 (2019). https://eprint.iacr.org/2019/1047

16. Damgård, I.: Towards practical public key systems secure against chosen ciphertext attacks. In: Feigenbaum, J. (ed.) CRYPTO'91. LNCS, vol. 576, pp. 445–456. Springer, Heidelberg (1992). https://doi.org/10.1007/3-540-46766-1_36

17. Daza, V., Ràfols, C., Zacharakis, A.: Updateable inner product argument with logarithmic verifier and applications. In: Kiayias, A., Kohlweiss, M., Wallden, P., Zikas, V. (eds.) Part II. LNCS, vol. 12110, pp. 527–557. Springer, Heidelberg (2020). https://doi.org/10.1007/978-3-030-45374-9_18

18. Fiat, A., Shamir, A.: How to prove yourself: Practical solutions to identification and signature problems. In: Odlyzko, A.M. (ed.) CRYPTO'86. LNCS, vol. 263, pp. 186–194. Springer, Heidelberg (1987). https://doi.org/10.1007/3-540-47721-7_12

19. Fuchsbauer, G.: Subversion-zero-knowledge SNARKs. In: Abdalla, M., Dahab, R. (eds.) PKC 2018 Part I. LNCS, vol. 10769, pp. 315–347. Springer, Cham (2018). https://doi.org/10.1007/978-3-319-76578-5_11

20. Fuchsbauer, G., Kiltz, E., Loss, J.: The algebraic group model and its applications. In: Shacham, H., Boldyreva, A. (eds.) Part II. LNCS, vol. 10992, pp. 33–62. Springer, Heidelberg (2018). https://doi.org/10.1007/978-3-319-76578-5_11

21. Gabizon, A.: AuroraLight: improved prover efficiency and SRS size in a sonic-like system. Cryptology ePrint Archive, Report 2019/601 (2019). https://eprint.iacr.org/2019/601

22. Gabizon, A., Williamson, Z.J., Ciobotaru, O.: PLONK: permutations over lagrange-bases for oecumenical noninteractive arguments of knowledge. Cryptology ePrint Archive, Report 2019/953 (2019). https://eprint.iacr.org/2019/953

23. Ganesh, C., Khoshakhlagh, H., Kohlweiss, M., Nitulescu, A., Zając, M.: What makes fiat-shamir zkSNARKs (updatable SRS) simulation extractable? In: Galdi, C., Jarecki, S. (eds.) Security and Cryptography for Networks. LNCS, vol. 13409, pp. 735–760. Springer, Cham (2022). https://doi.org/10.1007/978-3-031-14791-3_32

24. Garg, S., Mahmoody, M., Masny, D., Meckler, I.: On the round complexity of OT extension. In: Shacham, H., Boldyreva, A. (eds.) Part III. 10993, vol. 109933, pp. 545–574. Springer, Heidelberg (2018). https://doi.org/10.1007/978-3-319-96878-0_19

25. Goldwasser, S., Micali, S., Rackoff, C.: The knowledge complexity of interactive proof systems. SIAM J. Comput. 18(1), 186–208 (1989)

26. Groth, J.: On the size of pairing-based non-interactive arguments. In: Fischlin, M., Coron, J.-S. (eds.) EUROCRYPT 2016 Part II. LNCS, vol. 9666, pp. 305–326. Springer, Heidelberg (2016). https://doi.org/10.1007/978-3-662-49896-5_11

27. Groth, J., Kohlweiss, M., Maller, M., Meiklejohn, S., Miers, I.: Updatable and universal common reference strings with applications to zk-SNARKs. In: Shacham, H., Boldyreva, A. (eds.) CRYPTO 2018 Part III. LNCS, vol. 10993, pp. 698–728. Springer, Cham (2018). https://doi.org/10.1007/978-3-319-96878-0_24

28. Icart, T.: How to hash into elliptic curves. In: Halevi, S. (ed.) CRYPTO 2009. LNCS, vol. 5677, pp. 303–316. Springer, Heidelberg (2009). https://doi.org/10.1007/978-3-642-03356-8_18

29. Kate, A., Zaverucha, G.M., Goldberg, I.: Constant-size commitments to polynomials and their applications. In: Abe, M. (ed.) ASIACRYPT 2010. LNCS, vol. 6477, pp. 177–194. Springer, Heidelberg (2010). https://doi.org/10.1007/978-3-642-17373-8_11

30. Kohlweiss, M., Maller, M., Siim, J., Volkhov, M.: Snarky ceremonies. In: Tibouchi, M., Wang, H. (eds.) ASIACRYPT 2021 Part III. LNCS, vol. 13092, pp. 98–127. Springer, Cham (2021). https://doi.org/10.1007/978-3-030-92078-4_4

31. Lipmaa, H.: A unified framework for non-universal SNARKs. In: Hanaoka, G., Shikata, J., Watanabe, Y. (eds.) PKC 2022 Part I. LNCS, vol. 13177, pp. 553–583. Springer, Heidelberg (2022). https://doi.org/10.1007/978-3-030-97121-2_20

32. Lipmaa, H., Siim, J., Zajac, M.: Counting vampires: from univariate sumcheck to updatable ZK-SNARK. In: Agrawal, S., Lin, D. (eds.) ASIACRYPT 2022 Part II. LNCS, vol. 13792, pp. 249–278. Springer, Heidelberg (2022). https://doi.org/10.1007/978-3-031-22966-4_9

33. Maller, M., Bowe, S., Kohlweiss, M., Meiklejohn, S.: Sonic: zero-knowledge SNARKs from linear-size universal and updatable structured reference strings. In Cavallaro, L., Kinder, J., Wang, X., Katz, J. (eds.) ACM CCS 2019, pp. 2111–2128. ACM Press (2019)

34. NCC. Zcash overwinter consensus and sapling cryptography review (2019). https://research.nccgroup.com/wp-content/uploads/2020/07/NCC_Group_Zcash2018_Public_Report_2019-01-30_v1.3.pdf

35. Parno, B., Howell, J., Gentry, C., Raykova, M.: Pinocchio: nearly practical verifiable computation. In: 2013 IEEE Symposium on Security and Privacy, pp. 238–252. IEEE Computer Society Press (2013)

36. Ràfols, C., Zapico, A.: An algebraic framework for universal and updatable SNARKs. Cryptology ePrint Archive, Report 2021/590 (2021). https://eprint.iacr.org/2021/590

Author Index

A. Aly and M. Tibouchi (Eds.): LATINCRYPT 2023, LNCS 14168, pp. 397–398, 2023.
https://doi.org/10.1007/978-3-031-44469-2

Printed in the United States
by Baker & Taylor Publisher Services